Listen
to the
Music

Listen
to the
Music

A Self-Guided Tour
Through the Orchestral Repertoire

based on program notes
written for
the Cincinnati Symphony Orchestra, 1980–89;
adapted and reprinted with the
kind permission of the Cincinnati Symphony

JONATHAN D. KRAMER

SCHIRMER BOOKS
A Division of Macmillan, Inc.
NEW YORK

Collier Macmillan Publishers
LONDON

Schirmer Books
866 Third Avenue, New York, N. Y. 10022

Collier Macmillan Canada, Inc.

Library of Congress Catalog Card Number: 88-9248

Printed in the United States of America

printing number
    3   4   5   6   7   8   9   10

Library of Congress Cataloging in Publication Data
Kramer, Jonathan D., 1942–
    Listen to the music: a self-guided tour through the orchestral repertoire / Jonathan D. Kramer.
        p.   cm.
    "Based on program notes written for the Cincinnati Symphony Orchestra, 1980–88."
    Bibliography: p.
    ISBN 0-02-871841-0.
    1. Orchestral music—Analysis, appreciation.   I. Title.
MT125.K72   1988   88-9248
785'.01'5—dc19   CIP
                                                                        MN

dedicated to

Zachary Kramer

Stephanie Kramer

Contents

Preface

Why program notes? Shouldn't music speak for itself? Why this mania to explain, to attempt the impossibility of translating musical expression into verbal language?

Music isn't unique among the arts in being the subject of countless books and articles that explain or interpret. But with music the disjunction is particularly great. There's a difference between using the English language to discuss a poem in English and trying to talk about a non-verbal art by using normal language.

Yet program notes persist. Concertgoers, record collectors, radio listeners, and even musicians seem to enjoy them, rely on them, and want them, even if people are a little uneasy reading about an art that's supposed to have immediacy.

Part of the reason for program notes is that the symphony concert is an elaborate ritual. To those who don't know the rules, and even to those who do, it can be forbidding. Program notes should try to get around the ritual, to help people make direct contact with the music, to turn what looks like a formal and impersonal occasion into one with personal meaning and enjoyment.

Also, program notes give people who are bored with the music something to do while trapped in a seat they paid good money for. It's a funny paradox. The better the program notes are, the more people sit in concerts reading them when they're supposed to be listening.

This book is a series of essays on the orchestral music most often heard in the concert hall, on records and tapes and CDs, and on the radio. As the essays are aimed at the general music listener, they aren't too technical. Their purpose is simply to increase understanding and enjoyment of music, in what I hope is an entertaining fashion.

These program notes usually avoid guided tours through the music, such as: "The first theme is ushered in by the trumpets and strings; then, following a hushed transition in the violas, the lyrical second theme bursts forth in the wind choir, accompanied by string basses and timpani." Such banal descriptions do little to enhance understanding or enjoyment. They explain nothing. They merely tell the listener what he or she can perfectly well hear. Thus the tours here are self-guided. I prefer to excite your curiosity rather than correct your listening. "Tour" writing appears in this book only when it illuminates a unique aspect of a piece. For compositions where it's more appropriate to discuss non-technical matters, the focus is on how the pieces came to be, how they relate to other music, how they fit in with the general cultural milieu in which they were conceived, what aesthetic and/or sociological issues they speak to, etc. These notes try to demystify the listening experience. They try to show composers as ordinary (or in some cases eccentric) people with human concerns and aspirations.

The discussions of the music itself that I've included are, I hope, relevant and easy to follow. I've avoided being too detailed because I don't want to prejudice anyone. Listeners bring individual backgrounds, interests, and abilities to the concert hall. I want only to suggest ways to listen, not to force anyone to hear my way.

Program notes have three problems:

1. The things which are easy to talk about—thematic derivation or orchestration, for example—are not always the most salient to hear. When the music is really about harmony, tonality, large-scale form, etc., then it's best to talk about the composer's personality! Someone once told me a story about what happened when a major symphony orchestra was playing a difficult new work. The local critic wanted to help the audience understand the piece, so a few days before the concert he published a diagram of the piece in the newspaper. He was then horrified to see lots of people show up at the concert with his diagram in hand, carefully following it (while supposedly listening) and conferring with their neighbors about where in the piece they were. Can those people really have had a musical experience? Did following a map really enhance their understanding? They probably thought it did, which is a strong argument for avoiding charts in program notes.

2. It's impossible to talk about music in any substantial way without invoking a specialized vocabulary. The concepts and terminology of music theory aren't shared by many listeners, yet there is no other way to talk about a lot that really matters in music. What seems to the outsider as pseudo-scientific pretension often communicates to professionals real insights about how music works, how it's heard, and what it means. But there's simply no way to share these ideas with the general music-lover, no matter how accomplished he or she may be as a listener. That's a pretty serious problem, and I see no solution.

3. It's nearly impossible to refer to a particular place in a piece. I can't tell you to count the minutes and seconds, because each performance is different. I can't cite measure numbers, because few people listen with scores in hand. I won't print musical excerpts, because I don't assume that all readers of this book understand music notation. Furthermore, musical excerpts would have to be lengthy to be sufficiently substantive.

In Cincinnati I've dealt with the third problem, and to some extent the others, with radio broadcasts. On the radio I can point things out in recorded performances, and I can prepare special musical demonstrations. But this book is supposed to be self-contained. What I've done is to try to focus more on aesthetic, historical, and biographical issues than on analytic problems. When I discuss the actual music, I do use a small number of technical terms. Many readers will know what they mean. For others I've added a glossary.

Selecting the pieces to include hasn't been as straightforward as I'd expected. When I began to put this book together, I thought of it as a guide to the standard symphonic repertory. Today's composers all know what that repertory is: they're always complaining that orchestras, instead of playing *their* music, are forever repeating the same fifty pieces by the same twenty dead Germans! Actually, the standard literature is bigger than they think. It's more like five hundred pieces by fifty dead composers from several countries. Even so, the concept of the standard repertory is vague. The exact boundaries of this literature aren't clear. Most musically knowledgeable readers will find a few, possibly quite a few, favorite works omitted. This is inevitable, no matter how large the scope of the book.

In making my selection, I decided to exclude certain categories. For example, operas, opera excerpts, and opera overtures are expendable because they aren't, strictly speaking, symphonic. I've made a couple of exceptions where the music has become known as a symphonic work quite apart from its operatic origins (e.g., Hindemith's symphony *Mathis der Maler*, Kodály's *Hary Janos* Suite). I've also omitted orchestral songs (except when they're of truly symphonic scope, as with Mahler's *Das Lied von der Erde*). And I haven't discussed any large choral works (such as the Berlioz Requiem or the Bach B Minor Mass), other than choral symphonies (such as Berlioz' *Romeo and Juliet*, Beethoven's Ninth, or Stravinsky's *Symphony of Psalms*). These are included because of their relationship to the symphonic tradition. Furthermore, there are no "pops" compositions.

This book is for record collectors and radio listeners as well as symphony goers. The music that these three groups listen to is not always the same. Classical radio stations explore lesser known pieces more than orchestras do. Radio stations, after all, have to come up with as much as 140 hours of music a week, while orchestras manage on two. Record (or tape or CD) collectors are likely to have their own individual tastes. Certain works may be rare in the concert hall but popular otherwise. Mahler's Eighth Symphony, for example, isn't heard live too often, since it requires close to a thousand performers. Yet Mahler fans are likely to have a recording of it. This book tries to strike a balance between the interests of all three categories of listeners, with perhaps a slight leaning toward the music that concert-goers encounter most frequently.

There are pieces I've left out that are heard more often than ones that are included. Chabrier's *España*, for example, probably appears on more concerts than Webern's Six Pieces for Orchestra. A combination of factors has influenced what, in the final analysis, must be taken as a personal selection: historical importance, musical importance, whether something interesting and informative can be said about the piece, and the extent to which a program note would be helpful.

Audience members at Cincinnati Symphony concerts sometimes ask me whether my program notes include personal opinions. Because I don't want to prejudice listeners, I try never to express a negative judgement. I may, occasionally and mildly, say less than lofty things about some pieces that are so enshrined in the canon of Great Art that people may be afraid to listen to them just for enjoyment. When I have some real enthusiasm about a piece or some aspect of a piece, however, I let it shine through. Sometimes concertgoers have told me that they sense my enthusiasm, when in fact I was writing about some pieces that I don't particularly like. This pleases me a lot, because I don't really want to share my idiosyncratic dislikes, at least not in print. There are in this book essays on two or three pieces I thoroughly, even passionately, detest. I'm not saying that they're bad music, only that I would go out of my way to avoid hearing them. But I defy anyone to identify them.

There are disguised messages other than value judgements in some of these notes. While most of them don't have hidden political agendas, some do. When I was writing up the Mahler Ninth Symphony for a Cincinnati Symphony performance, for example, the music director was facing a decision on his reappointment. He was controversial, since he programmed a lot of new music, since he had brought a new level of discipline to the orchestra, since he had been hired without having guest conducted and without consultation with the orchestra players, and since his programming had a high level of intellectual content. I was fascinated to discover that Mahler had faced the same situation with the New York Philharmonic in 1909–10. So I included in the program note the story of Mahler's difficulties with the Philharmonic board. Up to a point, the stories are exactly the same. Just change the names, dates, and repertory. (The point at which the stories diverge is where Mahler's conversations were subject to eavesdropping; I don't think that Michael Gielen's meetings were ever bugged!) I thought it was really important for the symphony and for the city that Gielen be reappointed. So what I wrote explains the ramifications when a superb though controversial conductor, who has done a tremendous amount for an orchestra, is let go prematurely. The moral of my story is in the last paragraphs of the note. (By the way, Gielen was reappointed and went on to lead the Cincinnati Symphony in three more seasons of wonderful music-making.)

Another "political" essay is that on Dvořák's *New World* Symphony. Here the message is not at all disguised. The essay states blatantly that American arts organizations and audiences ought to accord greater respect to their own native musicians and not to be so eager to enshrine foreign artists.

There may also be other program notes in this collection with hidden agendas, though they are surely in the minority.

Sometimes being a program annotator has led to amusing incidents. In 1967–70 I wrote the concert notes for the San Francisco Symphony. On one occasion that orchestra was doing a new piece by a relatively unknown Europen composer. I could find nothing about him in any reference books. I wrote to him for biographical and program note materials, but he didn't answer. I was getting nervous. I wrote again. Still no answer. Finally, in desperation, I sent a telegram. A week later, as my deadline was breathing down my neck, I received a letter from him. He apologized for not having written sooner. You see, he said, I've been in an automobile accident. A car hit me and broke my leg. But don't worry, he wrote, I'll be fine. He went on to talk about his great pain and the inconvenience of being laid up in the hospital. Then he signed off: sincerely yours, etc., etc. That was it. Nothing about his professional life, nothing about his symphony. What was I supposed to do? I had no choice. I printed the only information I had on him, namely, his letter!

Then there was the time the San Francisco Symphony was playing a piece by a local composer. I called him up for program note information. He said that he preferred not to have any notes written. That was fine with me. As a composer myself, I could sympathize with his wish for his music to speak for itself. Anyway, I was facing severe space limitations. So I printed a one-sentence program note: at the composer's request, no notes will be provided for this performance. The day after the first performance, I received an angry phone call from the composer. "I didn't mean you should print *absolutely* nothing!" he complained. Did I say something earlier about composers being eccentric?

The Cincinnati Orchestra was doing a symphony by Swedish composer Franz Berwald (1796–1868). Since Berwald is not well known, I included a lot of human-interest information on him. I thought the audience would like to know that he had difficulty earning a living as a composer and had been forced to work at such jobs as an orchestral violinist, publisher of a music journal, founder of an orthopedic institute, manager of a glassworks, director of a sawmill, and author of articles on such social issues as popular education, forestry conservation, and rent control. At the concert, an audience member came up to me and told me that it wasn't suprising that the music was so terrible, since the composer was such a loser that he couldn't even hold down a steady job! So much for human interest.

Yo Yo Ma came to Cincinnati to play the Lutosławski Cello Concerto with Michael Gielen and the orchestra. There's one particularly busy passage for cello, in the middle of which there's a page turn. The soloist couldn't possibly negotiate a page turn while furiously flailing his instrument, so Michael leaned over from the conductor's podium and turned the page for him. A couple of days after the performance, I received a phone call from a woman who thought it was terrible that a conductor should have to turn a soloist's page. She thought I should look into the invention of a device by which someone could turn pages with his or her feet.

My favorite story is the one about the woman and her cat. In 1983–84 we performed Elliott Carter's Variations for Orchestra, a piece that some listeners find quite difficult. Several weeks after the performance, I received the following letter:

Dear Mr. Kramer:

Hi! Thought you might be interested in a little "tail" about my cat, the Music Critic.

In October my daughter and I attended the Cincinnati Symphony concert in order to hear violinist Itzhak Perlman. We were first held captive by the worst piece of music we had ever heard, namely Variations for Orchestra by Elliott Carter. The orchestra tuning up is easier to listen to.

Anyway, with some weeks to forget about it, we decided to listen to the rebroadcast on the radio. Now mind you, my cat can curl up on the table and listen to WGUC by the hour. Loves "catsical mewsic." When Variations for Orchestra came on, she jumped up and, with glazed eyes, wildly clawed at the door to get out. As it was very cold outside, she soon scratched to get back in. Hearing that Elliott Carter was still on, she clawed wildly to get out. This "in and out" business went on for the duration. Finally, after repeating this "cataplexy" behavior many times, she came in and heard that Itzhak Perlman was playing Beethoven's Violin Concerto, whereupon she hopped up on the dining room table in front of the stereo, put her head on her front paws, and, purring, fell into a contented sleep. This leads me to believe that she is one of the great music critics of all time.

I responded:

While I would take exception to your evaluation (devaluation?) of Elliott Carter's Variations for Orchestra, I did enjoy your cat story. I am confident Elliott Carter would be flattered to learn that his music had such a profoundly "moving" effect on "one of the great music critics of all time." Beethoven, on the other hand, would no doubt be chagrined to learn that his music had put the great critic to sleep.

I agree with you that your cat is a perceptive music critic, but I think you misread her signals. Clearly she was reacting vigorously to the challenge of Carter's knotty score but was hopelessly bored by Beethoven's concerto, even as performed by Itzhak Perlman. Is it hard to live with a cat who has musical tastes so completely at odds with your own?

I envy your association with such a musically sophisticated feline. I have two cats, but they are hopelessly oblivious to all kinds of music. This makes them rather agreeable, but I do not have the constant intellectual excitement of living with a great critic who responds directly to difficult contemporary music.

Sometimes Cincinnati Symphony subscribers complain that my program notes are too long. I suppose it *is* hard to read them completely before a concert begins. I usually answer, if the notes are too long, just don't read them all. But it can take several paragraphs to say what should be said. We've tried to deal with this problem at the CSO. Each season we publish all the program notes in advance, in the form of a *Handbook to the Season*. This book is a bonus for season subscribers. They can read the notes at home before coming to the concert. Some subscribers have confessed that they use the handbook to help them decide whether or not to come at all! The notes are reprinted in the regular weekly concert programs as well. We've had great success with the handbooks, and I recommend the idea to all orchestras.

The essays in this book are self-contained and may be read in any order. Duplication of material from one program note to another has been minimized. Therefore, in order to gain a broad understanding of a composer and his work, I suggest that you read all the essays about his music, whether they are primarily analytic, aesthetic, biographical, or historical.

I'm not a historian. Only a few of the historical and biographical insights in this book are original. I've read a number of sources on all the composers covered here, and I have a fairly good idea of which are the more reliable. The bibliography lists some of the books I've found the most useful. It's surprising how much biographies differ, on facts as well as interpretations. I've tried to sort out the truth as well as I can. I hope that these essays reflect the current state of historical knowledge about the composers and their works.

But I am a music theorist and analyst. A large percentage of the aesthetic and analytic ideas presented here *are* my own. As I've already said, I've tried to suggest ways of listening and ways of understanding, without imposing my own biases too rigidly. When accepted ideas are misguided, however, I've proposed my own thoughts in their place.

I'm also a composer. A composer's understanding of traditional music is somewhat different from that of a performer, musicologist, theorist, or aesthetician. I suspect that my more illuminating ideas come from my composer's perspective. I don't mean only ideas on the music, but also ideas on composers' lives, on their practical concerns, and on the processes of composing, copying, rehearsing, revising, publishing, promotion, collecting royalties, dealing with performers, dealing with critics, and dealing with other composers. The role of the composer, his or her problems, values, etc., may have changed a lot as society has evolved, but I'm continually fascinated by how much a composer's life—outer as well as inner—has remained the same.

Several people should be thanked for their help in putting this book together. I greatly appreciate the proofreading help of my wife Norma, my resident non-musician who never lets me get away with obfuscation, tedium, or jargon. C. B. White also did some very perceptive reading and criticizing; my thanks to her. And to Virginia Saya, for editorial assistance. Thanks also to Norma, Zachary, and Stephanie, and to Molly Myerowitz, for helping me come up with a title. My apologies for taking none of their suggestions.

Maribeth Anderson Payne, senior editor at Schirmer Books, encouraged me to do this book, and for that I'm deeply grateful. Her staff, including Michael Sander and Fred Weiler, has been most helpful, as has production editor Sylvia Kanwischer and copy editor Jeanne Ford.

My gratitude also goes to Steven Monder, general manager of the Cincinnati Symphony, for encouragement and for permission to reprint program notes in revised form. I also appreciate the tireless help of the two editors with whom I've worked on the *Cincinnati Symphony Orchestra Handbook to the Season:* Elizabeth Smart Runyon and Miriam DeJongh. And thanks to CSO concertmaster Phillip Ruder, who first suggested—and kept reiterating—the idea of publishing program notes in book form. And to Ann Santen, music director at Cincinnati's WGUC, for providing a radio forum for the discussion of symphonic music and for teaching me about program notes for broadcast.

Special appreciation must go to the two CSO music directors with whom I've worked, Jesús López-Cobos and Michael Gielen, for interesting and varied programming that has always been a joy to write about. I also thank associate conductors David Loebel and Bernard Rubenstein and numerous guest conductors for fine programming. And, finally, a special thanks to Stuart Schloss, for help in legal matters.

Jonathan D. Kramer
Montgomery, Ohio
1 January 1988

Johann Sebastian Bach

Born on 21 March 1685 in Eisenbach, Germany.
Died on 28 July 1750 in Leipzig.

◆　◆　◆

Brandenburg Concerto Number 1 in F Major, B.W.V. 1046
> [Allegro]
> Adagio
> Allegro
> Menuetto. Trio I. Menuetto. Polacca. Menuetto.
> Trio II. Menuetto

Brandenburg Concerto Number 2 in F Major, B.M.V. 1047
> [Allegro]
> Andante
> Allegro assai

Brandenburg Concerto Number 3 in G Major, B.W.V. 1048
> [Allegro]
> Allegro

Brandenburg Concerto Number 4 in G Major, B.W.V. 1049
> Allegro
> Andante
> Presto

Brandenburg Concerto Number 5 in D Major, B.W.V. 1050
> Allegro
> Affettuoso
> Allegro

Brandenburg Concerto Number 6 in B-Flat Major, B.W.V. 1051
> [Allegro moderato]
> Adagio ma non troppo
> Allegro

The Brandenburg *Concertos were composed in 1719 or 1729 and first performed shortly thereafter at the court of Cöthen.*

How compositions acquire their nicknames is often a mystery. No one is sure, for example, how Mozart's *Jupiter* Symphony or Beethoven's *Emperor* Concerto got their names. Several works have been named for people. The Kreutzer of Beethoven's violin sonata was a violinist, while the Waldstein of his piano sonata was a nobleman. Bach's *Goldberg* Variations were commissioned by Count von Kayserling to help cure his insomnia, but the music did not become known as the *Kayserling* Variations. Goldberg was the long-suffering clavierist who played the variations night after night in an attempt to put the Count to sleep. The *Brandenburg* Concertos are likewise named for a person — Christian Ludwig, Margrave of Brandenburg. It is ironic that history has given the *Brandenburg* name to this music, because Christian Ludwig had no use for it. Yet it is only because of these concertos that the Margrave is still remembered.

They were composed while Bach was employed at the court of Prince Leopold of Anhalt-Cöthen. As the Prince belonged to the Reformed Calvinist Church, in which music played only a small role, Bach was not required to compose for the church. His output during his Cöthen years consisted mainly of instrumental works.

In 1718, while in Berlin to order a new harpsichord, the composer met the Margrave of Brandenburg. Christian Ludwig cultivated the acquaintance of many musicians, and he collected scores, particularly of concertos. He heard Bach perform and, later, casually mentioned being interested in a series of concertos. The Margrave promptly forgot about his request and was no doubt surprised two years later to receive a beautifully autographed score of *Six Concertos for Diverse Instruments*. Bach had taken such a long time to write the music because he was probably less than enthusiastic about composing for the tiny court orchestra at Brandenburg.

Bach thought of himself as a humble servant; the era of the artist as independent genius was yet to come. Thus Bach's dedication to Ludwig — translated by an unknown hand into courtly French — seems by today's standards obsequious:

> Two years ago I had the good fortune to perform before Your Royal Highness at Your command, and I noticed then that You showed some pleasure at the small talent for music which Heaven has given me. When I took my leave, Your Royal Highness did me the great honor of ordering me to send Him some pieces of my own composition: therefore, and in accordance with His gracious order, I have taken the liberty of fulfilling my very humble duty to Your Royal Highness with these concertos, which I have scored for several instruments.

> Begging Your Highness most humbly not to judge their imperfection with the rigor of the fine and delicate taste which the

whole world knows Your Highness has for musical pieces; but rather to infer from them in benign consideration the profound respect and the most humble obedience which I try to show Your Highness therewith.

Further, Sir, I beg very humbly that Your Royal Highness will continue to have the goodness to hold me in His good favor and be convinced that I have nothing nearer to my heart than to be employed on occasions more worthy of You and Your service.

I am, Sir, with unparalleled zeal, Your Royal Highness's very humble and very obedient servant, Johann Sebastian Bach.

There is more than a little irony in one of the world's great composers effacing himself in dedicating some of the world's great music to someone who would not even bother to have it performed. Christian Ludwig did not think enough of the concertos to list them in his library catalog, which did include nearly two hundred concertos by other composers. Bach's manuscript lay unnoticed until 1734, when it was sold for a small sum after Ludwig's death.

The instrumentation is different in each concerto, but in every case the ensemble was too large for the Brandenburg musicians. Each piece did nicely fit the resources at Cöthen, however, and this fact suggests that perhaps the concertos were written for use at Leopold's court and only later dedicated to Christian Ludwig.

The *Brandenburg* Concertos are typical of their age, in that they use a variety of instrumental combinations within the *concerto grosso* format. Yet some aspects of the concertos are frankly experimental: the virtuosic treatment of the trumpet (Concerto 2), violin (Concerto 4), and harpsichord (Concerto 5); doing away with the contrast between a small group of soloists and a larger accompanying body of strings (Concerto 3 and first movement of Concerto 1); having soloists and continuo play a middle movement without orchestra (Concertos 2, 5, and 6). The *Brandenburgs* are both a summing up of the baroque *concerto grosso* tradition and a foreshadowing of the instrumental concerto of the upcoming classical era.

Cast in four movements rather than the usual three, the First Concerto is in many ways the most elaborate. Its orchestra includes solo violin, three oboes, and two *corni da caccia* (hunting horns) in addition to the usual strings and continuo (bass line plus harmonic filler, here probably best played by bassoon, low strings, and harpsichord). The solo violin Bach called for is the small, high-pitched *violino piccolo*.

A *concerto grosso* traditionally contrasts the orchestral mass, called the *ripieno*, with the solo group, called the *concertino*. In the

First *Brandenburg* there is considerable variety in the treatment of the *concertino*. The first movement is largely orchestral, with all instruments frequently playing together. There are short solo passages for the horns or some of the oboes, but the large-scale alternation of large and small groups typical of earlier baroque concertos is absent.

The slow second movement features, in turn, an oboe, the solo violin, and the continuo bass, each with an ornate solo. Toward the end the solo violin and oboe play in beautiful counterpoint. Again the approach to the orchestra is imaginative and atypical of the *concerto grosso* tradition — the *concertino* is not treated as a consistent group but rather as a number of soloists, each with its own opportunity to shine. Particularly imaginative is the very end, with its alternation of single chords in the continuo, winds, and strings.

The third movement is orchestral, like the first, except that Bach uses a variety of combinations of solo instruments. It is as if he conceived the movement as a *concerto grosso* for a variable *concertino*.

The fourth movement, a series of dances and interludes, has been called a treatise on baroque instrumentation. Its main section, a minuet, is scored for the full ensemble used in a massive, almost bland orchestration, with the winds constantly doubling the strings. This full sonority is a striking contrast to the delicate interludes with which it alternates: a trio for oboes and bassoons, a *polacca* (stylized dance of Polish origin) for strings featuring the first violins, and a trio for horns and oboes. The trios, each cast for some of the *concertino* instruments, are delectable moments of chamber music in the midst of a fully symphonic orchestral texture.

The Second Concerto has the most varied group of solo instruments in the set — trumpet, flute, oboe, and violin. Because of the spectacular sound of the high trumpet, the Second *Brandenburg* is known primarily for its brass solos. The instrument Bach called for was the small trumpet in F, which in his day had no valves. Thus the trumpeter had to project different notes, including rapid trills, primarily by varying lip pressure. The trumpet part was therefore considerably more challenging in 1718 than it is now. Even today, however, it is an impressive feat to play this virtuosic music.

The solo instruments are introduced at the beginning of the first movement. First an orchestral *tutti*, then the violin; another *tutti* is followed by the oboe, accompanied by the violin; after a third *tutti* the flute is featured, accompanied by the oboe; another *tutti* and we hear the trumpet, accompanied by the flute. By this time we understand that Bach is exploring not only each solo instrument and the solo quartet but also all possible duets within the group of four (actually he saves one duet — trumpet and oboe — for the beginning of the final movement).

The slow movement is scored for solo trio (the trumpet is silent) plus the continuo instruments. The full ensemble returns for the finale. It starts out as an accompanied fugue, with each of the four solo instruments given an opportunity to state the fugue subject. The accompaniment theme, heard at the beginning in the cello and harpsichord, eventually moves to other instruments. Thus the movement is really a double fugue — a fugue with two subjects, always stated simultaneously. Thus, behind the magnificent bravura of this forthright movement lies astonishing compositional subtlety and craft.

In contrast to the Second, the Third Concerto calls for no solo instruments. There are three violin parts, three viola parts, three cello parts, and a continuo (in this case probably string basses). The lack of a small solo group to be contrasted with this full string ensemble sets this work somewhat outside the *concerto grosso* tradition. It has some relationship to the Venetian *canzona*, composed in the late sixteenth century by Giovanni and Andrea Gabrieli, which features alternating choirs of like instruments. The Third *Brandenburg* divides its string ensemble into three groups of three. This three-by-three instrumentation gives a rich contrapuntal texture. At times Bach composes three-part counterpoint *within* each group, and at other times there is counterpoint *between* the three groups.

Another unusual feature of this concerto is its lack of a written-out slow movement. Instead, the two allegros are separated only by two chords. Scholars think that Bach himself improvised at the harpsichord a slow movement that ended with the strings playing these chords. If this speculation is true, it lends further evidence to support the claim that the *Brandenburgs* were really written for Bach himself to perform at Cöthen and not for Christian Ludwig's Brandenburg musicians. Sometimes modern conductors insert a slow movement from another Bach work, while other performers simply separate the two fast movements with the two chords.

The Fourth Concerto, in contrast to the orchestral Third and parts of the First, is a true *concerto grosso*. The *concertino* in this case consists of a solo violin and two *flauti d'echo*. Musicologists are unsure exactly what instrument these "echo flutes" might have been. In no other work did Bach call for them. Historian Thurston Dart believed that this was another name for the flageolet, a small, high-pitched instrument used to teach caged birds to sing tunes. Today the parts are played on recorders or modern flutes.

As in the Second and Fifth *Brandenburgs*, Bach singles out one instrument in the *concertino* for particularly virtuosic treatment. In the Fourth Concerto that instrument is the violin. The resulting texture of one solo violin contrasting with a pair of winds, all accompanied by the strings, is most clearly established in the first movement. Here the two winds nearly always form a pair, often playing the same music at the interval of a third. In the second movement the *concertino* is treated more as a unit, sometimes by itself and sometimes together with the *ripieno*. Even here, however, the two wind instruments are frequently paired. In the fugal finale the pairing of flutes gives rise to *stretti* — one flute enters with the theme before the other has finished it. The violin is again treated as a virtuosic solo.

The Fifth Concerto is also a real *concerto grosso*. The *concertino* consists of flute, violin, and harpsichord, and the *ripieno* is the strings. The concerto goes beyond the traditional form of the *concerto grosso*, however. Normally the *ripieno* is supported by the harpsichord, playing the continuo part. Thus the keyboard instrument usually has an essential yet background role. In the Fifth *Brandenburg*, however, the harpsichord is a member — the most prominent member — of the *concertino*. Thus the harpsichordist fills two roles — continuo player and soloist. Thus the Fifth *Brandenburg* is actually a harpsichord concerto.

Bach took full advantage of the harpsichord as solo instrument. The highpoint of its virtuosity occurs toward the end of the first movement, where it is given an extended unaccompanied cadenza. The middle movement, by contrast, is chamber music. The three soloists play what amounts to a trio sonata, while the *ripieno* remains silent. The final movement is a fugue, introduced at first by the *concertino*, which is then joined by the *ripieni*.

The Sixth Concerto, like the Third, is scored for strings and continuo. The sound of these two string concertos is completely different, however. The Sixth omits violins. Bach probably did not want the more brilliant violin sound to take attention away from the darker, more intimate sound of the solo violas.

Also in contrast to the Third, the Sixth *Brandenburg* is a true *concerto grosso*. The two solo violas, sometimes joined by the cello, are contrasted with the larger accompanying body of strings. The orchestra consists of two violas, two violas da gamba, cello, and continuo (probably harpsichord and string bass). Bach designated that the viola parts be played on violas da braccio — "arm" violas, held up as is the modern viola. The viola da gamba is a "leg" viola, held between the legs, somewhat like the modern cello.

The Sixth Concerto is a *tour de force* of counterpoint. In the first movement we hear all manner of imitation. Imitation occurs when different instruments play the same melody but not at the same time.

The round, canon, and fugue are three examples of imitative forms. But the concerto adheres to none of these strict forms for an entire movement. There are two variables in imitative music that Bach exploits fully: he alters both the pitch interval and the time interval between melodies presented imitatively. At the very beginning, for example, the violas play the same melody just a half beat apart. This procedure involves considerable compositional skill, since not only must the counterpoint sound good, but also the notes on the beat in one viola part must sound well off the beat when they are heard less than a second later in the other viola part. A little later Bach presents a variant of the opening melody in five-part imitation at the space of two full beats: cello, first viola, first viola da gamba, second viola, and second viola da gamba. Throughout the first movement we hear ever more ingenious imitations. This kaleidoscope of counterpoint is endlessly varied and fascinating. Bach helps the listener hear these intricacies by restricting the accompaniment to the simplest of materials — repeated notes articulating slowly changing harmonies.

The second movement, a trio for violas and cello accompanied by the continuo, is also imitative, with relatively long periods of time between entrances of the main theme. The final movement, a gigue, features imitation more as a detail of development than as a pervasive technique. The violas and cello have a few virtuosic passages, in which they are treated, in true *concerto grosso* fashion, like a trio of soloists accompanied by a small orchestra.

Prelude and Fugue in E-Flat Major, *St. Anne* (orchestrated by Arnold Schoenberg)
Ricercar Number 2 in C Minor, from the *Musical Offering* (orchestrated by Anton Webern)

The date of composition of the St. Anne *Prelude and Fugue is unknown; the work was published in 1739. The* Musical Offering *was composed between May and July 1747. Schoenberg's orchestration was begun in May and completed in October 1928; it was first performed in Vienna on 10 November 1929, with Webern conducting. Webern's orchestration was begun in 1934 and completed in 1935; he conducted the first performance in London on 25 April 1935.*

The Prelude in E-Flat and the Fugue in E-Flat are the outer pieces of the third part of the *Clavier-Übung,* a set of exercises for the organ.

These exercises were among the very few works of Bach published during his lifetime. Both the prelude and the fugue are symbolic of the Holy Trinity: each has three flats in the key signature, each has three sections, and each has three main themes. In addition, the fugue uses three versions of its first theme. This triple fugue is one of Bach's monumental works in this form; another of his massive fugues is the six-voice ricercar from the *Musical Offering.*

The *Musical Offering* is an abstract compendium of many of the contrapuntal forms Bach had mastered. It, like the subsequent *Art of the Fugue,* is a summary and a culmination of his compositional techniques. The theme which runs through all movements of the *Offering* was provided by King Frederick II of Prussia, an amateur composer and flutist. Bach had been invited to visit Frederick's court and, while there, was asked to improvise a fugue on this theme. The subtlety and beauty of "Old Bach's" improvisation astounded all who heard it. Upon returning home to Leipzig, the composer decided to make the royal theme the basis of a series of fugues, canons, and a trio sonata. He sent the finished collection to King Frederick with the dedication *Regis Iussu Cantio Et Reliqua Canonica Arte Resoluta* ("By command of the King, the theme and other things developed in canonical art"). The first letters of the words of this Latin dedication spell RICERCAR, which is the name of the fugal form that appears twice in the *Offering.* The ricercar Webern orchestrated is a six-voice fugue of extraordinary complexity (most Bach fugues have three or four voices, although the *St. Anne* Fugue has five voices).

A ricercar is a type of fugue cast usually in 4/2 time. The subject has a regular, slow rhythm. Ricercars often have several separate sections, based on variants of the same theme. Bach used the somewhat obsolete term "ricercar" only in the *Musical Offering,* which contains both the six-voice ricercar Webern used and also a three-voice ricercar which is thought to be the fugue Bach had improvised for King Frederick. There are a few other ricercars, not so named, in Bach's music; one of them is the fugue known as the *St. Anne,* which Arnold Schoenberg arranged for a full modern symphony orchestra in 1928.

Schoenberg frequently orchestrated works by earlier composers. He learned the skill of transcribing as a young man, when he earned his living orchestrating operettas. Later he continued to make arrangements to satisfy his interpretative instincts. He was not a proficient instrumentalist, but by reorchestrating he was able to put his personal stamp on the works of others in much the same way a performer does. Between 1897 and 1921 Schoenberg transcribed music by such composers as Rossini, Schubert, Beethoven, Busoni, Zemlinsky, Johann Strauss, Heinrich Schenker, and several others. In 1922 he began to take the art of transcription seriously, making it more

like recomposition than arranging. In that year he set two choral preludes of Bach for modern orchestra. Then, in 1925, he made an interesting chamber version of Johann Strauss's *Kaiser* Waltz. In 1928 he
turned again to Bach, orchestrating the Prelude and Fugue in E-Flat.
He wrote a Concerto for Cello and Orchestra in 1932, based loosely
on a harpsichord concerto by the eighteenth-century Viennese composer Georg Matthias Monn, and, in 1933, he completed a Concerto
for String Quartet and Orchestra which is a "free arrangement" of a
concerto grosso by Handel. Schoenberg's final such effort was the
1937 orchestration of Brahms' Piano Quartet in G Minor.

Schoenberg's transcriptions were controversial, but the composer defended his actions, citing the frequency with which Bach
himself rearranged music by others, most notably Vivaldi. Schoenberg felt that the primary musical interest in the Bach works lay in
their motivic procedures, which he felt were similar to his own
twelve-tone method of composition. He often jokingly called Bach the
first twelve-tone composer. There actually are passages in the music
of Bach that anticipate that of Schoenberg. Both composers were interested in the powerful unity that results when virtually all melodic
materials in a piece are derived from a single source, whether a Bach
fugue subject or a Schoenberg tone row. Schoenberg wanted to use
the vast resources of the modern orchestra to help make Bach's subtle
command of motivic derivation readily evident to the ear. Thus he
created an orchestration in which contrasting sonorities are used for
different strands in Bach's contrapuntal fabric.

Schoenberg wrote, "Our modern conception of music demands
clarification of the *motivic* procedures in both horizontal [i.e., me-
lodic] and vertical [i.e., harmonic] dimensions. . . . I think that, in
these circumstances, transcription in not a right, but a duty."

Anton Webern, Schoenberg's student and friend, shared his
teacher's love of Bach and enjoyment of reorchestration. Webern
made arrangements of music by Schubert, Johann Strauss, and
Schoenberg that do not depart radically from the spirit of the originals. But he wanted to do a transcription that would express his own
distinctive musical personality. He was attracted to Bach's Ricercar
from the *Musical Offering* because the Leipzig composer had never
indicated on what instruments he wished the music performed. Thus
Webern's work is not an arrangement so much as an orchestration of
an abstract skeleton.

Webern wrote to Schoenberg, "It would interest me extraordinarily to transform this abstraction (which probably has never been
performed except perhaps occasionally by an organist) into an
acoustically possible reality, if I may call it that. I . . . would be very
glad to hear your opinion beforehand or to receive some advice."

Schoenberg replied,

This is no easy task, for these pieces are very little known, and if one wants to make them palatable to the public, it will probably be necessary to help somewhat through the manner of their presentation. Actually, I do not beleve that this can be effected by merely bringing out the [fugal] "entries." ... I can only say what I have done myself in this regard in my Prelude and Fugue: I have, so to speak, modernized the organ, replaced its slow, rarely occurring change of colors, with a more richly varied one that establishes precisely the rendition and the character of the individual passages, and I have given attention to clarity in the web of voices. ... I have taken the position that I am making a *transcription* and that I should be allowed to take for myself at least as much liberty as Bach permitted himself in chorale transcriptions.

Webern took Schoenberg's advice. His liberties consisted of fragmenting Bach's themes in order to emphasize their constituent motives. Rarely does an entire melody remain in one instrumental color. Webern adapted his own technique of orchestration, in which melodic lines are passed around from instrument to instrument, to the otherwise continuous language of Bach. The result is a fascinating amalgamation of two very different styles. The late Arnold Elston (a teacher of the author of these program notes) recalled that he was a student of Webern when the latter was orchestrating the Ricercar: "Pointing to one of those long lines without pauses in Bach's score, Webern maintained that it was necessary to crystallize out the particles of such a line, to bring out the refined succession of impulses and articulations in the rhythmic values and melodic intervals through changes of tone color and fresh attacks by the instruments."

Webern, like Schoenberg, was seeking to popularize and to interpret Bach's music. He wrote to conductor Hermann Scherchen,

I am very glad that you are performing "my" (I think I can call it that) Bach fugue. ... My orchestration tries merely to reveal the motivic coherence. That was not always easy. Beyond that it shows my feeling for the character of the piece: what music it is! The ultimate object of my bold undertaking was to make it available by trying to show in my arrangement my view of the work! Yes, isn't it worthwhile awakening what still sleeps in the seclusion of Bach's own abstract presentation and so for most people remains either completely unknown or at least unapproachable?

In 1954, after the deaths of both Schoenberg and Webern, their two Bach orchestrations shared a concert program. Scherchen conducted them at the Darmstadt Summer School for New Music. The reaction was vehemently mixed, with some listeners opposing the supposed desecration of the music of Bach and others praising the ingenuity of Schoenberg and Webern. Some of the young composers and performers in the audience actually hissed and whistled during the performance, because they thought that Schoenberg and Webern were claiming that *only* by transcription can the music of Bach live today. Battle lines were drawn, and subsequently many musicians took strong stands in favor of or opposed to these transcriptions. The controversy has still not died down completely. Much of the rhetoric has been sensational, but two critics have truly understood the significance of these Bach arrangements:

Schoenberg biographer H. H. Stuckenschmidt wrote of Webern's treatment,

> The pointillistic process, i.e., the division of a melody between several instruments which appear to form the links in a chain, . . . [is an] endeavor to achieve the strongest possible accentuation [that] allows the motives to pass from one instrument to another, so that the aesthetic impression of a 'plane' of color is produced, in the same way that the neo-impressionistic painters Paul Signac and Georges Seurat used a large number of dots in close proximity. But with Webern there is not so much an impressionistic urge for expression behind this as a strong will to construct and dissect.

Webern biographer Walter Kolneder wrote that the

> sense of "dissection" is perhaps one of the chief characteristics of the development of Webern's style. . . . In the Bach arrangement we are confronted with an "orchestrated analysis" or an "analytical orchestration." We possess a sufficient number of fugues or fugal expositions orchestrated by Bach himself and know his own method of doing this; Webern naturally knew this perfectly well. But if he still let himself in for such a "bold undertaking," he did it with creative mastery and transformed the Bach work into one of his own. The phrase "my Bach Fugue" has a deeper meaning here: in the arrangement Webern has almost created an original work. Anyone who listens to the Ricercar as a work of Bach's is bound to be disappointed. In Bach the motives are the foundation stones of the long line: they fulfill their function in just being there without obtruding. Webern

teaches analysis with the searchlight of tone-color. So the motives acquire a life of their own at the expense of the line.

Thus, neither orchestral transcription sounds much like Bach. Hearing these works is instructive; we learn that musical style resides as much in the use of instruments as in the construction of melodies, harmonies, and rhythms. The two arrangements are very different from each other, reflecting the contrasting idioms of Schoenberg and Webern. Schoenberg's orchestration is rich, varied, and massive, while that of Webern is sparse and concentrated. To orchestrate a five-voice fugue Schoenberg uses an enormous ensemble, with winds and brass in fours, including such extravagances as *two* contrabassoons, *two* piccolos, *two* English horns, *two* bass clarinets, *four* trumpets, *four* trombones, crash cymbals, glockenspiel, harp, and string basses sometimes divided into four groups and utilizing an extended low range. Webern, working with a six-voice fugue, is content with strings plus one of each wind: flute, oboe, English horn, clarinet, bass clarinet, bassoon, horn, trumpet, and trombone. Schoenberg's work is full of imaginative combinations, while Webern uses each instrument more as an entity than as a member of a colorful sonority. The result is that Schoenberg's orchestration sounds like a sumptuous late-nineteenth-century interpretation of Bach, while Webern's is more a kaleidoscopic twentieth-century view of the high baroque. Both versions are fascinating, because of their combination of chronologically separated historical eras.

Concerto in A Minor for Violin and String Orchestra, B.M.V. 1041

      [Allegro]
      Andante
      Allegro assai

Concerto in E Major for Violin and String Orchestra, B.W.V. 1042

      Allegro
      Adagio
      Allegro assai

Concerto in D Minor for Two Violins and String Orchestra, B.M.V. 1043

      Vivace
      Largo ma non tanto
      Allegro

The Violin Concertos were composed at Cöthen, sometime between 1717 and 1723.

The concerto, an instrumental form that first appeared in the last two decades of the seventeenth century, soon became the baroque era's most important orchestral genre. There were three types of concertos in the late baroque: (1) the orchestral concerto, a relatively simple work for a unified body of instruments; (2) the *concerto grosso*, in which a group of three or four solo instruments (the *concertino*) alternated with a larger string orchestra (the *ripieno*); and (3) the solo concerto, in which one instrument, usually a violin, was featured in opposition to a larger body of strings. The solo concerto was destined to have a long and important history, culminating in the romantic concertos of the nineteenth century. During the baroque era, however, the *concerto grosso* and the solo concerto shared equal importance, while the orchestral concerto was of considerably less prominence.

The first important concerto composers were Italians, notably Giuseppe Torelli (1658–1709) and, following his model, Antonio Vivaldi (1678–1741). Bach understood the importance of the Italians in developing the *concerto grosso* and the solo concerto. Since he lived in the days before Xerox machines and copyright protection, he studied Vivaldi's concertos by copying out a number of them by hand, usually transcribing them in the process for a new medium. Bach reworked 16 Vivaldi violin concertos for harpsichord and orchestra and three more for organ and orchestra, and he recast Vivaldi's Concerto for Four Violins and Orchestra as a work for four harpsichords with strings. In each case he retained Vivaldi's structure and themes, but he strengthened the counterpoint, added bass motion, added other contrapuntal lines, translated violin figures into keyboard effects, and enriched the harmony.

Bach studied the typical three-movement, fast-slow-fast structure of Vivaldi's concertos. The first of these movements is often a rondo-like structure, in which large *tutti* passages alternate with solo interludes, sometimes based on materials from the *tutti* passages. The second movements frequently use ostinatos in the bass: a simple melodic pattern is repeated again and again. Finales tend to adhere to the rondo format of the opening movements. Bach saw great potential in the rondo idea, which he utilized in a number of his own concertos, and he used the ostinato idea for the slow movements of his only two extant violin concertos.

These two concertos, plus the one for two violins and orchestra, are surely not the only violin concertos Bach composed. During the six years he worked at the court of Prince Leopold of Anhalt-Cöthen, an accomplished amateur violinist, he was expected to supply music for weekly concerts. Years later he again used much of this same instrumental music when he was director of the Collegium Musicum in Leipzig. Seven harpsichord concertos from the Leipzig period are transcriptions of string works from the Cöthen years. Since Bach had had experience rewriting Vivaldi string concertos for keyboard and orchestra, he had no trouble recasting his own violin concertos as harpsichord concertos. Thus the Violin Concerto in A Minor became the Harpsichord Concerto in G Minor, the Violin Concerto in E turned up as the Harpsichord Concerto in D, and the Two-Violin Concerto in D Minor was tranformed into the Two-Harpsichord Concerto in C Minor. The reason for the changes in key is that the top harpsichord note was one step lower than the note accepted at the time as the violin's upper limit. Bach's typical method was to assign the original violin solo to the keyboard player's right hand, which might be given additional material as well, while the left hand played (and possibly elaborated) the bass line. It is easy to imagine the violin origins of many of the other harpsichord concertos of Bach's Leipzig period, and several lost violin concertos have been reconstructed from these harpsichord versions. While Bach's transcriptions are quite skillful, the original versions are generally preferable and more frequently played today.

The existence of two versions of the E Major Concerto does tell us one interesting thing. The solo violin has a brief adagio cadenza written out just before the recapitulation in the first movement. This passage should perhaps be played as written, but it may have been intended as a suggestion to improvise a more elaborate solo, using Bach's two measures as a starting point. But how are we to know? Looking at the harpsichord version, we discover there is, in fact, a more elaborate cadenza written in at this place.

The first movement of the A Minor Concerto is particularly rich in counterpoint. Not only do the different instruments in the string orchestra have quite independent melodic lines, but also, in typical Bach fashion, each of those melodies is actually made up of several interlaced lines. Consider, for example, the solo violin entrance. There are, in effect, two tunes played by the one instrument. One melody is represented by a quick three-note turn, heard again and again. Between these repetitions, a higher line presents a rising profile.

Although cast in the presumably sunnier key of C major, the andante is surprisingly poignant. The bass line, which is heard many times throughout the movement, revolves around a single note, repeated and ornamented. When the upper instruments' harmonies clash with that note, as they invariably do, the result can be pungent dissonance. Since the bass line is both restricted and pervasive, Bach provides variety by modulating frequently to new keys. Thus this ostensibly major-mode movement spends considerable time in minor keys: D minor, A minor, and C minor appear in succession between the opening and closing sections in C major.

The finale is a gigue, which is a dance cast in 9/8 time. This meter is particularly challenging for the composer, since each measure contains three beats subdivided in threes. A 3×3 metric scheme can be unsettling, since two-groupings tend to sound more natural than three-groupings. Bach meets this challenge ingeniously. He utilizes a mixture of two- and three-groupings, but of measures rather than of beats. Another factor that offsets this movement's "three-ness" is the occasional appearance of *four* successive beats repeating one note (B). All this adds up to a movement of considerable subtlety and vitality. Also of interest is the virtuosic violin figuration, particularly just before the final statement of the main theme. The solo instrument plays fast arpeggios that revolve around the special sound of the open E string.

Beneath its ebullience, the first movement of the E Major Concerto is a masterpiece of subtle construction. Notice, for example, how the fanfare-like triad of the first measure and the answering motive of the second measure combine (triad in the solo violin, motive in the orchestral violins) at the first solo entrance. There is even a hint of imitation here, as the continuo instruments echo the triad figure a half measure later. Notice also how these two opening figures pervade the movement and are elaborated in ever greater virtuosity.

Also impressive is the way the soulful second movement is pervaded by the figure initially heard in the bass. This line is repeated several times (as in the corresponding movement of the A Minor Concerto), although sometimes transposed and sometimes omitted, so that the movement is not quite a strict chaconne.

The rondo structure that Bach learned from Vivaldi is most evident in the finale (although also present to some degree in the opening movement). Throughout, a 16-measure *tutti* alternates with 16-measure solo interludes, which increase in ornamentation and virtuosity throughout. The final solo passage is twice the length of its predecessors, and the figuration is so rapid that we feel nothing more elaborate can be done. And thus the movement closes, with one final statement of the *tutti* passage.

With the addition of a second soloist, the D Minor Concerto becomes considerably more contrapuntal than its cousins. The opening, prior to the appearance of the solo lines, is elaborately fugal. When the two violins enter, they at first seem to begin a second fugue. The interweaving of melodic lines throughout the movement is intricate and ingenious.

The slow movement also suggests fugue. Its long, arching, intertwining lines in the two violins, with an orchestral accompaniment that remains in the background throughout, is the essence of lyricism. This movement is one of Bach's best known creations.

The vigorous finale is nearly as polyphonic as the first movement. The violins imitate one another, sometimes at the close interval of one beat. Elsewhere the imitation is more leisurely. Of particular interest are the passages where the solo violins, playing evenly repeated chords, accompany the orchestra.

◆   ◆   ◆

Suites for Orchestra

Suite Number 1 in C Major, B.W.V. 1066
Ouverture
Courante
Gavotte
Forlane
Menuet
Bourrée
Passepied

Suite Number 2 in B Minor, B.W.V. 1067
Ouverture
Rondeau
Sarabande
Bourrée
Polonaise
Menuet
Badinerie

Suite Number 3 in D Major, B.W.V. 1068
Ouverture
Air
Gavotte
Bourrée
Gigue

Suite Number 4 in D Major, B.W.V. 1069
Ouverture
Bourrée
Gavotte
Menuet
Réjouissance

Little is known about the origins or early performances of the orchestral suites, which were probably composed before 1725.

The term "suite," which first appeared in 1557, originally referred to a set of dances known as *branles*. By the late seventeenth century, the term had come to mean a group of varied dances, all in the same key, preceded by a prelude. Such pieces were at one time used to accompany social dancing at court balls, but the dances found in a typical suite soon went out of fashion. Late-baroque suites therefore consist of stylized dance movements meant for listening entertainment. Musicologists have tried to find a unifying principle common to all baroque suites, but the search has been fruitless. There is no universally shared characteristic. Even once a fairly standard sequence of dances (allemande, courante, sarabande, gigue) emerged, there were still many exceptions: added dances, movements omitted, extra movements that were not dances, changed order, etc. When the baroque suite became a concert form, composers' imaginations were no longer restricted by social convention. As baroque ideals gave way to classical-period aesthetics, the suite was gradually replaced by the sonata and the symphony. The minuet remained as the one link between the suite and the symphony.

The culmination of the baroque suite tradition lies in the music of J. S. Bach, who composed at least 45 such works. His solo violin and solo cello suites and his keyboard suites — *English* Suites, *French* Suites, and Partitas — are magnificently sophisticated examples of concert dances. Often the textural complexity is so great that it is difficult for a performer to project the underlying rhythmic patterns of the dance. Bach also composed several suites for orchestra, of which only four have survived. Each of these orchestral suites is divided into two parts. The first is a long overture and the second is a set of dance movements and other short pieces. The orchestral suites tend to be less complex than the solo and keyboard pieces, which implies that they were probably intended as entertainment music. Their often brilliant orchestration would seem to support this notion.

Little is known about the origins of the orchestral suites. Their different instrumentation implies that they were not composed for the same occasion or the same ensemble. It has been suggested that Suite Number 1, because it is in certain technical ways less advanced than the others, was composed earlier. It was probably conceived late in Bach's Cöthen period (1717–23) or early in his Leipzig years (1723–50).

When Bach entered the service of Prince Leopold of Anhalt-Cöthen, he was for the first time in his life expected to devote the major portion of his compositional efforts to secular music. Thus much of his chamber, keyboard, and orchestral music dates from this period. Prince Leopold, an accomplished violinist, viola da gambist, and harpsichordist, often held concerts for which Bach supplied the music. Several of the orchestral suites that have been lost were written for such occasions. After a few years the Prince married a woman who did not care for music, and his concert activites were diminished. Bach therefore took a new position at Leipzig, where he was expected to compose both sacred and secular music. The remaining orchestral suites date from the Leipzig period, when he was directing a series of weekly concerts with the Collegium Musicum. Bach worked with this ensemble in 1730–37 and 1739–44.

It has been suggested that, like Number 1, Suite Number 4 may have been composed between 1717 and 1723. The first version was scored for a small orchestra, such as that at Cöthen. The orchestra at Leipzig was larger than that at Cöthen. Thus Bach added not only voices but also three trumpets and timpani to the overture from Suite 4 when, in 1725, he used it as the introductory chorus of his *Christmas* Cantata (Number 110). The final version of the suite, with trumpets and drums in all movements except the minuet, was prepared in Leipzig about 1729. This suite is the most brilliant of the set, with three oboes, bassoon, strings, and continuo joining the brass.

Since Suite 3 is similar to the final version of Suite 4, some scholars feel that it too was composed in Leipzig. The use of three trumpets in the orchestra would seem to support this theory, since the ensemble at Cöthen had but two trumpeters.

The fact that Bach used the overture from Suite 4 as the introductory chorus of a cantata lends circumstantial evidence to the claim that he composed more than the four orchestral suites we know today. Other cantatas, nobably Numbers 61, 97, and 119, begin with choruses based on the model of the French overture, which was invariably (as far as we know) the form of the first movements of the orchestral suites. Cantata 61 was written too early (1714) to have had its origins in an orchestral suite, but what of the other two? Perhaps in Cantatas 97 and 119 we have all that remains of two additional Bach suites for orchestra. (There is a Suite in G Minor for orchestra that was once thought to be the work of Bach, but recent research has established it as a composition of a younger composer — possibly one of his sons — that Bach had copied for performance at Leipzig.)

The first movement of each of the suites is a French overture, which is an elaborate movement with a slow introduction featuring dotted rhythms. The allegro is fugal, and the introduction returns at the end.

The scoring of the First Suite recalls the *concerto grosso* format. A small group of instruments, in this case two oboes and bassoon, is treated like three soloists, accompanied by the larger force of strings plus continuo. The winds form the solo group in the fugal section of the overture and in the middle sections of the gavotte and bourrée.

The series of dances following the overture is more extensive than in most other Bach suites (except the orchestral Suite in B Minor). These movements are the courante (running dance in 3/4 or 3/2 time), gavotte (French court dance in 2/4 or 2/2 time, beginning on the second half of the measure), forlane (Venetian dance in 6/4 time, resembling a gigue, popular with opera baroque composers), minuet (stately French court dance in 3/4 time), bourrée (stately French court dance, similar to a gavotte, in 4/4, 4/2, 2/2, or 2/4 time, beginning with an upbeat), and passepied (lively Breton dance in 3/4 time).

Most of the dances in the C Major Suite, other than the courante and forlane, are "doubles." This means that they are cast in the time-honored ABA form. In the gavotte, for example, a strong dance is played first, followed by a tender gavotte, after which the strong gavotte is repeated. Traditionally the gentler middle sections were played by only three instruments and hence were called "trios." This name remained long after the custom of casting central dance sections for three players had disappeared. Thus, even today we find the middle parts of symphonic minuets or scherzos called trios, whatever their instrumentation. In Bach's Suite 1, the bourrée has a real trio performed by the three wind instruments. The trio of the passepied is played by the full complement of instruments but, in the strict trio tradition, consists of only three separate contrapuntal parts — one played by oboes, one by violins and violas, and one by bassoon and other continuo instruments. The middle section of the gavotte is a trio (for two oboes and continuo) which is repeatedly interrupted by a soft fanfare-like figure in strings. The central section of the minuet is not, strictly speaking, a trio; it is cast in four voices, played by the strings and continuo.

Suite Number 2 is a solo-instrument concerto for flute and string orchestra. The dance movements which follow the overture comprise a rondeau (which is, in effect, a gavotte in rondo form), sarabande (a stately dance in 3/4 time), bourrée, polonaise (a proud, striding dance of Polish origins, popular in the eighteenth century but rarely found in suites), minuet, and badinerie (a term meaning "frivolity"; the movement is a lively finale that is not, strictly speaking, a dance).

The Second Suite abounds with clever contrapuntal and other devices. The fast middle section of the overture, for example, is a fugue. The rondeau is characterized by an intriguing metric ambiguity: the movement begins seemingly on the strong first beat of the 2/2 measure, whereas in fact the opening is written on the weak second beat. In the course of the movement, the melody is eventually shifted so that the heard meter agrees with the written barlines. The sarabande is a strict canon: the bass line imitates the melody (flute and first violins) at the lower fifth after one measure. There are hints of imitation in the bourrée. The second part of the polonaise is a "double," in which the bass line is identical to the melody (flute and first violins) of the first part, which is subsequently repeated. During this double, the flute plays virtuosic scales and arpeggios while the upper strings remain silent. The badinerie utilizes the same metric ambiguity as the rondeau, with the resolution postponed until the last possible moment.

Suite Number 3 begins with the typical French overture, followed by an air. It is a well-known piece, since it was rewritten for violin and piano in 1871 by one A. Wilhelmj, who called it *Air on the G String*. In this bastardized form the movement has been played quite often as an encore piece in violin recitals.

The dances start with the third movement, a gavotte. The brilliance of the trumpets make this stately movement quite regal. The bourrée is a fast and lively dance in 6/8 time, as is the final gigue.

When Bach used the overture of Suite Number 4 as the basis of the initial chorus of Cantata 110, he used a text from Psalm 126: "Then was our mouth filled with laughter and our tongue with singing." It is not difficult to hear ripples of laughter in the running 9/8 figuration of the fugal middle section. The slow outer sections of the suite's overture became the instrumental prelude and postlude of the cantata's opening movement.

The series of stylized dances following the overture includes a gavotte, bourrée, and minuet. The work closes with a non-dance movement called *Réjouissance* ("Rejoicing").

Toccata and Fugue in D Minor (orchestrated by Leopold Stokowski)

Bach probably composed the Toccata and Fugue sometime before 1708. Stokowski made his orchestration in the mid 1920s.

Leopold Stokowski had an extraordinarily long career as a conductor. His orchestral debut took place in 1909, and he was still actively conducting at the time of his death at the age of 95, in 1977. He first achieved major stature as conductor of the Cincinnati Symphony Orchestra. He used his Cincinnati post as a stepping stone to the Philadelphia Orchestra, which he led with great flair and distinction for 29 years.

Frequently during his tenure in Philadelphia, Stokowski made and performed orchestral transcriptions of works by various composers, notably Bach. The best known of these transcriptions is of Bach's Toccata and Fugue in D Minor, originally for organ. Stokowski had often played this work during his early years as an organist. It was one of his first orchestral recordings with the Philadelphia Orchestra — it appeared on disc in 1927. The conductor-orchestrator wrote, "The Toccata and Fugue in D Minor is like a vast upheaval of Nature. It gives the impression of great white thunderclouds — like those that float often over the valley of the Seine — or the towering majesty of the Himalayas. The Fugue is set in the frame of the Toccata, which comes before and after. This work is one of Bach's supreme inspirations — the final cadence is like massive Doric columns of white marble."

As a preface to the Toccata and Fugue orchestration, Stokowski wrote:

Of all the music of Bach, this Toccata and Fugue is among the freest in form and expression. Bach was in the habit of improvising on the organ and harpsichord, and this Toccata probably began as an improvisation in the church of St. Thomas in Leipzig [the date of composition makes this statement most likely false]. In this lengthy, narrow, high church the thundering harmonies must have echoed long and tempestuously, for this music has a power and majesty that is cosmic. Its main characteristics are immense freedom of rhythm and plasticity of melodic outline. In the sequence of harmonies it is bold and path-breaking. Its tonal architecture is irregular and asymetric. Of all the creations of Bach, this is one of the most original. Its inpiration flows unendingly. In spirit it is universal, so that it will always be contemporary and have a direct message for all men.

On another occasion Stokowski wrote, "If Bach were alive today, he would undoubtedly write glorious music for the highly evolved modern orchestra — he would find no limits to his expression but would use every resource of the orchestra today as he used every resource of the organ in his own time."

The Toccata and Fugue is a particularly appropriate work for the modern orchestra. Its massive sonorities, brilliant figuration suggestive of improvisation, and overt emotional power make it seem to cry out for symphonic treatment. In addition, its figures that alternate rapidly between notes in two or three different registers suggest string writing more than organ music.

Stokowski's Bach transcriptions have always been controversial. Intellectual purists, on the one hand, have objected to the alleged desecration of Bach's masterpeces. On the other hand, some have doubted whether Stokowski himself ever made the orchestrations. He always maintained a very active conducting schedule, and it is hard to imagine him taking the time to write out painstakingly each entire orchestral score.

A clarinetist in the Philadelphia Orchestra, Lucien Cailliet, claimed to have made some of the Bach-Stokowski arrangements: "I orchestrated Bach's D-Minor Toccata and Fugue ... in connection with my job as orchestrator for the Philadelphia Orchestra. . . . Of course, we had some discussions before as, after all, he was an organist and a famous musician. . . . I must confide in you that as the situation developed, Stokowski asked me from the beginning not to mention or speak about it and keep the situation *entre nous* and adding, 'The people would not understand.' That is how the name of Stokowski appeared on the programs as orchestrator." The crucial phrase is "we had some discussions before." In what detail did Stokowski instruct Cailliet as to which instruments were to play what music? Several other musicians also have claimed to have "helped" Stokowski with his orchestral arrangements, working from detailed markings on original keyboard scores. The conductor, however, steadfastly maintained that he had done all of the orchestrations himself.

Even if these transcriptions horrify purists, and even if they are not wholly the work of Stokowski, they must be credited with having brought the music of Bach before a far larger audience than normally goes to organ, choral, and baroque concerts. Surely the biggest audience Bach has ever had was for the Toccata and Fugue in D Minor, as transcribed by Leopold Stokowski and performed by him and the Philadelphia Orchestra in Walt Disney's 1940 film *Fantasia*. Musical snobs may have felt it appropriate that Stokowski shakes hands with Mickey Mouse in this movie, but there is no denying the impact the film has had. Many people attend their first concert in order to hear more of the kind of music they first encounter in *Fantasia*. The animation accompanying the Toccata and Fugue is arguably the most imaginative in the movie, since its abstract lines (which become moving violin bows) beautifully mirror the character of the music. *Fantasia* has been re-released again and again, so that it still serves as an important introduction to symphonic music for many people.

The controversies surrounding Stokowski's transcriptions have been analyzed by composer-critic Eric Salzman:

> So much ink has been spilled and so much spleen vented over the issue of the Stokowski transcriptions that it is worthwhile to recall a few facts: Stokowski was a great interpreter of Bach and a real pioneer in introducing this music not only to orchestra programs but also to records. In effect, he helped bring a whole generation to Bach, and his arrangements, performances, and recordings were rapturously received even (or especially) by the cognoscenti in a day when Mozart was still considered a cute little fellow in a funny wig. And let us not forget that transcription was considered (as it still should be) a fine branch of the musical art. Schoenberg transcribed Bach, and so did Webern and Stravinsky. So, for that matter, did Bach — who also transcribed the music of his contemporaries so relentlessly that scholars are still arguing over who did what and to whom.

Comparable "transcriptions" are commonplace in the theater. If a contemporary theater group can, for example, perform Shakespeare's *Julius Caesar* in a setting suggestive of a Third World country at war in the mid-twentieth century, why cannot a modern symphony orchestra perform Bach's organ works?

Samuel Barber

Born on 9 March 1910 in West Chester, Pennsylvania.
Died in New York on 23 January 1981.

Adagio for Strings, Opus 11

The Adagio for Strings was composed in 1936 as the slow movement of a string quartet. The first performance of the string orchestra version took place in 1938 by the New York Philharmonic, conducted by Arturo Toscanini.

Samuel Barber was a child prodigy, having started to play the piano at six and to compose at seven. He was 14 when he enrolled at the Curtis Institute of Music in Philadelphia.

His career was so successful that Barber avoided the necessity that plagues almost all contemporary composers — having to make a living at something other than composing. Barber was a composition teacher only sporadically, except in 1939–42, when he returned to Curtis as a faculty member. This fact might account for there being relatively few younger composers who directly imitated his style. In contrast to his approximate contemporaries Walter Piston, Roger Sessions, and Milton Babbitt, he did not teach and thus did not imprint his musical personality on a new generation of composers.

Barber was a traditionalist who never abandoned tonality. He, like most major composers, maintained a healthy interest in all kinds of music. He studied scores by such stylistically divergent composers as Boulez, Schoenberg, and Webern, but he always remained stubbornly resistant to influences foreign to his own aesthetic. He pursued his own lyricism with integrity, unconcerned with whether his music happened to be in favor or out of favor at the moment. Barber was sometimes ridiculed by less-than-generous fellow composers, whose more austere music failed to gain the wide acceptance Barber's enjoyed. Barber was never swayed by petty jealousies. In 1971 he stated, "I write what I feel. I'm not a self-conscious composer. . . . It is said that I have no style at all, but that doesn't matter. I just go on doing, as they say, my thing. I believe this takes a certain courage." Ironically, now that Barber is dead many composers, including some of the very ones who scorned his neo-romanticism, are returning to romantic styles that are really quite similar to Barber's.

The Adagio for Strings, the composer's most popular work, is a prime example of his neo-romanticism. It works its way from a sub-dued beginning inexorably to a climax of great intensity, after which it quietly returns to the opening. Despite the work's romantic spirit, and despite the intense chromaticism at and just after the climax, the piece is remarkably diatonic for a composition written in 1936. Actually, Barber uses — loosely and in his own unique style — one of the medieval church modes (the phrygian). The neo-romanticism of this work, built on the simplest and most direct of materials, lends it a unique quality: contemporary in spirit, it nonetheless evokes both nineteenth-century romanticism and fifteenth-century modality.

The structure of the Adagio is straightforward. It consists of a series of phrases, each of which begins slowly (usually with one voice of the string choir entering on a note, followed by the remaining in-struments filling out the chord) and evolves into a lyrical, stepwise melody in even note values. What makes the piece build in intensity, despite the consistency of its phrase structure, are the subtle differ-ences between successive phrases.

When we hear the powerful climax, we may find it hard to imag-ine the piece as originally conceived for only four instruments. It was first composed as the middle movement of a string quartet. Barber changed little in transcribing it for string orchestra, a medium better able to sustain the Adagio's long lines and rich harmonies. In the late 1960s the composer made a third version of the piece, for chorus, using the traditional *Agnus Dei* text. The string orchestra version has been used effectively as film music, most recently in *Platoon*.

The Adagio is a beautiful work, well deserving of its position as one of the most popular of contemporary American compositions. Had Barber written nothing else, this piece would have guaranteed his importance in American music.

Béla Bartók

Born in Nagy-szentmiklos, Hungary, on 25 March 1881.
Died in New York on 26 September 1945.

Concerto for Orchestra
  Andante non troppo. Allegro vivace
  Giuoco delle coppie: Allegretto scherzando
  Elegia: Andante non troppo
  Intermezzo interrotto: Allegretto
  Finale: Presto

The Concerto for Orchestra was composed at Saranac Lake, New York, between 15 August and 8 October 1943. Serge Koussevitzky conducted the first performance with the Boston Symphony Orchestra on 1 December 1944.

Bartók's American years (1940–45) were not happy. He was continually plagued by problems of health and finances. Forced by the war to leave their native Hungary, Bartók and his wife Ditta arrived in New York in October 1940. They had to find a place to live and a means of support. The former problem was particularly difficult, because they needed an apartment large enough for both their pianos and quiet enough for Bartók to compose in peace — difficult requirements for a low-rent New York apartment!

It was hard for the Bartóks to adjust to the very different lifestyle in New York. They once spent three hours in subways, "traveling hither and thither in the earth; finally, our time waning and our mission incomplete, we shamefacedly slunk home — of course, entirely underground." They also suffered a typical travelers' nightmare: their luggage arrived in New York two months after they did.

The composer had hoped to earn money by giving duo-piano concerts with Ditta. Friends had been able to arrange some appearances, but reviews were often unfavorable, as critics had a difficult time with Bartók's unusual music. As a result their engagements for the following season were disappointingly meager — only one concerto performance, three two-piano recitals, and four lecture-recitals.

Soon after his arrival in New York, Bartók was awarded an honorary doctorate from Columbia University. This led, in turn, to his being hired part-time at that college to do research with a collection of recorded Serbo-Croatian folk music. The composer greatly appreciated this position, since it meant a steady, if small, income and because he had been active as a folklorist in Hungary. His grant paid $3000 a year. He was concerned because there was no guarantee that the grant would continue, and in fact his contract had to be renewed every six months. The university did eventually run out of money, but some of Bartók's friends quietly raised the funds among themselves to continue his salary. As Bartók was a fiercely proud man who would surely have refused the money had he known where it came from, his friends kept their charity a closely guarded secret. A brief lectureship at Harvard helped augment this income.

Bartók's health began to fail. He was weak and often feverish. He complained of pains in his shoulders and legs, and his weight dropped to 87 pounds. He collapsed while giving a lecture at Harvard. The diagnosis was grim. He had leukemia. ASCAP (American Society of Composers, Authors, and Publishers), the performing rights organization, assumed all costs of his medical care. The composer's spirits were low. He was suffering from a debilitating disease, he was across the ocean from his homeland and from the way of life he knew, the war weighed heavily on him, he was unable to perform, he had little income, and he could not compose. Although he had been in the United States for three years, he had written nothing.

Once again friends came secretly to his aid. His compatriots Joseph Szigeti, the violinist, and Fritz Reiner, the conductor, approached Serge Koussevitzky, music director of the Boston Symphony Orchestra. They worked out the details for a commission through the Koussevitzky Foundation. Koussevitzky visited Bartók in his hospital room and offered him a check for $500 as half payment for a work for orchestra. The composer was reluctant to accept. He felt that his composing days were behind him and that he could never regain sufficient strength to fulfill the commission. But he became excited about writing for a fine orchestra, and he agreed to try.

The stimulus of the commission caused his health to improve, and he was able to complete the Concerto for Orchestra the following summer. The symptoms of his illness came and went. He was able to obtain grudging permission from his doctor to travel to Boston for the rehearsals and performance of the concerto. Bartók thought the performance was excellent, and Koussevitzky felt that the concerto was the finest work to have been written by anyone in the past quarter century. The critics, for once, were enthusiastic, and the public hailed the work. As a result of this success, Bartók's fortunes began to improve.

Although previously all but neglected as a composer in this country, he suddenly found himself besieged with commissions. He was asked to write a seventh string quartet, a concerto for two pianos, and a viola concerto. His music began to be played more widely, and he began to receive royalty income. The Concerto for Orchestra rapidly entered the standard repertoire; just four years after its premiere, Bartók's orchestral music was more played in this country than that of Berlioz, Liszt, Dvořák, Mahler, or Schubert. But Bartók did not live to see this success. He died ten months after the first performance of the concerto. He had been unable to fulfill many of the new commissions, but, his confidence bolstered by the success of the Concerto for Orchestra, he did compose the Third Piano Concerto and most of the Viola Concerto.

It was gratifying for Bartók to achieve recognition and respect, however belatedly. It is tragic that he could not compose more of the music he had planned. When he died, he was mourned throughout the musical world. But it is a chilling fact that one of the few undisputedly great modern composers died in near poverty and came close to dying unknown in the middle of one of the largest cultural centers of the "enlightened" mid-twentieth century.

Bartók provided the following program note for the first performance of the Concerto for Orchestra:

> The general mood of the work represents, apart from the jesting second movement, a gradual transition from the sternness of the first movement and the lugubrious death song of the third to the life assertion of the last one. . . . The title of this symphony-like orchestral work is explained by its tendency to treat single orchestral instruments in a *concertante* or soloistic manner. The "virtuoso" treatment appears, for instance, in the fugato sections of the development of the first movement (brass instruments), or in the *perpetuum mobile*-like passage of the principal theme in the last movement (strings), and especially in the second movement, in which pairs of instruments consecutively appear with brilliant passages.

Bartók utilizes most of the techniques that he had developed in earlier compositions, although he applies them to less pungent materials, so that the concerto is more expansive, less dissonant, and possibly more approachable than many of its predecessors. We hear the careful derivation of most of the music from one common source, the interval of the fourth (heard most obviously at the beginning of the first and third movements). We hear a concerto cast in Bartók's typical arch form: substantial outer movements flank two scherzos, with the slow movement as keystone. We find the usual fugatos (particularly in the outer movements), motivic development, and inversions (notice how the motive that starts the first movement's allegro is immediately repeated upside-down).

The second movement is called "Game of Pairs." Pairs of instruments play in turn, each time locked together at a different interval. For example, after the drum introduction the bassoons enter, playing in sixths. They are answered by a pair of oboes playing in thirds. Next come the clarinets in sevenths, then the flutes in fifths, and finally the muted trumpets in seconds. After a chorale-like middle section, the pairs begin to be combined.

The folklike melodies of the third movement, "Elegia," "constitute the core of the movement, which is framed by a misty texture of rudimentary motives," according to the composer.

The fourth movement, "Interrupted Intermezzo," uses as its second theme the song "Hungary, Gracious and Beautiful," played by the violas. This melody is interrupted by a parody of Shostakovich's *Leningrad* Symphony. Bartók heard this symphony broadcast while he was composing the concerto, and he thought the march passage in the first movement (in which the same theme is repeated again and again in an inexorable evocation of war) ludicrous. His parody consists of a quotation of the second part of Shostakovich's march tune in the clarinet, followed by purposefully vulgar comments in the trumpets (trills) and trombones (*glissandi*). Bartók then repeats the parody, this time with the violins playing the march theme, accompanied brightly by the winds, with the cymbal added to the commentary. After this interruption, the Hungarian song and then the main theme return.

The finale is based on a "perpetual motion" figure in the violins and on Hungarian dance rhythms. It contains an elaborate fugue.

Concerto Number 1 for Piano and Orchestra
Allegro moderato. Allegro
Andante —
Allegro molto

Bartók composed the First Piano Concerto between August and November 1926. He continued to make changes and revisions until the second publication of the score, in January 1929. The composer was soloist and Wilhelm Furtwängler was conductor at the first performance on 1 July 1927 in Frankfurt at the annual festival of the International Society for Contemporary Music.

Bartók's four works for piano and orchestra span his creative lifetime. The Rhapsody is his Opus 1; the First Concerto dates from 1926, a time when he was exploring relentlessly driving rhythms; the Second

Concerto comes from his complex middle period, when he was at the height of his powers; the lyric Third Concerto is his last completed work. For a long time the First Concerto was the least played of these four compositions. Bartók composed it for his own use on concert tours, but it was too difficult for other pianists. When the Second Concerto took its place in the composer's repertory, performances of the First became rare. The First Concerto does lack the subtleties of the Second and Third, and this fact may have delayed its wide acceptance by pianists. But the work does not try to be subtle. Rather, its character lies in its hypnotic driving force.

Soon after playing the premiere of the concerto, Bartók made a two-month tour of the United States, his first visit to the country that would eventually become his adopted homeland. He traveled to New York, Philadelphia, Los Angeles, San Francisco, Seattle, Portland, Denver, Kansas City, St. Paul, Chicago, Washington, D.C., New York again, Boston, Detroit, Cleveland, Cincinnati, and finally Chicago again. Travel was exhausting, as were frequent performances as soloist with major orchestras and in chamber concerts. Bartók found American cities depressingly similar, American orchestras first-rate, and jazz America's most interesting music.

The composer was scheduled to make his New York debut with the First Concerto, which he was to play under the direction of Willem Mengelberg. Because of inadequate rehearsal time, however, the concerto had to be canceled. It was replaced by the far tamer Rhapsody, Opus 1. New York had to wait a few weeks to hear the exciting, almost frightening rhythms of the First Concerto. Bartók finally played the work in Carnegie Hall with the Cincinnati Symphony Orchestra, conducted by his friend and compatriot Fritz Reiner. The piece was greeted with derision by the press.

Today, when audiences accept Bartók's music readily, we may well wonder what made the First Concerto such a difficult work for its first audiences. Why did it take several years before other pianists would perform it?

One answer lies in the startling originality of the piano writing. In reaction to the nineteenth century, when the keyboard was a vehicle of intimate and lyric sentiments or else a means toward sometimes empty virtuosic display, Bartók showed that the piano could be used percussively. Every aspect of the concerto serves this unique conception of piano sonority: the driving rhythms are underlined by piano punctuations, and the melodic material is kept purposefully minimal, as is the counterpoint. Bartók apparently felt that any extended melody would detract from the brutally percussive character. In place of melody we hear fragments of scales. The music is built from these small fragments, not from tunes. Such a compositional strategy makes the music constantly exciting. Bartók learned this techique from the music of Stravinsky, which he greatly respected.

The concerto is dissonant, but the dissonance does not function expressively. In most music, particularly twentieth-century compositions, dissonance has strong emotional connotations. A dissonance is usually a tension-filled sound that needs to be (but may or may not actually be) resolved. The dissonance in the Bartók First Concerto, however, works differently. Dissonant notes are added to chords to increase their pungency, to give them a sound quality as sharp as that of a snare drum or cymbal. There is no need for resolution, because the dissonance does not work as harmony but rather as color. The underlying tonal language of the concerto is essentially consonant, with foreign notes grafted on to add spice. To almost tonal sounds Bartók added acid dissonances, which, without upsetting the clarity of the music, gives it its biting vitality. It was this quality of brutality that early audiences and performers found difficult to understand, but today we can readily understand it as a statement of the tensions of our times, and we can hear how truly engaging Bartók's fierce rhythms are. The barbaric qualities of the First Concerto were an extreme for the Hungarian composer. Although he continued his interest in percussive writing, he never again approached the raw force of the First Concerto.

In the center of this extraordinary concerto stands the middle movement, surely the most original part of the work. Here the elemental rhythms are quieted in favor of a delicate, but still percussive, piece of "night music." The piano is joined by the percussion instruments, playing sparsely. Eventually the winds join in, and the piano writing becomes ominously persistent. Bartók creates some beautiful textures, in which the mixed tone quality of piano plus percussion (supported by winds) seems to matter more than what the actual notes are. This unique movement offsets the driving, repetitive rhythms, which return in the finale to generate incredible excitement.

Concerto Number 2 for Piano and Orchestra
Allegro
Adagio. Presto. Adagio
Allegro molto

The Second Piano Concerto was composed between October 1930 and October 1931. Bartók played the first performance with conductor Hans Rosbaud in Frankfurt, on 23 January 1933.

To compare the *Hungarian* Rhapsodies of Liszt or the *Hungarian* Dances of Brahms with any of the folk-inspired works of Bartók is to realize the difference between an assumed nationalism and a deeply felt commitment to folk art that results from years of study and assimilation. Liszt was born in Hungary but spent little time there; Brahms had no claim at all to being Hungarian. The "Hungarian" compositions of these two composers were essentially impressions by tourists. Bartók not only grew up thoroughly imbued with Hungarian culture but also made a specific commitment to learn as much as he could about the music of his people. He lived among Hungarian peasants, listening to, recording, and writing down in his own special notation thousands of folksongs. He collected, catalogued, and analyzed this music. He penetrated the spirit of Hungarian music, which consequently colored his own compositional style. There is scarcely a page in any of his compositions that does not have the distinctive sound that is equally well characterized as Hungarian or Bartókian.

Bartók's folk art goes deeper than simply quoting tunes or inventing folk-like melodies, as Liszt and Brahms did. Bartók wrote:

> The appropriate use of this folksong material is not, of course, limited to the sporadic introduction or imitation of these old melodies, or to the arbitrary thematic use of them in works of foreign or international tendencies. It is rather a matter of absorbing the means of musical expression hidden in this treasury of folk tunes, just as the most subtle possibilities of any language may be assimilated. It is necessary for the composer to command his musical language so completely that it becomes the natural expression of his own musical ideas.

The Second Piano Concerto is a good example of what Bartók meant by a musical language indebted to a folk language. The concerto has an affinity for native Hungarian music, but the exact nature of that affinity is elusive. The composer did indeed have the command of his craft needed to assimilate the folk influence: there is no grafting of external nationalism onto a foreign style here. Although there is no overt quotation in the concerto, it is just as close to the folk tradition as are those Bartók pieces that use real folk tunes.

Bartók steadfastly refused to be a composition teacher, because he felt unable to divorce himself from the works of students. He feared stifling their originality with his own stylistic predilections. He had to earn his living instead as a concert pianist and piano teacher. He composed the Second Concerto for his own use on European concert tours. After its premiere in Frankfurt, he was able to secure engagements performing it at the International Society for Contemporary Music's annual festival in Amsterdam, and in London, Stockholm, Strassburg, Vienna, Winterthur, and Zürich.

Like many other Bartók works from the 1920s and '30s, the concerto is cast in an arch form. The scherzo section of the second movement is the keystone of the arch, the midpoint of the form. It is flanked on both sides by adagio sections that use the same material. The middle movement is in turn surrounded by two fast movements, which also share material. Bartók was fascinated by symmetry, and the use of arch forms is but one example of his interest in balance. Symmetries abound in all his works, from tiny details to entire formal plans.

The piano plays almost continuously throughout the first movement. It often functions in opposition to brilliant brass instruments, and it is frequently combined with percussion. The movement is scored without strings, in order to create the special sonority appropriate to this driving, forceful, flashy music.

The strings make their appearance in the second movement. Their sound at the opening is atmospheric, even mysterious. They play quiet, sustained chords with mutes and without *vibrato*. Their music is mostly its own mirror image — whenever the high strings move some interval, the low strings move the same interval in the opposite direction. This "mirror writing," as this device is called, is a further example of Bartók's fondness for symmetry.

The finale starts with the only fresh material in the movement. All other themes, transitions, and even the coda are new versions of music from the first movement. Except for one subdued interlude, the music moves relentlessly forward to its tumultuous conclusion.

Concerto Number 3 for Piano and Orchestra
    Allegretto
    Adagio religioso. Poco più mosso. Adagio
       religioso —
    Allegro vivace. Presto. Allegro vivace

Bartók worked on the Third Piano Concerto throughout the summer of 1945. He had finished all but the scoring of the last 17 measures by his death. The first performance was given by pianist György Sándor and the Philadelphia Orchestra, conducted by Eugene Ormandy, on 8 February 1946.

Bartók toured the United States in 1927. He came to Cincinnati to rehearse the American premiere of his First Piano Concerto, with conductor Fritz Reiner. As he knew little English and had few acquaintances in Cincinnati, it was natural that he spent most of his free time with Tibor Serly, a composer who played in the orchestra's viola section. Serly had met Bartók four years earlier while studying in Hungary.

When Bartók moved permanently to the United States several years later, Serly again came into his life. The violist had moved to New York to play in the NBC Symphony. It was he who met the Bartóks' boat in 1940. Serly remained close to the composer for his remaining years.

Those were difficult years. Bartók desperately missed his homeland, but he was unable to return because of the war. He had little money, and he and his wife were forced to live in a cramped apartment in New York. His health was failing, and he could no longer perform as a pianist. He gave his final concert in January 1943.

The composer was eager to receive commissions that might provide much-needed income. He was no doubt pleased to receive no fewer than four commissions in the first months of 1945, but his health was too precarious for him to accept them all. He did promise to write the Viola Concerto for William Primrose, and he did accept a cash advance on a seventh string quartet (which he never composed), but he turned down a commission for a two-piano concerto. When the summer came and he was able to leave his tiny apartment for a holiday at Saranac Lake, where he was much better able to work, Bartók planned to work on the Viola Concerto and, surprisingly, on a non-commissioned work.

Bartók's publisher had requested the Third Piano Concerto back in 1940, but the composer had not written it. Now he wanted to undertake it in addition to the Viola Concerto, despite the fact that he rarely composed two pieces at once. Tibor Serly explained,

> In America Bartók's main source of a steady income had been through lecture and concert engagements. But for two years he had been too ill to take on either and now he feared he might never be well enough to return to the concert stage. He considered his talented wife and former pupil, Ditta Pásztory Bartók, to be among his most representative disciples and greatly admired her interpretation of his piano works. Sensing the seriousness of his illness, Bartók determined to leave her the only inheritance within his power, a concerto for piano and orchestra made to order for her style, a work that would give her an opportunity both to exhibit her talents and at the same time carry on as a disciple of the Bartók tradition.

And, it might be added, to have an assured source of income as the concerto's principal performer.

Bartók worked as hard as his health would permit on both concertos throughout the summer. When he returned to New York in

September, the Viola Concerto was still in a fragmentary state (though his correspondence indicates that it was completely worked out in his mind). The Piano Concerto was completely sketched and much of the orchestration had been accomplished.

On 21 September Serly visited the composer in the small apartment. "He was obviously quite ill. When I spoke to him, he was lying in bed. By that time it was very well known that he was close to having completed the Viola Concerto for Mr. Primrose. But strangely, a totally different manuscript was in his lap. This was the Third Piano Concerto. I had some vague notion that he had been writing a piano concerto, but no one else knew about it." The very morning after Serly's visit, Bartók was taken to the hospital. He died five days later, having completed all but the final 17 measures of the Piano Concerto's orchestration. Serly realized that, had he not taken up the composer's time with a visit on that fateful night, the concerto would have been finished. Serly himself therefore undertook the minor task of filling in the orchestration in the final bars. Two years later he also took on the far more difficult job of putting the fragments of the Viola Concerto into playable order.

Ditta Bartók did not play the Third Concerto for a number of years. The composer had written the work particularly for her talents and personality, but it was left to György Sándor to introduce the concerto to the world. It is impossible to know to what extent Bartók's decision to write for Ditta was responsible for the very special nature of his last completed work. It is far simpler, more direct, more tonal, and less dissonant than his other mature compositions. Some commentators have suggested that Bartók was cultivating a more accessible style in his late works (the Viola Concerto shares this consonant idiom with the Third Piano Concerto) in order to capitalize on the public attention he was at last beginning to receive. Others have thought that the new simplicity was a result of Bartók's inability to handle complex forms while suffering from leukemia. Whether or not such unkind ideas are the true reasons for the newfound simplicity in the Third Concerto, the result is a music of beguiling beauty and sunny innocence.

The simplicity of the Third Piano Concerto extends beyond its consonant harmonies. Gone is the conflict between piano and orchestra found in the First and Second Concertos: in the Third the orchestra accompanies as a subordinate. Gone are Bartók's complex forms. And gone also is the elaborate counterpoint of the earlier music. Listen, for example, to the beautiful opening melody in the piano. The accompaniment is of elegant simplicity — string undulations, sustained clarinet notes, and rhythmic punctuations first in the timpani and then in the *pizzicato* low strings. The pianist plays the same music in both hands (two octaves apart), rather than a contrapuntal combination of figures. Although contrapuntal interplay between the piano and orchestra does increase throughout the first movement, the piano is always treated as virtually a single-line instrument, with all manner of clever doublings.

The second movement is based on the slow movement of Beethoven's String Quartet Number 15 in A Minor, Opus 132. This is the famous movement in which Beethoven sings a hymn of praise after having recovered from a serious illness. Perhaps Bartók was hoping that his composing a similar hymn might mean that he too would recover. Both movements begin — with almost identical themes — in the strings, entering from top to bottom. This material alternates (again in both movements) with the actual hymn, in block chords. Bartók's hymn is always in the piano, and its kinship to Beethoven's is more spiritual than melodic. Just as in the Beethoven movement, the concerto goes to a completely contrasting second section. Both composers chose to juxtapose the austerity of the hymn with highly ornamented, far more worldly music. Bartók turned to some bird calls, which he had written down two years earlier in North Carolina. After the bird-call section the hymn returns in an ornamented version, just as in the Beethoven Quartet, where the hymn of praise is elaborated on its final appearance.

The third movement is a rondo that provides the counterpoint missing from the earlier movements. It includes two fugues. Yet the mood is anything but learned. It is relaxed, almost carefree: hardly the type of music one would expect from a composer who knew that his life was coming to an end.

Concerto Number 2 for Violin and Orchestra
Allegro non troppo
Andante tranquillo
Allegro molto

The Second Violin Concerto was composed in Budapest between August 1937 and 31 December 1938. Willem Mengelberg conducted the first performance with violinist Zoltán Székely in Amsterdam on 23 April 1939.

Although an active concert pianist, Bartók wrote much music for violin. Part of the reason for his interest in the violin was its important place in Hungarian folk music. He was deeply interested in his native music. He was one of the first of many musical scholars to take folk music seriously as a genuine expression of national character. Bartók spent much of his life collecting, categorizing, and studying authentic folk tunes. As a composer he strove quite deliberately for a style that was an amalgamation of Hungarian folk idioms and contemporary European art music. His music is therefore unlike that of any of his contemporaries (although it has been imitated endlessly by subsequent generations, even down to the present crop of composition students — it seems as if every would-be composer must pass through a Bartók phase). Bartók's style is infused with Hungarian rhythms and scales. It is no coincidence, therefore, that the violin should play a large part in his output. It is tempting to hear behind the fiery dance-like virtuosity of the Second Concerto a gypsy violinist playing his people's traditional music.

Bartók wrote this concerto during a period of political turmoil throughout Europe. The German Reich Music Chamber decided that it needed proof that any composer whose music was to be played in Germany be of Aryan descent. Bartók, who had wanted to remain uninvolved in politics, could not bring himself to participate in such an invasion of artistic freedom. He refused to fill out the required questionnaire. He later demanded that his music not be broadcast where it could be heard in Hitler's Germany or Mussolini's Italy. This courageous public stance cost him much needed royalty money, yet it was impossible for a responsible artist to remain aloof from politics in those troubled times.

While Bartók was debating whether or not to stay in Axis-dominated Europe, he received a commission for a concerto from Hungarian violinist Zoltán Székely. Bartók preferred to compose a set of variations for violin and orchestra, but the virtuoso wanted a full-fledged concerto. Actually, the finished work does use variation techniques. The middle movement is cast as a theme and variations, and the materials of the first movement return in varied form in the finale.

When the composer sent the finished score to Székely, the soloist was dissatisfied: the ending did not display his prowess sufficiently. Bartók complied with the violinist's wishes and wrote a new ending, but he allowed himself the satisfaction of publishing the work with both endings. The original version is rarely used, however.

The composer did not attend the premiere by Székely in Amsterdam. Bartók had already gone to America to see whether or not he could make a life for himself and his wife on the other side of the Atlantic. He had to wait until 1944, a year before his death, after he had permanently emigrated to the United States, before hearing a performance of the concerto. The composer was finally able to hear

Tossy Spivakovsky perform it in New York. "What delighted me most was the fact that I found nothing amiss with the instrumentation. I did not have to change a thing. Whereas, we all know, orchestral 'accompaniment' of the violin is a very ticklish matter."

Székely received for his commissioning fee a concerto of major proportions, which treats the violin with great bravura. The violin part explores many special string techniques — tremolo, quarter tones, *glissando* — but there is not much of the *pizzicato* that is a hallmark of Bartók's string quartets. This plucked sound is instead given to the harp, which has unusual prominence. It opens the concerto and is never long absent, particularly in the first two movements.

The second theme in the first movement is somewhat notorious, because it uses all twelve tones of the chromatic scale, stated in order without duplication. Thus this theme is like a twelve-tone row, although it is used more like a melody than like a Schoenbergian row. The interesting question is, why did Bartók insert this isolated row into a non-twelve-tone piece? Halsey Stevens, in his comprehensive study of the composer's life and works, offers a plausible explanation: parody. Bartók is referring to an idiom with which he felt less than total sympathy, much as he did with the inane A-major tune in the finale of the Fifth Quartet or the Shostakovich quotation in the Concerto for Orchestra. The same reasoning may explain the quarter tones (intervals smaller than a half step) in the solo part before the end of the first movement. As quarter tones do not appear elsewhere in the concerto, perhaps they occur in this one place as a parody of the avant garde.

The second movement is a beautifully scored set of variations. Bartók uses the orchestra mostly as a delicate chamber ensemble. He comes up with some exquisite timbres, such as the timpani and string bass punctuations of the solo line in the first variation, or later the use of harmonics.

The finale must be heard with the memory of the first movement still fresh. Only then can the transformations of melodic materials from the first movement into the finale be readily followed. The final movement is a marvelous reinterpretation of the first. We hear two different movements based on the same materials.

Concerto for Viola and Orchestra
Moderato —
Adagio religioso —
Allegro vivace

The Viola Concerto was begun in January 1945 and remained un-finished at the composer's death. It was completed by Tibor Serly and first performed on 2 December 1949 in Minneapolis. William Primrose was soloist and Antal Doráti conducted the Minneapolis Symphony Orchestra.

On 22 January 1945 William Primrose, the distinguished violist, wrote to Bartók asking him to compose a concerto. In an interview in 1970, Primrose recalled:

> When I commissioned it, Bartók — if you can believe it — was an obscure composer. He was generally known to musicans, and he was reviled by the public. Aside from performances of the Concerto for Orchestra given by the Boston Symphony Orchestra under Koussevitzky, I don't recall many other performances of Bartók's works. When I commissioned the concerto, most people thought I had made a big mistake, including people in my manager's office. Who on earth was going to ask me to play a concerto by Béla Bartók? I paid him what he asked, $1000, and I played the concerto well over a hundred times for fairly respectable fees. So it was almost like getting in on the ground floor in investing in Xerox or the Polaroid camera.

The bulk of the work on the concerto was accomplished at Saranac Lake, where the Bartóks spent their summer vacation. When he returned to his small New York apartment in the autumn, the composer wrote to Primrose,

> I am very glad to be able to tell you that your Viola Concerto is ready in draft, so that only the score has to be written, which means a purely mechanical work, so to speak. If nothing happens I can be through in 5 to 6 weeks, that is I can send you a copy of the orchestral score in the second half of October, and a few weeks afterwards a copy (or if you wish more copies) of the piano score. Many interesting problems arose in composing this work. The orchestration will be rather transparent, more transparent than in the Violin Concerto. Also the somber, more masculine character of your instrument executed some influence on the general character of the work.

"If nothing happens. . . ." Unfortunately, something did happen. On 21 September Bartók was visited by his friend, composer Tibor Serly. Serly, who knew about the Viola Concerto, was surprised to see Bartók working on a totally different piece, the Third Piano Concerto. "I asked him, 'What about the Viola Concerto?' He pointed toward the other side of the bed, where another pile of manuscripts lay. That was evidently the Viola Concerto." The morning after Serly's visit, Bartók was taken to the hospital. He died five days later, leaving the final 17 measures of the Piano Concerto unscored and leaving the entire Viola Concerto in a fragmentary state. It fell to Serly to complete both pieces.

Serly received the sketches of the Viola Concerto in 1947. He worked two years on the difficult task of assembling a complete piece. In the preface to the published score, Serly explained the challenges he faced:

> First there was the problem of deciphering the manuscript itself. Bartók wrote his sketches on odd, loose sheets of music paper that happened to be on hand at the moment, some of which had parts of other sketches already on them. Bits of material that came to his mind were jotted down without regard for their sequence. The pages were not numbered nor the separation of movements indicated. The greatest difficulty encountered was deciphering his correction of notes, for Bartók, instead of erasing, grafted his improvements onto the original notes.
>
> The next problem involved the matter of completing harmonies and other adornments, which he had reduced to a form of shorthand. For, as Bartók observed in his letter [to Primrose]: "Most probably some passages will prove uncomfortable or unplayable."
>
> Finally, except for Bartók's statement that "the orchestration will be rather transparent," there were virtually no indications of the instrumentation. Strangely, this part presented the least difficulty, for the leading voices and contrapuntal lines upon which the background is composed were clearly indicated in the manuscript.

Whenever a composer leaves a work unfinished at the time of his death, controversy surrounds attempts by others to complete it. There are inevitable arguments about the propriety of another composer taking over; the musicological and/or compositional skills of the one who undertakes the task are usually questioned; the musical worth of the product is forever debated. There is no easy answer. Should the last statement of an important artist be withheld from the public, or should it be presented in an incomplete state?

The debate over the Bartók Viola Concerto has been less vehement than those surrounding, for example, the completion of the Mahler Tenth Symphony by Deryck Cooke, of the Mozart Requiem by Franz Süssmayr, or of Puccini's *Turandot* by Franco Alfano. Part of the reason is that there are relatively few viola concertos of comparable quality, so that soloists have welcomed the work into their repertory. Another reason is that the sketches have been largely unavailable for scholars to study just what Serly did in the process of preparing the concerto for performance. Serly's death in 1977 further complicated the matter by removing an important source of information.

Recently, Hungarian musicologist János Kovács has been able to compare Serly's score with Bartók's sketches, and, predictably, the controversy has begun to warm up. The "odd, loose sheets" Serly mentions turn out to be only 13 pages, unnumbered to be sure but, given the completeness of the solo part and much of the accompaniment in short score, easily placed in sequence. The randomly jotted "bits of material" appear on only one page. Most of Serly's work was orchestration, which he dismissed as presenting "the least difficulty." In fact, it is extremely problematic to orchestrate a viola concerto so that the solo line will not be covered. Bartók gave a very few clues, most of which Serly ignored. Yet Serly was able to accomplish a very clean and clear scoring. There are questionable passages, particularly in the last movement, on which Bartók spent the least time. The question of Serly's faithfulness to Bartók's surmised intentions will surely continue to be debated by scholars, while violists will continue to perform Serly's completion to the delight of audiences.

The Viola Concerto shares many features with its companion piece, the Third Piano Concerto. The slow movements of each — marked "Adagio religioso" in both cases — share a mood of serenity. The harmonic style of both concertos is more consonant, more triadic, than in Bartók's earlier works. This newfound simplicity makes both concertos extraordinarily beautiful compositions. The Viola Concerto, despite the lessening of Bartók's pungent dissonances, is typical of the composer, particularly in the finale, where we hear the Hungarian dance rhythms that are the hallmark of his style.

The Miraculous Mandarin

Bartók began the pantomime The Miraculous Mandarin *in October 1918 and completed the composition in May 1919. He revised it extensively in 1924, and in November of that year he finished orchestrating it. The work was staged in Cologne in November 1926, under the musical direction of Jenő Szenkár. In January 1927 Bartók extracted the orchestral suite, which was first performed by Ernö Dohnányi and the Budapest Philharmonic on 15 October 1928. The stage version was further revised in 1936.*

Bartók's third and final stage work, the pantomime *The Miraculous Mandarin*, was conceived in a period of political and economic turmoil. The composer began the piece during World War I. He completed the sketch a year later, just before he left his home to get away from the terrorist government of Béla Kún, who ruled Hungary for 133 bloody days.

The horrors of the war-torn second decade of this century were reflected in much European art. As Bartók's biographer József Ujfalussy explains,

> European art began to be populated by inhuman horrors and apocalyptic monsters. These were the creations of a bourgeois world in which man's imagination had been affected by political crises, wars, and the threat to life. . . . This exposure of latent horror and hidden danger and crime, together with an attempt to portray these evils in all their apocalyptic magnitude, was an expression of protest by twentieth-century artists against the obsolete ideals and inhumanity of contemporary civilization. In his study of *The Miraculous Mandarin*, Bence Szabolcsi has stated that feelings of "anger and despair" were largely responsible for the artistic protests which channeled all the furious currents of indignation. The avant garde of the artistic communities, especially during the war, considered no method too garish or shocking for use in their attempts to draw attention to their eleventh-hour warnings and cries for help. They cast aside all previous notions of propriety in order to dispel the illusions which prevented people from seeing what was really happening in the world. . . .
>
> The great majority of radical Hungarian intellectuals recognized in the imperial war the legacy of a hateful past and opposed it with all their might. . . . Bartók's social and artistic outlook caused him to be attracted towards those Hungarian writers, painters, and sculptors who held revolutionary views and were totally opposed to the maintenance of the old order. These were the ideas which possessed his mind when he came to read [Menyhért] Lengyel's libretto.
>
> It is easy to recognize in Lengyel's characters some reflection of the spectres haunting the imagination of the age — crime, eroticism, barbarism, and the mysteries of the Orient. The social criticism implicit in the text and its bitingly satirical style are undeniable. But there is an intrusive and pervading note of naturalistic brutality which arouses horror and revulsion and serves to conceal the object of criticism. The girl, who symbolizes humanity in the story, is caught in a conflict between two kinds of barbarity, which it is left to her to resolve if she is to end the horror of her situation. Once again Bartók was

expressing his hatred of the inhumanity of urban civilization. He does not see the Mandarin as a grotesque monster but rather as the personification of primitive, barbaric force, an example of the "natural man" to whom he was so strongly attracted.

The central character is the girl, driven by circumstances to prostitution. She reveals a different side of her character in each of her encounters. She is being used by three thieves to attract victims. During the course of the pantomime, she entices three men. The first is a penniless old man. The second is an adolescent to whom she is attracted in an impersonal way. But the youth is also penniless and is dismissed. Then comes the wealthy Mandarin, who is greatly aroused by the girl's seductive dancing. He is inflamed by passion, but the girl shrinks away in horror. The thieves overpower him and rob him, but still his desire for the girl remains unabated. The thieves try to kill him by smothering him, stabbing him, and hanging him. But his passion keeps him alive. Finally the girl gives herself to the Mandarin. His desire finally satisfied, the Mandarin dies.

The erotic and violent nature of *The Miraculous Mandarin* worked against its being performed. A 1921 production in Berlin fell through, as did one every year from 1922 to 1926 at the Budapest Opera. The violent music certainly did not help convince any producers of the work's viability on the stage.

Nonetheless, Bartók felt that the work was among his best, and he wanted to see it produced. He therefore set about revising and censoring it. He eliminated more than half of the suggestive scene between the girl and the youth. He also removed two of the three climaxes in the scene where the Mandarin's passion is finally satisfied. Finally a performance was scheduled — after repeated delays — in Cologne, almost a decade after Bartók had begun the piece.

The composer was not happy with the choice of city, because of Cologne's conservatism. Predictably, the premiere was a fiasco. One newspaper reported that the work

> roused opposition from a vast majority of the audience. The commotion which broke out in the auditorium and the disgusting plot caused the rows in front of the stage to be emptied out before the end. And, as the curtain went down, a hasty retreat ensued from the spaces that had been profaned by this (to put it mildly) inferior work. . . . The premiere of the Bartókian prostitute-and-pimp play with orchestral racket would have ended in a calm, noiseless rejection, had not small groups . . . tried through hand clapping and calling for the author to twist the incontestable failure of the work into a success. . . . Shouts resounded a hundredfold for minutes: "Shame! Vulgarity! Scan-

dal!" The applause was nearly drowned out. The noise mounted again when, in spite of the exodus, Mr. Bartók stepped onto the stage. It was now high time for the fire curtain to be rung down — which was done to the applause of the majority.

The mayor of Cologne, Konrad Adenauer, summoned and reprimanded the conductor, and all subsequent performances were banned. Other cities, fearing that the near-riot might be repeated, avoided staging the pantomime. Only in Prague did it play successfully, but there only briefly. The government-controlled Opera House in Budapest continued to vacillate about producing this controversial work by Hungary's greatest composer. Finally, after countless delays, a version that completely altered and emasculated the original conception was scheduled. When Bartók attended a rehearsal, he was horrified at the travesty of his work. His dissatisfaction was duly reported in the press, and the producers felt that a scandal was now inevitable, no matter how the work was presented. The performance was again delayed and then cancelled. Budapest had to wait until after Bartók's death to see this powerful work on the stage.

The composer was not unwilling to compromise, but he felt he had to retain the underlying social criticism of the pantomime. The explicit portrayals of sex were expendable, but not the grotesque picture of urban life. He made one further major revision, replacing the almost graphic sexual climax of the Mandarin with music describing, in the words of Bartók scholar John Vinton, "an experience more transcendental than physical." The composer then decided to extract an orchestral suite — essentially the first two-thirds of the music. He felt, rightly as it turned out, that the music by itself, without the grotesque and erotic plot, would fare much better with the public.

Musicologist Vinton feels that, "had the work been first performed in Berlin as Bartók wanted, or in Paris, and had [his publisher] Universal Edition been more adept at publicity, *The Miraculous Mandarin* might have gained a following comparable to that of [Stravinsky's] *Le Sacre du printemps*. But instead, public taste seems to have typed it as a period piece that was too blatantly grotesque for the twenties and is now too naïvely grotesque."

The following description of *The Miraculous Mandarin* is derived from the stage directions in Bartók's score and the interpretation in Ujfalussy's biography.

The work opens with a string rush and incisive repeated notes in the winds, brass, and percussion. Such notes, heard through much of the music, symbolize the urban background of the story. They appear whenever the thieves come out from their hiding places. The unchanging nature of this figure implies that the underworld of urban crime never changes.

The curtain rises as this violent opening subsides. Accompanied by low string tremolos, the violas play a rhythmic figure: the first thief rummages through his handbag looking for money, without success. The rhythmic figure transfers to the violins, as the second thief looks through a kitchen cabinet, finding nothing. The third thief jumps out of bed, goes to the girl, and orders her to stand by the window and entice men up from the street so that they can be robbed.

The music slows down and becomes less nervous. After a horn fanfare, the high violins announce that the girl disobeys. Her theme is derived from that of the thieves, showing that she is in their power, but it carries a hint of suffering. The thieves reiterate their order, and the girl gives up and goes reluctantly to the window. A halting clarinet solo indicates her unwillingness.

She sees a man, and, as the orchestra's repeated-note figures intensify, he comes up the stairs. The thieves hide. Sliding trombone music indicates that an old man, a shabby cavalier, enters. This jerky music is like that of a puppet, and indeed the girl mocks him as a fairy-tale princess might mock a wooden puppet. The cavalier makes comical sexual advances. The girl asks if he has money. An English horn solo indicates his reply: money is immaterial, for love is supreme. As the music slows down, he becomes increasingly insistent. Now the music accelerates and, as the repeated notes return, the three thieves suddenly spring from their hiding place, grab the old cavalier, and throw him out. They turn angrily to the girl and force her to go to the window again.

Again a clarinet solo implies her unwillingness, but this time the music is less halting. The girl loses hope of avoiding participation in the thieves' scheme. She sees someone else. The thieves hide again. To a lyrical oboe solo, a bashful youth appears at the door. He can scarcely hide his embarrassment. The girl caresses him to encourage him, feeling in his satchel. He has no money. She pulls him to her and begins timidly to dance with him. The five-beat rhythm of their slow dance implies their awkwardness: they are attracted to each other, but both realize the hopelessness of their situation. The music gets faster as the dance becomes more passionate, but suddenly, with the return of the violent repeated notes, the thieves reappear. They seize the youth and throw him out.

They order the girl to cooperate and find a suitable man. Again her clarinet music is heard as she goes a third time to the window. As the music becomes agitated, she sees with horror a sinister form in the street. His steps are already heard ascending. The thieves hide. A forceful two-note descent in the brass, with trombone *glissando*, announces that the Mandarin has arrived. He stands motionless in the doorway. The frightened girl runs to the other end of the room.

She overcomes her loathing for him and begins a slow, cautious dance. The dance becomes little by little more spirited, becoming at its climax wildly erotic. The immobile Mandarin stares with fixed gaze at the girl during the entire dance. His mounting passions are scarcely noticeable. Her dance reveals her true self, as her timid movements are transformed into a waltz. The waltz becomes an ecstatic dance of death, a savage march.

Finally the girl falls against the Mandarin. She begins to tremble in feverish excitement. Then she shudders in anticipation of his embrace. She tries to break away from him, as the trombones depict his mounting frenzy. The music breaks into stark repeated-note rhythms in the low instruments. The Mandarin begins his wild pursuit of the girl, who continually escapes. A frightened version of her theme is heard, starting in the violas and cellos but eventually pervading the orchestra.

This frenzied music breaks off, as the Mandarin stumbles, quickly gets up, and continues his pursuit ever more passionately. Finally, as her theme returns, he catches her. They struggle with one another.

Here, at the vehement climax, *The Miraculous Mandarin* Suite ends. But in the complete work, the thieves return. The music graphically depicts their three attempts to murder the Mandarin, the gratification of his desire, and his death. Bartók omitted this music from the suite because he undoubtedly felt that there had been about as much frenetic music as a listener can bear, without direct involvement in stage action.

Music for Strings, Percussion, and Celeste

Music for Strings, Percussion, and Celeste was composed in Budapest during 1936; it was completed on 7 September 1936. The first performance was given by Paul Sacher and the Basel Chamber Orchestra on 21 January 1937.

Bartók's extremely personal style draws on an incredible diversity of influences. His style can be traced to the sensuousness of Debussy, the orchestral brilliance of Strauss, the contrapuntal rigor of Bach, the melodic and rhythmic patterns of Hungarian folk music, the clarity of Mozart, and the structural drama of Beethoven. What is more amazing than the variety of his sources is the depth to which he studied and absorbed each one. Many composers have perused and then emulated Beethoven, Mozart, Bach, Debussy, and even Strauss, but few have penetrated beyond simple imitation or inspiration. Bartók truly understood what each of these composers had accomplished, yet he invariably expressed his understanding in terms of his own musical personality. Similarly, several composers have written pieces based on folk music, but no one has penetrated the music of his people with the depth that Bartók achieved. His thorough, lifelong study of Hungarian folk music became such an integral part of his art that its presence is felt even in his most abstract works, such as the Music for Strings, Percussion, and Celeste. We might speak of the synthesis of his diverse influences, but his success rests on more than that. His personal stamp is always foremost, and all the external influences are unified by it. It is *Bartók's* sensuousness, orchestral brilliance, contrapuntal rigor, folk melodies and rhythms, clarity, and structural drama that we hear.

Music for Strings, undoubtedly the composer's masterpiece, is a fine example of the way he integrates eclectic sources into a unified conception. The first movement is a strict fugue, in which all melodic material is a consequence of the opening viola line. The second movement is a scherzo in sonata form. The third movement is an atmospheric, impressionistic piece of "night music," as biographer Halsey Stevens calls such movements. The finale is a dance-like piece with obvious references to Hungarian and Bulgarian folk music. Such an overview of the work might suggest a diffuse composition, a potpourri of divergent techniques and sounds. But, in fact, Music for Strings is a tightly woven, intricately unified conception.

The opening fugue subject is the source of important themes in all the movements. But this factor is only one means of unification. Bartók also holds the piece together tonally, with an elegant scheme of conflicting and resolving tonal areas that is difficult to achieve in a fundamentally atonal musical language.

There are many other means of unification, some of which are heard only subconsciously. Perhaps the most interesting appears in the first movement (there is a similar structure in the third movement as well). The proportions of this movement — how long the sections last in relation to one another — are derived from a number sequence known as the Fibonacci series. This series of numbers is encountered in nature: it determines patterns of shell growth, numbers of petals on flowers, patterns of branches on trees, numbers of spirals of eyes (fruitlets) in pineapples, numbers of ancestors of bees, and ratios of distances of planets. It is encountered in art: it determines proportions in ancient Greek vases, poetry of Vergil, Minoan architecture, and Greek and Gothic cathedrals. It appears in science: Fibonacci numbers are approximated in certain structures of atomic and subatomic particles, they have played a part in cancer research, and they have been useful in water pollution control. And, in the music of Bartók (and certain other composers), Fibonacci numbers have been used to determine the durations of sections.

The Fibonacci series is 1, 1, 2, 3, 5, 8, 13, 21, 34, 55, 89, ... Each number is the sum of the previous two. Listeners may doubt the relevance of a seemingly arbitrary mathematical structure to a piece of music, yet let anyone who is skeptical listen to the accumulated emotional power of the fugue, to its integration, and to its unmistakable balance and symmetry despite the differing lengths of sections. Bartók was fond of symmetry, and he, more than any other twentieth-century composer, knew how to turn symmetry into powerful musical expression. The fugue's total span of 89 measures (actually 88 plus the final silence) is subdivided 55 + 34 by the climax of the movement. The first 55 measures are grouped 34 + 21 by the removal of mutes and the entrance of the timpani. The last 34 measures are grouped 13 + 21 by the replacement of mutes. The exposition of the fugue is 21 measures long. The last 21-measure span is subdivided 13 + 8 by a textural change. And so on, down to the smallest details. This pervasive structure is not a gimmick. It is a unique way to integrate the music, and it is the source of its power and drive. No matter that the Fibonacci proportions are not consciously perceived: they are all the more powerful because they are subliminal, reaching us through our intuition and emotion.

This extraordinary piece is unified in yet another way. There is a progression over the course of its four movements from the intense chromaticism of the fugue to the exuberant diatonicism of the finale. This change from dissonance to consonance may be characterized as a move from pessimism to optimism, or from obscurity to clarity. Whatever labels we attach to this development, it enables the listener to hear four very different movements as stages of dramatic growth.

The orchestra in Music for Strings is unusual. There are two identical string sections, seated at opposite sides of the stage. Between them are two percussion groups, one containing timpani, snare drums, celeste, and piano, and the other including bass drum, cymbals, xylophone, and harp. Bartók requires this special seating to help emphasize the antiphonal nature of the music. The string groups answer each other from opposite sides of the stage, particularly in the second and last movements.

The fugue subject, which is destined to appear in all movements, is first stated in the violas. It is a tortuously chromatic melody that remains within a narrow range. One by one, other instrumental groups enter playing this tension-laden line. The intensity builds gradually yet inexorably, until it is almost unbearable. The music reaches its climax — a unison high E-flat, the note farthest away tonally from the A which begins and ends the movement. After this high point the fugue melody is played in inversion (i.e., upside-down): the climax has shattered the theme, forcing it to be changed yet allowing it to remain fundamentally the same. Gradually tension subsides. An ethereal texture emerges near the end, where high and low violins play the theme and its inversion simultaneously. When the music returns to its initial note, the arch has been completed.

The two string groups alternate antiphonally at the opening of the second movement. The second group plays a cleverly disguised variant of the first movement's fugue subject. This movement abounds in contrasts and in rhythmic vitality. It also includes some attractive special effects, including *pizzicato glissandi*, "snap" *pizzicato* (letting the string hit the fingerboard loudly), bowed *glissandi*, etc.

The atmospheric third movement is, like the first movement, an arch. After the delicate opening in which the xylophone plays an acceleration and then deceleration on one high note to the accompaniment of the timpani, the strings enter with a dirge-like melody related to the first movement's fugue theme. A more overt quotation of a fragment of the fugue leads to the colorful second section. After another reference to the fugue, the music becomes even more colorful. After the faster center section of the arch, the sections are heard in reverse order, until the xylophone and timpani return to end the movement.

The main theme of the finale is a dance in Bulgarian rhythm. This melody and other dance-like tunes are developed, until we hear a strong restatement of the fugue theme. This melody, which begins life (in the first movement) as an other-worldly abstraction, joins (in this movement) the real world, as represented by folk music. All that remains is the coda, which drives to its conclusion using the Bulgarian melody.

The Wooden Prince

The one-act ballet The Wooden Prince *was begun early in 1914 and completed early in 1916. The first performance was conducted by Egisto Tango at the Hungarian State Opera House on 12 May 1917. In 1921 Bartók extracted a short suite, consisting of three dances; this suite was first performed on 23 November 1931 by the Budapest Philharmonic Orchestra, conducted by Ernö Dohnányi. The composer then constructed a longer suite in 1931–32.*

Bartók's only three works for the stage were written in close succession, between 1911 and 1919. They were the opera *Bluebeard's Castle* and the ballets *The Wooden Prince* and *The Miraculous Mandarin*.

The composer related how he came to compose *The Wooden Prince*:

> It may sound strange, but I must confess that the impulse to compose this ballet came from the neglect of my one-act opera *Bluebeard's Castle*. . . . I was so pleased with the opera that, when I received the script for a dance pantomime from [*Bluebeard's* librettist] Béla Balázs, I immediately thought that the ballet, with its spectacular effects as well as its colorful, rich, and varied plot, would make an excellent companion piece. The two works could be performed the same evening, I thought. . . . I started to compose the dance pantomime before the war, but I left it for a long time, as I had gone through a great deal of emotional upheaval. At one point I heard István Strasser conduct my symphonic work *Two Portraits*. The second movement, "Grotesque," I was hearing for the first time. It inspired me to continue with the composition of *The Wooden Prince*, which in fact I completed in a short time.

The Wooden Prince was a success. Part of the reason was that the conductor, Egisto Tango, demanded and was given permission to hold thirty rehearsals. Because the choreographer could not understand the music, Tango had to supervise the dances as well as be stage director and conductor. Bartók, who had been accustomed to poorly rehearsed performances, was delighted with the quality of the production. "At last I was lucky enough to hear a major work of mine in a musically perfect performance, thanks to Maestro Egisto Tango." The public reacted favorably, despite previous indifference to his music. One result was that *Bluebeard's Castle*, which had not yet been performed, was mounted a year later, and, as if to fulfill Bartók's wish, it shared the bill with *The Wooden Prince*.

The principal characters of the ballet are a prince, a princess, and a fairy. The setting is an enchanted land, where there is a forest, flower garden, stream, and two hills with tiny castles atop them. At the beginning the princess dances alone in the forest. The prince is in love with her, but he is unable to reach her because the fairy has put a spell on the river. He tries many times to get to the princess, but he repeatedly fails. Finally he succeeds in catching her attention, but she is not interested in him. He tries one last idea: from his staff he carves a wooden doll in the shape of a prince, and he clothes the doll with his own cloak. He cuts his hair off to attach to the doll.

The trick works only too well. The princess is intrigued by the doll. The wooden prince gains her affection, while the real prince stands by forlorn, without raiment or hair. The fairy breathes life into the doll, who begins a demonic dance with the princess. The fairy takes pity on the prince and causes a crown and new clothes to be made from flowers. The doll dances more slowly, and the princess turns her attention to the real prince.

The original roles have now been reversed: the princess pursues the prince, but he spurns her. She finally realizes that she can be worthy of his love only once she gives up her crown, or her own free will. She takes off her crown and cloak and cuts her own hair; she is humbled before the prince. Now the prince and princess can be united, and, once they are, everything returns to its original state.

Librettist Balázs explained the symbolism of the story: "The wooden prince, which my prince makes in order to attract the princess, symbolizes the creative work of the artist, who puts all of himself into his work until he has made something complete, shining, and perfect. The artist himself, however, is left robbed and poor. I was thinking of that very common and profound tragedy when the creation becomes the rival to the creator, and of the pain and glory of the situation in which a woman prefers the poem to the poet, the picture to the painter."

Bartók scholar János Kárpáti has described how the music elaborates Balázs's basic theme:

> The motive of the trial is pervaded by another motive, the conflict of true and false values. . . . The music of the wooden puppet is none other than a "distorted" variation of the prince's theme. . . . The composer wishes to present contrasting "ideal-grotesque" pairs developed out of identical material, but of course in a new context. But in Bartók the "artistic tragedy" projected by Balázs broadens into general human tragedy, since in a wider sense the meaning of the ballet is essentially that an empty, inhuman, or alienated world stands between the natural encounter of man and woman, or between human beings in general. Their happiness can only be reached by overcoming this dehumanized world. . . . The prince and princess are both put to the test by the world that surrounds them, which is both their friend and their enemy. Even though the prince successfully conquers the forest, he is unable to cross the brook. He stands up to this ordeal by stripping himself of all worldly embellishments in order to make the wooden puppet. The princess in turn cannot come to grips with the forest — this really requires mas-

culine strength — but she proves herself morally by "discarding her crown and royal mantle and finally even cutting her hair." . . . The concept which brings them together, that of inner strength and values, . . . is reinforced by a connection expressed only in music: the dance of the wooden puppet, which is both grotesque and fearful, is closely related to the dance of the forest. Thus, in this sense, the animated forest is . . . the same cold, alientated world which gave rise to the wooden puppet.

Ludwig van Beethoven

Born on 16 December 1770 in Bonn, Germany.
Died on 26 March 1827 in Vienna.

◆ ◆ ◆

Concerto Number 1 in C Major for Piano and Orchestra, Opus 15

> Allegro con brio
> Largo
> Allegro scherzando

Little is known of the history of the First Piano Concerto. It was probably composed in 1798 and first performed by Beethoven in the same year in Prague.

Beethoven moved to Vienna in 1792 and immediately began a spectacularly successful career as a pianist. Since he arrived with an introduction from Count Waldstein and with an invitation to study composition with Haydn, he entered musical circles with no trouble. It did not take the Viennese long to realize that they had gained an exciting new virtuoso. However, in composition Beethoven was viewed only as Haydn's student.

There were some three hundred pianists in Vienna, all competing for prominence and all making a living teaching the more than six thousand keyboard students in the city. The rivalry among these pianists was fierce. Beethoven spoke of his "desire to embarrass" his opponents, whom he referred to as his "sworn enemies." He feared that some of his rivals would copy the "peculiarities of my style and palm them off with pride as their own." On such pianists he would "revenge myself."

The pianists competed like gladiators, and the most successful had large followings. In fact, virtuosos were considered more like freaks than like artists: child prodigies were exhibited publicly along with jugglers and tightrope walkers. Pianists engaged in what were more like duels than recitals. Beethoven, who went quickly to the top of every competition, received support from a large number of aristocratic families. They lavished money and gifts on the young performer in their attempt to establish their own high social standing. So great was this attention that Beethoven was often embarrassed by excessive generosity.

By the mid-1790s Beethoven's fame had spread beyond Vienna, and he was able to make concert tours to other countries. He played his First Piano Concerto in Prague in 1798. His reputation as a composer began to grow as he played his own compositions more and more. His earliest works composed for his own use were solo sonatas and chamber pieces, but he was also beginning to write music for piano and orchestra.

His First Piano Concerto was not really his first such work. The Concerto Number 2 in B-flat preceded it by a couple of years, but the C Major was published first and hence numbered first. In addition there is a Concerto in E-Flat that Beethoven wrote at the age of 14, long before coming to Vienna. There is also a Concerto in D and a Rondo in B-Flat for Piano and Orchestra, dating from about 1795.

He tried to keep the so-called First Concerto for his own private use, not allowing its publication until 1801. By then he was beginning to turn away from a career as soloist and more exclusively toward that of a composer.

Beethoven's model was Mozart, a pianist-composer who had written a long series of concertos for his own use. Mozart had become (ironically, only after his death) the pride of Vienna. Beethoven's strongest competitor was a memory. From the Mozart piano concertos Beethoven took his ideas of balanced opposition between soloist and orchestra, clarity of form, and keyboard virtuosity designed to show off the soloist. This First Concerto was the last in which Beethoven adhered closely to his models. In the subsequent Third Concerto he expanded the scope and emotional range. This process reached its culmination in the *Emperor* Concerto.

The dramatic opposition at the heart of the First Concerto appears immediately, as the strings contrast a forceful motive with a rapid scale, both starkly separated by silences. A further source of contrast is the large number of different themes introduced during the orchestral exposition. When the piano finally enters, it becomes the catalyst for reconciling the extremes. The scales become the source of pianistic virtuosity, as they fill in the silences. Particularly compelling is the transition to the recapitulation: piano and horns alternate repetitions of the opening motive, which is gradually reduced to barest essentials.

The second movement explores florid piano writing. Despite the extremely slow tempo, the piano moves in elegant fast figurations. This studied sophistication is soon dispelled, however, by the carefree innocence of the main rondo theme of the finale, introduced in the piano. The first subsidiary theme is equally engaging, particularly because of its off-beat accents. The second subsidiary theme is also attractive: it is in minor, and it is treated as a miniature rondo in itself, complete with secondary ideas. Toward the end, the music gradually slows down as it repeats the opening motive. A small cadenza over a sustained string chord brings the tempo down to adagio, for an oboe solo. We may not suspect it, but the piano has already made its final exit and the concerto is about to end. It does so just six measures later, after a sudden return to the allegro tempo. A thoroughly delightful ending to a thoroughly delightful movement!

Concerto Number 2 in B-Flat Major for Piano and Orchestra, Opus 19

Allegro con brio
Adagio
Molto allegro

The B-Flat Piano Concerto was begun in 1794 and completed in 1795. Beethoven played the first performance in Vienna on 29 March 1795. He subsequently revised the work for a 1798 performance in Prague.

Beethoven's Second Piano Concerto, which was composed before his First, is actually his third work in the genre. He was 14 years old when he wrote a Concerto in E-Flat, of which all that survives is the solo part and a piano reduction of the orchestral preludes and interludes. Sometime later he composed a Concerto in D Major, of which the first movement has survived. The B-Flat Concerto was written for the composer's first public concert in Vienna. He had been living in that city for two years, and, even though he had previously performed only in private recitals, his fame as a pianist was considerable. The public was eager to hear the phenomenal young performer.

The occasion of his public debut was the annual concert for the benefit of widows and orphans of the Society of Musicians. As the day of the performance neared, the concerto remained unwritten, at least on paper. Beethoven probably had planned the work quite thoroughly in his head. The final movement was written down only two days before the concert, while the composer was suffering a severe attack of colic. Wegeler, Beethoven's doctor, described the scene of Beethoven working furiously on his score, Wegeler himself working equally diligently on the colic, and four copyists in the anteroom awaiting each page of music.

The first rehearsal took place the next day, in Beethoven's rooms. After the orchestra had assembled, it was discovered that the piano was tuned a semitone flat. With no difficulty Beethoven played the challenging piano part in B major rather than the intended B-flat major.

The concerto was probably the first orchestral work of Beethoven to be performed. It is also his nearest approach to the style of Mozart, whose piano concertos he greatly admired. Even the purpose of the work (a display piece for a pianist-composer) and its manner of composition (first in his mind and then at the last minute onto paper) recall the Salzburg master.

Beethoven was never totally satisfied with the Second Concerto, perhaps because of its reliance on the concertos of Mozart. He revised it for a subsequent performance and then revised it again in preparation for its 1801 publication. In his dealings with his publisher, he referred to it as "a piano concerto which, to be sure, I do not claim to be among my best."

Echoes of Mozart are heard most strongly in the elegant and sophisticated first movement. The later Beethoven is more evident in the slow movement, which begins dramatically. The sophisticated finale is delightfully witty.

The fun starts immediately, as the main theme seems somehow askew. The notes which should be on the beat (long, accented) are off the beat, and the ones that should be off (short, unaccented) are on. This syncopation is developed at length in the second subsidiary section. There is a brilliantly imaginative moment just before the final statement of the theme: the piano reverses the syncopation so that what seems as if it should be on the beat really is. By now, however, we have heard the syncopated version so many times that the "right" version sounds wrong. Since it is also in the wrong key for a final statement, this delightful gesture is a doubly false recapitulation.

Concerto Number 3 in C Minor for Piano and Orchestra, Opus 37

>Allegro con brio
>Largo
>Allegro. Presto

The Third Concerto began to be sketched in 1797, although the bulk of the work on it was accomplished in 1800, the year of its completion. Beethoven continued to revise it until the day of the first performance. The composer was soloist at that premiere, which took place in Vienna on 5 April 1803.

Mozart was more than an influence on Beethoven, who felt himself heir to Mozart's talents and achievements and sought not only to equal but also to surpass him in every way possible. Beethoven's first two piano concertos, as well as an early concerto composed at the age of 14, are thoroughly Mozartian, taking their inspiration from the Salzburg master's major mode, sunny works for piano and orchestra. Beethoven approached the darker, more intense world of the minor mode concertos when he wrote his own Concerto Number 3. The direct influence was Mozart's Concerto Number 24. Both works share not only mood but also the key of C minor, with its connotations of heroic tragedy and powerful drama.

In 1801 Beethoven entered into an agreement with the director of the new Theater-an-der-Wien, which allowed him full use of the hall and its orchestra in exchange for the composition and production of a new opera. The composer took advantage of this arrangement by mounting a concert for his own benefit in 1803. This huge concert included a performance of the First Symphony plus premieres of the Second Symphony, the Third Piano Concerto, and the oratorio *Christ on the Mount of Olives.*

The concert was fraught with difficulties. The director of a competing theater hired all of Vienna's best musicians for a performance the same evening of Haydn's *The Creation.* Beethoven had to make do with second-rate players. And, as is often the case with composers and their premieres, the day of the concert came and the music was not yet finished.

Beethoven's star pupil Ferdinand Ries arrived at the composer's lodgings in the theater at 5:00 a.m. He found Beethoven furiously working. "What are you working on?" asked Ries. Beethoven shouted back, "Trombones!"

The only rehearsal began at 8:00 a.m. By the middle of the afternoon, the musicians were tired, frustrated, angry, and hungry. There were no musicians' unions in 1803 to protect players from impossibly demanding rehearsal schedules, but Beethoven's patron Prince Lichnowsky saved the day by providing a lunch for the musicians. Spirits improved, and the rehearsal continued. The concert began at 6:00 p.m., with Beethoven conducting and playing the piano.

Although the Third Concerto had been completed a few years earlier, Beethoven had been revising it continually. Thus he had not had time to write out the solo part of the final version prior to the premiere. All he had was a pile of papers, each adorned with jottings in his private shorthand, to remind him of what he was supposed to play. To Ignaz von Seyfried fell the strange task of turning these pages during the rehearsal and performance. "Heaven help me, that was easier said than done! I saw almost nothing but empty leaves. At the most, on one page or the other, a few Egyptian hieroglyphs wholly unintelligible to me were scribbled down as clues for him, for he played nearly all the solo part from memory. As was so often the case, he had not had time to put it all down on paper. He gave me a secret glance whenever he was at the end of one of the invisible pages. My scarcely concealed anxiety amused him greatly."

The parallel to Mozart's C Minor Concerto is evident from the outset. Both works begin with the strings playing softly in octaves an ascending triad from C. In both concertos the winds join in to lead the music to a loud statement by the full orchestra. The parallels are striking, perhaps even intentional. If you listen carefully you can even hear Mozart's main theme quoted almost literally in the lower strings shortly after the opening. Beethoven was paying homage to a work he knew well and had himself performed. In both compositions there is a lyrical second theme featuring the winds. Beethoven's melody has a thoroughly Mozartian grace. According to pianist Charles Rosen,

> Most striking is the imitation of the coda of K. 491, with its exceptional use of the solo instrument playing arpeggios at the end of the first movement. Beethoven omits a final ritornello after the cadenza and leaps directly to the coda; the Mozartian arpeggios are made almost melodramatic with timpani playing part of the main theme. In this superbly effective coda, only the arpeggios are not thematic, and this makes their borrowed character all the more apparent. In the development section, a curiously beautiful non-thematic passage also turns out to be inspired by Mozart, this time the B-flat Piano Concerto, K. 450. But it is the C minor K. 491 again which dominates many of the thematic details, at least of the first movement.

After the serene middle movement, the concerto again recalls Mozart in the finale. Like K. 491, but unlike most classical period pieces in the minor mode, the concerto casts its final movement in the minor. Both works close with a coda in 6/8 time based on a variant of the main theme. The mood is different, however. Beethoven's coda moves to C major, in order to end brightly, while Mozart remains in the minor to the end.

Despite the many similarities between these two C Minor Concertos, it would be a mistake to think of the Beethoven Third only as an imitation of the Mozart work. Beethoven's composition is powerfully original, despite its gestures of respect toward an older masterpiece. Beethoven was trying to move beyond the classical elegance of his earlier concertos, and thus he turned away from the models of Mozart's usual piano concertos and looked instead toward Mozart's least typical work in the genre. Thus the Third Concerto was a transitional work into Beethoven's second style, in which he overthrew the elegant restraints of classicism, as inherited from Mozart and

Haydn, in favor of the overtly emotional aesthetic heard in such C-minor works as the *Coriolan* Overture and the Fifth Symphony.

Concerto Number 4 in G Major for Piano and Orchestra, Opus 58

Allegro moderato
Andante con moto —
Vivace

The Fourth Piano Concerto was composed in 1805–06. Beethoven was soloist at the first performance, which took place at the palace of his patron Prince Lobkowitz in March 1807.

Beethoven worked on the G Major Concerto at about the same time he was composing several other large pieces, including the opera *Fidelio*, the Triple Concerto, the *Appassionata* Sonata, the *Razoumovsky* Quartets, and the Fourth and Fifth Symphonies. This flood of masterworks is truly astonishing, especially when one realizes how many of them are pathbreaking works. Beethoven was expanding his musical language at an amazing rate.

The composer set himself the task in the Fourth Concerto of replacing the virtuosically conceived concerto of the classical period with a more lyrical genre. Most previous concertos had been composed to display the skills of some pianist, often the composer. There were certainly musically significant works of this type, despite the tendency toward superficiality of showpieces, but Beethoven's Fourth was the first concerto completely to overthrow virtuosity in favor of pure artistic expression.

This concerto is often labelled an original work for quite another reason: the piano starts alone. There was a precedent in Mozart's K. 271 (Concerto Number 9 in E-Flat Major), but even that piece has a brief *tutti* before the piano enters. The significance of Beethoven's idea lies not in the mere novelty of beginning with a solo but rather in the consequences of such an opening. The typical classical concerto begins with a long orchestral exposition that prepares for the entrance of the solo instrument. The orchestral texture comes to need contrast, and the soloist provides it. The usual means of achieving this sense of expectancy is for the music to remain in the tonic key long enough almost to suggest monotony, which the solo entrance subsequently dispels. The situation is entirely different in the G Major Concerto, however. After the opening phrase on the piano, the solo instument falls silent for the entire orchestral *tutti*. Thus the orchestral music must justify a re-entrance rather than an entrance. The piano opening is left unresolved, so to speak, and the resultant tension is relieved only by the reappearance of the solo. Given this new strategy, Beethoven no longer felt that the *tutti* had to remain in one key. The orchestral exposition in this concerto is therefore unusually developmental and tonally unstable. Because of the innocent simplicity of the opening solo, we subconsciously equate the piano with stability. We await the piano's return to resolve the tension of instability.

What seems a mere detail in the concerto's opening becomes a significant force in the entire piece. Beginning with piano alone followed by orchestra alone suggests dialogue. This implication is fulfilled in the slow movement, which is entirely a conversation by alternation. Such a procedure is reminiscent of the texture, though hardly the spirit, of the baroque concerto. The piano and orchestra almost never play together until the final measure. Such a form might produce fragmentation in the hands of a lesser composer, but Beethoven avoids this pitfall by varying the length of each statement in the dialogue. Notice how the movement proceeds, in a very general sense, from long statements to short and back again to long.

The finale, which follows the slow movement without pause, continually tries to establish the wrong key as tonic (Beethoven used this same device in the finale of the Second *Razoumovsky* Quartet, written at about the same time). It also deals with dialogue, although in not as single-minded a fashion as the andante. The culmination of the dialogue process occurs in the cadenza, where two different textures in the solo piano alternate. The dialogue goes on, but now it is between the solo instrument and itself, while the orchestra remains silent.

Placing such a strategic event as the culminating solo dialogue in the cadenza shows how far Beethoven had come from the virtuosic piano concerto of his predecessors. The cadenza is traditionally the place where the soloist displays technical prowess. In earlier concertos it has little structural function but rather acts as if in parentheses: after the soloist finishes showing off, the piece gets underway again. Thus Mozart and others traditionally left the cadenza for the soloist to improvise or write, so little did it matter to the concerto's structure what music the cadenza contained. But Beethoven, reluctant to leave any part of his mature compositions to chance, wrote out the cadenzas for use in the G Major Concerto (he did, however, provide two different alternatives for the first movement).

The virtuosity of these cadenzas is largely absent elsewhere in the concerto. Although a greater percentage of bravura passage work might have been expected from the finest pianist of his day composing a concerto for his own use, Beethoven sought to transcend the display concerto of the classical period. The serene and reflective mood of this work tends to preclude pianistic acrobatics, and thus the Fourth Concerto is unique for its time.

Concerto Number 5 in E-Flat Major for Piano and Orchestra, Opus 73, *Emperor*
Allegro
Adagio un poco mosso —
Allegro

The Emperor *Concerto was composed between February and October 1809. Friedrich Schneider was pianist at the first performance in Leipzig on 28 November 1811.*

No one knows how Beethoven's Fifth Piano Concerto came to be known as the *Emperor.* The composer did not give it that title; he would surely not have chosen to honor Emperor Napoléon Bonaparte, whose army occupied Vienna while Beethoven was composing the concerto. Of Napoléon the composer said, "It is a pity that I do not understand the art of war as well as I do the art of music. Then would *I* conquer *him!*"

Napoléon's armies invaded Vienna on 12 May 1809. A week later they seized the island of Loban, near the city. The battle of Wagram took place on 6 July, and from then until Vienna surrendered on 14 October hostilities continued in and around the city. Beethoven's lodgings were in the midst of the fighting, and the noise and commotion often kept him from working on the concerto. At one point he had to seek safety in his brother's basement. The composer described his difficulties:

"We have passed through a great deal of misery. I tell you that since 4 May I have brought into the world little that is connected — only here and there a fragment. The whole course of events has affected me, body and soul. Nor can I have the enjoyment of country life, so indispensable to me. . . . What a disturbing, wild life around me! Nothing but drums, cannons, men, misery of all sorts!"

Beethoven had been ambivalent about Napoléon for years. It is well known that he originally dedicated the *Eroica* Symphony to the French general and then angrily tore off the dedication page when Bonaparte declared himself emperor. Beethoven identified with this powerful, self-made man but was repulsed by Napoléon's willingness to use his strength for destruction and personal gain. The composer was enough of a nationalist to hate Napoléon for invading Vienna, yet at the same time he conducted a performance of the *Eroica* in the hopes that the Emperor would take it as homage. The composer considered accepting a well-paying post at the court of Bonaparte's brother Jerôme, who had recently become king of Westphalia.

Despite the fact that most of Vienna's aristocracy had fled the city, several remaining noblemen banded together to offer Beethoven a substantial honorarium not to accept the position in Westphalia. Archduke Rudolph, Prince Lobkowitz, and Prince Kinsky felt it would be a national disgrace for Beethoven to accept employment at the enemy's court. The aristocrats drew up a contract:

"As it has been demonstrated that only one who is as free from care as possible can devote himself to a single department of activity and create works of magnitude which are exalted and which ennoble art, the undersigned have decided to place Herr Ludwig van Beethoven in a position where the necessities of life shall not cause him embarrassment or clog his powerful genius."

Beethoven was elated. He felt his financial worries were over, and he was able to return to work on the concerto, at least to the extent that the war permitted. He turned down the offer from Westphalia. But his monetary troubles were not at an end. The war led to a devaluation of Austrian currency, so that his annuity became worth far less than his patrons had intended. Furthermore, in the aftermath of the war Prince Lobkowitz went bankrupt. Also, Prince Kinsky died.

Some commentators have heard in the *Emperor* Concerto suggestions of war. Alfred Einstein noted the "apotheosis of the military concept" in what Maynard Solomon later called the "warlike rhythms, victory motives, thrusting melodies, and affirmative character." Einstein attributed the enormous popularity of the work at its first performance to the public taste for military music. Audiences "expected a first movement in 4/4 time of a 'military' character, and they reacted with unmixed pleasure when Beethoven not only fulfilled but surpassed their expectations."

The concerto opens dramatically with the orchestra playing a series of broad, simple chords, each of which the piano extends with wide arpeggios. After three chords the orchestra re-enters with the main theme, and the piano falls silent. Instead of waiting for a dramatic entrance by the solo instrument, as we do in most classical concertos, we await instead a re-entrance. The suspense of waiting for the piano to return casts a psychological tension onto the listening process. The piano finally comes back, just after a restatement of the opening chords.

The second movement alternates lyric melody in the orchestra with accompanied piano figurations. Eventually the two types of music are combined. The entire movement is understated, in preparation for the dramatic shift in key toward the end. This sudden move forms the transition to the finale.

The piano begins the last movement with the main theme, which contains quirky rhythmic irregularities. These rhythms pervade much of the movement. Of particular interest is the duet for piano and timpani just before the end.

It is curious that Beethoven, who was 39 years old when he wrote the *Emperor*, never composed another concerto, although 18 years of life remained to him. His only other attempt was the unfinished Piano Concerto in D (not to be confused with the odd transcription of the Violin Concerto he made for piano and orchestra), of which about sixty pages were scored in 1815. Thus the *Emperor* is the culmination of Beethoven's work in a form that places two forces, solo and orchestra, into dramatic opposition. He never completed another concerto because his later works are not based on the confrontation of musical opposites. The concerto form came to be inappropriate to his style.

Concerto in D Major for Violin and Orchestra, Opus 61
Allegro ma non troppo
Larghetto —
Allegro

The Violin Concerto was begun in 1806 and finished just in time for its first performance on 23 December 1806. The soloist for this Vienna premiere was Franz Clement.

Violinist Franz Clement was one of the most gifted musicians in Beethoven's Vienna. He had made his mark as a child by performing at the Vienna Imperial Opera House from the age of nine, and by playing concertos under the baton of Haydn in London two years later. He made frequent international concert tours. When Beethoven first heard the 14-year-old boy perform in 1794, the composer wrote to the prodigy:

"Continue along the road on which you have already made such a fine and magnificent journey. Nature and art have combined to make a great artist of you. Follow them both and, never fear, you will reach greatness, the highest goal that an artist can desire in the world. All my good wishes for your happiness, dear child, and come back soon so that I can hear your clear, magnificent playing once again."

Clement fulfilled Beethoven's hopes. He grew up to become concertmaster and conductor of the Vienna Opera. Beethoven entrusted
to him conducting the first performance of the *Eroica* Symphony.

Clement had a phenomenal musical memory. The composer Ludwig Spohr recalled how Clement perfectly reproduced long stretches
of an oratorio having heard only two rehearsals and one performance. Clement made a piano reduction of Haydn's large oratorio
The Creation — from memory! And, when the first version of Beethoven's opera *Fidelio* was a failure and a group of musicians met to
decide how to salvage the work, Clement sat at the keyboard and
played the entire score from memory.

Clement decided to give a benefit concert in December 1806. He
asked Beethoven to contribute a violin concerto, and the composer
readily agreed, for Clement was one of the few musicians in Vienna
he respected, — and from whom he would accept criticism. The numerous changes in the manuscript bear witness to their frequent editorial sessions. Since the composer was not himself a violinist, he
had to rely on Clement's expertise in practical matters.

As was often the case with Beethoven, the work was completed
only at the last minute. Clement had often gone over the solo part
with the composer, but there was not enough time for even a single
full rehearsal with orchestra. Miraculously, the performance was not
a fiasco, as Clement's keen memory of the sketches compensated for
the lack of practicing time. But it could not have been a completely
convincing performance either, as the unfavorable reviews would
seem to indicate. The situation was furthermore not helped by Clement's tendency to show off. He actually played a sonata of his own
between the first and second movements of the concerto, and, in order to keep the audience's interest, he played it on only one string of
a violin held upside down!

The audience reaction was lukewarm. Even if the performance
had been well rehearsed and not interrupted by Clement's silly display of ego, the concerto still might have puzzled its original listeners. It was far longer and more complex than any previous violin
concerto. The concertos of Mozart, for example, are modest in comparison. But Beethoven's work is expansive and symphonic. One
critic, while praising Clement's performance, wrote of the concerto,
"The musical argument is often quite loose, and the unending repetition of certain rather ordinary passages might easily become wear-
isome."

There was a second, somewhat more successful performance a
year later, but in the following thirty years there were no more than
a half dozen performances. It was not until another boy, Joseph
Joachim, played the concerto in 1844 (at the age of 13) under the

direction of Felix Mendelssohn that the work was fully appreciated. Henceforth it entered the standard repertoire of every concert violinist.

The critic's "unending repetition of certain rather ordinary passages" no doubt refers to the principal motive of the first movement. Heard quietly at the outset in solo timpani, this figure is the simplest possible musical gesture: five evenly played repetitions of the same note. The figure may be commonplace, but its subsequent development is hardly simplistic. The simplicity of the motive allows it to be used in a variety of contexts, lending an undercurrent of tension to this otherwise gentle movement. Beethoven unifies the movement by the pervasive use of this figure. There is scarcely a page of the movement that does not contain this motive, whether blatantly orchestrated as at the recapitulation, tucked away within a melodic line as in the second theme, speeded up as in repeated sixteenth-note passages, or hidden in an accompanimental line.

The first movement creates inner tension in another manner. It makes us wait as long as possible before the violin enters. We must wait even longer before hearing the entire lyrical second theme played by the solo instrument: it comes directly after the cadenza, with a wonderfully peaceful feeling.

These undercurrents of tension subtly disturb the beautifully melodic, wonderfully lyrical, almost pastoral melodies of this movement. Despite these tensions, though, the movement moves at a leisurely pace. Notice, for example, how long the music remains on one harmony (the dominant) when the soloist first enters. It is almost as if Beethoven stops time for a moment, to let the violin slowly assert itself.

The slow movement is a dialogue between the solo instrument, which usually plays florid figures, and the orchestra, whose music is generally unadorned. At the end, the music turns suddenly almost operatic in what turns out to be a direct transition into the finale.

The finale opens with a straightforward rondo tune for the solo instrument. Beethoven instructs the soloist to play this melody solely on the G string, the lowest string on the violin, despite the tune's frequent rise into the registers of the A and D strings. The result, besides being difficult to perform well, is a special nasal timbre which lends this folk-like tune its special character. The movement presents contrasting ideas but returns inevitably to this main theme.

The ending is particularly clever. The music seems to have nothing more to say. It simplifies and seems about to die away, when the solo instrument returns for one final quiet suggestion of the main tune. Then, at the last possible moment, the full orchestra plays two short concluding loud chords.

Concerto in C Major for Violin, Cello, Piano, and Orchestra, Opus 56, *Triple*

Allegro
Largo —
Rondo alla polacca

The Triple Concerto was begun late in 1803 and completed in the summer of 1804. It was first performed in Vienna in May 1808, on a concert for the nobility beginning at 6:00 a.m.

Beethoven began to sketch the Triple Concerto while he was at work on the *Eroica* Symphony. It is hard to imagine two more different works composed by one person at the same time. The symphony is powerful while the concerto is restrained; the symphony is strikingly original, foreshadowing the symphonic developments of the entire nineteenth century, while the concerto looks backward to the classical era's *sinfonie concertante.*

The concerto was written for Archduke Rudolph, who at age 16 had recently become Beethoven's piano student. The composer was eager to provide the Archduke with an opportunity to perform as a soloist, yet he knew his student's musical limitations. Beethoven once said that Rudolph could play well only "when he is feeling just right." The Archduke could never manage a solo concerto, but he could function adequately as a member of a solo trio, provided the piano part was less demanding than the violin and cello parts, which were to be played by professionals. The simplicity of the piano part (a few passages do achieve a degree of virtuosity) is indicated by the fact that there are arrangements of the work for trio alone, in which the string parts remain intact while the piano plays the original piano *and* orchestra music. Beethoven's generous compromise for the sake of Rudolph's modest abilities helped create a lifelong friendship between the composer and the young Archduke, who in later years became one of Beethoven's major patrons.

Beethoven tried several times to secure publication for the concerto. He offered it to Breitkopf and Härtel as early as 14 October 1803, when only a few sketches existed. Nothing came of this attempt, but the composer renewed his efforts with the same publishing house on 26 August 1804 and again on 10 October 1804. The work was finally printed by a different house in 1807. For unknown reasons, the dedication was not to Archduke Rudolph but to another patron, Prince Lobkowitz. Only after the work was published was it finally performed, by players other than the trio for whom it was composed. The soloists at the premiere had not learned their music particularly well, and their poor performance helped make the concerto rather unpopular with listeners. It was not played again during Beethoven's lifetime, and it remains to this day one of the composer's least performed large-scale works.

Writing a triple concerto presented Beethoven with several orchestrational challenges. Was the trio to be treated as a single soloist or as three solo performers? If the former, the work might be too frequently dense, which would be inappropriate to the delicate nature of its themes. But if the trio were really three separate soloists, then each would "want" a turn at playing all the main themes, thus creating a work of considerable length. Beethoven chose a compromise solution: the trio is usually treated as two solo groups: a string duet and a piano solo. This idea gave the concerto its large but not unmanageable scope, it allowed for sufficient variety of tone color, and it made it possible for Archduke Rudolph sometimes to be featured as piano soloist.

Another challenge was to allow all three solo instruments to be heard equally. The piano is unlikely to be covered by the orchestra, because the two media have such different colors. The violin is also unlikely to be obscured, because that instrument can sound quite high. But the cello is in danger of being buried. Beethoven's solution was to write the cello frequently high in its own register, so that it often plays on its penetrating A-string. Thus the cello part became more virtuosic than either of the other solo parts.

A further consequence of the special scoring is the nature of the themes in the outer movements. They are made up mostly of short fragments; only rarely are they full-fledged tunes. Thus the trio can pass around bits of melody, and the concerto can utilize every combination of one, two, or three soloists, often in rapid alternation. The slow movement, by contrast, explores the lyricism of one expansive theme. By the time it is heard in the solo cello and then again in the solo violin (accompanied by the other solo instruments plus a few winds), the movement is nearly complete. Thus the lovely middle movement is hardly more than an introduction to the finale (a practice Beethoven also used in the *Waldstein* Sonata, composed at about the same time).

The last movement is a *polacca,* which is a Polish folk dance also known as a polonaise. The polonaise dates back at least to the seventeenth century, when it was danced by nobility to a sung accompaniment. The musical style of this dance remains part of Polish folklore to the present day. Perhaps because it signified Polish style and taste, German composers (notably J. S. Bach) used it in their instrumental dance suites. Beethoven followed the traditional model by casting the main theme in 3/4 time without upbeat and by using the characteristic polonaise rhythm.

Coriolan Overture, Opus 62

The Coriolan *Overture was composed in 1807. Beethoven conducted the first performance at Prince Lobkowitz's palace in Vienna in March 1807.*

Beethoven needed to compose a concert overture. He had written only one, other than the overtures belonging with his opera *Fidelio*. The *Prometheus* Overture was frequently used to open his concerts, and the composer wanted a fresh piece for this purpose. He found an appropriate subject in his friend Heinrich von Collin's tragedy *Coriolanus*. This play had premiered in 1802 and had been performed frequently during the next three years. The public knew it well. It was revived for one performance in April 1807, specifically for the purpose of uniting Beethoven's music with Collin's drama.

The overture is not truly programmatic. Beethoven rarely wrote music that followed a specific story. The *Pastorale* Symphony is about as close as he came to descriptive instrumental music. But he often was inspired by the character of a particular person, especially if that person was a hero. Thus the *Eroica* Symphony is not a musical portrait of Napoléon but rather the result of the composer identifying with the titanic character of the Frenchman. Similarly, the music to *Egmont* reveals more of the composer than it does of Goethe's hero.

Beethoven knew the legendary character Coriolanus not only in Collin's treatment but also from Plutarch's account of the Roman general and from Shakespeare's play *Coriolanus*. Collin's drama concerns the exiled general, who joins the Volscians, the traditional enemies of Rome, and marches against his own people. The Volscians lay seige to Rome, and the Romans, in desperation, send to Coriolanus a delegation led by his mother and wife. The general's pride and determination are eventually worn down by his mother's pleas. He yields and withdraws his forces, thus incurring the wrath of the Volscians. He is finally driven to suicide.

Beethoven felt an affinity for Coriolanus' qualities of daring, individualism, pride, and recklessness; he knew the loneliness of one who would yield to none; yet he understood the power of feminine persuasion to undermine all those noble qualities. The struggle between love and patriotism must have been especially meaningful to the composer, who held both qualities high. He also understood the alarm and humiliation of a city beseiged and forced to resort to pleading with the enemy: Vienna had just fallen to the French.

The conflict between pride and love in the tragic figure of Coriolanus corresponds to the contrast of the two main themes of the overture, one impetuous and one lyrical. The impetuous mood is proclaimed immediately, with the strings playing a single note followed by a short loud orchestral chord and a dramatic silence. Notice how stridently dissonant the short chord is when the gesture is repeated, as the trumpets and timpani stubbornly repeat their notes from the preceding chord despite the changed harmony. The overture's quiet ending signifies the hero's death.

The Creatures of Prometheus Overture, Opus 43

The Creatures of Prometheus was composed in 1801. The first performance was given in Vienna on 28 March 1801.

Beethoven composed ballets only twice. His first such work, the *Ritterballett,* he wrote at the age of 21. He acted as ghostwriter for his patron Count Waldstein, who was listed as composer at the first performance. Ten years later Beethoven returned to music for the dance for his *Creatures of Prometheus,* a ballet with overture, introduction, and 16 scenes.

The producer of *Prometheus* was Salvatore Viganó, who was renowned for bringing dignity and realism to the dance. Beethoven and Viganó experienced differences typical of a composer working with a ballet master. Beethoven complained that the choreographer did not pay enough attention to the music, while Viganó felt that the composer was trying to treat the dance as background to the music. Nonetheless, the production was a huge success. It was given 29 times in 1801–02 and thus contributed greatly to Beethoven's emerging reputation as a major artist. The popularity of his first major effort for the theater led directly to his receiving a commission for a full-length opera, *Fidelio.*

When composing *Prometheus* Beethoven had to obey certain ballet conventions. He was required to produce a series of relatively short, independent pieces, each of which derived its rhythm precisely from stylized dance gestures. The music thus had to enhance the stage movement and could not be too dramatic itself. Probably because of these strictures, and also because public tastes eventually turned away from Viganó's style of ballet, the music fell into disuse.

Beethoven never again wrote for the dance, and in fact it was not until 1875, the year of Tchaikovsky's *Swan Lake*, that any other major composer wrote a full-length ballet.

Of the *Prometheus* music only the overture remained in the concert repertoire. It was, for a time, the only overture Beethoven had composed, and thus it was often used to open his concerts. He did, however, retain a fondness for some of the other music of the ballet. One number is a direct ancestor of the storm movement of the *Pastorale* Symphony. Another movement presages the *larghetto* of the Second Symphony, written the following year. Beethoven recast two of the ballet pieces as ballroom dances. The theme of one of these dances he also used for his Variations and Fugue for Piano, Opus 35. This melody is best known, however, as the theme of the finale of the *Eroica* Symphony.

The story of the ballet concerns Prometheus, the god who fashions the first man and woman from clay and water. He models them after the best qualities of animals and then gives them life with fire stolen from heaven. He finds himself unable to give his creatures the power to reason, and he decides to destroy them. But he is stopped by a higher power. Prometheus then brings man and woman to hear the music of Apollo, which creates in them the ability to reason. Melpomene, the Muse of Tragedy, gives them tragic emotions, and Thalia, the Muse of Comedy, teaches them to laugh. They learn to dance from Terpsichore, the Muse of Dancing, and Bacchus shows them the pleasures of wine. Only then are the creatures ready to begin life's journey.

The delightful overture is thoroughly Mozartian. It scarcely hints at the musical dramas to come in Beethoven's subsequent orchestral music. It opens in an interesting manner. The forceful first four measures sound more like the end of an adagio introduction than a beginning: after the loud *fermata* in the fourth measure, we expect to go into a rollicking allegro. But instead we hear music which sounds more like the real beginning — a soft, slow, melodic statement of the tonic chord. The dramatic first measures are never again heard, as the adagio is replaced by an allegro that begins with a rapid string theme.

Leonore Overtures
Number 1 in C Major, Opus 138
Number 2 in C Major, Opus 72a
Number 3 in C Major, Opus 72b

The non-chronological numbering of the Leonore *Overtures, all intended but then rejected as the prelude to the opera* Fidelio, *derives from long-standing confusion over the date of composition of Number 1. Since it is shorter and less complex than Numbers 2 and 3, it was once thought to have been written first. Because it was never performed during Beethoven's lifetime and never at all with* Fidelio, *knowledge of its origins was minimal. Only in 1977 was the actual date established by musicologist Alan Tyson, in part by studying the watermarks on Beethoven's manuscript papers.*

The first Leonore *Overture was actually composed early in 1807. Bernhard Romberg conducted the first performance, in Vienna, on 7 February 1828. The second* Leonore *was composed in October and November 1805 and first performed (with the opera) in Vienna on 20 November 1805. The third* Leonore *was composed early in 1806 and first heard (with the opera) on 26 March 1827 in Vienna.*

Beethoven experienced no end of difficulties in composing and producing his only opera, *Fidelio.* He revised it many times for different performances, some of which never took place. Some parts of the opera, such as the introduction to Florestan's aria, were revised as many as 18 times. Beethoven wrote no fewer than four different overtures for the work. In addition, he used a totally different prelude for one production and actually sketched a fifth overture.

The main reason for all the changes was his inexperience in writing for the stage. In contrast to Mozart and Cherubini, the two opera composers Beethoven most admired, he had never served an apprenticeship in an opera house. His first music drama was destined to be his only one. It was a work of his mature years, when he was already expected to be a master of his craft. *Fidelio* eventually became a beautiful stage work with considerable dramatic impact, but even in its final form it is admittedly uneven.

Fidelio is a "rescue opera," a genre quite popular in the late eighteenth and early nineteenth centuries. Rescue operas combine suspense, loyalty, and the triumph of virtue over evil in stories that involve the escape of a central character from a dire fate. Particularly in the violent aftermath of the French Revolution, rescue operas were well liked because of their many exciting escapes from death (and, as well, many tragic failures to be rescued).

Musicologist Donald Grout gives the following brief outline of the plot:

Florestan has been unjustly imprisoned. His wife Leonora, disguised as a man under the name of Fidelio, obtains the post of assistant to Rocco, the jailer. There are two subsidiary characters: the jailer's daughter Marzelline and her lover, the porter Jaquino. Pizarro, governor of the prison, has been warned that Don Fernando, the minister of state, is coming to investigate the cases of the prisoners. Pizarro therefore determines to murder Florestan, but Leonora prevents him. At that instant Don Fernando arrives, sets Florestan free, and punishes Pizarro.

Beethoven, who was in constant search of the ideal drama for an opera, was taken by this story's themes of unselfish love, loyalty, courage, sacrifice, endurance, and heroism. He was apparently unable at first to discern the dramatic weaknesses in the libretto. He began work on the project in 1804, and he composed virtually nothing else for the next year and a half. The first performance of the opera was scheduled for 15 October 1805, under the title *Leonore,* but Beethoven had not finished the music and the premiere had to be postponed. The overture was one of the numbers not yet ready. This first overture, now known illogically as *Leonore* Number 2, was eventually completed for the actual performance on 20 November. By this time Napoléon's armies had occupied Vienna, so that many Austrians had fled and the audience included several officers of the enemy forces. With few friends but several real enemies in attendance, Beethoven had little chance of success. *Fidelio,* as the work was now called, met with an indifferent response.

The difficult political climate and the unfavorable reviews combined to keep audiences away from the theater for two subsequent performances. *Fidelio* closed a failure. Beethoven was not easily defeated, however, and he set about revising the work extensively. The long, undramatic first act was cut severely, the first and second acts were combined, and the overture was rewritten. The new overture, today known as *Leonore* Number 3, was heard when the new *Fidelio* made its debut on 29 March 1806. The revised version of the opera fared somewhat better than the original had, but it closed after only two performances, in part because of strained relations between composer and performers.

There was talk of a Berlin performance in 1806 and a Prague production in 1807, but neither materialized. For the latter Beethoven provided yet another overture, now called *Leonore* Number 1. But the opera lay dormant until a revival in 1814, for which the composer again rewrote the score extensively. He intended once again to provide a new overture, but was unable to complete it in time for the performance on 23 May. Rather than return to one of the earlier overtures, Beethoven substituted *The Ruins of Athens.* By the second performance three days later, he had completed the final overture, the one that has remained with *Fidelio* until the present: the *Fidelio* Overture. The opera was at last a success. It played several times, although the composer continued to make revisions.

Beethoven's search for an integrated dramatic statement in the opera parallels his struggle to find the right overture. It is interesting to compare the three *Leonore* Overtures in order to understand the evolution of Beethoven's conception of the proper way to introduce the opera.

Overture Number 2, Beethoven's first attempt, is long and dramatic — too much so, in fact, to serve as just a prelude to a real drama. The overture begins with an enormous introduction, which starts forcefully yet soon gives way to an extensive quotation of Florestan's aria. There follows a gradually building passage based on rising triads and figures from the Florestan theme. The crescendo reaches an enormous outburst, followed by silence, both of which are repeated. The music subsides into a mysterious progression in the low strings, which serves as transition to the allegro: after a considerable time, the main part of the overture has finally arrived.

Beethoven sought to tighten this somewhat diffuse structure when he rewrote the overture for the 1806 production. *Leonore* Number 3 is thus more concise, more compact, more logically developed, and shorter than Number 2. And therein lay a problem, because Number 3 became actually more dramatic than Number 2, and the ensuing opera seems pallid by comparison.

The crucial dramatic moment of both Numbers 2 and 3 is the appearance of an offstage trumpet. The music is taken from the opera. It is the call of the watchman in the tower warning Pizarro of the arrival of the Minister. In Number 2 the trumpet call arrives at the end of an extensive development section. This moment is late in the overture, and thus Beethoven wisely chose not to attempt a full-scale recapitulation afterwards. That would have made this already lengthy overture far too long. Instead, Florestan's theme returns, followed by a swift coda. In Number 3, however, the trumpet call occurs several minutes earlier. There is still time for more development. The trumpet call is more an interruption than the culmination it is in Number 2. The development resumes and leads dramatically to a full-scale recapitulation.

Comparing the codas of Numbers 2 and 3 shows Beethoven's strategy of revision. In Number 2 we hear a relatively brief whirlwind that closes the overture in typical theatrical fashion. The coda even includes a speeded-up version of the main theme. The drama in Number 2 has led up to the trumpet call. There is little left to do other than to end. But Number 3 has been restrained up to this point, saving its drama and energies for the coda. It too is a whirlwind *presto*, but it is twice as long. For once Number 3 takes its time. It has earned the right to develop carefully, to build excitement, to be subtle — all qualities used up by this point in Number 2. Tremendous excitement builds throughout the coda in Number 3, culminating in a fiercely dissonant chord shortly before the end.

In *Leonore* Number 3 Beethoven composed a shorter and in some ways less complex overture, but he also created a highly integrated composition that cannot serve as introduction to a larger work. Number 3 is a complete and totally self-contained concert piece, but it is not an opera overture. Thus he had to try once again, and the result was *Leonore* Number 1. This overture continued Number 3's trend toward brevity and simplicity, but it too did not go far enough. It was only in 1814, with the short, light *Fidelio* Overture, that Beethoven finally avoided undue length and complexity.

In order to prevent excessive drama in *Leonore* Number 1, the composer bypassed the quintessential dramatic form, the sonata-allegro. Thus Number 1 is in no sense a revision of Numbers 2 or 3, although it does share with them Florestan's theme. (Only the *Fidelio* Overture, paradoxically, contains no thematic reference to the opera it so aptly introduces.) Number 1, like Numbers 2 and 3, begins with an introduction: a slow rising figure in the violins, which soon leads to a full chord in the orchestra. Listen carefully to this chord. Beethoven has some of the instruments enter after the others. This syncopation casts its spell on much of the remaining music. For example, when a lyric theme gives way to a transition to the allegro, syncopations increase, so that the main allegro theme both contains and is accompanied by off-beats. After a second theme the music unexpectedly stops on three sustained chords. Florestan's adagio theme then follows. It is treated at some length, before the allegro resumes with the main theme. This return constitutes a recapitulation: the Florestan melody has replaced the traditional development section. Hence there is little trace here of the developmental tensions of Overtures 2 and 3.

The lack of development and drama has made Number 1 less frequently played than Numbers 2 or 3 or even the *Fidelio* Overture. Beethoven himself never had Number 1 performed, even after he realized that it too, like Numbers 2 and 3, could not serve as prelude to the opera. In fact, Number 1 was all but unknown until after the composer's death, when it was offered for sale along with several obscure minor works. *Leonore* Number 1 was first performed nearly a year after Beethoven died.

Symphony Number 1 in C Major, Opus 21
Adagio molto. Allegro con brio
Andante cantabile con moto
Menuetto: Allegro molto e vivace. Trio. Menuetto
Adagio. Allegro molto e vivace

The First Symphony was composed in 1799–1800, with sketches dating from 1795. Beethoven conducted the first performance in Vienna on 2 April 1800.

"A caricature of Haydn pushed to absurdity." So one reviewer criticized Beethoven's C Major Symphony when the composer introduced it at his first large-scale concert in Vienna. Beethoven's reaction to this harsh criticism is not known, but the inevitable comparison with Haydn must have irked him. Haydn had been his teacher as well as a principal influence, and the years around 1800 were marked by a struggle to get beyond this influence and to establish his own style and career. Beethoven's relations with his former teacher were as strained during these years as they had been during his student years, 1792–93.

At that time Haydn, recognizing the genius and potential of his pupil, had requested that Beethoven publicly call himself "student of Haydn." The headstrong young composer, feeling that Haydn envied him, refused. Beethoven, who was a less than ideal student, insulted his mentor a second time: while he went to Haydn for counterpoint lessons, he secretly sought out another teacher for help with his homework. Haydn eventually found out about Beethoven's duplicity and was understandably annoyed. Beethoven was less than honest with Haydn in another way: he presented his teacher with "new" works that were really pieces he had written years earlier in Bonn. Haydn furthermore resented Beethoven's rapid rise in Viennese society. This young musician was not about to spend two-thirds of his life as a servant to nobility.

Even if Beethoven was less than conscientious with his counterpoint exercises, and even though Haydn was apparently equally lackadaisical about correcting them, the younger composer learned important lessons from the master's works. The treatment of sonata form, of large-scale harmony, of the emotional power of contrast, of ways to achieve unity within variety — these characteristics of Haydn's finest music were models for the compositions of Beethoven's early maturity. While the First Symphony does not quite sound as if Haydn could have written it, Beethoven could never have made such an auspicious entry into the ranks of symphonists without a deep understanding of what Haydn had achieved in his own symphonies.

Haydn had planned to take his young protégé with him when he made his second triumphant journey to London in 1794, but the increasingly difficult relations and mistrust between teacher and pupil made Haydn reconsider. The counterpoint lessons ceased when Haydn left, and the two men never resumed a formal teacher-student relationship. Once Haydn returned to Vienna in 1795, Beethoven brought music to him occasionally for criticism, which he alternately appreciated and resented. Beethoven respected his older colleague, but he felt himself potentially in competition with him. This sense of rivalry surfaced around 1800, when Beethoven could no longer be content as the composer of Haydnesque trios and sonatas. He openly challenged Haydn's reputation as the greatest living composer when he brought before the public his First Symphony.

Today it is difficult to appreciate the boldness of the First Symphony. Compared to the powerful *Eroica* or Fifth, the C Major seems tame. But to turn-of-the-century listeners it suggested a frightening new vision of music as an art of strong emotions rather than of social graces. To be sure, some works of Mozart and Haydn had already exceeded the emotionalism of the First, but their most popular music was not such *Sturm und Drang* ("storm and stress") pieces but rather their elegantly refined and classical cousins. Now that we know Beethoven's other symphonies, the First does seem to belong more to the era of Haydn than to the romantic century, and thus it is no surprise that the C Major long remained Beethoven's most popular symphony with conservative Viennese audiences.

Nonetheless, the radical newness of some features of the First Symphony was not missed by its first listeners. In the very first chord contemporary ears might well have heard the dawning of a new age. It was virtually unprecedented in 1800 to begin a symphony with a dissonance; it was all the more bold to open not in the proper key of C major but rather with a suggestion of F major. The orchestration — *pizzicato* strings giving an extra bite to the beginning of each wind chord — adds to the novelty of the passage. From this dramatic beginning the music starts an inexorable and intense drive toward the allegro, which arrives with an enormous sense of resolution: C major at last!

There are other bold strokes beyond this "off-key" opening. The pulsating of timpani in the slow movement (which seemingly cannot decide whether it wants to be a fugue or a sonata form) is quite original, as is the character of the third movement. Although marked "minuet" in the usual manner, the movement is more a scherzo, like those in Beethoven's later symphonies. The composer realized that, as the symphony became more dramatic in his hands than it had been in Haydn's and Mozart's, the stately minuet (left over from stylized baroque dance suites and roccoco serenades) had no place. With Beethoven the third movement functions as light-hearted or even comic relief after the emotional depths of occasionally turbulent first and sometimes soulful second movements. In this scherzo-minuet the 3/4 time moves so rapidly that we feel not three beats but one to the measure. As a result the opening eight-measure phrase, which is in reality only eight beats long, seems maddeningly truncated when, in the traditional manner, it is not repeated on its final appearance.

Another innovation in the First Symphony occurs in the introduction to the finale. The violins keep going up the same scale, unaccompanied, achieving one higher note with each successive ascent. This seemingly simple-minded gesture borders on the absurd, thus making it an extreme contrast to the sophisticated allegro that follows, in which the ascending scale becomes a pervasive motive that is now anything but obvious. It is known that some early conductors actually omitted the introduction for fear that it would make audiences laugh!

The contrast of such obvious humor with the refined wit of Haydn symbolizes the differences between the two composers' aesthetics. Beethoven was capable of both more obvious and more subtle gestures than was his mentor. By comparing Beethoven's First Symphony with the last works of Haydn in that genre (composed five years earlier), we can observe in embryo some of the basic differences between classic and romantic music.

Haydn's reaction to the First Symphony is not recorded, but one would like to think that he understood the potential for future greatness contained in its modest innovations. The confluence of homage toward and revolt against Haydn's music that we hear in the symphony surely reflects the composer's ambivalent feelings at the time toward his old teacher, whom Beethoven consulted less and less frequently. In his last years Haydn expressed both disappointment over his former pupil's neglect and bewilderment with Beethoven's overtly revolutionary compositions, such as the *Eroica* Symphony. Once Haydn died in 1809, however, Beethoven stopped making disparaging comments and expressed nothing but admiration for the composer whose music had helped to shape his own.

Symphony Number 2 in D Major, Opus 36
Adagio molto. Allegro con brio
Larghetto
Allegro
Allegro molto

The Second Symphony was composed in 1802. Beethoven con-
ducted the first performance in Vienna on 5 April 1803.

For some time Beethoven had been alarmed over the weakening of
his hearing. How could he function as a musician if he were to become deaf? What chagrin he would feel if he, the world's greatest
composer, could not hear! He consulted several doctors, each of
whom prescribed a different remedy. Nothing worked. He had days
of good hearing and days when he could barely make out conversations. There were times when he could hear music perfectly and other
times when he could not even rehearse, because all he could perceive
were high notes.

One of his doctors felt that a few months away from the tumult
of Vienna might help. So the composer went for six months to the
small town of Heiligenstadt. There he composed the Second Symphony. Also, he had time and solitude to reflect on the consequences
of his loss of hearing. He faced up to the inevitability of eventual
deafness, he contemplated suicide, and he wrote down his anguished
concerns in a document known as the "Heiligenstadt Testament." The
testament is ostensibly addressed to Beethoven's brothers, although
at times he seems to speak to all of humanity, sometimes to God, and
at other times to one special, unnamed person.

Oh you men who think or say that I am malevolent, stubborn,
or misanthropic, how greatly do you wrong me. You do not
know the secret cause which makes me seem that way to you.
From childhood on, my heart and soul have been full of the tender feeling of goodwill, and I was ever inclined to accomplish
great things. But, think that for six years now I have been hopelessly afflicted, made worse by senseless physicians, from year
to year deceived with hopes of improvement, finally compelled
to face the prospect of a *lasting malady* (whose cure will take
years or, perhaps, be impossible). Though born with a fiery, active temperament, even susceptible to the diversions of society,
I was soon compelled to withdraw myself, to live life alone. If at
times I tried to forget all this, oh how harshly I was flung back

by the doubly sad experience of my bad hearing! Yet it was impossible for me to say to people, "Speak louder, shout, for I am deaf." Ah, how could I possibly admit an infirmity in the *one sense* which ought to be more perfect in me than in others, a sense which I once possessed in the highest perfection, a perfection such as few in my profession enjoy or have ever enjoyed. Oh, I cannot do it; therefore forgive me when you see me draw back when I would have gladly mingled with you. My misfortune is doubly painful to me because I am bound to be misunderstood; for me there can be no relaxation with my fellow men, no refined conversations, no mutual exchange of ideas. I must live almost alone, like one who has been banished; I can mix with society only as much as true necessity demands. If I approach near to people, a hot terror seizes upon me, and I fear being exposed to the danger that my condition might be noticed. . . . What a humiliation for me when someone standing next to me heard a flute in the distance and I heard nothing, or someone heard a *shepherd singing* and again I heard nothing! Such incidents drove me almost to despair; a little more of that and I would have ended my life — it was only *my art* that held me back. Ah, it seemed to me impossible to leave the world until I had brought forth all that I felt was within me. . . .

That fond hope, which I brought here with me — to be cured to a degree at least — this I must now wholly abandon. As the leaves of autumn fall and are withered, so likewise has my hope been blighted. I leave here — almost as I came — even the high courage, which often inspired me in the beautiful days of summer, has disappeared. Oh Providence, grant me at last but one day *of pure joy*. It is so long since real joy echoed in my heart.

One might expect such anguished feelings to be reflected in the music composed at the time of the Heiligenstadt Testament, but the Second Symphony is surprisingly happy, carefree, and innocently sunny. One might expect that Beethoven's concern over his hearing would eat away at his creativity, but he was composing at breakneck speed. One might expect that the composer would give up, but instead he plunged himself into composing with renewed ardor, and soon his music matured into his extraordinary second-period style.

His deafness actually may have helped more than harmed his work. He was forced to retire from the concert stage, and so he devoted more time to composition. Also, as his deafness increased, he kept more and more to himself, thereby developing the strong inner personality that shines through in his mature works. Although he did have occasional periods of normal hearing almost to the end of his life, his deafness made him more and more withdrawn. He shunned the company of all but his close friends, and he compensated for his isolation with an incredible intensity in his music.

People often wonder how someone can compose if he is deaf. Composers imagine the sounds of their music in their minds. They usually do not need to rely on the actual physical sounds of instruments. If they compose at the piano at all, for example, it is more for convenience than necessity. Beethoven was already an experienced composer when he began to lose his hearing. He knew exactly what his music sounded like, without having actually to listen to it. Occasional slips in orchestration in his later works have been attributed to his deafness, but his sense of melody, harmony, and counterpoint — the essentials of his art — never wavered.

A later composer, Hector Berlioz, provided an interesting and useful description of the Second Symphony:

> In this symphony everything is noble, energetic, and proud. The introduction is a masterpiece. The most beautiful effects follow one another without confusion and always in an unexpected manner. The song is of touching solemnity, and it at once commands respect and puts the hearer in an emotional mood. The rhythm is already bolder, the instrumentation richer, more sonorous, more varied. An *allegro con brio* of enchanting dash is joined to this admirable adagio. The *grupetto* [the rapid figure that forms the principal motive], which is found in the first measure of the theme, given at first to the violas and cellos in unison, is taken up again in an isolated form, to establish either progressions in a crescendo or else imitative passages between wind instruments and strings. . . .
>
> The *larghetto* is not treated after the manner of the First Symphony. It is not composed of a theme worked out in canonic imitation, but it is a pure and frank song, which at first is sung simply by the strings and then is embroidered with a rare elegance by means of light and fluent figures. Their character is never far removed from the sentiment of tenderness which forms the distinctive personality of the principal idea. It is a ravishing picture of innocent pleasure, which is scarcely shadowed by a few melancholy accents. . . .
>
> The scherzo is as frankly gay in its fantastic capriciousness as the second movement has been wholly and serenely happy, for this symphony is smiling throughout. The warlike outbursts of the first allegro are completely free from violence; there is only the youthful ardor of a noble heart, in which the most beautiful illusions of life are preserved untainted. The composer still believes in love, in immortal glory, in devotion. What abandon

in his gaiety! What wit! What sallies! Hearing these various instruments disputing over fragments of a theme which no one of them plays in its complete form, hearing each fragment thus colored with a thousand nuances as it passes from one to the other, it is as though you were watching the fairy sports of Oberon's graceful spirits. . . .

The closing movement is of like nature. It is a second scherzo, in 2/2 time, and its playfulness has perhaps something still more delicate, more piquant.

Berlioz' descriptive terms — noble, energetic, proud, touching solemnity, enchanting dash, rare elegance, tenderness, ravishing picture of innocent pleasure, frankly gay, serenely happy, delicate, etc. — certainly do not suggest the turmoil of Beethoven's mind as revealed in the Heiligenstadt Testament. The human mind, particularly that of a genius like Beethoven, is complex. It is capable of operating on independent planes at once. Beethoven demonstrated this fact more than once. His Eighth Symphony, for example, is just as carefree and witty as the Second, yet it too was written during a difficult period.

Beethoven had a strong character, and he always managed to emerge the victor in his internal struggles. That he surmounted his deafness to go on composing is more important than the degree to which his struggles were manifested in the music. Eventually his inner strength did gain expression in, for example, his next symphony, the *Eroica*. Perhaps, at the time of the Second, his musical personality was not yet ready to express the anguish over his deafness because he had not yet mastered his fate. As a result the Second Symphony could become a happy creation, although written at the unhappiest of times.

Symphony Number 3 in E-Flat Major, Opus 55, *Eroica*
Allegro con brio
Marcia funebre: adagio assai
Allegro vivace
Allegro molto. Andante. Presto

The Third Symphony was composed in the summer of 1803. The first public performance was given in Vienna, conducted by Franz Clement, on 7 April 1805.

Perhaps the most popular image of Beethoven is of a heroic humanitarian who used music as a force for freedom and against tyranny, as the "man who freed music" (actually the title of a popular biography of the composer). One source of this view is the *Eroica* Symphony, the work with which Beethoven ushered in a new style that completely and permanently changed the very nature of music. The symphony was intended to be an homage to Napoléon Bonaparte, the general who had led the struggle for freedom in France, but the composer angrily removed the dedication when Bonaparte had himself crowned Emperor. The powerful, liberating, heroic nature of the Third Symphony is unmistakable, whatever the degree of influence Bonaparte really had on its composition.

Beethoven was deeply ambivalent about Bonaparte. He identified with this self-made man who, at least early in his career, fought for freedom, justice, and equality. He admired the Frenchman's courageous leadership and, like many European intellectuals of the time, applauded Bonaparte's restoration of order in post-Revolutionary France. But Beethoven also deplored Napoléon's continual wars of conquest. As early as 1796 Beethoven was composing anti-Napoléonic patriotic songs. He reacted strongly against the suggestion of a publisher that he compose a sonata celebrating Napoléon:

"Has the devil got hold of you all, gentlemen, that you suggest that *I should compose such a sonata?* Well, perhaps at the time of the Revolutionary fever, such a thing might have been possible, but now, when everything is trying to slip back into the old rut . . . , to write a sonata of that kind? . . . But good Heavens, such a sonata — in these newly developing Christian times — ho, ho — there you must leave me out. You will get nothing from me."

Yet Beethoven soon started not a sonata but an enormous *Bonaparte* Symphony, even though the French general had two years earlier invaded and defeated Austria. It was impossible to live in Vienna and remain neutral about Napoléon; to compose a work in honor of the conquerer (especially at a time when renewed war was imminent) would have been pointedly anti-patriotic. Why, then, did the composer decide to dedicate a symphony to Bonaparte?

The easy reason is that he was considering a permanent move to Paris, and he thought such a work would provide an entry into French social and intellectual circles. But there were deeper reasons. Beethoven despised the way Vienna's artists had to depend on patronage from the aristocracy, and he thought that the dedication of a major symphony to Vienna's enemy, coupled with a well-timed move to the enemy's capitol, would be an appropriate slap in the face to those who wielded artistic power through wealth. His recent anti-Napoléonic songs and dedications to Austrian nobility had been acts of a faithful servant of the state. But, deep down, he was an independent spirit who hated Viennese society. He saw the French general, who had proclaimed the liberty of all people, as the symbol of his own desired independence from an aristocratic society that supported him financially. The inner manifestation of his struggle to be free of a social system on which he depended for his livelihood was his intense ambivalence toward Bonaparte; the outer manifestation of this ambivalence was the *Eroica* Symphony.

Shortly after finishing the symphony, Beethoven received the news that France's First Consul had declared himself emperor. Beethoven's friend Ferdinand Ries recounted the composer's reaction:

> Beethoven esteemed him greatly at the time and likened him to the greatest Roman consuls. I as well as several of his more intimate friends saw a copy of the score lying on his table with the word "Bonaparte" at the extreme top of the title page. . . . I was the first to bring him the intelligence that Bonaparte had proclaimed himself emperor, whereupon he flew into a rage and cried out: "Is he then, too, nothing more than an ordinary human being? Now he, too, will trample on all the rights of man and indulge only his ambition. He will exalt himself above all others and become a tyrant!" Beethoven went to the table, took hold of the title page by the top, tore it in two, and threw it on the floor.

Napoléon's personal ambition may have enraged and disillusioned Beethoven, but it cannot have been a total surprise. The act of removing Bonaparte's name from the title of the Third Symphony represented the victory of Beethoven's patriotism over the heady influence of Napoléon. By his rejection of Bonaparte, Beethoven announced that he would remain in Austria and that he would accept, albeit with misgivings, the Viennese patronage system. The composer entitled the symphony simply "Heroic."

It was clear that Beethoven had made an important decision, but it was equally clear that his conflicting feelings toward Napoléon had not been resolved. In later years, the composer said, upon hearing of yet another Napoléonic victory, "It is a pity that I do not understand the art of war as well as I do the art of music. Then *I* would conquer *him*!" Yet, at the very time when Vienna was (yet again) under attack from Napoléon, Beethoven befriended Bonaparte's Council of State, who noticed the composer's admiration for the emperor beneath the facade of resentment. At about the same time, Beethoven came close to accepting a post at the court of Bonaparte's brother, who was the newly installed ruler of Westphalia. Also at that time, Beethoven conducted the *Eroica* at a concert he had hoped Napoléon would attend. The next year the composer contemplated dedicating his Mass in C to the despot.

Beethoven's ambivalence toward Napoléon never abated during the Frenchman's life. As Beethoven's biographer Maynard Solomon explains,

> It is a pity that we have only the insufficient word "ambivalence" to describe such total reversals of emotional attitude — surely too tame a word for so turbulent a set of feelings. What is involved, actually, is not merely a series of reversals but an insoluble conflict which can be resolved only through a change in the balance of forces. This was to come later, with Napoléon's defeat at Waterloo, his exile to St. Helena, and his death. On hearing of Napoléon's death on May 5, 1821, Beethoven remarked, "I have already composed the proper music for that catastrophe."

The composer was referring to the Funeral March, which forms the *Eroica's* second movement. The symphony was not simply an act of homage but also a portrayal of death. Biographer Solomon is particularly eloquent on this point:

> The *Eroica* Symphony, therefore, may not, after all, have been conceived in a spirit of homage, which was then superseded by disillusionment; rather, it is possible that Beethoven chose as his subject one toward whom he already felt an unconquerable ambivalence containing a strong element of hostility. The symphony, with its Funeral March, is centrally concerned with the death of the hero as well as with his birth and resurrection: "Composed," Beethoven wrote on the title page, "to celebrate the memory of a great man." Striving to free himself from his lifelong pattern of submission to the domination of authority figures, Beethoven was drawn to the conquerer who had confounded the venerable leaders of Europe and set himself in their place. If homage is on the surface, the underlying themes are patricide and fratricide, and these are mingled with the survivor's sense of triumph. . . . Beethoven . . . fixed upon one towards whom he had mixed feelings, one he had already rejected as an ideal prince/legislator. Thus the choice of Bonaparte as his subject and the rending of the inscription were part of the same process. Beethoven disposed of Bonaparte twice — once in composing the symphony and again in removing his name from the title.

The true hero of the *Eroica* was not Napoléon. Beethoven's ambivalence toward the French leader became transformed into a subjective statement on heroic birth, death, and rebirth. What Beethoven really buries (with his Funeral March) is not Bonaparte, nor even his own conflicting attitudes toward Napoléon, but the classical style in music. What is born is an overtly emotional music of unprecedented power and immediacy. The real hero of the *Eroica* is music itself.

Only rarely in the history of art have external and internal stimuli interacted within the psyche of one creator to produce such striking originality. (The twentieth-century analogues of the *Eroica* — powerful compositions that completely changed the face of music — are Schoenberg's *Erwartung* and Stravinsky's *Rite of Spring*.) It is no surprise that the strength and originality of the *Eroica* (and of its counterparts a century later) should come from an external source, as the existing musical styles (those of Mozart, Haydn, and the early Beethoven) were designed, so to speak, for less extreme expression. The current vocabulary of music was incapable of matching the forceful persona of Bonaparte. To interpret such power in music required new means, and thus the originality of the symphony was an inevitable consequence of its intended meaning.

We listen to the *Eroica* and hear one strikingly original gesture after another. The first such event is the opening sound — a tremendous chord played and reiterated, followed by a melody which simply presents the notes of this chord one by one. Later in the first movement we hear intense rhythms, strongly accented (!) silences, an other-worldly derivative of the opening theme in the far-off key of E minor, a mysterious horn statement of the tonic theme against dominant harmony in the strings (just before the recapitulation), exciting rhythmic interactions of twos and threes, and two final tonic chords that mirror the opening. The Funeral March is equally original, from its very nature through its poignant fugue to its shattering climax. The third movement contributes an enormous vitality that comes from wonderfully inventive rhythms: the opening metric ambiguity and its extraordinary resolution, the unexpected move into two-beat rhythms during the restatement after the trio, and the interplay of twos and threes (even more involved than in the first movement). The originality of the affirmative finale lies in its form. It starts as a series of variations on a simple theme, which becomes the bass line of a more melodic theme and eventually disappears.

This list of unprecedented gestures in the symphony could go on and on, but it is not the novelty of materials to which we should listen. Rather it is the originality of conception that matters. Beethoven had a unique idea for his Third Symphony, and in the process of finding music appropriate to that idea he created an expansive, integrated, and powerful work.

Once the *Eroica* existed, no subsequent composer could ignore it. The development of nineteenth-century symphonic music is traceable more to the *Eroica* than to any other single work, and it took composers more than a century to exhaust its implications.

Symphony Number 4 in B-Flat Major, Opus 60
Adagio. Allegro vivace
Adagio
Allegro vivace. Un poco meno allegro. Allegro
vivace
Allegro ma non troppo

The Fourth Symphony was begun in the summer of 1806 and completed that fall at the estate of Prince Karl Lichnowsky in Silesia. The first performance was given in March 1807 at the palace of Prince Joseph Lobkowitz.

Virtually all of Beethoven's compositional efforts in 1804–06 went into his only opera, *Fidelio.* That work caused him countless problems and required repeated revisions. He was never totally pleased with it. "This whole opera business is the most tiresome affair in the world, for I am dissatisfied with most of it, and there is hardly a number in it which my present dissatisfaction would not have to patch up here and there with some satisfaction."

Although he was destined to return to *Fidelio* in later years, Beethoven put it aside in the spring of 1806. He acted like a prisoner released. In rapid succession he produced a number of large-scale instrumental works. He put the finishing touches on the *Appassionata* Sonata and then wrote the Fourth Piano Concerto, the three *Razoumovsky* Quartets, the Fourth Symphony, the Violin Concerto, the *Coriolan* Overture, the C Minor Piano Variations, the Fifth Symphony, the Sixth Symphony, the A Major Cello Sonata, and the *Ghost* Trio — an amazing amount of work, completed in less than two years!

The beginning of this period of amazing productivity was marked by an event which was destined to have enormous repercussions throughout Beethoven's later life. His brother, Caspar Carl, married Johanna Reiss on 25 March 1806. The composer, having no use for this woman, tried to prevent the marriage. That Reiss was already three months pregnant only intensified Beethoven's ill feelings. "My brother's marriage was as much an indication of his immorality as of his folly." The marriage was loveless, marked by physical abuse of both Johanna and her son, Karl, and by frequent intense quarrels with the meddlesome Ludwig. After Caspar Carl's death in 1815, Beethoven entered into a five-year fight to take from Johanna the legal guardianship of Karl. The composer's struggle to gain the possession and affection of his nephew became his overriding obsession, the outward manifestation of an intense creative struggle toward his sublime final style. Biographer Maynard Solomon writes of Beethoven's "attempt to surmount — indeed to survive — a personal and creative crisis that threatened to overwhelm his personality. We may be better able to understand this story if we view the appropriation of his nephew as not merely one manifestation of this crisis but as the primary means by which Beethoven struggled toward a new psychological and creative equilibrium."

In 1806, however, the composer could hardly have realized that the child Johanna Reiss was carrying was destined to change his life. Nor is there anything in the music of the Fourth Symphony to presage the impending turmoil of Beethoven's constant interference in the lives of Carl Caspar, Johanna, and Karl. The symphony, in contrast to Beethoven's life at the time, is elegant, sophisticated, high spirited, and witty.

◆　◆　◆

Symphony Number 5 in C Minor, Opus 67
Allegro con brio
Andante con moto
Allegro —
Allegro

Beethoven first sketched some ideas for the Fifth Symphony in 1804. He began to compose in earnest in 1806 and completed the work early in 1808. The first performance took place in Vienna on 22 December 1808.

The Fifth Symphony dates from a period of feverish compositional activity. Several of the fruits of this fertile period were exhibited before the public for the first time at Beethoven's benefit concert of 22 December 1808. The concert included premieres of the C Minor Symphony (listed as Number 6), and *Pastorale* Symphony (listed as Number 5), the Third Piano Concerto (replacing the scheduled Fourth at the last minute), and some vocal works. Although the triumphant nature of the C Minor Symphony made it a natural candidate to close the concert, Beethoven placed it earlier because he wisely wanted his audience to be alert when they heard this utterly original symphony. He needed a different rousing work to close the concert, so he hastily composed the Fantasy for piano, orchestra, and chorus.

Beethoven had trouble with the orchestra musicians. There had been problems during the preparations for another concert a month earlier, when Beethoven had gotten carried away while conducting a rehearsal and had knocked over a choirboy who had been holding some lighted candles. The players were infuriated, and they agreed to perform the December concert only if Beethoven would not conduct the rehearsals. The composer was forced to listen from another room and after each movement to report his suggestions to the concertmaster.

Despite the precautions, there was more ill will between composer and orchestra. The *Choral* Fantasy had been finished too close to concert time for any rehearsals. There was some confusion during the concert over whether certain of its repeats were to be observed. Some of the players repeated, and some went on. The result was chaos. Beethoven shouted out to the orchestra to stop, and when it did he made the musicians start again. They felt they had been publicly humiliated.

Given all these and other problems, the concert must have been a nightmare. The Fifth Symphony, a work of such startling originality that it needed an accurate performance before an attentive audience, was lost on its listeners. Since then, however, it has become the best known and best loved symphony in the entire repertoire.

It is difficult to know exactly why the Fifth has become supremely popular, perhaps the most performed of all symphonies as well as the source of several popular and disco arrangements. The work is a masterpiece, but hardly in a class by itself. No one could reasonably claim that it is the world's best symphony simply because it is the most famous. Does its popularity stem from its unrelenting power? Or from the fact that its opening motive, which stands for "V" in Morse code, became the symbol of victory during World War II? Or from the way that Beethoven integrates the entire symphony with recurrences of that motive? Or, perhaps, simply from the coincidence of repeated programming begetting increased demand for more performances?

Whatever the reason, it testifies to the monumentality of the symphony that it has survived its overexposure. Not many compositions could retain their freshness after the repeated hearings this work has had.

The opening of the symphony is powerful. No melody is heard, but rather only the forceful "V" rhythm. "Thus Fate knocks at the door," Beethoven is supposed to have said. Of course, such a simple motive is not unique to this piece. It can be found, for example, in the Fourth Piano Concerto, which is not a particularly forceful work. The twentieth-century music theorist Heinrich Schenker, noting that both works use the same motive, asked, "Was this another door on which Fate knocked or was someone else knocking at the same door?" Schenker's point is that it is the treatment of the motive throughout all four movements, not its inherent shape, that makes it fateful. The motive pervades the symphony as part of accompaniment figures (throughout the first movement), subtly disguised (in the second movement), overtly stated (by the horns in the scherzo), and embedded within a melodic line (such as the finale's last theme).

The pervasiveness of the opening motive is but one aspect of the symphony's integrated structure. The incredible unity of four quite different movements also has to do with implications and with when and how they are fulfilled. For example, the headlong thrust of the first movement, broken only by a wistful oboe cadenza just after the start of the recapitulation, makes the movement seem almost too short — not too short to be a movement, but too brief to resolve all its accumulated tension. We know that another movement must follow. As if by compensation, the slow second movement seems almost too long. Compensating for a compact movement with a leisurely one is only part of the structuring process, however. The scherzo is dynamic, like the first movement, yet its thrust becomes mysterious and covert as it heads toward the finale. The beginning of the last movement, coming without pause after the scherzo, is surely one of the great moments in music. The reason for this magnificent arrival, this tremendous release of tension, has to do not only with the incredibly powerful drive during the transition from the scherzo but also with the remembered tensions from the curtailed first movement and overly drawn out resolutions in the second. Thus the three first movements point to and prepare for the triumphant beginning of the finale.

This moment, incidentally, marks the first appearance ever of trombones in a symphony orchestra. Their wonderfully strong sonority underlines the extroverted mood of the finale, which gives way only to an abbreviated restatement of the transition from the scherzo. Exultation returns at the recapitulation and continues to the coda, which becomes progressively faster and simpler: eventually there is nothing left but tonic and dominant chords, then tonic chords, then finally a powerful tonic note. Such a dramatic close is appropriate, given the relentless driving motion in much of the symphony. Unfortunately, this kind of ending did subsequently become a cliché in the hands of several nineteenth-century orchestral composers, such as Tchaikovsky and Dvořák.

Symphony Number 6 in F Major, Opus 68, *Pastorale*

Awakening of Serene Impressions on Arriving in
   the Country
Scene by the Brook
Jolly Gathering of Country Folk —
Thunderstorm —
Shepherd's Hymn and Thankful Feelings after the
   Storm

The Pastorale *Symphony was composed mostly in 1808, with
sketches dating from 1806. Beethoven conducted the first performance in Vienna on 22 December 1808, on a program that also
included the premiere of the Fifth Symphony. The two symphonies
were listed with their numbers reversed.*

Among Beethoven's very earliest works is a set of three piano sonatas,
written when he was twelve years old. When they were printed two
years later, the publication was advertised in Bossler's music journal.
On the same page of the journal there appeared a notice for a new
symphony by one Justin Heinrich Knecht.

Knecht's symphony was subtitled *A Musical Portrait of Nature.*
Its movements bore the following descriptions:

1. "A beautiful countryside where the sun shines, the soft breezes
blow, the streams cross the valley, the birds twitter, a cascade murmurs, a shepherd pipes, the sheep leap, and the shepherdess lets her
gentle voice be heard."

2. "The heavens are suddenly darkened, all breathe with difficulty and are afraid, the black clouds pile up, the wind makes a rushing sound, the thunder growls from afar, the storm slowly descends."

3. "The storm, with noise of wind and driving rain, roars with
all its force, the tops of the trees murmur, and the torrent rolls down
with a terrifying sound."

4. "The storm is appeased little by little, the clouds scatter, and
the sky clears."

5. "Nature, in a transport of gladness, raises its voice to heaven
and gives thanks to its Creator in soft and agreeable song."

Since the advertisements of his and Knecht's works appeared together, it is reasonable to assume that Beethoven knew of Knecht's
symphony, a typical classical-period attempt at literal tone painting.
Beethoven may even have studied the work. We know from his sketch

books that he thought long and hard about the challenges of program music. To what extent should the musical meaning depend on the listeners' knowledge of what is being portrayed? In other words, should the tone painting be as literal as Knecht apparently believed?

As he began to sketch the *Pastorale*, Beethoven jotted down several ideas about program music: "The listeners should be allowed to discover the situations themselves." "People will not require titles to recognize the general intention to be more a matter of feeling than of tone painting." "*Pastorale* Symphony: no picture, but something in which emotions are expressed that are aroused by the pleasure of the country." "All painting in instrumental music, if pushed too far, is a failure." "*Sinfonia caracteristica*, or a recollection of country life."

According to musicologist F. E. Kirby, what Beethoven probably meant by "characteristic symphony" was

> a composition possessing certain typical features that mark it as belonging to a particular genre or type. Such a piece, then, must make use of a musical style that has explicit associations with a definite expressive character. . . . Hence, when Beethoven used the designation *sinfonia caracteristica* or, later, *sinfonia pastorella*, it is obvious that he intended a particular kind of characteristic work, one associated with the pastoral character. . . . As the principal elements in the pastoral style we may mention bird-call themes, hunting-horn themes, shepherds' pipes (*pifa* or *pifferari*) and shepherds' calls (*ranz des vaches* or yodeling), country dances, the representation of flowing water and of bleating sheep, and the imitation of that characteristic instrument of country life, the bagpipe with its drone bass.

The Sixth Symphony was completed nearly a quarter century after Knecht's work, but its program is remarkably similar. Beethoven's indebtedness to Knecht (in the programmatic outline and in the five-movement format) is obvious, but the differences are equally significant. Beethoven avoided the detailed programmatic descriptions of his predecessor. Knecht's symphony was squarely within the tradition of literal representation, a tradition that included music of Bach, Vivaldi, Boccherini, Handel (there is a "Pastoral Symphony" in the *Messiah*; mosquitoes, frogs, and a hailstorm are depicted in *Israel in Egypt*), Haydn (we hear a lion's roar, whinnying horse, and heavy-footed animals in *The Creation*), and — twenty years after the *Pastorale* — Rossini (the *William Tell* Overture is in four sections, respectively portraying dawn, a storm, a pastoral, and a quick march). But Beethoven's goal differed from these composers' intentions.

"More an expression of feeling than tone painting," he wrote on the title page. This simple statement was the distillation of all his aesthetic musings while composing the *Pastorale*. He was afraid that excessively literal representation might trivialize the music. But he did not fulfill his intentions entirely. The bird calls toward the close of the second movement, the village band of the scherzo, the yodeling theme in the finale, the bagpipe-like drones in the outer movements, and the storm are all as much tone painting as expression of feeling. Beethoven did not totally transcend the tradition of pastoral music.

How did he attempt to convey the characteristic *feelings* as well as the *sounds* of the countryside? Consider the first movement. Everything is leisurely, like country life. The piece unfolds in an un-hurried manner. The harmonies are for the most part simple, and the music remains in each harmonic area for a rather long time. This means that there are many passages with long sustained pitches (the bagpipe drones) or repeated notes. In addition, there is a lot of repe-tition of small motives, whole melodies, and even entire sections. The leisurely pace of seemingly endless repetition is established shortly after the beginning, where one string figure is heard ten times in succession with no change other than a crescendo then diminuendo (Beethoven subtly adds the bassoons just for the one loudest repeti-tion). Although there are several passages for full orchestra, there is not much sense of climax. Even at the recapitulation, where in many of his other works Beethoven delivers a huge release of tension, the music keeps moving along gently. A listener of today who does not know the symphony's title may not recognize that the countryside inspired this movement (although a listener in 1808 probably could readily recognize the conventions of pastoral music), but the gentle character is unmistakable. This movement, at least, perfectly exem-plifies Beethoven's preference for expression over tone representa-tion.

The second movement is somewhat more literal, as pervasive six-teenth-note undulations represent the babbling brook. Explicit tone painting emerges near the end, with the bird calls. Beethoven labels the flute part "nightingale," the oboe "quail," and the clarinets "cuc-koo."

There is literal tone painting of another sort in the third move-ment. Beethoven enjoyed hearing amateur bands play Austrian folk dances, even when their playing was less than accomplished. His friend Anton Schindler recorded in 1819, "Beethoven asked me if I had not noticed how village musicians often played in their sleep, occasionally letting their instruments fall and keeping quite still, then waking up with a start, getting in a few vigorous blows or strokes, usually in the right key, and then dropping off to sleep again. He had tried to portray these poor people in the *Pastorale* Symphony." The fun starts just after the horn calls. First we hear an inanely simple accompaniment figure in the violins. Then the oboe enters with the melody, but a beat late, as if the player had not been quite ready for his entrance. Four measures later the (second!) bassoon apparently awakens, enters unexpectedly for three notes, then falls back to sleep, only to reawaken five bars later. The melody is passed to the clarinet — still a beat off — which is accompanied suddenly by the violas and, seemingly a bar late, the cellos. It is as if the viola player suddenly awoke and began to play, and his entrance woke up the cellist. The melody then passes to the horn player, who also enters a beat off. Eventually the string basses and finally the first bassoon awaken and join in with sustained notes. The gentle humor of this movement turns dark toward the end, in order to symbolize the gathering clouds of the storm.

The thunderstorm (fourth movement) begins its ominous threat by an unprepared move to a distant key. The scherzo does not end, but the storm interrupts it with this modulation. The violence of the storm is depicted by thundering timpani, string tremolos, and strident dissonances. The tempest eventually subsides, and the final movement follows without pause.

The finale's shepherd's hymn returns to the unhurried atmosphere of the first movement. Before we hear the main theme, a clarinet and then a horn play yodeling figures over bagpipe drones in the strings. The melody, which is introduced in the violins (the drone moves to the clarinets and bassoons), is actually a Swiss yodeling tune. Each time this melody is heard it is repeated, usually twice. This repetition suggests both an unhurried atmosphere, as in the first movement, and also successive hymn verses sung to the same music. The movement ends with a typically pastoral gesture: horn yodeling accompanied by a wind drone.

Symphony Number 7 in A Major, Opus 92

Poco sostenuto. Vivace
Allegretto
Presto. Assai meno presto. Presto
Allegro con brio

The A Major Symphony was composed in 1811–12 and first performed on 8 December 1813 in Vienna.

To define in words the uniqueness of any Beethoven symphony is difficult, no matter how well we know intuitively what makes it special. Yet many who have fallen under the spell of Beethoven's masterpieces have felt compelled to try the impossible — to express verbally the essence of the music. The Seventh Symphony has, more than other pieces, suffered the platitudes of well-meaning critics, interpreters, composers, and program annotators. Carl Iken, a contemporary of the composer, wrote an essay "demonstrating" that the symphony portrays a political revolution. A. B. Marx saw it as a story of Moorish knighthood, including a warriors' festival. Ludwig Nohl also visualized a knights' festival. Alexandre Oulibischev labelled it a masquerade of drunkards. Paul Bekker called it a "bacchic orgy." Ernest Newman described it as "the upsurge of a powerful dionysiac impulse." Vincent d'Indy and Wilhelm von Lenz believed it to be a second *pastorale* symphony. Robert Schumann recognized a rustic wedding in the second movement. Emil Ludwig found in it a woodland festival, a priest's march, dance ceremonies, and a bacchanale. Richard Wagner dubbed it "the apotheosis of the dance." Hector Berlioz found in the work a peasant dance. D'Ortigue thought the second movement contained a procession in an old cathedral. Dürenberg described the same movement as the love-dream of a sumptuous odalisque. Teetjen discerned a picture of feudal times. For Serov the piece was full of military pomp.

To discover in a piece of instrumental music a political revolution, Moorish knights, a concubine's love-dream, or a picture of feudal times is at best idiosyncratic and at worst silly. But some of these interpretations are somewhat less whimsical, since there *is* something a masquerade, a procession, a rustic wedding, a peasant dance, etc., have in common. What these commentators heard in the Seventh was echoes of the dance and the march, both rhythmic types of music. And that is the true magic of this symphony: its incessant, captivating, varied rhythmic drives.

There is another common denominator to many of these quaint interpretations. As Beethoven's biographer Maynard Solomon explains,

A work that so powerfully symbolizes the act of transcendance, with its attendant joyous and liberating feelings, can be represented in language by an infinity of specific transcendent images — which may tell us as much about the free associations of their authors as about Beethoven and his music. But the apparently diverse free-associational imagery of these critics — images of masses of people, of powerful rhythmic energy discharged in action or in dance, of celebrations, weddings, and revelry — comprises, at bottom, variations upon a single image: that of the carnival or festival, which, from time immemorial, has temporarily lifted the burden of perpetual subjugation to the prevailing social and natural order by periodically suspending all customary privileges, norms, and imperatives.

Whether or not Beethoven had in mind an image of a festival is irrelevant. Whether or not he consciously intended a theme of freedom does not matter. For whatever reasons, he created a symphony with extraordinarily liberating rhythmic drive. In order to emphasize the rhythm, Beethoven limited his melodic muse. Thus we find figures based on the reiteration of single tones: the main motive of the opening movement is a telegraphic repeat of one pitch, the second movement is pervaded by a simple rhythm on one note, and the finale starts with a reiterated rhythm. The third movement, the most overtly dance-like part of the symphony, has a trio section in which one pitch is sustained with only the slightest ornamentation throughout, first in the violins and then in the trumpets. It is this emphasis on rhythm, often at the expense of melody, that gives this composition an impetuous, exuberant vitality that has reminded many commentators of carnivals.

Is this most beautiful of symphonies being accused of melodic impoverishment? What heresy! Yet it is true. When we leave the concert hall humming strains of Beethoven's Seventh, it is more their rhythmic sweep than their melodic shape that we are remembering. Consider, for example, the main theme of the second movement: almost a Johnny-one-note. (Of course, a lyrical counter-melody does eventually accompany this non-tune, but the counter-theme is always treated as secondary.) Also, how many listeners can sing the second theme of the first movement, which in most other symphonies is a melody of great lyricism? Or, for that matter, how singable are the main tunes of the third and fourth movements?

What counts in the Seventh is not what the melodies are but how they are used. They are understated and rarely lyrical, in order to focus our attention on the rhythmic drive. They are the way they are to project the drama and unity of Beethoven's conception. The listener is rarely given the respite that a truly lyrical melody might provide from the inexorable rhythmic progression.

Rhythm is the temporal aspect of music, and for Beethoven time was of paramount importance. Music reflects the way we perceive time, and Beethoven's music structures its listeners' time experience in deeply meaningful ways. Thus the melodies and rhythms in the Seventh are significant for how they create and resolve the tensions that drive the music forward. This is a music more of time than of sound (if commentators of previous generations could indulge their fancies for creative interpretations, so perhaps can a program annotator of today). Every element of this composition exists to create a dynamic, kinetic, living, integral work.

Listen to the temporal structure of the first movement. During the long slow introduction, tension mounts as the music searches for stability. When the music eventually dissolves into repeated notes, more and more isolated, it slips almost unnoticed into the fast tempo of the main portion of the movement. Where was the long-sought arrival? Somehow the allegro gets going without a resolution, without a well-defined starting point. And so it goes throughout the movement: at every place where we expect a resolution of the rhythmic drive, Beethoven finds a new way to frustrate that expectation. In this way he keeps the tension growing until very close to the end of the movement, where, with horns soaring, he allows the music at last to reach its goal. This tremendous arrival, this enormous "structural downbeat" (as music theorists call such events), is one of the great moments in all music, not (once again) for what it is but for what it means *in context*.

As another example of dramatic architecture in time, consider the second movement. The outlines of the form are common enough: five sections, the first, third, and fifth of which are based on one set of themes and the second and fourth of which are based on another (though there is the same incessant rhythm underlying the whole). Within this abstract frame the composer has created one of his most original conceptions: an arch form. After the opening woodwind chord, the low strings play three phrases of seemingly inconsequential simplicity (the Johnny-one-note melody). This three-phrase group is repeated three more times, each time with something new added to it. The build-up to a full texture is powerful. After the second section temporarily relieves the tension, the middle section returns to the original materials, which continue to grow in complexity. The climax is a fugue, the keystone of the arch. The music then falls away from the climax by reversing the order of the steps used in the ascent. Since the opening section is a gradual accumulation of melodies, the last section must somehow break them apart. Beethoven achieves this goal by fragmenting the materials of the first section. The opening woodwind chord returns at the end to complete the arch.

Not only is each movement a powerfully rhythmic conception, but also the whole symphony interrelates through a complex network of tensions and resolutions. Each movement depends on, and has implications for, the others. We remember during the entire piece, for example, the enormous feeling of expectancy of the introduction. When the wildly abandoned finale carries us along at breakneck pace, we at last feel the complete resolution of this expectancy. Thus the unity of the symphony depends on the temporal relationship of every segment of the music to every other and also on the meaningful placement of all events within the forty-minute block of time that constitutes the very special world of Beethoven's Seventh Symphony.

Symphony Number 8 in F Major, Opus 93
Allegro vivace e con brio
Allegretto scherzando
Tempo di menuetto
Allegro vivace

The Eighth Symphony was begun late in 1811 and completed in October 1812. The first performance took place under the composer's direction on 27 February 1814 in Vienna.

Johann Nepomuk Mälzel was an inventor of musical gadgets. In 1812 he perfected his panharmonicon, a mechanical combination of the instruments in a military band, and his chronometer, a predecessor of his metronome. Beethoven visited Mälzel's workshop often, and their friendship was strengthened when the inventor made an ear-trumpet for the partially deaf composer.

Mälzel joined other friends of Beethoven in a farewell dinner for the composer, who was about the embark on a journey late in the spring of 1812. Beethoven was in one of his fun-loving moods, which he described as "unbuttoned." During the party Mälzel described his chronometer, by means of which he hoped to give composers a way to indicate tempo exactly and to provide performers with an aid to steady playing. Beethoven applauded the idea gaily, and then he launched into a seemingly spontaneous song based on the "ta ta ta" of Mälzel's instrument. The others joined in making the song into a round. This inconsequential tune found its way into the second movement of the Eighth Symphony, which Beethoven was working on at the time. The melody is given a ticking accompaniment suggestive of the chronometer.

The inclusion of this metronomic theme is not the only example of humor in the symphony. The work abounds with unexpected pauses, surprising notes, and unprepared gestures. The sudden outbursts in 2/4 time within the 3/4 first movement are one example of the symphony's good-natured fun. Also witty is the way the first movement ends, with the sudden cutting short of what seems to be a restatement of the prinicpal theme.

The incessant repeated notes that pervade the second movement, even up to its final measure, are a further instance of the symphony's humor. Any piece that lacks a slow movement but has instead both a scherzo and a minuet is bound to be good-humored. Thus the wit continues in the minuet, which begins with a delightful ambiguity over which beat is really the first of each measure.

The finale starts with a similar ambiguity and with a purposefully inconsequential theme. We are continually amazed at the sophisticated developments that grow from such an unpromising beginning. The Haydnesque false recapitulation, almost as soon as the development section has begun, is a delightful *non sequitur.* The overly grandiose ending is one final bit of humor.

There is a lesson in the story of the Eighth Symphony for anyone who believes that a piece of music is necessarily a direct expression of the composer's innermost emotions. This happy, "unbuttoned," thoroughly delightful symphony was written during one of the most tortured periods of Beethoven's life. It was composed at the time of his involvement in the only truly passionate love affair of his life, an affair that was doomed to all but destroy his spirit.

The woman has been known mysteriously as the Immortal Beloved, on the basis of an agonized, half-rational love letter Beethoven wrote to her. The letter is not dated, and the composer apparently never sent it. The date and the identity of the Beloved have eluded generations of musicologists and biographers, until quite recently. Beethoven scholar Maynard Solomon, writing in 1977, gave conclusive proof that the Beloved was Antonie Brentano and that Beethoven was hopelessly in love with her at the time he was working on the Eighth Symphony.

Beethoven had been in love many times, but every other involvement had led nowhere. The composer was repeatedly rebuffed by the women he chose, who were either not interested in him or else attached to other men. So often had the composer chosen unavailable or uninterested women that biographer Solomon is confident he did so for deep-seated psychological reasons. Beethoven may have consciously thought he wanted a normal sexual and family life, but in reality he was incapable of sustaining either. And so he repeatedly chose women whom he could blame for his own failings. But then he met Antonie, and everything changed.

Antonie Brentano was a happily married mother of four children. She moved with her family to Vienna in the fall of 1809. Beethoven met the family and became friendly with both husband and wife. Franz Brentano wanted to move back to Frankfurt, but Antonie loved Vienna and wanted to stay. As Franz became more insistent, Antonie became more desperate. She leaned on Beethoven for support, and their friendship gradually turned to love. He dedicated several pieces to her. By the spring of 1812, there was a true affair in progress.

After the farewell dinner with Mälzel, Beethoven left for Prague, where he joined Antonie. She confessed her love openly and offered to leave her family to live with him. She and Franz were going to be at the Karlsbad spa in July, and Beethoven planned to meet her there.

But, prior to leaving for Karlsbad, he wrote the famous Immortal Beloved letter. In it he pleaded with Antonie not to destroy her family, yet to continue loving him. He went to Karlsbad, where he tried to resume normal friendly relations with Antonie and her husband. She realized that Beethoven would never make a commitment to her. By November, when the Eighth Symphony was finished, the Brentanos had moved away from Vienna. Beethoven was thoroughly shaken by the entire incident, and he never again became more than casually involved with a woman.

What moved Beethoven was the unselfishness and totality of Antonie's love. She had no reservations, and she was willing to risk social condemnation to be with him. His letter to the Beloved reflects his tremendous inner conflict. He was torn between the desire for a life with Antonie and the strong pull of his old habits. He was a loner who had always *thought* he wanted a woman and a family. Now, confronted with the real possibility, he was far from sure. Beethoven had allowed himself to fall in love because, subconsciously, he had thought Antonie was "safe" — she was married happily and she was a mother. While they were together in Prague, however, he found out that she was willing to go to any lengths to be with him. His reaction was painfully ambivalent, and his pain was increased by his friendship with Antonie's husband. As there was none of the rejection Beethoven had been accustomed to, he was forced to confront reality. The affair shattered his lingering illusions that he could lead a normal life with a woman. He ceased thinking of himself as a real man, and therein lay his deepest tragedy. Having found unselfish love, he was forced to admit that he was incapable of returning it.

Having rejected Antonie, he stayed away from Vienna in the fall while she was preparing to leave. He went instead to Linz to visit his younger brother Nikolaus Johann and to finish the Eighth Symphony. Nikolaus had been having a blatant affair with his housekeeper, Thérèse Obermayer. Beethoven sought to break up the affair. His underlying motive seemed to be, why should he allow his brother to have a woman if he could not himself? The liaison between Nikolaus and Thérèse had been going on for some time, but only now was Beethoven, agonized by the events of his own life, determined to do something about it. He brought the matter before the bishop and the police in Linz, and he came to physical blows with Nikolaus. But Beethoven's actions had an effect opposite to what was intended: Nikolaus married Thérèse. The composer never forgave his brother, and he retained his hatred of his new sister-in-law for the rest of his life. The incident was so upsetting to Beethoven that his health suffered.

And so, at a time of his life when he was forced to face very painful truths about himself, when he had to give up the only deep love he had ever known, when he had a profound falling out with his brother, when he contemplated (if not actually attempted) suicide — at that time he composed his happiest, wittiest, most carefree symphony, a work totally devoid of the dark emotions of his life. The relationship between an artist and his work is complex, as the story of the Eighth Symphony should always remind us.

Symphony Number 9 in D Minor, Opus 125, *Choral*
Allegro ma non troppo, un poco maestoso
Molto vivace. Presto. Molto vivace
Adagio molto e cantabile. Andante moderato
Presto. Allegro assai. Alla marcia. Andante
       maestoso. Adagio ma non troppo, ma divoto.
       Allegro energico. Allegro ma non tanto.
       Prestissimo

While materials for the Ninth Symphony date back as far as 1815, Beethoven did not start to work in earnest on the piece until 1822. It was completed in February 1824. Michael Umlauf conducted the first performance in Vienna on 7 May 1824.

"To arrive at a solution even in political problems, the road of aesthetics must be pursued, because it is through beauty that we arrive at freedom." This motto of poet Friedrich Schiller might well have been Beethoven's own. His belief in music as a political force was lifelong. The history of the *Eroica* Symphony is perhaps the most obvious manifestation of the idea of freedom from political tyranny through the beauty of art.

Beethoven's belief in the humanity of art became particularly pronounced in his late music. His final years were a time of social isolation. No longer able to function as a performer, increasingly separated from his fellow men because of his deafness, no longer the center of Vienna's musical life, Beethoven compensated by making music that was vitally concerned with communication. What we sometimes hear about his late string quartets and piano sonatas — that they are abstract and hermetic — is nonsense, a half-truth born a century and a half ago when this unfamiliar music *was* indeed perplexing. But the impulse motivating the late works of Beethoven is a reaching out to humanity: hence, for example, the simple, almost folk-like tunes that pervade the last works. Musicologist Joseph Kerman writes of Beethoven's "determination to touch common mankind as nakedly as possible. Never in the past had Beethoven reached so urgently for immediacy. There is something very moving about the spectacle of this composer, having reached heights of subtlety in the pure manipulation of tonal materials, battering at the communications barrier with every weapon of his knowledge. The great exemplar of this drive is the Ninth Symphony."

The need to communicate led him to the directness of words. The symphony, which starts from a veiled murmuring of strings, finishes as an operatic finale. From the vague to the concrete, from mystery to joy, from the abstract to the human, the Ninth cannot remain content with instrumental sound. Thus Beethoven introduced Schiller's "Ode to Joy," a text in which the poet (and hence the composer) predicts the brotherhood of all men. Although the text is naïve and sentimental (Schiller's poem was, at least in part, a drinking song), the juxtaposition of this praise of joy with the tragedy, demonic satire, and sublimity of the first three movements is deeply meaningful. Beethoven seems to be not simply embracing the millions, but saying that by believing in the joy of brotherhood mankind can rise above the pain of life and of living.

The sentiments of Schiller's lines may seem quaint to a world that has known Hitler and Stalin, that has seen Auschwitz and Vietnam, but Beethoven's interpretation of those words remains a beacon of hope. This is because Beethoven uses Schiller's words as a *solution* to the universal problems of mankind hinted at in the first three movements. He does more than join Schiller in praising joy. Beethoven implies that in the *belief* in brotherhood and joy lies man's salvation. Beethoven has his chorus sing not of what is but of what might be, not of mankind's condition but of its potential. He utters this message of hope after giving full voice to other sides of human emotions, in the darkly tragic first movement, the obsessive scherzo, and the tranquil adagio.

A dozen years separate the completion of Beethoven's Eighth and Ninth Symphonies. During that interval he wrote primarily chamber music, solo piano music, songs, and the *Missa Solemnis*. He established his intimate late style, which was in many ways antithetical to large orchestral forces (and to concertos and operas). The Ninth Symphony, which brought together certain ideas he had been toying with his entire mature life, looks back to the heroic middle period through the filter of the personal late style. The first three movements are, in their own way, as extroverted as the Fifth Symphony, while the choral finale approaches the forthrightness of the concertos and the opera *Fidelio*.

Beethoven had expressed as early as 1793 his intention to compose a setting of Schiller's *Ode to Joy*. In 1798 he made a preliminary setting of the Schiller text, as a song. In 1808 he wrote the *Choral* Fantasy, which turned out to be a study piece for the Ninth Symphony finale. In the fantasy he experimented with a form in which the chorus enters after an extended orchestral section. The main choral theme, which he took from a song he had composed in 1795, is quite similar to the symphony's *Joy* melody. In 1812 he contemplated a symphony using the Schiller text in the finale. In 1815 he jotted down what was to become the scherzo theme of the Ninth.

Beethoven continued to sketch, but he set to work in earnest only in 1822. He was still planning a totally instrumental finale as late as the summer of 1823. The theme for that rejected movement eventually became the main melody of the last movement of the String Quartet in A Minor, Opus 132. Once he decided definitely on the choral finale, the composer felt the most difficult task was how to move from the instrumental portions of the symphony to the choral ending. He worked out the variations on the *Joy* theme well before he composed the finale's instrumental introduction. According to his friend Anton Schindler, "When he reached the development of the fourth movement, there began a struggle such as is seldom seen. The object was to find a proper manner of introducing Schiller's *Ode.* Entering the room one day, he exclaimed, 'I have it! I have it!' He showed me the sketchbook bearing the words, 'Let us sing the song of the immortal Schiller,' after which a solo voice began directly the hymn to joy."

Owing to his deafness, Beethoven was unable to conduct the first performance. He did supervise rehearsals, however. He angrily refused requests from singers that he alter the music to make it easier. Knowing he could not hear, they simply omitted the high notes. The real conductor instructed the musicians to pay no attention to the composer, should he begin to beat time.

Beethoven could not hear the performance, but he followed it in a copy of the score, imagining in his head the sounds everyone else was hearing. At the end of the performance, he was still engrossed in his score, unable to hear the applause. One of the soloists touched his sleeve and turned him so he could see the clapping hands and waving handkerchiefs. Only then did he bow to the audience. Whether or not many in the audience could comprehend this utterly original music, no doubt played poorly, few could have failed to be moved by the sight of the greatest genius of music acknowledging applause, which he could not hear, for his music, which he also could not hear.

The opening of the Ninth Symphony is celebrated in the symphonic literature. Although it may seem commonplace today, the manner in which the music grows from nothingness was unprecedented in 1824. The reason this kind of opening is familiar to us is that it was often imitated by later nineteenth-century symphonists. Bruckner's final symphony, sharing key and number with Beethoven's Opus 125, is an obvious example. Another is Strauss's *Also Sprach Zarathustra.* In an ideal performance of the Beethoven Ninth, it is impossible to pinpoint the exact instant when the sound starts. There is no sharp delineation between silence and sound, and the symphony begins as if it has been going on and the volume just happened to be increased. As musicologist Leo Treitler explains, "The silence is not broken; it is gradually replaced by sound. The listener is not drawn into the piece; he is surrounded by it as the orchestra fills and expands its space. . . . Probably the sense of the cosmic that has become a commonplace about the Ninth Symphony is a response to this condition of the opening."

Several aspects of this opening — the stillness, the stark and unmoving harmony, and the absence of any melody — create an atmosphere of expectancy. As the music unfolds, as it gradually takes on a more definitive character, it lives up to these expectations. Tentatively, the music acquires a personality. First the skeleton of a melody appears in the violins, gradually expanded, until the harmony changes (but in an understated manner). Finally the full orchestra combines for a unison statement of a powerful falling figure that plunges the music back to its point of origin.

Since the first movement is cast in sonata form, we might wonder how such a tentative opening might return, in accordance with the form's traditional dictates, as a triumphant resolution at the beginning of the recapitulation. Beethoven transforms the hushed opening into an apocalyptic catastrophe. We are shocked by the full orchestra playing loudly the same music that had constituted the hushed opening. We are moved by this sidestep into D major, where D minor had been expected. Treitler calls this moment the finest "display anywhere of the horrifying brightness that the major mode can have. It is, all in all, the shock of being now pulled into the opening with great force, instead of having it wash over us."

At the end of the movement, the powerful descending theme is stated one final time. Now it includes two rapid ascending scales, which prevent the descending motion from closing off the music completely. These two rushes upward linger in the memory, yet to be resolved. And thus we move on to the second movement of this extraordinary symphony.

The scherzo is cast in sonata form, with a fugal exposition. This is a most unusual fugue, however, since each theme and countertheme has virtually the same rhythm. The result, as these similar melodies pile on top of one another, is a relentless *perpetuum mobile.* Clever rhythmic irregularities, sometimes involving timpani punctuations of the opening motive, add grim humor. The trio section is faster and lighter.

The slow movement is a series of variations on two alternating themes, at two different tempos. The tender lyricism of this movement is a marked contrast to darker emotions of the opening movements and to the joyful finale.

The form of the finale is unusual. Like the second movement, it is an experiment in combining different traditional forms into a single movement: sonata, variations, cantata, concerto, fugue, and opera. It is a complete four-movement symphony in miniature, onto which is grafted the outlines of sonata form. The sonata's exposition is a set of variations, its development is a fugue, and its coda is an operatic finale. The form, as pianist and analyst Charles Rosen points out, is actually modeled after the classical concerto, with its double exposition, rather than the typical symphony.

Before this fascinating amalgamation of forms can begin, memories of the other movements must be laid to rest. The finale starts with a massively dissonant fanfare, which alternates with a recitative-like line in the lower strings. This recitative is a surprise. What is such an operatic gesture doing in the midst of a symphony? As Treitler explains, "It signals a breakdown in the purely musical means of expression." It implies that only through words will the symphony reach its full meaning. Brief references to each of the other movements alternate with the recitative. The first three references are reminiscences and the fourth is an anticipation of the upcoming finale.

Finally the exposition begins with the famous *Joy* theme. The vocal quality and balanced construction of this melody make it unlike any of the symphony's earlier materials. Three variations on this theme follow, and then a transition brings us back to the opening fanfare. The form resembles that of a classical concerto in that the main material is presented first by the orchestra and then by the "soloist" with orchestra. In this case the "soloist" comprises the vocal soloists plus chorus. Before they can enter with the main theme, however, the previous instrumental symphony must be completely dispelled. After the fanfare, the recitative returns, now actually sung. The words are, "O friends, no more these sounds! Let us sing more cheerful songs, more full of joy!" With this exhortation to song, the chorus enters with three additional variations on the *Joy* theme.

When the music modulates to B-flat major for the second theme, the character changes to that of a Turkish march, complete with drum and triangle beats. This section functions like a scherzo movement within the finale's pseudo-four-movement structure. The full chorus and orchestra follow with an additional variation on the *Joy* theme, to the original words "Joy, bright sparks of divinity, daughter of Elysium." After a break the fugue begins: "You millions, I embrace you!" This section functions like a slow movement and also like the finale's development section. The *Joy* and fugue themes are combined in a grand recapitulatory move back to D major: the finale's finale commences. But this extraordinarily conceived movement is not ready to end. The implications of having begun with a recitative must be fulfilled. As the text sings of joy one final time, the music begins to sound very much like an opera finale. And so it ends, about as far as imaginable from the mysterious and abstract opening of the first movement, in a thoroughly operatic, extroverted, joyful song of praise.

Alban Berg

Born in Vienna on 9 February 1885.
Died there on 24 December 1935.

Concerto for Violin and Orchestra
Allegro. Allegretto
Allegro. Adagio

The Violin Concerto was begun in April 1935 and completed on 11 August 1935. Louis Krasner was soloist at the first performance, which was conducted by Hermann Scherchen at the International Society for Contemporary Music festival in Barcelona on 19 March 1936.

Louis Krasner, an American violinist who performed some of the most advanced contemporary compositions, became interested in twelve-tone music in the 1930s. He began to think about a concerto written especially for him by one of the three great twelve-tone composers — Arnold Schoenberg or one of his two disciples, Alban Berg and Anton Webern. Krasner knew Berg's music and felt that, of the three, Berg was the best choice because his lyrical style was well suited for the violin. (Krasner later approached Webern for a solo piece, but it was never written.)

After making discreet inquiries about the violinist, Berg agreed to meet him. The composer was not particularly interested in the project, because he was deeply involved in the composition of the opera *Lulu* and because he doubted his ability to compose a virtuoso concerto. Krasner convinced him that he was not interested in an empty showpiece but rather in a substantial work in the tradition of the concertos by Brahms and Beethoven. Krasner argued that a lyrical solo work would help the public understand that twelve-tone music is not cerebral, abstruse, or mathematical. In addition, the commission was lucrative and Berg was having financial difficulties. With some trepidation he accepted the commission; this was only the second time he had written for a fee.

Soon after Berg agreed to write the concerto, something occurred that was to have a profound impact on it. He was friendly with Alma Mahler Gropius and her family. Alma, the widow of composer Gustav Mahler, was then married to architect Walter Gropius (she later married novelist Franz Werfel). She had two daughters, Anna Mahler and Manon Gropius. Berg was particularly close to Manon. Mutzi, as Berg called her, was 18 years old when she was struck with polio. As her mother subsequently explained,

> Alban Berg loved my daughter as if she were his own child from the beginning of her life. My daughter became more and more beautiful as she grew into young girlhood. When Max Reinhardt saw her, he asked if I would allow her to play the part of the first angel in the *Grosses Welttheater* in Salzburg. But before everything could be arranged, she was stricken with infantile paralysis. So she lay for one year and died on Easter day, 1935. She did not play the angel, but in reality she became one. After her passing Berg could not finish his own opera, *Lulu.* He composed the Violin Concerto and dedicated it to the memory of Manon.

Berg wanted the concerto to portray first Manon's personality and then her suffering, death, and transfiguration. It is probably not coincidental that his idea is similar to that behind Strauss's *Death and Transfiguration,* since that was the only work of Strauss that Berg respected.

While working on the concerto, Berg wrote to Willi Reich asking for some Bach chorales. Berg wanted to include a chorale because of Manon. Reich sent the music, and Berg found that one of the chorales began with the final four notes of the tone row with which he was working. He was thus able to integrate the chorale into the concerto in a logical manner, without the sudden appearance of tonality in a twelve-tone work seeming arbitrary. The chorale he chose is *Es ist genug!* ("It is enough!") The text reads: "It is enough! Lord, if it is Thy pleasure, relieve me of my yoke! My Jesus cometh: now good night, O world! I am going up into the house of heaven, surely I am going there in peace; my great distress remains below. It is enough, it is enough!"

Berg's work begins in an elemental fashion: the soloist plays on the four open strings of the violin. It is as if the concerto grows from this most basic of violin sounds. The second part of the first movement portrays Manon's happiness and vivacity. There are sections marked *scherzando, wienerisch* (in a Viennese manner), and *rustico*; there are waltz rhythms and yodeling figures; and there is an actual Carinthian folk song.

The first part of the second movement is purposely harsh and dissonant, in order to depict Manon's illness. Later the Bach chorale is intoned as a memorial for the dead girl. After two variations on the chorale, the Carinthian folksong is recalled with great pathos, and the work ends tenderly as the solo violin rises into its highest register, symbolizing Manon's ascent into heaven.

This portrayal of Manon is what might be called the concerto's public program. There is considerable evidence that Berg also intended an additional, private meaning. In the Violin Concerto as in most of his other mature works, he indulged in mystical numerology. Tempo markings and lengths of phrases and sections are often determined by three "magic" numbers — 23 (which was Berg's own fateful number), 10 (which he used in several works to symbolize Hannah Fuchs-Robettin, the woman with whom he carried on a secret affair for the last ten years of his life), and the as yet unexplained number 28. Calculations in the margins of Berg's manuscript confirm his preoccupation with these three numbers. In particular, the variations on the Bach chorale are stuctured according to lengths of 10, 23, and 28 beats. Why should Berg use symbols of his love for Fuchs-Robettin in a concerto conceived as a memorial to Manon Gropius?

Another puzzle, according to Berg scholar Douglas Jarman, concerns the (unheard) text of the Carinthian folksong Berg quotes. Since the words of the Bach chorale are appropriate to the concerto, and since in other Berg works the original texts of quotations always refer to the meaning of the music, is it not reasonable to assume that the folksong text is relevant? Yet the words of this innocent tune have nothing to do with either Hannah Fuchs-Robettin or Manon Gropius. They speak of a girl named Mizzi. As it happens, there was a Mizzi in Berg's life. When he was 17 the composer had an affair with Marie Scheuchl, whose nickname was probably Mizzi. Berg and Mizzi had a daughter, born in 1902.

Perhaps the folksong refers not only to Manon's innocence but also, more secretly and more specifically, to Berg's first love. Perhaps the secret number 28 refers to Mizzi Scheuchl or to their illegitimate daughter. Perhaps Berg identified his only child, to whom he could never be a true father, with Manon Gropius, whom he loved "as if she were his own child." Since the composer may have sensed that the concerto was to be his final work, it is at least likely that he included in it hidden references to his real daughter and to his surrogate daughter, as well as to his first and last loves — the one remembered (in a folksong heard "as if from afar") as an involvement of youthful innocence and the other (as symbolized in the phrase lengths of the chorale variations on "It Is Enough") tinged with the pathos of impending death.

Fearing the worst, Berg worked rapidly. He nonetheless conferred frequently with Krasner. Rather than have Krasner play over passages on which he was working, Berg asked him to improvise for hours. Berg would seem not to be listening, but whenever the violinist would stop the composer came into the room and urged him to continue. In this manner Berg learned what kind of technical devices came most easily to Krasner. Nonetheless, when the concerto was finished, the soloist thought several parts too difficult. Berg was about to revise, when Krasner asked for time to work out these challenging passages. The violinist found he could master them, and nothing was changed.

Berg's health was not good. According to his wife, "Alban, ill in bed and tortured with pain, worked frantically and without interruption to conclude the composition of his Violin Concerto. Refusing to stop for food or sleep, he drove his hand relentlessly and in fever. 'I must continue,' Berg responded to [my] pleadings, 'I cannot stop — I do not have time.'"

The concerto was finished in August. Berg was 50 years old. By December he was hospitalized, apparently the victim of blood poisoning from abscesses. Despite two operations and blood transfusions, he did not improve. He tried to maintain his good humor, for the sake of his wife. He asked, for example, to meet the young man who had donated blood, who turned out to be an ordinary, unconcerned Viennese. Berg remarked, "If only I don't now turn into a composer of operettas!" On 23 December he announced, "Today will be a decisive day." He died shortly after midnight on the 24th. His death mask was taken by Anna Mahler. The Violin Concerto became his own requiem.

Berg never heard the concerto, which Krasner first played the following March in Barcelona. The composer's close friend, Anton Webern, was to have been the conductor, but he was too upset by Berg's death to rehearse effectively. He spent the first two of three scheduled rehearsals on the opening of the concerto, taking time to explain in detail (in his hesitant Spanish) Berg's compositional intentions. Finally Webern withdrew, leaving Hermann Scherchen one rehearsal to prepare the parts of the concerto that the musicians had still not even sightread. Two years later Webern wrote to Scherchen, "To think that absolutely no one understood me! No one understood how I felt so soon after Berg's death, and that I was simply not up to the task of conducting the first performance of his last work."

Three Pieces for Orchestra, Opus 6
Prelude
Rounds
March

Three Pieces for Orchestra was begun in 1913 and completed in 1915. The first two movements were first performed on 5 June 1923 in Berlin under the baton of Anton Webern. Berg revised the orchestration slightly in 1929. Johannes Schüler conducted the first complete performance on 14 April 1930.

Alban Berg had a peculiar relationship with his teacher, Arnold Schoenberg. Schoenberg was a decade older, and Berg revered him. The younger composer learned enormously from the older, but the student also was the victim of what must be called abuse. Schoenberg was dictatorial, demanding, and authoritarian. Berg, who had far less self-confidence than his teacher, went to great lengths to remain in Schoenberg's good graces.

Schoenberg made his students not only work on extensive projects in traditional harmony and counterpoint but also attend concerts, proofread his scores, make piano reductions of his orchestral works, conduct rehearsals, and write extensive program notes. Berg was an apprentice, if not a slave. Yet the student willingly took on all this work — some of it for no payment — even though he was left with far less time than he needed for composition. Schoenberg required Berg to make a piano version of the massive *Gurrelieder*, to copy most of the orchestral parts for this work's first performance, to rehearse the chorus, and to write a hundred-page booklet analyzing the piece. Although Berg needed more than a year to complete these projects, Schoenberg was not satisfied with the results. Rather than show gratitude, the elder composer contemptuously ignored Berg, in one case by leaving him waiting a long time on the doorstep before agreeing to see him.

Berg was hurt by his teacher's moodiness, but he accepted whatever abuse Schoenberg threw at him. Berg was particularly offended when Schoenberg, having decided to move from Vienna to Berlin, at the last moment ordered his pupil to take care of all the arrangements for the move and to look after his legal affairs in Vienna. The younger composer did all that was required of him, without complaint. He even went so far as to raise money for his teacher. He referred to Schoenberg as a genius whose music was a miracle. If Berg felt any resentment, he kept it to himself.

Once Schoenberg had moved to Berlin, Berg was on his own as a composer. He continued to correspond with Schoenberg, and he tried to arrange performances of Schoenberg's music in Vienna. After some time he visited Schoenberg in Berlin, where he received some scornful criticism of his *Altenberg* songs and Four Pieces for Clarinet and Piano — the first music he had written away from his teacher. Schoenberg also complained about Berg's low rate of productivity (for which he was partly responsible). The former student wrote to his master with characteristic self-effacement: "I must thank you for your censure just as much as for everything you ever gave me; I know it was meant for my own good. I need not tell you that the great pain it caused me is proof that I have taken your criticism to heart."

"Every student of mine should have written a symphony," Schoenberg once said, and thus Berg, determined to win back his

former teacher's approval, set to work on a large orchestral composition to be dedicated to Schoenberg on the latter's fortieth birthday.
Berg wrote: "You know yourself, dear Mr. Schoenberg, how I am always conscious — I could never be conscious of anything else — of
being your pupil who obeys you in every respect and knows that anything he might do *against* your wishes would be wrong. If in the last
few weeks I have thought so much and so intensely of the symphony,
this was largely because I wanted to catch up with all that I would
have written *under you if you had stayed in Vienna.*"

The work, which actually was not completed until Schoenberg
was nearly 41, became the Three Pieces for Orchestra, Opus 6. For
his fortieth birthday Schoenberg received, instead of the symphony
he had all but demanded, a letter of apology from the still less than
prolific Berg:

> For years it has been my secret but persistent desire to dedicate
> something to you. The works composed under your supervision
> . . . do not count for this purpose, since I received them directly
> from you. My hopes of writing something more independent and
> yet as good as these first compositions (something I could con-
> fidently dedicate to you without incurring your displeasure)
> have been repeatedly disappointed. . . . I cannot tell you today
> if I have succeeded or if the attempt has failed. Should the latter
> be the case, then, in your paternal benevolence, you will have to
> accept the good intention of the deed. I have really tried to give
> of my best and to follow your advice. In this endeavor the un-
> forgettable experiece of . . . the close study of your orchestral
> pieces was an immense help and has sharpened my self-criti-
> cism more and more. *This* is the reason why I have not been able
> to compete the score of the second of the three pieces, Rounds,
> in time and why I have had to leave it until later, when I shall
> probably succeed in changing what is wrong with it.

Schoenberg apparently never responded to this letter or to the
dedication of the complete score, which arrived a year later.

It is difficult to explain adequately the strange relationship between these two great masters of early twentieth-century music.
Schoenberg was a paranoid, who would turn on even his most trusted
friend at the slightest provocation. Yet he also deeply believed in
Berg's genius and saw himself as a demanding teacher entrusted with
molding the talents of his younger colleague. Berg, on the other hand,
was insecure and seems to have thrived on Schoenberg's criticisms
as much as on his teaching. The psychological interaction between
these two men was complex, as is their music. The interesting thing
is that there was not more actual musical influence. Perhaps what
really irked Schoenberg was that Berg's style took as much from De-

bussy and Mahler as it did from him. Although Berg professed to have learned greatly from Schoenberg's Five Pieces for Orchestra, Opus 16, when writing his own Three Pieces, Berg's music sounds closer to the expressive world of Mahler's Sixth and Third Symphonies and sometimes to the harmonic and orchestral world of the French Impressionism.

Berg, Schoenberg, and Webern are often called the Second Viennese School (the first comprises Haydn, Mozart, and Beethoven). When their dissonantly expressive music was new, it seemed a revolutionary break with the past. In their later music these composers used the twelve-tone method of composition to create works clearly related to tradition: examples include the Violin Concertos of Berg and Schoenberg. It is sometimes suggested that Schoenberg was the innovator, Berg related Schoenberg's advances to the past, and Webern related them to the future. There is some truth in this oversimplification. As Berg's biographer Karen Monson points out, in the Three Pieces "Berg managed to produce the work that was so necessary, but that neither Schoenberg nor Webern had been able to find; the work that drew the line between the mainstream of the late nineteenth and early twentieth centuries and the avant garde faction called the New Viennese School."

The strongest link to the immediate past in the Three Pieces is to Mahler, a composer whom Berg revered and who had died two years before Berg began the Three Pieces. There are superficial similarities to Mahler in some of Opus 6's melodic lines, some of the scoring, the size of the orchestra (although Berg's counterpoint is denser, even after he thinned out the orchestration in the 1929 revision), and the use of hammer blows in the finale (recalling the powerful finale of Mahler's Sixth Symphony, of which Berg once said, "There is but one Sixth, in spite of [Beethoven's] *Pastorale*"). The percussion at the opening and closing of the first piece recalls Mahler's Third Symphony, and the stylized waltz figures in the second piece are not far removed from the folk-like *Ländler* movements in several Mahler symphonies. The final piece, the March, comes closest to the earlier composer, with its fanfares, drum rolls, and march rhythms.

The Prelude begins with the indistinct noises of soft percussion. The sonority gradually gets clearer and more focused, culminating in a beautiful violin melody. The movement continues to build, reaching a huge climax in the middle. It then gradually dies away, ending as it began with percussion alone. The arch form thus created suggests Berg's later interest in retrogrades — music that is the same when played backwards.

Berg declared that Rounds was a study for the Inn Scene in his opera *Wozzeck*. The atmosphere of the Austrian waltz is never far away in this movement, which at times sounds like a surreal treatment of the idiom of Johann Strauss.

The final piece is as long as the other two put together. It is a fierce and agitated version of the march: dense, complex, and potent. Berg's biographer Mosco Carner sees a relationship in this movement not only to Mahler but also to Schubert: "Both [Mahler and Berg] appear to have interpreted the march as the symbol of an inexorable, cruel fate, [but] the first to see in the march rhythm the embodiment of a poetic idea, namely life as an interminable and sad wandering on earth, was Schubert." Several influences — the poignant lyricism of Schubert, the unique vision of Mahler, the free dissonance of Schoenberg, and the sensuous colors of Debussy — converge to make Berg's Three Pieces for Orchestra extraordinarily powerful and beautiful.

Hector Berlioz

Born on 11 December 1803 in Côte-Saint-André, Isère, near Grenoble.
Died on 8 March 1869 in Paris.

◆ ◆ ◆

Le corsaire Overture, Opus 21
King Lear Overture, Opus 4

Both overtures were begun in Nice in April 1831. Le corsaire *was first completed 13 years later and then premiered in Paris in January 1845. Berlioz subsequently revised it. The final version was heard in Paris on 1 April 1855. The* King Lear *Overture was finished in Rome in 1831. It was first performed in Paris on 22 December 1833.*

On his fourth try Berlioz managed to secure the coveted Rome Prize, which provided a stipend to a promising young composer to spend 18 months in Rome. He had been eager to receive the prize not only for its prestige and monetary reward but also because his winning it was a condition of his betrothal to the attractive pianist Marie ("Camille") Moke. Camille's mother had not been too happy over the match, but felt she could give her consent if it seemed that Berlioz might actually amount to something as a composer. Berlioz, on the other hand, was reluctant to go to Italy, because he did not want to leave either Camille or Paris, which was the center of his musical career. He tried a number of schemes to have the rules of the prize changed, but to no avail. He left for Rome on 29 December 1830.

The trip took several weeks. Berlioz heard nothing from Camille during this time. He was understandably uneasy. Finding no letters from her awaiting him when he arrived in Rome, he was tempted to return to Paris immediately to find out what was happening. Yet he knew that he would have to forfeit the prize money, and with it any hope of marrying Camille, if he returned. Why had he received no letters? Had not Madame Moke publicly called him her son-in-law? He was tormented, lovesick, and depressed. Finally, in the middle of April, a letter arrived from Madame Moke, in which she informed the ill-fated composer that Camille was to marry the piano-maker Pleyel. Berlioz' depression turned instantly to rage. He sent his clothes to his father and the score of his *Symphonie fantastique,* which he had been revising, to conductor F. A. Habaneck, with instructions on how to complete the revisions. Then he set off for Paris.

He had decided on a bizarre scenario of revenge against Camille,

Mme. Moke, and Pleyel. His account (in his memoirs) of his self-in-dulgent plan of retribution is as bemused as it is tragic; the story could serve well as the plot of a melodrama. He decided to go "immediately to Paris and there kill without compunction two guilty women and one innocent man. As for subsequently killing myself, after a coup on this scale it was of course the very least I could do. . . . They would be expecting me to come back. Therefore I must take every precaution and go in disguise."

First the composer bought a maid's outfit and then set off on his journey.

At Genoa the police examined his passport and concluded that he was a dangerous character. "Which of us was the more splendidly idiotic," he wrote later, "The police, who saw in every Frenchman an agent of the revolution, or I, who imagined I must not set foot in Paris without having first disguised myself as a woman, as though every-one who met me would instantly read my intentions in my face?"

Berlioz was allowed to continue on to Nice. Later he recalled, "I rehearsed in my mind every detail of the little comedy I intended to enact when I reached Paris. I go to my friends' house. . . . I say I am the Countess M's personal maid with an urgent message. While it is being read, I draw my double-barrelled pistols, blow out the brains of number one and number two, seize number three by the hair, re-veal myself and, disregarding her screams, pay my respects to her in similar fashion, after which, before this cantata for voices and or-chestra has had time to attract attention, I present my right temple with the unanswerable argument of the remaining barrel."

The composer eventually began to have second thoughts. He weighed the advantages of suicide against those of continuing to live. "I realized that I was hungry, having eaten nothing since Florence. Oh blessed, base human nature! It was clear that I was cured. . . .

"I remained in Nice for a month. . . . I wrote the overture to *King Lear.* I breathed, I sang, I believed in God. A convalescence indeed. These were the three happiest weeks of my life."

As he stayed on in Nice, Berlioz began to compose a second over-ture, which evenutally became known as *Le corsaire.* He did not finish it, however, as he was forced to leave Nice and return to Rome. He left at the "invitation" of the chief of police, who was suspicious be-cause the composer had become friendly with the two officers of the Piedmontese garrison.

The chief reasoned, "This young French musician . . . spends whole days on the rocks at Villefranche; he must be waiting for a signal from some revolutionary vessel. He never dines at the table d'hôte. Of course — because he does not wish to be drawn into con-versation by our agents. And now he is surreptitiously entering into relations with the officers of our regiment — undoubtedly in order to open negotiations with them — negotiations with which he has been entrusted by the leaders of Young Italy. A flagrant case of conspiracy!"

Berlioz was formally interrogated:

"What are you doing here?"

"Recovering from a painful illness. I compose, I dream, I thank God for the glorious sun, the blue sea, and the great green hills."

"You are not a painter?"

"No, sir."

"Yet you are seen everywhere, sketchbook in hand, drawing. Are you by any chance making plans?"

"Yes, I am making plans for an overture on *King Lear*: in fact I have made them. The drafting and the instrumentation are complete. . . ."

"Who is this King Lear?"

"Alas, a poor old English king."

"English! . . . This word instrumentation?"

"A musical term."

"The same excuse again. Now, sir, I know perfectly well that's not the way people compose, without a piano, simply wandering about the beach with a sketchbook and a pencil. Tell me where you wish to go and your passport will be made out. You can't stay in Nice any longer."

"Very well, I'll return to Rome, and by your leave continue to compose without a piano."

And that was that. Next day I left Nice, very reluctantly but with a light heart and in the highest spirits. I was alive and cured.

Berlioz never indicated how explicitly programmatic he intended his *King Lear* Overture to be. Several commentators have found parallels between the music and the drama. Biographer Jacques Barzun, for example, likens the thrice repeated opening theme with its three "answers" to King Lear's three questions to his daughters. Critic Irving Kolodin considers the allegro's oboe melody to be a characterization of Cordelia. Richard Strauss suggested that the two *pizzicato* chords in the coda represent the snapping of Lear's mind. Arthur Smolian believed that "we hear in the principal theme of the allegro the gathering pride and fury of the deeply wounded royal heart against all the outrageous ingratitude of his children." Berlioz himself admitted that the timpani beats at the end of the introduction depict the king's entry into his council chamber.

The accuracy of these interpretations need not concern the listener, since *King Lear* is, after all, a concert piece. It was not meant as prelude to or incidental music for Shakespeare's drama, nor was it intended as introduction to any larger work (e.g., an opera) based on the play. It is simply a tone poem inspired by Shakespeare's tragedy.

When Berlioz returned to Nice 13 years after his banishment, his interest in the unfinished *Corsaire* Overture was rekindled. Sitting atop the Martello Tower, inspired by the sea, he finished the piece. He called it *The Tower of Nice*. It was performed in Paris in January 1845.

The composer was not satisfied when he heard the overture, and he set it aside for revision. He did not get around to making changes until 1851–52, however. At that time he gave the overture a new name — *Le corsaire rouge* ("The Red Corsair") — after the novel by James Fenimore Cooper. Berlioz had probably recently reread this sea tale by one of his favorite authors, who had just died. In Cooper's story a tower on a rocky coast plays an important role, and Berlioz made the association with the Martello Tower.

He subsequently removed the word *rouge* from the title, feeling that people who did not know the Cooper book would be confused and those who did would look for exact programmatic correspondences. Also, the new title suggested Byron's Corsair, a sea-roving bandit who harbored contempt for all men and gallantry for all women.

The revised version, with its final title *Le corsaire*, was finally performed in 1855, 24 years after it had first been sketched.

The form of the overture is traditional, except for the unusual way it begins. The impetuous allegro opening sounds as if we were suddenly thrust into the midst of a performance. This rapid music gives way almost immediately to an adagio. The fiery beginning remains in our memories, like an unanswered question. The psychological resolution comes when the allegro returns and eventually works its way back to a restatement of the opening. Then Berlioz' purpose becomes clear: the overture, begun in such a headlong manner, suddenly stops because the traditional slow introduction has been, so to speak, forgotten. Once this "omission" is corrected, the fast music can resume.

Throughout the remainder of the overture, we are treated to Berlioz' brilliant orchestration, inventive rhythms, exciting syncopations, and wonderful melodies. The overture is carefree, witty, and thoroughly delightful.

Harold in Italy, Opus 16

Harold in the Mountains: Scenes of Sadness,
Happiness, and Joy

March of the Pilgrims, Singing Their Evening
Prayers

Serenade of a Mountaineer of the Abruzzi to His
Mistress

Orgy of the Brigands: Memories of Past Scenes

Harold in Italy *was begun early in 1834 and completed on 22 June*
of the same year. It was first performed on 23 November 1834 by
violist Chrétien Urban at the Paris Conservatoire.

Harold in Italy owes its origins to the great violin virtuoso Niccolò
Paganini. Paganini's incredible abilities were legendary. His style of
playing influenced pianists and composers as well as violinists. He
was more than a violinist, however. He was an accomplished composer, violist, and (like Berlioz) guitarist. When he acquired a Stra-
divarius viola in 1833, he was eager to display its wonderful sound
in concerts. There was a problem, however. There was no music of
sufficient virtuosity written for the instrument. When Paganini heard
a performance of Berlioz' brilliant first symphony, the *Symphonie*
fantastique, he was immediately struck with the answer: he would
get Berlioz to compose a viola concerto for him.

Berlioz protested that Paganini himself would be the logical
choice of composer, but the violinist insisted, "You are the only one I
can trust for such a work." Berlioz accepted the commission. He had
been planning to compose a second symphony, and the stimulus of a
commission made him think about "a solo piece for viola, but a solo
combined with orchestra in such a manner that it would not injure
the expression of the orchestral mass. . . . My idea was to write a series of scenes for the orchestra in which the solo viola would be involved as a more or less active character, always retaining its own
individuality. By placing the viola in the midst of poetic recollections
of my wanderings in the Abruzzi, I wished to make it a sort of melancholy dreamer after the manner of Byron's *Childe Harold.* Thus the
title *Harold in Italy.*"

Berlioz in fact followed none of the scenes in Byron's poem. The
composer had read the work while in Rome, and he identified with
the poet wandering through Italy, recording his impressions. The colorful titles that Berlioz gave to the four movements constitute all that
he was willing to disclose about the program.

Harold is represented by a theme, heard when the viola makes its first entrance. This theme recurs in all movements, as Harold observes the different scenes. Thus it is like the *idée fixe* in the *Symphonie fantastique*. But there is a difference. Berlioz explained, "The *idée fixe* intrudes itself obstinately, like a passionate, episodic idea, into scenes wholly foreign to it, disrupting them, while Harold's strain is added to the other orchestral strains, with which it contrasts both in movement and character, without hindering their development."

Part of the reason for the vagueness of the program is that Berlioz had already composed some of the music before receiving Paganini's commission. The Harold theme and the second theme of the first movement were both previously used in the *Rob Roy* Overture, which he had written in 1831–32 and subsequently discarded. The Harold theme had been a lyrical English horn solo. Partly for this reason, there is not much outright virtuosity in the solo line of the first movement. Also, there are many passages in which the soloist does not play at all. Paganini was not very happy when Berlioz showed him the finished score of this movement. "That's not it at all!" he cried. "I am silent too long. I must be playing the whole time." Paganini withdrew his support, but Berlioz carried the work through to completion nonetheless. He dedicated it to another violist, Humbert Ferrand.

In 1838 Paganini, who was by then old and feeble, heard *Harold* for the first time. He told Berlioz, "Never before have I been so powerfully impressed at a concert. If I did not restrain myself, I should have to go down on my knees to thank you for it." Shortly thereafter Berlioz received a huge sum of money, which he thought to be a gift from Paganini. In fact, the violinist was a skinflint, and the money came from Berlioz' friend Armand Bertin, who wanted to give the composer something to help free up his time. As Bertin knew Berlioz would never accept a gift from him, he arranged for the composer to think that it had come from Paganini. With this money Berlioz took time off from other duties to compose his third symphony, *Romeo and Juliet*, which he dedicated to Paganini.

Harold is a special work. Not really a concerto, not quite a symphony, it has aspects of both. The use of the soloist as a commentator rather than as the featured performer is quite unusual. The orchestration is, as always with Berlioz, extraordinarily imaginative, colorful, and exciting.

The first movement begins with an enormous introduction divided into four subsections. Even once the tempo quickens to allegro, we are still in the introduction. The main part of the movement begins when the viola introduces the main theme, one note at a time.

The second movement is an extraordinarily original conception. After an introduction of isolated chords, a melody is sung by the first violins. It continues in the violas and then the winds. And so it goes, again and again the same pattern repeated. Eventually the solo viola enters, playing the Harold theme. But the rest of the orchestra keeps on going as if the viola were not even there. Interestingly, the phrase lengths of the orchestra and those of the viola are not equal. A subtle tension is thus created. After the viola exits, the orchestra still continues as it has been. After a middle section, marked *Canto religioso,* the main section returns. There is an extended coda, in which the winds and harp seem unable to decide on which of two notes to settle. The passage suggests two distant tolling bells. This utterly simple yet endlessly fascinating movement is like none other in all of music.

The third movement is scarcely less original. It begins with a scherzo theme played on oboe and piccolo (a sonority imitative of a rustic oboe Berlioz heard in Italy). Once the viola enters with the Harold theme, the orcehstra ignoes it, much as in the slow movement. Gradually, step by step, the viola music becomes more like that of the rest of the orchestra, until the two are fully integrated. The movement closes with an elaborate coda that superimposes the scherzo rhythm, a lyrical melody previously heard in the English horn, and the Harold theme — all moving simultaneously at seemingly different tempos.

The finale starts impetuously with its main theme, which is cut short as abruptly as it begins. There ensues a series of recollections, always in the solo viola, of themes from the earlier movements (a device Berlioz borrowed from the finale of Beethoven's Ninth Symphony). Alternating with these reminiscences are forceful attempts by the orchestra to start the finale moving with its own material. Finally, the orchestra is free to develop into a frenzied bacchanal, aided by a second theme of even greater abandon than its predecessor. During this entire long "Orgy of the Brigands," the solo viola is silent, almost forgotten. Finally, the frenzy subsides and three distant string instruments intone one further reminiscence (the main theme of the second movement). Only then can the viola reappear, after having been absent for almost all of the movement. All it gets to play, though, is one beautifully extended phrase, after which the orchestra resumes its orgy and pushes forcefully toward the conclusion. An extraordinary movement, cast in a unique form, serves as a fitting conclusion to this thoroughly unique symphony-concerto.

Roman Carnival Overture, Opus 9

The Roman Carnival *Overture was composed late in 1843 and first performed under the composer's direction in February 1844 in Paris.*

Early in 1844 Berlioz published one of his most influential works. It was not a composition but a textbook. The *Treatise on Modern Instrumentation and Orchestration* was the first manual of scoring written by a major composer. Several generations of musicians learned orchestral craft from this book. In fact, it is still consulted today. For a textbook to remain useful for a century and a half is as impressive as it is unusual.

Berlioz was a master orchestrator. Writing music for instruments was for him an art, not a technique. He was the first to differentiate between the "science" of instrumentation (the study of what various instruments can and cannot do well) from the art of orchestration (the creative combination of instrumental colors). He believed that the instrumental garb of a musical idea was an intrinsic part of both its affect and its effect. This idea was radically new in 1844. Previous composers had conceived their music apart from its orchestral color: witness the readiness with which a Bach or a Schubert transferred works cast in one medium to another. Not so Berlioz, at least for the most part. A work like the *Symphonie fantastique* or the *Roman Carnival* Overture can exist only as orchestral music.

Berlioz' biographer Jacques Barzun points out that the *Treatise on Orchestration* could have made Berlioz (and his estate) wealthy, had copyright protection been as strong as it is today. The book was soon translated into German, Italian, Spanish, and English. Later such accomplished orchestrators as Felix Weingartner and Richard Strauss thought highly enough of Berlioz' treatise to modernize it rather than undertaking to write their own texts. Among other composers who acknowledged indebtedness to the book were Mahler, Delius, Elgar, Mussorgsky, Busoni, d'Indy, Debussy, Bruckner, and Saint-Saëns.

It is instructive to compare the orchestration lessons Berlioz offered in the book with the orchestral music he was composing at the same time. The *Roman Carnival* Overture was written just as the *Treatise* was going to press. The book calls for rescuing from neglect certain instruments, such as the violas. In the overture, there is a sumptuous passage for violas. After a lyrical melody is stated in the English horn, it is repeated with a fuller orchestration. Notice the special quality of the violas as they sing this tune, to the accompaniment of violins, cellos, horns, clarinets, flutes, and bassoons — instruments violas typically accompany. Berlioz' text also calls for orchestral clarity, even in dense passages. The overture's subsequent passage for full orchestra is a model of transparency: everyone is playing, yet we have no trouble following simultaneously the Italianate repeated rhythms (in the brass, percussion, clarinets, and one flute), the lyrical theme in imitation (bassoons, violas, and cellos answered by violins, oboe, English horn, and the other flute), and the sustained note in the string basses.

The *Roman Carnival* Overture did not come into existence to demonstrate principles developed in the *Treatise*. The overture does show, however, that the mind and ear of the composer and of the pedagogue were working in tandem. The overture is wonderfully alive, marvelously sonorous — because of its orchestration. Despite the prevalence of the piano as the instrument of choice in the mid-nineteenth century, a piano transcription of the *Roman Carnival* would surely sound pale (although a performance by four pianists, including Franz Liszt, did once evoke thunderous applause). The music must be orchestral because its expressivity is actually *in*, not simply conveyed by, its sonorities.

The two main melodies of the overture come from Berlioz' opera *Benvenuto Cellini,* completed a few years earlier. These themes are taken from the grand chorus "Come Ye All, People of Rome" and the carnival scene "Ah, Sound the Trumpets, Sound the Bagpipes, Sound the Gay Tambourines." The *Roman Carnival* was probably not intended to be performed with the opera, however, although there is some speculation that Berlioz wished it to precede the second act. The situation is similar to that of Beethoven's *Leonore* Overtures, which belong in a fundamental way to the opera *Fidelio* but are not intended to be played with it.

Berlioz may have been thinking about *Benvenuto Cellini* because some music from that opera had recently been performed on his concert at the Paris Conservatoire. This concert, unlike most he had given, was a smash success. "Woe to anyone hereafter who shall dare deny M. Berlioz' genius," wrote one reviewer. Certain members of the Parisian musical establishment felt threatened by Berlioz' unexpected success. They retaliated by arranging for Berlioz to be denied use of the concert hall henceforth. Furthermore, the conductor of the Paris Opéra managed to force the cancellation of a concert by Berlioz' newly founded Association of Musical Artists.

The *Roman Carnival* rose to enormous popularity, despite these political intrigues against Berlioz' music. The overture had to be played again at its premiere, and it was soon being performed widely. Even in the face of this public acceptance, however, Berlioz' enemies would not concede the artistic worth of his music. One opponent, conductor F. Seghers, happened to hear a rehearsal of the overture. He actually liked it, until he found out who the composer was. "What is the fascinating overture you have been playing?" Seghers asked the leader of the rehearsal. "That was the *Roman Carnival* by Berlioz," was the reply. Seghers stammered, "Well! I must say!" One of the composer's friends interrupted, "I agree with you that Berlioz ought to be ashamed to go against an honest man's prejudices in that way."

The delightful overture begins with a headlong rush, which is twice interrupted by silence. The music seems to falter, as if it has realized that it forgot its slow introduction (Berlioz used a similar strategy in *Le corsair* Overture). The tempo then changes to andante for the lyrical English horn theme. This melody develops at length before the return of the allegro and, eventually, the first theme — now properly introduced.

In a few places the dance-like 6/8 of the allegro is interrupted by a sudden shift to 2/4. The final time this happens, shortly before the end, the music comes precariously close to chaos — but just for a brief moment. Berlioz presents in quick succession eleven of the twelve notes of the chromatic scale, with no duplications. This procedure, which eventually became a major technique of twelve-tone composers a century later, is deliberately incongruous in the *Roman Carnival* Overture. The passage is not so much prophetic as special in itself; Berlioz would no doubt have been as surprised as anyone by twelve-tone music. But these brief three measures sound wonderfully imaginative, if a bit quirky or even bizarre, in a piece composed in 1843. But the *Roman Carnival* Overture is not a typical mid-nineteenth-century composition. Rather, it is a work of a true original, whose orchestral craft and melodic imagination were unlike those of any other composer.

Romeo and Juliet, Opus 17

Combat. Tumult. Intervention of the Prince

Romeo Alone. Sadness. Distant Sounds of
    Music and Dancing. Festivities at the Capulets

Night. The Capulets' Garden, Peaceful and
    Deserted. The Young Capulets on Their Way
    Home. Love Scene

Queen Mab, the Spirit of Dreams

Juliet's Funeral. Romeo at the Tomb of the
    Capulets. Finale

The dramatic symphony Romeo and Juliet *was composed mostly in 1839, although it was planned as far back as 1827 and it was revised through 1847. It was first performed in Paris in November 1839 under the direction of the composer.*

Nearly twenty years passed between the initial conception of *Romeo and Juliet* and its completion in final form. When Berlioz was a young man of 27, he traveled to Italy and, under the spell of the country that had given artistic inspiration to many composers, he decided on what turned out to be almost his entire life's work. He wrote down descriptions of several dramatic works: the symphony-concerto *Harold in Italy* (completed four years later), the opera *Benvenuto Cellini* (eight years later), the dramatic symphony *Romeo and Juliet* (17 years later), the opera *The Trojans* (28 years later), and the opera *Beatrice and Benedict* (32 years later). These were the subjects that interested him, and he was committed enough to his youthful ideas to see them through to completion.

Berlioz' interest in *Romeo and Juliet* actually started three years before his Italian trip, when he first saw the play. He had read Shakespeare in translation, and he was eager to see it on stage when a troupe from England toured France. Shakespeare's plays took Paris by storm. His dramas were heralded by the French romantic movement as an exciting alternative to academic classicism. Berlioz joined the intellectual elite that turned out to see *Romeo*. He was as overwhelmed as the rest of the audience, despite the fact that he knew no English. He was taken not only with the play but also with Harriet Smithson, the actress who played Juliet. He also saw her astounding performance as Ophelia in *Hamlet*, and he fell instantly in love with her. He idolized and idealized her before even meeting her. In his mind her person merged with that of Juliet; both represented "the true meaning of grandeur, beauty, and dramatic truth" in Shakespeare. Berlioz saw in Shakespeare implications for "the entire development of the music of the future," and he saw in Harriet a symbol of Shakespeare's supreme artistry. He decided to pursue his unattainable dream: he supposedly said after first seeing *Romeo and Juliet*, "I shall marry Juliet and I shall write my biggest symphony on the play."

He accomplished both goals. After considerable effort he persuaded Smithson to meet him and eventually to marry him. Only then did he begin to learn that one cannot marry a dream. Harriet was not a Juliet, and Berlioz was for years burdened by a demanding, self-centered wife who constantly embarrassed him.

Berlioz thought about a symphony based on *Romeo and Juliet* for years. He knew it would be a major undertaking. He was finally able to find time to compose it in 1839, thanks to a large grant he thought was from violin virtuoso Niccolò Paganini, who had been deeply impressed with Berlioz' music (the money actually came secretly from the composer's friend Armand Bertin). After three performances, Berlioz decided to revise the work. It was ready for publication in 1847, twenty years after he had first seen Shakespeare's play.

Berlioz called *Romeo and Juliet* a "dramatic symphony." This subtitle is a good clue to the real nature of the work. Since it has voices, it follows in some ways Beethoven's Ninth Symphony, which Berlioz admired. The choral parts are more integrated with the entire piece than in Beethoven, because the work is specifically dramatic: it is based on a play, not a poem. But it is not simply a setting of the play. The music does not accompany the drama, as it does in opera or incidental music. In fact, when Berlioz had the opportunity to use some of the music in a production of Shakespeare's tragedy, he found the idea ludicrous. *Romeo and Juliet* is a programmatic symphony, in the tradition of Berlioz' own *Symphonie fantastique.* Like the *Fantastique,* the *Romeo and Juliet* Symphony tells a story *within the music.* A listener who does not know Shakespeare's play cannot learn the plot just from hearing symphony. Yet someone who does know Shakespeare can hear themes from the play echoed and commented upon by the music.

The concept behind *Romeo and Juliet* was without precedent. It is not an opera and not an oratorio, but a true symphony. It is a fusion, not a hybrid, of lyric and dramatic elements. It represents a new genre, which led eventually to Wagner's music dramas (Wagner traveled to Paris to hear *Romeo and Juliet*, and he was deeply impressed), in which a continuous instrumental fabric encloses an unfolding drama.

Berlioz' work is indeed a symphony. After the extended choral prologue there are three orchestral movements corresponding to first movement, slow movement, and scherzo of a conventional symphony. The piece closes with a large choral finale.

Part I summarizes the drama to come and introduces the main themes. It begins with a fugal prologue, followed by a low brass recitative. Then a solo contralto and small chorus explain the subject of the drama to follow: the feud between two families and the star-crossed love of two of their children. The contralto then sings of love, after which Queen Mab is introduced in a small scherzo. At the end of the movement, the chorus foretells the tragic death of Romeo and Juliet and the eventual reconciliation of the families.

Part II is a true symphonic movement, complete with slow introduction and elaborate allegro. It depicts Romeo's contrasting moods of lonely sadness and gaiety while at the concert and the ball. Romeo's motive, introduced at the beginning, is subjected to various transformations as the protagonist moves as if in a dream through despondency, happiness, and the exuberance of the crowd. Particularly interesting is the simultaneous statement of the slow Romeo motive and the boisterous crowd music. As Berlioz' biographer Jacques Barzun explains, "The rhythms of revelry mix, clash, go to pieces, and resurge, ceasing only near the end, to permit a fragment of the oboe theme to be heard at the throbbing close."

Part III, the adagio, expresses the tragic and passionate love at the heart of the play. The setting is the solitary night in the Capulet's garden after the ball. Berlioz felt that he could give a fuller and truer expression of love in the abstract world of instrumental sound than he could hope to achieve with words. "The instrumental idiom [is] a richer, more varied, less limited language, and by its very unliteralness infinitely more powerful." This movement could well have been inspired by these lines from Shakespeare's Act II:

> How silver sweet sound lovers' tongues by night,
> Like softest music to attending ears!

Barzun hears in this movement "the purity that comes not from reticence but from incandescence, from the tragic, not the sultry, acceptance of fate. The music also conveys a sensation of limpid depths which may be associated with nature in stillness, young love, or night-time."

Part IV is the famous "Queen Mab Scherzo," the first part of the symphony Berlioz conceived. Queen Mab is, according to English legend, a fairy midwife who delivers man's dreams into the world. The atmosphere of this scherzo parallels that of Mercutio's speech:

> She is the fairies' midwife, and she comes
> In shape no bigger than an agate stone
> On the forefinger of an alderman,
> Drawn with a team of little atomies
> Athwart men's noses as they lie asleep —
> Her wagon spokes made of long spinners'
>   legs;
> The cover, of the wings of grasshoppers;
> Her traces, of the smallest spider's web;
> Her collars, of the moonshine's watery
>   beams;
> Her whip, of cricket's bone; the lash, of film;
> Her wagoner, a small gray-coated gnat
> Not half so big as a round little worm
> Pricked from the lazy finger of a maid.

These elfin lines correspond beautifully to Berlioz' fairy-like scherzo. He once told Mendelssohn about his idea for a Queen Mab scherzo, and then he worried that his friend might compose it himself, since such airy music is typical of Mendelssohn's scherzos. But the German composer left it to the Frenchman to compose a musical picture of the fairy queen. The delicate scherzo rarely rises above the level of *piano,* yet it is brilliantly and imaginatively scored.

Part V depicts Juliet's funeral, Romeo at the tomb of the Capulets, Juliet's awakening, the frenzied joy and despair of the lovers, their last words, their agony and death, the brawling between the Capulets and Montagues, Friar Laurence's recitative and aria, and finally the reconciliation of the feuding families. Juliet's funeral music is played by the orchestra while the chorus intones a dirge on a single note. Halfway through, the roles are reversed: the orchestra takes the monotone while the Capulets sing the dirge. After the lovers die, the two families resume their feud in the cemetery, but the Friar comes forward and, singing first to the Capulet chorus and then to the Montagues, persuades them that the deaths of the lovers teaches what comes of fighting. The two families finally agree to reconcile.

Symphonie fantastique, Opus 14a
>   Reveries, Passions
>   A Ball
>   Scene in the Country
>   March to the Scaffold
>   Dream of a Witches' Sabbath

The Symphonie fantastique *was composed in 1830 and first performed on 5 December 1830 under the baton of François-Antoine Habaneck in Paris.*

Three important influences entered Berlioz' life during his 24th year. The first was Goethe's *Faust,* which the composer read and reread in a translation by Gérard de Nerval. According to Berlioz' biographer Jacques Barzun, Faust represented for the impressionable French romantic "genius in all its greatness." The second influence was the symphonies of Beethoven, particularly the *Eroica,* heard for the first time in Paris. Berlioz was overwhelmed by the power and originality of the Bonn master's orchestration. And, finally, there was Shakespeare, known in Letourneur's translation and experienced in performances by an English troupe of actors that toured France in 1827. The young Frenchman understood Goethe, Beethoven, and Shakespeare as kindred romantic spirits. No matter that these perceptions were one-sided and colored by what Berlioz was looking for — these three artists seemed to answer a great longing the composer felt for seriousness of purpose, depth of vision, bold originality, and all-encompassing humanity. The inspiration he drew from their works coalesced two years later in one of the most original pieces ever composed, the *Symphonie fantastique.*

Actually, there was a fourth influence, that turned out to be more significant for the composer than Goethe, Beethoven, or Shakespeare. There was in the Shakespearean acting company a young woman named Harriet Smithson, who had a strikingly beautiful face, a moving voice, and an enchanting stage manner. Her Ophelia held Parisian audiences spellbound. Berlioz was more than spellbound. He fell in love with Smithson immediately. "The impression made on my heart and mind by her extraordinary talent, nay her dramatic genius, was equalled only by the havoc wrought in me by the poet she so nobly interpreted."

Berlioz was an unknown student composer and Harriet was a famous actress. Did the composer have any hopes of ever winning her love? He felt the first step was to make himself at least known to her. He began to give concerts with the main purpose of making his name better established, hoping that Harriet might hear of him. After a few months of touring the provinces, Smithson's company returned to Paris and Berlioz ventured backstage after a performance, but she refused to see him. He wrote her love letters, which she took as fan mail and left unanswered. She returned to England without ever having even acknowledged the existence of her strange suitor. She still had only a vague idea of who he was.

Somehow Berlioz convinced himself that she had been impressed with his letters and was testing his sincerity by a few months of silence. His feelings for her began to wane, but then they returned with great intensity as he decided to make his love for her the subject of his new symphony.

> I have just been plunged again into all the tortures of an endless and unquenchable passion, without cause, without purpose. She is still in London, and yet I seem to feel her around me; I hear my heart pounding, and its beats set me going like the piston strokes of a steam engine. Each muscle of my body trembles with pain. Useless! Frightening! Oh, unhappy woman! If she could for one moment conceive all the poetry, all the infinity of such a love, she would fly to my arms, even if she must die from my embrace. I was on the point of beginning my grand symphony *Episode from the Life of an Artist,* in which the development of my infernal passion is to be depicted; I have it all in my head, but I can write nothing.

Soon after writing this letter on 6 February 1830, Berlioz heard and believed a rumor that Harriet was having an affair with her manager. The composer was disgusted, and he snapped out of his lovesick lethargy. Now he was able to compose the symphony. It was ready for its first performance the afternoon of 5 December 1830.

Smithson, in the meantime, had fallen on hard times, although the rumor of her affair had proven false and her good name had been restored. The acting company had gone bankrupt in London, and the actress was forced to accept walk-on parts at the Opéra-Comique. Since she did not have a singing voice and did not speak French, her roles were minor, and she was barely able to make a living. By coincidence Harriet gave a benefit performance a few hours after the *Symphonie fantastique* premiere. Berlioz, who was moved by Harriet's plight and still felt tenderness for her (though he had still never even met the woman), stayed away: he did not want to fuel the rumors (quite true, of course) that she was the beloved woman mentioned in the published program of the *Symphonie fantastique.*

A few weeks after the premiere of the *Symphonie,* Berlioz left for a year and a half in Rome. There he revised the second and third movements of the piece, and he composed a sequel called *The Return to Life.* He returned to Paris in November 1832 and rented an apartment across from where Smithson used to live.

> I asked [the housekeeper] what had become of Miss Smithson and whether she had heard any news of her. "But sir, . . . she's in Paris. She was staying here only a few days ago. She left the day before yesterday and moved to the *rue de Rivoli.* She was in the apartment that you have now. She is director of an English company that's opening next week." I stood aghast at the extraordinary series of coincidences. It was fate. I saw it was no longer possible for me to struggle against it. For two years I had heard nothing of the fair Ophelia; I had had no idea where she was, whether in England, Scotland, or America; and here I was, arriving from Italy at exactly the moment when she reappeared after a tour of northern Europe. We had just missed meeting each other in the same house; I had taken the apartment that she had vacated the previous evening.

Berlioz was arranging for a concert that would include the revised *Fantastique* and its new sequel. He had a man named Schutter see to it that Smithson attended the concert. Harriet was distressed at the time because Shakespeare was no longer popular in Paris and attendance was low at her company's productions. She decided to spend an afternoon at a concert as a diversion from her financial troubles. By now she knew who Berlioz was, but she still had never met him and she had no idea of her intimate connection with the music she was about to hear. In the cab to the concert, she studied the concert program and "she learned that I was the originator of the proceedings. The title of the symphony and the headings of the various movements somewhat astonished her; but it never so much as occurred to her that the heroine of this strange and doleful drama might be herself."

Every eye was on her as she arrived. Everyone in Parisian music circles knew the truth, but Harriet did not. She took the stares as directed at a famous actress. During the intermission (after the *Fan-*

tastique but before *The Return to Life*), Schutter made "veiled allusions to the cause of this young composer's well-known troubles of the heart. [She] began to suspect the truth." The second half began, and the actor playing the part of Lélio (the hero who represents Berlioz in *The Return to Life*) delivered this line:

> Oh, if I could only find her, the Juliet, the Ophelia for whom my heart cries out! If I could drink deep of the mingled joy and sadness that real love offers us, and one autumn evening on some wild heath with the north wind blowing over it, lie in her arms and sleep a last, long, sorrowful sleep!"
>
> "God!" she thought. "Juliet-Ophelia! Am I dreaming? I can no longer doubt. It is of me he speaks. He loves me still." From that moment . . . she felt the room reel about her; she heard no more but sat in a dream and at the end returned home like a sleepwalker, with no clear notion of what was happening.

This was Berlioz' account of how Harriet finally came to understand that the irrational young man who had written her love letters two years earlier had actually made a monumental musical composition based on his hopeless love for her. Finally, the day after the concert, the inevitable happened: the two met. Thus ended a fairy tale and began life's reality. Several months later they were married, but within a few years they were miserable. They separated after a decade of marriage. Berlioz married his mistress when Harriet died in 1854.

Berlioz actually made two different versions of the program for the *Symphonie fantastique*. The original one is printed here; the revised version was intended for use when *The Return to Life* is also performed. But that strange second work is rarely heard today.

> *Reveries, Passions.* . . . A young musician . . . sees for the first time a woman who embodies all the charms of the ideal being he has imagined in his dreams, and he falls desperately in love with her. Through an odd whim, whenever the beloved image appears before the mind's eye of the artist, it is linked with a musical thought whose character, passionate but at the same time noble and shy, he finds similar to the one he attributes to his beloved. . . .
>
> The passage from this state of melancholic reverie, interrupted by a few fits of groundless joy, to one of frenzied passion, with its movements of fury, of jealousy, its return to tenderness, its tears, its religious consolations — this is the subject of the first movement.
>
> *A Ball.* The artist finds himself in the most varied situations — in the midst of the tumult of a party, in the peaceful

contemplation of the beauties of nature. But everywhere — in town, in the country — the beloved image appears before him and disturbs his peace of mind.

Scene in the Country. Finding himself one evening in the country, he hears in the distance two shepherds piping a *ranz des vaches* in dialogue. This pastoral duet, the scenery, the quiet rustling of the trees gently brushed by the wind, the hopes he has recently found some reason to entertain — all concur in affording his heart an unaccustomed calm. . . . He reflects upon his isolation; he hopes that his loneliness will soon be over. But what if she were deceiving him! This mingling of hope and fear, these ideas of happiness disturbed by black presentiments, form the subject of the adagio. At the end one of the shepherds again takes up the *ranz des vaches*; the other no longer replies. Distant sounds of thunder — loneliness — silence.

March to the Scaffold. Convinced that his love is unappreciated, the artist poisons himself with opium. The dose of the narcotic, too weak to kill him, plunges him into a sleep accompanied by the most horrible visions. He dreams that he has killed his beloved, that he is condemned and led to the scaffold, and that he is witnessing his own execution. The procession moves forward to the sounds of a march that is now somber and fierce, now brilliant and solemn, in which the muffled noise of heavy steps gives way without transition to the noisiest clamor. At the end of the march, the first four measures of the *idée fixe* reappear, like a last thought of love interrupted by the fatal blow.

Dream of a Witches' Sabbath. He sees himself at the sabbath, in the midst of a frightful troop of ghosts, sorcerers, monsters of every kind, who have come together for his funeral. Strange noises, groans, bursts of laughter, distant cries which other cries seem to answer. The beloved melody appears again, but it has lost its character of nobility and shyness; it is no more than a dance tune, mean, trivial, and grotesque. . . . Funeral knell, burlesque parody of the *Dies irae* (hymn sung in the funeral rites of the Catholic Church), sabbath round-dance. The sabbath round and the *Dies irae* combined.

The drug-induced fantasy world of this program is only one of many utterly original aspects of the *Symphony fantastique.* The degree of detail in the program and the composer's insistence on its importance for the listener are also unprecedented. The most original aspect of the work, however, is its orchestration. The use of four bassoons, four types of clarinets, large bells, and cornets as well as trumpets lends this score a unique sound. But it is mainly Berlioz' uncanny sonic imagination that gives the piece its utterly unique quality, that makes it sound as fresh today as it must have in 1830. The finale in particular abounds in incredible sonorities — from the parody of the *idée fixe* tune in the C and then E-flat clarinets, to the bells that announce the ancient Gregorian chant *Dies irae,* to the subsequent woodwind distortion of that melody, to the weird sound of the wooden parts of bows hitting the strings just before the end. The work consistently demonstrates Berlioz' incredible originality as an orchestrator.

The *Symphonie fantastique* is a work like none other. Its reason for being is odd. Its sound palette is unprecedented. Its forms are fresh. Its program is grotesque. And the result is a composition that creates its own world in sound. The influence of Goethe, Beethoven, and Shakespeare, plus the irrational love for Harriet Smithson, all worked on the mind of the 27-year-old composer, and what resulted was completely new, amazingly fresh, wholly personal — and a masterpiece.

Alexander Borodin

Born on 12 November 1833 in St. Petersburg.
Died there on 27 February 1887.

Symphony Number 2 in B Minor

Allegro
Scherzo: Prestissimo. Allegretto. Prestissimo
Andante —
Allegro

The B Minor Symphony was begun early in 1869 and completed in December 1875. Edward Napravnik conducted the first performance at a concert of the Russian Musical Society in St. Petersburg on 10 March 1977. Borodin subsequently revised the symphony, and the final version was first conducted by Nikolai Rimsky-Korsakoff in St. Petersburg on 4 March 1879.

Borodin was both a composer and a scientist. Although he was more committed to science and did make some important contributions to chemistry, he is of course remembered today mainly as a composer.

Both interests manifested themselves early. As a teenager Borodin composed, played chamber music, experimented with galvanism, and made fireworks. In 1850 he entered the Medico-Surgical Academy, where he studied botany, zoology, crystallography, anatomy, and chemistry. After graduating with honors, he was appointed an assistant in general pathology and therapy. He attended international scientific congresses, at one of which he presented a paper called "On the Action of Ethyl-iodide on Hydrobenzamide and Amarine." He received his Ph.D. in 1858 with a dissertation entitled *On the Analogy of Arsenical with Phosphoric Acid.* He then went to Germany for post-doctoral studies in chemistry. After a subsequent period doing research in Italy, he returned to Russia to assume a faculty position at the Academy. At this time he was investigating the condensation of the aldehydes of valerian, enantol, and vinegar. After a few years Borodin discovered that German scientists were duplicating his work using superior apparatus, so he changed the focus of his research and concentrated more on administration at the Academy. In this capacity he traveled again to Germany to study how different chemical research laboratories were structured.

The above *curriculum vitae* hardly sounds like that of a composer. Borodin was an active and respected scientist, and thus it is not sur-

133

prising that his compositional output was small. He composed mainly in his spare time, of which he had little. Not only did his work keep him from music but also his propensity for involvement with attractive young women.

While pursuing his post-doctoral studies in Germany, Borodin became enchanted with Ekaterina Sergeyevna Protopopova, a 29-year-old pianist. When she had to go to Italy for her health, he followed her, managing to find scientific work there. While in Italy he met a different young woman, who fell in love with him. He thought of her as a daughter, but he did keep up a regular correspondence with her for the next eight years. This minor involvement did not deter Ekaterina from marrying him when they returned to Russia together the following spring. But this was hardly the end of Borodin's being distracted by beautiful women. A few years later Anna Kalina, sister of composer Nikolai Lodyzhensky, fell in love with him. He was quite taken with her and spent a lot of time in her company (much to the annoyance of Ekaterina — he described to her every detail of his relationship with Anna), but the friendship remained platonic. Borodin tired of Kalina eventually. A few years later another young woman threw herself at the composer. He was again enchanted, and he used this involvement in his opera *Prince Igor.* Again he remained faithful to Ekaterina but spent a lot of time with his new friend.

Borodin's active scientific career and frequent long-term involvements with young women were two factors that took time away from composition. A third was his chaotic household. Historian Richard Anthony Leonard describes it thus:

> No account of the career of Alexander Borodin would be complete without some descripion of his home life, the incredible domestic symphony amid which the artist-scientist lived and worked for a quarter of a century. The apartment at the Academy was a large one and was supplied to the Borodins rent-free; but there its advantages ended. Rimsky-Korsakoff said that it was like a corridor, for it never permitted Borodin to "lock himself in or pretend he was not at home to anyone." In consequence people swarmed through it all hours of the day or night — students seeking advice, friends seeking company, relatives (both near and distant) seeking shelter. The relatives especially came often and in large numbers, sometimes choosing Borodin's home as a convenient hospice in which to "fall in or even lose their minds." When all the beds were taken, they slept on couches or on the floor or dozed in chairs; not infrequently they took Borodin's bed. The apartment itself was usually a litter of disorder and disarray. Five years after they moved in the Borodins still

picked their way around piles of books and music, half-unpacked trunks and suitcases; on one occasion when carpenters and plumbers came to repair defective drain-pipes they left holes in the floor that remained uncovered for months.

Since Borodin seemed never to remember whether or not he had eaten, meals were fantastically irregular, with dinner often begun as late as eleven o'clock at night. Along with transient guests, relatives, and partial strangers, the Borodins shared their meals with a colony of cats — bold animals of both sexes and varying sizes which walked on the tables, examined the food, leaped onto the backs of the diners and in general treated the Borodin ménage as a feline liberty hall.

It is not surprising that someone living in such chaos, frequently distracted by flirtatious women, and employed outside of music should leave several compositions unfinished and should require a long time to compose those he did finish. The history of the Second Symphony is typical. He began the work in early 1869, but he soon turned his attention to an opera. When that failed to materialize, he transferred some of its music to the symphony. By the fall of 1871 the first movement was done. In November he completed the sketch of the finale. A piano score of the entire symphony was ready in the spring of 1873. He completed the orchestration two years later. When he learned, in 1876, that the work was under consideration for performance, he could not find the score! He finally located the middle movements, but he had to re-orchestrate the outer ones. The symphony was finally heard in March 1877. This performance was not successful, largely because the scoring was too heavily dominated by brass. He reworked the orchestration, and the final version was premiered in March 1879, a full decade after he had begun the piece — ten years of research, innocent flirtations, household chaos, and (when time allowed) composition.

Borodin was one of a group of composers who tried consciously to make their music sound Russian. These composers were suspicious of the influence of western Europe, and thus Borodin's training in science rather than in European music theory was actually an asset. Although real folk tunes are not used in the Second Symphony, the contours of the melodies and the rhythms have a decidedly Russian feeling.

The melodic language is unique, contributing to this being one of the most original of nineteenth-century symphonies. Virtually all of the melodies in the four movements are mosaics of cells — too long and with too much individual character to be motives, yet too short and too concentrated to be complete melodies in themselves. The first such cell is heard at the beginning, just after the sustained first note. After this string figure alternates with *fermate*, a contrasting cell enters in the winds. We hear the influence of Russian folk music but still no true melody. The two cells alternate until a third one appears in the cellos — somewhat longer, more lyrical, quite beautiful, but still not a real tune. These three cells are juxtaposed and varied, but true thematic development is not possible with such fragmented materials.

The whirlwind scherzo is based on two ideas that are closer to real melodies than anything in the first movement. The second is particularly interesting for its engaging syncopations. The lightness of this movement is implied by its tempo marking of *prestissimo* and by its unusual time signature of 1/1.

The horn plays the symphony's only full-length melody at the beginning of the third movement. The finale is again a mosaic of cells. It is amazing that a work with few real tunes should strike us as wonderfully melodic. The cells are folk-like and even singable, but structurally they are unlike folksongs.

Borodin thought of this symphony as a picture of old Russia. The first movement is supposed to depict the assembling of Russian princes, the slow movement recalls the old Slavonic *bayans* (the Russian equivalent of troubadours), and the finale portrays a celebration banquet of heroes.

Johannes Brahms

Born in Hamburg on 7 May 1833.
Died in Vienna on 3 April 1897.

Academic Festival Overture, Opus 80
Tragic Overture, Opus 81

The Academic Festival *Overture was composed in 1880 and first performed, conducted by Brahms, on 4 January 1881 in Breslau. The* Tragic *Overture was also composed in 1880, but sketches date back as far as 1869. It was first performed on 20 December 1880 in Vienna.*

Brahms never went to college. His only experience with university life as a young man was the month he spent with his friend, violinist-composer Joseph Joachim, who was attending philosophy and history lectures at the University of Göttingen. Brahms enjoyed the student life-style, from the drinking sessions to the debates to the lectures.

In later life he became involved with universities in quite a different way. He received honorary doctorates from Cambridge University and, some time later, the University of Breslau. When he heard from the latter, in March 1879, he expressed his thanks — by sending back a postcard! The Director of Music in Breslau, who was Brahms' friend, suggested that the proper way to express his gratitude was with a new composition.

Thus Brahms wrote the *Academic Festival* Overture. The piece is hardly the serious work the officials in Breslau undoubtedly expected from a musician receiving their university's highest academic honor. The overture is based on four college drinking songs, which the composer recalled from his month in Göttingen years earlier. He referred to the overture as "a cheerful potpourri of student songs à la Suppé." (The reference is to Franz von Suppé, composer of such pops concert favorites as the *Light Cavalry* Overture.)

At the same time, as if to make up for his frivolousness, Brahms wrote a companion piece, the appropriately sober *Tragic* Overture. Yet it was the *Academic Festival* that he presented when he went to Breslau to receive his degree in January 1881. He conducted both works at the degree ceremony, but the *Tragic* had already been performed. The *Academic Festival*, being premiered on this occasion, was Brahms' offering to the academic community. How the professors re-

137

acted to this send-up is not known. They surely did not suspect any mischief when the overture began, with a hushed and mysterious introduction. But then the college tunes came along. The students in the audience were delighted to recognize songs popular with their generation: *Wir hatten gebauet, Der Landesvater, Was kommt dort von der Höh'*, and, as the coda, the well-known *Gaudeamus igitur.* Much to Brahms' delight, the students joined in singing, using their own irreverent words. The light-heartedness of the overture was underlined by the comic treatment of *Was kommt dort von der Höh'*, first played by bassoons and then by oboes.

Today it is difficult to appreciate the humor in the *Academic Festival,* since the drinking songs are no longer current. But we can imagine Brahms' mischievousness as he introduced, one after another, inappropriate tunes into an overture conceived for a most solemn occasion.

"One laughs, the other weeps," Brahms said of the two overtures. The *Tragic* is as serious as its companion is humorous. Whereas the *Academic Festival* was composed quickly, materials for the *Tragic* had been gestating for over a decade. There is an elaborate portion of it amongst the sketches for the *Liebeslieder* choral pieces (composed in 1868–69) and the *Alto Rhapsody* (written in 1869). In the overtures we can hear the difference between a piece worked out carefully over many years and one all but tossed off for a specific occasion. While the *Academic Festival* is skillfully done — all fine humor requires first-rate craftsmanship — we understand from its immediacy that it was quickly composed. The *Tragic* came not in one outpouring but, as its studied intensity suggests, with considerable difficulty.

There is some evidence that Brahms may have at one point intended the *Tragic* as part of some incidental music for a production of *Faust.* But he was not particularly interested in theater music, nor in descriptive music of any kind. He was even indifferent over the title of the overture. To conductor Bernhard Scholz he wrote, "You can put on the program *Dramatic* or *Tragic* Overture, or *Overture to a Tragedy.* You see, this time, too, I cannot find a title."

The piece is in D minor, the tragic-heroic key of Beethoven's Ninth Symphony, Schumann's Fourth, Mozart's Piano Concerto Number 20, and Brahms' own First Piano Concerto. The work is cast in sonata form, with a fugato in the development section. Notice the unusual prevalence of open sounds (e.g., perfect fifths with no thirds).

Concerto Number 1 in D Minor for Piano and Orchestra, Opus 15

Maestoso
Adagio
Allegro

The First Piano Concerto was composed between 1854 and 1858. Brahms was soloist in the first performance, which Joseph Joachim conducted in Hanover on 22 January 1859.

Brahms was just twenty years old when he first showed some of his compositions to Robert Schumann. Schumann was so impressed that he came out of retirement as a music critic to write a special article in praise of Brahms. In this review he prophesied that the younger composer would "reveal his mastery not by gradual development but would spring, like Minerva, fully armed, from the head of Jove. . . . If he will dip his magic wand where the powers of the choral and orchestral masses will lend him their strength, then there will appear before us more wonderful glimpses into the secrets of the spiritual world."

This was enormous praise for a young composer who had thus far written mostly chamber music and piano works. He was suddenly thrust before the musical world with a reputation to uphold. He felt that he had an obligation to try to compose a symphony, and so he wrote to Schumann in January 1854, "I have been trying my hand at a symphony during the past summer and have even orchestrated the first movement and composed the second and third."

The next month Schumann, suffering from mental illness, threw himself into the Rhine. He was rescued, but he had to spend the remaining two and a half years of his life in an asylum. Brahms was devastated. He moved into Schumann's home to try to help take care of Clara Schumann and her children. He developed a deep feeling for Clara, with whom he was in love but who was also a mother figure for him. He continued to work on his symphony, and he painted a musical portait of Clara into the slow movement.

Brahms received help with the orchestration from his friend Julius Grimm. The composer was dissatisfied, however. He felt that he was not yet ready to attempt such a monumental form as the symphony. His actual First Symphony was not to be finished for 22 more years. He changed the early, partially completed symphony into a sonata for two pianos, which he played with Clara. He also listened to her play it with Grimm. Still he was not satisfied. Grimm suggested he combine his two ideas and make it a piano concerto. The notion seemed plausible, and the composer set to work revising again. He rescored the first two movements for piano and orchestra, but he replaced the third movement with a new finale. The discarded movement eventually became the chorus "Behold All Flesh" in the *German* Requiem.

The concerto was nearly ready by the spring of 1858. Brahms had the opportunity to try it out in rehearsal. He made more changes. He was still not totally satisfied, and he was unsure of bringing it before the public, but he finally decided to go ahead with two performances in January 1859. At the first performance, conducted by Joseph Joachim, the audience listened politely but with little understanding or appreciation. Five days later Brahms played it in Leipzig, and he wrote to Joachim about its failure.

> My concerto has been a brilliant and decisive — failure. . . . The first rehearsal excited no kind of feeling either in the performers or the audience. No audience at all came to the second, however, and not a performer moved a muscle of his face. . . . In the evening . . . the first and second movements were listened to without the slightest display of feeling. At the conclusion three pairs of hands were brought together very slowly, whereupon a perfectly distinct hissing from all sides forbade any such demonstration. . . . This failure has not impressed me at all. After all, I am only experimenting and feeling my way. All the same, the hissing was rather too much. In spite of everything the concerto will meet with approval when I have improved its bodily structure, and the next one will sound quite different.

Several reasons have been offered for the lukewarm reception. The work was too boldly passionate for the conservatives, yet not colorful enough for the radicals. The piano part had far less virtuosity than audiences expected. The piece was exceptionally long for a concerto. Some of the orchestration was rather clumsy, such as the opening, where the modest scoring seems too thin for the passions expressed.

Still, the work eventually gained approval and enthusiasm. Today it is popular with audiences, though perhaps less so than the Second Concerto. We understand its excesses and occasional awkwardness as products of a young composer's inexperience.

The concerto's emotionalism is arguably its most interesting trait, because this was the last work of Brahms' passionate early stage. Never again did he let his romantic spirit have such free rein. After this concerto he began to explore the restraints of classicism, which he learned through careful study of the works of Beethoven, Mozart, and others, but the First Concerto as a whole makes little attempt to harness its emotions. Burnett James, in his book *Brahms: A Critical Study,* clearly sums up this issue:

> The D Minor Concerto is a direct and authentic transcript of Brahms' deepest and most tortured experiences at the time of its production. It also marks the end of Brahms' youthful romantic period. Never again was he to let himself go with such uninhibited passion; never again to wear his heart so unashamedly on his sleeve; never to let his guard so down that all the turbulence of his heart and mind would appear in his music, or in his life. Never again was he to seek open battle with life through his public art on terms of exposed blood, sweat, and tears. . . . He did henceforth turn his back finally upon all extravagance and only allow as much of his inner life to appear on the surface as he quite consciously and deliberately wished to appear. If the openly passionate and impetuous side of his nature ever had the chance of taking command of him, its last full fling was in the D Minor Concerto.

The turbulent, dramatic nature of the piece is evident immediately. The forceful opening motive, though absent for much of the first movement, casts its spell over even the most lyrical of secondary themes, so that we can never quite believe in the apparent peacefulness. For most of the exposition, the piano and the orchestra have separate themes. The process of development is in part the process of integration. Particularly beautiful is the second theme, first heard in the piano alone. Although this vast movement passes through many moods, its underlying brooding passion is felt throughout.

The second movement tries, by its expansive gentleness, to dispel the intensity of the first. But there is an undercurrent of remembered tension, because the slow movement is cast in the opening movement's meter (6/4) and key (D major as opposed to D minor, although the first movement spends a long time in the major just before the end). The steady rhythm suggests a hymn.

The finale is a Hungarian gypsy rondo, with several themes, two cadenzas, and a developmental fugato. There is a transformation of the main theme into a major-mode slow march in the coda.

Concerto Number 2 in B-Flat Major for Piano and Orchestra, Opus 83

Allegro non troppo
Allegro appassionato
Andante
Allegretto grazioso

Brahms began the Second Piano Concerto in the spring of 1878 and finished it in the summer of 1881. The composer was soloist in the first performance, which Hans von Bülow conducted in Zürich on 27 November 1881.

Brahms fell heir to a golden opportunity in 1881. The distinguished conductor Hans von Bülow, who had been a champion of the music of the "other camp" — Wagner and Liszt — had recently come under the spell of Brahms' music. Von Bülow, partly for musical reasons and partly for personal reasons, now threw his whole energies into the promotion of Brahms' works. One result was that the conductor placed at the composer's disposal the Meiningen Orchestra, not just for performances but also as a test laboratory for works in progress. Such an opportunity was (and still is) almost unheard of for a composer, and Brahms was quick to take advantage of von Bülow's extraordinary generosity.

The composer was at work on his Second Piano Concerto, and he moved to Meiningen in order to utilize the orchestra's services. Von Bülow and the Meiningen musicians gave the first performance. Von Bülow's enthusiasm for this music was great, and he arranged subsequent concert tours to bring the new work before audiences all over Europe.

Brahms thought of the concerto with characteristic self-deprecation. He wrote to his friend Elisabeth von Herzogenberg, "I want to tell you that I have written a tiny little concerto with a tiny little scherzo. It is written in the key of B-flat major, and I fear that I have made too heavy and frequent a demand on this udder which has on many occasions provided such excellent milk."

This "tiny little concerto" is probably the longest piano concerto in the standard literature. The "tiny little scherzo" is a fully developed movement between the first and slow movements. The number of movements is thus an atypical four.

A lot of nonsense has been written about the Second Concerto. Because it has four movements, many writers have placed it in the symphonic tradition, some even calling it a "symphony-concerto." While it is true that its scope is symphonic and that it lacks a concerto's cadenzas, and while it does have a scherzo-like movement, it is based on concerto concepts throughout. The idea of dialogue, established at the outset with the piano answering the French horn, is the essence of both the classical and the romantic concerto.

Another unfounded idea about the concerto is that it is a latter-day instance of classicism. While it is surely true that Brahms yearned to be a classicist and that he followed the model of Beethoven in many works, the concerto is not one of them. The titanic spirit of Beethoven may be felt lurking behind the B-Flat Concerto, but the influence is far less pronounced than in many of Brahms' other compositions. The Second Concerto is thoroughly romantic. Any gestures toward classicism are superficial. It is a large, often rhapsodic work, with many themes that appear at times loosely interwoven (the structure is not really as free as it seems, but the effect is decidedly rambling). In fact, Brahms had originally indicated frequent slight changes of tempo, in the romantic manner, but he later deleted them because he felt performers would follow them too literally.

Another misconception about the concerto is that it is not a pianistic showpiece. While it is true that the tone of intimacy is never long absent, Brahms had sufficient craft to convey this intimacy even through dazzling pianistic figuration. The piano writing is marvelously varied and extraordinarily difficult, and it often does show off the purely physical accomplishments of the soloist.

Commentators have sometimes accused Brahms of bland orchestration. This is an overstatement. His use of the orchestra is invariably clear and functional, and in some works quite colorful. But it is true that his orchestral palette in this concerto does not contain the inventive combinations of a Berlioz or a Mendelssohn. Brahms' style of orchestration is perfectly suited to the ideas of the concerto, however. The piano writing *is* brilliant and varied, subtly nuanced, and beautifully realized — in fact, the piano "orchestration" is quite marvelous. But even the most beautiful piano writing cannot compete for variety with the orchestra. By avoiding extremes of color in the orchestra, however, Brahms places the two forces — piano and orchestra — on equal footing. Each has a comparable range of colors. The result is a balanced dialogue of equals, an ideal approached in many concertos but rarely achieved as well as in this one.

The enormous first movement contains many themes, which are united by the simple three-note figure that opens the work. The second movement, the "added" scherzo, is full of Brahms' usual rhythmic finesse. The slow movement continues the exploration of rhythmic irregularities, though in an understated manner — the six beats in a measure are sometimes grouped 3 + 3 and sometimes 2 + 2 + 2. The finale, with its Hungarian tunes and rhythms, comes closest to being an all-out fast movement, but even here the amosphere of intimacy prevails.

After the not totally successful premiere of his First Piano Concerto, a far more overt work, Brahms had said, "My second one will sound quite different." Twenty-two years later he fulfilled his prophecy with a beautiful, tranquil, intimate, yet large and powerful work very different from its passionate predecessor. The Second Piano Concerto deserves to be heard for what it is — a large romantic concerto for piano and orchestra. It is not a classical concerto, it is not a symphony with piano, and it is not a reincarnation of a Beethoven piano concerto. It is thoroughly Brahmsian, and it is a major work in the concerto literature, despite what the composer may have said about its being a modest effort.

Concerto in D Major for Violin and Orchestra, Opus 77
Allegro non troppo
Adagio
Allegro giocoso, ma non troppo vivace. Poco più
    presto

The Violin Concerto was composed in the summer of 1878 in the village of Pörtschach, in the Austrian Alps. Joseph Joachim was soloist when Brahms conducted the first performance on 1 January 1879 in Leipzig.

The violin concertos of Tchaikovsky, Brahms, and Beethoven have certain things in common. Each was considered all but unplayable when it was new. Each is now in the standard repertory of virtually every violinist. All three are in D major.

The fact that these concertos are in the same key is not a coincidence. The four violin strings are tuned to the notes G, D, A, and E respectively. These are the so-called open notes, which means that they can be produced without placing a finger on the string. Open strings are easy to play (which can be useful in the middle of fast figuration), and they have a resonant sound. Thus a key which includes all four open notes is useful for a violin concerto. D major is such a key: the main notes of D major are the open strings of the violin.

The reason for the difficulty of the three concertos is that each composer had an abstract idea of violin virtuosity rather than a performer's practical perspective. Therefore each concerto has passages so unlike anything performers had had to play previously that it took quite a lot of thought and practice before they could master them. By writing difficult music that nonetheless sounded right on the instrument, each composer expanded the range of what was accepted as typical violin music.

Brahms sought the advice of his friend Joseph Joachim, an accomplished violinist, while composing his concerto. He frequently asked about the difficulty of various passages. Joachim's advice about simplifying some of the music often went unheeded, although, paradoxically, his purely musical criticisms were usually followed.

While working on the piece, Brahms wrote to Joachim: "After having written it out, I really do not know what you will make of the solo part alone. It was my intention, of course, that you should correct it, not sparing the quality of the composition, and that if you thought it not worth scoring that you should say so. I shall be satisfied if you mark those parts which are difficult, awkward, or impossible to play. The whole affair is in four movements." (The final version has three movements.)

Joachim wrote back: "It gives me great pleasure to know that you are composing a violin concerto — in four movements, too! I have had a good look at what you sent me and have made a few notes and alterations, but without the full score I cannot say much. I can, however, make out most of it, and there is a lot of really good violin music in it, but whether it can be played with comfort in a hot concert hall remains to be seen." It was apparent from this letter that Joachim was a first-rate musician. He was reluctant to pass judgement on the violin part alone, although that was what he would play as soloist, without knowing how it would fit into the entire ensemble.

Brahms wrote back that he would send the score. He also mentioned that "the middle movements are failures. I have written a feeble adagio instead." Although the composer was still not completely satisfied, Joachim wanted to perform the work. Brahms agreed reluctantly. After the performance Joachim made further suggestions. Brahms was beginning to get annoyed. He tried to conceal his displeasure in a joke: "Your sole means of impressing the world is by making alterations and suggestions!"

Joachim was apparently not bothered by the nastiness in Brahms' humor. He kept the concerto and performed it several times in England. The composer was beginning to think he ought to ask another violinist's opinion about the proposed changes. He wrote to Joachim, "I am eager to see what alterations you have made in it and whether they will be convincing to me or whether I shall have to consult someone else — a thing I do not want to do. Tell me, is the concerto fit to be printed?"

Some weeks later Brahms wrote again. "You will think twice before you ask me for another concerto! It is a good thing that your name is on the copy, as you are more or less responsible for the solo violin part." Brahms actually did begin a second violin concerto shortly thereafter, but he never completed it.

The Violin Concerto is dedicated to Joachim, despite Brahms' misgivings over the criticisms. He trusted Joachium to write his own cadenza. (Subsequent violinists have written new cadenzas.)

The concerto's difficulties made it hard to secure performances. Conductor Hans von Bülow called it "a concerto against the violin." Only a few violinists other than Joachim were able to play it. Some soloists were less than enthusiastic because the work's difficulties were not always apparent to the ear. Technical feats that are supposed to sound as though played with ease rather than with commanding bravura do not show of a soloist's virtuosic flair.

A few others did play the concerto, including Richard Barth, Hugo Heerman, and Adolf Brodsky (who had courageously premiered Tchaikovsky's formidably difficult concerto a few years earlier). A young woman of 19, Marie Soldat, then played the piece for the composer, who was enormously impressed with her talent. He decided to give a concert with her, and he succeeded in having her admitted to Joachim's master classes.

Two years before his death, Brahms heard a Polish boy of twelve play the concerto. This young violinist was Bronislaw Huberman, who went on to become one of the great virtuosos of the early twentieth century. If a work which had been condemned as unplayable when it was new could now, 17 years later, be played by a young boy, then the concerto must have a future. So Brahms must have thought, and of course he was right.

Huberman improved on conductor von Bülow's inane comment on the concerto: "Brahms' concerto is neither *against* the violin, nor *for* the violin with orchestra. It is a concerto for violin *against* orchestra — and the violin wins." The violinist realized that, in the Brahms concerto, there is a dramatic opposition between two forces: soloist and orchestra. This kind of drama, typical of piano concertos from Mozart on, was actually relatively rare in violin concertos. Only the Beethoven concerto, prior to the Brahms, utilized the prinicple of opposition. Other concertos were more technical and/or emotional display pieces for a violinist accompanied by an orchestra. In Brahms' and Beethoven's works, the two forces are treated as equals.

Three examples demonstrate this point.

1. Brahms' orchestral exposition in the first movement is exceedingly long. Once the violin finally enters, it has to assert its equality with an orchestra that has already been playing for quite

some time. It does so by performing not the main theme but an extended quasi-cadenza, with the orchestra temporarily relegated to a subservient role. This passage balances the orchestral exposition. Once the violin has asserted its independence, it can at last play the main theme, in its beautiful high register.

2. Another example occurs in the second movement. The opening melody belongs to the orchestra (initially, just to the winds.) The violin never plays more than the first three notes of it. The function of the violin is to ornament that theme, to comment on it, but never to quote it. To do so would be to invade the territory of the orchestra.

3. As in the Tchaikovsky concerto, the finale uses the violin as a gypsy instrument. The Hungarian folk music that Brahms loved and immortalized in his Hungarian Dances is the inspiration behind the main rondo theme. The violin and orchestra trade this tune back and forth, as if to show that their previous competition has turned to cooperation.

Concerto in A Minor for Violin, Cello, and Orchestra, Opus 102, *Double*
Allegro
Andante
Vivace

The Double *Concerto was composed in the summer of 1887 at Hofstetten, on Lake Thun, in Switzerland. It was first performed at a private gathering on 23 September 1887 at the Kurhaus in Baden-Baden. Joseph Joachim was the violinist, Robert Hausmann was the cellist, and Brahms conducted. The same principals participated in the public premiere on 18 October 1887 in Cologne.*

Brahms' Opus 102 was his fourth essay in concerto form. He wrote it for his friend, violinist Joseph Joachim, for whom he had composed his Violin Concerto nine years earlier. In the interim the two artists had had a falling out, because the composer had sided with Joachim's wife in a marital dispute. The violinist continued to perform Brahms' music, but the two refused to speak to each other for several years. It was in part to mend the friendship that Brahms undertook the composition of the *Double* Concerto.

As the work was nearing completion, Brahms wrote to Joachim about it. The violinist expressed interest and asked the cellist in his quartet, Robert Hausmann, to perform it with him. Rehearsals and editing went smoothly. Joachim suggested changes, usually in an attempt to increase the virtuosity of the violin music. Brahms was a skillful diplomat: he found solutions that did not insult his friend but that preserved the musical integrity of his concerto.

At first, neither Brahms' friends nor the public were overly enthusiastic. Even Joachim had reservations, though he performed the work several times and eventually came to love it. Clara Schumann thought it had little future. Eduard Hanslick, the critic who was Brahms' strongest supporter, admired the concerto's construction but found little creative feeling in it.

Brahms himself had doubts, even while composing it. To Franz Wüllner he wrote: "I must inform you that I have had the strange notion of writing a concerto for fiddle and cello!" To Clara Schumann: "I have some queer news to tell you about myself. I have had the happy notion of writing a concerto for violin and cello. . . . I might better have left the idea to someone who understands fiddles better than I do." To Joachim: "After you have seen the piece, you may send me a card which simply says, 'I disown it.' That will be quite sufficient for me, and I shall know what to do." To his publisher, Fritz Simrock: "I must inform you of my latest piece of folly, which is a concerto for violin and cello! Owing to the relations between myself and Joachim, I tried to give up the job, but it was no use." Later, again to Simrock: "I warn you not to ruin yourself! Offer me a small sum!" To Elisabeth von Herzogenberg: "I can give you nothing worth being called information about the undersigned musician. True, he is just now writing down a thing that does not yet figure in his catalog — but neither does it figure in other people's catalogs. I leave it to you to guess the particular form of the idiocy."

Why was Brahms so unsure of himself? There is a clue in the last quotation. He was not particularly innovative in matters of genre. Most of his music follows classical (his symphonies, sonatas, and chamber music) or romantic (his songs, piano pieces, and concertos) models. But there was little precedent for a double concerto. The similarities to the baroque *concerto grosso* are superficial, because that form deals more with the alternation of small and large ensembles than with the dramatic interplay of soloists and orchestra. The *Double* Concerto is closer to the *symphonie concertante* genre, which flourished in Paris from about 1770 to 1830. Despite a substantial literature, few of these *symphonies concertantes* had any lasting value. Two exceptions were works for four winds and orchestra by Mozart and Haydn. But writing a concerto for four winds presents very different challenges from composing for two strings. The only direct ancestor of Brahms' Double Concerto is the magnificent *Symphonie concer-*

tante for violin, viola, and orchestra of Mozart. Even Beethoven's Triple Concerto (violin, cello, piano, and orchestra) could not have provided a terribly useful model, because the presence of the piano makes an enormous difference. Thus Brahms felt he was, to a large extent, working in virgin territory.

The uniqueness of the genre — a romantic concerto for two soloists and orchestra — offered difficult challenges. Should the two solo instruments be treated as equals despite their different registers? Given the octave and a half gap between them, might it not seem that a middle instrument (such as a viola) was missing? Can both soloists be treated as virtuosos without having to sacrifice the richness of the orchestra? Should the two solo instruments be treated as a unit or as opposing forces in a three-character drama? Can the orchestra be used symphonically (as it is in the other Brahms concertos) without covering either of the solo instruments? Can the solo parts be givien enough prominence to satisfy both soloists?

Brahms succeeded. He created a work of sufficient scope and stature to solve all these problems. The solo instruments are sometimes used separately and sometimes together. When together, they may be in dialogue, they may play the same music in octaves, or they may be in opposition. Frequently they are silent, as the orchestra establishes itself as a full-fledged participant in the concerto's drama.

The three protagonists are understood as equals almost from the start. The powerful opening orchestral *tutti* soon gives way to the dramatic cello entrance. After the cello cadenza, the orchestra reappears briefly, with winds only. Then comes the violin's dramatic entrance. The cello soon joins in for a duo-cadenza. This cadenza establishes the two solo instruments as equals. It is only during the duo-cadenzas that the orchestra is silent. Traditionally cadenzas appear toward the ends of concerto movements, but here Brahms uses them to expose his two soloists. After the first extended duo-cadenza, the orchestra has its turn. The roles and interactions established at the beginning of the first movement continue through the tender andante and the energetic finale.

The *Double* Concerto has a haunting beauty not only (or even primarily) because of Brahms' elegant solutions to the problems inherent in the double concerto genre, but also because it was written toward the end of his life, at a time when his expression was turning inward and his music was becoming more simplified and intimate. It is no coincidence that this, the least virtuosic of the Brahms concertos and the least extroverted of his orchestral compositions, should be his last work for orchestra. He spent the remaining ten years of his life composing the chamber music, piano music, and songs that many feel are his greatest achievements.

Quartet Number 1 in G Minor, Opus 25 (orchestrated by Arnold Schoenberg)

Allegro
Allegro ma non troppo
Andante con moto
Presto

The Quartet was composed in 1859 and subsequently revised. The first public performance took place in Hamburg in November 1861, with Clara Schumann as pianist. Brahms himself played the piano part on 16 November 1861 in Vienna. Schoenberg worked on his orchestration of the quartet from 2 May to 19 September 1937. It was first performed on 7 May 1938 by the Los Angeles Philharmonic Orchestra conducted by Otto Klemperer.

Brahms' Quartet in G Minor for Piano and Strings was his first mature chamber composition. After it received a few private performances, pianist Clara Schumann and violinist Joseph Joachim expressed doubts about it. Joachim found insufficient depth in its thematic materials, and Schumann felt tonal imbalance in the first movement and did not care for the trio of the second movement. Brahms revised the composition, although it is not known how extensively or how much under the influence of his friends' criticisms. It was first played publicly two years later.

The most popular movement has always been the finale — the Gypsy Rondo. Although German by birth, Brahms had an affinity for Hungarian folk music. His *Hungarian* Dances are the most obvious example of this influence. The finale of the quartet is just as thoroughly imbued with the rhythms and melodies of Hungarian folk dances, so much so that early audiences questioned its appropriateness in a piece of serious chamber music.

Brahms would surely have been surprised had he known that another composer was to recast the quartet as an orchestral composition 78 years after its composition. On the surface one would hardly expect there to be much in common between Brahms, the conservative nineteenth-century composer who sought his inspiration in the music of Beethoven, and Schoenberg, the twentieth-century innovator credited with the "emancipation of the dissonance" and the invention of the notorious "twelve-tone method" of composition. Schoenberg's early tonal music followed not Brahms but rather the chromatic harmonies and free forms of Wagner. Schoenberg's later music, such as the monodrama *Erwartung,* is dissonant, intense, and in its compositional procedures quite revolutionary. Why would a composer once influenced by Wagner and subsequently involved in twelve-tone music want to orchestrate a chamber piece of Brahms?

In fact, Schoenberg felt a deep affinity with Brahms. Among his earliest musical experiences were hearing performances of Brahms' late works and playing his chamber music. Although his own early music was written under the spell of Wagner, Schoenberg knew what few other musicians of the late nineteenth century understood — that the styles, procedures, and aesthetics of Brahms and Wagner were not really opposed.

Schoenberg felt that it was misleading to dismiss Brahms as a conservative. In 1933 he wrote an extended essay (revised in 1947) called "Brahms the Progressive." He points to certain aspects of Brahms' music that proved to be signposts toward the future. He mentions the independence of the instruments in the chamber music, the near avoidance of fixed tonality in some pieces, the structural unity achieved by deriving much of a composition from a few basic ideas, the metrical asymmetry, and the pervasiveness of variation procedures. The latter point is particularly enlightening, since the twelve-tone system comprises perpetual variations on a series of notes.

Schoenberg saw himself, like Brahms, as a progressive, not a radical. He constantly sought ways to integrate his twelve-tone procedures into traditional tonal forms. In addition, he periodically returned to tonality in his mature years, writing pieces that do not use the twelve-tone method at all. Schoenberg disliked being cast as a revolutionary; he saw himself as continuing the grand tradition of German music which he inherited from Brahms and Wagner.

Around 1920 Schoenberg planned to write an orchestration textbook. Among the sketches for this book is a quotation from the slow movement of Brahms' G Minor Quartet. The textbook was never written, as Schoenberg came to believe that orchestration should be a part of composition and thus cannot be taught separately. He did, however, retain his interest in orchestrating the Brahms work. In 1937 he decided to make a version of the quartet for full orchestra. This was not the only time he orchestrated works by earlier composers. With the Brahms Quartet, however, he remained more faithful to the original than he had with the music of Bach, Monn, or Handel.

Schoenberg gave the following reasons for orchestrating the Quartet:

1. I like the piece.
2. It is seldom played.
3. It is always very badly played, because the better the pianist the louder he plays and you hear nothing from the strings.

I want at once to hear everything, and this I achieve. My intentions:

1. To remain strictly within the style of Brahms and not go further than he himself would have gone if he lived today.

2. To watch carefully all these laws which Brahms had made and not to violate any of those which are only known to musicians educated in his environment. How I did it:

For almost fifty years I have been very thoroughly acquainted with Brahms' style and his principles. I have analyzed many of his works for myself and for my pupils. I have played this work as violist and cellist and many others numerous times: I, therefore, knew how it should sound. I had only to transpose this sound to the orchestra and this is in fact what I did.

Of course there are weighty problems. Brahms likes very low basses, of which the orchestra possesses only a small number of instruments. He likes the full accompaniment with broken chord figures, often in different rhythms. And most of these figures cannot easily be changed, because generally they have a structural meaning in his style. I think I have resolved these problems, but this merit of mine will not mean very much to our present-day musicians because they did not know about them, and if you tell them there are such, they do not care. But to me it means something.

For several reasons Schoenberg's idea of orchestrating Brahms' quartet is rather curious, as is the resulting work: (1) Brahms' work is an intimate chamber piece, except for the overt finale, while Schoenberg's orchestra is large and therefore hardly conducive to intimate expression. (2) Schoenberg's and Brahms' styles of orchestration are quite different: Schoenberg was a colorist, creating many special effects and frequently subdividing instrumental groups and utilizing unusual combinations, while Brahms orchestrated in a functional manner in order to bring out the contrapuntal structure of his music. (3) Schoenberg chose a work dominated by the piano, which is difficult to translate faithfully into the orchestra. (4) In Schoenberg's attempt to orchestrate as Brahms might have in 1937, he included instruments that Brahms never actually used: English horn, E-flat clarinet, bass clarinet, glockenspiel, and xylophone. These instruments were available to Brahms, but he chose not to employ them in any of his orchestral works. (5) It is curious that Schoenberg, who beleved that composition and orchestration ought to be inseparable, should feel no contradiction in orchestrating a completed work by another composer.

Schoenberg's orchestral technique comes from Wagner and Mahler, not Brahms. What Schoenberg did was to orchestrate the quartet not in the style of Brahms, nor in the style of Schoenberg, but in a style somewhat like that of Mahler. The piece is thus a twentieth-century orchestration of a composition by one nineteenth-century composer in the style of another nineteenth-century composer. Despite his claim to the contrary, Schoenberg's work is not really an extension of Brahms' style and it is not Brahms brought up to date. Yet it is not a trivial exercise. Schoenberg lavished great care on the details of his work, and the result is a stunning orchestration. It is an example of a most intriguing style that never existed but well might have.

The special, non-Brahmsian sound of the orchestra is evident right from the beginning. The work opens with the three clarinets — the small E-flat, the regular B-flat, and the large bass — playing in octaves. Before long we hear other sounds unlike anything Brahms would have done — chromatic lines in the valve trumpet (an instrument for which Brahms refused to write), subdivided violas, winds used in threes for three-part harmony, and extensive use of string mutes. The coda of this movement is exceptionally well conceived for orchestra, although it is utterly unlike anything Brahms composed. Here Schoenberg's mastery of the orchestra creates a thoroughly delectable texture. The strings are divided into four very different functions — sixteenth-note figurations in the first violins, *pizzicato* eighth notes in the seconds and violas, sweeping eighth-note arpeggios in the cellos, and isolated *pizzicato* notes in the basses. Later we hear triple stops (three notes played at once by each player) in the violas and cellos plus the second violins divided into three groups — scoring procedures typical more of Richard Strauss than of Brahms. Later on in the coda there are several string solos and then alternating wind solos — a thoroughly imaginative and very beautiful passage, yet unlike a Brahms orchestration.

The coda of the second movement is also a *tour de force* of orchestration, in a delicate texture. We hear subdivided strings again, prominent solos on two non-Brahmsian instruments — the E-flat clarinet and the piccolo — and, toward the end, string harmonics.

The opening of the third movement is Brahmsian in spirit but not in technique, again because of extensive subdivisions in the strings. The middle section is a march-like 3/4 passage, orchestrated with trumpets and drums. Is Schoenberg suggesting parody?

The finale, the Gypsy Rondo, is the least like Brahms in orchestration, although in spirit it is akin to his Hungarian Dances. Some of the sounds typical of Schoenberg's (but not Brahms') orchestral palette include xylophone, tambourine, flutter-tongued stopped horns, glockenspiel, trombone *glissandi*, and brass trills. Just before the coda in the Brahms original, the piano plays a brief virtuosic cadenza — a real challenge to transfer to the orchestra. Schoenberg comes up with a wonderfully imaginative solution, involving solo E-flat clarinet and rapid string *pizzicato* arpeggios.

Schoenberg liked to think of this work as Brahms' "fifth symphony." The orchestration is indeed symphonic, but at heart the piece is still chamber music. It is thus an anomaly, but a fascinating one. It differs, in its subtle way, from other music written by either Brahms or Schoenberg. Purists may complain about the discrepancy between Schoenberg's and Brahms' orchestral styles, but the piece remains not only intriguing but also a spectacular example of orchestral technique. Schoenberg was a master orchestrator, and he gave the Brahms quartet a wonderfully new sound.

Symphony Number 1 in C Minor, Opus 68

Un poco sostenuto. Allegro
Andante sostenuto
Un poco allegretto e grazioso
Adagio. Allegro non troppo, ma con brio

The First Symphony was completed in September 1876. It was first performed on 4 November 1876 in Karlsruhe under the baton of Felix Dessoff. Brahms himself conducted a performance in Mannheim three days later.

When a composition by the 20-year-old Brahms received a press review of enviable praise, he was understandably pleased. The reviewer was no less a personage than composer Robert Schumann. Yet Schumann laid a heavy burden on the young composer. There was a veiled comparison with Beethoven. Brahms, who had not yet written anything for orchestra, was being told — publicly — that he could, should, and probably would take up where Beethoven had left off.

It was only a few weeks later that Brahms accepted the challenge. He began to compose a symphony in D minor. But he was not ready to tackle the enormous form in which Beethoven had excelled. Parts of this symphony eventually found their way into the *German Requiem*, other parts into the First Piano Concerto — a work that cost Brahms five years to complete — but there is no symphony in D minor in Brahms' catalogue. During those five years he also wrote two serenades for small orchestra. He had decided to approach the orchestra gradually. The composition of a symphony would have to wait. After he had written for small orchestra and for piano and orchestra, he wrote for chorus and orchestra. Finally, in 1873, he composed the Variations on a Theme of Haydn. Now at last he felt ready to start — and *finish* — a symphony.

Actually, some of the materials of the First Symphony had already been in existence for a number of years. Brahms had sent Clara Schumann a sketch of the first movement, minus its famous introduction, in 1862, and he had sent her a birthday song in 1868 using the horn theme from the finale. But it was only in 1876 that the composer completed the Symphony in C Minor. That was 22 years after Schumann's review had prompted Brahms to think about composing in symphonic form.

Why did it take him so long to finish a symphony? The answer lies in the influence of Beethoven. As Schumann's review implied, the figure of Beethoven loomed over the entire nineteenth century like that of Big Brother. Beethoven's compositions were studied, admired, misunderstood, emulated, and canonized not only by every composer but also by other artists. The titanism of Beethoven, his image as the great liberator of art from the constraints of classicism, became a rallying cry for the self-consciously free spirit of romanticism.

This nineteenth-century view of Beethoven was necessarily colored by contemporary values. Most romantic composers failed to recognize the classicism in his music, a self-made classicism that counterbalanced the fiery and temperamental side of Beethoven's genius. The only composer who really understood the balance of classic and romantic in Beethoven was Brahms. Brahms was the proverbial wise man who feared to tread where fools rushed in. He knew what others failed to realize — that writing a free-spirited symphony was not a profound response to the implications of Beethoven's music. Brahms would not allow himself superficial emulation of the Bonn master. It took Brahms 22 years to find a way to cope with the implications of his predecessor, to keep classicism and romanticism in balance, and yet to remain original.

When the C Minor Symphony was first performed, conductor Hans von Bülow dubbed it "The Tenth" (Beethoven had completed nine symphonies), thereby declaring Schumann's prophecy fulfilled. Bülow recognized the affinity between the two great composers who, reaching across the intervening half century of romanticism, established contact as romantic classicists.

Brahms was also influenced by the romantic composers — Schubert, Mendelssohn, Berlioz, Chopin, Weber, Schumann, and even his "rivals" Wagner, Liszt, and Bruckner. One result of this romantic influence was that Brahms' classicism was more self-conscious than that of Beethoven. The First Symphony works on a tightly constructed musical logic, which is never quite spontaneous. Brahms was too self-critical to be spontaneous. A further aspect of romanticism that could not fail to touch Brahms was its brooding melancholy. Thus the First Symphony contains restless music, especially in its first movement.

Brahms was attempting an all but impossible task, that of living up to the genius of Beethoven. In 1870 he said, "I shall never compose a symphony! You have no idea how the likes of us feel when we hear the tramp of a giant like him behind us." Yet he succeeded. He did not recapture Beethoven, but in trying to do so he found himself.

Neither Brahms' allegiance to the spirit of Beethoven nor his self-imposed classicism should be thought of as an inhibition to his creativity. The First Symphony is in many ways an original work, despite its adherence to traditional aesthetics and techniques. Consider, for example, the third movmement. Brahms replaced the traditional dance movement with a more abstract intermezzo. The minuet or scherzo as symphonic third movement was a holdover from the baroque dance suite. It serves a useful purpose in a symphony: it usually functions as a lighter and simpler piece between a possibly sober slow movement and an often elaborate finale. This function could also be served by movements not derived from the dance, as Brahms realized. Thus the replacement of Haydn's minuet and Beethoven's scherzo with Brahms' intermezzo was a stroke of originality that owed nothing to the past. The result was sufficiently satisfactory and interesting for Brahms to continue to include intermezzos in place of scherzos in nearly all of his subsequent four-movement symphonic works.

The exceptionally long introduction to the finale — as long as the entire intermezzo — is another original idea. This introduction contains material that is utilized in different parts of the ensuing finale: even the lyrical C major melody that opens the allegro is foreshadowed (in minor) near the beginning of the introduction. This introduction also belies the commonly heard complaint that Brahms was not an imaginative orchestrator. Here we find the composer utilizing particularly beautiful orchestral colors in order to sustain interest in an uncommonly long introductory section. Some examples: the gradually accelerating *pizzicato* passageheard twice, the horn call with muted strings shimmering in the background, and the trombone-bassoon chorale. Brahms was indeed capable of creating coloristic orchestration when the occasion demanded it.

It took Brahms 22 years to learn how to use the orchestra symphonically. That period was hardly an apprenticeship, considering the long list of fine works composed while he struggled to create a symphony. During those years he worked to tame and control his romanticism, to merge inspiration and intellect, to understand Beethoven deeply, and to mold his own symphonic thoughts. The result of this incredible struggle for self-discipline is undoubtedly the greatest first symphony ever composed.

Symphony Number 2 in D Major, Opus 73

Allegro non troppo
Adagio non troppo
Allegretto grazioso. Presto ma non assai. Allegretto
    grazioso
Allegro con spirito

The Second Symphony was started in June 1877 in the small Austrian town of Pörtschach. It was completed the following fall and first performed on 30 December 1877 by the Vienna Philharmonic Orchestra conducted by Hans Richter.

Brahms had a special relationship with Clara Schumann, wife of composer-pianist Robert Schumann and herself an accomplished pianist. The friendship began when Brahms helped the Schumann family during the older composer's hospitalization and after his death. Brahms often sought Clara's advice on the music he was composing or her opinion of pieces he had just finished. The Second Symphony was no exception.

It is difficult to understand completely the nature of Brahms' feelings for Clara. When he was in his early twenties and still a protégé of Schumann, he loved Clara at a respectable distance. While Schumann was confined in an asylum during his last years, Brahms expressed his affection more openly, but he restrained himself from acting on it. He wrote, "My dearest Clara, I wish I could write to you as tenderly as I love you and do as many good and loving things for you as I would like. You are so infinitely dear to me that I cannot express it in words. I should like to call you darling and lots of other names, without ever getting enough of adoring you."

Once Schumann had died, Brahms could think realistically about a union with Clara. But it did not feel right. She was his friend and he loved her, but she was also the widow of Schumann. Furthermore, Brahms knew that a domestic life would interfere with his creative work. He wrote to his friend Joachim: "I believe that I do not respect and admire her so much as I love her and am under her spell. Often I must forcibly restrain myself from just quietly putting my arms around her and even — I don't know, it seems to me so natural that she would take it ill. I think I can no longer love a young girl. At least I have quite forgotten about them. They but promise heaven while Clara reveals it to us."

Clara and Brahms had been in constant daily contact, but then she moved to Berlin and he returned to Hamburg. They kept up a steady correspondence, and Brahms sent her every one of his compositions for criticism. But love was not openly discussed. Brahms never cared as deeply for another woman, but he was unable to bring himself to make a decisive commitment to Clara. Many years later he insisted they return each other's letters and destroy them. Clara complied reluctantly, managing to save a few of her favorites. Because most of the correspondence was burned, we will probably never have sufficient information to understand fully the odd relationship between these two artists.

After years of struggle composing the First Symphony, with many preliminary versions sent to Clara for suggestions, Brahms found it far easier to compose his Second. He did his best work away from the city in the summer, and so he wrote the Second Symphony in a few months at a small town on Wörther Lake. When it was done, he sent Clara the first movement, which she praised. She predicted that it would have more immediate success with the public than the First had had, and she was right. The third movement was so popular at the premiere that it had to be repeated.

The Second Symphony offers an interesting parallel to Beethoven. Brahms was constantly aware of the earlier composer, whose music was a model and an inspiration. Beethoven had written his Fifth and Sixth Symphonies closely togther, as did Brahms with his First and Second. The Fifth is brooding yet passionate, emotional yet triumphant, and it is in the appropriate key of C minor. Brahms' First shares key and mood with Beethoven's Fifth. Brahms' next symphony shares mood (but not key) with Beethoven's subsequent *Pastorale.* Both are idyllic, untroubled, and peaceful (although there is plenty of inner drama in both works).

Brahms, who did not believe in program music, would never have called a symphony *Pastorale,* and he would no doubt be annoyed with those commentators who find in the D Major Symphony reflections of the peaceful countryside in which it was conceived. But there is no denying that, if any of Brahms' symphonies deserve to be thought of as pastoral, this is the one. It occupies roughly the same position in Brahms' output as Beethoven's Sixth, Schumann's First, Dvořák's Eighth, Schubert's Fifth, Mahler's Fourth, Bruckner's Fourth, and Mendelssohn's Third do in their respective composers' catalogues. It would seem that writing a peaceful symphony was something that any self-respecting romantic composer had to do.

Brahms' Second is a masterpiece of tight construction and rhythmic inventiveness, qualities not necessarily associated with peaceful music. Consider the technique of motivic derivation, for example, which Brahms borrowed and expanded from Beethoven (notably in the Fifth Symphony). The first movement is pervaded by two extremely simple figures, heard at the very beginning: the three-note turn in the cellos and string basses (heard upside-down a moment later in the third measure of the horn melody) and the rising two-note figure that begins that horn tune. One would be hard put to think up any simpler material. Yet the manner in which almost everything in this complex movement comes from these two basic figures is amazing. But derivation of the movement from its opening is only part of Brahms' sophisticated technique.

The three-note figure is also the source of wonderful rhythmic developments. In its original form it fits nicely the 3/4 measures as 1 + /2 + /3 + ("+" indicates off-beats, not actually heard until later in the movement). In other words, the quarter note is the basic beat. But the motive can be (and eventually is) played slower: 1 + 2 + /3 + 1 + /2 + 3 +, with the half note (two beats long) now serving as the basic pulse. Thus a conflict is set up between the two-beat pulse of the tune and the three-beat measure. Further complications arise when the figure is speeded up so that the eighth note becomes the basic unit. It is too fast to be heard as the beat, so the entire three-note motive (now one and a half beats long) provides the pulse unit: 1 + 2 /+ 3 +. What all this means is that there are three different rates of speed in the movement, represented by three different pulse units, respectively 1, 1½ and 2 beats long. This conflict is intensified when Brahms plays these different speeds in alternation or even, in the development section, simultaneously. This rhythmic subtlety gives rise to further complexities, and the result is a movement that is endlessly intriguing beneath its placid surface.

The second movement also is full of unusual rhythms which are derived from its beginning, although here they are based not on different speeds but on different placements of the opening melody with the 4/4 measures. Listen carefully to that first tune — it sounds as if it fits the measure exactly: 1 2 3 4. The next four beats seem to confirm this interpretation, but then there is somehow an extra beat before the third measure. It somehow sounds like: 1 2 3 4 / 1 2 3 4 / 4 1 2 3 4. In actuality, the music begins on the fourth beat: 4 1 2 3 / 4 1 2 3 /4 1 2 3 4. From this initial displacement comes the movement's frequent emphasis on the fourth beats of measures and its tendency to start melodies anywhere within the measure. The opening tune, for example, later starts on a third beat. It is not placed "properly" within the measure until the very end, and there Brahms achieves regularity by an ingenious means: listen to it!

The deceptively innocent opening of the third movement actually contains the greatest rhythmic sophistication thus far. The suggestions of 2/4 and 4/4 within this 3/4 section are too complex to trace here. As a total contrast, the ensuing *presto* in 2/4 time is devoid of complication: its straightforward simplicity is welcome. After a return of the opening *allegretto*, a second *presto*, now in 3/8 time, is less innocent.

Although much of the finale is rhythmically regular, there are several stunningly imaginative passages: syncopations at different rates, 1½ and 2½ beat patterns within a 2-beat framework, and mixtures of speeds as in the opening movement. The result is a movement full of life and vitality, a fitting conclusion to this happiest of Brahms symphonies.

Brahms was a strange combination of humility and self-assuredness, of secretiveness and candor. He was unable to speak directly about himself or his work, but he was willing enough to communicate in riddles, ambiguities, or false modesties. Thus he could call the Second Symphony a collection of waltzes. His underlying self-confidence sometimes came through his put-on modesty: he told his friend Schubring that the symphony was "a quite innocent, gay little one." Brahms went on to compare it favorably, in his typical understated manner, to other composers' music: "Expect nothing, and for a month before drum nothing but Berlioz, Liszt, and Wagner; then its tender amiability will do a lot of good." After the successful premiere of the Second, the composer said, with his usual pseudo-self-effacement: "Whether or not I have a pretty symphony I do not know; I will have to ask some wiser people." Of course there were no wiser people, as Brahms well knew. He also knew that the symphony is indeed "pretty," as do all of us less wise music lovers.

Symphony Number 3 in F Major, Opus 90
   Allegro con brio
   Andante
   Poco allegretto
   Allegro. Un poco sostenuto

The Third Symphony was begun in 1882 and completed in the summer of 1883. Hans Richter conducted the first performance with the Vienna Philharmonic Orchestra on 2 December 1883.

Brahms was a man of contradictions, the greatest of which was the conflict between his passionately romantic personality and his classically oriented intellect. He was a product of his times, and his times were the turbulent years of nineteenth-century romanticism. His early works, such as the First Piano Concerto, are filled with pessimism, triumph, and a brooding bordering on sensationalism. These emotions were natural to the composer. Yet he had the intelligence to realize the underlying fallacy of romanticism: an overabundance of feeling can become undisciplined.

Brahms strove mightily to distance himself from the romantic aesthetic, but he was too much a man of his cultural environment to make a complete break. He tried to achieve a measure of objectivity by involving himself with his musical heritage. He tried to counteract his innate romanticism with the understated balance of classicism. Thus, he necessarily had to come to grips with the legacy of Beethoven. He was remarkably successful in his attempt to reconstruct the symphonic values of Beethoven.

But the art of Brahms was just that — a reconstruction. He was not so much the inheritor of Beethoven's titanic classicism as the reinterpreter of it. This fact does not detract from the stature of Brahms, who achieved his goal better than anyone else could have. But it does define the underlying tragedy of his creative existence. As musicologist Paul Henry Láng explains,

> The very currents that stream backwards from Brahms surged forward in Beethoven. Since the times could no longer furnish him with the antitheses Beethoven once found, he could only conjure them up. And thus classicism became in him a beautiful gesture, whereas in Beethoven it was fulfillment and synthesis. His tragedy was that Beethoven's shadow followed him everywhere. . . .
>
> To him who carries the past in himself, the essence of conscientiousness is a faithfulness and a moral obligation to the past, for the dissension between past and present means new wounds and eternal remorse. This is at the basis of that extraordinary sensitiveness which made Brahms' life the life of Hamlet, made him hesitant and chaste . . . , for he to whom every seemingly innocent action may become the source of new regrets shuts himself in and shuns action. If, however, he is enticed onto the field of action, he longs for solitude as the sick man for his bed. And he endeavors to live a blameless life, a life that can remain blameless only if others are not intimately involved in it. Thus Brahms remains a genius in the mask of a morose middle-class professional man.

All the other contradictions in Brahms the man and Brahms the composer stemmed from his desperate attempt to make his past less remote. Thus, there was the contradiction between the composer's apparently genuine modesty, bordering on self-deprecation, and his equally genuine pride in his accomplishments. He wrote to a friend, for example, about the newly completed Third Symphony, a masterpiece that exudes self-confidence, "Wrap it daily in a cloth moistened with the best Rhine wine — and do whatever else one does for such dry products."

Another contradiction was Brahms' unwillingness to speak or write about himself in any but the most elliptical or obscure manner. He once wrote to his publisher Fritz Simrock, for example, "Only one thing is sure: soon I'll not have a *groschen* of money left! Now, I am counting on the appreciation and gratitude of you and all your fellow publishers. You will pass around the hat and send me an eminent reward — because I leave you so nicely in peace and you need not run any risks for me." Simrock, who knew his composer-friend well, immediately understood that Brahms was telling him about a newly completed major work, namely the Third Symphony.

Another contradiction: Brahms was a man of both politeness and rudeness. He was considerate enough to remove his shoes for fear of disturbing the lady living below him, yet he was rude enough to reply in kind to this question, asked him just before a performance of the Third Symphony: "And where are you going to lead us tonight, Herr Doctor? To Heaven?" Brahms replied, "It is all the same to me where you go!"

The contradiction between his gentle humor and naïve rudeness is illustrated by a remark made upon leaving a gathering of his friends: "If there is someone here whom I have neglected to insult, I apologize."

One final contradiction: Brahms occasionally felt, despite his consistently high level of productivity, that he was too old to compose any more. At the age of 49, for example, he solemnly assured Simrock that he would never again write or publish a piece. The very next year saw the premiere and immediate success of the Third Symphony.

After that premiere, which had been conducted by Hans Richter, there was competition among conductors for the right of second performance. Brahms entrusted his old friend Joseph Joachim with this honor. Hans von Bülow, not to be outdone, programmed the work second *and* fourth on a concert of five pieces played by his Meiningen Court Orchestra. The symphony was hailed at each new performance, and it made Brahms' name as a symphonist resound as never before.

The work is the composer's only cyclical symphony. The opening theme returns at the end "like a rainbow after a thunderstorm," as Brahms' biographer Karl Geiringer expresses it. Also, the second theme of the slow movement finds its way into the finale.

The introductory motive, F A-flat F, stands for Brahms' motto *frei aber froh*, "free but happy." He was in actuality neither free nor happy. Joachim's motto *frei aber einsam*, "free but lonely," came closer to the truth. But Brahms characteristically felt the need to say the opposite.

He could not admit the tragedy that was his deep secret, that he was lonely, not happy, because of his isolation from his age and because only he fully realized the fatal fallacy of romanticism. He longed for the impossible return to an age of pure classicism. The Third Symphony does not disclose this tragedy. It hides behind its motto "free but happy." Brahms did not write a programmatic piece, least of all one in which he revealed his darkest secret. He knew the futility of denying his age, and he admitted it with characteristic understatement, but he never let it become a part of his music: "That people in general do not understand and do not respect the greatest things, such as Mozart's concertos, helps our kind to live and acquire renown. If they would only know that they are getting from us by drops what they could drink there to their hearts' content!"

The "free but happy" motive, which pervades the first movement, suggests conflict, since its notes imply the key of F minor while the symphony is actually in F major. Thus, when the beautifully lyrical second theme arrives in the clarinet in A major, the A-flat is replaced by the "correct" A-natural in the most definitive manner. Ironically, the happiness of this theme is increased by the way it contradicts the "free but happy" motive. The ultimate consequence of this motive is that much of the finale is cast in F minor. The coda, however, moves into the peaceful key of F major and closes with a beautiful reminiscence of the opening of the first movement.

Symphony Number 4 in E Minor, Opus 98
>   Allegro non troppo
>   Andante moderato
>   Allegro giocoso
>   Allegro energico e passionato. Più allegro

The Fourth Symphony was composed during the summers of 1884 and 1885 in Mürzzuschlag, Austria. Brahms conducted the first performance in Meiningen on 17 October 1885.

Brahms liked to retreat to small rural towns for the summer months, in order to work close to the natural settings he deeply loved. In 1884 he decided to spend the summer in Mürzzuschlag, in the Austrian Alps, a town he had visited 17 years earlier with his father. Brahms made several friends in the village and received many guests from Vienna, but he nonetheless had ample time to finish the first two movements of a symphony. Since he liked the town, he returned the following summer to complete it.

The composer went home to Vienna in the fall with the completed score of what he knew to be a most unusual symphony. He was eager to have his friends hear it, so he made a four-hand piano arrangement, which he played with the help of his friend Ignaz Brüll. Critic Max Kalbeck, who was Brahms' first biographer, related the awkwardness of first hearing this confusing piece:

As Brahms was out of practice and Brüll had never seen the work, the performance was less than perfect. The first movement was received with dead silence, into which at last Eduard Hanslick, the critic who had previously championed each new work of Brahms, interjected, "Throughout the entire movement I had the sensation of being flailed by two fearfully ingenious persons." The composer's friend Elisabeth von Herzogenberg complained of the "tangled overgrowth of ingeniously interwoven detail." The performers passed on to the second movement, which met with no reaction at all. At last Kalbeck spoke, uttering some banality in order to break the tense silence. The performers continued. Kalbeck felt that the "shaggy, grimly joyful scherzo seemed far too insignificant in comparison to the preceding movements, and the mighty passacaglia of the finale — the crowning glory of all of Brahms' variation movements — did not appear a proper conclusion for a symphony." The critic went to visit the composer the next day, to implore him to destroy the scherzo, preserve the finale as a separate work, and write two new movements. Uncharacteristically, Brahms did not get angry. He defended his use of variation form in a finale, citing the precedent of Beethoven's *Eroica* Symphony.

The composer, as usual, had his own doubts about the new composition. He wrote to conductor Hans von Bülow in typically self-deprecating fashion: "A few entr'actes are lying here ready — the thing one usually calls a symphony." To another friend Brahms wrote, "It is very questionable whether I will ever expose the public to this piece." But he was confident beneath this facade of self-effacement. He believed in his unusual new symphony, and he wanted to hear it played by an orchestra. That was the real reason for the letter to von Bülow. It continued,

I often indulge myself by imagining how nicely and comfortably I could work on this piece with you and the Meiningen Orchestra while on tour. I am thinking now — and at the same time pondering — whether the symphony will find more of a public. I fear it smacks of this country — the cherries are not sweet here and you would certainly not eat them! In Rhenish or Dutch towns, where my other things are heard often enough and liked, the new symphony would probably be quite a good item. How amusing it would be if I were to travel with you as a sort of extra conductor!

Von Bülow had been a strong supporter of Brahms for several years. Previously he had allied himself with the rival faction, led by avant-gardists Wagner and Liszt. He had married Liszt's daughter Cosima, but she left him to live with, have children by, and eventually marry Wagner. These events caused the most proper von Bülow public embarrassment and private chagrin. He abandoned the cause of avant-garde music and began to champion Brahms, the latter-day classicist. It was von Bülow who had coined the phrase "the three B's," equating the genius of Brahms with that of Bach and Beethoven. The conductor supported Brahms' music as ardently as he had that of Wagner and Liszt: "I have [Brahms] to thank for being restored to sanity — late, but I hope not too late — in fact, for being still alive. Three quarters of my existence has been misspent on my former father-in-law, that mountebank, and his tribe, but the remainder belongs to the true saints of art and above all to him." Bülow offered Brahms his orchestra, for first performances and even for trying out passages of works in progress. Bülow readily agreed to allow Brahms to tour with the orchestra as "extra conductor."

Bülow had learned from Wagner that composers can be hard to deal with. His friendship with Brahms subsequently suffered a rift that might well have reminded him that geniuses can be temperamental and not always trustworthy. First of all, Brahms insisted that no other work of any substance precede the Fourth Symphony on tour concerts. Then the composer asked to conduct the piece on nine different occasions, including the premiere (which Bülow had rehearsed). Bülow began to wonder who was really the "extra" conductor. The final blow came when Brahms absented himself from the orchestra for a few days in November, in order to conduct the Fourth Symphony in Frankfurt. Bülow had scheduled a performance in Frankfurt a few days later, and he was insulted when the composer stole his thunder with a prior performance. Bülow felt that Brahms was showing a lack of confidence in him and that his professional honor had been compromised. He over-reacted by resigning his post as conductor of the Meiningen Orchestra. The composer and the conductor maintained a stony silence for a year.

Eventually the friendship was restored. Bülow came to Vienna and Brahms sent him a card with a musical quotation from Mozart's opera *The Magic Flute*, the words of which are, "Shall I never see thee again, beloved?" Bülow was touched and immediately called on Brahms, and the friendship was renewed.

The Fourth Symphony, despite the doubts of Brahms' friends,

was popular with audiences, eventually even in staid Vienna. The unusual nature of the symphony did not detract from its impact. Its strangeness lies in its combination of modern (for 1885) harmonies and suggestions of old music. This tendency toward the archaic is evident in the opening and closing of the slow movement, which implies one of the renaissance era's church modes (the phrygian), and in the finale. The last movement is cast as a passacaglia, a form popular with baroque composers. In a passacaglia a short theme is repeated again and again, with different variations and ornamentations. Not only the form but also the actual theme Brahms chose suggest the baroque period. The dynamism of the fourth movement comes from the insistent presence of this theme and from the ingenious variations constructed on it. Since the theme is only eight measures long, the careful listener can usually follow it. It is heard 31 times in a row, yet always in new guises, so that it never becomes tedious. This movement, in addition to being a *tour de force* of compositional technique, is unprecedented in a symphony: many movements in earlier symphonies are cast in variation forms, but none has so short and simple a theme.

"Tragedy with unsurpassable variety of expression and power of climax." "A funeral procession moving in silence across moonlit heights." "Elegaic and meditative." "Shadowy desolation and mystically supernatural atmosphere." "Vigor and nobility that is indeed often heroic." "The realms where joy and sorrow are hushed." "Sturdy gaiety." "Under the shadow of an inevitable fate." "Boisterous and sportive." "Quiet tragedy and uncanny merriment." "Deeply earnest." These are just some of the ways commentators have characterized the E Minor Symphony. The far-flung variety of these descriptions indicates not only the range of moods found in the symphony but also its elusive character. The Fourth is a deeply meaningful and profoundly communicative work, yet it is absolute music of the highest order. It is not really "about" anything that can be readily characterized verbally, and these quotations attest to the futility of trying to translate its rarefied world of tones into the concreteness of language. The emotions of the Fourth are there to be heard and experienced, whatever labels an individual may want to attach to them.

The symphony begins with a two-note motive, repeated and developed immediately and extensively. It almost seems as if the music had been playing already when we happened to tune in on it. In an early sketch Brahms had, in fact, preceded this opening with a brief introduction. Notice how the weak-strong rhythm of the two-note figure pervades the entire movement. The development section of this sonata form begins like a relaunching of the opening — a reference to procedures of the classical period, when composers generally indicated that exposition sections were to be repeated. Having begun the development like the opening, Brahms could hardly also start the recapitulation in the same manner. So he disguises the return. Only in the fifth measure of the theme does it regain its original form.

In the second movement Brahms creates a subtle undercurrent of tension by a sophisticated compositional strategy. The listener may well not be aware of it consciously, but the effect is unmistakable. Tension is maintained by continually stating the opening horn theme in the "wrong" key or on the "wrong" degree of the scale. At the beginning, for example, the melody seems to suggest the key of C major, with an emphasis on the note E. But the movement is destined to be in E major, not C major. The clarinets and *pizzicato* violins take up the theme in the "correct" key of E, but emphasizing the note G-sharp. After a hint of G major, the theme is again stated in E with G-sharp emphasized. At long last, resolution is felt as the violins, played bowed for the first time in the movement, state the theme (slightly disguised) in the key of E major *and* emphasizing the note E. To underline this sense of arrival, Brahms orchestrates sumptuously: oboe and bassoon commentary, violin and cello arpeggios, and horn and trumpet syncopations accompany the melody. Now that the theme has finally achieved the stability it has sought from the beginning, the music is free to move on to other matters. After an interlude the opening theme returns, sometimes in the "right" key and sometimes in a distant (e.g., B-flat major) "wrong" key. The movement ends quietly with a reminiscence of the opening, the melody still suggesting C major but the harmony firmly in E major. The tensions of the movement never reach full resolution.

The colorfully orchestrated third movement is the only true scherzo in all the Brahms symphonies. It is cast in C major, not unexpected after the hints at that key in the slow movement.

The theme of the finale is only eight notes long. For those who may like to follow this simple tune through its numerous variations, they are listed below. It is suggested that you not try to follow these transformations, however, unless you are already quite familiar with the movement. You could well miss the music while listening too carefully to the notes.

(1) The first series of variations begins with the exposition of the theme in full brass and woodwind chords. (2) The theme is played *pizzicato* in the violins, accompanied by the horns, trombones, timpani, and other strings. (3) The theme is played *pizzicato* in the violas and cellos accompanying a flowing melody in the winds. (4) An ornamented version of the theme is played by the full orchestra, with the original version sounding in the violins, violas, trumpet, and

trombone. (5) The theme in low strings accompanies a new melody in the upper strings. (6) The theme, in *pizzicato* string basses and at the bottom of cello arpeggios, accompanies an elaborated version of the new melody from (5). (7) Continuation of (6), with the theme still in string basses (now bowed) and cello arpeggios. (8) The theme is in the string basses and bassoon arpeggios (in a dotted rhythm) against dotted-rhythm melodies in the upper and lower strings. (9) The theme is again in the string basses and cellos, accompanying sixteenth-note figurations in the violins. (10) The figurations speed up, becoming sixteenth-note triplets; the theme is embedded within these figurations in the violas and cellos while it is also heard unadorned in the string basses. (11) The theme is heard as the bass line of block chords that alternate between the strings and winds. (12) The theme is the bass line (bassoons, cellos, and violas), but it is also in the horn, accompanying a melody in the flutes and violins. (13) The theme starts to move twice as slowly (the time signature changes from 3/4 to 3/2) as the solo flute plays a lyrical melody derived from the theme. (14) The music changes from minor to major for the first time, as the theme becomes the basis of a dialogue among the winds. (15) The theme is the bass line of a chord progression in the low winds and brass. (16) The chord progression of (15) is repeated in an elaborated version.

(17) After a brief pause the music returns to minor and to 3/4 time for a recapitulation of the theme in its original chordal version, in the brass and winds, joined eventually by the strings. As this variation marks the midpoint of the movement, it initiates a second series of variations that loosely parallels the first. (18) The theme is heard tremolo in the cellos, while the upper strings also play tremolo in accompaniment to two-note figures in the winds, reminiscent of the first movement. (19) An elaborated version of the theme becomes the melody in the upper winds, accompanied by most of the orchestra. (20) A forceful ornamented version of the theme is played in eighth-notes by the violins, alternating with the winds. (21) Continuation of (20) with further ornamentation of the theme. (22) A forceful treatment by the full orchestra, with the theme in the violins and flutes — the beginning notes of each rapidly ascending scale and the top notes of some of the staccato chords comprise the theme. (23) The theme is embedded within the bass line of a quiet, staccato version in the strings and winds. (24) The theme is stated powerfully in the horns, while the winds alternate triplet figures. (25) A forceful statement by the full orchestra, with the theme in the violins and upper winds. (26) The forceful statement continues with a counter-melody in the oboes, bassoons, violins, and violas, while the theme is heard in the upper trombones, trumpets, and horns. (27) The theme is ornamented slightly in the horns, switching to the oboes, and is accom-

panied by a quiet string undulation. (28) The theme is embedded within an arpeggiated melody in the violas and cellos, accompanied by soft wind chords and *pizzicato* lower strings. (29) A wind melody is accompanied by upper string arpeggios that contain the theme and by lower strings playing *pizzicato*. (30) The full string section plays *pizzicato* arpeggios based on the theme, accompanying two-note figures in the winds. (31) The arpeggios (and hence the theme) are treated in canon by the nearly full orchestra. (32) A brief transition to the coda, which is faster. It starts with a forceful statement of the beginning of the theme, and it goes on to develop parts of the theme rather than varying the whole theme.

What is amazing about the finale is not only its strict adherence to one theme (sometimes prominent, sometimes buried in an accompanimental figure) but also the way in which Brahms continually creates variety. He achieves this variety while playing the same melody again and again, never even allowing himself the relief of a key change. The inexorable momentum built up in this manner makes the finale a powerful and unique listening experience (whether or not you choose to follow the transformations of the theme consciously) and a fitting conclusion to an extraordinary symphony — and to a series of four magnificent symphonies.

Variations on a Theme of Haydn, Opus 56a

The Variations was composed in the summer of 1873; the version for two pianos was completed in July and the orchestral version in October. Brahms conducted the first performance of the latter in Vienna on 2 November 1873.

Brahms' *Haydn* Variations is an important work for many reasons. As his first composition for large orchestra without soloist, it prepared him to tackle the monumental task of composing a symphony (his First Symphony appeared three years later). More significantly, the variations mark a turning point in Brahms' development from an impressionably young romantic to a fully disciplined latter-day classicist. The composition is important also because it is apparently the first set of independent (not part of a larger work) variations ever composed by anyone for orchestra. That Brahms thought highly of the work is evidenced by the fact that he kept his preliminary sketches, which he otherwise almost never did. That he labored hard on the piece is shown by the numerous changes and careful calculations in those sketches.

Brahms first encountered the theme on which he based the variations in 1870, when it was shown to him by his friend C. F. Pohl, biographer of Haydn. It comes from the slow movement of one of six divertimentos for wind instruments that Pohl had recently discovered. Neither Brahms nor Pohl could have known that latter-day scholars were to pronounce the six divertimentos spurious, probably the work of one of Haydn's students, such as Ignaz Pleyel. Furthermore, the tune, which is labelled *Chorale St. Antoni*, was not original with the divertimento composer. No one has explained the title or the exact origin of the melody, but current speculation is that it was an old folk tune that might have been sung by penitents in honor of St. Anthony's Day.

Whatever the origin, the theme made an excellent candidate for variations. The original composer of the divertimento so used it, and Brahms resolved to do likewise. He was attracted to its irregular phrase structure: each of the first two phrases (which are both repeated) is five, rather than the standard four, measures long.

Brahms planned from the start to make the variations an orchestral work, perhaps because he was taken with the wind scoring that Pohl had shown him. He does, in fact, retain much of this orchestration for the opening statement. Because the composition turned out to be difficult and complex, he first wrote a version for two pianos. This is not simply an unorchestrated sketch but rather a full-fledged piece. He probably intended it as a birthday gift to Clara Schumann.

The composition consists of a theme, eight variations, and a coda. Each variation retains the irregular phrase structure of the theme, as well as certain melodic contours and important harmonies. Yet each also has its own particular mood, tempo, orchestration, and figuration.

The *andante* theme (as well as each variation) is divided into two parts, each repeated. The second half starts with a brief development of the material of the first part, followed by a restatement of the basic melody with its irregularities somewhat smoothed out.

Variation I, *poco più animato*, presents wide-ranging string figures against repeated notes (from the theme) in the winds. Variation II, *più vivace*, develops the theme's opening dotted rhythm. Variation III, *con moto*, contains a version of the theme in even eighth notes, to which sixteenth notes are added. Variation IV, *andante con moto*, is in the minor, and in it winds and strings constantly trade off melody and accompaniment. Variation V, *vivace*, returns to the major for a scherzo-like interlude. Variation VI, *vivace*, is march-like, featuring brass and woodwinds. Variation VII, *grazioso*, is stately. Variation VIII, *presto non troppo*, is in the minor. It starts in the low strings and moves in continuous motion into higher instruments.

The finale, *andante,* is a *tour de force* of compositional technique. It is, in effect, another set of variations, based not on the full 29-measure theme but on a five-measure derivative of it. This phrase is repeated, usually in the bass, some twenty times. This form, called passacaglia or thorough bass or chaconne, was to serve Brahms also in the finale of his Fourth Symphony. Against this repeating phrase is heard a wonderfully varied series of contrapuntal lines, so that the excitement and interest build to the end.

Max Bruch

Born in Cologne on 6 January 1838.
Died at Friedenau, near Berlin, on 20 October 1920.

◆　◆　◆

Concerto Number 1 in G Minor for Violin and Orchestra, Opus 26

Allegro moderato —
Adagio
Allegro energico

The First Violin Concerto was sketched in 1857 in Cologne and finished in 1866 at Koblenz. Otto von Königslöw premiered the work, with Bruch conducting, at a benefit concert for the Evangelical Women's Society in Koblenz on 24 April 1866. The work was subsequently revised, and the final version was premiered by violinist Joseph Joachim in October 1867.

Bruch had an extremely long creative life. He began composing at the age of eleven, with some chamber pieces and an orchestral overture, and his last works — a set of songs with piano and a large work for chorus and orchestra — were written shortly before his death at the age of 83.

His first instruction was from his mother, a well-known music teacher and soprano. At the age of twelve, Bruch composed a symphony and won a prize for a string quartet. The prize money enabled him to study composition, theory, and piano with some of the leading teachers in his native Cologne. By age 20 he was himself employed as a teacher, and he had composed his first of three operas. He left Cologne in 1861 and traveled extensively, finally settling in Koblenz to accept a position as music director. Later he moved to Sondershausen, Berlin, Bonn, Liverpool, and Breslau. In the latter two cities he held positions as conductor of the local orchestras. In 1891 he at last achieved a degree of fame, as he was appointed professor of composition at the Berlin Academy, a position he held until his retirement in 1910. He also served as vice-president of the Academy after the death of violinist Joseph Joachim in 1907.

Most of Bruch's music is seldom heard today. During his lifetime his large secular choral works were considered his most significant compositions, but today he is remembered mainly for his violin pieces and *Kol Nidre* and *Shelomo* for cello and orchestra. His works for violin and orchestra include three concertos, the *Scottish* Fantasy, and six smaller pieces.

It is hard to understand the differing degrees of popularity of the three concertos. They are all tuneful, competent, idiomatic works that utilize the solo instrument in both lyrical and dazzling passages, yet the First has long remained a concert favorite, the Second is rarely played, and the Third remains virtually unknown.

Bruch wrote as follows about his interest in the violin:

> In my youth I studied the violin for four or five years, and, although I did not become an adept performer, I learned to know and love the instrument. The violin seemed to me even at that time the queen of instruments, and it was quite natural that I early had the inclination to write for it. Thus my First Concerto, Opus 26, which was introduced to the musical world by Joseph Joachim during the season of 1867–68, gradually grew. It was not at that time my intention, so far as I can remember, to write further works for the violin, and indeed for years I devoted myself to writing compositions in large form for chorus and orchestra. In 1873 I wrote *Odysseus* and in 1875 *Arminius* (which is better known in America than in Germany) and in 1877 *The Song of the Bells*. During the year 1877 I made the acquaintance of the eminent Spanish violinist Pablo de Sarasate at the time when his star was in the ascendancy in Germany. We were together a great deal and became firm friends, and it was at his urgent request that I wrote for him in 1877 my Second Concerto in D Minor, Opus 44, and in 1880 the *Scottish* Fantasy. After a considerable pause I then wrote, in 1890, the Third Concerto in D Minor, Opus 58, for Joachim, who played it for the first time on 31 May 1891 at a music festival I gave in Düsseldorf. I never had any special interest in the piano, and I wrote only a little for it in my youth. I was destined by nature to write compositions for the voice, and I always studied singing with special interest and have associated largely with singers. This tendency has, of course, also been displayed in my violin works.

The revised version of the First Concerto is dedicated to Joachim, who provided valuable advice on recasting the work. Because of the unorthodox opening (violin playing rhapsodically in alternation with chordal phrases) and because of the avoidance of sonata form in the opening movement, Bruch wanted to call the piece "fantasy" rather than "concerto." Joachim dissuaded him, pointing to the solidly classical structure of the other two movements.

The first movement of this romantic concerto really has no extended themes. The opening woodwind motive returns in many contexts to bind the movement together, but it is hardly a melodic line. The intervening violin figurations introduce the instrument and its capabilities, but they are too florid to be melodic. Once the introduction ends, a new motive — a simple, restless rhythm in the bass instruments — takes over as an almost constant undercurrent. The music builds in excitement, with the solo violin contributing fiery chords, until there is a gentle return to the opening of the movement. This time the entrance of the full orchestra sends the music in a new direction tonally, in preparation for the second movement.

After this transition the solo instrument re-enters with a lyrical melodic line. The second movement thus immediately establishes the melodiousness that is absent from the first. This opening theme gives way to a second tune of even greater beauty. Despite the lyricism of this piece, the solo violin does play some striking passages with rapid notes.

The finale begins with murmurings in the low instruments, suggesting the upcoming first theme. The solo violin enters with the first full statement of this gypsy-like melody, played with great flair across all four of the instrument's strings. After considerable development of this impetuous and irresistable melody, a second, more expansive tune is heard. These two themes alternate. Toward the end, the main theme returns twice in unexpected keys. The final few measures are a furious *presto*.

The concerto is a mesmerizing display of violin virtuosity. Bruch utilizes open strings, high registers, four-note chords, rapid double and triple stops, etc., with great understanding. The resulting work is a virtuoso's dream. When well played it shows off the instrument to great advantage. The piece is also dramatic, fiery, and melodic, and thus it has remained popular with soloists and audiences alike.

Anton Bruckner

Born on 4 September 1824 in Linz, Austria.
Died on 11 October 1896 in Vienna.

◆　◆　◆

Symphony Number 1 in C Minor
Allegro
Adagio. Andante. Adagio
Scherzo: Schnell. Trio: Langsamer. Scherzo
Bewegt, feurig

The First Symphony was begun in January 1865 and completed on 14 April 1866. Bruckner conducted the first performance on 9 May 1868 in Linz.

Like most of Bruckner's symphonies, the First went through many revisions, and as with many of the other symphonies the original version is superior to the composer's later reworkings. Bruckner had already written two "apprentice" symphonies, but the C Minor is the first one he felt deserved to be numbered. This decision was appropriate, because the First decisively convinced him that his future lay in composing symphonies. He had previously been known mainly as an organist who wrote liturgical music, but with the First he created a boldly original, non-religious work for orchestra. And he believed in it enough to perform it in his native Linz.

The performance was not very good. The orchestra was a pick-up group that included theater orchestra musicians, members of two regimental bands, and local amateurs. There were only twelve violins, three violas, three cellos, and three basses. Furthermore, few people attended, since the previous day the bridge across the Danube had collapsed and the people of Linz were too involved with the aftermath of this disaster to show much interest in an afternoon concert. Nonetheless, the few people who came seemed to like the music.

Bruckner, as usual, had second thoughts. And third thoughts. He returned to the symphony in 1877 and made changes in the phrase structure, adding a measure here, removing one there, sometimes repeating one. A year or so later the composer decided to revert to the original versions of the third and fourth movements. He continued to tinker with the symphony through 1889. In 1890–91 he made another thorough revision for a performance by conductor Hans Richter. Although another conductor, Hermann Levi, implored Bruckner not to revise the work, the composer went ahead and made major changes.

He spent a whole year revising, time that he could more profitably have spent working on his Ninth Symphony, which he subsequently left unfinished at his death. Richter conducted the new version on 13 December 1891. This revision, known as the Vienna version, differs significantly in scoring and counterpoint. Bruckner added a lot of fussy details that obscured the original freshness of the Linz version. His additions often clouded the materials with unnecessary textural densities. Some of the revisions were real improvements, based on what he had learned about orchestration in the intervening years, but they often sound at odds with the compositional style of the symphony. As composer and Bruckner scholar Robert Simpson has written,

> Of the revisions he is known to have made himself, that of the First Symphony is the worst. . . . It is true that the Vienna version of Bruckner's First contains refinements and subtleties that the composer of the Linz version would not have thought of, but most of them are of a kind that could have been apt only in his later works. If we want to know what the symphony is really like, we must turn to its bold, clean Linz version, and it is unlikely that its bluntness will now strike us (as it must have done the agitated old man of the 1890s) as crudeness. Such impurities as it has are less disturbing than the anachronisms that were afterwards imposed upon it.

Bruckner's First is less solemn than its better known siblings. "I was never again so bold and daring as I was in the First Symphony. I challenged the whole world," Bruckner is reported to have said. He referred to this stormy symphony as *das kecke Beserl* ("the impudent urchin"), a nickname Viennese students often gave to fresh young girls.

Symphony Number 2 in C Minor
Ziemlich schnell
Adagio: Feierlich, etwas bewegt
Scherzo: schnell
Mehr schnell

The Second Symphony was begun late in the summer of 1871. The first version was completed on 11 September 1872. Bruckner conducted the first performance in Vienna on 26 October 1873. He subsequently revised the work, and the new version was first performed on 20 February 1876. There were minor revisions made in 1879 and 1891.

When Simon Sechter, Bruckner's old counterpoint teacher, died in 1867, the composer's friend Johann Herbeck suggested that Bruckner apply for Sechter's position on the faculty of the Vienna Conservatory. The job was his if he wanted it, but Bruckner was hesitant to leave his home town of Linz, he was uneasy about taking such a responsible teaching post, and he was afraid that a conservatory salary would not provide sufficient income to live in Vienna. He kept putting off making his decision. He had recently been turned down for a post at the University of Vienna, and he feared that teaching music in Vienna was not for him. Immobilized by indecision, Bruckner went into a depression and even wrote to Herbeck that he was thinking about ending his life.

Herbeck responded, "You have no one to fear but yourself, particularly if you start writing hysterical letters to anyone else like the one I received from you today. Far from 'leaving the world,' you should go into the world!" After deliberating for several months (!), the composer accepted the offer. In October 1868, at the age of 44, he moved to Vienna and thereby began a new phase in his life. He left behind a career as a composer mainly of church music and became a symphonist. It is true that he had already completed three symphonies (two youthful works and the First), but his real maturity as a symphonic composer started with the Second Symphony.

Bruckner was able to supplement his income by serving as organist at the Imperial Chapel. His fame as a performer outweighed his reputation as a composer. He was invited to represent Austria at an international contest of organists in France, where he succeeded in winning first prize. As a result he was the only Austrian invited to perform at the International Exhibition of 1871 in London. Bruckner's trips to France and England turned out to be the provincial musician's only international journeys.

In London Bruckner was excited to see "everywhere my name in letters bigger than myself." Unfortunately, the British public was incensed that many foreign organists had been invited while English performers had been neglected. As a result the reviews were unfavorable, although Bruckner fared better than the other organists. He was given the opportunity to pay for a favorable review, which he angrily refused to do.

While he was in England, Bruckner began to compose the Second Symphony. He made a conscious effort to write a simpler piece than the First Symphony, because several critics had complained of that work's complexities. The composer's willingness to accept and act on criticism from less than knowledgeable musicians foreshadowed his lifelong acquiescence to suggestions for cuts and changes in his symphonies. Bruckner was a strange mixture of self-confidence and self-doubt. He always spoke of his unshakable belief in his symphonies, yet he repeatedly bowed to requests for "improving" them. His biographer Edwin Doernberg believes that the problem lay with Bruckner's "deep-rooted and humble respect for 'authorities.'" Everyone who had achieved a respectable position, whether a newspaper critic or an orchestra conductor, was an authority, and the composer, although almost fifty years old, bowed to the opinions of those whose positions he respected. His desire to write the simple symphony the critics had demanded caused him great difficulty. He admitted, "They frightened me so much that I feared to be myself."

He decided that simpler meant clearer, and he composed a first movement with numerous pauses between sections in order clearly to delineate the sonata structure. When the symphony was completed, it was rehearsed by the Vienna Philharmonic Orchestra, under the direction of Otto Dessof. The conductor dismissed the work as nonsense, and one of the orchestral musicians dubbed it the "Symphony of Pauses." The composer was asked to make some cuts, and he agreed to removing some thirty or forty measures. But this gesture was hardly enough for Dessof, who wanted the symphony substantially shortened. The score was returned to the composer.

Bruckner did not give up in his attempt to find a performance for the work. With the help of a patron, he hired the Philharmonic and conducted it himself. The orchestra members continued to dislike the work, but they acted as professionals and did their best. Since Bruckner's patron had paid for a large number of rehearsals, the performance went well. And it was well received, although the critics nonetheless did complain about the music. Bruckner wrote a letter of thanks to the orchestra:

"Never in all my days can I put into words — still less repay — all that you did for me yesterday with such infinite kindness, and in all the vast range of your artistic accomplishment, in which (if it were possible) you excelled yourselves. But at least I can try to express my deep emotion and my unending gratitude towards you. I ask you, then, gentlemen, to accept my profound and heartfelt thanks." The composer asked permission to dedicate the symphony to the Philharmonic.

As the orchestra management never replied to this letter, Bruckner decided to dedicate the symphony to Liszt instead. Liszt had never liked Bruckner very much, and he wrote him a perfunctory letter of thanks. Soon thereafter the Hungarian composer lost the manuscript, which luckily found its way back to the symphony's offended composer. Liszt apparently never even realized he had lost the score. Bruckner finally decided to dedicate the work to no one.

Bruckner's friend Herbeck suggested extensive cuts and revisions, to try to make the symphony easier for conductors and critics. Herbeck hoped to make it more conventional, whereas in reality it is the first work in which Bruckner's unique musical personality emerged fully. Surely Herbeck had Bruckner's best interests at heart, but he was not the musican that the composer was, and he was unable to recognize the uniqueness of the music. Bruckner's self-doubts surfaced, and he reluctantly agreed to removing large sections and making other changes. Thus began his lifelong struggle with revisions and with well-meaning friends who wanted to prettify his symphonies.

The new version was finished in 1876. By this time Bruckner had completed the first versions of the Third, Fourth, and Fifth Symphonies. Subsequent revisions of the Second were minor, so that there exist essentially two different scores: the original version and the Bruckner-Herbeck revision.

Both versions are performed today, and there are passionate advocates of each. The original version is more structurally balanced but in some ways more crude. The revision was made after the composer had gained more experience in writing for orchestra, and thus some of the scoring is more sonorous. But the cuts obscure some of the formal proportions, so that the revised version is less satisfying as a totality. The feelings of the composer himself are no help. He stated flat out that he would stand by the revision, but he might have been speaking out of loyalty to Herbeck, who had died soon after their collaboration ended. On the other hand, Bruckner never destroyed the original score, which he might have done had he really believed that it was, as he called it, just an "old arrangement."

The notorious pauses in the first movement, which the Vienna Philharmonic players ridiculed, serve not only to delineate the form. They also create a block-like structure typical of all subsequent Bruckner symphonies. Each section is internally continuous, but the junctures, marked by pauses (literal silences or soft sustained notes) are disquieting. The result is a music of wonderfully romantic lyricism and calm on the surface but with an unmistakable undercurrent of intensity. While there is no reason to look for a programmatic source of this contradiction, it does parallel Bruckner's personality. A calm, placid man, he was consumed by an inner turmoil that several times erupted in nervous disorders. Similarly, the symphony's almost Schubertian grace is many times interrupted by discontinuities that are foreign to its lyricism but that hint at darker emotions beneath the surface. The composer explained this movement simply: "When I want to present a new, momentous idea, I must stop to catch my breath." But there is a much deeper significance in the pauses than Bruckner consciously realized.

The slow movement has almost as many pauses as the *moderato*, though they are somehow less disruptive. Thus the inherent lyricism is allowed to soar, especially in the last third of the movement. Interestingly, Bruckner uses in the coda music from the *Benedictus* of his F Minor Mass, composed shortly before the symphony.

Because of its dance-like character, the third movement has fewer pauses. Particularly continuous (though not totally devoid of pauses) is the idyllic trio section, a wonderfully nostalgic *Ländler*.

The finale is the most discontinuous of the movements. Different materials and different moods confront each other, often not even across pauses like those of the earlier movements. Fanfares, an intimate slow passage (another quotation from the F Minor Mass, this time from the *Kyrie*), lyrical melodies, passages of great fullness, even an impish scherzo (in which instruments alternate rapidly, note-by-note) — the movement contains great variety.

Symphony Number 3 in D Minor, *Wagner*

Gemässigt, misterioso
Adagio: Feierlich
Scherzo: Ziemlich schnell
Allegro

The Third Symphony was begun in the fall of 1872 and completed on 31 December 1873. The composer conducted the first performance on 16 December 1877 with the Vienna Philharmonic.

Bruckner's Third Symphony has an extraordinarily complicated and confused history. Bruckner was a shy, reclusive man who was a curious mixture of determination and vacillation. He continued to compose symphony after symphony, despite often hostile reception from conductors, critics, and audiences. Yet he all too often acquiesced to requests from conductors and publishers to cut down the extreme length of his works. Thus most Bruckner symphonies exist in several versions, which represent the composer's inability to commit himself to one definitive version. His biographers cite his mania for revising, particularly in his later years.

Even today the question of which versions of Bruckner's symphonies ought to be performed is not settled. Original versions represent the composer's often idealistic first conception, untarnished by practicalities and uninfluenced by others. Original versions, on the other hand, are sometimes problematic, because Bruckner mastered symphonic form slowly, and many of his earlier works are flawed. Later versions at best represent the more mature composer's second or third thoughts, but at worst they are products of other hands, well-meaning but ill-advised performers who sought and all too readily received Bruckner's reluctant blessing for extensive cuts. Bruckner himself was sometimes prevailed upon to and sometimes even decided himself to alter his symphonies years after their completion, thereby introducing into a work in an earlier style music of a later idiom.

There are practical musicological questions of finding all the versions, deciding which revisions were actually made by the composer, and making available to conductors each separate version. The Complete Bruckner Edition, most fortunately, is dedicated to publishing every authentic version of each symphony. In the case of the Third, there are no fewer than three distinct versions, each made by the composer at a different period in his life. In addition, two versions of the symphony were published during Bruckner's lifetime, yet neither of these publications corresponds exactly to any of the three manuscript versions.

There is an early Bruckner Symphony in D Minor, composed in 1864, which the composer ultimately came to regard as an apprentice work that should not be performed. He called it his Symphony Number 0. He started to revise it in 1869 but left off that task. Eventually some parts of the Symphony Number 0 found their way into the Third Symphony.

Bruckner greatly admired Wagner. His early symphonies were obviously cast under the influence of the Bayreuth master. In the Third Symphony the imprint of Wagner went beyond mere influence, however. Bruckner paid homage by quoting parts of two of Wagner's music dramas: *Die Walküre* and *Tristan und Isolde.* Bruckner gathered up his courage and wrote to Wagner, requesting an interview. As Wagner never replied, Bruckner, tenacious though shy, resolved to pay Wagner a visit. He showed up one day in September 1873 in Bayreuth, armed with the score of the recently completed Second Symphony and portions of the Third. Perhaps he hoped that he would find a champion in Wagner, who would help him secure performances: the Second Symphony had been rehearsed by the Vienna Philharmonic and declared unplayable.

At first Wagner refused to see this unknown composer who impudently knocked at his door, but eventually he acquiesced. He was not particularly impressed by the Second, but when he took up the score of the unfinished Third, he became very excited. Bruckner timidly asked him if he would accept the dedication of the work, and

Wagner, after studying the score further, agreed to the honor. Bruckner was overjoyed at meeting his idol, receiving praise from him, and having the dedication accepted. In his excitement Bruckner got confused and the following day could not remember which symphony Wagner had accepted. He sent Wagner a hastily written card: "Symphony in D Minor, where the trumpet begins the theme? Anton Bruckner." Wagner jotted down at the bottom of the card, "Yes! Yes! Best wishes! Richard Wagner," and sent it back. From then on the symphony was known as the *Wagner* Symphony.

Bruckner's alliance with Wagner proved to be of no help politically. Wagner represented the avant garde, and his music was deeply resented in Vienna. The fight against Wagner was led by the powerful critic Eduard Hanslick. Bruckner, by allying himself publicly with Wagner, incurred the wrath of the previously supportive Hanslick.

The Third Symphony was completed on the last day of 1873. Two days later Bruckner began his Fourth. The flow of his lyricism was nearly constant, despite increasing difficulties securing performances and recognition. Conductor Otto Dessof, who had pronounced the Second Symphony impossible, cancelled a scheduled performance of the Third in 1874. Bruckner tried again the following year to interest the Vienna Philharmonic in performing an "improved version" of the symphony, but it was rejected. It is likely that the conservative Viennese musical establishment would have nothing to do with a work that did not have Hanslick's stamp of approval.

Bruckner decided to revise the symphony thoroughly in 1876. He removed all the Wagner quotations, feeling that such an obvious gesture of allegiance was detracting from recognition of his own originality. He also felt that the huge length of the work was making conductors timid about bringing it before their audiences, so he shortened it from its original 2056 to 1815 measures. Johann Herbeck now agreed to conduct the work with the Vienna orchestra, but he died unexpectedly. The performance was cancelled, but finally the Philharmonic agreed to let Bruckner conduct the work himself on 16 December 1877.

Bruckner's bad luck continued. He was neither an effective conductor nor did he have an engaging personality on the podium. The orchestra was as hostile as the public. The audience gradually walked out during the performance, and at the end the orchestra immediately exited, leaving the shattered composer alone on stage to receive the derisive laughter and antagonistic hissing of the few audience members who had remained to the end. There were, however, cheers from high in the balcony, where a group of students — among them the 17-year-old Gustav Mahler — heard the work as a masterpiece it is. (It is interesting to note how the trio of the third movement anticipates several of Mahler's folk-like symphonic dance movements.)

The composer's fortunes began to change, however, when Theodore Raettig, trusting his own musical instincts and disregarding Hanslick's harsh review, decided to publish the symphony. Bruckner made a few changes, and the symphony appeared in print in 1878 in its second version. The publication sat on the shelf, however. There were no further performances.

Bruckner returned to the Third again in 1888. He had just received another devastating rejection. Hermann Levi, who had been a staunch supporter of Bruckner's music, refused to conduct the new Eighth Symphony. As he was despondent and unable to compose, Bruckner turned to extensive revisions of several earlier works. Franz Schalk, a conductor, and his brother Joseph, a pianist, urged the composer to revise the Third Symphony, making it still shorter. Franz Schalk himself suggested certain cuts, which Bruckner accepted, although the composer refused the most extensive cut, preferring to compose a new passage. Several sections were replaced, with the result that the Third Symphony acquired several passages written in the style of the Eighth Symphony. This curiously amalgamated version, which brought the total length down to 1644 measures, was to be published by Raettig. Mahler, hearing of Bruckner's intention to revise the Third again and knowing full well that Bruckner's revisions tended to introduce more problems than they solved, persuaded Bruckner to have the second version reprinted. Bruckner agreed and demanded that Raettig destroy the plates that had already been engraved. No sooner had the long-suffering Raettig complied than the brothers Schalk convinced Bruckner to go ahead with the revision. The third and final version appeared in print in 1890. It was conducted by Hans Richter on 21 December 1890, this time to tumultuous applause. Bruckner was called out for twelve bows.

Hanslick's review was as scathing as ever, but Bruckner's fame seems to have been established. He began to pursue an old dream: to obtain an honorary doctorate. As Austrian universities did not grant the Ph.D. in music, Bruckner had to search for other institutions. He was refused by several American universities, where he was quite unknown. Finally, the University of Vienna broke with tradition and awarded him an honorary Doctor of Philosophy in 1891.

Bruckner scholars often criticize the Third Symphony because of alleged problems of form. The sources of these problems are undoubtedly the revisions and cuts in the second and third versions. The original version, which Wagner had praised, was never performed nor published during the composer's lifetime. This first version, the longest of Bruckner's symphonies, remained unknown to those who criticized the symphony's pacing and proportions. In fact, the form of the Third as originally conceived is quite successful.

Performances of the symphony were usually of the third version until the second was reprinted in 1950. The first version, with its quotations from Wagner, had been searched out and readied for publication in 1944 by Robert Haas, but this edition was destroyed during the Second World War. It was possible to piece together enough of Haas' work for a performance of the original version by Joseph Keilberth in Dresden in 1946, but it apparently remained unperformed thereafter until the International Bruckner Society published the work in 1977. Now authentic publications of all three versions are available, and conductors may choose among them.

Symphony Number 4 in E-Flat Major, *Romantic*
Bewegt, nicht zu schnell
Andante, quasi allegretto
Scherzo: Bewegt. Trio: Nicht zu schnell. Scherzo
Bewegt, doch nicht zu schnell

The Romantic *Symphony was begun on 2 January 1874 and completed in November 1874. Bruckner worked on revisions between January 1878 and June 1879. It was first performed by conductor Hans Richter in Vienna in 1881. More revisions were made in 1881 and 1886.*

The history of Bruckner's Fourth Symphony is as complicated and confused as that of his Third. There are no fewer than five versions. (1) Bruckner first composed the Fourth in 1874, while he was revising the recently completed Third Symphony. The original version was never performed or published. (2) He rewrote the symphony between January and September 1878. Then, in December, he replaced the scherzo with a completely new movement, the one that we know today. Between November 1879 and June 1880 he completely recast the finale. The resulting version was performed by Hans Richter in Vienna in 1881. (3) Bruckner made small revisions after hearing the work, in preparation for another performance in 1881 conducted by Felix Mottl in Karlsruhe. This version was published by the Bruckner Society in 1936. (4) The composer again revised the work in 1886, this time for a performance in New York by Anton Seidl. This version has minor changes in about 140 measures (7% of the total); the only major alteration is the quotation of the main motive from the first movement in the last bars of the finale (strangely orchestrated so that it is quite difficult to hear). The Bruckner Society also published this version. (5) In 1886–87 Bruckner's friends Franz Schalk and Ferdinand Löwe made an extensive revision of the Fourth Symphony, which was

performed in 1888 by Hans Richter in Vienna. This version was published in 1890 and became the only publication available for performance for many years.

The totally spurious (5) has not been totally supplanted by the
publication of two versions approved by the composer, (3) and (4). In
1954 a new edition of (5) was printed, freed from obvious errors.
Schalk and Löwe, the first editors of (5), were no doubt trying to help
their friend attain more performances and greater recognition, but
they in fact mutilated his conception. They made drastic cuts in the
scherzo and finale, and they completely altered the orchestration.
These editors were deeply influenced by the music of Wagner, as was
Bruckner, but their understanding of Brukner's art was superficial.
Thus they changed Bruckner's scoring to make it sound less stark and
more sumptuous — a quality surely more appropriate for Wagner
than for Bruckner. Hans Redlich, editor of the 1954 republication of
the Schalk-Löwe edition, gives examples of the questionable orchestration: "It is difficult to believe that Bruckner could have sanctioned
the blatant sonorities of piccolo-flute and cymbals, suddenly and er-
ratically introduced for the first time in movement IV. . . . Both instruments introduce an element of theatricality, totally alien to
Bruckner's world of sonorities. Equally suspicious are the *pp* cymbals
(à la *Lohengrin*) . . . and the effect of muted horns."

There are only two authentic versions: (3) and (4). Which of these
represents Bruckner's final thoughts? Actually, it is possible to answer this question with reasonable certainty. Bruckner made a new
copy of (3) in 1890, the year of the publication of (5). No one knows
for sure why the composer went to the huge effort of recopying his
score, but perhaps this act was a protest against the emasculation of
the symphony by Schalk and Löwe. He had acquiesced in the publication of (5), but he must have disapproved. He refused to give the
publisher written authorization. When he chose to make a new copy
in reaction to the publication of (5), Bruckner went back to (3) rather
than to (4). This fact indicates that his final preference must have
been for (3).

Today three versions are in print: (3), (4), and (5). Different conductors choose to perform different editions, and many decide to
make their own versions, borrowing from each of the three publications. Thus it is possible to hear two performances of Bruckner's
Fourth Symphony in which the music itself is quite different.

One of the reasons Bruckner was willing to allow revisions (by
himself and others) of his symphonies was that he desperately craved
recognition. He thought that proper retouching — especially if it involved cuts — would increase the likelihood of performance. Again
and again he was frustrated, yet he kept on composing, revising, and

submitting his symphonies to conductors. He kept a diary that chronicles his repeated rejections. When he did receive a performance, he was deeply grateful — even if it was a poor reading of a truncated version.

Hans Richter was a prominent conductor in Vienna. He was not a close friend of Bruckner, but he believed in his music. When Richter agreed to premiere the Fourth Symphony, the composer was elated. Bruckner had had so little experience in the social world of musicians that he did not know how to show his gratitude. In his naïveté he demonstrated his appreciation in touchingly inappropriate ways. At a rehearsal the conductor asked the composer to clarify what a particular note was, and Bruckner replied that it did not matter — Richter could choose whatever note he wanted! Later Bruckner actually offered Richter a tip! The conductor recalled, "For the first time I conducted a Bruckner symphony, at rehearsal. Bruckner was an old man then. His works were performed hardly anywhere. When the symphony was over, Bruckner came to me. He was radiant with enthusiasm and happiness. I felt him put something into my hand. 'Take it, and drink a mug of beer to my health.'" Richter did not want to insult Bruckner, so he accepted the coin. He had it attached to his watch chain, as a "memento of a day when I wept."

Richter's performance was well received, which was quite unusual for a Bruckner symphony. As a result there were further performances of the Fourth. It was the first Bruckner work to be presented in America. It was done in New York twice within a year, by Walter Damrosch and Anton Seidl. Its success led to further performances of Bruckner's works in this country. The *Te Deum* received its United States premiere in 1892 in Cincinnati, which also became the first American city to hear the Ninth Symphony (in 1904, eight years after the composer's death).

After completing it (the first time), Bruckner named his Fourth Symphony the *Romantic*. No one knows why he singled out this work from his eleven symphonies for a descriptive title. There is nothing particularly programmatic about the piece. Its harmonies and melodies are no more romantic than those of any of his other symphonies, and the piece seems as far removed from descriptive music as anything he ever wrote. Perhaps he was referring to the almost pastoral character of the music. Once the composer was asked what the title meant, and his reply was so out of character (for the man and for the music) that it must be taken as a joke, as a satire on overly descriptive music: "A citadel of the Middle Ages. Daybreak. Reveille is sounded from the tower. The gates open. Knights on proud chargers leap forth. The magic of nature surrounds them." On another occasion the composer was less whimsical. Asked what he had in mind while writing the finale, he replied, "I do not know myself what I had in mind."

The pastoral mood is present from the beginning, where a solo horn intones the principal theme over hushed string tremolos. This theme is destined to dominate the movement, as is the horn. The symphony is, in fact, almost a horn concerto. Another pervasive element is the "Bruckner" rhythm of two quarter notes followed by a quarter-note triplet: 1-2/1-2-3.

Bruckner specialist Robert Simpson feels that the slow movement "has something of the veiled funeral march about it, as if it were dreamt; sometimes we seem close to it, even involved, sometimes we seem to see it from so great a distance that it appears almost to stand still. It is hard to explain subjectively the uncannily poised nature of this movement." The beautiful opening cello theme, with an almost Schubertian grace, is actually a transformation of the first movement's horn tune. When this melody returns on the horn, the correspondence is unmistakable.

The pastoral character of the music is most obvious in the scherzo. The horns, still prominent, now sound hunting calls, especially prominent at the beginning, where they are accompanied (as at the beginning of the first movement) by string tremolos. These fanfares are based on the 1-2/1-2-3 rhythm. The rustic simplicity of the brief trio — reminiscent of the Austrian folk dance known as a *Ländler* — completes the pastoral image.

Like the first and third movements, the finale begins with a horn melody (with clarinets) over a string accompaniment (featuring tremolos), building to an enormous *tutti*. Before this *tutti* has run its course, the main theme of the first movement makes a triumphant appearance. The finale, in contrast to the earlier movements, is fragmented and disjointed, a stylistic feature of several other Bruckner symphonies. Schalk and Löwe apparently felt that this characteristic was a defect, and they made extensive cuts in an attempt to graft an artificial continuity onto a fundamentally discontinuous piece. While some of their connections are smooth, others are ludicrously incongruous. Their version of this movement, more than their revisions of the other parts of the symphony, is a travesty. Now that Bruckner's original intentions can be heard, we can understand the power that accumulates throughout this massive mosaic that ends the Fourth Symphony.

Symphony Number 5 in B-Flat Major
Adagio. Allegro. Adagio. Allegro
Adagio
Molto vivace
Adagio. Allegro moderato

The Fifth Symphony was composed between 14 February 1875 and 16 May 1876. Bruckner started a revision early in 1877, which he completed on 4 January 1878. Franz Schalk conducted the first performance on 8 April 1894 in Graz.

When in 1932 the original versions of Bruckner's symphonies began to be published and performed, the musical world was astounded at the differences between the revisions that had been accepted as Bruckner's music and what the composer had actually intended. Numerous distortions had been introduced into his scores by well-meaning editors and by Bruckner himself. As he lacked self-confidence and was highly self-critical, the composer repeatedly revised his works, often to their detriment. Some compositions, such as the Third Symphony, exist in as many as four different versions. There are five versions of the Fourth. Bruckner all too readily yielded to demands from conductors for cuts. He wrote to conductor Felix Weingartner, for example, concerning a performance of the Eighth Symphony: "Please apply radical cuts to the finale, as indicated, for it would be much too long and is valid only for a later age."

Now that the "later age" has arrived, we are faced with some 34 published versions of the nine symphonies. Bruckner's first conceptions were sometimes naïve, yet his final opinions were also not always reliable, since many years often separated the first version and the final revision. In addition, as he was an organist with little practical orchestral experience, the composer's command of scoring came slowly and painstakingly. Since performances of his symphonies were infrequent, he only occasionally had the opportunity to judge his orchestrations by actually hearing them. Thus some of the revised instrumentation suggested by such conductors as Franz Schalk, Joseph Schalk, and Ferdinand Löwe actually does improve the sound. But many of their other revisions all but destroy the sense of the music. The raw power of Bruckner's language does not survive being artifically refined or prettified.

No sooner had Bruckner completed the Fifth Symphony than he

began to revise it, completing the procedure two years later, in 1878. These revisions were not substantive. Even in this improved state, the score remained unperformed for many years. As the composer never returned to it, it might be assumed that editorial problems of the Fifth are less vexing than with other Bruckner symphonies. Not so. Other hands than the composer's meddled with the piece.

A performance of a two-piano reduction by Joseph Schalk and Franz Zottman in 1887 kindled interest in the possibility of an orchestral performance of this massive work. In 1894 Franz Schalk dared to conduct the piece in Graz. But he was unwilling to use Bruckner's score. He felt obliged to introduce huge revisions — cuts, re-orchestrations, changed rhythms, and so forth. Schalk's motives were above reproach: he wanted the symphony to be appreciated, yet feared that it was too large and too austere in its original form. He made it sound, in effect, like the sumptuous music of Wagner, which was in great vogue at the time. Schalk added an extra brass choir at the crowning chorale in the finale — a spectacular effect, no doubt, but hardly appropriate to the symphony or its composer. The conductor removed 122 of the 635 measures of the last movement, in addition to making cuts in the other movements. As a result, the symphony lost about twenty minutes, the length of many entire symphonies by earlier composers. There is hardly a measure in the Bruckner Fifth that Schalk left untouched.

The composer was two years from his death at the time of Schalk's performance. Bruckner was too sick to travel to the performance, and he was too busy trying to complete the Ninth Symphony to be bothered with Schalk's changes. He neither approved nor disapproved them, because he never even looked at them. He seemed to have realized, although too late, that time spent reworking old pieces was time taken away from finishing the Ninth.

Schalk believed that he was doing a real service for the music and its composer. He wrote to Bruckner after the performance: "Honored master, you surely must have heard of the enormous impression which your great and wonderful Fifth has made. I can only add that this night will remain among the most wonderful memories in my entire life. Deeply moved, I blissfully felt myself walking in the realms of eternal greatness. No one who has not heard it can imagine the crushing power of the finale. Thus, my dearly beloved master, I lay all my admiration to your feet in ardent enthusiasm and bring hail to him who created such a work."

When the Fifth Symphony was published in 1896, it was printed in Schalk's version. For many years this was the only available edition of the work. Fortunately, the Bruckner Society published the original version of the Fifth (including Bruckner's own minor revisions) in 1939. The Schalk mutilation has now fortunately fallen into disuse.

The Fifth was a major stylistic and technical advance for Bruckner. It is his first unquestionable masterpiece. What in the earlier symphonies sometimes seems mannered, clichéd, or overblown is now invested with unerring emotional power. For the first time Bruckner seems in total control of his slow pacing, frequent pauses, juxtapositions of different material, and block-like construction. Thus the symphony, despite its great length, is taut and economical.

The work is a unified conception, largely because there are implications that operate across the whole span of the symphony. The magnificent slow introduction, for example (no other Bruckner symphony has one), creates an underlying tension that is resolved only in the finale. The introduction presents several independent ideas, starkly separated by silence. They refuse to meet, to mingle, or even to acknowledge one another. This fragmentation resonates throughout the first movement, which is similarly terraced. As the movement progresses, ideas congeal, but Bruckner carefully avoids permitting any melody to spin itself out totally without interruption. In this manner the discontinuous character of the introduction casts its influence over the subsequent allegro: the entire first movement functions as introduction to the symphony.

This situation is different from that in the typical classical symphony, where the first movement, far from being an introduction, is the center of gravity, the emotional core, of the work. But Bruckner's Fifth is a "finale symphony." Because the first movement is an introduction, we are forced to wait until the last movement to discover the essential meaning of the work and to experience complete resolution.

Bruckner reminds us of still unresolved tensions when he opens the finale with the exact same material that begins the symphony (a theme, by the way, that appears in inversion in the middle section of the scherzo movement). Much of the first movement's music shows up again in the finale, but now it participates in a continuous development toward the apotheosis of the symphony, the final chorale. This chorale dispels fragmentation permanently and thus brings resolution.

The similarity of the outer movements is mirrored in the inner movements. They too share opening material, although the mood differs. Thus movements II and III share themes, as do movements I and IV. By contrast, movements I and III are fragmentary, while movements II and IV are continuous. The pairing of moods thus does not correspond to the pairing of melodies.

The symphony is more contrapuntal than most by Bruckner. Shortly after the opening of the second movement, we hear what amounts to two different tempos simultaneously. The most complex counterpoint, however, is found in the finale, and it is because of the resulting intensity that the last movement is the heart of the symphony. After the finale begins with reminiscences of the first two movements, a fugal exposition is heard. The fugue gets swallowed up in a march, however. This march eventually gives way to a chorale, which becomes the basis of a second fugue. This fugue acquires considerable complexity and intensity: at last the music can develop continuously. The themes of both fugues are combined during this development. Eventually the main theme from the first movement joins in for some staggeringly complex triple counterpoint, which is resolved as the chorale comes back full force.

Thus an extraordinary symphony ends. It is extraordinary because of the myriad ways it is integrated and because of the powerful progression from a deceptively simple, mysterious opening in *pizzicato* low strings to the peroration of brass that penetrates the orchestral fabric in the final chorale.

Bruckner knew before he started to compose the Fifth Symphony that a performance was unlikely. The First, Second, and Third Symphonies had repeatedly been rejected by the Vienna Philharmonic. The Fourth Symphony was given a trial reading before it too was rejected. It was called "idiotic," and the composer was advised to throw away his manuscripts and try to make a living making piano arrangements of other composers' symphonies.

Bruckner was hurt by these rejections. Because of them his mania for revising his earlier works increased. But he also stubbornly embarked on the composition of the Fifth Symphony.

It was a difficult time for the composer. He was in a precarious financial situation. He had lost one of his teaching positions, and he had to make do with a poorly paid job at the Vienna Conservatory plus a bit of supplemental income from private students.

I have only my place at the Conservatory, on the income from which I find it impossible to exist. I have been compelled to borrow money over and over again, or else accept the alternative of starvation. No one offers me any help. The Minister of Education makes promises but does nothing. If it were not for a few foreigners who are studying with me, I should have to become a beggar. Had I even dreamed of such terrible things, no earthly power could have induced me to come to Vienna. Oh, how happy I would be to return to my old position in Linz!

Finally a friend found him a position teaching piano at a seminary for women teachers. But his gruff country manner was misinterpreted by two students, who accused him publicly of having insulted them. His innocence was proved, but not before the incident was reported in the press. As a result of the unfavorable publicity, he was transferred to the seminary's men's section and his salary was lowered. Soon thereafter his position was abolished.

He applied repeatedly to the University of Vienna for a teaching post, but he was always turned away. The composer naïvely wrote in his letters of application that he wanted the job so that he would have time to compose. The university, understandably, was more interested in people who wanted to spend their time teaching. Finally, with the help of some newspaper publicity (this time favorable), Bruckner did receive a faculty appointment, but it was *unpaid.* So he gained no increase in income but only a decrease in composing time.

Nonetheless, Bruckner enjoyed his post at the university. He liked lecturing, and he appreciated the company of people who were devoted to him and to music. But his finances were still a shambles. He applied for a job as music director of a church, but he was refused. Finally his prospects improved in 1878, when he was elected to membership in the Imperial Chapel, thus becoming eligible for an annual stipend.

With little time to work uninterrupted and with little reason for optimism, Bruckner composed the Fifth Symphony. He dedicated it to Karl von Stremayr, the Minister of Education who had tried to obtain for him a paid position at the university. Bruckner was right about the future of the symphony. It had to wait 15 years for a performance, and he never heard it. But the composer was resilient. He simply went on composing, one symphony after the next.

Symphony Number 6 in A Major
Maestoso
Adagio: sehr feierlich
Scherzo: nicht schnell. Trio: langsam. Scherzo
Bewegt, doch nicht zu schnell

The Sixth Symphony was begun in August or September 1879 and completed on 3 September 1881. The two middle movements were first performed by Wilhelm Jahn and the Vienna Philharmonic on 11 February 1883. The complete symphony was first heard in a version drastically cut and revised by Gustav Mahler, who led the Vienna Philharmonic on 26 February 1899.

Bruckner was obsessed with numbers. He carefully numbered the barlines in his scores. He kept track of how many measures each phrase he wrote contained and how many times he repeated various figures in his symphonies. His fascination went beyond music. He would count the statues he passed during his long walks, and, if he suspected he had missed one, he would retrace his steps to check his counting. He tried to find out how many of various things there were, such as municipal towers in Vienna. He also kept lists of the numbers of prayers he said each day, the number of times he repeated particular prayers, how often he had danced with certain young women at balls, and to how many women he had felt attracted.

The latter list grew considerably during his vacation in 1880. Rarely a traveler, Bruckner did make a summer journey while working on the first movement of his Sixth Symphony. He visited Zürich, Geneva, Chamoix, and Berne, where he performed on the cathedral organ. He also went to Oberammergau, where he saw the Passion Plays. He was charmed by a girl named Marie Bartl, who played one of the Daughters of Jerusalem. He waited for her after the performance, introduced himself, and proceeded to spend the evening with her at her aunt's house. Once again he was in love; once again he added the name of a young woman to his list; once again he proposed marriage to a teenager. Bartl was seventeen and Bruckner was fifty-six. She was flattered, but he was more like a grandfather than a lover. Her parents were horrified. The marriage never took place, although Bartl did continue to correspond with the composer for about a year. Bruckner was hurt, but he never learned his lesson. Almost to his death he continued to add to his list of young women to whom he had proposed.

Bruckner was a deeply inward man and, as this incident shows, not particularly adept with social conventions. His inner and outer lives hardly touched one another. Thus no critic tried to find in the Sixth Symphony reflections of his thwarted love or of the wondrous Swiss mountains he saw for the first time on his trip. Most other composers, particularly of the nineteenth century, suffer frequent attempts to interpret their music in terms of their lives. But Bruckner's inspirations came from deep within himself, often from his unquestioning religious faith.

The only performance of the Sixth that took place during his lifetime was given by the Vienna Philharmonic in 1883. Wilhelm Jahn conducted the middle two movements on the first Philharmonic concert ever to include a piece by Bruckner. He was so excited that he absent-mindedly showed up for the dress rehearsal wearing unmatched shoes.

Brahms attended this performance and applauded enthusiastically. But Eduard Hanslick, the powerful critic Bruckner both feared and despised, sat through the performance in stony silence and then wrote a typically scathing review. Critic Max Kalbeck wrote, "It is as though a pack of wolves met on Walpurgis Night, such stamping and raging, roaring and screaming goes wildly on. If the future can relish such a chaotic piece of music, with sounds echoing from a hundred cliffs, we wish that future to be far away from us."

The Sixth Symphony is the only work (apart from the unfinished Ninth Symphony) that Bruckner never revised. It did, like most of his symphonies, suffer at the hands of well-meaning but misguided editors, but for once Bruckner himself was not one of them.

The first performance of the entire symphony took place three years after the composer's death. Gustav Mahler led the Vienna Philharmonic in a version that cut out huge portions and reorchestrated much of what remained. Mahler's decision to tamper with Bruckner's score is curious, since the Sixth is one of the shorter Bruckner symphonies, since Mahler himself was a composer of gigantic symphonies and surely could have appreciated the importance of the Sixth's proportions, and since he had earlier been instrumental in resurrecting the original, unrevised version of Bruckner's Third Symphony. In 1899 the Sixth was published in an edition by Bruckner's former student Cyril Hynais. This version, which was subsequently reprinted several times, contained many unfortunate revisions, had been shortened, and included suggestions for additional cuts.

In 1919 musicologist Georg Göhler became suspicious while examining this published version of the Sixth Symphony. He had heard rumors that the publications of the Bruckner symhonies varied considerably from their original manuscripts. Göhler urged scholars to study the manuscripts and to correct discrepancies. Since the two main editors of Bruckner's symphonies — Franz Schalk and Ferdinand Löwe — were still alive, Göhler consulted them. To his astonishment, they claimed that an investigation of the manuscripts was unnecessary, as all revisions had been done under the composer's supervision or at least with his consent. This could hardly have been the case with the Sixth, however, as it was edited for publication (not by Schalk or Löwe) only after Bruckner's death. Rightly suspecting that their professional ethics were being questioned, Schalk and Löwe refused to cooperate. Furthermore, several manuscripts were (conveniently?) missing. An elaborate series of intrigues ensued, involving charges and countercharges of slander and libel. As late as 1927 another *revised* version of the Sixth appeared. The scandal erupted in full force in the early 1930s, with the performance of the original versions of the Fifth and Ninth Symphonies. Schalk and

Löwe had by this time died, but their tenuous position was perpetuated by conductors who had known the Bruckner symphonies only in the revised editions. With the establishment of the Bruckner Society, the musical world made a commitment to finding, publishing, and encouraging performances of Bruckner's unedited originals. In 1935 and again (with minor corrections) in 1952, the Society issued the original version of the Sixth Symphony. Today only this score is performed.

The Sixth has always been the least known of Bruckner's mature symphonies. Writing on a record jacket in the early 1950s, Paul Affelder offered the extraordinary revelation that the Sixth had been performed in America only "once or twice" since its American premiere in 1912. The reason for the relative obscurity of the symphony is hard to fathom. It is no more abstruse, no more difficult, and no longer than other Bruckner symphonies. Actually, it is readily approachable and, frankly, on a higher artistic level than some of his earlier, better known works.

The composer's favorite rhythm, known as the "Bruckner rhythm," consists of a beat divided in a duple manner followed by a beat divided in a triple manner: 1-2/1-2-3. "Duple" refers to subdivisions into halves and quarters; "triple" refers to thirds or sixths. The composer used the Bruckner rhythm in many compositions. In the Sixth Symphony it is more than an interesting detail. It is possible to understand the entire symphony in terms of the interplay and contrast between duple and triple rhythms.

The Sixth Symphony's version of the Bruckner rhythm is the first thing heard. The violins play a repeated note in alternating duple and triple patterns. The duple in this case is a dotted figure (a dotted eighth-note followed by a sixteenth-note); the triple rhythm is a simple eighth-note triplet. The importance of this rhythm is apparent because it is repeated again and again in some part of the orchestra 92 times in succession. A figure that prominent is bound to have consequences.

We begin to understand the implications of the duple/triple opposition when the second theme arrives. Over a steady triplet bass line, we hear a decidedly duple melody. The bass line seems so regular that we almost accept it as the beat, rather than as a triplet against the beat. If we hear the melody in terms of this triplet beat, the effect is strangely unsettling, as if there are two different tempos going on simultaneously. Bruckner subsequently explores all manner of duple/triple interactions, some obvious and some subtle. At the climax of the development section, with the full orchestra playing, the original version of the Bruckner rhythm, again in the strings, punctuates the texture like an insistent Morse code message. The conflict between duple and triple rhythms continues through to the triplet-dominated triumphant ending.

The remaining movements explore one rhythm or the other, rather than their conflict. In the beautifully lyric adagio, for example, the movement is half over before a single triple rhythm is heard. Even the meter is thoroughly duple: 4/4 time heard as two groups of two beats per measure. The triple rhythms, when they arrive (after a complete silence) as soft string undulations accompanying an oboe melody, have the effect of opening up the music. The mood becomes expansive and free. At the recapitulation the triple rhythms disappear, never again to return during the slow movement.

If the adagio is a study in duple, the scherzo is — appropriately — a study in triple. There are three beats per measure, and often each beat is subdivided into a triplet. We do hear triple and duple rhythms simultaneously, but the effect is not conflict, as in the first movement, but rather cooperation. The slow middle section is exclusively duple, utilizing dotted rhythms reminiscent of the first movement.

The finale, like the adagio, concentrates on duple rhythms, sometimes dotted and sometimes even. When the rhythm that opens the symphony returns toward the end, we understand it in terms of the rhythmic procedures of the entire piece. It is more than simply one of the finale's quotations of earlier movements. It is heard as the source and the goal of the rhythmic language of the symphony.

There is more to the Sixth Symphony than its rhythmic activity. Its massive climaxes, lovely melodies, powerful drives, subtle modulations, and beautiful harmonies make it a special piece. The rhythmic procedures provide a scaffolding that unifies, in a most intriguing and original manner, the work's melodies, harmonies, and textures.

Symphony Number 7 in E Major
Allegro moderato
Adagio: Sehr feierlich und sehr langsam
Scherzo: Sehr schnell. Trio: Etwas langsamer.
    Scherzo
Bewegt, doch nicht schnell

The Seventh Symphony was begun in September 1881 and completed on 5 September 1883. Artur Nikisch conducted the first performance on 30 December 1884 in Leipzig.

The external events in Bruckner's life were seldom noteworthy. He composed one large symphony after another, with rarely time out between them (he started the Seventh within days of completing the Sixth). He repeatedly suffered frustrations in his attempts to find performances for these compositions. When they were played, critics usually condemned both them and their creator in the harshest terms. Audiences were often equally disapproving. The composer reluctantly resorted to cuts and revisions, sometimes on his own initiative yet often at the urging of friends, to try to make the symphonies more approachable.

With the Seventh Symphony Bruckner's fortunes changed. It was performed readily and often, it was hailed by audiences and by most critics, and consequently Bruckner felt no need to revise it extensively. It became a turning point for the formerly despondent composer. It opened the door to the international fame he coveted.

Bruckner composed the scherzo first. It is the only movement in the symphony to adhere to classical sonata form principles. Next he wrote the opening movement, with its long, arching first theme. He then turned his attention to the adagio. At this time he heard of the poor health of his idol, Richard Wagner. He thought of the adagio as a memorial for the Bayreuth master whose music had always been his inspiration. Bruckner wrote to his friend Felix Mottl, "I felt very sad. I did not think the master would live much longer. Then I conceived the adagio in C-sharp minor." He had composed most of the movement, up to its large climax, when he received the news of Wagner's death. He then wrote the serene coda "in memory of the immortal and dearly beloved master who has departed this life." Last he composed the relatively brief finale.

Bruckner's friend Josef Schalk showed the finished score to the young conductor Artur Nikisch. Schalk reported, "We had hardly finished the first movement of the Seventh when Nikisch, usually so sedate and calm a person, was all fire and flame. . . . 'Since Beethoven there has been nothing that could even approach it!' 'What is Schumann in comparison?' That is how he talked all the time. . . . He said, 'From this moment I regard it as my duty to work for Bruckner's recognition.'"

Nikisch kept his word. In the intervening months, while he learned the score, he played the work at the piano several times for influential critics, preparing them for the orchestral performance. This attention paid off handsomely, although Bruckner, accustomed to harsh treatment from critics, still feared the worst.

The premiere took place in Leipzig. Although he had lived in Vienna for most of his life, Bruckner was unable to secure performances there because of the powerful critic Eduard Hanslick, who detested Bruckner's music. Hanslick saw the musical world as divided into two camps: the Wagnerians and the Brahmsians. He praised the latter as much as he reviled the former. Bruckner belonged to the Wagnerian camp. It may be hard today to understand the influence wielded by one critic, but it seems that he all but dictated what would and would not be played.

The new symphony met with success in Leipzig. When a second performance took place in Munich under the baton of Hermann Levi, the success was still greater. Bruckner's fame began to spread, and more performances of the Seventh Symphony were projected. Even the Vienna Philharmonic considered a performance. Bruckner, still sensitive to abuse from Vienna critics, asked the orchestra to cancel the performance "for reasons which arise from the sad local situation, referring to the criticisms of authorities which come my way and may damage my recent successes in Germany." It is a sad situation when critics are so vicious that a composer feels he must cancel performances.

Vienna did eventually hear the symphony, when Hans Richter conducted it on 21 March 1886. The public was wild with enthusiasm, but Hanslick and other critics under his influence reacted as Bruckner had predicted. Hanslick wrote, "The music is antipathetic to me and appears to me unnaturally exaggerated, sick, and perverted." Another Viennese critic, Gustav Dömpke, wrote, "We recoil in horror before this rotting odor which rushes into our nostrils from the disharmonies of this decomposing counterpoint. His imagination is so incurably sick and warped that anything like regularity in chord progressions and period structure simply do not exist for him. Bruckner composes like a drunkard . . . , [with] an excessively ugly mixture of coarseness and over-finesse." If such abuse had been printed even a year earlier, it would have prevented further performances of the symphony. But the successes in Leipzig and Munich had already been widely reported, and Vienna was no longer able to dictate the future of a Bruckner symphony. During the same year the Seventh was played in Cologne, Graz, Hamburg, Chicago, New York, and Amsterdam. Bruckner at last achieved the recognition that had long eluded him. He was 62 years old.

Once the Seventh Symphony had had some successful performances, Bruckner wanted to capitalize on his newly won fame by receiving an honorary doctorate in music from a major university. He wrote first to Cambridge University and then to the University of Pennsylvania, with no success. Then, in 1885, a swindler apparently convinced him that, for a price, he could receive a doctorate from the University of Cincinnati. The swindler got his money, and Bruckner sent a letter of application and a copy of his baptismal certificate to the university. Incidentally, it is only from this copy that we know that the composer's full name was Joseph Anton Bruckner. There was no doctorate forthcoming from Cincinnati. Finally, in 1891, after his successes had at last begun to quiet the Vienna critics, Bruckner received his honorary degree from the University of Vienna.

The Seventh, like most Bruckner symphonies, is quite long. The music states right from the outset what its proportions are to be. The opening expansive melodic line arches upward in a long span — 21 measures — taking the cellos into their high register. This enormous melody is repeated, with a fuller orchestration featuring high winds and strings. We are two minutes into the movement before we hear anything other than this melody. In a classical period symphony, we might be a third or a quarter through the movement at the two-minute mark, but here we have barely begun. Thus we already know we are dealing with a work of massive size.

The first contrasting idea, which follows in the winds, also moves upward. There is a reason for the yearning upward thrust in both of the first two themes: later in the movement, when the opening theme is inverted (that is, turned upside down), we readily recognize a new direction for an old theme.

For a movement as long as this one, two thematic ideas would hardly suffice. The third melody is a more sprightly, almost dance-like tune that descends. It is followed by a powerful brass fanfare, which leads to the beginning of a developmental section that introduces the process of inversion.

This development is long and complex. It utilizes all thematic ideas and passes through many different keys, thus creating a sense of restlessness. The music is struggling to return to the opening melody in an unequivocal E major. Bruckner keeps us waiting for this arrival until almost the end, where it comes with serene confidence. With string tremolos as background, the brass intone the theme again and again, as the sonority builds to an organ-like fullness by the end.

The second movement is equally massive. This extended elegy to Wagner rises to two powerful climaxes. It is based on two ideas. The first, heard at the opening in the strings, has a long sweep reminiscent of the first movement's main idea. It grows in intensity until most of the instruments drop out, leaving the high violins playing with great intensity over a brass chord. The music dies down, and then the extraordinarily beautiful, lyrical second idea enters at a faster tempo in the strings. The music alternates and develops these ideas at length, until the enormous second climax occurs in the foreign key of C major. The coda, which was written in reaction to Wagner's death, has a restrained beauty that is a fitting dénouement to this powerful movement.

The scherzo is a simpler piece. Throughout it contains without exception dance-like four-bar groupings. The main scherzo theme is of utmost simplicity: a rising octave and falling fourth and fifth in the trumpet. This motive (there is really not enough of it to call it a melody) is readily susceptible to contrapuntal manipulation. It is overlapped with itself and inverted.

The finale utilizes a regularized, shortened, faster version of the long melody from the opening movement. The second theme is a chorale that, in its continual modulations (changes of key), is a complete contrast to the main idea. The movement ends, as does the first movement, with a long coda on E major building to a wonderfully sonorous closing.

One may wonder why this particular symphony catapulted the composer to fame. How does it differ from his earlier, initially less successful efforts? Sympathetic performance was undoubtedly part of the reason for its success: it was introduced by one of the world's best conductors, who had spent months learning the score. In addition, the work is more obviously unified and continuous than the early symphonies, and hence its form is easier to follow. The melodies have a wonderful lyricism that keeps the music moving along despite long stretches of slow music in each movement. The orchestration is more imaginative than in some of Bruckner's earlier symphonies. For these reasons it is understandable why the first audiences for the Seventh were wildly enthusiastic, calling Bruckner back to the stage again and again. Bruckner's special world of slow-moving intensity, overpowering climaxes, and intimate lyricism nowhere found a more coherent or beautiful statement than in the Seventh Symphony.

Symphony Number 8 in C Minor
Allegro moderato
Scherzo: Allegro moderato. Trio: Langsam.
  Scherzo
Adagio: Feierlich langsam, doch nich schleppend
Feierlich, nicht schnell

The Eighth Symphony was begun in July 1884 and first completed on 10 August 1887. Bruckner revised the work between 4 March 1889 and 10 March 1890. Hans Richter conducted the first performance in Vienna on 18 December 1892.

Bruckner's outward life was as simple and uneventful as his inner life was complex and turbulent. He had no adventures, no love life, few travels. He was a simple country man, out of place during his later years in the sophisticated metropolis of Vienna. He had a few friends and he was very religious (he was said to possess only two books, the Bible and a biography of Napoléon, both of which he read again and again), but he existed for and through his teaching and composing. Internally he lived with a single-minded, all-consuming passion for one thing: his symphonies. He worked intensively on each of these monumental works, and when he finished it he went on to the next. His pride was fierce, as can be seen in his careful noting of the exact dates on which he finished each movement. He labored on behalf of his symphonies, even after he had finished them, by trying to get them performed and by endlessly revising them.

His pride in his music was contradicted by huge insecurities. Whenever one of the symphonies was badly received or whenever a conductor refused to perform one, Bruckner went into a depression. He was obsessed with achieving recognition. Thus he was all too susceptible to well-meaning but ill-founded suggestions from friends who wanted to make the symphonies more palatable by cutting and revising. His insecurity confronted his pride when he made or supervised these revisions: in the interests of having his works performed, he readily acquiesced to his friends' shortening and thereby mutilating them, always hoping that his *own* conceptions would be favored by posterity.

As a result of this constant conflict between Bruckner's outer calm and inner turmoil, between his pride and his insecurity, we find that the greatest dramas of his life center around the often-repeated scenarios of compulsive revisions. Nothing in the composer's routine outward existence can rival his emotions as the history of each symphony played itself out, from the first to the last times it was "finished." Bruckner's biography is the story of composing, revising, searching for performances, revising again, elation or depression over critics' and audiences' responses, and revising still again. It should not be surprising, therefore, that program notes for Bruckner symphonies often deal with the history of revisions, a topic that with most other composers comprises musicological trivia of little interest to listeners.

The "Bruckner Problem" continued for more than a half century after the composer's death, as conductors and scholars searched for and argued about the most appropriate version of each symphony. The debate over which revisions were made by or sanctioned by Bruckner, plus the argument over which score represents Bruckner's final intentions, led to sometimes acrimonious disagreements. And these disagreements have in turn led to the existence, for some symphonies, of several quite different, equally authentic versions. The history of no symphony is more problematic than that of Bruckner's Eighth.

His previous work, the Seventh, had brought him long wished for recognition. Its many well-received performances excited the composer, who started the Eighth in the highest of spirits. Reports of further performances of the Seventh and other symphonies kept arriving, and Bruckner at long last knew he had achieved widespread recognition. He was decorated by the Emperor, and he received a series of grants as well.

After three and a half years of work, he completed the Eighth in August 1887, and he looked forward to new triumphs when it was performed. He sent the score to Hermann Levi, who had conducted a successful performance of the Seventh in Munich two years earlier. Bruckner's cover letter was optimistic: "I simply cannot describe my feeling of elation at the prospect of its being performed under your masterly direction." While he awaited Levi's reply, he began to sketch the Ninth Symphony.

Levi believed in Bruckner, but he could not muster any enthusiasm for the new work, which was totally different from the popular Seventh. Levi asked their mutual friend Joseph Schalk to break the news gently to the aging composer that the Eighth would not be played. Schalk reported back, "It is hardly surprising that Professor Bruckner has taken your verdict very badly. He is still very unhappy about it and refuses to listen to a word of comfort. . . . I only hope he will soon calm down and follow your advice by attempting a revision, which, by the way, he has already started for the first movement. For the time being, of course, it would be better if he stopped work on it because he is desperately worked up and has lost all confidence in himself."

Because of Levi's refusal to program the Eighth, Bruckner went into a depression which precluded his continuing work on the Ninth for the next three years (with the result that he left that symphony unfinished at his death). Instead, he embarked on a series of largely disastrous and usually unnecessary revisions of earlier symphonies. He spent a full year revising the Eighth, with Schalk's occasional assistance. If Bruckner was trying to make the work acceptable to Levi, he probably worked in vain. The conductor had found the conception of the entire work, not just of certain passages, problematic. Nonetheless, Bruckner made extensive revisions, including: (1) an enlarged orchestra, with triple instead of double woodwinds plus harp(s); (2) a new ending for the first movement, soft rather than loud; (3) a completely new trio for the scherzo; (4) the climax of the slow movement recast in another key; (5) extensive changes in orchestration; and (6) about 150 measures deleted.

By the time Bruckner completed these revisions, Levi was no longer conducting in Munich. The composer instead approached Felix Weingartner, conductor at Mannheim. Weingartner, although not particularly fond of Bruckner's music, agreed to try the symphony. The composer wrote a letter that reveals his pathetic insecurity:

"How fares the Eighth? Have there been any rehearsals yet? How does it sound? I do recommend that you shorten the finale severely, as indicated. It would be much too long and is valid only for later times and for a circle of friends and connoisseurs."

The Mannheim performance never took place. Weingartner was appointed to conduct the Berlin Philharmonic and left Mannheim hurriedly. He assured Bruckner, vaguely and emptily, that he would perform some work of his in Berlin "as soon as possible."

Thus it fell to Vienna to hear the first performance of the Eighth. Bruckner had always dreaded having his music performed in the city where he lived, because the local music critics, led by the powerful and vindictive Eduard Hanslick, invariably condemned his work, no matter what the public reaction. Since the critics wielded considerable influence over what was performed, Bruckner had all but given up on Viennese performances. Nonetheless, the composer decided to take his chances, and he allowed Hans Richter to introduce the Eighth in December 1892. Hanslick was true to form, although he did mention the public's "tumultuous acclamations, waving handkerchiefs, innumerous calls, laurel wreaths, and so forth. No doubt whatever, for Bruckner the concert was a triumph." But his own evaluation spoke of "unrelieved gloom," "the misery of dream-troubled cats," "hideous length," and "interminable, disorganized, and violent" music; the critic concluded that "it is not impossible that the future belongs to this nightmarish . . . style, a future which we therefore do not envy."

Hanslick confounded Bruckner a few weeks later by sending him a New Year's card, signed "To my sincere friend." Yet, two weeks after that, the critic published another article condemning Bruckner's music.

The revisions of the Eighth Symphony must be given special consideration. With most other Bruckner symphonies, preference should go to the composer's original version over revisions made by him and/or others years after the works were completed. But, with the Eighth, the revisions were done while the work was still fresh in the composer's mind and before any major style changes had appeared.

The problem of which version of the Eighth to perform would not seem too complicated. There would appear to exist only two choices, the original or the revised score. Furthermore, since the original version was first published in 1972, one would suspect that only recently has there even been a choice. Not so. There is another version, published in 1939, in which editor Robert Haas attempted to combine the two versions by Bruckner.

Haas felt that some of Bruckner's revisions were distinct improvements, while some of the cuts had been done only in an attempt to make the symphony more appealing to conductors. Haas restored 48 of the 150 bars Bruckner and Schalk had removed, and he reverted to some of the original scoring. Haas' successor as editor of the International Bruckner Society's complete edition, Leopold Nowak, rejected his predecessor's work on the grounds that an authentic version could not logically consist of materials drawn from two different sources. Haas' edition, according to Nowak, cannot "be said faithfully to represent Bruckner's own directives." Nowak printed two separate scores (in 1955 and 1972, respectively), each corresponding to one of the Bruckner versions, and advised against using the Haas score at all. Although the composer's revision has been frequently played, Nowak asked that conductors also remember Bruckner's hope that the original version would eventually find favor.

If Bruckner had done his revisions on his own, one might support Nowak's position that only authentic versions should be performed. But Bruckner was, as often, influenced against his better judgement. Some of the changes Schalk suggested (or actually made) are musically questionable, such as truncating a passage from the finale's recapitulation but not the comparable place from the exposition.

The debate over which of the three versions to perform continues. As a curiosity, one might choose the original version (edited by Nowak, 1972); for historical accuracy, one might prefer the Bruckner-Schalk final version (edited by Nowak, 1955); on musical (but historically untenable) grounds one might choose the compromise version (edited by Haas, 1939). Or one might make yet another version, combining aspects of the three published possibilities. Although the orchestral sonority of all three versions is similar, the structural differences are considerable.

Symphony Number 9 in D Minor
Feierlich
Scherzo: Bewegt, lebhaft. Trio: Schnell. Scherzo.
Adagio: Sehr langsam

The Ninth Symphony was begun in August or September 1887. Bruckner was still working on it the day of his death. The first performance of the three completed movements was conducted by Ferdinand Löwe on 11 February 1903.

Bruckner began to compose his final symphony virtually as soon as he had completed the Eighth, yet the Ninth remained unfinished at the composer's death nine years later. Although he always worked meticulously, and although his gigantic symphonies did require long periods of gestation, nine years on a single work was unprecedented. There were several reasons why, despite a fervent wish to complete the symphony, he was unable to do so. His health was declining, and he showed distinct signs of mental instability. One manifestation of his illness was a mania for revising several of his previous symphonies. Furthermore, another fanaticism overtook him and sapped his energy. His devotion to religion, always strong, got out of hand during his final years. His wish to dedicate the Ninth Symphony to God is symptomatic of his obsession. He spent several hours each day in fervent prayer, hours that might more profitably have been spent composing. Ironically, what he prayed for was time — time to finish the D Minor Symphony.

The doctor who attended Bruckner during his declining years reported, "Often I found him on his knees in profound prayer. As it was strictly forbidden to interrupt under these circumstances, I stood by and overheard his naïve, pathetic interpolations into the traditional texts. At times he would suddenly exclaim, 'Dear God, let me get well soon; you see, I need my health to finish the Ninth.'" The composer often said, "If God does not spare me to finish this Symphony, He must take responsibility for its incompleteness." Bruckner's religious fervor is apparent also from the phrases of the Lord's Prayer that he jotted down on several pages of the finale.

The composer suffered another obsession, which intensified during his final years — a macabre fascination with death. His interest went beyond the typical morbidity of an elderly person in failing health. He was drawn not only to death but also to the dead. He made a journey to Bayreuth to pray at the graveside of Richard Wagner, the composer he revered above all others. While there he lost (but later recovered at the police station) the sketches for the Ninth Symphony. Why would a composer bring the only copy of an important work on a long journey to a cemetery? Years earlier, his obsession with the dead had manifested itself in his frantic attempt to catch a glimpse of the remains of Schubert and Beethoven when they were reinterred long after their deaths. Bruckner once rushed to a mortuary to view the charred remains of several people who had perished in a theater fire, and earlier he tried to gain possession of the skull of his teacher and cousin, composer Johann Baptist Weiss. He once contemplated a trip to Mexico for the sole purpose of seeing the body of the slain Emperor Maximilian. The composer's will included detailed instructions for the disposal of his remains.

Bruckner's mental stress intensified shortly after he began the Ninth Symphony. He learned that conductor Hermann Levi would not perform the recently completed Eighth. The composer had been counting on this performance, and he was crushed by Levi's failure to comprehend the work. Bruckner's reaction went beyond all reason, however. He went into a deep depression, contemplated suicide, stopped working on the Ninth Symphony for three (!) years, and embarked on a series of major revisions of the Eighth and earlier symphonies.

One further obsession: although Bruckner appears never to have been deeply involved with a woman, he was fascinated with women and continually proposed marriage to young girls. He kept a list in his diary of every woman toward whom he had ever felt an attraction. His frustrations in love continued practically until his death. In 1891 and again in 1894 he proposed to a hotel chambermaid, but she refused to convert to Catholicism and the unlikely marriage never took place. At about the same time he proposed to a young lady in Salzburg, whose parents would not allow the union.

All these obsessions — women, religion, the dead, revisions — conspired to prevent Bruckner from completing the Ninth Symphony. Yet he did finish the first three movements, and he had completed a good portion of the finale by the time of his death. The last movement exists in no fewer than six different versions, some of them complete (except for a few gaps and some crucial missing inner voices) up to the beginning of the coda. The substantial fragment includes 72 pages of score, representing perhaps 75% of the movement.

The Ninth had to wait six years after Bruckner's death for performance. The composer's friend Ferdinand Löwe conducted the first performance of the symphony, but in a version he had drastically (and anonymously) revised. Although he felt he was performing a service to his departed friend by making the work more approachable, his reworking displays little understanding of the symphony's extraordinary originality. Löwe removed measures, inserted others, changed harmonies, rewrote transitions, and changed innumerable details in the orchestration. In addition, he performed Bruckner's earlier *Te Deum* in lieu of a finale, thereby perpetuating the myth that Bruckner had, on his deathbed, expressed the wish that the *Te Deum* be used as the final movement if he died before finishing the symphony. The fact that the finale fragment actually quotes the *Te Deum* (along with a number of other Bruckner works) seemed adequate justification to Löwe.

It was not until 1932 that the original version of the three-movement Ninth became available. On 2 April of that year, Siegmund von Hausegger conducted on the same concert the well-known Löwe version and the then unknown original version. The verdict was unanimous. The Löwe rewriting was retired, and Bruckner's original intentions were soon published and now are always performed.

But what of the finale? The parallel with Mahler's Tenth Symphony is striking. Both composers devoted nearly their entire outputs to large-scale symphonies; both completed ten symphonies (Mahler refused to number his song-symphony *Das Lied von der Erde,* and Bruckner did not count his two youthful efforts in F minor and D minor); both left their eleventh symphonies nearly complete. Scholars have been working on reconstructions of the Mahler Tenth for two decades, and finally a viable performing version is available and frequently heard. The problem with Bruckner's Ninth is more difficult, however, because of the total absence of the coda. Reconstructions of the Mahler were possible because there was enough music to permit understanding the overall framework. But any attempt at completing the Bruckner Ninth must deal with the total absence of even a hint of what the coda was to be.

Nonetheless, attempts have been made. There are at least two different completions of the Bruckner finale in existence, both of which have been performed. They are controversial (as were the first reconstructions of the Mahler Tenth). Some people have praised efforts to make available as much of the finale as exists, while others have felt that these versions were not even close to the level of Bruckner's inspiration. Time will determine whether a viable reconstruction of the Ninth is possible. Until one appears, most orchestras will continue to perform the symphony as a three-movement work. The frequently voiced sentiment that the adagio third movement is really Bruckner's farewell to life, while clearly not true in any literal sense, does reflect a sense of completeness in the three movements that is quite unlike what any other symphony offers after only three of its four movements have been heard.

As several commentators have mentioned, Bruckner defined both his style and his conception of symphonic form early in his career and subsequently refined but never altered them. Unlike a composer such as Beethoven, whose understanding of the symphony and whose personal style changed over the years, Bruckner found his unique artistic vision early and then explored, with ever greater subtlety, the implications and possibilities of his idiom. The Ninth Symphony is the culmination of this development. Outwardly it has many features in common with earlier Bruckner symphonies — four-movement form, wealth of themes, religious undertones, persistent triplet rhythms, massive orchestral sonorities, subtle modulations, lyrical melodies, merging of recapitulation and development, discontinuities. But what in certain earlier works was overused and mannered here comes through with mastery and sophistication. The result is music of tremendous emotional impact, from the powerful first movement through the demonic scherzo to the tortuous adagio.

Within Bruckner's self-imposed limits, there is considerable originality in the Ninth. Both the extensive tonal wandering very near the beginning of the first movement and that movement's withholding of a truly melodic tune for an incredibly long time are striking and dramatic gestures. The dissonances and colorful orchestration of the scherzo are also quite new for Bruckner, as is his casting the trio section at a pace faster than that of the scherzo proper. The adagio, however, contains the greatest originality. It lies not with any novel details but rather with the whole conception, with successive climaxes that seem to build one upon the next, until the final shattering outpouring. After this enormous outburst, the subsequent tranquil close seems to come from another world. It is hard to imagine anything coming after this transcendant resolution. But, of course, we do not know the symphony as Bruckner conceived it. We still do not know, despite the recent attempts at reconstruction, exactly what the finale might have been.

Frédéric Chopin

Born at Zelazowa Wola, near Warsaw, on 1 March 1810.
Died in Paris on 17 October 1849.

Concerto Number 1 in E Minor for Piano and
Orchestra, Opus 11
>   Allegro maestoso
>   Romanze: Larghetto —
>   Vivace

Concerto Number 2 in F Minor for Piano and
Orchestra, Opus 21
>   Maestoso
>   Larghetto
>   Allegro vivace

*The First Concerto was begun in 1829 and completed in September
1830. Chopin first performed the work in Warsaw on 11 October
1830. Carlos Evasio Soliva conducted.*

*The Second Concerto was begun in 1828, during Chopin's final
year as a conservatory student, and finished early in 1830. Chopin
played the first performance at a private concert with conductor Ka-
rol Kurpinski in Warsaw on 3 March 1830. The first public performance was given by the same performers on 17 March.*

Much music history in the first half of the nineteenth century can be
traced through the piano literature. The piano was the romantic instrument *par excellence*. Capable of extremes of expression, from the
fiery to the tender, from the bombastic to the intimate, this instrument became the favorite of such pianist-composers as Liszt, Schumann, and Chopin, as well as such all but forgotten figures as Kalkbrenner (to whom Chopin's E Minor Concerto is dedicated), Thalberg,
Henselt, Hummel, Elsner, and Field. The piano was in addition a social instrument, for which a lot of salon music was written. It was
also the means by which musicians and music lovers learned new
orchestral and operatic scores. In this way it was the nineteenth-century equivalent of our phonograph.

A musician such as Chopin could have flourished only at such a
time. He wrote virtually all his music for the piano. His intimate personality found its best expression at the keyboard. A few works for

piano and orchestra and a few for piano and cello emphasize the keyboard member of the team. All other Chopin pieces are for piano alone.

The quality of intimacy in Chopin's music reflects his own piano playing. In an age when pianists were competing with one another to find the most dazzling virtuosic techniques, Chopin raised his quiet yet firm voice in opposition. His playing was free of excesses, as is his music. It is reported that he never played above the level of *forte,* yet he conveyed dynamic subtleties with greater sensitivity than any other pianist.

Chopin's two piano concertos are early works, dating from his final years in Warsaw. They are not concertos in the tradition of Beethoven's mature masterpieces, which are dialogues between two opposing but equal forces: soloist and orchestra. Chopin's concertos derive from a different tradition, represented by J. C. Bach, the early Mozart, Hummel, Field, Kalkbrenner, and Moscheles. In the concertos of these composers, the orchestra is subservient to the solo instrument. Chopin's concertos are conceived for piano *with* orchestra rather than piano *and* orchestra.

Chopin never totally mastered the art of orchestration. In fact, beyond the age of 21 he never wrote for orchestra. The relative unimportance of the orchestra in his concertos is proven by the fact he once performed the F Minor Concerto as a piano solo, to good effect. Hector Berlioz, who was very sensitive to the use of the orchestra and who never himself wrote a true concerto, had harsh words for the accompaniments in the Chopin concertos: when the orchestral instruments "play *tutti,* they cannot be heard, and one is tempted to say to them: why don't you play, for heavens sake! And when they accompany the piano, they only interfere with it, so that the listener wants to cry out to them: be quiet, you bunglers, you are in the way!" Nonetheless, once the piano enters, it takes our complete attention and we hear the keyboard magic that is uniquely Chopin's. Then the orchestra hardly matters.

Berlioz was perhaps overly critical. Although he eventually became disinterested in it, Chopin did know how to use the orchestra. The opening *tutti* of the E Minor Concerto, for example, is solidly scored. The instrumentation may not be unusual or imaginative, but it is functional. Similarly, the staggered entrances of muted strings at the beginning of the slow movement of the same concerto are attractive and they serve their purpose: to introduce the ensuing piano solo.

The First Concerto was actually composed after the Second. The discrepancy in numbering occurred because Chopin lost the orchestral parts to the Second before it could be published. By the time they were recopied, the E Minor Concerto had been composed and published as the First.

The concertos were written soon after Chopin completed his education. At the time, he was eager to promote his career by moving to Vienna, which was, after Paris, the musical center of Europe. A preliminary visit in the summer of 1829 was most successful. His music impressed a Viennese publisher, who hastily arranged for Chopin to give some recitals. The press and public were enchanted with the perfection and originality of his playing. His fame spread rapidly. He had invitations not only to move to Vienna but also to visit Berlin and Italy.

When he returned home to Warsaw, a small incident showed him how pointless it was for him to remain in Poland. A Warsaw newspaper, purporting to reprint one of the reviews of his Vienna concerts, actually (perhaps deliberately) mistranslated it so that it said the opposite of what the Austrian critic had intended. The "translation" read: "He is a young man whose desire to please the public comes before the endeavor to make good music."

With this kind of publicity at home, Chopin understandably felt drawn to more cosmopolitan European cities, where his art was genuinely appreciated. Another factor, however, was keeping him in Warsaw. Chopin was in love (for one of many times in his life). He was painfully shy, a condition not helped by the fact that Konstancja Gladkowska had many admirers. He could not bring himself to confess his feelings to Gladkowska, a young singer who was his classmate at the Warsaw Conservatory. Instead he spoke of his love in a letter to his friend Tytus: "Perhaps to my misfortune I have met my ideal and have served her faithfully for six months, without speaking to her of my feelings. I dream about it. Under her inspiration have been born the adagio of my Concerto in F Minor and, this morning, the little waltz I am sending you. No one will know about it except you. . . . I tell to the piano what I confide in you."

Because of the distractions of love, Chopin was for a long time unable to finish the F Minor Concerto. His fame had begun to spread, however, and a critic announced that the composer was at work on a new concerto. "It is hoped that he will not delay any longer in confirming our conviction that Poland too can produce great talent." Under the pressure of public scrutiny, Chopin at last finished the piece. It was played in private to an enthusiastic audience, then two weeks later before eight hundred listeners, the largest group the composer had played for yet. The reception was again favorable, and the critics were both perceptive and generous.

Despite this favorable press, Chopin remained firm in his conviction to leave Warsaw. He turned his attention to the E Minor Concerto, because he felt he had to have two concertos in hand when he moved to Vienna. The work was at last ready to be performed — at one of Chopin's farewell concerts in Warsaw.

Before he left Poland, the composer and Gladkowska exchanged friendship rings. He had still not declared his love, and Konstancja thought of him merely as a friend. She married a year after Chopin left. She gave up her operatic career and moved with her husband to the country, where they raised five children. In 1845 Konstancja went blind and in 1878 she was widowed. When a biography of Chopin was read to her, late in her life, she was astounded to learn how much she had meant to the young composer. "I doubt whether Chopin would have been such a good husband as my honest Józef," she said, "for he was temperamental, full of fantasies, and unreliable." One of her last acts, before her death in 1889, was to destroy all of Chopin's letters and mementos to her.

Despite its early date, the E Minor Concerto exhibits Chopin's original approach to the piano. He takes typical keyboard ornamentation and gives it deeper meaning than it had ever before had. It is no longer accurate to speak of piano arpeggios and runs as figuration. In Chopin's music they become genuinely expressive musical gestures. Chopin was able to do this because of two factors: (1) a deep understanding of the piano, so that the arpeggios and runs have exquisite sonorities, and (2) a wonderful harmonic sense, which makes the figuration carry subtle underlying meaning rather than functioning solely as a vehicle for the soloist's dexterity. The harmonic nature of the ornamental piano writing is demonstrated by the fact that we readily understand whether a passage is fast or slow on the basis not of the rapidity of its notes but rather of the rate of the underlying harmonies. Thus, for example, the concluding passage of the slow movement consists of fast piano figuration over slowly changing harmonies.

The tonal plan of the E Minor Concerto is unusual, if not eccentric. Throughout the orchestral exposition, the music does not wander far from the home key: the first theme is in E minor, the second in E major. This much is typical of the classical concerto. But, once the piano enters, both main themes are again presented in the key of E. It is not until the development section that there is a large-scale change of key (to C major). In the recapitulation, where the second theme is normally in the tonic, it appears in G major — the key it "should have" taken in the exposition. Furthermore, both the slow movement (a *romanze*) and the finale (a Polish dance known as a *kra-*

kowiak) are cast in the first movement's key of E — another most unusual procedure.

What, if anything, do these patterns of key mean to the listener? The lack of traditional key contrast serves to heighten certain special modulations, such as the side-stepping to E-flat major that occurs briefly in the outer movements. Whether the concerto is tonally traditional or innovative, however, is not the issue. What matters is that the traditional dynamic confrontation between tonal areas is absent from this piece. It is thus less dramatic than, for example, the concertos of Beethoven or Mozart. There is little opposition of tonalities, just as there is little confrontation between piano and orchestra. The impulse behind the work is lyrical. We are led to listen not for a titanic struggle of opposites, not for an eventual resolution of tensions, but rather to lovely details of melody, harmony, and figuration. These gestures are in the concerto for one reason only: for their beauty. They are not the vehicles for large dramatic conflicts. Beauty, not drama, is the essence of the E Minor Concerto.

Chopin's affinity for the piano also pervades the F Minor Concerto. It is nicely demonstrated by the first theme. When it is introduced in the strings, with wind and brass interjections, it is quite forceful, but we cannot appreciate its real beauty until it is restated by the piano. The piano adds attractive ornamentation, causing the melody to come to life. The same comparison holds for the second theme. Once the piano enters, it keeps our attention. The typical orchestral accompaniment, when there is one, is simple string chords. The winds and brass remain silent until the orchestral interludes.

The *larghetto* begins ambiguously. At first the music seems still to be in the first movement's key of F minor, but then it moves toward A-flat major. In order confirm A-flat as the real key, Chopin reiterates the wind cadence in the strings. Curiously, the result sounds more like a movement ending than an opening. The piano enters at this moment, and the orchestral style reverts to that of the first movement: slowly moving string chords with occasional wind contributions. The piano writing is in Chopin's typically florid style: lyrical melodies ornamented with fast figuration. This figuration seems almost improvisatory, since the beat is subdivided in many different ways. For example, we hear 29 notes evenly spaced across two beats, 27 equal notes in two beats, 15 even notes in one beat, 14 in one, 21 in two, 9 in one, 10 in one, 21 in four, 7 in two, 19 in one, etc. The integrity of the beat is maintained by most of these figures, but the variable subdivisions make the piano writing rhapsodic. At the end of the movement, the opening returns to fulfill its implied closing function.

The orchestra finally is given some prominence in the finale. There are even a couple of special effects that suggest that Chopin might have developed into an imaginative orchestrator had he continued to compose for the medium: the *col legno* passage that annouces the *scherzando* in the middle of the movement (the strings are hit with the wood rather than the hair of the bow) and the horn call that announces the coda. The movement has great vitality, especially the main theme, which contains several metric ambiguities. The music seems unwilling to decide whether its meter is 2/4 or 3/4 and also just where the barlines fall.

Aaron Copland

Born on 14 November 1900 in Brooklyn, New York.

Appalachian Spring

Appalachian Spring was composed in 1943–44 as a ballet for Martha Graham, who first performed it with her company at the Library of Congress in Washington, D.C., on 30 October 1944. Copland expanded the original instrumentation from 13 players to full orchestra when he made a condensed version in 1945.

Like most composers of his generation, Aaron Copland was at first excited by the dissonant harmonies and jagged rhythms that he heard in the 1920s. But he was also concerned about the inaccessibility of modern music. He preferred to create a musical language that was essentially American, in order to speak directly to an American audience. At first he tried to incorporate elements of jazz into his symphonic works, but with only limited success. A more drastic approach was needed. Therefore, in the late 1930s, the composer deliberately turned his back on his earlier dissonant style. He created a series of simple, straightforward, largely consonant works.

> During these years I began to feel an increasing dissatisfaction with the relations of the music-loving public and the living composer. The old "special" public of the modern music concerts had fallen away, and the conventional concert public continued to be apathetic or indifferent to anything but the established classics. It seemed to me that we composers were in danger of working in a vacuum. Moreover, an entirely new public for music had grown up around the radio and phonograph. It made no sense to ignore them and to continue writing as if they did not exist. I felt that it was worth the effort to see if I couldn't say what I had to say in the simplest possible terms.

Thus was born Copland's aesthetic of musical populism. He realized that the communications media had vastly increased the size, but not the sophistication, of the music-listening public. He felt that the way to reach this large audience was to make music not only for concerts but also for radio, movies, records, and ballets. His populist style used such items of Americana as cowboy songs, Latin-American rhythms, folksongs, and New England and Shaker hymns. The resulting music was as immediate as it was simple. It is probably only a coincidence, but surely an interesting one, that the crowning achievement of Copland's musical populism — the ballet *Appalachian Spring* — includes (in its next to last section) a set of variations on a Shaker hymn tune that praises simplicity:

> 'Tis the gift to be simple,
> 'Tis the gift to be free,
> 'Tis the gift to come down
> Where we ought to be,
> And when we find ourselves
> In the place just right,
> 'Twill be in the valley of
> Love and Delight.

Despite its direct appeal, *Appalachian Spring* is realized with consummate skill and subtlety, so that its simplicity is not trivialized. It typifies the philosophy of many American composers of the 1930s and '40s: "We wanted to find a music that would speak of universal things in a vernacular of American speech rhythms. We wanted to write music on a level that left popular music far behind — music with a largeness of utterance wholly representative of the country that Whitman had envisaged."

The music Copland wrote for Martha Graham's ballet *Appalachian Spring* reflects his desire to create a non-elitist music, a music that expresses the experiences and visions of an American artist. Several years earlier he had written: "The conviction grew inside me that the two things that seemed always to have been so separate in America — music and the life about me — must be made to touch. This desire to make the music I wanted to write come out of the life I had lived in America became a preoccupation."

The immediacy of *Appalachian Spring* is evident right from the beginning. The first section, and many subsequent passages as well, uses a technique sometimes called "pandiatonicism." All seven notes of a particular key (in this case, A major) are freely combined in traditional and non-traditional ways, but the other five notes of the chromatic scale are studiously avoided. The resulting sound is open and consonant without being much like traditional tonal music, in which notes foreign to the prevailing key invariably appear sooner or later.

The rhythms of *Appalachian Spring* are as direct and engaging as its pandiatonic harmonies. Sometimes their vitality comes from clever irregularities, but often Copland's means are simpler: repeatedly coming to rest on the fourth beat of a measure in one section, or interruptions by silences of varying length in other places.

The composer explained the relationship of this music to the folksong tradition of the Shakers:

Appalachian Spring is generally thought to be folk inspired. But . . . the Shaker tune "Tis the Gift to Be Simple" is the only folk material I actually quoted in the piece. Rhythms and melodies that suggest a certain American ambience . . . and the use of specific folk themes . . . are, after all, not quite the same thing.

You know, *Appalachian Spring* took me about a year to finish, and it was originally scored for only 13 players. I remember thinking how crazy it was to spend all that time, because I knew how short-lived most ballets and their scores are. But the suite for symphony orchestra that I derived from *Appalachian Spring* was awarded a Pulitzer Prize in 1945 and took on a life of its own. Actually, it had a lot to do with bringing my name before a wider public.

According to Graham, the ballet concerns "a pioneer celebration in spring around a newly-built farmhouse in the Pennsylvania hills in the early part of the last century. The bride-to-be and the young farmer-husband enact the emotions, joyful and apprehensive, their new domestic partnership invites. An older neighbor suggests now and then the rocky confidence of experience. A revivalist and his followers remind the new householders of the strange and terrible aspects of human fate. At the end the couple are left quiet and strong in their new house."

By 1943 Martha Graham was recognized as the country's leading modern dance choreographer, but she had not yet created a dance to original music. Thanks to the generosity of arts patron Elizabeth Sprague Coolidge, Graham was able to commission a score from Copland. She decided to base the ballet on the childhood memories of her 90-year-old grandmother, who had spent most of her life on a Pennsylvania farm. The music was completed long before Copland learned the title Graham had chosen. He found out only just prior to the premiere that she had selected the name of the dance (and hence of his piece) from a poem by Hart Crane.

The premiere took place at the Library of Congress, where many works commissioned with funds provided by Elizabeth Sprague Coolidge found their first audiences. The concert was a special eightieth-birthday tribute to the lady who had made a tremendous impact on contemporary American music. As the World War II was still raging, everything brought into the Library of Congress had to be inspected. Graham's costumes, iron, ironing board, and dress were thoroughly searched for bombs.

The performance was a complete success. Copland subsequently made a concert suite from the ballet, which was recorded by conductor Serge Koussevitzky. Because it was this recording that first brought Copland's music to a wide audience, *Appalachian Spring* fulfilled the composer's ideal of a music of and for the American people disseminated to them through the media of the phonograph and radio.

Arcangelo Corelli

Born in Fusignano, Italy, on 17 February 1653.
Died in Rome on 8 January 1713.

Concerto Grosso in G Minor, Opus 6, Number 8, *Christmas*

Vivace. Grave. Allegro
Adagio. Allegro. Adagio
Vivace
Allegro. Pastorale

Little is known about the composition of the Christmas *Concerto; it is possible that it was written as early as 1690, although it may date from somewhat later.*

Although his output was small, Corelli was an important and influential musician. He helped bring a new high standard to violin and ensemble playing, and he was a skilled conductor. He insisted, for example, that all string players move their bows in the same direction together, so that they would produce a homogeneity of sound as well as a pleasing visual spectacle. In addition, he was the first composer ever to gain a substantial reputation exclusively for instrumental music, the first whose fame was a product of his published music, and the first whose instrumental works were studied, admired, performed, and imitated long after his death. In England, for example, his music remained in the active repertoire until well into the nineteenth century.

Corelli's fame as the leading composer in Rome led to his works being played elsewhere as well. Once, when one of his sonatas was performed in Bologna, musicians there were puzzled by a passage that seemed to violate certain musical rules (it contained parallel fifths). When one of the Bolognese musicians wrote to Corelli for an explanation, the composer defended his music indignantly. Accusations went back and forth between the musicians of the two cities, and the dispute actually lasted several months.

Nearly all of Corelli's works fall into one of three categories: solo sonata, trio sonata, and *concerto grosso*. He did not invent the *concerto grosso* form but rather inherited the genre he was to perfect from Alessandro Stradella. The characteristic that distinguishes this structure — the alternation of small (*concertino*) and large (*ripieno*) instrumental groups — derives from overtures and instrumental interludes in the operas of Stradella and others. It remained for Corelli to free the concerto from the theater and to codify the principles that were to nourish its future composers.

To listeners today a *concerto grosso* by Corelli may sound like run-of-the-mill baroque instrumental music. The reason for this apparent lack of distinction, actually, is that many of Corelli's contemporaries and successors directly followed his style. Among his imitators, three in particular stand out as having taken his model and added their own distinct contributions: Vivaldi, Handel, and Bach. Handel's Opus 6 concertos were inspired by Corelli's Opus 6; similarly, Bach's *Brandenburg* Concertos trace their ancestry to Corelli's collection.

Corelli composed two kinds of *concerto grosso*: secular works that include numerous dance movements and concertos intended for use in church. The former are related to baroque dance suites. The latter type, which includes the *Christmas* Concerto, is more important. Both kinds include a large number of movements, in contrast to the three-movement fast-slow-fast pattern preferred by other composers. The twelve concertos of Opus 6 exhibit a wide structural variety. They contain different numbers of movements, which are cast in different forms and use diverse tempos.

Like its sister works, the G Minor Concerto calls for two violins and continuo in the *concertino*, plus *ripieno* comprising two violin parts, viola part, and continuo part (the continuo, which carries the bass line and supplies the implied harmony above it, is usually played by bass instruments and harpsichord or organ). In some movements the *ripieno* accompanies, usually by punctuation, while in other movements the two groups play together. Corelli indicated that a *concertino* could play the piece alone.

Vastly different sized ensembles played the concertos on different occasions. Anyone is mistaken who thinks that a Corelli *concerto grosso* is necessarily chamber music and that a performance by a modern symphony string section violates the original spirit. Performances of baroque instrumental music by large orchestras took place on many occasions, including one when Corelli directed a string orchestra numbering a hundred fifty.

A distinguishing feature of Opus 6, Number 8, is the lovely pastorale that closes the work. The style of this movement, with its drones (foreshadowed toward the end of the preceding allegro) and siciliano rhythms, dates back to the renaissance, although this type of music appeared in early baroque operas as an imitation of shepherd music. This movement was probably included in the concerto when it was performed during midnight mass at Christmas but omitted on other occasions.

The solemn *grave* movement is thought to depict the crucifixion and the pastorale to represent the nativity. The peaceful joy of the angels hovering over Bethlehem is conveyed by casting this final movement in G major, after all preceding movements have been in the darker keys of G minor and E-flat major.

Claude Debussy

Born on 22 August 1862 in St. Germain-en-Laye, outside Paris.
Died on 29 March 1918 in Paris.

◆　◆　◆

Images

　　　Gigues
　　　Rondes de printemps
　　　Ibéria
　　　　　Par les rues et par les chemins
　　　　　Les Parfums de la nuit
　　　　　Le Matin d'un jour de fête

The composition of the orchestral Images *occupied Debussy from 1906 to 1912.* Ibéria *was completed on 25 December 1908 and first performed on 20 February 1910 at the Concerts Colonne in Paris, conducted by Gabriel Pierné.* Rondes de printemps *was finished on 10 May 1909 and first performed on 2 March 1910 at the Concerts Durand in Paris, under the direction of the composer.* Gigues *was completed in a version for two pianos on 4 January 1909, but the orchestral version had to wait until 1912 before it was finished, with the help of André Caplet, who did much of the orchestration owing to the composer's ill health. Caplet conducted the first performance at the Concerts Colonne in Paris on 26 January 1913.*

"I am getting to believe more and more that music is not, in its essence, a thing which can flow within a rigorous and traditional form. It is composed of colors and rhythmic moments of time. All the rest is a fraud, invented by cold-blooded imbeciles riding on the masters' backs." So wrote Debussy to his publisher about *Rondes de printemps.* These words may well be taken as the key to all the composer's later works. It surely applies to all the orchestral *Images.* These pieces do not adhere to classical formal molds, but rather they generate their structures seemingly spontaneously.

The *Images* were conceived as works for piano four-hands or for two pianos. Debussy originally thought of them as separate pieces. There is little literal interrelationship between them, and in fact they are often performed separately. *Ibéria* — itself a three-movement composition — is frequently heard by itself, while *Gigues* and *Rondes de printemps* are played less often. The order Debussy designated for performance is not the order of composition.

The composer is often called a musical Impressionist. He deplored the term. In *Images* he was "trying to achieve something different," he wrote, "an effect of reality." This effect was, he explained, "what some imbeciles call 'Impressionism,' a term that is utterly misapplied, especially by critics." Yet the term has remained a convenient label for much of Debussy's music, in which he tries not to create musical equivalents of scenes or stories, as in nineteenth-century program music, but rather to put into music his impressions of visual stimuli. To this end he incorporated folksongs, sometimes literally and sometimes only in spirit, in *Images. Gigues,* for example, uses an actual folksong, "The Keel Row." This tune, familiar in northern England and Scotland, was known to Debussy with words by the French poet Verlaine under the title *Dansons la gigue* ("Let's Dance the Jig").

Just as *Gigues* is English, so *Rondes de printemps* is French. It uses two French folksongs. Debussy prefaced the score with a quotation from a recent book by Pierre Gauthier: "Welcome May and the woodland banner." Gauthier was describing a medieval May Day scene in Tuscany, impressions of which Debussy apparently wished to portray in *Rondes.* Gauthier writes, "On the first day of May, the whole country scene awakens and rejoices. Women and girls form processions and pair off with joyous dancers or musicians, their heads encircled with garlands of flowers. Games and contests take place and lovers carry the May banners — branches brought from the woodlands — leaving them at their sweethearts' doors and proceeding to sing the May song."

The third *Image, Ibéria,* has a decidedly Spanish flavor. In 1920 Spanish composer Manuel de Falla wrote an explanation and appreciation of this Spanish influence:

> Claude Debussy wrote Spanish music without knowing Spain, that is to say without knowing the land of Spain, which is a different matter. Debussy knew Spain from his readings, from pictures, from songs, and from songs danced by true Spanish dancers.
>
> At the World Exposition held on the Champs de Mars, two young French musicians were to be seen going about together, listening to the exotic music of many countries. Mingling with the crowd, these young musicians abandoned themselves to the magic of this strange music, and later they were able to discover new fields of expression. These two musicians were Paul Dukas and Claude Debussy.
>
> Our knowledge of this simple fact will help us to understand many aspects of Debussy's work. His first-hand knowledge of new types of music, including Chinese and Spanish music, ex-

cited his imagination. "I have always been an observer," he declared, "and I have tried in my work to put my observations to good account." Debussy's manner of conveying the essential spirit of Spanish music shows how successful he was. . . .

Only once did he cross the Franco-Spanish frontier, to spend a few hours at San Sebastian, where he watched a bullfight. This was hardly knowing Spain! He remembered, however, the light in the bull-ring, particularly the violent contrast between the one half of the ring flooded with sunlight and the other half deep in shade. The *Matin d'un jour de fête* from *Ibéria* is perhaps an evocation of this afternoon spent just over the French border. But this was not the Spain that was really his own. His dreams led him farther afield, and he became spellbound by an imaginary Andalucía. We have evidence of this in *Par les rues et par les chemins* and *Parfums de la nuit* from *Ibéria*. . . .

So far as *Ibéria* is concerned, he made it clear that he did not intend to write Spanish music but rather to translate into music the associations that Spain had aroused in him. This he triumphantly achieved. A sort of *Sevillana*, the generating theme of the work suggests village songs heard in the bright, scintillating light; the intoxicating magic of the Andalucían nights, the light-hearted holiday crowds dancing to chords struck on guitars and *bandurrias* — all these musical effects whirl in the air while the crowds, as we imagine them, approach or recede. Everything is constantly alive and extremely expressive.

Gigues is an essay in discontinuity. Rarely does the piece proceed for more than a few measures without a major contrast. Nonetheless, it is held together by consistency of motivic materials and by an overall shape that builds to a large climax and then dies away to a quiet ending. A prominent role is given to the oboe d'amore, a baroque instrument that is a lower-pitched and mellower version of the modern oboe. It is first heard playing the English folk tune after the atmospheric opening, and it returns frequently throughout *Gigues*.

Rondes de printemps combines the fragmented temporal world of *Gigues* with the sonorous textures of *Les Parfums de la nuit*. The orchestral sonorities that Debussy invented are extraordinarily beautiful. He all but avoids outright melodies in much of the piece, as if he feels that an extended tune would take attention away from these sonorities. Eventually a wonderful melody does arrive in the strings — in the unusual meter of 15/8 — but it lasts only two measures. Other melodies, which are French folk tunes, are disguised or buried within large textures. Contrasts are frequent, yet the music drives, inexorably if circuitously, towards its dramatic close.

Ibéria is more continuous, more developmental, less a mosaic than either *Gigues* or *Rondes*. The first movement is pervaded by Spanish dance rhythms. The frequent use of castanets and tambourine complete the effect. The movement is melodic. The second section, on the other hand, is more textural than tuneful. It is wistful and dream-like. Debussy here creates some exquisite ethereal sonorities, often involving high strings, celeste, and harps. The third section is once again dance-like. What seems to be an accompanimental figure keeps growing in complexity and volume of sound. When real melodies do finally arrive — first with the whole string section playing *pizzicato* and then in the high clarinets — the Spanish flavor is unmistakable. At the close the music becomes brilliantly animated.

◆ ◆ ◆

Jeux

Jeux was composed during August 1912. It was first performed as a ballet by the Ballets Russes at the newly opened Théâtre des Champs-Elysées in Paris on 15 May 1913.

The original idea for the ballet *Jeux* ("Games") came from the dancer Vaslav Nijinsky. He wanted no large group of dancers, but rather only three soloists. There were to be no traditional ballet dances, but just a game of tennis interrupted by an airplane crash. The impresario Serge Diaghilev wanted Debussy to write the music, but the composer thought that whole idea silly. He cabled back, "No, it is idiotic and unmusical. I would not dream of writing a score for this work."

Debussy was at the time having severe financial problems, and when Diaghilev offered to double the fee, the composer acquiesced. Even after Nijinsky eliminated the airplane crash, Debussy had trouble working up much enthusiasm for the project. He spent only three weeks composing the music. Nijinsky and Diaghilev had hoped that *Jeux* would be a uniquely contemporary marriage of the arts of music, plot, costume, scenery, and dance, yet each of these elements was commissioned separately, and the participating artists collaborated but little. What is amazing, given the dubious conditions under which *Jeux* was created, is not that it was a failure with its first audiences but that the music turned out to be one of the most startlingly original and most influential compositions of all times.

Nijinsky tried to create a new type of dance in *Jeux*. According to his wife Romola, "In this new work the freize was almost alive and moved in space, the gestures were split up so that it would give the impression of many small movements consecutively following each other as they logically developed, and through this it gave the impression, as some called it, of a *ballet cinématographique*. Each limb made a different movement and followed a different rhythm." Nijinsky explored abstract visual effects. He was trying to create a dance of pure movement, only superficially connected with the scenario, decor, or music.

Debussy was outraged when he first saw Nijinsky's choreography, which he had not viewed in its entirety prior to the first performance. The composer did not even stay to see the entire ballet. The public was mystified, if not derisive. This negative reception was all but forgotten, however, when precisely two weeks later the same dance company premiered in the same theater Stravinsky's notorious *Rite of Spring*, which provoked a riot in the audience. Both works were equally revolutionary, both were based on minimal plots, and both were musically discontinuous. But Stravinsky's music was aggressive, even barbaric, while Debussy's was sophisticated and subtle. Thus the *Rite* caused a scandal while *Jeux* engendered only puzzled silence. It took audiences far longer to learn to understand *Jeux*. Its first performance as a purely orchestral work the following year also perplexed its listeners, while Stravinsky's piece soon became a popular success in the concert hall. It was not until relatively recently that performers, audiences, composers, and critics have come to appreciate *Jeux* fully.

The program at the first performance provided the following synopsis of the action: "The setting is a garden at twilight. A young man and two girls have lost their tennis ball and are searching for it. The dusk and the garish light from the huge electric lamps pique their senses, and their search turns into an amorous game of hide and seek. They try to catch one another, they quarrel, and they embrace in a passionate triple kiss. A ball thrown from the shadows startles them. Realizing they are being spied on, they vanish in alarm into the deepening shadows of the garden."

It is hardly surprising that Debussy was at first uninterested in a virtually plotless scenario. But its strangeness seems to have acted subliminally on the composer, so that he produced uniquely powerful music. What is so special about it? What first strikes the listener is not so much what it contains as what it avoids. There is almost no melody, only rarely do sections return, and there seems to be no continuity. One section follows another without transition or warning, and the contrasts between succeeding passages are disturbingly abrupt. In virtually all previous music, continuity was the foundation of form. Music moved logically from the beginning to the end of a work. But *Jeux* is a mosaic of ideas, many of which seem only half-formed. Yet there is an underlying sense of balance. The parts do seem to belong together, but in what manner this unity is accomplished is anything but obvious.

Debussy created a unique section for each of the scenario's events. Although some passages share motivic material, no section returns literally until quite close to the end. This lack of section repetitions removes one of the traditional means composers employed to delineate form. Instead, Debussy relies on balance between lengths of sections and on the density of materials they contain, but not particularly on their orderly progression. Thus *Jeux* seems more like a free association than a linear development.

Each section is characterized by its constituent motives, which are repeated several times, with subtle variation. Also important are the particular tone colors and rhythms of each passage. Debussy constantly invented new sonorities, all related to one another in subliminal ways but at the same time contrasting sharply one with the next. The composer called this new approach to musical form a "cinematography of instants through which the author moved while he was composing his piece."

The middle sections are the most overtly discontinuous. Here different meters, as well as different instruments, represent the three dancers. As the dancers come into various relationships with one another, the music changes abruptly. For example, each of three meters — 3/4, 3/8, and 2/4 — stands for one of the characters. The interaction of these meters reflects the interaction of the dancers. When two of them embrace, their 3/4 and 3/8 meters are heard simultaneously, while the third dancer, who is temporarily rejected, is represented by a 2/4 that alternates with the superimposed meters. At the loud climax motives associated with each meter are combined into a grand reconciliation — visual and musical. At this point, according to Debussy, "in a passionate gesture, the young man unites their three heads and a triple kiss allows them to merge in an ecstasy that lasts until the 3/8." The dancers remain in their mutual ecstasy until another tennis ball intrudes.

In the original piano score to *Jeux*, Debussy provided the following guide to the dances:

> After a slow prelude of several measures — a first scherzando motive in 3/8 appears, soon interrupted by the return of the prelude — then the scherzando resumes with a second motive. At this point the action begins: a ball falls on stage; a young man crosses the stage — disappears. Then two girls come — start to dance — notice the young man — he persuades one of them to dance with him — scorn and jealousy cause the other girl to begin an ironic and mocking dance (2/4) and thus attract the

attention of the young man: he invites her to a waltz (3/8) — the first girl wants to leave but the second holds her back (3/4, very moderate) — all three dance (3/8) faster and faster up to the moment of ecstasy (3/4, very moderate), which is interrupted by another tennis ball — return of the chords of the prelude — and that's it.

There are some 25 different motives in *Jeux*, but only two fully developed melodies, which appear only at the middle of the piece. This concentration on short wisps of melody rather than on long lines contributes to the fragmentary nature of the music. The resulting discontinuity surely had a lot to do with the puzzlement of audiences in 1913 and the work's subsequent neglect.

Today *Jeux* is frequently performed in concert and occasionally danced. In addition, several avant garde European composers of the 1950s — Pierre Boulez, Karlheinz Stockhausen, Herbert Eimert, and others — have acknowledged an indebtedness to *Jeux's* unique approach to musical time.

The temporal world of *Jeux* is not one of eternally flowing time, nor one of logical progression. Rather, the music symbolizes a disjointed, seemingly irrational time in which events interrupt other events and in which an underlying linear thrust is difficult to find. In this manner the music anticipates certain developments in later twentieth-century art. Contemporary culture is characterized by fragmentation, by an illogicality called "absurdity" by existential philosophers. Even in our daily lives we pointedly sense the irrationalities of constant interruption, because discontinuity is understood against a backdrop of orderly, predictable progression. And so it is in *Jeux*. The temporal mosaic makes sense, and the piece coheres, but not in the simple linear fashion typical of earlier of music. It is no coincidence that *Jeux* influenced later composers, who were trying quite consciously to find new definitions of time appropriate to twentieth-century thought. And it is not surprising that today's listeners, who have lived through much of the tumultuous twentieth century, can appreciate the discontinuities of such music.

La Mer

From Dawn to Noon on the Sea
Games of the Waves
Dialogue of the Wind and the Sea

La Mer was begun in July 1903 and completed at precisely 6:00 p.m. on 5 March 1905. Camille Chevillard conducted the first performance at the Concerts Lamoureux in Paris on 15 October 1905.

La Mer was composed during a difficult time for Debussy. The composer wanted to write about the sea, but he felt that actually being at the ocean would distract him and make the act of composition seem superfluous. So he and his wife Lily went to the mountains of Burgundy, where "my old friend the sea, always innumerable and beautiful," was but a sensuous memory. The compositional process went slowly, and there were many delays. A year later the work was far from done, and the Debussys again prepared for the summer. But on 14 July 1904, the day on which the French celebrate Bastille Day (comparable to our Fourth of July), Debussy walked out on Lily.

For the preceding three years he had become increasingly fascinated with Emma Bardac, a prominent member of the intellectual and artistic elite of Paris and wife of a wealthy banker. The Debussys had often been invited to dine with the Bardacs, but Lily continually felt out of place. The others treated her as an intellectual inferior. When Lily found out that Debussy had left her for Emma, she shot herself, almost fatally.

An enormous scandal ensued. The wife of the best known composer in France had shot herself because he had run off with the wife of one of the most prominent men in Paris. Everyone was interested, and the gossip flew. Most of Debussy's friends sympathized with Lily. They started a fund to pay her hospital bills. When the composer found out about this, he broke his friendships with everyone involved. His remaining friends disapproved of his behavior and broke with him. Debussy had Emma, but otherwise he was alone.

Debussy and Emma went away for the summer, and he continued to work on *La Mer*. He returned to Paris in October, took an apartment, and, unknown to anyone, started to visit Lily regularly. One evening several months later, he told Lily that Emma was going to bear his child. He then showed Lily to the door and, after that, saw her only at the bitter divorce hearings the next summer. The divorce settlement went against Debussy. In October *La Mer* was premiered and, two weeks later, a daughter was born to Emma and Debussy. They tried to start a new life, but they were boycotted by Parisian society, even after they finally married three years later.

It is impossible to assess the impact of his personal difficulties on *La Mer*. It is true that the composer was able to complete the piece only after two years of continually interrupted work, and it is true that in it his style changed from his previous thin, almost nebulous textures to a thicker, more concrete, more dissonant, more polyphonic language. Such changes might, of course, have occurred even under happier circumstances; they were in fact what Debussy probably believed appropriate in a work related to the sea.

The composer felt a basic identity between the mysterious omnipresence of natural phenomena and the subjective pathos of the human spirit. He was interested in portraying in music the subtle nuances of the tiniest details and most majestic triumphs of nature. Since the soul of nature was for him fundamentally the same as the soul of man, neither interpretation nor introspection was necessary. To evoke the sea was automatically to evoke the most profound of human emotions. In his interest in portraying the extramusical, Debussy was a romanticist; in his desire to remove himself and let nature speak directly he was a classicist. The essence of his Impressionistic style lies in the balance between these romantic and classic sides of his musical personality.

The composer's love of nature extended to water, snow, fog, clouds, fish, rain, and, above all, the sea, all of which he made subjects of his compositions. While starting to write *La Mer*, Debussy wrote to André Messager, "You may not know that I was destined for a sailor's life and that it was only quite by chance that fate led me in another direction. But I have always retained a passionate love for the sea. You will say that the ocean does not exactly wash the Burgundian hillside, and my seascapes might be studio landscapes; but I have an endless store of memories, and to my mind they are worth more than the reality, whose beauty often deadens thought."

Debussy is really the first composer to create music of pure sonority. Certain earlier musicians composed intriguing orchestral textures, but these sonorities were always in the service of articulating or enriching melodic, harmonic, and rhythmic structures. In Debussy's mature music the actual sound is more important than the melodies or rhythms. He created extraordinarily beautiful sonorities, which he allowed simply to exist, without having constantly to progress toward goals. Sonorities change to other sonorities, but always there is ample time given to appreciate each one for itself. It is appropriate that *La Mer*, one of the important works in this highly original style, should be symbolic of the sea. Just as sea waves move toward the shore while the actual water bobs up and down in place, so the melodies in *La Mer* move forward in time while the underlying harmonies and sonorities are nearly static.

Debussy understood full well what he was doing and how it differed from earlier practices. In 1915 he complained, "We are still at the stage of 'harmonic progressions,' and there are very few musicians who are satisfied with beauty of sound alone." Earlier he spoke revealingly about his orchestral technique: "Musicians no longer know how to decompose sound — to give it in all its purity. . . . [For me] the sixth violin is just as important as the first. I try to employ each timbre in its purest form." This statement applies well to *La Mer*, in which the orchestration is clear despite frequent subdivisions of the strings into up to 15 parts, as opposed to the traditional five.

The first movement, "From Dawn to Noon on the Sea," opens with a gradual awakening of sonority from the lowest sounds in the orchestra to its full sonority (though rarely particularly loud). There are melodic fragments — most notably the figure heard on the muted trumpet and English horn (an inspired combination!) shortly after the beginning — but these never quite become real tunes. The movement is a mosaic of such fragments and of endlessly varied orchestral textures. It is like the sea: always the same yet continually changing.

"Games of the Waves" is more animated, but melodic fragments rather than fully developed lyrical melodies still abound. Rapid figures suggest splashing waves. Debussy's biographer Oscar Thompson described this movement as a "world of sheer fantasy, of strange visions and eerie voices, a mirage of sight and equally a mirage of sound. On the sea's vast stage is presented trancelike phantasmagoria so evanescent and fugitive that it leaves behind only the vagueness of a dream."

The final movement, "Dialogue of the Wind and the Sea," uses some materials from the first movement plus some new fragments in an active seascape. The music reaches an intensity perhaps suggestive of a storm. Debussy allows himself to utilize the full resources of the orchestra, with brasses blaring — a rather rare overt gesture in a work usually delicately scored.

Anyone approaching *La Mer* with expectations of specific imagery will be disappointed. Debussy was not a programmatic composer like, for example, Richard Strauss, whose music he abhorred. Nowhere in Debussy do we find explicit events or plot comparable to those in *Till Eulenspiegel*. Rather, Debussy recorded impressions — a series of fleeting emotions, an evocation of the magic of the sea more than of its appearance, a meditation on its character.

◆   ◆   ◆

Nocturnes
    Nuages
    Fêtes
    Sirènes

Nocturnes was composed in 1897–99, but earlier versions go back at least to 1892. The first two movements were performed by Camille Chevillard on 9 December 1900 in Paris. The first complete performance was given by the same performers on 27 October 1901, also in Paris.

Nocturnes has a complicated history. Debussy started it in preparation for a projected tour of the United States in 1892. The work was then known as *Trois scènes au crépuscule* ("Three Twilight Scenes"). He put it aside after the tour fell through. He returned to it two years later to transform it, surprisingly, into a violin concerto for the Belgian virtuoso Eugène Ysaÿe. The composer wrote to the violinist in 1894: "The orchestra of the first [movement] consists of strings; of the second, flutes, four horns, three trumpets, and two harps; of the third, both these groups. It is an experiment with the different combinations that can be obtained from one color — like a study in gray in painting."

In 1896 Debussy informed Ysaÿe that the work was finished, but a year later the composer had second thoughts. Ysaÿe never got to see the concerto, and the score has been lost. Debussy started once again to recast the three movements, and by 1899 they were complete in final form. There was no longer a solo violin, and the severe timbral contrast between the first two movements was softened. The third movement acquired a wordless women's chorus.

The composer wrote the following program note for the final version:

> The title *Nocturnes* is to be interpreted here in a general and, more particularly, decorative sense. Therefore it is not meant to designate the usual form of the nocturne, but rather all the various impressions and the special effects of light that the word suggests. *Nuages* ["Clouds"] renders the immutable aspect of the sky and the slow, solemn motion of the clouds, fading away in gray tones tinged with white. *Fêtes* ["Festivals"] portrays the restless dancing rhythms of the atmosphere, interspersed with sudden flashes of light; the episode of the procession (a dazzling, fantastic vision) passes through the festive scene and becomes merged in it. But the background remains persistently the same: the festival, its blending of music and luminous dust participating in cosmic rhythms. *Sirènes* ["Sirens"] depicts the sea and its innumerable rhythms; presently, amid the waves ensilvered by the moon, the mysterious song of the Sirens is heard; it laughs and passes on.

Nocturnes displays three typical influences on Debussy: (1) Russian music, (2) the imagery of poetry, and (3) Impressionism in painting.

1. The best-known Russian music in Paris in the 1880s was that of Tchaikovsky, notably his Fourth Symphony. Tchaikovsky visited Paris seven times between 1883 and 1892. Prior to that, Debussy had been employed in Russia by Tchaikovsky's patron Nadezhda von Meck, with whom the young Frenchman played the Fourth Symphony at the piano. The fanfares of *Fêtes* are perhaps reminiscent of

those in the symphony. More important, however, was the visit of Tsar Nicholas II and Tsarina Alexandra Feodorovna to France in 1896. Debussy attend the festivities and heard numerous Russian fanfares.

2. The first version of *Nocturnes* was named after a set of ten poems by Henri de Régnier: *Scènes au crépuscule.* Debussy was friendly with the poet, with whom he shared aesthetic values. The composer wrote, "When he spoke to me of the debasement through usage of certain words in the French language, I thought that this also applied to certain chords which had become vulgarized in the same way." Debussy's biographer Edward Lockspeiser explains the relationship between *Nocturnes* and Régnier's poetry: The poems

> are the product of an imaginary theater of the mind in which action is sacrificed to poetic associations. Twilight is neither hopeful day nor deathly night; it represents disillusionment. . . . The imagery of the first poem is associated with musical instruments, trumpets and flutes, suggesting Debussy's *Fêtes*, and also with a female choir, as in *Sirènes*. It is true that the flutes in Régnier's poem, "deep flutes weeping in vanity," do not suggest the brilliant opening of *Fêtes*. But contrasted with the flutes and trumpets is a "wan choir" (*choeur qui s'étoile*) which may well have planted in Debussy's mind the idea of the female choir in *Sirènes*. Elsewhere in this collection [of poetry] . . . Régnier speaks of "a procession of flutes" and "the brilliance of angry tambourines and sharp trumpet calls.". . . Debussy surely knew [these poems] at the time of their publication in 1890.

3. The title of the work derives from the "Nocturnes" of James Whistler, whose paintings the composer knew and loved. Debussy's remark about a study in gray indicates that he might have intended the composition as a set of "color studies" in the manner of Whistler. As Debussy's biographer Léon Vallas explains, in the work of both Whistler and Debussy "the lines seem to resolve themselves into an atmosphere, luminous and sonorous, colored or harmonic, that seems more essential to the composition than either the subject or the landscape." Debussy's *Nocturnes*, like Whistler's paintings, are about psychological states. Thus, despite the descriptive titles and program notes, *Nocturnes* is not really program music. *Nuages*, for example, is not about what clouds are like or what happens to them. It is about personal responses to clouds, and it is an attempt to create a kind of music that evokes similar responses. Vague harmonies, wisps of melody, sensitive colors, ethereal sonorities — these qualities are the essence of Debussy's impressionism, and nowhere are they more beautifully used than in *Nocturnes*.

Prelude to *The Afternoon of a Faun*

The Prelude was begun in 1892 and completed in September 1894. Gustave Doret conducted the first performance on 22 September 1894 in Paris.

It was all but inevitable that late nineteenth-century French composers would become interested in the Symbolist poets. The Symbolists, led by Stéphane Mallarmé, sought to duplicate in literature the effects of music by using vague images, elusive syntax, and fleeting ideas. Mallarmé envied music for the mystery of its notation (in contrast to the commonality of the written word) and for its power to evoke deeply human yet non-specific meanings. His own work, such as the poem "The Afternoon of a Faun," is heavily metaphorical and, in its own way, musical. He once said of "Faun," in his typically elliptical manner, "Such a poem is suggested by music proper, which we must raid and paraphrase if our own music, struck dumb, is insufficient." Also, "I have found an intimate and peculiar manner of depicting and setting down very fugitive impressions. What is frightening is that all these impressions are required to be woven together as in a symphony."

In 1865 Mallarmé wrote the first version of the poem that was destined to be widely studied and interpreted throughout the subsequent century. The poet attempted, with no success, to arrange for a staged reading of "Monologue of a Faun." In 1875 a revision entitled "Improvisation of the Faun" was rejected for publication. The final version appeared in 1876, and soon its fame and that of its author began to spread. In 1884 the young Debussy wrote a song using a text of Mallarmé, who by then was widely regarded as the leading experimental poet in France.

Mallarmé began to conduct informal seminars at his home. At these regular Tuesday evening gatherings, he would expound and develop his unique concept of poetry. Debussy was a frequent participant in these seminars, and by the time of the poet's death in 1898 the two men were close friends. In 1892 Debussy formulated the idea of attempting to reflect in music the fleeting emotions of "Faun" — which, in turn, had been derived from music. Just as the poem is not a specific translation of music into words, so Debussy's idea was to write not a programmatic piece but rather a musical equivalent of the mysterious world of the poem. The composer originally planned a more extensive work, which was listed (but never played) on an all-Debussy concert in Brussels in March 1894 as *Prelude, Interludes, and Final Paraphrase for the Afternoon of a Faun.*

The composition was in its final form by the following fall, and it was heard in September. The music excited its first listeners by its daring; this evocative paraphrase of Symbolist poetry was as unprecedented as the poem itself had been 15 years earlier. Debussy provided an interesting program note: "The music of this Prelude is a very free illustration of the beautiful poem of Mallarmé. By no means does it claim to be a synthesis of the latter. Rather there are the successive scenes through which pass the desires and dreams of the faun in the heat of this afternoon. Then, tired of pursuing the fearful flight of the nymphs and the naiads, he succumbs to intoxicating sleep, in which he can finally realize his dreams of possession in universal Nature." After hearing the music Mallarmé told Debussy, "I was not expecting anything of this kind! This music prolongs the emotion of my poem and sets its scene more vividly than color." Later the poet wrote to the composer, "Your illustration of 'The Afternoon of a Faun' would present no dissonance with my text, unless to go further, indeed, into the nostalgia and the light, with finesse, with malaise, with richness."

Debussy's biographer Edward Lockspeiser has written perceptively about the correspondence between the poem and the music:

> Certain interpretations that have been made of Mallarmé's aesthetic also illuminate the inspiration of Debussy. Mallarmé's poem goes far beyond its theme of abduction. Buried in its abstruse language is a philosophical treatise on the life of the senses and the psychology of sublimation. It is also an exploration of the borderlands between the conscious and the half-conscious, the waking state and the state of reverie.... There is a difference between the dreams of sleep and the musings of reverie. The latter are considered by Mallarmé to be adolescent and even impotent. And from one viewpoint the faun, too, is the adolescent artist anxious to make amorous conquests but remaining more truly a poet....
>
>   The heart of the poem is in a definition of sublimation. Mallarmé attempts to trace the process in which desire first vanishes into the dream and is then transformed into music:
>
>> And further that we might, no matter how high love
>> May be transposed, distill from vulgar thought of shoulder
>> Or thigh, which I pursue with leering scrutiny,
>> A single line of sound, aloof, disinterested.
>
>   I think we may see in the last line the origin of the flute solo at the opening of Debussy's score. In the preceding lines the faun's flute-playing is actually described as "a long solo":

Which, taking to itself my cheek's hot agitation,
Dreams in a long soliloquy that we did entertain
The beauty all around us by deceitfully
Confusing it with that of our credulous song.

These four lines, which bring us to the heart of Debussy's inspiration, are interpreted by [critic Wallace] Fowlie thus: "In the high notes of the flute, the entire experience of love may be reduced into a single melodic line, vain and monotonous as all art is when contrasted with the immediacy and necessity of experience. As he plays thus on his instrument, the faun is master of himself and his feelings. . . ." In the end *L'Après-midi* is seen to be a poem about how a poem, or indeed, music, is written.

The elusive world of Mallarmé's *Faun* called for a new kind of music: apparently vague, more suggestive than assertive, fleeting, non-dramatic. Debussy's unprecedented world of sounds and colors is often called the beginning of modern music. As composer-conductor Pierre Boulez explains, "The flute of the *Faun* brought new breath to the art of music; what was overthrown was not so much the art of development as the very concept of form itself, here freed from the impersonal constraints of [classical forms], giving wings to a supple, mobile expressiveness, demanding a technique of perfect instantaneous adequacy. Its use of timbres seemed essentially new, of exceptional delicacy and assurance in touch."

The opening flute line, for example, is not a melody in the traditional sense. It is a wistful wandering down and then back up a scale: evocative, suggestive, but not really lyrical. As this line returns again and again it is placed in new contexts by its colorful accompaniments. Eventually a true melody is sounded (first in the oboe), but still it is more the mood of this tune than its actual melodic shape to which we respond. Even a contrasting melody (in the full orchestra playing softly) furthers rather than supplants the atmosphere of mystery. Atmosphere is indeed what this music is creating — not a definite set of emotions and certainly not a specific story. Debussy shares with his listeners the very special world suggested to him by the Mallarmé poem.

Antonín Dvořák

Born on 9 September 1841 in Mühlhausen, near Prague.
Died on 1 May 1904 in Prague.

Concerto in B Minor for Cello and Orchestra, Opus 104
Allegro
Adagio ma non troppo
Allegro moderato. Andante. Allegro vivo

The Cello Concerto was composed between 8 November 1894 and 9 February 1895. Revisions were completed on 11 June 1895. Dvořák conducted the first performance with the London Philharmonic Orchestra and cellist Leo Stern in London on 19 March 1896.

The romantic era produced relatively few cello concertos. Since the cello has neither the penetrating high range of the violin nor the sharp percussive sonority of the piano, its sound can easily be overpowered by a full orchestra. In the classical period, by contrast, orchestral ensembles were small. It is unlikely that an orchestra of a dozen or so players would cover a cello. Thus Haydn, for example, wrote cello concertos without any problems of balance. Twentieth-century composers, on the other hand, thrive on difficult challenges, such as composing for cello and large orchestra. In the nineteenth century, however, the standard orchestra was large but composers were not yet deliberate experimenters. It is therefore no surprise that there are no cello concertos by Beethoven, Brahms, Mendelssohn, Berlioz, or Liszt. (Schumann did compose one, however.) Dvořák, on the other hand, was tempted by the challenging medium twice.

At the age of 24 he composed the large but immature Concerto in A Major, which he never orchestrated. At the time he had just begun teaching, and he had fallen in love with one of his students, a 16-year-old named Josefina Čermák. Josefina did not return the composer's love, but he thought that he might win her heart by composing some songs for her. So he spent his time writing the cycle *Cypresses* instead of orchestrating the concerto. But Josefina remained cool, and Dvořák dedicated the songs to someone else. Later he became enamored of Josephina's younger sister, whom he eventually married. But Josephina's connection with Dvořák's cello music was not yet ended.

Since he never orchestrated the A Major Concerto, the composer never had to face the problem of balancing a cello with a full orches-

237

tra. It was thirty years before he again turned his attention to the medium. In the B Minor Concerto he faced the challenge head on.

In 1892 Dvořák began a three-year tenure as director of the National Conservatory in New York. The founder of the conservatory, Jeanette Thurber, hoped to increase the prestige of her school by adding to its faculty one of Europe's leading composers. Thus she began a practice that has remained typical to the present — attracting prominent foreign composers to teach in American schools. The composer was offered a salary 25 times (!) what he had been making at the Prague Conservatory. He was promised a four-month summer vacation. The Conservatory orchestra was placed at his disposal for ten concerts, which were expected to include much of his own music.

Dvořák became something of a celebrity in New York society, but he missed his homeland. After his first season he spent the summer vacation in the small town of Spillville, Iowa, where several Czech families lived. But that atmosphere made him more homesick. After his second season in New York, he spent the summer in Prague. When he again returned to New York, he missed his country still more. After his third season he could no longer bear the thought of living abroad, and he resigned.

His compositions of the period reflect these emotions. The first works written in the United States are full of references to American folk music. The *New World* Symphony is the best known of these pieces. But, by his last American work — the B Minor Cello Concerto — his homesickness prevailed. There are no hints of Americana here, but rather the concerto is full of the spirit of his native Bohemia.

Despite his early attempt at composing a cello concerto, Dvořák continued to think of the instrument as more suited to orchestral and chamber music than to solo treatment. He changed his mind, however, when he heard composer Victor Herbert perform his own Second Cello Concerto in Brooklyn in 1894. Herbert was solo cellist of the New York Philharmonic and also composer of concert works and shows, such as *Babes in Toyland*. Dvořák was impressed with the manner in which Herbert employed a large orchestra, even including trombones, despite the weakness of the cello sound in certain registers. The Bohemian composer decided to use in his own concerto such penetrating instruments as piccolo, triangle, tuba, and trombone — tone colors he had avoided in previous concertos for violin and for piano.

A second stimulus toward the composition of the Cello Concerto came from Hanuš Wihan, a friend of the composer who played cello in the Bohemian String Quartet. Wihan was considered the finest Czech cellist of the day, and Dvořák wrote the concerto especially for him.

The first movement shows the different ways Dvořák solved the problem of balance between cello and orchestra. When the solo instrument finally enters, after a series of themes presented by the orchestra, we hear a long succession of imaginative treatments of its special timbre. The cello, for example, plays the main theme over an understated wind and string accompaniment. For part of this theme, it plays triple stops (three notes at once) to help its sound carry over that of the orchestra. As the solo line becomes more virtuosic, the orchestra enters into a dialogue with the cello, so that the orchestral instruments play only when the cello is performing sustained notes or trills. When the cello plays fast runs, the orchestra is silent. As the two forces join together, the cello plays in its penetrating high register, so that it is readily heard above the orchestra. Other times, the cello plays rapid arpeggios that accompany (and hence blend in with) the orchestral texture. When it comes time for the orchestra to assert its full sonority, the cello is silent: it cannot and hence does not compete with the massive sound of the full ensemble.

The second movement uses most of the same techniques to overcome the balance problem, although in a more lyrical and subdued context. While Dvořák was composing this movement, he received word that his sister-in-law Josephina — the woman with whom he had been in love many years earlier — was seriously ill. He was deeply concerned and therefore decided to use the melody of one of his songs, "Leave Me Alone," in the slow movement of the concerto. This song, one of Josephina's favorites, has certain similarities to a song from the early cycle *Cypresses*, which he had composed in his futile attempt to woo her. The second movement develops both the song melody and the main theme.

The finale is more dance-like than the preceding movements. The cello is utilized in typical fashion: carrying the melody when lightly accompanied, providing a fast-moving accompaniment, or sitting out for the more forceful passages. Later on, the gentle lyricism of the earlier movements reappears, allowing the cello's songful voice to be heard once again in its beautiful high register. Toward the end, the music slows and thins for an ethereal reminiscence of Josephina's song from the second movement. Only at the last possible moment, after the final cello exit, does the music swell and return to its original fast tempo.

Interestingly, this magical ending was not Dvořák's original idea for concluding the concerto. He returned to Bohemia after his American sojourn with a somewhat different concerto in his suitcase. When he arrived home, he learned that Josephina had died, and he decided thereupon to revise the concerto to include a final memorial to the woman who had been his first love. He removed four measures near the end of the finale and replaced them with an extended quotation from Josephina's song. (The composer would no doubt be flabbergasted if he could see a very different association of his Cello Concerto with romantic love: in the 1987 film *The Witches of Eastwick*, the playing of this music leads to such passionate love making between actors Jack Nicholson and Susan Sarandon that her cello bursts into flames!)

Dvořák made further small revisions, as suggested by cellist Wihan. But Wihan also wanted a major alteration: the insertion of a large cadenza just before the end. Dvořák was annoyed, not only because the cellist wished to tamper with the piece merely to show off his virtuosity, but also because such a change would have ruined the passage memorializing Josephina. The composer wrote a strongly worded letter to his publisher, denouncing the cadenza and demanding that the work never be printed with this spurious addition.

Wihan did not play the premiere. For a long time it was believed that the cellist's attempt to insert a cadenza had sufficiently irked Dvořák that the composer was unwilling to allow his friend the privilege of the first performance. But correspondence has recently been discovered that indicates other reasons. Dvořák had been engaged to conduct the premiere in London, with Wihan as soloist, in March 1896. But Wihan developed a schedule conflict and tried to have the date shifted to April. The composer agreed to the date change, but the London Philharmonic management had already planned its season and thought the best solution was to let the March date stand but to engage another cellist. But Dvořák wanted Wihan, and he wrote to the Philharmonic, implying that he would not come at all if another cellist was hired: "I am sorry to announce you that I cannot conduct the performance of the celo [*sic*] conzerto [*sic*], the reason is I have promised to my friend Wihan — *he will play it*. If you put the conzerto [*sic*] into the programme I could not come at all, and will be glad to come another time."

The secretary of the Philharmonic wrote back, "We should have been most happy to have had Mr. Wihan to play your concerto. But as you told me he could not come on the 19 March we thought to please you by including the work, and have engaged Mr. Leo Stern who says he knows the work. Now when all this is done you write to say you cannot come if we include the concerto. It is very embarrassing for us, but as you wish it we will take the concerto out."

Dvořák decided to go to England after all and conduct the premiere with Stern as soloist. Wihan did eventually perform the concerto, and the work was published with a dedication to the cellist for whom it had been written.

Concerto in A Minor for Violin and Orchestra, Opus 53
Allegro ma non troppo —
Adagio ma non troppo
Allegro giocoso, ma non troppo

The Violin Concerto was composed between 5 July and the middle of September 1879. Violinist František Ondříček played the first performance in Prague with the Orchestra of the National Theater, conducted by Mořic Anger, on 14 October 1883.

The crucial event in Dvořák's rise from obscurity to international fame was meeting Johannes Brahms. Brahms had been a member of the jury that awarded Dvořák the Austrian State Prize several years in succession. The two composers admired each other's work. Brahms helped his younger colleague in several ways: he introduced him to Fritz Simrock, who subsequently published much of Dvořák's music, and to the distinguished violinist Joseph Joachim. Joachim had long been an admirer of Brahms' work; in fact, Brahms had just the year before composed his own Violin Concerto for Joachim. When Brahms mentioned that Joachim ought to look at some of Dvořák's music, he played several of the chamber works. As Joachim liked what he heard, he thought of commissioning a concerto.

The composer set to work in July 1879. He traveled to Berlin at the end of the month to confer with Joachim. By September the concerto was completed, and Dvořák sent the score to Joachim in November. The violinist replied in a letter,

> The mail had just arrived with your parcel containing the Violin Concerto, and I feel obliged to thank you for the honor you have done me by the dedication. My sincere interest in your excellent and genuine musicianship, which I hope I have proved with my careful performance of your beautiful, really exquisite Sextet in A Major, makes me the more appreciative of your dedication and the camaraderie for which it speaks! I shall now try to increase the demanded sincerity and am looking forward to inspecting soon, *con amore,* your work.

When Joachim got around to studying the score, he was not totally pleased. He had several suggestions for improvements. Dvořák respected Joachim's opinion, since the latter was not only a first-rate violinist but also a composer, and the concerto was revised.

In May 1880 Dvořák wrote to his publisher Simrock, "According to Mr. Joachim's wish I worked most carefully over the whole concerto, without missing a single bar. He will certainly be pleased by that. I put the greatest effort into it. The whole concerto has been transformed. Besides retaining themes I wrote several new ones. The whole conception of the work, however, is different. The harmonization, the instrumentation, the rhythm, the whole course of the work is new. I shall get it ready as soon as possible and give it immediately to Mr. Joachim in Berlin."

Joachim received the revised score and remained silent for another two years. Finally he wrote to the composer in August 1882.

Recently I made use of some time I had to spare to revise the violin part of your concerto and to make some of the passages, which were too difficult to perform, easier for the instrument. For even though the whole proves that you know the violin very well [Dvořák was himself a violinist], from some single details it may still be seen that you have not played yourself for some time. While making this revision I was pleased by the many true beauties of your work, which it will be a pleasure for me to perform. Saying this with utmost sincerity, I may — without the danger of being misunderstood — confess that I still do not think the Violin Concerto in its present shape to be ripe for the public, especially because of its orchestral accompaniment, which is still rather heavy. I should prefer you to find this out for yourself by playing the work with me. Would it suit you to come here in the middle of September? We could rehearse the composition at the beginning of October with the orchestra of the High School of Music [which Joachim conducted].

The rehearsal took place, and Simrock sent a representative, who made further criticisms. Dvořák was no doubt losing patience. He wanted to have the concerto performed, and if Joachim was not going to do it, he would find someone else. He compromised on some suggested alterations, then he insisted that Simrock publish it. Once it was in print, Dvořák gave up on Joachim and had the work premiered by František Ondříček in October 1883. Joachim never played the concerto, although there were tentative plans for such a performance in London in 1884.

Several historians have speculated on the underlying reasons for Joachim's equivocation. He was a classically oriented, conservative musician, and there were aspects of Dvořák's concerto that must have puzzled him. The structure of the first movement is unusual: the violin enters rather early, the recapitulation is drastically curtailed, it goes without pause into the second movement, and there is no cadenza. The last movement is more like a series of dances than an organically developed symphonic conception. These innovations help to make the piece the fresh, spontaneous work that has endeared it to generations of violinists, but the conservative Joachim might not have recognized these qualities.

The dance-like character of the finale is typical of Dvořák's folk-inspired music. He had recently composed his first set of *Slavonic* Dances, which had more than any other work brought him international fame. Simrock had reaped a small fortune from the dances, as Dvořák had found a style with enormous popular appeal. The finale of the concerto continues in the same tradition, by including such folk dances as the furiant and the dumka.

The opening furiant, which recurs often, has a delightful ambiguity: it can be heard in either 3/4 or 6/8 time (actually it is written in 3/8). Dvořák plays on this dichotomy throughout the movement, thereby creating exciting cross rhythms. When the first theme recurs, the delectable scoring (solo violin, timpani, sustained horns and flutes, *pizzicato* violas, oboes playing a two-note figure, and violins and cellos playing a faster two-note alternation) is reminiscent of Czech bagpipes. Another theme is like a waltz. Each of its phrases ends with what sounds like a Slavonic dancer's three foot-stomps. In the middle of the finale we hear the somber dumka.

Symphonic Variations, Opus 78

The Symphonic Variations was composed between 6 August and 28 September 1877. Ludevít Procházka conducted the Orchestra of the Provisional National Theater of Prague in the first performance, which took place on 2 December 1877 on Sophia Island (now known as Slavonic Island) in Prague.

When Dvořák composed his Opus 38, the Symphonic Variations, in 1877, he considered it one of his finest achievements. His opinion was seconded by the audience at the premiere a few months later, when the work was for some reason listed as Opus 40. Despite its favorable reception, the composer subsequently put the piece aside, and it was not performed again for a decade. The reason, paradoxically, was that Dvořák had become well known. In 1878 some small, simple nationalistic pieces — the first set of *Slavonic* Dances and the *Moravian* Duets — plus some chamber music made the composer's name famous throughout his native Bohemia. Brahms, who knew and respected Dvořák's music, had recommended it to his publisher Fritz

Simrock two years earlier. At that time Dvořák had only a small handful of works in print, but Simrock saw a potential gold mine in the *Moravian* Duets and similar compositions. His publication of this music opened up to Dvořák the wider European market. But the contract with Simrock also began several years of uneasy relations between composer and publisher. Simrock was a shrewd businessman, and he knew the music market far better than the naïve Dvořák. The publisher was interested in songs and small piano pieces, not in large symphonic works. And so, as he got more and more deeply involved with Simrock, Dvořák was pressured to shelve large projects like the Symphonic Variations and turn his attention to smaller works.

Ten years later, once Dvořák's fame had spread, he found renewed confidence in his larger works. He wanted them performed and published. He returned to such earlier compositions as the Symphonic Variations, which he conducted in Prague in 1887. He then approached Hans Richter, one of the great conductors of the day, about the work. Richter wrote from London, "Before fixing my London program, I had intended to ask whether you had something new for me. Now your Symphonic Variations come as a splendid addition to my program — and so they are *definitely* accepted with my warmest thanks. Please send the score and parts as soon as possible."

A few weeks later Richter wrote again: "I have just returned entranced from the first rehearsal for the concert at which we are playing your Symphonic Variations. It is a magnificent work! I am happy to be the first to perform it in London, but why did you hold it back for so long? These variations can take their place among the best of your compositions. . . . They will also be on the program for the next Philharmonic concerts in Vienna."

With such a reception, Dvořák naturally expected that Simrock would eagerly publish the variations. The publisher was reluctant, however, still feeling that small character pieces were more profitable. Simrock and Dvořák were also haggling at this time over the fee for the Seventh Symphony. The publisher furthermore held out for additional *Slavonic* Dances, but Dvořák wanted mainly to see several earlier symphonic works, including the variations, in print. Simrock wrote:

> If only I did sufficient business with your symphonies to be repaid for my enormous expense! But this is far from being the case, and I am thousands down on them. That is how it is — and nothing can change it. What use is it if I make money on one or six works and lose it again on four others? I cannot carry on my business like that! If the performances are successful, the composer always thinks his works will sell. You were successful over

Bülow's performance of your D Minor Symphony, but subsequently not a single copy, not even a piano duet version, was sold. . . . So, unless you also give me small and easy piano pieces (and even these will sell almost exclusively in Bohemia . . .), it will not be possible to publish big works.

Relations became even more strained, but Simrock finally agreed to publish the variations in 1888. Much to Dvořák's consternation, the publication was labelled as Opus 78. Simrock felt that a purportedly new work would sell better than one obviously ten years old. Dvořák understandably wanted his opus numbers to reflect the order of composition, not of publication.

Dvořák's uneasy relationship with Simrock is typical of business dealings between composers and publishers. Today, a hundred years later, the problem is even more acute. Publishers are unwilling to print costly works that will be performed rarely, and composers are reluctant to compose easy pieces that will sell well. Dvořák's troubles are common and, to some extent, inevitable. By the time a work like the Symphonic Variations has gained such widespread popularity that it is played by orchestras worldwide, the copyright period is likely to be close to an end, so that the publisher will be unable to reap huge sums from his earlier investment.

The theme of the variations was taken from a piece for men's chorus called *I Am a Fiddler*, that Dvořák wrote in January 1877. This tune, stated immediately at the outset, is followed by 27 variations and a finale. Since this is an unusually large number of variations, it is not surprising to find them grouped into sections.

One facet of the theme that no doubt attracted Dvořák to it is its irregular phrase structure. Its three parts are respectively 7, 6, and 7 measures long (as opposed to the more standard 8, 8, and 8). Several of the variations, however, regularize these lengths. Another striking feature is the unusual harmony in the second measure, where the fourth degree of the scale (the third note of the tune) is raised despite the descending melodic line. It is possible to follow this alteration through most of the variations. Sometimes it is blatantly melodic, yet other times it is half hidden in the harmony.

The first three variations simply repeat the theme, with embellishments. The real process of variation starts with Variation 4, although Variation 5 brings back the theme in the horn and cellos toward the end. The subsequent variations move progressively farther from the theme. Of particular interest is the quiet *lento* of Variation 14, followed by the trombone *maestoso* of Variation 15. With Variation 17 the time signature changes to 3/4 for a scherzo, and in the next variation the music finally changes key. Variation 19 is a waltz, and Variations 20–24 are in the minor. The music begins to move back toward the theme with the bassoon at the end of Variation 26, followed by a slight variant of the theme, back in the home key of C major, in Variation 27.

The finale follows, in which the theme is treated first in an elaborate fugue and eventually as a polka. The ending is typically grandiose.

Symphony Number 5 in F Major, Opus 24 (76)
Allegro ma non troppo
Andante con moto —
Andante con moto. Allegro scherzando
Allegro molto

The Fifth Symphony was composed between 15 June and 23 July 1875. It was first performed on 25 March 1879 in Prague by the Orchestra of the Czech National Theater, conducted by Adolf Čech.

Dvořák was an unknown, impoverished, 32-year-old composer when his lady-friend informed him that she was pregnant. Despite poor financial prospects, the couple hastily married. Dvořák felt the acute need for money, and he did what most unknown, impoverished composers of today do: he applied for a grant. The composer was Bohemian, and, as Bohemia still belonged to the Hapsburg Monarchy, he was eligible for the Austrian State Prize. He submitted a couple of early symphonies, neither of which had been performed, plus some chamber music. He did not know any of the judges. They included some of the most distinguished musicians of the day: the critic Eduard Hanslick, the conductor Johann Herbeck, and the composer Johannes Brahms. This committee was impressed, and Dvořák received the grant. And he received a renewal for each of three successive years. Dvořák reacted as many composers a century later react upon receiving similar news. He gave up his hated post as an organist, he took a trip, he and his wife moved into a larger apartment, and he started to compose at a feverish pace. His son was born soon thereafter.

The grant led to further opportunities. Dvořák met the judges and became friendly with Brahms. Brahms in turn introduced him to his publisher, Fritz Simrock, who expressed considerable interest in Dvořák's music. It was several years before the publications actually began to appear, but Dvořák knew at last that he was coming out of obscurity.

Simrock was responsible for the confusion in the numbering of Dvořák's symphonies. The F Major Symphony, one of the first works Dvořák composed after learning of the grant, was actually his fifth, but the composer thought of it as his Symphony Number 4 because he had discarded an immature first symphony called *The Bells of Zlonice.* The first symphony Simrock published, however, was the subsequent Symphony in D Major, now known as Number 6. But Simrock printed it as Symphony Number 1, Opus 60. This was in 1881. In 1885 the publisher brought out Dvořák's next symphony as Symphony Number 2, Opus 70. When these works became popular, Dvořák told Simrock about the earlier pieces that lay on his shelf. The publisher agreed to print the F Major, but he wanted to number it in sequence of publication as Symphony Number 3. Furthermore, he wanted to assign it the opus number 76, because he hoped to suggest to prospective purchasers that it was the composer's latest effort. Dvořák protested strenuously, since he did not want the work judged against the standards of his latest compositions. But business won out over art, and Dvořák's fifth symphony, which the composer wanted to call his Fourth Symphony, Opus 24, was published as Symphony Number 3, Opus 76.

It was not until the mid-twentieth century that all the confusion was cleared up, with the publication of all nine Dvořák symphonies, including *The Bells of Zlonice.* Now they are numbered in their proper chronological sequence. Thus, for example, the *New World* Symphony, long known as Symphony Number 5, is now recognized as Symphony Number 9.

The real Fifth Symphony begins with an arpeggiated theme in the clarinets that sounds more like an introduction than the main idea. This impression is strengthened by a grand crescendo to a full statement of what seems to be a main theme — stable, melodic, and forceful. There is also a chromatic second theme, which, in part because it is cast in the distant key of D major, is bright and peaceful. The opening idea dominates the development section, proving that less melodic themes can be better candidates for development than tunes that are already fully developed melodically. This arpeggiated theme has the last word, as the movement closes peacefully. And so an unpromising idea does indeed turn out to be the main theme.

The slow movement begins with a beautiful, melancholy cello theme, coincidentally similar to the famous opening of Tchaikovsky's First Piano Concerto. Dvořák derives accompaniment figures from this tune, which also finds its way into the brighter middle section. The somber mood returns at the end. Without pause the music moves into a transition to the scherzo, a boisterous, colorfully scored piece full of delightfully unexpected contrasts.

After such a brilliant scherzo, a more serious finale seems appropriate. The last movement is dramatic and exciting. Just as the earlier movements have played with distant or "wrong" key relations, so the finale starts out and long remains in the "wrong" key of A minor. When the music finally moves to the tonic F major, it does so with great impact. After a tempestuous development section, the recapitulation begins — again in A minor, but remaining in this unstable area a far shorter time. Before the coda there is a magical passage in which the tonic chord is sustained softly, as if to compensate for all the foreign keys earlier in the movement. Against this chord the strings play reminiscences of the opening theme of the first movement.

The Fifth Symphony is a powerful, beautiful, finely crafted work. It is the first symphony of Dvořák's maturity, and it deserves to be heard far more often than it is. It can easily stand beside his better known, later symphonies. Perhaps Simrock's inclination, to publish it as a later work than it really was, actually had merit.

Symphony Number 6 in D Major, Opus 60
Allegro non tanto
Adagio
Furiant: Presto. Trio: Poco meno mosso. Furiant
Allegro con spirito

The Sixth Symphony was composed between 27 August and 15 October 1880. Adolf Čech conducted the first performance in Prague on 25 March 1881.

Soon after the birth of his first son and his receipt of the Austrian State Prize, Dvořák embarked on a period of intense compositional activity. His style matured as his performances increased. The Austrian Prize was renewed three times. The composer was elated by these successes.

But there was tragedy at home. A daughter was born but died within a few days. Another daughter was born a year later. When this daughter was one year old, she and her brother (age three) both died within a month of each other. The Dvořáks were again childless.

After several months of depression, the composer began to work again. Soon his compositional pace was as rapid as ever. His first widely circulated works, the *Moravian* Duets and *Slavonic* Dances, began to spread Dvořák's reputation abroad. Because his first internationally known music was of folk origins, the composer became known primarily as a Czech nationalist. He responded by making his music even more self-consciously Bohemian. He saw himself as the musical spokesman for his country's culture. But he was not content being known only for short compositions of national flavor. He was eager to write a new Czech symphony. And he was eager for it to be published, so that his reputation would not be solely for short pieces.

The opportunity came when Dvořák attended the Vienna premiere of his Third Slavonic Rhapsody, which received an enormous ovation. He promised to write a symphony for the Vienna Philharmonic Orchestra and its conductor, Hans Richter. Several months later, Dvořák returned to Vienna with the score of his newly completed Symphony in D Major. He played it at the piano for Richter, who embraced the composer after each movement. The conductor promised a performance in Vienna the following month.

As the date approached for Dvořák again to travel to Vienna, he received a letter from Richter, in which the conductor apologized for having to postpone the premiere, owing to the orchestra's fatigue. Three months later Richter again put off the performance, this time citing his wife's confinement, his children's illnesses, his mother's death, and his own overwork. Dvořák began to suspect there were other reasons. In fact, members of the orchestra, who had some say in programming, were opposed to the Austrian ensemble too frequently playing music by a contemporary Czech composer (the Vienna Philharmonic played six pieces by Dvořák between 1882 and 1887).

The composer decided to entrust the premiere to his old friend, Adolf Čech, who conducted the symphony in Prague in March 1881. In April, August Manns introduced the work in London. A month later Richter conducted it, but in London, not Vienna. Vienna heard the work a year later, when Wilhelm Gericke directed it. Richter never played the symphony in the Austrian capital, although he retained his enthusiasm for Dvořák's music and conducted 16 different pieces by the composer.

As the symphony's performances were highly successful, Dvořák's publisher decided to print it. He was usually more interested in shorter works, which were less costly to produce and more likely to be performed, but he was sufficiently impressed with the symphony to take a chance on it. Since it was the first symphony of Dvořák to appear in print, it was published as Symphony Number 1. This illogical numbering remained in effect until about 1955, when the earlier Dvořák symphonies were published and began to be heard regularly.

The nationalistic flavor of the Sixth Symphony is apparent at the outset, where the main theme appears gradually from the spacious consonance of the opening. The triadic nature of the melody is typical of Czech folk music, as is the subsequent interplay between 2/4 and 3/4 rhythms.

The lyricism of the glowing, soulful second movement also has its origins in the folk music of Dvořák's native land. The most direct reflection of Bohemian music in the symphony, however, is found in the third movement. This rhythmically inventive scherzo is a furiant, a vigorous Czech folk dance. The constant intrusion of 2/4 groupings within the 3/4 meter has an effect different from that of the comparable rhythms in the first movement. Because the tempo is fast, we do not primarily feel changing groups of two and three beats but rather an alternation of two different tempos. Sometimes the two speeds are superimposed simultaneously, with an irresistible, buoyant effect. The middle trio section avoids rhythmic complexities and is therefore calmer. Its piccolo solos suggest a rustic scene with shepherds' piping.

The finale, like the first movement and the third movement's trio, starts with a diatonic, almost triadic theme. This initial simplicity gradually gives way to increased chromaticism. This rollicking movement delights the listener with several unexpected turns of phrase.

Symphony Number 7 in D Minor, Opus 70
Allegro maestoso
Poco adagio
Vivace. Poco meno mosso. Vivace
Allegro

The Seventh Symphony was composed between 13 December 1884 and 17 March 1885. Dvořák conducted the first performance with the London Philharmonic Orchestra on 22 April 1885. He revised the symphony the following month.

When fame began to come to Antonín Dvořák, his reputation spread rapidly. Brahms, who knew the Czech composer and his music, introduced him to the publisher Simrock, who subsequently brought out several of his scores. Brahms also secured performances of Dvořák's music in Germany. These successes in Germany led to exposure in England, which in turn led eventually to an invitation to the United States.

The composer was ambivalent about this rapidly achieved fame. He was grateful that his music was widely appreciated, and he was pleased with the additional income from conducting engagements.

But he felt that he still remained "a simple Czech musician." The more he saw of foreign cultures, the stronger his own nationalistic identity became. Although never deeply involved in politics, he found himself increasingly in sympathy with movements aimed at preserving his homeland and its culture. His music reflected his identification with Bohemia.

In the early 1880s, the time of his rise to fame, Dvořák was involved with opera. His opera *Dimitrij* had been a success in Prague, and a performance was contemplated in Vienna. But, as there were just then strong anti-Czech feelings in Austria, the promoters decided not to risk mounting a Czech nationalist opera. The composer was instead urged to write a new opera, specifically for Vienna. He was given two German librettos from which to choose. At the same time the influential critic Eduard Hanslick advised him to drop the new national traits in his compositions if he wanted increased appreciation in Vienna. Brahms suggested that he move to Vienna, which was considered (by Austrians, at least) the musical center of the world. Furthermore, Dvořák had trouble convincing his new publisher Simrock to print the titles of his works in Czech as well as German, and the two had heated exchanges over whether to publicize the composer's name in its German form (Anton) or in the original Czech (Antonín).

Something was wrong, Dvořák felt. He had gained fame partly because of his Bohemian nationalism, but now everyone wanted him to renounce it. After some thought, the composer decided not to write a German opera. He thereby sacrificed a major career advancement in order to remain faithful to his musical nationalism. He stayed a resident of Prague, and he insisted that his compositions be published as Czech music by a Czech composer. He refused to speak German unless necessary, and he declined an invitation from the German Artists' Club. He wrote to Simrock, "May the nations never perish that *possess art* and represent it, however small they may be. Forgive me for this, but I simply wished to tell you that an artist also has a fatherland in which he must have firm faith and for which he must have a warm heart."

The energies he could have put into writing a German opera went instead into his very Czech Seventh Symphony. This work was commissioned by the London Philharmonic Society, which had elected Dvořák an honorary member. But there is nothing English about the symphony. He wanted the new piece to further his reputation in England without compromising his national identity. He wanted it to be his finest effort. He wrote to his friend Antonín Rus, "Just now a new symphony (for London) occupies me, and wherever I go I think of nothing but my work, which must be capable of stirring the world, and may God grant that it will!"

The work in fact did turn out to be what is generally considered Dvořák's best symphony. Several factors combined to make it his symphonic masterpiece: the composer's determination to compose on the highest level for England; the model of Brahms' Third Symphony, which Dvořák had recently heard premiered and which had impressed him; his deepening Czech nationalism, which is expressed in the piece; the dedication and hard work he had intended to put into the composition of a grand opera. With this symphony the composer seemed to be saying: I am bringing into the world a musical statement of myself, a Czech composer; this work is also a statement of the Czech spirit; it compromises nothing to the tastes of German or English musicians or audiences; I was asked to forsake my homeland and its music, and this composition is my response.

The forceful yet brooding quality of the music can be traced to these strong emotions. Nationalism is everywhere evident in its melodies — not quite folk tunes, they nonetheless share with Bohemian peasant songs certain inflections, certain scales, certain rhythms that come perhaps from the speech patterns of the Czech language. The music does express the spirit of the Czech people, more deeply than more self-consciously nationalistic music (such as Dvořák's Slavonic Dances). The themes of the first movement, for example, seem to show the many-sided character of Dvořák's people. The first theme — sometimes dark, sometimes mysterious, sometimes triumphant — contrasts with the second theme, alternately gentle, dance-like, and happy.

These folk influences do not preclude compositional sophistication. Notice, for example, the often intricate interweaving of elaborate figurations in the second movement, which is rich in counterpoint and pungent dissonances.

The third movement betrays its national origins most clearly. The Czech dance called the furiant provides the basic rhythm, in which six-beat measures are subdivided sometimes 2 + 2 + 2 and sometimes 3 + 3. From these conflicting rhythms comes great excitement: we never quite know which grouping will come next. Particularly engaging are the passages in which both rhythms are played simultaneously.

The finale, without overtly referring to the materials of the earlier movements, sums up the variety of moods in the symphony. We hear a contrast of the tragic with the carefree (as in the first movement) in the two main themes. The sophisticated counterpoint from the second movement is often heard as well, as is the rhythmic vitality from the scherzo.

Not always does a composer succeed when he sets out to create a substantial work. Pretentiousness is one of the dangers of self-confidence. But in the Seventh Symphony Dvořák did indeed make a deeply felt and finely crafted artistic statement. That he wanted to give the London Philharmonic a work worthy of their commission was no doubt a secondary inspiration. More significant was his sense of obligation to express his people's spirit in his music. The national identity of Bohemia flows through this music.

Symphony Number 8 in G Major, Opus 88
Allegro con brio
Adagio
Allegretto grazioso. Molto vivace
Allegro ma non troppo

The Eighth Symphony was begun on 26 August 1889 and completed on 8 November of the same year. Dvořák conducted the premiere in Prague on 2 February 1890.

Many composers, at least since Beethoven, have written one symphony that stands out in their *oeuvre* as peaceful, simple, and natural. Beethoven called his the *Pastorale.* Other composers may not have borrowed Beethoven's title (although Vaughan Williams did for his Third Symphony) nor his programmatic linking of an untroubled symphony with images of the countryside, but there is a certain idyllic mood shared by Brahms' Second, Schumann's *Spring,* Schubert's Fifth, Mahler's Fourth, Prokofiev's Seventh, Nielsen's *Espansiva,* Bruckner's *Romantic,* Mendelssohn's *Scottish,* and Dvořák's Eighth.

The Eighth Symphony reflects not only Dvořák's happiest spirits but also a continuation of the commitment to Czech nationalism in his music. Because the work was composed at his summer home in Vysoká, away from the professional pressures of urban life, and possibly because the composer intended to invoke folk music, the symphony was composed effortlessly. He felt his head overflowing with musical ideas: "If only one could write them down straight away! But there — I must go slowly. . . . Melodies simply pour out of me." Because the music flowed easily, the composer was able to start the symphony only one week after completing his previous work, a piano quartet. It took him only 12 days to compose the first movement, another week for the second, four days for the third, and six days for the finale. The orchestration was completed six weeks later.

Two months after completing the work, the composer presented it to the Bohemian Academy for the Encouragement of Art and Literature, to which he had recently been elected. He also presented the symphony as his "exercise" when, in 1891, he was given an honorary degree by Cambridge University. It was played at the presentation ceremonies along with his *Stabat Mater*. Dvořák recalled the incident:

> I shall never forget how I felt when they made me a doctor in England. Nothing but ceremony, and nothing but doctors. All faces were serious, and it seemed to me as if no one knew any other language but Latin. I looked to the right and to the left, and I did not know to whom I was to listen. And when I realized that they were talking to me, I had quite a shock, and I was ashamed at not knowing Latin. But when I think of it today, I must laugh, and I think that to compose the *Stabat Mater* is, after all, more than to know Latin.

The Eighth Symphony, despite its untroubled surface, exhibits several novel approaches to symphonic form. The first movement begins with a theme that is a cross between an introduction and an exposition. Like an introduction, it leads into the symphony by moving toward the main key. But unlike an introduction, it is played at the same fast tempo as the remainder of the movement. What turns out to be the main theme is heard somewhat later: a tune of folk-like simplicity, played by the solo flute. The second theme, characterized by upward leaping octaves in the winds, utilizes a device typical of Czech folk music: it repeats its opening measure two times before proceeding.

The second movement also has an unusual structure. It begins with a somewhat solemn, somewhat poignant theme that at first seems to hover between E-flat major and C minor. What seems to be a contrasting theme arrives in C major: to an accompaniment of violin scales, the flute and oboe play an exquisitely peaceful melody. This tune seems too tranquil to offer the traditional conflict with the main theme. And so it is, for never again does the music return to E-flat major or C minor. In retrospect we understand that the opening, like that of the first movement, is as much an introduction as an exposition. The self-assured nature of the C major melody pervades the music. It is this second theme, not the first, that returns after the development section. Even when the opening theme eventually does come back, it is in the key of the second theme.

The third movement is traditionally structured. It consists of a waltz of distinctly Czech folk character, with a middle section that is also folk-like. At the start of this trio, the flute and oboe play a beautiful tune to a delectable accompaniment in strings and timpani. This melody is taken from Dvořák's opera *The Stubborn Lovers*. After the waltz returns, the middle section is transformed into a fast dance to conclude the movement. In its simplicity this movement recalls the composer's Slavonic Dances.

The finale is a set of variations. After a trumpet fanfare we hear the main theme in the cellos. This melody begins, like the flute theme in the first movement, with an ascending tonic triad. The composer had difficulty constructing this melody. He actually wrote ten different versions of it. It is fascinating to compare them in order to see its eventual shape emerge step by step. The variations move progressively farther from the initial theme, passing through a delightful flute variation and a section in C minor, before the trumpet fanfare signals a return to the theme in its original guise.

Symphony Number 9 in E Minor, Opus 95, *From the New World*

Adagio. Allegro molto
Largo
Molto vivace
Allegro con fuoco

The New World *Symphony was composed in New York between 19 December 1892 and 24 May 1893. Anton Seidl conducted the first performance on 16 December 1893 with the New York Philharmonic Orchestra.*

Jeanette M. Thurber, wife of a wealthy wholesale grocer in New York, had a vision. She wanted to foster an American style of music composition. Her first step was to found the National Conservatory of Music in 1885. The school failed at first to attract much attention or many talented students. Mrs. Thurber, feeling that a major initiative was needed to further her dream, decided to appoint to the Conservatory faculty one of the world's great composers. As Antonín Dvořák was considered by many second only to Brahms among living composers, she invited him to become director of the school. At first he had little interest, but assurances that his music was known and respected in America began to sway him, as did a most attractive contract. He was offered a two-year commitment, with only eight months a year of official duties (administration, conducting, and teaching). The remaining four months would consist of paid vacation. His conducting was to include several of his own works each season. The financial offer was hard to refuse: $15,000 a year, which was 25 times the salary he had been earning at the Prague Conservatory! He accepted. He left for New York, with his wife and two of their four children, in September 1892.

Aside from occasional bouts of homesickness, Dvořák enjoyed his stay in the United States. He was readily accepted into New York society. He found the level of professional performance there high, although he was disappointed in the quality of the Conservatory orchestra. Several of his composition students impressed him. He took a five-room apartment at 327 East 17th Street, and there he composed a number of new works, including the Ninth Symphony.

Hiring Dvořák proved to be a wise decision by Mrs. Thurber. He agreed with her that American composers needed help finding their own musical identity. He saw that most American musicians were far more influenced by the music of the European masters than by their native folk music. At the very time that many European composers, including Dvořák himself, were striving to create musical styles reflecting the national spirits of their homelands, most American composers remained unaffected by American music. The visiting composition professor resolved to help American musicians learn to appreciate and use the wealth of indigenous music on this continent:

> My own duty as a teacher, I conceive, is not so much to interpret Beethoven, Wagner, or other masters of the past, but to give what encouragement I can to the young musicians of America. I must give full expression to my firm conviction, and to the hope that just as this nation has already surpassed so many others in marvellous inventions and feats of engineering and commerce, and has made an honorable place for itself in literature in one short century, so it must assert itself in the other arts, and especially in the art of music.

The composer felt that the key to future developments in American music lay in the study and assimilation of native music. "The music of the people is like a rare and lovely flower growing amidst encroaching weeds. Thousands pass it, while others trample it under foot, and thus the chances are that it will perish before it is seen by the one discriminating spirit who will prize it above all else. The fact that no one has as yet arisen to make the most of it does not prove that nothing is there."

He went further than teaching and writing articles in his promotion of American music. He incorporated into his first major composition in the New World several of the style traits he had discovered in American folk music. He tried to reflect the sounds of Negro and Indian music by using scale patterns common to the two kinds of American music he had studied.

Dvořák learned Negro spirituals and plantation songs from one of the faculty members at the Conservatory, James Huneker. Also, one of his composition students, Harry T. Burleigh, was black, and Dvořák frequently asked him to sing spirituals. The composer studied American Indian music in transcription. His exposure to this music was superficial, since writing down the folk music of one people (American Indians) in the musical notation of another (Europeans) removes the all-important first-hand contact with the live performance tradition. Dvořák actually heard Indian music only once, when he saw Buffalo Bill's Wild West Show. The commercialized songs in that production could hardly have had much to do with authentic Indian melodies. Hence it is not surprising that Dvořák had little in-depth knowledge of American Indian music.

Dvořák composed many pieces while in this country, both in his New York apartment and during a summer sojurn in the small town of Spillville, Iowa. The public warmly received these compositions as acts of homage by the distinguished foreigner. The *New World* Symphony is the best known of these works. While Dvořák strongly denied the use of actual folk music, the character of the music made it hard for audiences to accept that there were no actual Negro or Indian melodies used. The composer was trying only to reflect the character of native music: "It is this spirit which I have tried to reproduce in my new symphony. I have not actually used any of the melodies. I have simply written original themes embodying the peculiarities of the Indian music and, using these themes as subjects, have developed them with all the resources of modern rhythms, harmony, counterpoint, and orchestral color."

William Fisher, one of Dvořák's Conservatory students, subsequently made an arrangement for chorus of the theme from the slow movement, putting to it words that expressed a nostalgia seemingly implied in the music. This arrangement, called "Goin' Home," became so widely known that it was mistakenly assumed (and still is to this day) by many to be a Negro spiritual that Dvořák had quoted in his symphony.

There are other Americanisms in the *New World*. The second theme of the first movement (in the winds), with its lowered seventh scale degree and its drone accompaniment, is decidedly folk-like. The third theme of the same movement (first heard as a flute solo), which is recalled in the third movement, sounds something like the spiritual "Swing Low, Sweet Chariot." There is also an American programmatic element. Henry Wadsworth Longfellow's poem "Song of Hiawatha" was, according to Dvořák, the direct inspiration for the second and third movements. The *largo* was suggested by the scene "Funeral in the Forest," and the scherzo was intended to depict "a feast in the wood where the Indians dance."

Elsewhere in the symphony, however, the composer's nostalgia for his homeland is evident. The two dance-like subsidiary themes of the scherzo and the lyrical second theme (first heard in the clarinet) of the finale suggest Bohemia more than America.

The *New World* Symphony was a gesture of respect toward our native music and toward the American spirit by a great and generous European. He emphasized his admiration for our music: "These beautiful and varied themes are the product of the soil. They are American. They are the folksongs of America, and your composers must turn to them. In the Negro melodies of America, I discover all that is needed for a great and noble school of music."

The American public appreciated Dvořák's love of their native music. Perhaps they appreciated it too much. That the National Conservatory should have to search abroad for its director, that the American press should lionize a visiting composer while all but neglecting native composers, that listeners should learn to legitimatize their native music only after they have encountered it in the respectable garb of a symphony by a European — these factors point to a feeling of cultural inferiority in America. This feeling has abated in recent decades, but it has not totally disappeared. Dvořák was certainly entitled to take inspiration from our music, and he is hardly the only composer to have written travelogue music. And, even if the *New World* is not his finest symphony, it is beautiful and significant. But his understanding of American folk music *was* superficial. Our music was not in his blood. Yet the American public immediately loved the symphony, while they continued to ignore compositions by Americans who reflected their native heritage with greater purity and understanding. Most American composers, however, were as guilty as the public of reverse chauvinism: it took the presence of a European composer writing "American" music to show them the cultural values of their own country.

As our culture has grown stronger, our audiences and composers have slowly come to accept American music as just as viable as the imported music that still fills the majority of our concert programs. That our national identity in music in the late nineteenth century should be more linked to the *New World* Symphony than to music composed by Americans or to the folk music itself simply shows how tied to our European lineage we still were. Today the United States has begun to come of age culturally. Now we value our own artistic creations as much as "postcards" by visiting artists who have become enchanted with our culture. Although on purely musical grounds the *New World* Symphony surely deserves the popularity it has achieved in this country, its initial successes served to underline America's cultural naïveté a century ago.

Edward Elgar

Born in Broadheath, near Worcester, England, on 2 June 1857.
Died in Worcester on 23 February 1934.

Variations on an Original Theme, Opus 36, *Enigma*

Sketches for the Enigma *Variations date from the fall of 1898. The
work was completed on 19 February 1899. Hans Richter conducted
the first performance on 19 June 1899 in London. Elgar subsequently revised the piece, extending the finale. Revisions were completed by 12 July 1899.*

Elgar's *Enigma* Variations was his first major work. It was, in fact,
the first important large orchestral piece by a British composer ever.
The composition served to bring English orchestral music into international prominence, just in time for the twentieth century.

It is fitting that the variations should be known as *Enigma*, since
several mysteries surrounded it at its first performance. In the program note for the premiere, Elgar excited his listeners' curiosity with
one puzzle. "The enigma I will not explain — its 'dark saying' must
be left unguessed, and I warn you that the apparent connection between the Variations and the Theme is often of the slightest texture;
further, through and over the whole set another and larger theme
'goes,' but is not played. . . . So the principal Theme never appears,
even as in some late dramas — e.g., Maeterlinck's *L'Intruse* and *Les
Sept princesses* — the chief character is never on the stage."

People have been wondering about the identity of the enigma
theme past the point where it matters. Some scholars suggested that
Elgar meant by "theme" not a melody but rather a programmatic or
philosophic idea. His friends, however, insisted that there was a real
tune involved. The composer told the secret to only three people, all
of whom carried it to their graves. Late in his life Elgar admitted that
the theme "was so well known that it was strange no one had discovered it." This statement prompted several musicians to try to fit popular melodies contrapuntally to the variation theme. Tunes from
Wagner, Mozart, Chopin, and Leoncavallo were found to work, as
were "God Save the Queen," "Pop Goes the Weasel," and "Auld Lang
Syne." One friend of the composer, who knew well Elgar's penchant
for puzzles and practical jokes, suggested that he was merely playing
a joke on posterity by claiming that there was a hidden melody when,

in fact, there was none. If this suggestion is true, then Elgar may be congratulated on having successfully led generations of musicologists on a wild-goose chase.

There is a second enigma. Since the composer did disclose the programmatic reference of each variation, just what is the meaning of the theme? Elgar did eventually admit, although not publicly, that he was himself the subject of the theme. Actually, as Elgar's biographer Michael Kennedy points out, the opening four notes of the theme seem a natural setting of the syllables "Ed-ward El-gar." Furthermore, in his later work *The Music Makers*, Elgar quotes this theme to illustrate the loneliness of the creative artist.

A third enigma concerns the identities of the friends depicted in the Variations. The score is dedicated to "my friends pictured within." As he was finishing the work, Elgar wrote, "I just completed a set of Symphonic Variations (theme original) for orchestra — thirteen in number (but I call the finale the fourteenth, because of the ill fate attaching to the number). I have in the Variations sketched portraits of my friends — a new idea, I think — that is, in each Variation I have looked at the theme through the personality (as it were) of another Johnny." Each variation is prefaced by the initials or nickname of the friend whom it depicts. When the work was new, Elgar refused to disclose who the individual friends were, thereby compounding the mysteries. He subsequently did publish an extensive explanation, however:

Theme. *Enigma* (andante). Since the theme is an "enigma," Elgar offers no explanation.

Variation 1. *C.A.B.* (andante). The composer's wife, C. Alice Elgar, is portrayed in "a prolongation of the theme with what I wished to be romantic and delicate additions."

Variation 2. *H.D.S.-P.* (allegro). The friend is Hew David Steuart-Powell, a pianist with whom Elgar used to play chamber music. "His characteristic diatonic run over the keys before beginning to play is here humorously travestied in the semiquaver passages; these should suggest a Toccata, but chromatic beyond H.D.S.-P.'s liking."

Variation 3. *R.B.T.* (allegretto). This variation is a caricature of Richard Baxter Townshend, whose deeply resonant bass voice is portrayed by the bassoon. The variation refers to "R.B.T.'s presentation of an old man in some amateur theatricals — the low voice flying off occasionally into 'soprano' timbre."

Variation 4. *W.N.B.* (allegro di molto). The subject is William Neath Baker, "a country squire, gentleman, and scholar. In the days of horses and carriages, it was more difficult than in these days of petrol to arrange the carriages for the day to suit a large number of guests. The Variation was written after the host had, with a slip of paper in his hand, forcibly read out the arrangements for the day and hurriedly left the music-room with an inadvertent bang of the door. . . . [There] are some suggestions of the teasing attitude of the guests."

Variation 5. *R.P.A.* (moderato). Richard Penrose Arnold was the son of poet Matthew Arnold. The younger Arnold "was a great lover of music, which he played (on the pianoforte) in a self-taught manner, evading difficulties but suggesting in a mysterious way the real feeling. His serious conversation was continually broken up by whimsical and witty remarks."

Variation 6. *Ysobel* (andantino). This was Elgar's nickname for Isabel Fitton, who studied violin with Elgar. She switched to viola — hence the prominence of that instrument in this variation. The opening "is an 'exercise' for crossing the strings — a difficulty for beginners." The composer was fully aware of Ysobel's charms and quite taken with her beauty, so that the variation is "pensive and, for a moment, romantic."

Variation 7. *Troyte* (presto). Arthur Troyte Griffith was an architect who had a gift for saying the unexpected — hence the cross-rhythms in his variation. This section is not so much a portrait as a remembrance of Troyte's "maladroit essays to play the pianoforte; later the strong rhythm suggests the attempts of the instructor (E.E.) to make something like order out of chaos, and the final despairing 'slam' records that the effort proved to be vain."

Variation 8. *W.N.* (allegretto). Winifred Norbury and her sister Florence were music lovers. Winifred was employed as a secretary to the Worcester Philharmonic Society. "The gracious personalities of the ladies are sedately shown. W.N. was more connected with music than others of the family, and her initials head the movement; to justify this position a little suggestion of a characteristic laugh is given."

Variation 9. *Nimrod* (adagio). Nimrod was a hunter, and the German word for "hunter" is *Jäger.* Elgar is depicting his friend, the critic August J. Jaeger. The Variation "is the record of a long summer evening talk, when my friend discoursed eloquently on the slow movements of Beethoven and said that no one could approach Beethoven at his best in this field, a view with which I cordially concurred. It will be noticed that the opening bars are made to suggest the slow movement of the Eighth Sonata (*Pathétique*)."

Variation 10. *Dorabella* (intermezzo: allegretto). Dora Penny was a close friend whom Elgar nicknamed Dorabella, from the Mozart opera *Così fan tutte.* "The movement suggests a dancelike lightness." Dorabella wrote an entire book on the *Enigma* Variations and the people portrayed therein.

Variation 11. *G.R.S.* (allegro di molto). The subject is George

Robert Sinclair, a cathedral organist. Some injustice is done, Elgar notes, since the variation has "nothing to do with organs or cathedrals or, except remotely, with G.R.S. The first few bars were suggested by his great bulldog Dan (a well-known character) falling down the steep bank into the River Wye . . . , his paddling up stream to find a landing place . . . , and his rejoicing bark on landing. . . . G.R.S. said, 'Set that to music.' I did; here it is."

Variation 12. *B.G.N.* (andante). Basil G. Nevinson was an amateur cellist and a member of a trio with Elgar and H.D.S.-P. "The Variation is a tribute to a very dear friend whose scientific and artistic attainments, and the wholehearted way they were put at the disposal of his friends, particularly endeared him to the writer." Predictably, the variation includes a wonderful cello solo.

Variation 13. * * * (romanza: moderato). "The asterisks take the place of the name of a lady who was, at the time of composition, on a sea voyage. The drums suggest the distance throb of the engines of a liner over which the clarinet quotes a phrase from Mendelssohn's *Calm Sea and Prosperous Voyage.*" The timpani were supposed to be played with snare drum sticks, but at the first rehearsal the timpanist tried using coins instead, and Elgar liked the sound. The mysterious woman was Lady Mary Lygon, who was on her way to Australia when Elgar wanted to ask her permission to use her initials.

Variation 14. *E.D.U.* (finale: allegro). E.D.U. stands for "Edoo," Alice Elgar's pet name for the composer. He paints himself "bold and vigorous in general style." Just before the first overt restatement of the original theme, the woodwinds play a phrase which is also hidden in Alice's variation. Elgar used to whistle this tune as his special signal to Alice. The Nimrod variation is also recalled.

Manuel de Falla

Born on 23 November 1876 in Cádiz, Spain.
Died on 14 November 1946 in Alta Garcia, Argentina.

◆　◆　◆

El amor brujo

The ballet El amor brujo *was composed between November 1914 and April 1915. Moreno Ballesteros conducted the first performance in Madrid on 15 April 1915. Falla subsequently revised the work considerably. The first concert performance of the final version was given on 28 March 1916 by the Madrid Philharmonic Orchestra, conducted by Bartolomé Pérez-Casas.*

Falla took what was supposed to be a week-long vacation to Paris in 1907, but he was so charmed with the French capital that he ended up staying seven years. The first work he wrote upon his return to Spain was the ballet *El amor brujo,* composed at the time he was completing *Nights in the Gardens of Spain.* In fact, the ballet's tango movement was originally conceived as part of *Nights.*

The impetus for *El amor* came from Pastora Imperio, a singer and dancer who wanted a piece in which she could perform in both capacities. She approached Falla and dramatist Gregorio Martínez Sierra. Both men were interested in the project. Sierra provided a scenario based on an authentic folk tale. Imperio came from a family of gypsies, several of whom became involved with the first performance. Her mother instructed Falla about gypsy folksongs and legends, her brother danced the role of Carmelo, and her sister-in-law and daughter also appeared in the production.

As the work was initially a failure, the composer subsequently rewrote it by combining its two scenes into one, expanding its chamber ensemble to an orchestra, and removing several songs and recitatives. The new version was heard in concert in 1916, but it had to wait for a staged production until 1925, when it was performed in Paris by the celebrated dancer La Argentina. Falla extracted an orchestral suite from the ballet by omitting the vocal numbers.

Through its popular songs and dances, *El amor brujo* reflects the mysticism of the gypsy culture. Particularly Spanish is the manner in which the "brute forces of unregenerate nature," as Falla biographer Burnett James explains the symbolism of the Specter, are overwhelmed by "resolute human mind and spirit," as represented by the love of Carmelo and Candelas. As James explains, the music grew out of the background and the songs and dances of the Andalucían gypsies, and it has about it for much of the time a strangely primitive quality; or rather, a kind of emotional and spiritual elementalism contained within a highly sophisticated technical and stylistic cask. There is also a frequent Oriental flavor, not surprisingly in view of the known and acknowledged Oriental derivation of many aspects of flamenco. . . . Falla understood, although he still had not been there, the significant differences between Andalucía and gypsy Andalucía, and composed accordingly. But he didn't use a single traditional tune, Andalucían or gypsy, although he did employ with great skill and understanding several of the rhythms of popular dance. In the matter of thematic material, he remained true to his own belief that folk music is of most value to the cultivated musician who does not use authentic folk tunes but comes to "feel" the spirit and essence of them and that way allows them to inform but not take over his own compositions. . . . The mystical, mysterious, and modal character of *El amor brujo* set a particular stamp on its music, for it derived from the very heart of the subject matter.

The title *El amor brujo* is usually given in English as "Love, the Magician," but in fact the Spanish is untranslatable. The setting is probably the southern coast of Spain, near Cádiz. Both the subtitle "The Fisherman's Tale" and the seven-beat Cádiz tango in the "Pantomime" movement strongly suggest this locale. The following synopsis appears in the published score of *El amor:*

Candelas, a young, very beautiful, and passionate woman, has loved a wicked, jealous, and dissolute, but fascinating and cajoling gypsy. Although having led a very unhappy life with him, she has loved him intensely and mourned his loss, unable ever to forget him. Her memory of him is something like a hypnotic dream, a morbid, gruesome, and maddening spell. She is terrified by the thought that the dead may not be entirely gone, that he may return, that he continues to love her in his fierce, shadowy, faithless, and caressing way. She lets herself become a prey to her thoughts of the past, as if under the influence of a Specter; yet she is young, strong, and vivacious. Spring returns, and with it love, in the shape of Carmelo.

Carmelo, a handsome youth, enamored and gallant, makes love to her. Candelas, not unwilling to be won, almost unconsciously returns his love, but the obsession of her past weighs against her present inclination. When Carmelo approaches her and endeavors to make her share in his passion, the Specter returns and terrifies Candelas, whom he separates from her lover. They cannot exchange the kiss of perfect love.

Carmelo being gone, Candelas languishes and droops. She feels as if bewitched, and her past love seems to flutter heavily round her like malevolent and foreboding bats. But this evil spell has to be broken, and Carmelo believes to have found a remedy. He has once been the comrade of the gypsy whose Specter haunts Candelas. He knows that the dead lover was the typical faithless and jealous Andalucían gallant. Since he appears to retain, even after death, his taste for beautiful women, he must be taken by his weak side and thus diverted from his posthumous jealousy, in order that Carmelo may exchange with Candelas the perfect kiss against which the sorcery of love cannot prevail.

Carmelo persuades Lucia, a young and enchantingly pretty gypsy girl, the friend of Candelas, to simulate acceptance of the Specter's advances. Lucia, out of love for Candelas and feminine curiosity, agrees. The idea of a flirtation with a ghost seems to her attractive and novel. And then, the dead man was so mirthful in life! Lucia takes up the sentinel's post. Carmelo returns to make love to Candelas, and the Specter intervenes — but he finds the charming little gypsy and neither can nor will resist the temptation, not being experienced in withstanding the allurements of a pretty face. He makes love to Lucia, coaxing and imploring her, and the coquettish young gypsy almost brings him to despair. In the meantime, Carmelo succeeds in convincing Candelas of his love, and life triumphs over death and over the past. The lovers at last exchange the kiss that defeats the evil influence of the Specter, who perishes, definitely conquered by love.

Nights in the Gardens of Spain
En el Generalife
Danza lejana
En los jardines de la Sierra de Córdoba

Nights in the Gardens of Spain was begun in Paris in 1909 and completed in Sitges, near Barcelona, in 1915. José Cubiles was piano soloist when Enrique Fernandez Arbós conducted the premiere in Madrid on 9 April 1916, on a concert that also included El amor brujo. *Falla subsequently revised the score.*

While living in Paris from 1907 to 1914, Falla began a set of nocturnes for solo piano. Two other Spanish musicians also residing in Paris — composer Isaac Albéniz and pianist Ricardo Viñes — urged him to expand the work. When Falla explored their suggestion, the piece became a work in which the piano is an integral, though featured, part of a large orchestra. The gestation process was long, and, according to Jean Aubrey, Paris "waited in vain for the first performance. These nocturnes began to be legendary in the Parisian musical world." But France was not destined to hear the premiere. The work remained unfinished when Falla left for Spain.

Upon his return to his native land, the composer took up residence in the coastal village of Sitges. There he composed at an old piano in the luxurious villa of Catalán painter Santiago Rusiñol. Rusiñol had painted about thirty pictures depicting Spanish gardens, and some Falla experts believe that the inspiration behind *Nights in the Gardens of Spain* came from an exhibition of these paintings that Falla attended. Others disagree, citing the fact that Falla had been working on *Nights* several years before seeing this exhibition. Henri Collet, who knew the composer in Paris, suggested that an atmospheric French poem by Francis Jammes was the real impetus behind the composition.

In fact, both French and Spanish influences are evident. The Spanish scales, rhythms, and motives are cast in a thoroughly French orchestration. As Vladimir Jankélévitch explains, the three movements "would not have this brightness, this unmatched liquidity, this impressionist freshness of sight, sound, and smell, if Ravel's *Rapsodie espagnole* and Debussy's *Ibéria* had not existed. . . . It is the same mystery — the mystery of voluptuousness and a scented darkness — which suffuses the *En el Generalife*, Debussy's *Parfums de la nuit*, and Ravel's *Prélude à la nuit*, just as it is the one and the same vernal intoxication which leaps up from the orchestra of Ravel's *Feria* and the orchestra of *Nights*."

At one point Falla planned to include a fourth movement, based on the tango of Cádiz. But that projected movement found its way instead into *El amor brujo*.

By a strange coincidence, the main motive that appears throughout *Nights* was also used prominently by composer Amadeo Vivès. The reason was that Vivès and Falla had been living in the same house and every day had heard a blind old beggar play this motive on his out-of-tune violin. They both unconsciously adopted the street musician's tune. Neither composer realized that the motive was not original until long after they had completed their respective pieces.

Falla biographer Burnett James explains the aesthetic behind *Nights*:

[It] reveals very clearly from a particular standpoint the dualism inherent in the Spanish temperament and consciousness and therefore in Spanish art. The score contains as perhaps no other does, at least as directly and with the utmost subtlety, the twin poles of Moorish charm and sensuality and Gothic intellectual idealism. The floating arabesques, the nocturnal warmth and emotive poetry complement perfectly the beautiful architecture of the Alhambra, with its gardens and fountains and cypress trees, the supreme legacy in southern Spain of the Moorish occupation. Yet underlying this there is an outline of strong, lean, rhythmic structure; the crisp accents and occasional asperities of harmony and texture pay their tribute to the great tradition of the Spanish Gothic. . . . If the charm and sensuality are the most immediately striking elements in the seductive "Symphonic Impressions," as the subtitle of the score has it, that is because of its poetic origins in the mind of the composer, origins that go back to Paris, where the embryonic ideas first came to him.

The composer wrote about *Nights* as follows:

If these "symphonic impressions" have achieved their object, the mere enumeration of their titles should be a sufficient guide to the listener. Although in this work — as in all which have a legitimate claim to be considered as music — the composer has followed a definite design, regarding tonal, rhythmic, and thematic material, . . . the end for which it was written is no other than to evoke [the memory of] places, sensations, and sentiments. The themes employed are based (as in much of the composer's earlier works) on the rhythms, modes, cadences, and ornamental figures which distinguish the popular music of Andalucía, though they are rarely used in their original forms. The orchestration frequently employs, and employs in a conventional manner, certain effects peculiar to the popular instruments used in those parts of Spain. The music has no pretensions to being descriptive; it is merely expressive. But something more than the sounds of festivals and dances has inspired these "evocations in sound," for melancholy and mystery have their part also.

More expressive than descriptive, evocations in sound, melancholy and mystery — these terms suggest musical impressionism, and *Nights in the Gardens of Spain* is no doubt Falla's most impressionistic work. It is easier to explain what impressionism is not than what it is. The term, borrowed from the visual arts, refers to composers' attempts to portray feelings and impressions associated with places, scenes, events, or people. It stops far short of literal tone painting, such as Richard Strauss's bleating sheep in *Don Quixote* or Charles Ives' conflicting brass bands in *The Fourth of July.* Yet impressionism is equally far removed from absolute music, such as the symphonies of Brahms, that claims to be about nothing beyond itself. Impressionistic music is concerned with something specific but intangible, with something elusive and abstract, with human feelings.

Each of the three movements of *Nights* refers to a different Spanish garden. The first is "In the *Generalife.*" The *Generalife* (which means "Garden of the Architect") is part of the Alhambra, the ancient fortress of the Moorish kings of Grenada. This hillside garden contains fountains and ancient cypresses. Falla never divulged in what garden the "Dance in the Distance" takes place. The third movement's locale is "In the Gardens of the Mountains of Cordova."

The Three-Cornered Hat

The Three-Cornered Hat was originally a two-act pantomime entitled The Corregidor and the Miller's Wife, *composed in 1916–17 and first performed in Madrid on 7 April 1917 under the direction of Joaquín Turina. Falla expanded the work to a two-act ballet in 1918–19. This version was first produced by the Ballets Russes, conducted by Ernest Ansermet, on 22 July 1919 in London.*

Falla had long wanted to compose a stage work based on the novel *The Corregidor and the Miller's Wife,* by Pedro Antonio de Alcarcón. This story, based on a folk tale, is full of comical misunderstandings and adventures. Composer Hugo Wolf had already used the novel as the basis of his opera *Der Corregidor,* performed in 1896 and subsequently forgotten.

Serge Diaghilev, the Russian impresario who had commissioned ballets from such composers as Stravinsky, Debussy, Ravel, and Prokofiev, was interested in the project. World War I intervened, however. Falla wrote in the meantime a preliminary version in the form of a pantomime with chamber ensemble. Diaghilev, who traveled to Madrid to see this work, was enthusiastic. He suggested certain modifications, and Falla began the complete ballet. By the time it was finished, the War was over and Diaghilev's Ballets Russes was again functioning.

For the production, which took place in London, Diaghilev assembled some of the top talents of the day. The leading dancers were

Karsavina, Woizikovsky, and Massine, who was also choreographer. The conductor was Ernest Ansermet, and the sets and costumes were designed by Pablo Picasso, who had never before done ballet design. He finished painting the drop curtain during the final rehearsals. Diaghilev was so taken with this curtain that he asked Falla to compose an introduction, during which the audience could admire Picasso's work. The composer completed this prelude in 24 hours.

The setting is outside a mill. There are vines covered with grapes, a well, and a cage containing a blackbird. On the wall is a sundial. Inside the mill can be seen a large bed, which can be hidden by drawing some curtains. We hear a distant voice singing:

> Little wife, secure your door; the Devil may now be sleeping, but you can be sure he will awaken!

The Miller and his Wife are working happily at their mill. The Miller tries to make the blackbird announce that it is *two* o'clock (three-note rising figure played twice on muted trumpet). The blackbird responds by whistling *three* times (piccolo and solo violin). The Miller tries again. This time the blackbird responds with *four* whistles. The Miller is furious (upward rush in full orchestra). The Wife, who is on a chair gathering grapes, laughs (woodwind, then solo violin, trills). She jumps down (downward run in harp and celeste). She offers the blackbird a grape and gently echoes the Miller's exhortation (three-note figure twice in low flute). The blackbird responds with *two* whistles. The Wife claps her hands and leaps with joy (full orchestra).

The Miller and his Wife exchange love teases (3/4 dance in full orchestra). He goes to the well to draw water for the garden (fast, high piccolos, violins, and violas). He whistles as he waters the plants (piccolo alone). A well-dressed, handsome man comes by and ogles the Wife. The Miller interrupts his work and his whistling to watch (the orchestra continues the whistling tune). By finishing the orchestra's tune (single piccolo note), he seems to be telling the man that the beautiful woman is *his* wife. The Wife laughs good-naturedly (winds and strings).

A procession approaches (timpani and then other low instruments). It is the Corregidor (local magistrate) with his retinue. The Corregidor drops his gloves, which the Wife returns to him (march music). He is taken with her beauty.

As soon as the procession has passed, the couple return to their work (3/4 dance). A girl comes by with a pitcher of milk on her head (trills in the flute and clarinet). The Miller smiles at the girl and throws her a kiss, but his Wife is jealous. She becomes angry and starts to cry (high strings). The Miller consoles her with gallant bows, as he swears that he loves only her. The Wife's tears gradually turn to smiles, and the Miller kisses her to seal their reconciliation. The steps of the approaching Corregidor are now heard again (solo bassoon). The Miller and his Wife hastily separate, and the Corregidor appears (*pizzicato* string march). The Wife mocks him (woodwind interjections). The Corregidor has returned to woo her. She protests to the Miller that she loves only him and that she scorns the Corregidor's advances. At her suggestion, the Miller hides behind a tree to watch.

The Miller's Wife begins her dance, a fandango, pretending not to notice the approaching Corregidor (the characteristic fandango rhythm — a mixture of 3/4 and 6/8 — in the full orchestra). The Wife dances ever more passionately, until suddenly she pretends to be startled by the Corregidor (interruption by two horns holding a single note). He comes forward, inflamed by the dance he has witnessed (bassoon solo, playing a well-known Andalucían dance, the *olé gaditano*). The Miller's Wife pretends to be honored by his visit (full string section playing a minuet). She gives a long, ceremonious curtsy and laughs (flute solo).

The Wife offers her grotesque admirer some grapes and indulges in all manner of flirtation as she circles around him. The Corregidor tries in vain to catch a grape in his mouth and at the same time to kiss the woman. He chases her and falls down (groans in the horns and *glissandi* in the cellos). The Miller appears (fast violin run), in order to investigate the commotion. The Corregidor, fearing that the Miller may have witnessed his advances, begins to tremble (fast bassoon solo). The Miller and his Wife help the Corregidor up and shake off his clothes, a little more vigorously than necessary. The Corregidor goes off angrily, and the couple is joyous at this prank. A Constable appears menacingly (trumpet solo), but the couple refuses to let this premonition spoil their fun. They dance the fandango to end the first act.

The second act takes place that night. Some neighbors have joined the Miller and his Wife to celebrate St. John's Night. They dance a *seguidillas* based on two folksongs — one a gypsy tune (violins at the beginning), the other a melody Diaghilev once heard a Spanish fiddler play (introduced in the cellos and string basses). The Wife asks her husband to dance for their friends. He complies with a farruca, a flamenco dance (introduced by a horn solo). The Miller begins almost motionless, dancing only with his heels, and gradually becomes more and more frenzied.

Constables interrupt the festivities (vigorous dance). They show the Miller a paper that says he is arrested on orders from the Corregidor. They refuse to say why. The Constables lead the Miller away and refuse to let his Wife follow. She is alone, gazing into the distance. She hears from afar a song:

In the night the cuckoo sings, warning husbands to secure their latches, for the Devil is vigilant. In the night the cuckoo sings: cuckoo! cuckoo! cuckoo!

The cuckoo clock strikes nine (clarinet, low violins, and glockenspiel), echoed by the blackbird (piccolo and solo violin). The Wife puts out the lights and draws the curtains.

The Corrigedor suddenly appears (bassoon). He tries to seduce the Wife again, but she eludes him. In the ensuing chase he falls into the stream (descending bassoon solo) and yells (trills in full orchestra). He comes out of the water, and the Wife is indignant. Every time he tries to speak, she interrupts him by stamping her foot (clarinet and English horn continually interrupted by orchestra). Aroused by anger and passion, he chases her. She threatens to shoot him. He falls to the ground in fear (horn and cellos interrupt). She runs off, and the Corregidor takes off his clothes and puts them on a chair to dry. He hides in the bedroom. The Miller, who has escaped, reappears (flute alone) and, seeing the Corregidor's clothes, writes a note saying that he will avenge himself by seducing the Corregidor's wife. The Miller goes off dressed as the Corregidor, and the Corregidor, reading the note, puts on the Miller's clothes in order to run after him.

The final scene is full of confusion. The police appear, in pursuit of the escaped Miller, just as the Corregidor is coming out of the mill dressed in the Miller's clothes (strings and trumpets play the Corregidor's march). The police tackle the Corregidor. The despairing Wife returns (high strings) and sees what she thinks is an attack on her husband by the police. She joins the fray to protect him, not realizing that he is actually the Corregidor. The neighbors reappear to add to the confusion. Since it is still St. John's Night, they dance a *jota* (the full orchestra plays an actual folk dance that Falla had heard in Aragon). The Miller reappears, pursued by more police (soft wind tremolos and low string figures, punctuated by brass playing a children's song whose words are "You won't catch me!"). The *jota* continues as more neighbors join in the confusion. The Miller sees his Wife defending the Corregidor (the orchestra plays the "grapes" music), and he becomes furiously jealous. The Miller attacks the Corregidor. Confusion mounts (the orchestra plays several motives in turn — the *jota*, the Miller's dance, the Constables' motive, the "grapes" dance, the children's hide-and-seek tune). During the melee the true identities of the two men are discovered, and the Miller and his Wife are reconciled. The Corregidor is scoffed by the crowd and, in true Spanish tradition, tossed in the air on a blanket. The crowd is joyous.

In his book on the composer, Burnett James explains the nationalistic themes of the ballet. The three-cornered hat, worn by the Corregidor, is the symbol of authority in Spain; and nothing delights a Spaniard more than the debunking of authority. . . . Falla's ballet is very properly devoted to making the local representative of law and order look ridiculous; aided of course by the representative himself, who is determined to put himself in a ridiculous situation. But it is also something more than that. Basically, it upholds the pride and dignity of the individual, both in the obvious sense and at deeper levels. It is by no means a simple case of good and evil, which is so easy as not to be worth the trouble. It is more subtle, more complex. The Corregidor, gross and coarse though he is, can hardly be called evil so much as pompous, muddle-headed, lecherous, and stupid — a fairly alarming combination in anyone who wields authority over others and by no means uncommon; but hardly satanic. He is the epitome of all blundering, scheming, self-satisfied officialdom. Although he uses his authority, via his . . . [Constables], for the purpose of trying to seduce another man's woman (the Miller's Wife, who is not at first all that averse to the exercise, in a general and non-specific way), he is no Scarpia. For one thing, he is not nearly clever enough. No heads are cut off, no one gets a knife between the ribs or faces a firing squad. And the Corregidor himself comes to no particularly bad end. The worst that happens to him is a dousing in the mill stream, much enthusiastic ridicule, and an honest taste of blanket-tossing after the honorable Spanish custom. And because he is not evil, only preposterous, we can feel for him a kind of reluctant sympathy. . . . His stupidity, incompetence, and pomposity lead to his undoing. He is laughed out of court, not trampled down in hatred. The chortling bassoon tells us so. The traditional Spanish faith in individual dignity and personal freedom is vindicated, its traducers ceremoniously and uproariously defeated.

César Franck

Born on 10 December 1822 in Liège, Belgium.
Died on 8 November 1890 in Paris.

◆　◆　◆

Symphony in D Minor

Lento. Allegro non troppo. Lento. Allegro. Lento
Allegretto
Allegro non troppo

The D Minor Symphony was begun in 1886 and completed on 22
August 1888. It bears a dedication to Franck's student, composer
Henri Duparc. It was first performed on 17 February 1889 at Paris
Conservatory under the direction of Jules Garcin.

In order to appreciate why Franck's Symphony in D Minor was a failure at its first performance, it is necessary to understand the musical
climate in Paris in the 1880s. There were essentially three factions.
The general public was interested nearly exclusively in opera, often
of the most trivial sort. The progressives, who included Franck and
his students, were excited by the radical new music of Wagner and
Liszt. The Paris Conservatory, at which Franck was a professor, represented the musical establishment. Through their teaching and their
control over what was performed at the Conservatory, the other faculty composers sought to uphold the symphonic tradition of Beethoven and Haydn. Since he taught not composition but organ,
Franck was considered an outsider. The composition professors could
not sympathize with his interest in Wagnerian harmonies, despite
the current rage in Paris for Wagner's music, especially among the
younger composers. Franck's D Minor Symphony (actually not his
only one: fifty years earlier he had composed a large G major symphony, which was performed in 1841) owes allegiance to both traditions: its symphonic form is Beethovenian while its harmonic language is Wagnerian.

Wagner wrote music dramas, not symphonies. Thus his popular
appeal in France was understandable, since opera dominated French
musical life in the second half of the nineteenth century. Most of the
French Wagnerians — including Franck's pupils Vincent d'Indy and
Henri Duparc, plus the young Emmanuel Chabrier (who decided to
become a composer upon hearing a performance of the Bayreuth
master's *Tristan und Isolde*) — composed operas, programmatic music, and vocal music. They, like Wagner, understood the intensities of

chromaticism and modulation as means to express specific emotions. But could a symphony with no story, with no text, be an appropriate vehicle for Wagnerian harmonies? According to the Parisian musical establishment, the answer was a resounding no. A symphony was supposed to follow the model set down by Beethoven (and carved in granite in Conservatory theory classes). An orchestral work in three rather than the traditional four movements, which used Wagnerian harmonies and modulations, and whose form was loose and rhapsodic — this was no symphony at all in the eyes and ears of the Conservatory establishment. No matter that Franck thoroughly used and extended Beethoven's principle of thematic consistency, no matter that the D Minor Symphony adhered to the outlines of classical form: the work was destined to be condemned.

It would have been strategically wiser for Franck to have the symphony performed outside the Conservatory, away from the reactionaries on the faculty and the conservatives in the subscription audience. Conductor Charles Lamoureux, who had included in his own concerts many of the Wagnerian works of Franck's students, considered performing the piece, but in the end he refused, presumably because it was cast in symphonic form rather than in the genres favored by Wagner and Liszt. "Let [Franck] take it to the Conservatory," Lamoureux proclaimed. "That is the sanctuary of the symphony."

Franck did just that. The first performance was given by the orchestra of the Paris Conservatory. The audience of conservatives and pedants thought they knew what a symphony was supposed to sound like, and Franck's new piece did not come close to their ideal. They dismissed it, often for the silliest of reasons.

Composer Vincent d'Indy recalled:

The performance was quite against the wish of most members of the famous orchestra, and was only pushed through thanks to the benevolent obstinacy of the conductor, Jules Garcin. The subscribers could make neither head nor tail of it, and the musical authorities were much in the same position. I inquired of one of them — a professor at the Conservatory, and a kind of factotum on the committee — what he thought of the work. "That a symphony?" he replied in contemptuous tones. "But, my dear sir, who ever heard of writing for the English horn in a symphony? Just mention a single symphony by Haydn or Beethoven introducing the English horn. There, well, you see — your Franck's music may be whatever you please, but it will certainly never be a symphony." That was the attitude of the Conservatory in the year of grace 1889.

(This "learned" professor was apparently unacquainted with Haydn's Symphony Number 22, which has two English horns, nor with Saint-Saëns' Second Symphony, which also includes one in its orchestra.)

Other pedantic criticisms included that of composer Charles Gounod, who was overheard saying, "It is the assertion of impotence pushed to the lengths of dogma." Also, Conservatory composition professor Ambroise Thomas asked how a symphony can be in D minor "when the principal theme at the ninth bar goes into D-flat, at the tenth C-flat, at the 21st F-sharp minor, at the 25th B-flat minor, at the 26th C minor, at the 39th E-flat major, and at the 49th F minor?" Actually, this criticism is misleading, since these keys are merely touched upon briefly, while the main keys of the movement are quite traditional: the second theme starts in F major and the recapitulation, which begins in D minor, presents the second theme in D major.

Franck's problem was more political than musical. Outside his circle of devoted students and admirers, he was virtually unknown. As one unkind critic put it, "Why play this symphony here? Who is this Mr. Franck? A professor of harmonium, I believe." The composer was recognized, if at all, as an organ teacher who in his spare time created pieces that were rarely performed. In fact, up to the age of 57 he had written only a couple of substantial works. Virtually all his music that is known today was composed in the last four years of his life. Thus, the D Minor Symphony greeted an audience that was both suspicious of the composer's credentials and skeptical of his aesthetics, even before the first note was sounded. The concert subscribers assumed there must be a good reason why the 66-year-old composer of the work they were about to hear was not established either as a Conservatory composer or as the creator of popular concert or operatic works.

So great was the prejudice against the symphony that, at the dress rehearsal, Franck's loyal students had to surround him to protect him from the vocal criticisms of other faculty members and students at the Conservatory. The composer's wife could not bring herself to attend the concert and witness the expected derision. At the actual premiere, reactions were mixed. The public was bewildered, the Conservatory professors were hostile, and the critics were divided, but Franck's circle of disciples was enchanted.

Tastes change, however. Before too many years passed, Franck and his school became the conservative establishment in France, against which still younger composers rebelled. The Symphony in D Minor was then seen as an upholder of tradition, because it utilized polyphony, classical forms, and Wagnerian harmonies — musical values that the younger generation sought to overthrow. This generation, which included Debussy, Ravel, and Satie, cultivated an indigenous French musical language that had little to do with either Wagner or his French counterpart.

Yet the music of Franck continued to attract an ever wider public, especially as it was vigorously promoted and defended by the composer's former pupils. As historian Paul Henry Láng explains, "The ecstatic yet sensuous and disquieting quality of Franck's music pleased the overrefined aural senses of the public, no longer capable of subsisting on diatonic harmonic logic; at the same time they beheld the saintly devotion of the man, his indifference to success and financial returns, his apostolic zealousness to move a public indifferent to pure music, and his love of the faithful disciples gathered around him. Franck has been at once perhaps the most overrated and the most calumniated of composers of recent times."

In the hundred years since the premiere of the symphony, opinions of it have continued to vacillate. Some writers have praised its vitality, while others have criticized its looseness of form (perhaps traceable to Franck's background as an organ improviser) and its squareness of phrase structure. The Symphony in D Minor has enjoyed periods of enormous popularity with conductors, orchestras, and audiences, and it has suffered periods of neglect. But latter-day musicians and music lovers judge the work by its intrinsic merit, something that seems to have eluded its first listeners. They were too caught up in the typically French polemics for and against the symphony and its composer to be able to respond to its inherent beauty.

Franck, in contrast to his colleagues on the Conservatory faculty, thought of the work as very much within the symphonic tradition, despite its harmonic boldness. Although he admitted that the work was "very daring," he wrote the following explanation of its traditional spirit:

The work is a classical symphony. At the end of the first movement there is a recapitulation, exactly as in other symphonies, for the purpose of more firmly establishing the main subjects, but here it is in an alien key. Then follow an andante and scherzo. It was my great ambition to construct them in such a way that each beat of the andante movement should be exactly equal in length to one bar of the scherzo, with the intention that after the complete development of each section one could be superimposed on the other. I succeeded in solving that problem. The finale, just as in Beethoven's Ninth Symphony, recalls all the themes, but in my work they do not make their appearance as mere quotations. I have adopted another plan and made each of them play an entirely new part in the music.

The main motive, which is destined to pervade the symphony, opens the first movement. It is, interestingly enough, virtually the same figure as that which opens two other works, which represent the two traditions Franck sought to merge: Liszt's symphonic poem *Les Préludes* and the finale of Beethoven's Haydnesque String Quartet in F Major, Opus 135. When Franck's slow introduction gives way to an allegro, we hear this figure speeded up but otherwise unchanged. The slow version is heard thrice more, twice in imitation: at the recapitulation and at the end of the movement.

The second movement begins with a tune that turns out to be the accompaniment for the lyrical English horn theme. Franck's description of the two moods of this movement is accurate. The middle section's scherzo proceeds at exactly three times the speed of the slow first part, so that no change of tempo or meter needs to be notated. Thus Franck could combine the slow and fast ideas simultaneously toward the end of the movement.

The finale has its own two main melodies, but it also treats extensively the lyric theme from the middle movement and, eventually, the two themes of the first movement. Franck takes his inspiration from both Beethoven and Wagner. Beethoven often unified multi-movement works by having themes of earlier movements recalled later. Wagner's system of *leitmotiven* provided a means by which a network of distinct motives could pervade and unify an entire large composition. Franck's contribution, most noticeable in the D Minor Symphony's last movement, was to apply Wagner's operatic technique to a Beethovenian symphonic structure and thereby to extend Beethoven's methods of thematic derivation.

Although his contemporaries may have deplored the intrusion of Wagnerian techniques and harmonies into the hallowed symphonic tradition of Beethoven, Franck's ideas have both integrity and power. Thus the symphony has survived far longer than the petty polemics that confronted it at its premiere.

Alexander Glazunov

Born in St. Petersburg (now Leningrad) on 10 August 1865.
Died in Paris on 21 March 1936.

Concerto in A Minor for Violin and Orchestra, Opus 82

The Violin Concerto was composed in 1904 at St. Petersburg and at Glazunov's summer retreat in Oserki. Mischa Elman was soloist at the first performance, which took place in London on 17 October 1905.

Glazunov belonged to what is sometimes called the "second generation" of Russian composers. He came after and to a large extent continued the work of the "Mighty Five" — Mussorgsky, Rimsky-Korsakov, Borodin, Balakirev, and Cui — and their contemporary Tchaikovsky. This first generation had struggled, both in their compositions and in their professional activities, to establish a Russian national school of composition. They were concerned to what degree their music should be like that of the West (mainly Germany and Italy) and to what extent it should use native Russian folk idioms and coloristic harmonies and orchestrations. Opinions ranged widely, and the composers of the first generation succumbed in varying degrees to the temptation to imitate their Western colleagues. Nonetheless, they did succeed in building a native symphonic repertoire. By the time Glazunov reached his maturity, the battle for an indigenous style had been won.

Several factors contributed to a subsequent decline in Russian nationalism during Glazunov's lifetime. As Western Europeans became more aware of Russia's nationalist spirit, cross fertilization became inevitable. Travel was now easier, and the nationalism which had reached its height in the 1860s was facing the onslaught of an internationalism brought to Moscow and St. Petersburg by travelers from the West. Furthermore, the older generation was dying. By 1890 novelists Dostoevsky and Turgenev were dead and most of Tolstoy's major works had been written. Nineteenth-century cultural liberalism was beginning to give way to twentieth-century conservatism. In music, Tchaikovsky was writing his last works, Rimsky-Korsakov was becoming an academic pedant who taught his students mainly the German classics, and Borodin and Mussorgsky were dead. The

278

future of Russian music lay in the hands of Glazunov and his contemporaries Taneyev, Arensky, Ippolitov-Ivanov, and Liadov.

These composers did not have to struggle to establish the validity of their art; they inherited it. They did not have to forge a new style; that too was handed to them. Thus they did not create music with the unbridled vitality that comes from creating a new idiom. Their task was rather to reconcile Russian nationalism with the centuries-old traditions of Western music. This was a more intellectual than spontaneous challenge, and, not surprisingly, many of these composers retreated into academicism. It is also not surprising that within this desire for integration with Western Europe lay the seeds for the destruction of Russian nationalism. It is typical of his generation that most of Glazunov's major works were written before he was forty, and that his late works are less colorful and less exciting than his early pieces. The Violin Concerto is virtually his last work composed before this decline began.

Glazunov had an enormous talent. He began composing at the age of eleven. By the time he was 14 he was taking lessons from Rimsky-Korsakov, who said that his young pupil progressed "not day to day but hour to hour." When Glazunov was 16, his First Symphony was performed. His teacher reported, "The public was astounded when the composer came forward in his high school uniform to acknowledge the applause. But there were a few snarls from the critics. And there were caricatures in the newspapers depicting Glazunov as a child at the breast. Rumor had it that the symphony had not been written by him but commissioned by his wealthy parents from 'you know whom.'"

As a result of this premiere, Glazunov became, despite his youth, a member of an informal circle of Russia's leading composers. In 1884 he traveled to Germany, where Liszt was impressed by a performance of the First Symphony. Glazunov was much taken with the innovations in the music of Liszt, Wagner, and Brahms, and, as a result of his studying their scores, the Russian nationalism in his own works gave way somewhat to a more international style.

A few years later, when his friend Borodin died, Glazunov undertook to complete and edit several of his unfinished works. Glazunov was able to write down from memory the *Prince Igor* Overture, which he had heard Borodin play once at the piano.

In 1899 Glazunov became a professor at the St. Petersburg Conservatory. He composed his Violin Concerto, which he dedicated to the great violinist Leopold Auer, in 1904. It was premiered, first in England by the young Mischa Elman and then in Russia by Auer, in 1905. That same year Glazunov resigned from the Conservatory as a protest to the firing of Rimsky-Korsakov, who had been dismissed for sympathizing with striking students. Both men were reinstated after a few months, and Glazunov was made director of the Conservatory. He was then at the height of his fame: his music was performed in many countries, he had traveled in the West, and he had received honorary degrees from Cambridge and Oxford Universities.

The hectic life of an academic administrator took its toll. Glazunov's works fell sharply in number and quality after he assumed the directorship of the Conservatory. He nonetheless remained in that position until 1930. He was a dedicated teacher, and he helped many students, including Prokofiev and Shostakovich. In time, however, he came to be regarded by the Conservatory students as hopelessly old-fashioned. His position had become that of a guardian of tradition against the threats of such Western modernists as Stravinsky, Schoenberg, Strauss, and Mahler.

The Russian Revolution of 1917 made life difficult for Glazunov. He was forced to move, with his aged mother, into an unheated two-room apartment. There the famous composer received many distinguished visitors, including author H. G. Wells. Wells recalled, "He used to be a big, florid man, but now he was pallid and much fallen away, so that his clothes hung loosely on him. . . . He told me that he still composed but that his stock of music paper was almost exhausted." Despite his hardships Glazunov remained active as a conductor, administrator, and composer.

In 1928 he took a leave of absence from the Conservatory to go to the West. He guest conducted in many countries, including the United States. As his health was deteriorating, he resigned from the Conservatory and remained in Paris for his final years.

The structure of the Violin Concerto shows the influence of Liszt. Like Liszt's Second Piano Concerto, it is written as one extended movement that contains sections corresponding to the traditional three-movement concerto. The first "movement" is interrupted after the exposition of two main themes by a slow "movement" in the distant key of D-flat major. After this andante the opening "movement" resumes with a development of its themes, culminating in a written-out cadenza. Instead of recapitulating the opening themes, the music goes into a rondo, which serves as the finale.

The concerto is a good example of Glazunov's fondness for both Russian and Western elements. The themes do have faint echoes of Russian folk melodies, but their manner of development is more intricate than in most nineteenth-century Russian symphonic music. The final "movement," however, is more like the nationalist music of, for example, Borodin. This section has a wealth of wonderful melodies, again with more than a hint of old Russia in them. Furthermore, the section unfolds more through variation and alternation of these themes than by true development. This procedure is reminiscent more of the music by the "first generation" of Russians than of that by their Western counterparts.

Edvard Grieg

Born on 15 June 1843 in Bergen, Norway.
Died in Bergen on 4 September 1907.

Concerto in A Minor for Piano and Orchestra, Opus 16
Allegro molto moderato
Adagio —
Allegro moderato molto e marcato. Quasi presto.
Andante maestoso

The Piano Concerto was composed in 1868. Grieg continued to revise it, completing the definitive final version shortly before his death in 1907. Grieg conducted the first performance in Copenhagen in the fall of 1869; the pianist was Edmund Neupert.

Grieg owed his lifelong commitment to creating a Norwegian national musical style to the early influence of two men: Ole Bull and Rikard Nordraak. Bull, a violin virtuoso and composer, was something of a folk hero in Norway. He was a symbol of the free spirit of the new Norway, which had recently broken away from four hundred years of Danish domination. Bull was enterprising, independent, and aggressive. Among his activities were frequent international concert tours, an attempt to establish a Norwegian colony in Pennsylvania (an adventure which cost him most of his money and almost his life), and the founding of a Norwegian national theater (as distinct from those performing Danish plays), for which he hired an obscure young playwright named Henrik Ibsen.

Grieg was 15 years old when he met the most famous man in Norway. Bull asked to hear some of the boy's compositions, with which he was suitably impressed. He recommended that young Edvard be sent to Germany to study at the Leipzig Conservatory. The aspiring composer and the famous violinist remained in contact. Some years later Bull, who liked to imitate folk fiddlers on his violin and who had transcribed fiddle tunes for piano, introduced Grieg to authentic Norwegian folk music.

Grieg also met the young composer Rikard Nordraak, a passionate advocate of anything Norwegian — saga literature, old ballads, mountain scenery, traditional costumes, festivals, folk music, and folk dances. Nordraak modeled his musical career on that of Ole Bull, whom he revered to the extent of hoarding the violinist's discarded cigar butts. His compositions owed more to Norwegian folk music than to academic training, for which he had little patience.

The two young composers agreed to make their life's work the carrying forward of Ole Bull's belief in a Norwegian national style based on the wonderful music of the people. Nordraak's death at the age of 24, two years after he and Grieg had become close friends, made Grieg even more determined to carry out his musical commitment to Norway.

The folk element is less focused in Grieg's small pieces and songs of the time than it might have been, had the influence not come second-hand through Nordraak. The themes of the Piano Concerto, written soon after Nordraak's death, also sound somewhat Norwegian, although no folk music is quoted directly. Soon after completing the concerto, Grieg came upon a collection of Norwegian folk music called *Mountain Melodies Old and New,* many of which Nordraak had used in his own compositions. This book proved to be just what Grieg needed — a first-hand source of melodies he could draw upon as he continued to forge a distinctively Norwegian style of art music. His first composition after the Piano Concerto was an arrangement of 25 of these tunes. He often returned to this book for source materials. His success in using folk music confirmed Grieg's belief that he was not cut out for composing in large forms. He began to concentrate on miniatures, in which he could make a folk melody serve not simply as the theme but as the entire basis of a short character piece. In fact, he completed only three more works in classical molds during his remaining 38 years: a string quartet and two sonatas. His major effort went into composing Norwegian dances, incidental music to accompany Norwegian plays, isolated movements, sets of brief piano pieces, songs, and short choral pieces. Thus the Piano Concerto turned out to be Grieg's largest work, and it marks the culmination of his early period, during which he had tried to force his lyrical gifts into the essentially foreign structure of large, traditional forms.

One of the great strengths of the concerto is its beautiful themes. Grieg's attempt to develop them according to sonata principles caused him considerable difficulty. Notice, for example, the textbook-like adherence to sonata form in the first movement, even to the point that the recapitulation is a nearly literal restatement of the exposition. He found it helpful to model the first movement on that of an existing work, Robert Schumann's Piano Concerto, also in A minor. Furthermore Grieg, never totally satisfied with his concerto, continued to revise it until his final year, despite frequent performances.

Musicologist Gerald Abraham traces the concerto's debt to Schumann: "In both [first] movements we find an introductory chordal passage for the soloist, descending from the high to the middle register. In both, the main theme is then stated by the winds and re-peated exactly by the soloist; both naturally have the second subject in the relative major, though Grieg does not follow Schumann in fashioning first and second subjects from the same basic idea." Grieg was perhaps too much a natural melodist to be content with one main theme for an entire movement. Abraham continues:

> Both expositions conclude with an *animato*; both developments fall into two main sections, in the first of which woodwind soli play with fragments of the main theme over piano arpeggios, while the soloist comes to the fore in the second . . . ; in both the cadenza is followed by a coda quicker than the rest of the move-ment, Schumann's on a new form of the motto-theme, Grieg's on an entirely new theme [which gradually reveals its deriva-tion from the opening chordal passage]. There is no resemblance between the actual ideas; it was simply that Grieg, at the high-est stage of his development as a composer in sonata form, still felt the need for a formal model.

Grieg tinkered with the orchestration even more than with the structure, and he was able to produce a definitive version only some forty years after first completing the concerto. For a while he fol-lowed suggestions by his friend and mentor, Franz Liszt, who was greatly impressed with the concerto. Liszt suggested, among other things, that the second theme of the first movement be given not to cellos but to a solo trumpet! After he decided against Liszt's more outlandish suggestions, Grieg still continued to perfect the scoring. The final version differs markedly from the version originally pub-lished in 1872.

In addition to the melodies, the exquisite piano writing contrib-utes to the beauty of this music, particularly in the slow movement. Grieg knew his instrument well, had studied the keyboard works of Chopin and Schumann, and usually composed at the piano. Thus he was able to imbue even the most ornate and figurative passages with a sensitive lyricism. Listening to the less bombastic runs and arpeg-gios, we have the feeling that every note counts, not just the sweep of the gesture. This is an impressive achievement, rare among romantic piano concertos, that has assured the concerto its position of enor-mous popularity.

Perhaps even more than in the melodies and piano figurations, the attractiveness of the concerto lies in its harmonies. Grieg had a wonderful sense of coloristic chords and progressions, liberally spiced with dissonances. The most famous, but hardly the most sub-tle, is the use of the lowered seventh scale degree (G-natural) in the final triumphant measures, in A major. It was this passage, more than anything else, that convinced Liszt of the concerto's importance. At one of their first meetings, Liszt was sight-reading the concerto, when, as Grieg later recalled, he

> suddenly jumped up, stretched himself to his full height, strode with theatrical gait and uplifted arm through the great monastery hall, and literally bellowed out the theme. At that particular G-natural he stretched out his arm with an imperious gesture and exclaimed: "G, G, not G-sharp! Splendid! That's the real thing!" And then, quite *pianissimo* and in parenthesis: "I had something of the kind the other day from Smetana." He went back to the piano and played the whole ending over again. Finally, he said in a strange, emotional way: "Keep on, I tell you. You have what is needed, and don't let them frighten you."

George Frideric Handel

Born in Halle, Germany, on 23 February 1685.
Died in London on 14 April 1759.

◆　◆　◆

Royal Fireworks Music
    Overture
    Bourrée
    La Paix: Largo alla siciliana
    La Réjouissance: Allegro
    Menuet

The Royal Fireworks *Music was completed on 21 April 1749 and first performed in Green Park, London, six days later.*

On 7 October 1748 the Treaty of Aix-la-Chapelle ended the war for Austrian succession, and peace returned temporarily to England. Several months later King George II ordered a large celebration, ostensibly in honor of the peace but in reality to entertain his subjects. The celebration centered around the completion of a building, begun just after the treaty was signed, whose sole purpose was to serve as a setting for an enormous fireworks display. The building was finished on 26 April 1749. It stood 410 feet long and 114 feet high. The Duke of Montagu, who was in charge of the celebration and who paid for much of it, was represented, as were Greek gods and King George himself, on the face of the building. At the top of a two-hundred-foot pole was an enormous artificial sun. There were also steps, pillars, passageways, arched colonnades, and extended walkways.

The King commissioned Handel to provide music for the occasion. The composer reluctantly agreed to the King's request that he use military instruments only. Handel arranged some music from two earlier concertos and wrote some original music to go with it, and he scored the piece for an enormous band: 24 oboes, twelve bassoons, nine trumpets, nine horns, three pairs of timpani, a contrabassoon, a serpent, and snare drums (not indicated in the score). The strings he had been forced to omit remained in his mind for future performances. Not every one of the 58 players had an independent part, but the sound was nonetheless massive.

This huge group excited public curiosity. The very day the building was completed, an outdoor rehearsal brought a crowd of 12,000 spectators, which caused a three-hour traffic jam on London Bridge and very nearly led to a riot. The next day even more people turned out for the festivities.

The event started well enough, but it soon turned into a fiasco. Handel's overture, the most elaborate piece in the suite, began the evening. At its conclusion there was a deafening salute by 101 cannons. Then the building appeared suddenly lighted by fireworks. Handel's bourrée was heard. A firework design depicting peace was accompanied by the slow movement, followed by the section called "Rejoicing." By this time the fireworks had gotten out of hand. They kept going off at the wrong times. Several men climbed the building to try to fix things, and there were long delays. Then the entire building burst into flames. The crowd began to panic as the heat became intense. A brisk wind carried flames across the park. Tempers flared as well, and arrests were made. Several people were injured, two fatally. The remaining movements of the *Fireworks* Music were played, but no one could hear them. The image of the King caught fire and fell ignominiously into the cauldron of fire.

Handel's music provided the only shred of dignity, and thus he rose considerably in King George's estimation. When the composer repeated the *Fireworks* Music on 27 May at a benefit concert for the Foundling Hospital, George donated a large sum. For that concert, incidentally, Handel used the instrumentation he had always preferred: a wind band of normal size plus the usual complement of strings.

The suite has been arranged for modern performing forces many times. For some time the most popular version was the one by Sir Hamilton Harty, who omitted the "Rejoicing" movement and orchestrated for a normal contemporary orchestra. Recently conductors have chosen to return to Handel's original conception, either with or without strings.

The work follows the pattern of the baroque dance suite. The overture is the largest and most substantial movement. The pompous, fully scored introduction ends with a chordal adagio that leads to the faster, military portion of the movement. This section contrasts different instrumental choirs. The motion intensifies, reaching the incredible sound of a mass of oboes all playing sixteenth notes. A big cadence leads directly to an interlude marked *lentement*, after which the main part of the piece is recapitulated.

The second movement is an elegant dance. The third features 12/8 dotted rhythms that develop into trill figures. The "Rejoicing" allegro adds snare drums to the ensemble, in order to increase the military atmosphere. The final minuet, with its contrasting middle section in the minor, begins as a canon. Each section of this movement is scored differently.

Water Music

Suite Number 1 in F Major
  Overture
  Adagio e staccato
  Allegro. Andante. Allegro
  Menuet
  Air
  Menuet
  Bourrée
  Hornpipe
  Allegro
Suite Number 2 in D Major
  Allegro
  Alla hornpipe
  Lentement
  Bourrée
  Menuet
Suite Number 3 in G Major
  Sarabande
  Rigaudon
  Menuet
  Gigue

The Water *Music was originally composed in 1715, although some movements already existed as parts of other pieces. The work was premiered in London on 22 August 1715. A version first heard on 17 July 1717, also in London, probably included newly composed movements.*

Handel's employer, the Elector of Hanover, granted him leave to go to England in 1712. Georg was willing for his *Kapellmeister* to become known in London, but he did expect that Handel would return before too long. The composer's operas met with such tremendous success in the British capital, however, that he was reluctant to return. As he kept delaying his trip home, Georg became increasingly annoyed.

In 1714 an unexpected turn of events saw Georg crowned King George I of England. When the new ruler came to London, Handel was understandably worried. He dreaded the inevitable confrontation with the employer he had been ignoring for two years. The King was still miffed at the composer, but he recognized that Handel was the most important musician in England. Important composers warrant respect, especially from a monarch who considers himself a connoisseur of music. A reconciliation was necessary.

Just how Handel returned to George's good graces is not clear. According to one popular story, the *Water* Music played a role. George had brought Baron von Kielmansegge with him from Hanover. The Baron came up with a plan that would heal the wounds between the composer and the King. George had decided to have a water party. The festivities were to take place on a barge, floating down the Thames from Whitehall to Limehouse, where the royal party would stop for dinner. Kielmansegge convinced George to have a second barge following close behind, on which musicians would provide suitable entertainment. The Baron secretly arranged for Handel to compose the music.

George found the music enchanting and praised it extravagantly. He asked the identity of the composer. When he found out it was Handel, the King forgave him, congratulated him, and restored him to favor.

How much of the music played that August night actually belongs to the *Water* Music as we now know it is unclear. A performance of the complete music did take place two years later, however, on a similar river party. On this occasion nearly an hour's worth of music was played, which the King commanded to be repeated twice.

The approximately twenty pieces (there are various ways of counting movements vs. sections of movements) that comprise the *Water* Music divide musically into three suites, possibly intended for the journey downstream, the dinner, and the return trip. The Suites in F Major and D Major are heavily scored, with horns (in both suites) and trumpets (only in the D Major). Handel used this full a sound so that the music could be heard across the water. The remaining suite is more intimate, suggesting that it was intended to accompany dinner, while the barges were moored.

The original order of the movements within each suite is not known. Today, the movements are heard in various sequences. For many years the music was known mainly in the versions by Sir Hamilton Harty and Sir Thomas Beecham, each of whom rescored a selection of the movements for modern orchestra. Recent conductors have tended to prefer Handel's original version, however.

The Suite in F begins with a typical baroque overture: a slow introduction is followed by a fugal allegro. In keeping with the *concerto grosso* tradition, this movement features a small *concertino* of two violins and oboe alternating with the full orchestra. The subsequent *adagio e staccato* movement features an exquisite oboe solo. The festive music gets underway with the entrance of the horns, in the next movement. Particularly engaging are the syncopated rhythms toward the end of the allegro. Several of the following movements consist of a theme with two or three variations. Handel's means of variation is primarily changing the instrumentation. Sometimes variations are separated by contrasting material.

The Suite in D contains the most festive music. The more intimate Suite in G includes beautiful movements in the minor.

The *Water* Music is an international piece. The hornpipe, which appears in two of the suites, is an English dance popular at the time. The rigaudon is a French dance native to Provence. The bourrée is also French, as are the gigue and sarabande.

Franz Joseph Haydn

Born on 31 March 1732 in Rohrau, Austria.
Died in Vienna on 31 May 1809.

Concerto in C Major for Cello and Orchestra
Moderato
Adagio
Allegro molto

*The C Major Cello Concerto was probably composed in 1761 or 1762
and first performed by cellist Joseph Franz Weigl with the Esterházy
Orchestra in Eisenstadt, Austria.*

Until relatively recently, it was believed that Haydn — composer of
countless symphonies, string quartets, and piano sonatas — had produced only a handful of concertos. Since World War II, however, close
to two dozen additional concertos have been discovered. The Cello
Concerto in C is one of these works.

In 1761 Haydn left behind ten years as a free-lance composer to
join the court of Prince Anton Esterházy, where he remained for over
three decades. The Prince employed a resident orchestra that was
considered large: it initially had eleven string players. Haydn was
allowed to hire extra players from the Prince's military staff and from
local churches. Taking full advantage of these additional resources
and of the Prince's enthusiasm for music, Haydn boosted the size of
the orchestra to as many as 28 instrumentalists, including pairs of
flute, oboe, bassoon, trumpet, and horn players.

He was impressed with the quality of the Esterházy musicians,
and he began to compose concertos for them. The C Major Cello Concerto was one of the first such works. Haydn wrote it for Joseph Franz
Weigl, a cellist and composer employed at Esterháza from 1761 to
1769.

At some point a copy of the concerto found its way into the library of Count Kolowrat of Prague, who liked to collect cello concertos. He had about thirty of them copied for performance by his resident orchestra. The Count, like most music enthusiasts of the day,
cared a lot about the latest compositions (a striking contrast to the
situation today!), but the importance of preserving music for posterity never occurred to him. The work was not published, and, once it
no longer had the appeal of newness, it disappeared. All that was
known of it was the listing in a catalogue of his compositions Haydn

began in 1765. For two centuries it was believed that the concerto (plus possibly another C Major Cello Concerto, also listed in the catalogue) was lost. Even in 1937 Anthony van Hoboken listed it as missing in his monumental Haydn catalog. But in fact the music had remained in private libraries in Prague.

The other Cello Concerto in C has never surfaced. Its opening theme, listed in Haydn's catalogue, is similar enough to that of the present concerto for scholars to suspect that the two may have been different versions of the same work. Neither piece should be confused with the later Cello Concerto in D Major, composed in 1783 and never lost.

After World War II many private collections in Czechoslovakia were confiscated by the government and placed in the National Library. It was there, in 1961, that musicologist Oldrich Pulkert discovered the concerto. Haydn scholars quickly established its authenticity, and it was given its modern premiere by cellist Miloš Sádlo and the Czechoslovak Radio Symphony Orchestra, conducted by Charles Mackerras, on 19 May 1962.

This early work (it is contemporaneous with Symphonies 6, 7, and 8) already shows Haydn as a master of instrumental writing. The solo cello part is thoroughly idiomatic. The concerto reflects the ritournello form of the baroque concerto as well as the emerging structure of the sonata-allegro form. As in the baroque *concerto grosso*, the accompanying ensemble is small: strings, two oboes, and two horns. It is possible that Weigl was the only cellist in the Esterházy Orchestra when Haydn composed the concerto, since there is only one cello line in the score, marked alternately "solo" and "tutti." There is also, however, a *basso continuo* line that might have been played by another cellist, or by Haydn himself on the harpsichord, or by a string bass player.

The soloist's virtuosity is exploited as soon as the cello enters. After the orchestral introduction, the solo instrument plays the opening theme with full chords that use all four strings. Virtuosity is developed further in the use of rapidly repeating notes, the very high range, and quick contrasts of register. Haydn entrusted his soloist with a solo cadenza toward the end of the first movement.

In the slow movement (scored without winds), the cello enters dramatically on a long note, played while the orchestral strings relaunch the opening theme. Two measures later the cello goes on to imitate this melody. Haydn was fond of this gesture: several times in the movement the cello enters on a sustained pitch. This movement, like the first, calls for a cadenza toward the end.

The breezy, good-natured finale also has the cello enter on a long note, after an extended orchestral introduction. After playing this tone, the cello seems to get stuck on that pitch, returning to it again and again. This is an early example of Haydn's sly wit. The virtuosity of the solo instrument is exploited in this movement, especially in passages where the cello alternates rapidly from low to high, so that two instruments seem to play in counterpoint. Haydn utilizes the sustained-note entrance several times, the final one on a very high, penetrating G.

Concerto in D Major for Cello and Orchestra
Allegro moderato
Adagio
Allegro

The D Major Cello Concerto was composed in 1783 and first performed that year by cellist Anton Kraft at the Esterházy Estate in Austria.

The court orchestra of Prince Esterházy, which Haydn led, included some extremely accomplished musicians. In particular, solo cellist Anton Kraft (1752–1820) was a true virtuoso. Haydn wrote his famous D Major Concerto for Kraft, who was also his composition student.

It is interesting to compare this concerto with the one Haydn wrote a decade earlier for Kraft's predecessor, Joseph Franz Weigl. The C Major Concerto is far less virtuosic than the later one. Perhaps the reason is that Weigl was a less proficient player than Kraft, or perhaps, as has been suggested by several musicologists, Kraft worked carefully with Haydn to insure that the D Major Concerto showed off his most dazzling skills.

Twenty years after its composition, the piece was first published by Johann André, who had obtained the manuscript from Kraft. André gave the work the opus number 101. The *Lexicon der Tonkunst*, a music dictionary published in 1837, claimed that the "Haydn Cello Concerto" was really by Kraft. The source of this information was apparently Kraft's son, who had probably heard his father speak of how he had collaborated with Haydn in the composition of the work. Since spurious pieces were often published under Haydn's name in order to increase publication sales, the suggestion was readily accepted that the D Major Concerto was just another forgery.

The situation was further complicated in 1890, when the work was again published, this time in an edition by G. A. Gevaert. Gevaert's re-orchestrated and shortened version is a travesty on the original, but, ironically, it became widely played and loved during the early decades of this century. This bastardized version was for a while the most performed of Haydn's orchestral works.

For a long time Haydn's manuscript was thought to have been lost. When historians compared the cello part in the André publication to other cello music by Haydn and his contemporaries, they saw that the concerto's virtuosity went far beyond the normal eighteenth-century demands on a soloist. These musicologists surmised that the *Lexicon der Tonkunst* must have been correct in asserting that the concerto was Kraft's. Even as late as 1932 an article entitled "Is Haydn's Cello Concerto Authentic?" answered in the negative. Three years later the André version was reissued, and the world learned how far from the original Gevaert's revision had been. But still no one knew for sure who the real composer was. In 1953 the original manuscript was discovered in Vienna, and all the problems were solved. It was unquestionably in Haydn's hand, and it largely agreed with the André publication. The work *was* by Haydn, despite the atypically spectacular solo part. Today the concerto retains its popularity, but in its authentic form.

Its virtuosity includes very high cello music, harmonics, elaborate counterpoint played on the solo instrument, melodies in octaves, fast runs and arpeggios, and leaps from one register to another. Even today, in an age when many cellists are extremely proficient, negotiating these obstacles can be treacherous. If Anton Kraft could play this concerto correctly, in tune, and with the appropriate flair, then he must indeed have been an incredible musician. And if, in fact, he advised Haydn on how to write the solo line, then his virtuosity has been immortalized in the D Major Concerto.

Concerto in E-Flat Major for Trumpet and Orchestra
Allegro
Andante
Allegro

Haydn's only Trumpet Concerto was composed in 1796. Soloist Anton Weidinger first presented the work on 28 March 1800 in Vienna's Burgtheater.

The newspaper advertisement for the premiere of Haydn's Trumpet Concerto proclaimed the soloist's "intention to present to the world for the first time, so that it may be judged, an organized trumpet which he has invented and brought — after seven years of hard and expensive labor — to what he believes may be described as perfection. It contains several keys and will be displayed in a concerto specially written for this instrument by Mr. Joseph Haydn, Doctor of Music." The soloist was Haydn's friend Anton Weidinger, and his new trumpet was indeed an important advance in musical instrument technology.

Previously, the tonal resources of most brass instruments had been limited to notes of the natural harmonic series. An old trumpet pitched in, for example, the key of E-flat could produce only those tones in the overtone series of the note E-flat. The performer changed from one pitch in the overtone series to another by varying lip and breath pressure. In a high register, most notes of the diatonic scale were available, but in a low range there were significant gaps. As a result, music written for the trumpet had to be carefully restricted. Furthermore, a performer had to own a different instrument for nearly each different key in which he might be asked to play.

Brass instruments do not have this problem today, because of the invention in 1813 of valves (it took more than a half century before valves became commonplace). Valves allow the performer's fingers to change the effective length of the tubing through which his breath goes. Prior to the adoption of the valve system, however, Weidinger's invention of a keyed trumpet seemed to hold out great promise. Weidinger and others experimented with adapting from the woodwinds the idea of drilling several holes in the side of the tubing. Uncovering a hole raised the pitch a semitone. Weidinger's trumpet had five holes, which were covered by keys operated by the player's left hand.

Although not as versatile as the valve trumpet that supplanted it, Weidinger's keyed trumpet was capable of what must have seemed, in 1800, an astonishing variety of notes. The concerto's frequent chromatic passages represent music that could never have been played on the natural trumpet.

Weidinger built his first keyed trumpet in 1793. Prior to that, there had been other makeshift experiments to increase the notes a trumpet could play — for example, adding a slide that would lower the pitch a semitone, or adding a system of coiled tubing that would make available some extra notes. The ideal, toward which Weidinger made considerable progress, was a fully chromatic instrument.

(Incidentally, a musicologist embarrassed herself in 1962 by publishing an article about a concerto for "chromatic trumpet" by Johann Georg Albrectsberger, dated 1771. Her thesis was entirely based on a mistaken understanding of the work's title page, on which the solo instrument is abbreviated "tromb." This designation actually stands for "trombola," or Jew's harp! There were *no* chromatic trumpets in 1771.)

Having a versatile instrument is not much use to a trumpeter until there is music to play on it. Weidinger approached Haydn, who had recently returned from his triumphant visits to London. The composer was intrigued by the new instrument and impressed with the soloist's virtuosity. He composed what was destined to become his last surviving purely orchestral work (a lost bassoon concerto may have been written later).

We do not know why Weidinger waited four years to introduce the concerto to the public; perhaps he was still perfecting his new instrument and/or his performance technique on it. After the premiere the work was apparently not heard again for 129 years. Like most of Haydn's concertos, it was conceived as a piece for a particular friend. No one gave much thought to preserving this music for later performers. Thus the majority of Haydn's concertos were never published during his lifetime, and consequently several were lost. Only one copy of the Trumpet Concerto — the original manuscript — survived beyond Haydn's day.

Today the concerto is far from obscure. It is undoubtedly the world's best known work for trumpet and orchestra, and it is among Haydn's most performed compositions. Its resurrection to popularity was occasioned not by a modern publication but by recordings. Although the work was published in an arrangement for trumpet and piano in 1929 and the full orchestral score appeared in 1931, interest was not sparked until the mid-1930s, when trumpeter George Eskdale and conductor Walter Goehr recorded the last two movements. They used a version with a drastically re-orchestrated accompaniment. This record became an enormous best seller, as did a 1950 recording of the entire work in its original orchestration by soloist Helmut Wobisch and conductor Anton Heiller. The latter disc sold thirty thousand copies in its first four years. Today there are numerous recordings and performances of Haydn's Trumpet Concerto.

As in most classical-period concertos, the main entrance of the solo instrument is delayed until after the orchestra has introduced the principle themes of the first movement. The trumpet is heard briefly prior to its thematic entrance, however. Soon after the orchestral *tutti* gets under way, the solo instrument plays a single loud note, followed by two fanfare-like arpeggios. Perhaps the composer was providing the soloist with an opportunity to warm up within the performance, so that his instrument is not cold (and hence out of tune) by the time of the thematic entry.

Before long we hear what Weidinger's keyed trumpet could do. Haydn gave his soloist not only high-register virtuosic passages typical of baroque trumpet concertos but also lyrical lines in the low register. Shortly after its thematic entrance, the solo instrument plays gently chromatic music that must have surprised listeners accustomed to the natural trumpet's diatonicism. Haydn scholar H. C. Robbins Landon feels that this passage marks the beginning of a long tradition of nostalgic and poetic Austrian trumpet music, which includes later compositions by Bruckner, Mahler, and Johann Strauss. Fanfare-like trumpet music, more typical of Haydn's day, is heard closer to the end of the movement.

Baroque trumpet concertos often omit the solo instrument from the middle movement, which is generally cast in a different key and which, as a slow movement, usually eschews virtuosity. But Weidinger's instrument could both produce lyricism and play in A-flat major. Therefore the andante assigns its beautiful and gentle melody to the trumpet. Furthermore, Haydn allows himself a modulation to C-flat major, a key in which no trumpet could previously have performed.

In the finale Haydn treats the trumpet in a more typical fashion, with virtuosic fanfares and grand bravura. Even here, though, there are passages of lyric chromaticism, which remind us that with this single work Haydn and Weidinger ushered in a new age of trumpet music.

The London Symphonies

Symphony Number 93 in D Major
Adagio. Allegro assai
Largo cantabile
Menuetto: Allegretto. Trio. Menuetto
Presto ma non troppo

Composed in 1791. First performed in London on 17 February 1792, with Haydn conducting.

Symphony Number 94 in G Major, *Surprise*
Adagio cantabile. Vivace assai
Andante
Menuetto: Allegro molto. Trio. Menuetto
Allegro di molto

Composed in 1791. First performed in London on 23 March 1792, with Haydn conducting.

Symphony Number 95 in C Minor
Allegro moderato
Andante cantabile
Menuetto. Trio. Menuetto
Vivace

Composed in 1791. First performed in London in March 1791, with Haydn conducting.

Symphony Number 96 in D Major, *Miracle*
Adagio. Allegro
Andante
Menuetto: Allegretto. Trio. Menuetto
Vivace assai

Composed in 1791. First performed in London in February 1791, with Haydn conducting.

Symphony Number 97 in C Major
Adagio. Vivace
Adagio ma non troppo
Menuetto: Allegretto. Trio. Menuetto
Presto assai

Composed in 1792. First performed in London on 3 May 1792, with Haydn conducting.

Symphony Number 98 in B-Flat Major
Adagio. Allegro
Adagio cantabile
Menuetto: Allegro. Trio. Menuetto
Presto

Composed in 1791–92. First performed in London on 2 March 1792, with Haydn conducting.

Symphony Number 99 in E-Flat Major
Adagio. Vivace assai
Adagio
Menuetto: Allegretto. Trio. Minuetto
Vivace

Composed in 1793. First performed in London on 10 February 1794, with Haydn conducting.

Symphony Number 100 in G Major, *Military*
Adagio. Allegro
Allegretto
Menuetto: Moderato. Trio. Menuetto
Presto

Composed in 1794. First performed in London on 31 March 1794, with Haydn conducting.

Symphony Number 101 in D Major, *Clock*
  Adagio. Presto
  Andante
  Menuetto: Allegretto. Trio. Menuetto
  Vivace

Composed in 1793–94. First performed in London on 31 March 1794, with Haydn conducting.

Symphony Number 102 in B-Flat Major
  Largo. Allegro vivace
  Adagio
  Menuetto: Allegro. Trio. Menuetto
  Presto

Composed in 1794. First performed in London on 2 February 1795, with Haydn conducting.

Symphony Number 103 in E-Flat Major, *Drum Roll*
  Adagio. Allegro con spirito
  Andante più tosto allegretto
  Menuetto. Trio. Menuetto
  Allegro con spirito

Composed in 1795. First performed in London on 2 March 1795, with Haydn conducting.

Symphony Number 104 in D Major, *London*
  Adagio. Allegro
  Andante
  Menuetto: Allegro. Trio. Menuetto
  Spiritoso

Composed in 1795. First performed in London on 4 May 1795, with Haydn conducting.

Haydn's career took a dramatic new turn in 1790. His employer, Prince Nicholas Esterházy, died at the age of 76. The last months of the Prince's life were filled with grief over the death of his wife and with apprehension concerning his own end. He withdrew into himself and thought of no one else. As a result, Haydn was not allowed to leave the Esterházy estate, since Nicholas thought that music might restore his happiness. The composer felt like a prisoner. "Now I'm caught yet again and have to remain here. . . . It is a sad thing always to be a slave, but Providence will have it so, poor wretch that I am! [I am] constantly harassed with much work and all too little leisure. . . . There are no real friends left."

The death of Prince Nicholas set Haydn free, since the new Prince Anton cared little for music. The court orchestra was dismissed, and only the wind band was kept. Haydn's only obligation to Anton was to use his title, "*Kapellmeister* to Prince Esterházy." In this way Anton retained a stake in the composer's fame.

Haydn left for Vienna and took up lodgings with his friend, Johann Nepomuk Hamburger. Offers for the composer's services began to pour in from all quarters. He was about to accept an offer of employment from King Ferdinand of Naples when Johann Peter Salomon arrived with a better deal.

Salomon, a native of Bonn, had been active for nine years as a violinist and impresario in England. He had unsuccessfully tried to lure Haydn away from Prince Esterházy in the 1780s. He happened to be in Cologne when the old Prince died, and he hurried to Vienna to try to persuade Haydn to return to London with him. His offer was too generous to refuse: 300 pounds for an opera, 300 more for six new symphonies, 200 pounds for their publication, 200 pounds for twenty other works, and at least 200 pounds for a benefit concert.

Haydn's friends tried to dissuade him from going, since he was advanced in age. Mozart felt that Haydn knew too little of the world and its languages to undertake such travel, but the latter replied, "All the world understands *my* language."

Thus he went to England, and the results of his two visits were his last twelve symphonies, known as the *Salomon* or *London* Symphonies, the crowning achievements of his already distinguished career. When Haydn went to England, he left behind forever the life of a high-class servant. He placed his fortunes in the hands of the general public, for whom he composed and performed. Haydn's decision was prophetic: the day of the composer as servant was drawing to a close. Composers were soon to take responsibility for their own success, as true artists rather than functionaries.

Haydn arrived in London on New Year's Day, 1791, and remained there for a year and a half — two concert seasons. During that time he produced six new symphonies: for the first season Numbers 95, 96, and 97, and for the second season Numbers 93, 94, and 98. The composer was pleased with a long overdue change of environment and with his new freedom. He won many admirers and friends in the new land. The personality of the man, the quality of his music, and the quality of his performances brought him great acclaim and affection and made Salomon's venture a resounding financial success.

Successful financial ventures spawn competition. During Haydn's second season in London, a rival concert series, known as the Professional Concerts, tried with the offer of a higher salary to lure him away from Salomon. The tactic failed, as Haydn remained loyal to the man who had been responsible for his London successes.

Next the rivals tried spreading rumors that Haydn's health was deteriorating. This attempt was also to no avail. Finally, the manager of the Professional Concerts announced that he had secured the services of another prominent composer, Haydn's former student Ignaz Pleyel. Haydn wrote, Pleyel "arrived here with a lot of new compositions, but they had been composed long ago; he therefore promised to present a new work every evening. . . . I announced publicly that I would likewise produce twelve different new pieces. In order to keep my word, and to support poor Salomon, I must be the victim and work the whole time."

Haydn was prolific, but even he could not produce twelve symphonies in a single season. Luckily, he had written two (Numbers 94 and 98) during the summer between his first and second London seasons

Everyone in London seemed to have an opinion about whether Haydn or Pleyel was the better composer. The newspapers were filled with articles praising one or the other. Haydn referred to the whole affair as a "murderous harmonious war." The Professional Concerts wisely planned to program some of Haydn's music, but Salomon would schedule no more than one of Pleyel's compositions. The battle lines were drawn at the beginning of the 1792 concert season.

Haydn competed with his greatest compositional skill. He used even more than his usual quotient of wit and delectable scoring in his newest symphonies of the season. In Symphony Number 94, for example, "it was my wish to surprise the public with something new, and to make a debut in a brilliant manner so as not to be outdone by my pupil Pleyel, who at the time was engaged by an orchestra in London . . . which had begun its concert series eight days before mine. The first allegro of my symphony was received with countless bravos, but the enthusiasm reached its highest point in the andante with the kettledrum beat. *Ancora, Ancora!* sounded from every throat, and even Pleyel complimented me on my idea."

The great enthusiasm was over the insertion of a sudden, unexpectedly loud chord, for full orchestra with timpani, halfway through the theme of the slow movement. Slow movements were supposed to be soft and delicate, and the utter simplicity of the symphony's quiet theme — it is innocent enough to be a nursery tune — hardly prepares the listener for this bold stroke. Haydn wittily returns to this chord, at the *beginning*, not the middle, of the first variation. This wonderfully humorous idea is what gave the symphony its title: the *Surprise*.

In June 1792 Haydn left London to return to Vienna. Haydn's two concert seasons had been satisfying in every way. He was a popular figure in society and his compositions had been received enthusiastically. Among other works, he had introduced to the London public six new symphonies.

When he returned to Vienna, Haydn was reunited with his wife, bought a new house with the money he had earned in England, and took on a new student: the young Ludwig van Beethoven. But Haydn longed for the exciting life in London and therefore entered into negotiations with Salomon about a return visit. Salomon was a shrewd businessman, who knew there was more profit to be gotten from Haydn in England. The two men signed a contract for the composer to produce six more London symphonies in 1794–95.

Haydn had some difficulty in obtaining permission from Prince Anton to make his second trip. The Prince was on good terms with Haydn and had gladly let him go the first time. He had followed reports of Haydn's successes with pride and interest, but he felt that the composer had reaped enough fame and that he was too old (he was 61) to undertake another strenuous journey. Haydn pointed out that he had signed a contract with Salomon and that he had made advantageous contacts with several English publishers. The Prince finally consented.

While staying at an inn on his return trip, Haydn heard someone playing the andante from the Symphony Number 94 on the piano. He followed the sound and discovered several Prussian officers playing and enjoying his music. He told them who he was, but they refused to believe it. One responded, "Impossible! Impossible! You Haydn? A man of such advanced years! How does that correspond with the fire in your music? No, we'll never believe it." Haydn had with him a letter from the King proving his identity, which he showed to them. They showered him with affection and stayed with him well past midnight.

The composer arrived back in London on 4 February 1794. He found everything in readiness for his first concert, which took place a week later. As usual, the reception from the audience and press was warmly enthusiastic. Haydn picked up his string of London triumphs exactly where he had left off two years earlier.

On this concert Haydn premiered Symphony Number 99. There was one new aspect of Haydn's art that the London audience heard: clarinets. Haydn had become interested in the instrument from studying some of Mozart's scores, and he had arranged with Salomon for the inclusion of clarinetists in the orchestra. This was the first Haydn symphony with clarinets, and it was no doubt the first symphony Londoners heard with them.

Shortly after this premiere, Haydn received the news that Prince Anton had died unexpectedly at the age of 56. Once again within the space of four years there was to be a new ruler at Esterháza. Under the circumstances, the composer felt confident he would encounter no difficulty remaining in Britain for the two seasons he had promised Salomon. He finally left in August 1795, never again to experience his London triumphs.

The greatest success of Haydn's 1794 season was the premiere of the *Military* Symphony. The critics, always generous with their praise, outdid themselves. One wrote: "The middle movement was ... received with absolute shouts of applause. Encore! encore! encore! resounded from every seat: the Ladies themselves could not forbear. It is the advancing to battle; and the march of men, the sounding of the charge, the thundering of the onset, the clash of arms, the groans of the wounded, and what may well be called the hellish roar of war increased to a climax of horrid sublimity! which, if others can conceive, [Haydn] alone can execute." As the composer's fame spread beyond London, several concerts were arranged in the provinces to acquaint Britishers with this symphony.

After the 1794 season, Salomon was forced to discontinue his series for political reasons. Haydn nonetheless remained in London for one more season, as he had planned. In 1795 he premiered his new works in Giovanni Battista Viotti's new series, called Opera Concerts. Viotti was an excellent violinist and himself a composer. He had an unusually large and accomplished orchestra, numbering some sixty musicians. As a gesture of appreciation for Viotti, Haydn included a long violin solo in the slow movement of Symphony Number 103, which was premiered at the second Opera Concert.

Haydn's final London symphony, Number 104, was introduced at a concert that may have been the greatest triumph of his life. It included, in addition to the premiere of the new D Major Symphony, some of his vocal music performed by the greatest singers in Europe and a repeat performance of the *Military* Symphony, which was his most popular work. The audience loved the concert and the reviews, as usual, were ecstatic. Haydn gave a few more concerts before the summer, but no more symphonies were forthcoming. On 8 June he made his last public appearance in England.

He remained in London for two more months, quietly composing music he had promised to a British publisher. He left England on 15 August to return to his duties under Prince Nicolaus II Esterházy in Austria. Through his renown in England he had become famous throughout Europe. Soon after returning he conducted the Symphony Number 104 in Vienna. Eventually all twelve of the symphonies he composed for England were heard in Austria. They were appreciated, but they never met with the wild enthusiasm they had provoked in London.

After his return to Austria, Haydn's commissions were for different kinds of music. Thus he composed no more symphonies, despite the fact that he lived another 14 years. The twelve symphonies he premiered in England form a triumphant conclusion to a series of over a hundred symphonies. No composer since Haydn's time has matched this output. In the eighteenth century, when composers' reputations depended more on groups of compositions than on single works, it was not unusual for someone to create vast numbers of works in a single genre. Haydn's symphonic output was surpassed, for example, by those of Johann Baptist Vanhal, Carl Ditters von Dittersdorf, and Carlos Ordoñez. But Haydn's symphonies, in contrast to those of his obscure contemporaries, were known and played throughout Europe. Thanks in large part to his extraordinary success in London, he spent the remainder of his life as a renowned and frequently performed composer.

What became of the London symphonies after their premieres was not always a happy story, however. In the days before copyright protection, as soon as a composer let a work out of his possession it was no longer his in any sense. Anyone could, and usually did, copy the work. Hand copies of the orchestral parts were made for various orchestras to use. Usually these copies were followed by competing editions by different publishers. Every time a new edition appeared, it was in effect a new version. The publishers' editors had little respect for Haydn's original ideas. These people were motivated by the practicalities of the marketplace: they printed editions in forms they felt would sell.

For example, composer-publisher Simon le Duc brought out a version of Symphony 98 that simply omitted the trumpets and drums — certainly a practical idea to help ensure performances by small ensembles, but a total mutilation of the symphony. Well after Haydn's death, sets of parts such as le Duc's were reprinted by various publishers. Since the practice of conducting from the harpsichord was giving way to the use of an independent conductor, it was necessary to have scores as well as parts. To make scores from existing parts when different sets of parts disagreed with each other, sometimes drastically, was a challenge. It required editorial decisions, which were made with apparent abandon. Orchestrations, melodies, and harmonies were freely changed. Anonymous editors made several of the London symphonies sound somewhat like Beethoven's works, which were quite popular. For example, they added heavy brass and timpani accents to the minuet of Symphony Number 98, rendering an otherwise elegant movement ponderous. Haydn's high trumpet parts were lowered, the timpani parts were tamed, and the dynamics were softened, so that the symphony ended up sounding as if it had been orchestrated in 1815 — which, in part, it had! In addition, a beautifully poignant harmonization at the final entrance of the main theme in the same symphony's second movement was simply eliminated, as was a prominent harpsichord solo near the end.

Thus many of the London symphonies entered the standard orchestral repertory in versions that were decidedly different from what Haydn had presented in London. Generations of audiences and conductors learned them from these bastardized editions. The fact that such popularly accepted versions were in reality falsified did not become widely known until the mid-twentieth century. Even then, old habits died slowly, as conductors were unwilling at first to switch to the authentic versions. They knew and loved the incorrect versions too well. Even as recently as 1963 an incorrect version of one of the symphonies was reprinted. But now, thanks in large part to the meticulous editorial work of Haydn scholar H. C. Robbins Landon, original versions are published, known, and often performed. Now we can at last hear Haydn's symphonies as he wrote them.

The powerful unison that begins Symphony Number 93 must surely have electrified Salomon's audiences. The allegro gets underway with a main theme that may sound familiar, since it has subsequently been used as a Protestant hymn tune in several American churches. There ensues a delightful interlude, in which the violins play a rising arpeggio thrice, each time joined by a different wind instrument. The development section utilizes a five-note motive that is derived from both main themes. The ending is unusually dramatic for Haydn.

Always the experimenter, Haydn cast the second movement in a combination of rondo and variation forms. The subsidiary themes are derived from the main theme, and some of the statements of the main idea are varied. Toward the end there is a delightful comic effect. The music dies down to a series of isolated chords, quiet and delicate. Then, just when we expect one more gentle chord, we hear instead one very low, very loud, unaccompanied bassoon note — a grotesquely incongruous noise.

The theme of the minuet is related to the second theme of the first movement, an unusual procedure for Haydn. The trio section is announced by winds, brass, and timpani playing a fanfare-like series of repeated notes, which continually recur throughout the section. Each time, the fanfare is answered by the strings, sometimes in surprisingly distant keys.

Haydn is reported to have revised the finale after the first performance, feeling that it was weak in comparison with the other movements. Here the composer plays witty games with our expectations. He presents a main theme and then a long transition to a new key, the dominant, where we hear the original theme again. So far the form is not unusual; Haydn's pieces often have only one theme, stated in two conflicting keys. But then, just when we have accepted the movement as monothematic, he does give us a totally new theme, in the oboe and bassoon. The return to the recapitulation is also delight-ful: the cellos alone play a rising octave twice, a move the full oches-tra then echoes a step higher. Then the tonic key and the main theme slyly return.

It was not Haydn but rather an English flutist named Andrew Ashe who gave Symphony Number 94 its nickname. "I christened it the *Surprise* when I announced it for my benefit concert [in 1795]. . . . My valued friend Haydn thank'd me for giving it such an appropriate Name."

The name has determined much of the work's subsequent history. Once a piece of music has a catchy title (plus a good story to explain that name), its popularity is all but guaranteed. The result in this case was that the *Surprise* became the most played of all Haydn sym-phonies. Preference for this work has extended even into the present century. Frequent performances inevitably lead to overexposure, and musicians began to tire of the *Surprise.* They dismissed it as unwor-thy of its popularity. There followed a period of rediscovery, during which people wrote learned articles about how the *Surprise* Sym-phony really does deserve respect. Of course, it *is* an excellent com-position, one of Haydn's finest, but it does not tower above (nor fall below) the other symphonies Haydn wrote for London. There has been a lot of needless energy expended both for and against the work, all because of its title.

The story of how Haydn came to incorporate a rude chord into an otherwise stately second movement has been, inevitably, disputed. The one sure fact is that the chord was an afterthought added to a completed symphony. According to Albert Christian Dies, one of Haydn's early biographers, the composer wanted to startle those who dozed off at his concerts. He carefully instructed the timpani player to use his sticks without mercy. Dies claimed that Haydn's idea worked perfectly, with several slumbering audience members star-tled out of their reveries and a few ladies even fainting.

Others have disputed Dies' account. Composer Johann Christian Firnhaber, writing in 1825, claimed that Haydn was too much a gentleman to play such a prank. Firnhaber did admit, however, that several listeners were startled.

One of Haydn's students, Sigismund von Neukomm, wrote that the loud chord was intended to awaken one particular old man, who invariably took the same seat and slept through every one of Salo-mon's concerts.

Composer Adalbert Gyrowetz believed that Haydn knew exactly what reactions he wanted. The composer played the slow movement on the piano for Gyrowetz, before it had been performed by an orchestra. As he played the famous chord, Haydn said, "There the women will jump." Gyrowetz agreed that Haydn intended the chord to awaken slumberers. He noted that Salomon's concerts often lasted past midnight.

The story, in almost any version, is delightful, and it has contributed as much to the ongoing popularity of the *Surprise* as has its name. It is unfortunate, however, that knowing the story tends to make people listen mainly for the naughty chord in the second movement. The entire symphony teems with delectable turns of phrase, clever orchestrations, and all-round good humor. The piece should be appreciated as an integrated whole, not just as the context for a single joke.

One Londoner in particular must have liked Symphony Number 95: the orchestra's first cellist. There is a lovely, lyrical solo that starts the slow movement's first variation, and the entire trio of the third movement is also a cello solo. In fact, the entire symphony is a study in string orchestration. The winds are relegated to a more background role than in many of Haydn's symphonies, as the string section is treated with great sensitivity and imagination. This is especially true in the second movement, where each variation seems to find yet another beautiful way to employ the strings.

The symphony, perhaps because of its minor key, is one of the composer's more serious works. There is much learned counterpoint, somewhat reminiscent of the baroque era. We hear this primarily in the first theme and its subsequent development in the first movement, and in the fugal tendencies of the developmental passages of the finale.

The seriousness of the symphony does not preclude glimpses of Haydn's wit, however. As in many of his works, there is a delightful use of silence: not just the silences between phrases but, more importantly, the unexpected pauses that interrupt the flow of the music. Interestingly, these silences occur only when the piece is in minor and at its most serious, and hence they are more dramatic than humorous. When the music becomes lyrical and goes into the major, it is inevitably continuous. We hear dramatic stops several times near the beginning of the first theme. In the second movement they are absent until the second variation, the only one in minor. There are two dramatic silences during the third movement's C minor minuet, but none at all in the cello solo that comprises the C major trio. Dramatic pauses are minimized in the finale.

Symphony Number 96 was the first of Haydn's new symphonies to be premiered in London. It marked an auspicious beginning for his new career in England. The symphony's subtitle, *Miracle,* is inappropriately applied. There was indeed a "miracle," but it was associated with the performance of another symphony, Number 102. At the conclusion of that work, the audience enthusiastically surged toward the stage. The noise of the applause was so great that it caused a chandelier to fall. Since everyone had moved forward, nobody was hurt. No one seems to know how this event came to be associated with the wrong symphony.

The *Miracle,* like most of Haydn's London symphonies, begins with a slow introduction, starting with a forceful unison on a descending tonic triad. When this gesture is repeated in the seventh measure, a new third note is added to make the triad minor — a fine dramatic stroke. The introduction ends with a delicate oboe cadenza. The allegro begins with three repeated upbeat eighth notes. This motive becomes increasingly important throughout the movement. It is heard in every section. Toward the end of the development section, we hear a delicious instance of Haydn's famous wit. The music stops dramatically for a long, indeed a *very* long, rest. We expect the recapitulation to follow, and what we next hear is in fact the main theme, but in the wrong key. This "false recapitulation" leads to the proper return a few bars later. Toward, the end, the music plunges dramatically into D minor (recalling the similar move in the introduction) before closing triumphantly in D major.

The slow movement begins with a string theme with many silences. When it is repeated, wind figures fill in the gaps. After a contrasting idea, the first section is rounded out by a return of the original theme, its silences filled in in a different manner. Then comes an unexpectedly dramatic middle section, highly contrapuntral, rather long, and in the minor. After a return to the major for a recapitulation of the opening section, we encounter something totally unexpected. The orchestra holds a "6/4" chord, suggesting a concerto movement with cadenza about to start. And that is exactly what happens! Haydn makes a solo grouping of flute, two oboes, two bassoons, and two violins, which he accompanies with the rest of the orchestra. The group cadenza ends, as is proper in a concerto, with trills.

The minuet is a typical Austrian dance movement. The oboe solo in the trio section recalls the prominence of that instrument in the first movement's introduction.

The whirlwind finale begins quietly and, except for a few dramatic interjections, remains soft for quite some time. Although it is a rondo, there is really only one theme. It is played in the minor in the second section, thus recalling the minor-mode parts of the first two movements. The middle section consists of a contrapuntal development of the theme. Toward the end there is a dramatic pause, after which the winds start the final drive to an exhuberant conclusion.

Symphony Number 97 also begins with a slow introduction, the main theme (heard in the violins in the second measure) of which is destined to be transformed in the ensuing vivace. The fast section starts forcefully with the entire orchestra playing a descending triad in unison. After a transition of considerable complexity, a second theme of comical simplicity is heard. It is a waltz-like tune in violins accompanied with an "oom-pah-pah" in the *pizzicato* lower strings and bassoons. The development section is concerned mainly with the forceful first theme, but there is a magically intimate middle part featuring woodwind solos in intricate counterpoint.

The adagio is a set of variations that moves progressively farther away from the original theme. After a variation in minor, the music returns to the major for a passage that Haydn originally designated to be played *sul ponticello* — bowing near the bridge to create a metallic, nasal sound. He knew Salomon's orchestra could produce this special effect, and he knew English audiences loved unusual orchestration. But he suppressed the designation when he had the symphony played in Austria. In fact, nothing was known of his original intention until the manuscript appeared in 1951. A version including the *ponticello* indication was published in 1965, yet even today many conductors do not perform it as Haydn wished.

All the traditional repeats in the minuet are written out, so that Haydn can vary the instrumentation on each recurrence of each melody. Surely the most delightful orchestration is the sudden interruption by a series of repeated timpani strokes. The trio section is a rustic peasant dance. Particularly subtle is the orchestration of the final statement of this melody, with trumpets and drums playing softly and first violins an octave higher than usual. Haydn marked this part "Salomon solo, but soft," referring to the fact that Salomon played violin in the orchestra. In his book *The Classical Style* Charles Rosen says of this passage: "The oom-pah-pah of a German dance band is rendered with the utmost refinement, amazingly by kettledrums and trumpets *pianissimo*, and the rustic *glissando* (a sort of glottal stop on the first beats) is given a finicky elegance by the grace notes in the horns as well as the doubling of the melody an octave higher with the solo violin. These details are not intended to blend, but to be set in relief: they are individually exquisite."

The finale is a rollicking movement which contrasts key areas but not thematic ideas. There are many wonderful surprises, such as a passage that alternates *pizzicato* with regular bowing, and a passage where the violins play nothing but repeated G's unaccompanied. This music shows Haydn at his wittiest and happiest.

Symphony Number 98 is more serious than many of its companions. But this seriousness does not preclude several clever devices, products of Haydn's ever-fertile imagination. The introductory theme, for example, is the same as the first theme of the allegro. In the introduction it is slow and in the minor, while in the allegro it is fast and in the major. The second movement's opening theme is based on the British national anthem, "God Save the King." By including this well-known tune Haydn was paying homage to the monarch of his host country. At several places in the finale, the first violin is given a solo — a gesture toward Salomon, who was concertmaster of his own orchestra. The ending of the last movement is a delightfully witty stroke: the music is obviously approaching the end, when at the last moment we hear the wrong chord. It is followed by a dramatic silence, while we wonder what went wrong. Two more chords, and then another silence. And a delightful unexpected passage in which Haydn provided a keyboard solo for himself to play on an English piano. These wonderfully imaginative eleven measures a nineteenth-century editor saw fit to re-orchestrate for strings alone!

The novelty of the clarinets in the orchestra of Symphony Number 99 can be heard immediately in the loud chord which opens the symphony. Notice how Haydn has the low second clarinet hold onto its note after everyone else has dropped to silence or gone on to the introductory theme. This adagio section is quite involved, but it eventually gives way to the vivace.

The reviews of the first London performance singled out the fine woodwind writing, which is particularly evident in the slow movement. At the outset the wind choir alternates with the strings. The culmination of this alternation is a long, delicate passage for flute, two oboes, and bassoon.

The stately minuet moves consistently in quarter notes before shorter or longer note values are introduced. The oboes play five repeated notes as a link to the trio section, which is rather wistful, especially in its extended transition back to the minuet.

The finale includes, after its first full section, a delightful passage that alternates strings and winds, both treated delectably lightly. Elsewhere the brass join in to create considerable power. The development section becomes quite serious, as it engages in learned counterpoint, including the theme played against itself in inversion.

The *Military* Symphony begins with a slow introduction, followed by an allegro that starts in the most delicate way: just one flute and two oboes play the sprightly main theme. The equally carefree second theme sounds like a folk tune or popular march. In fact, Johann Strauss quoted it in his *Radetzky* March, composed in 1848. The development section begins dramatically with silence, after which the innocent second theme is developed in a less than innocent fashion. It begins to sound quite ominous. Toward the end of the development, the texture thins and a small group of winds alternate with the strings. The recapitulation is quite truncated, and, as if in compensation, the coda is extensive.

Symphony Number 100 takes its title from its second movement. Its special effects include triangle, cymbals, drum, martial trumpets, "Turkish" music, and strident clarinets. The composer arranged for these special sonorities to have maximum impact by omitting most of these instruments prior to their appearance midway through the movement. Once these instruments have joined the orchestra, they alternate with a more delicate treatment of the basic material. The movement seems to end, but then there is a trumpet fanfare, followed by a dramatic drum roll which leads to a final statement of the military music, played loudly by the full orchestra. Haydn composed this "military" movement first and then went on to write the companion pieces. It is hardly surprising that the second movement had to be played again before the first audiences would allow the symphony to go on.

The minuet is in standard form. There is a contrapuntal development of the main material. The trio section emphasizes dotted rhythms with a martial character, particularly in the second part, where the full orchestra reiterates that rhythm.

The main theme of the finale so delighted English audiences that it became a popular tune. It was frequently played on mechanical organs, along with English country dances. The development section is quite complex, and there are many examples of Haydn's deft scoring. Particularly engaging is a quiet passage for first and second violins that sounds as if it is going to be a fugue and then turns out not to be. In the coda Haydn brings back the percussion battery for a rousing close.

The slow introduction of Symphony Number 101 is mysterious, extensive, and involved. Psychologically it prepares us for the airy *presto* first theme in 6/8 time. Such a time signature and tempo Haydn usually reserved for finales, where the music is essentially light-hearted. But first movements are generally more substantial, as the D minor introduction to this one implies. The second subject is similar to the first. Thus the intricate motivic workings out in the development section seem to relate to both main themes.

The symphony gets its nickname from the second movement, which begins with the tick-tock of bassoons and *pizzicato* strings accompanying the main tune. Like the *largo* movement of Symphony Number 93, this andante is a mixture of variation and rondo forms. The main interlude is a section in G minor that reaches an impassioned climax before giving way to the innocent tick-tock motive and the main theme. After this restatement, the music ceases for what seems like a very long silence (actually, it lasts but one measure), after which the tick-tocking resumes, but in the far-off key of E-flat major. Haydn had originally closed this movement with a single soft chord followed by a single loud chord. He perhaps came to feel that such an ending lacked subtlety. He changed it to three soft chords.

The substantial third movement is by far the longest minuet in the London symphonies. Its trio section is full of humor. It is a picture of a village band with less than competent musicians. Some of Haydn's wrong entries, delayed entrances, and hurdy-gurdy effects (as musicologist H. C. Robbins Landon calls them) so offended later musicians that editors "fixed" these "mistakes."

The simple opening theme of the finale hardly seems like the beginning of one of Haydn's most profound movements. But the movement does include a powerful section in the minor, followed immediately by a sprightly fugue based on the main theme, at just the point where we expect a literal recapitulation.

Symphony Number 102, which musicologist H. C. Robbins Landon calls Haydn's "loudest and most aggressive," begins with the full orchestra playing a sustained octave. We remember this bold opening and relate back to it not only its repetition a few measures later but also the dramatic lone octave in the allegro. This gesture, preceded and followed by silence, comes where we expect quite the opposite: it is at the supposed start of the second theme group, which is traditionally lyrical and gentle. Haydn repeats this striking idea before allowing the new theme to commence. The development also starts with this gesture, which subsequently casts its influence over the entire section. The development is unprecedented in its intensity. Contrapuntal density, fragmentation, and a false recapitulation add to the accumulating momentum. When the recapitulation finally arrives (prepared by a timpani roll), it does so with an enormous sense of release.

Haydn calls for muted trumpets and muffled timpani in the adagio. These designations may well be the first time such sounds were called for in a symphony. The London brass players were, in fact, unable to obtain mutes, and the symphony was probably first heard with mutes in later performances in Austria. Other aspects of the movement are even more forward looking. Robbins Landon mentions the formal freedom in this movement, which "sounds like a rhapsody. . . . Part of this rhapsodic atmosphere comes from the eccentric theme, with its constant rhythmic displacement; part comes from the equally eccentric orchestration [including a solo cello part]; part from the harmonic range, which surpasses anything Haydn had written in a symphony; and part comes from the exaggerated dynamic marks — orgies of *crescendi, decrescendi, forzati,* little accents, and so forth. The score sometimes looks like a work written fifty years later."

The minuet is also prophetic. The tendency of simple rhythmic figures to be placed at odds with the barlines creates a metric ambiguity worthy of a Beethoven or even a Brahms. Also Brahmsian, according to Robbins Landon, is the scoring of the trio, with "its doubling of the oboe and bassoon at the octave with the first violin in between."

The finale is unusual as well, in part as a consequence of its amusing and unexpected hint of D minor in just the eighth measure. The tendency of the music to get caught on reiterations of the opening three-note motive is equally witty. Haydn continually comes up with new ways of telling this same joke. Particularly delightful is the final time, shortly before the end, where the theme keeps trying — and failing — to start up one last time. The effect is the musical equivalent of stuttering. Robbins Landon calls this passage "the next thing to Shakespearian humor. . . . It is the most sensational of all Haydn's 'joke' finales, and we have completely forgotten how the symphony began; the solemn profundity has turned to midsummer madness."

Symphony Number 103 takes its title from the quiet timpani roll that opens the first movement. The thematic material of the lengthy adagio introduction plays an important role in the subsequent allegro. It is heard in a disguised, syncopated, accelerated version in the transition from the first theme (a Croatian folk tune) to the waltz-like second theme. It is the subject of the second of three main parts of the development section. It returns at its original tempo, once again preceded by a drum roll, in the coda. The connection between the adagio theme and its allegro derivative is made explicit in this coda, as one version follows the other immediately.

The second movement is a set of variations, based on two Croatian folksongs. The first tune is in C minor, the second in C major. Despite their origins as two distinct melodies, they are closely enough related to seem like variants of one another. In order to preserve the individuality of these two similar themes, Haydn allows the variations to depart less from the original themes than he does in monothematic variation movements.

The third movement is a standard minuet and trio. The finale begins with a horn call that recurs throughout as the accompaniment to the main theme, also of Croatian origin. Although the movement is quite elaborate, it has only one basic theme. Contrast comes from the varied treatments of this melody.

The *Drum Roll* was Haydn's penultimate symphony. It shows his complete mastery of the form in which he had written over one hundred works. Yet it also shows the old master continuing to try out new ideas, such as the monothematic finale, the bithematic variation movement, and the return of the slow introduction in the coda of the first movement.

The relationship between the opening adagio and the allegro of the first movement of Symphony Number 104 is more dramatic than motivic. The stern inexorability of the introduction is vital to the sense of the allegro. As the fast section begins, pay close attention to the third and fourth measures of the main theme — where the first violins play four repeated notes followed by a note a step higher and a return to the original note. This motive, innocuously embedded within the tuneful theme, is later extracted as the source of much of the development section's intense counterpoint. When the main theme returns in the recapitulation, it no longer seems quite so innocent, because we remember, even once the motive has returned to its original place, the power it generated in the middle of the movement.

After a beautifully warm and sensitive slow movement comes a boisterous minuet. The characteristic accents on the third beat of each measure lead eventually to a wonderfully witty two-measure pause, coming immediately after one of those accents.

The finale is based on a tune introduced at the beginning by the violins playing over a drone note in the horns and cellos. This melody is quite similar to a Croatian folksong sung in the region around Esterházy. There is some evidence that this tune was also a London street song known as "Hot Cross Buns." The drone accompaniment serves to underline the folk character. The movement that develops from this delightful tune is a typically fun-filled Haydn finale, which turns somewhat sober for its wistful second theme.

Paul Hindemith

Born in Hanau, near Frankfurt, on 16 November 1895.
Died in Frankfurt on 28 December 1963.

❖　❖　❖

Symphony *Mathis der Maler*
Angelic Concert
Entombment
Temptation of Saint Anthony

The opera Mathis der Maler *was begun in 1933. Later that year Hindemith decided to extract a symphony from the opera. The symphony was completed in 1934, before the opera. Wilhelm Furtwängler conducted the first performance with the Berlin Philharmonic Orchestra on 12 March 1934.*

How can an artist remain aloof, serenely and privately creating his works in the midst of a world of suffering and oppression? What right does anyone have to say, "I am an artist and will serve mankind only through my art"? Yet to devote less than full effort to artistic creation is to compromise that which requires total commitment. Thus an artist must selfishly sacrifice everything to art. A very few artists — those we consider great — are vindicated for this selfishness. What about the multitude of other, less than great creators, who are destined for obscurity? Their lives are selfish without redemption. The artist, by turning inward to give full concentration to the creative act, assumes an enormous responsibility.

Many artists are tormented by the inescapable selfishness of their lives. Hindemith was no exception. He composed an opera on the theme of the isolation of the artist. He chose the character of the sixteenth-century German painter Matthias Grünewald to represent all artists of all times who have felt the conflict between art and life. Hindemith extracted a three-movement symphony from the opera. Both works are entitled *Mathis der Maler* ("Matthias the Painter").

Grünewald lived from 1460 to 1528. Since little is known of the events of his life, the composer, who wrote his own libretto, freely invented episodes. Grünewald sympathizes with peasant revolts and feels he must join the struggle. This temptation causes him considerable inner turmoil, but he finally decides to leave the service of the Cardinal and join the revolution. He discovers that his life as an artist has been so divorced from the life of the peasants that he cannot communicate with them. When they are defeated, Grünewald flees in

315

confusion. His attempt to be useful to his fellow man has failed. The painter begins to doubt the validity of art and the depth of his commitment and genius. What does a single great painting mean if there is still suffering in the world? Grünewald has a vision of his finest work, "The Temptation of Saint Anthony." He realizes that his faith in himself, like Saint Anthony's, has been shaken by the outside world. Once the painter realizes the parallel between himself and the Saint, his faith is restored. He comes to understand that only by creating beauty can he serve humanity.

Each of the three movements of the symphony depicts one of Grünewald's paintings and symbolically represents an aspect of his inner struggles. The "Angelic Concert" is the opera's overture. The music was inspired by Grünewald's famous painting for the Isenheim Altar, in which a consort of angels sings hymns to the birth of Christ. The second movement, "Entombment," is an interlude in the final scene of the opera. The music is derived from a painting that shows the interment of Jesus. In this scene of the opera, Grünewald withdraws from the world of strife back into his private world as an artist. The finale, "Temptation of Saint Anthony," depicts the struggle between art and the outside world for the painter's soul. The movement bears the motto, "Where wert Thou, good Jesus, where wert Thou, wherefore didst Thou not give aid and heal my wounds?" In this scene Grünewald's temptations, doubts, and desires, which parallel those of the Saint, build to the emotional peak of the entire opera. Toward the end of the movement, the intoning of the chorale "In Praise of Zion that Shall Save Us" indicates that faith has conquered anguish and doubt for Saint Anthony, for Grünewald, and perhaps for Hindemith.

In the composer's words, Grünewald embodies "problems, wishes, and doubts, which have occupied the minds of all serious artists from the remotest times. For whom are works of art created? What is their purpose? How can the artist make himself understood to his adversary?"

While Hindemith was composing *Mathis,* the political situation in Germany was becoming progressively more dangerous. Both personal and artistic freedoms were threatened. At first the composer refused to believe the seriousness of the situation. He tried, like Grünewald at the beginning of the opera, to remain aloof and simply to do his art. Political noninvolvement became more and more difficult, however, and Hindemith's oppression ironically came to center around the *Mathis* Symphony.

Many other composers had already left Germany. Hindemith, as one of the few remaining, was highly valued by the Nazis in 1934. They felt it important to have cultural heroes. But problems were brewing. A broadcast performance of *Mathis* was canceled because someone thought the composer had once made a remark critical of Hitler. The allegation had to be investigated. Even if Hindemith were cleared of the charge, there was a standing order that permission had to be obtained from radio headquarters in Berlin for any Hindemith broadcast. Then there appeared in an official newspaper a review condemning the composer for allowing *Mathis* to be performed at an Italian festival "which is dominated by Jews." The composer protested, threatening to leave the country if he were not treated with more respect.

As the Nazis still valued Hindemith's presence in Germany, they gave in, and criticism turned briefly to praise. His name was linked with those of Hans Pfitzner and Richard Strauss as "the outstanding creative personalities in furthering the reputation of German music abroad."

With the opinion of Hindemith's work high in official circles, the conductor Wilhelm Furtwägler asked for permission to stage the operatic version of *Mathis.* Hermann Goering told him that only Hitler could give that permission, and that it was unlikely since Hitler had many years earlier walked out of a performance of Hindemith's opera *Neues vom Tage*, because it included a scene with a nude woman singing in her bathtub. The conductor and the composer thought that a newspaper article explaining Hindemith's loyalty would be useful. But the plan backfired. The article tried to dismiss the composer's early remarks against Hitler as "sins of youth," but in so doing the author admitted that the allegations were true. The wrath of all of Nazi officialdom came down on Hindemith. The following statement was issued: "In the rejection of Hindemith by the Ministry of Culture, the value or lack of value of his creative work is beside the point. National Socialism puts the personality of a creative artist before his work. The fact that before the new regime Hindemith showed signs of an un-German attitude disqualifies him from taking part in the movement's cultural reclamation work."

Later Goebbels made a speech denouncing the composer:

Purely German his blood may be, but this only provides drastic confirmation of how deeply the Jewish intellectual infection has eaten into the body of our own people. To reach that conclusion has nothing in the least to do with political denunciation. Nobody can accuse us of trying to inhibit true and genuine art through petty or spiteful regulations. What we wish to see upheld is a National Socialistic outlook and behavior, and no one, however important he may be in his own sphere, has the right to demand that this be confined to politics and banished from art. Certainly we cannot afford, in view of the deplorable lack of truly productive artists throughout the world, to turn our backs on a truly German artist. But he must be a real artist, not just a producer of atonal noises.

Goebbels then read a telegram, purportedly sent by the president of the German Music Group, Richard Strauss, congratulating him on the "weeding out of undesirable elements."

It was impossible to remain aloof. Hindemith the artist had become a political figure. Just like Grünewald, he felt the social importance of the artist in a directly personal way. Hindemith tried to regain favor in Germany, but his cause was doomed. He had to look to other countries for performances, and inevitably he had to leave his homeland. He and his wife eventually settled in the United States, where he became Professor of Music Theory and Composition at Yale University from 1940 to 1953.

Arthur Honegger

Born in Le Havre, France, on 10 March 1892.
Died in Paris on 27 November 1955.

◆ ◆ ◆

Pacific 231

Pacific 231 *was composed in 1923 and first performed on 8 May 1924, at the Paris Opéra, under the direction of Serge Koussevitzky.*

Honegger's early musical training took place in Le Havre and Zurich. In 1913 he entered the Paris Conservatory, where he studied with Charles Widor and Vincent d'Indy. Toward the end of World War I, he became one of a group of composers known as *Les Six*: Darius Milhaud, Francis Poulenc, Germaine Tailleferre, Georges Auric, and Louis Durey. The members of this group actually had little in common other than friendship, and Honegger fit in least of all. While other members of *Les Six* (named after the Russian Five of the nineteenth century) felt a spiritual affinity for the irreverence of Erik Satie, were strongly anti-Debussy, and cultivated a light, almost popular style, Honegger was a more serious artist. He had no respect for Satie's music (the feeling was mutual), and he did admire Debussy. Honegger was as sympathetic to German music as to French.

He readily assimilated a plethora of influences, including Gregorian chant, twelve-tone techniques, jazz, and Bach chorales. Honegger was never an experimentalist, and his music is always firmly rooted in tonality.

Many composers of the 1920s were fascinated with the sounds of industrial society. In some cases the influence was quite direct. Edgard Varèse, for example, used two sirens in his *Amériques* and George Antheil included airplane motors in his *Ballet mécanique*. Other composers responded by imitating the sounds of machinery with traditional orchestral instruments. Examples include Alexander Mossolov's *Iron Foundry* and Honegger's *Pacific 231*. The aesthetic shared by all these pieces is a modern romanticism, a fascination with the artistic qualities of machines whose primary purpose was surely not artistic. Honegger, for example, loved speed and the rhythms of locomotives, and he endeavored to put these sounds into his music.

I have always had a passion for locomotives. To me they are living beings whom I love as others love women or horses. In

Pacific 231 I have not aimed to imitate the noise of an engine but rather to express in terms of music a visual impression and a physical enjoyment. The piece opens with an "objective" contemplation, the quiet breathing of the engine at rest, the straining at starting, the gradually increasing speed — finally reaching the lyrical yet pathetic state of a fast train, 300 tons of weight, thundering through the silence of the night at a mile a minute. The subject of my composition is an engine of the "Pacific" type, number 231, used for heavy loads and built for great speed."

   Pacific 231 is the first of three "symphonic movements" that Honegger composed. The second, written five years later in 1928, also celebrates one of the composer's fascinations: sports. It is called *Rugby.* Four years later he added the final movement, *Mouvement symphonique, no. 3.* When he wrote his book *I Am a Composer* in 1955, Honegger had second thoughts about the programmatic nature of *Pacific 231*:

So many, many critics have so minutely described the onrush of my locomotive across the great spaces that it would be inhuman to disabuse them! One of them, confusing *Pacific* with the Pacific Ocean, even evoked the smells of the open sea. To tell the truth, in *Pacific* I was on the trail of a very abstract and quite ideal concept, by giving the impression of a mathematical acceleration of rhythm, while the movement itself slowed. Musically, I composed a sort of big, diversified chorale, strewn with counterpoint in the manner of J. S. Bach. . . .

   I first called the piece *Mouvement symphonique.* On reflection, I found that a bit colorless. Suddenly, a rather romantic idea crossed my mind, and when the work was finished, I wrote the title *Pacific 231,* which indicates a locomotive for heavy loads and high speed (a type unfortunately disappeared, alas, and sacrificed to electric traction). . . .

   I composed . . . three "Symphonic Movements," which were *Pacific 231, Rugby,* and, to conclude, *Mouvement symphonique, no. 3.* As a matter of fact, I lacked an idea for the third. But you must know that as regards *Pacific* and *Rugby,* the press turned out to be very prolix. People of great talent wrote wonderful articles, describing the driving-rods, the noise of the pistons, the grinding of brakes, the oval balloon, the release of steam, the commotion of the front wheels, etc., etc. All these images gave birth to copious studies. But my poor *Symphonic Movement, No. 3* paid dearly for its barren title: it barely harvested here and there a few evasive and polite lines. Moral: — but no, I have been a music critic myself, and I prefer not to speak ill of a profession which has fed me.

In purely musical terms, *Pacific 231* deals with accelerating rhythms and increasing density of textures. From the atmospheric opening with string harmonics, trills, and tremolos, punctuated by low horn notes, an incessantly accelerating rhythm emerges. Once the tempo reaches its fastest plateau, brass interjections suggest other speeds. In this middle section the tempo gets gradually slower, but the level of activity — measured by the speed of the notes and the number of layers of sound played simultaneously — increases. This is the "mathematical" relationship Honegger was exploring. Our impression is of consistency, because the slowing tempo and accelerating density counterbalance each other. A climax of maximum density is reached shortly before the end. The tempo has by this time returned almost to the level of the slow, atmospheric opening, but there is so much more activity at the climax that the two passages sound utterly different. To end the piece, Honegger gradually slows down not the tempo but the rhythm — the opposite procedure from the acceleration at the beginning — until two broad chords bring this unique work to a close.

Charles Ives

Born in Danbury, Connecticut, on 20 October 1874.
Died in New York on 19 May 1954.

◆ ◆ ◆

Symphony Number 2

> Andante moderato —
> Allegro
> Adagio cantabile. Andante. Adagio cantabile
> Lento maestoso —
> Allegro molto vivace

The Second Symphony was begun in 1897, using sketches that date back as far as 1889. The work was completed in 1902, but Ives continued to revise it. The first movement was performed around 1914 by Edgar Stowell and the string orchestra of New York's Music School Settlement. Leonard Bernstein conducted the first complete performance with the New York Philharmonic on 22 February 1951.

Like most of Ives' music, the Second Symphony has a complicated history. Much of it was written in 1897, while Ives was an undergraduate at Yale. A passage from the last movement, however, dates back to 1889, when he was 15. Parts of all five movements either originated as music that the composer played as a church organist in New Haven or came from overtures he wrote for a pops orchestra and a brass band during his college days. The symphony was finished in 1902, but he continued to tinker with it until 1909. A few years later Ives sent it to Walter Damrosch, who had once conducted — with little enthusiasm — three movements from Ives' First Symphony at a rehearsal of the New York Symphony. Damrosch neither acknowledged nor returned the score.

The third movement was originally part of the First Symphony, which Ives composed as his senior project at Yale. His composition teacher, Horatio W. Parker, objected to the movement, since it was in F major but began on the note G-flat, and since it quoted popular hymn tunes. According to Ives, Parker believed that "the hymn tune was the lowest form of musical life." He insisted that Ives write a more conventional slow movement. The discarded movement found its way into the Second Symphony, but not before it was revised, in part according to Parker's criticisms: the movement now begins on the proper note. But Ives came to regret having made the movement more conventional. He felt that Parker had forced him to turn out an imitative rather than an original work. Although he never changed the movement back to its original version, he did write on the manuscript, "It was made 'better' and spoiled (by advice HWP). . . . P said — a movement in Key of F should start in Key of F. So change and weaken it!!!!!!!!!"

During the first half of this century, Ives' music was virtually unknown and unplayed. Although a performance in 1939 of his extraordinary Second Piano Sonata rescued his name from total oblivion, the virtual isolation in which he lived his last 15 years made it all but impossible for interested performers to get access to his unperformed music. Except for a performance of two movements from *Three Places in New England* by the Los Angeles Philharmonic in 1932, no major orchestra played any of Ives' music until 1948. In that year *Three Places* was done by the Boston Symphony.

The next major orchestral performance was the premiere in 1951 — half a century after its completion — of the Second Symphony by Leonard Bernstein and the New York Philharmonic. Considerable work had to be done, largely by composers Henry Cowell and Lou Harrison and a team of copyists, to decipher Ives' messy manuscript.

The composer, who as a young man had frequently heard the New York Philharmonic, had often hinted how much he would like to hear a work of his in Carnegie Hall. But, as the premiere approached, he became increasingly nervous. He was 76 years old and in frail health, and he had been living completely apart from music for years. He could not bring himself to attend the performance. Bernstein offered to conduct a special rehearsal at which Ives could sit alone and unobserved in the darkened hall, but Ives declined. Mrs. Ives and other relatives attended the performance.

According to Ives' first biographers, Henry and Sidney Cowell, "At the end of the performance, Bernstein applauded the players and then turned toward the Ives box to join in the wild and prolonged applause that rose from the hall. Realizing that Mrs. Ives was not grasping its extent, a guest touched her arm to suggest she turn away from the stage to see the cheering, clapping audience below her, which rose in the distance to the remote galleries. The warmth and excitement suddenly reached her, and she said in a heart-breaking tone of pure surpise, 'Why, they *like* it, don't they!'"

A week later the symphony was broadcast, and Ives listened on a small radio in his kitchen.

The public and critical response to the symphony was overwhelming. Ives' biographer Frank Rossiter has an interesting theory about the lavish praise the work received:

Fondly recalling his father's musical life in Danbury, Ives in this symphony had glorified the life of the Connecticut country people of his childhood. With its naïve American awkwardness and its quotation of the old religious and secular tunes, the symphony seemed in 1951 a thin, threadlike connection between the present and a beloved but forever vanished past. And how democratic to incorporate popular American tunes into [what was essentially] a nineteenth-century European symphony! It was now pointed out that Ives alone had spoken in the true accents of America even back at the turn of the century, but that he had never been able to find an audience among other Americans because the musical institutions of the country had been monopolized by conservative and Europe-worshipping pedants. That the Second Symphony had lain neglected for fifty years while its composer had remained indifferent to self-promotion and had apparently even treated his music nonchalantly, but that this same composer was still alive and that after long years of neglect his countrymen were finally discovering that he had all along embodied the American spirit magnificently in his music — these circumstances gave the Ives Legend a compelling power over the imagination. Ives could now truly be hailed as the father of American music. As for the American national culture, it could be flayed for having so long neglected its most original composer, but also congratulated for having produced him in the first place.

On the occasion of the premiere, Leonard Bernstein offered some perceptive remarks on the Second Symphony:

Let us try to identify ourselves with young Ives, a mere 27 years old, living in a country and a community where being a musician was then considered vaguely reprehensible, and trying withal to record the sound images of his world. Those images were a combination of the great works of the German tradition — Beethoven, Brahms, Wagner — plus the local music he lived with — hymns, folksongs, patriotic songs and marches, college songs, and the like. All of this can be found in this Second Symphony — from Beethoven's Fifth to "Turkey in the Straw." But it all comes out Ivesian, somehow transmogrified into his own personal statement. It's really astonishing. . . .

There are other references: to Brahms' Third Symphony, to Wagner's *Tristan* and his *Walküre*, to Bach, to Bruckner, and even to Dvořák's *New World* Symphony — an odd interchange of nationalism, that one. But the Ives symphony never *sounds* like Brahms and Wagner and the rest — it sounds like Ives. It has all the freshness of a naïve American wandering in the grand palaces of Europe, like some of Henry James' Americans abroad, or perhaps more like Mark Twain's innocents. . . .

The list of these oddments of Americana is very curious. Besides "America the Beautiful" and "Turkey in the Straw," you'll also hear "Columbia, the Gem of the Ocean" used here and there as a *bass line* and finally emerging triumphant at the end. You'll hear "The Camptown Races" [in the horns near the beginning of the finale, and then several more times in that movement], five or six hymn tunes, including "Bringing in the Sheaves" [second theme of the second movement] and "When I Survey the Wondrous Cross." Then you'll hear phrases that sound very Stephen Fosterish, like a mixture of "Swanee River" and "Old Black Joe." There's a delicate little touch of "Long, Long Ago" [flute solo in the finale], a wild sudden reference to "Reveille" [as the finale approaches its close], and a number of college songs, including one old Dartmouth favorite ["Where, Oh Where, Are the Verdant Freshmen?"] that turns out to be the trio of the second movement.

And all this, alongside Bach, Brahms, and Wagner, instead of making a hodge-podge, turns out to make a real work, original, eccentric, naïve, and as full of charm as an old lace valentine, or a New England village green. . . .

In short this symphony adds up to a sort of personal memoir of Ives' own musical experience. . . . When you hear "Turkey in the Straw" in this symphony, you are not supposed to visualize a barn dance. Rather, try to feel the impact of such a tune on one particular composer's consciousness, at a given moment in American cultural history, when anything that was any good at all *had* to come from Europe. That's what's so touching about all this use of Americana. It comes to us full of Ives' brave resolve to be American, to write American music in the face of a diffident and uninterested world.

One of the more intriguing aspects of Ives' process of quotation was his ability to compose original material in the spirit of his models. He could vary, paraphrase, and transform, and thereby create a unified composition in which we cannot — and should not — always tell whether a melody is a direct quotation, a distorted quotation, or an original theme composed in the manner of some other piece. The horn tune in the manner of Stephen Foster in the last movement is an obvious example.

As we listen to the symphony, we are sometimes not sure whether a certain melodic fragment is a quotation or not. The melody that starts shortly after the beginning of the third movement is a typical example. It begins in the strings with what is apparently original material (since several hymn tunes well known in Ives' day are unknown now, it is difficult to prove that a hymn-like melody actually is by Ives). After three measures the melody quotes "Beulah Land," followed by a brief fragment from "America the Beautiful" and then, in the flute, a clear reference to the slow movement of Brahms' First Symphony. Rather than producing a collage, these fragments blend into one another with utmost musicality. Ives had an uncanny knack for seeing how unrelated materials might be combined, and this melodic amalgamation of original music, hymn tunes, and a Brahms symphony testifies to his powers of integration.

The difficulty of identifying quotations with certainty becomes obvious when we try to find all the references mentioned by Leonard Bernstein. Most of his citations are accurate, but there are no instances in Ives' Second that *literally* quote the music of Bruckner or the *New World* Symphony. There are, as musicologist Sydney Robinson Charles points out, tunes that sound distinctly like Bruckner and Dvořák, but no direct quotes. Furthermore, the alleged use of the opening of Beethoven's Fifth Symphony in the second movement is more directly linked to the "Missionary Hymn," which contains a five-note version of Beethoven's famous four-note motive.

Ives was no doubt trying to draw a parallel between the "Missionary Hymn" and the Beethoven Fifth. In doing so he weaved a web of associations — both musical and programmatic. The motive carries with it associations from both sources as it is wanders from one context to another.

Some quotations appear on the surface just once or twice, but others become recurrent unifying themes. In particular, "Columbia, the Gem of the Ocean" and "Massa's in de Cold, Cold Ground" occur in several movements. Thus the use of quotations is more than a collage of personal reminiscences or folksy Americana mingled with the grand heritage of German music. Quotation is *the* central idea of Ives' music. Musicologist J. Peter Burkholder explains, "Ives viewed his musical sources, by and large . . ., as models to be reworked into new pieces, new themes, and new forms, rather than as a grab bag of available themes and motives, as whole cloth to be stitched into a patchwork. . . . Understanding the . . . themes of the . . . Second Symphony . . . as paraphrases — restructurings — of hymns and popular tunes explains [its] countless puzzling 'quotations.'"

Burkholder's point is that much more of the Second Symphony than meets the eye — or the ear — is based on borrowed materials. Sometimes folk tunes and classical excerpts surface and we hear them directly. But they are nearly always present. They are sources for Ives' own melodies, models for his forms, and even suggestions for the moods and character of his music. If we understand the symphony in this manner, then we realize that the quotations are not merely incongruous surprises but that they are the most obvious manifestation of Ives' pervasive and unique compositional technique. Burkholder concludes, "Ives is remodeling his sources rather than making a crazy quilt, [and] the intelligibility of the music depends on its internal logic rather than on the fusing together of disparate elements."

The complete list (as thus far discovered) of sources quoted in Ives' Second Symphony is as follows: "Turkey in the Straw," Beethoven's Fifth Symphony, Brahms' Third Symphony, *Tristan*, "Where, Oh Where, Are the Pea-Green Freshmen?," Brahms' First Symphony, "America the Beautiful," *Die Walküre*, "Columbia, the Gem of the Ocean," "Camptown Races," "Bringing in the Sheaves," "Long, Long Ago," "When I Survey the Wondrous Cross," "Reveille," "Joy to the World," Bach's Fugue in E Minor from Volume I of *The Well-Tempered Clavier*, "Nettleton," "America," "Naomi," "Hamburg," "Massa's in de Cold, Cold Ground," and "Beulah Land."

Symphony Number 4
Prelude: Maestoso
Allegretto
Fugue: Andante moderato
Largo maestoso

The Fourth Symphony was composed in 1909–16, but it uses materials that date back as far as 1897. The first complete performance, conducted by Leopold Stokowski, was given by the American Symphony Orchestra in New York on 26 April 1965.

Charles Ives has arrived. During his creative life his music was mostly ignored or scorned; in his final years it was "discovered" and provoked a mighty controversy. Today the controversy has still not completely ended, as people hotly debate the ultimate significance of his unique contribution. But now Ives' music is performed, it is popular, and it is profitable for record companies. We even occasionally see a T-shirt or bumper-sticker proclaiming, "Ives thrives!"

Ives was a total American. He was one of our first composers not to think of himself as carrying on the musical heritage of central Europe. Thus the hymn tunes, marches, and patriotic songs of this country were more natural to him than the traditional masterworks he had studied (and, it must be stressed, mastered) under his composition teacher at Yale, Horatio Parker. To Ives the compositions of Beethoven and Brahms represented but one type of music, in no way superior to American folk music. He regarded the main characteristics of European art music — tonality, unity, progression, resolution — as optional, and he frequently chose not to exercise those particular options.

Yet he loved certain compositions written in the inherited tradition, just as he loved the native music with which he had grown up. He paid homage to all this music by quoting it, often quite literally, in his compositions. Encountering a fragment of a familiar tune, whether by Beethoven or Stephen Foster, in the midst of a dense texture in the Fourth Symphony, for example, can have an enormous impact — possibly humorous (especially when the quotation is distorted), sometimes sentimental, often jolting. If we recognize the music quoted, then we bring our own associations to Ives' context. If it originally had a text, we can relate its verbal meaning to the special world of Ives.

The collaging of well known tunes into chaotic textures was but one of Ives' incredible innovations. He claimed to have anticipated virtually all of modern music. A decade before Stravinsky he was supposedly working with changing meters and contradictory rhythms; a decade before Schoenberg he may have been writing dissonances that refuse to resolve and freely combining the notes of the chromatic scale; half a century before Penderecki he was said to be experimenting with quarter tones and dense textures; several decades before Cage he was composing open forms and incorporating chance into performance; he may have anticipated Bartók in the use of complex chords for percussive effect; he was superimposing different rates of motion when Carter was a child; he was using divided orchestras generations before Stockhausen. The list goes on and on. Every one of these so-called innovations can be found in the second movement of the Fourth Symphony.

Ives claimed that he knew virtually none of the music of other avant gardists and that he had arrived at his original language totally on his own. When he was informed that his innovations had anticipated virtually every significant development in twentieth-century music, he replied, "That's not my fault."

Musicologist Maynard Solomon has discovered convincing evidence that Ives may not in fact have been the highly touted innovator we have long believed him to be. Solomon demonstrates that the composer actually changed dates on manuscripts and forged other evidence, in an apparent attempt to become known as the foremost inventor in modernist music. Solomon writes that Ives' book *Memos* may be viewed as a brief to establish Ives' priority as a modernist innovator, an audacious and pathetic attempt, backed almost entirely by the conposer's own word and little, if any, external circumstantial documentation. Ives' lack of generosity toward his fellow composers strongly suggests the kind of rivalrous personality for whom such issues may become an obsessive preoccupation. . . . Ives somehow came to believe that originality lay in being up-to-date, in the patenting of techniques and procedures. He did not realize (or could not acknowledge) the extent of his own originality, the individuality of his style, the uniqueness of his voice. Ives' deceptions are wishes — attempts to reshape an unsatisfactory reality in accordance with his desires.

Ives' music had no audience at the time it was written (Solomon suggests that, contrary to popular belief, he did not stop composing after a heart attack in 1918). The few performances that took place were usually ridiculed. Anticipating such reactions, Ives had made an important decision upon graduation from Yale in 1898. He chose not to try to make his living in music. "Assuming a man lives by himself and with no dependents, no one to feed but himself, and is willing to live as simply as Thoreau, he might write music that no one would play prettily, listen to, or buy. But — if he has a nice wife and some nice children, how can he let the children starve on his dissonances?"

Ives went into the insurance business. The firm of Ives and Myrick was, at the time of the composer's retirement from the business world in 1930, the most successful agency in the country. He believed passionately in insurance, and he wrote an influential pamphlet called "The Amount to Carry: Measuring the Prospect," which remained in active use by insurance agents for decades. The concept of estate insurance originated with Ives.

He made this wonderful statement on the relationship between business and music:

It is my impression that there is more open-mindedness and willingness to examine carefully the premises underlying a new or unfamiliar thing before condemning it, in the world of business than in the world of music. It is not even uncommon in business intercourse to sense a reflection of a philosophy — a depth of something fine — akin to strong beauty in art. To assume that business is a material process, and only that, is to undervalue the average mind and heart. To an insurance man there *is* an "average man" and he is humanity. I have experienced a great fullness of life in business. The fabric of existence weaves itself whole. You cannot set an art off in the corner and hope for it to have vitality, reality, and substance. There can be nothing "exclusive" about a substantial art. It comes directly out of the heart of experience of life and thinking about life and living life. My work in music helped my business and my work in business helped my music.

As the musical times began to catch up with Ives, his fame spread. But the composer remained aloof, usually refusing to go to hear the music of latter-day progressives, or even his own. He was as indifferent to recognition as he had been to obscurity. When, in 1948, his Third Symphony (composed in 1910) was awarded a Pulitzer Prize, he said, "Prizes are the badge of mediocrity. They are for little boys. I'm grown up." He gave away the money.

Ives usually worked on many compositions at once. The Fourth Symphony, for example, was first completed in 1916, but some parts of it date back to his student days. During the seven years while he was putting the symphony together, he also was working on dozens of other pieces. The final score allows many options and hence is not really "final": the most famous is the designation that the first movement, scored for chamber orchestra and chorus, should be performed "preferably without voices"! He did not really believe in the idea of a finished piece. Most of his works exist in many forms, and parts of some compositions find their way into other pieces. Latter-day editors of Ives' music have had an extraordinarily difficult time deciding what version of a work to consider authentic.

The Fourth Symphony is Ives' last completed large work. It is both a summation and a consummation. It contains instances of virtually all of the composer's innovative techniques, which may have been added long after the alleged date of the work's completion. It has its share of wonderfully inventive chaos (second movement) but also of direct simplicity (third movement). If the music has unity, its source is not consistency of themes or motives but rather a philosophical idea. Ives believed in the inescapable unity of all things, and thus, when he created a symphony with as much diversity as can be imagined, he did so with complete confidence in the music's underlying coherence.

Ives' friend Henry Bellaman prepared a program note, with the composer's assistance, in 1927. This note is reproduced here, with additional comments on each movement.

PRELUDE. "The aesthetic program of the work is . . . the searching questions of What? and Why? which the spirit of man asks of life. This is particularly the sense of the prelude." In the first movement a unison chorus sings the words of the hymn "Watchman, Tell Us of the Night":

Watchman, tell us of the night,
What the signs of promise are:
Traveler, o'er you mountain's height,
See that glory-beaming star!
Watchman, aught of joy or hope?
Traveler, yes; it brings the day.
Promised day of Israel.
Dost thou see its beauteous ray?

This brief movement is full of quotations, the connotations of which enrich the associative meanings of the music. In his article "Charles Ives and the Meaning of Quotation," Christopher Ballantine analyzes the web of connotations:

The opening of the work immediately presents a conflict: a passionate two-measure outburst on strings, piano, and trumpet — fiercely chromatic and destructive of tonal sense, and rhythmically complex — is contrasted immediately with a disguised fragment of Lowell Mason's [hymn] "Bethany," sounded very quietly by some of the prescribed "distant choir" of two solo violins, solo viola, and harp, together with an *ad libitum* flute. The fragment is ephemeral, elusive, and fragile, and after only one measure is submerged in the resumed passionate outburst. "Bethany" (a hymn beginning "Nearer my God to Thee . . .") is to play an important part in the work, a role that is vital to an understanding of the symphony. . . . In fact the fragment hangs over most of the prelude statically, not developing or gaining in precision, and, according to Ives' instructions, "scarcely to be heard, as faint sounds in the distance"; it is always played by the so-called "distant choir." But its symbolic function grows in definition during the movement.

The introduction of Mason's "Watchman" . . . reaches its most significant moment for the symphony at the Watchman's exhortation, "Dost thou see its beauteous ray?" The several repetitions of this phrase are followed by moments during which nothing but the pervasive "Bethany" fragment is faintly heard. The fragment thus clearly assumes the extra symbolic function of the "Glory-beaming star.". . . It is this promise of joy or hope, still distant, small, and elusive like the star, that the symphony is to bring to fulfillment in the final movement. . . .

The "Watchman" tune brings with it a few accessories, the most notable being the first phrase of Sir Arthur Sullivan's "Propior Deo," which appears as a counterpoint. As another setting of the hymn text "Nearer my God to Thee . . . ," its appearance here will emphasize, for those who know this verbal connection between it and "Bethany," the desired identification between "Watchman" and "Bethany," between the promise of the former and the fulfillment — though as yet unattained and elusive — of the latter.

ALLEGRETTO. Bellaman's program note continues:

The three succeeding movements are the diverse answers in which existence replies. . . . [The second movement] is not a scherzo. . . . It is a comedy in the sense that Hawthorne's *Celestial Railroad* is comedy. Indeed this work of Hawthorne's may be considered as a sort of incidental program in which an exciting, easy, and worldly progress through life is contrasted with the trials of the Pilgrims on their journey through the swamp. The occasional slow episodes — Pilgrims' hymns — are constantly crowded out and overwhelmed by the former. The dream, or fantasy, ends with an interruption of reality — the Fourth of July in Concord — brass bands, drum corps, etc.

This amazing movement is like a circus, with its nearly constant overlays of complex rhythms, dense textures, and quoted fragments, including "Tramp, Tramp, Tramp," "In the Sweet By-and-By" played in quarter tones, "The Red, White, and Blue," "Columbia the Gem of the Ocean," "Beulah Land," Stephen Foster's "Massa's in de Cold Cold Ground," "Martyn," "Yankee Doodle," "Marching through Georgia," "Turkey in the Straw," "Long Long Ago," "Reveille," and "The Irish Washerwoman." The movement seems to be saying that all manner of things, even incongruous things, can and do happen, often at once. This collage of life is so complex that extra conductors are sometimes needed to sort out its contradictory rhythms.

FUGUE. "An expression of the reaction of life into formalism and ritualism," according to Bellaman's program note. This double fugue, which originated as an assignment when Ives was in college, uses as its subjects two hymn tunes, "From Greenland's Icy Mountains" and "All Hail the Power." At the end we are treated unexpectedly to a fragment of "Joy to the World." The rhythmic simplicity, the unambiguous tonality, and the diatonicism of this movement provide the greatest imaginable contrast to the preceding movement. Ives is not being ironic. He believed in simplicity as much as in chaotic complexity, and he enjoyed tonality as much as atonality. By putting two such different movements into the same symphony, he was stating his belief in the fundamental unity of all things.

LARGO MAESTOSO. Ives called this movement "an apotheosis of the preceding content, in terms that have something to do with the reality of existence and its religious experience." This finale, perhaps the most original in all of Ives' music, is one large gesture. It begins with distant percussion, which continues at its own independent speed until the end of the movement, when it is again alone. The final answer to the big questions posed in the prelude is outright, not merely implied, unity.

As this music evolves, slowly and carefully, fragments of well-known songs (plus the famous motive from Beethoven's Fifth Symphony) are woven into its continuous texture: "Bethany," "Martyn," "Missionary Chant," "Westminster Chimes," and "As Freshmen First We Came to Yale." These sometimes commonplace materials are raised to a spiritual plane by the religious overtones of this music, made most evident when the voices return wordlessly toward the end. The unity of this unbroken music symbolizes the equality of all things musical (and, by extension, human), from the most trivial college song to the loftiest of symphonic conceptions.

Three Places in New England
The "St. Gaudens" in Boston Common
Putnam's Camp, Redding, Connecticut
The Housatonic at Stockbridge

Three Places in New England was composed in 1912–14, with sketches dating back to 1903. It was premiered, in a revised version for chamber orchestra, on 10 January 1931 at New York's Town Hall. Nicolas Slonimsky conducted his Boston Chamber Ensemble. A private reading had taken place earlier, on 16 February 1930, before the American section of the Inernational Society for Contemporary Music. The version for full symphony orchestra was restored and edited by James Sinclair in 1972–73 and first performed in New Haven, Connecticut, on 9 February 1974 by the Yale Symphony Orchestra conducted by John Mauceri.

Three Places in New England has a convoluted history. In 1903 Ives composed two pieces, probably to serve as incidental music to a play by his uncle Lyman Brewster. These works, *Country Band March* and *Overture and March: 1776,* were combined into "Putnam's Camp" in 1912. The process of combining two existing works was extraordinary, as the newer composition weaves continually back and forth between the two older ones. Such a procedure could work only in an episodic, non-developmental style such as Ives'. In 1908 he sketched "The Housatonic at Stockbridge," inspired by a Sunday morning walk along the misty river with his new wife. In 1911 he began to sketch a "black march" as a tribute to the first black regiment in the Union Army, the 54th regiment. He subsequently called this movement "The 'St. Gaudens' in Boston Common," referring to the monument in front of the Massachusetts State House commemorating "Colonel Shaw and his colored regiment." In 1912, the same year he combined *Country Band* and *1776* into "Putnam's Camp," he orchestrated "St. Gaudens." "The Housatonic" was orchestrated the next year, and the following year he set "Putnam's Camp" for full orchestra. Thus, by 1914 several previously independent pieces had found their way into one work, now called *Three Places in New England.* He set the score aside.

In 1929 Nicolas Slonimsky offered to perform the work with a chamber orchestra of 24 Boston Symphony musicians. Ives made an arrangement for this ensemble, largely by transferring many of the brass parts into a difficult piano part. He may have added a lot of the work's dissonance at this time. The work was premiered by Slonimsky in New York in 1931. It was subsequently played in Boston, Havana, and Paris. It became Ives' first major orchestral work to be published.

It was not until 1948 that a full-sized orchestra played *Three Places.* Richard Burgin conducted it with the Boston Symphony, but only the chamber orchestra version was then available. Burgin augmented the string section but was otherwise unable to restore the piece to its original full orchestration. Thus it was the chamber version that became widely played and recorded. In 1972, conductor James Sinclair, working in the Ives Archives at Yale University under the supervision of John Kirkpatrick, the pianist who had been Ives' personal friend and one of his earliest champions, began to work on reconstructing a version for full orchestra. He sifted through many manuscripts and much correspondence. He was forced to make educated guesses in passages where the original score was missing. He also had to deal with the fact that Ives' 1929 version was based on old sketches rather than on the full orchestral score of 1914; yet the 1929 score contained many important revisions. Now, at last, a reasonable approximation of the full-size *Three Places in New England* is available.

The three movements are quite different. Ives was not particularly interested in overt musical unity, because he believed that all experience was of necessity unified. "St. Gaudens" is like a free association of ideas, floating by but rarely progressing. There are quotations of "Old Black Joe," "The Battle Cry of Freedom," and "Marching through Georgia." In the margins of one sketch, Ives wrote, "When a mass of men march up a hill, there is an unconscious slowing up; the drum seems to follow the feet rather [than] the feet the drum ... as on level ground." Elsewhere in the score Ives wrote, "That music can never get along with stickin' to one key and steady rhythm and time beats — this St. Gaudens can never be played or make sense to anyone."

The second piece is a dissonant collage of well-known tunes, including "The British Grenadiers," "Marching through Georgia," "Hail Columbia," and Sousa's *Semper Fidelis.* There is a lot of humor, as one type of music follows another unexpectedly. The movement is supposed to depict a Fourth of July picnic, where a child falls asleep and dreams of the Goddess of Liberty, soldiers marching, and General Putnam coming over the hills. There is a celebrated passage, very difficult to conduct, in which two bands are heard playing different marches in different tempos and different keys *simultaneously.*

"The Housatonic at Stockbridge," unlike the other movements, is a steady progression, a careful growth, from the quiet opening to an enormous climax, just a few bars before the quiet ending. In marked contrast to the other pieces, it is a unified and single-minded conception. On the score Ives wrote, "This is to picture the colors one sees, sounds one hears, feelings one has, of a summer day near a wide river — the leaves, waters, mists, etc., all interweaving in the picture, and a hymn singing in church across the river."

Charles Ives was an extraordinary composer, and *Three Places* is an extraordinary work. Luckily we now have a true representation of the piece as Ives wrote it. We also now have the advantage of temporal distance to enable us to put aside our puzzlement about Ives' alleged innovations and over his sometimes raucous, sometimes sentimental sound world. We are able to hear *Three Places* as the beautiful and meaningful composition it is.

Leoš Janáček

Born in Hukvaldy, Moravia, on 3 July 1854.
Died in Moravská Ostrava, near his birthplace, on 12 August 1928.

◆　◆　◆

Sinfonietta

Allegretto
Andante. Allegretto
Moderato
Allegretto
Andante con moto. Allegretto

The Sinfonietta was begun in 1925 and completed on 1 April 1926. Václav Talich conducted the Czech Philharmonic Orchestra in the first performance on 26 June 1926 in Prague.

Janáček's Sinfonietta is a youthfully vigorous work, full of life, optimism, and originality. It is surprising to learn, therefore, that the composer was 72 years old when he wrote it. It was conceived during a final burst of creativity that produced Janáček's best music. There were several reasons for this increased activity:

1. His opera *Jenufa*, published in 1917, was performed with success in several countries. As a result, his music was suddenly in demand beyond the borders of Czechoslovakia. There were now performers, listeners, and an ever-ready publisher eagerly awaiting each new composition.

2. As Janáček's fame grew, he had increased opportunities to travel to hear performances at new music festivals in various countries. He reacted to the latest music from different cultures more like a young man of 25 than an old man of 70. He was excited by what he heard, and he returned home eager to try out new sonorities and techniques in his own works.

3. He felt a patriotic pride in the newly won independence of his country, and, as a nationalist composer, he wanted to express that pride in music.

> I am filled with the young spirit of our republic, with a young music. I do not belong to those who have stayed behind, but to those who would rather look forward. I know that we have grown, and I do not see this growing process in terms of pains, in reminiscences of subjugation and suffering. Let us cast all

this from us! Let us imagine that we have to look to the future. We are a people that must take their place in the world. We are the heart of Europe. And the beating of this heart should be audible to Europe.

Janáček spoke these words of youthful optimism at the age of 72, soon after completing the Sinfonietta. Two years later he was dead.

4. He became enamored of Kamila Stösslová, wife of a merchant and 38 years his junior. He developed a compelling passion for this robust, warm young woman. As this passion grew, Janáček seemed to become younger. He composed music feverishly for this woman. He even considered leaving his wife for Stösslová. Although he never followed through with this idea, he did cause his wife considerable pain.

Janáček first met Stösslová and her husband in 1915, when she was 23 and the composer was 61. He was immediately attracted to her youthful and lighthearted personality, which contrasted greatly with that of Zdeňka Janáčková. The composer's wife was dignified, restrained, and sophisticated; Kamila was sensuous, feminine, and vital. Although Kamila never loved the composer, his desire for her grew steadily over the 13 years they knew each other. They saw each other infrequently, but Janáček wrote to her daily, pouring out his inmost thoughts and, in the process, idealizing Kamila beyond all plausibility. She responded only occasionally, always asking him to burn her letters. Her husband knew of the strange relationship and approved of it, but Zdeňka was intensely jealous and suspected the worst. Actually, the friendship always remained strictly platonic, but Zdeňka refused to believe it.

Kamilla Stösslová became at least the indirect inspiration for most of the composer's magnificent late works. One day, for example, he was with her at an outdoor band concert. He was enchanted with her company and with the sounds of the band. He was particularly intrigued by the manner in which the brass players stood to perform their fanfares. Since he had recently been asked to provide fanfare music for a gymnastics festival, he resolved to use these outdoor sounds to express his happiness. Thus began the Sinfonietta.

As Janáček grew older, his passion for Kamila intensified. Early in his last year he composed for her a string quartet called *Intimate Pages* (the original title was *Love Letters*). He wrote to her, "I have begun something beautiful. Our life will be contained in it. I shall call it 'Love Letters.' I think it will sound marvelous. How many treasured experiences we have had together! Like little flames, these will light up in my soul and become the most beautiful melodies."

Stösslová agreed to spend the summer of 1928 with the composer at his retreat. Janáček was elated. Caring little for his wife's feelings, the composer left on her birthday with Kamila, her son, and her husband. After a few days the husband tactfully left, and the composer settled into his newly decorated house with Kamila and her 11-year-old. She and her son stayed in the new rooms on the second floor, and the composer slept and worked on the ground floor. Only one week after the trio settled down to this odd domesticity, tragedy struck. Kamila's son got lost in the woods, and Janáček walked all over looking for him. The composer overexerted himself and had to lie down to rest. The boy wandered back a while later, but Janáček caught pneumonia. His condition worsened, and he was moved to a hospital, where he died a few days later. To Kamila fell the task of informing Zdeňka.

The commission for fanfare music provided Janáček with an opportunity to voice his patriotism. The Sinfonietta, he felt, expressed "the contemporary free man, his spiritual beauty and joy, his strength, courage, and determination to fight for victory." The composer wanted to represent his pride in the newly formed Czechoslovak state and in the struggle that had been necessary to achieve independence. At first calling the work *Military* Sinfonietta, he dedicated it to the Czechoslovakian Armed Forces. The festive fanfares comprise the introductory movement, which is played by an extra military brass section, consisting of nine trumpets, two tenor tubas, two bass trombones, and timpani.

Originally the movements were entitled "Fanfares," The Castle," "The Queen's Monastery," "The Street," and "The Town Hall." The references are to the city of Brno, which had been under German dominance but had recently been returned to the Czechs.

Janáček's style in the Sinfonietta is utterly unique, unlike that of any other composer. Part of the reason is his deep involvement with Slavic folk music. Many of the themes sound like folk tunes, and a few are actually adapted from folksongs. Another reason is that Janáček tried to let the rhythms and pitch patterns of the Czech language influence the curves of his melodic lines. A third aspect of the Sinfonietta's originality lies in its inordinately large amount of repetition.

Many phrases are heard twice, yet these repeats do not become tedious. Why? The primary reason for the constant freshness is the irregularity of phrase lengths. We never quite know how long a segment will be until it is repeated. Consider the opening fanfares, for example. The repeated phrases are respectively 7, 5, 5, 9, and 3 measures long — an odd assortment of lengths that totally avoids normal four-bar phrases.

Each of the remaining movements is a mosaic of brilliantly orchestrated passages of varying speeds and moods. Some sections are powerful, some are humorous. The third movement, for example, starts as if it is the slow movement, with an impassioned (and repeated) string melody. But the movement evolves to the blatant humor of a trombone solo and its subsequent exciting development. When the string opening returns at the end (mirroring, by the way, the structure of the entire Sinfonietta, which closes with a restatement of the opening fanfares), we realize how far this movement has traveled.

The fourth movement is almost a passacaglia — one theme, stated at the beginning by unison trumpets, is heard more than a dozen times in succession — with changing accompaniments and different interludes between restatements. Janáček's subtle wit is heard in this movement as well, when trumpets and bells seem to start the theme a beat too early.

The finale features intense high woodwinds. It works its way toward a triumphant recapitulation of the entire first movement, announced by cymbal clashes and all twelve trumpets (nine from the military brass group, which has been silent since the first movement, and three from the orchestra) playing a forceful motive in unison. The fanfares are accompanied by wind and string trills, so that at the end both ensembles at last play together.

Zoltán Kodály

Born in Kecskemét, Hungary, on 16 December 1882.
Died on 6 March 1967 in Budapest.

◆　◆　◆

Dances of Galánta

The Dances of Galánta *was composed in the summer of 1933 and first performed on 23 October 1933 by the Budapest Philharmonic Orchestra.*

Kodály spent his third through tenth years in the small village of Galánta, in western Hungary. He later described those years as the happiest of his childhood. It was in Galánta that he had his first musical experiences, involving both classical and folk music. As his father was an amateur violinist and his mother an accomplished pianist and singer, the boy heard a fair amount of chamber music. But he was equally fascinated by the songs and ballads he heard other children singing. These tunes represented the unspoiled heritage of the Hungarian countryside. The young Kodály also listened to a famous gypsy band that toured from Galánta. He described this band as the first orchestral sonority he had ever heard. He befriended the children of the band musicians, who fascinated Kodály with their little fiddles.

The young musician retained his interest in folk music even after his family moved away from Galánta in 1892. Three years later he heard about the work of Béla Vikár, the first man to use a phonograph to record folk music. As a teenager, Kodály compared early wax cylinder recordings of folk music to written transcriptions of the same music. He found the written versions to be inaccurate distortions of what the recordings revealed. He thereupon resolved to use the new technology to preserve folk music in its authentic state. He sought Vikár out and learned from him how to make folk music recordings.

About this time Kodály met a musician who was destined to become his lifelong friend — Béla Bartók. The two young men decided to dedicate a major effort to collecting and preserving Hungarian folk tunes. They understood that, since Hungary was a small country that had long been subject to political and cultural domination from more powerful neighbors, its traditional music was in constant danger of extinction. That old Hungarian folk music still exists today is due largely to the efforts of Kodály and Bartók.

For his first expedition in search of the true music of his people, Kodály returned to Galánta in 1905 and recorded about one hundred fifty folksongs. He later recalled, "Knapsack on back and stick in hand, and with fifty crowns in my pocket, I set out . . . to roam the countryside without any very definite plan. Sometimes I would just buttonhole people in the street, invite them to come and have a drink, and get them to sing for me; or sometimes I would listen to the women singing as they worked at the harvest. But the most exhausting part was the nightly sessions in the smoky atmosphere of the village pubs." In Galánta he recorded his former schoolmates singing the songs he remembered from his childhood.

The music he collected on this trip formed the basis of his Ph.D. dissertation, "The Stanzaic Structure of Hungarian Folk Song." This work was greeted with interest not only by musicians but also by literary scholars and philologists. In the thesis Kodály wrote, "It is impossible to study folksongs satisfactorily, particularly to investigate their rhythms, unless one hears them actually performed. Moreover, however extensive our knowledge and experience may be, it is only through hearing them sung by the peasants themselves that we can be certain as to their correct interpretation."

The folk music Kodály collected often included dance tunes. Hungarians have always been a dancing people. It is known that, as far back as the eleventh century, they celebrated their victories through dancing. During the eighteenth century one of the important Hungarian dances was the *verbunkos,* which accompanied the induction of enlisted men into the military. This dance originated from Turkish, Viennese, and gypsy elements. Musically it is characterized by syncopation, wide melodic skips, dotted rhythms, and the alternation of fast and slow figures. Its popularity caused the *verbunkos* eventually to become a purely musical form, divorced from the dance — particularly once conscription eliminated the need for a ceremony to accompany the recruiting of army volunteers.

In the late eighteenth century several authentic *verbunkos* were published in performing editions, and also many classical-period composers wrote concert works cast in this traditional folk form. In 1804 a two-volume collection of *verbunkos* from the region around Galánta appeared in Vienna.

It was to this old collection that Kodály turned in 1933, when he was asked to compose a dance suite in honor of the eightieth anniversary of the Budapest Philharmonic. In this set he found music from the almost forgotten world of the Magyars. In order to help preserve this ancient tradition, Kodály took melodies from the collection and dressed them in traditional harmonies and colorful orchestrations.

The vigorous sections of the *Dances of Galánta* reflect Hungarian folk singing. According to historian Adjoran Atvos, "No people on earth are as unmusical as the Magyars. Meeting in a convivial spirit, they do not sing; they whoop it up. No one in Hungary has ever heard peasants singing quietly, much less in harmony. Each voice improvises its own variations." Thus many of the wonderful melodies Kodály used are not singable but instead are dance tunes played by gypsy instrumentalists.

Several characteristics of the *verbunkos* tradition are evident throughout the *Dances of Galánta.* As the folk dance usually has at least two sections, the first of which is slow, Kodály's work begins with a slow introduction pervaded by the typical Hungarian dotted rhythm. The cellos start the piece with this rhythm — long notes alternating with pairs of short notes. A cadenza for the clarinet, an instrument often found in gypsy bands, leads to a somewhat faster section. This music uses a different, syncopated *verbunkos* rhythm. This rhythm pervades both the clarinet melody and its string accompaniment. Considerably later an oboe solo ushers in a new dance, which is also characterized by syncopations. Eventually other dance features are heard: fast figuration, wide leaps, Hungarian scales, etc. Thus the brilliant performing style of the gypsy violinists — who accompanied recruiting dances two centuries ago — lives on in the *Dances of Galánta.*

Háry János Suite
      A Fairy Tale Begins
      Viennese Musical Clock
      Song
      The Battle and Defeat of Napoléon
      Intermezzo
      Entrance of the Emperor and His Court

The opera Háry János *was composed in 1925–26. It was first produced at the Royal Opera of Budapest in the fall of 1926. Kodály extracted the orchestral suite in 1927.*

Kodály made a lifelong study of Hungarian folksongs. The music he studied found its way into his own compositional style. His music is thoroughly infused with the spirit of his culture, and several of his compositions use actual folk melodies. Because of the immediacy of theatrical performances, he felt it better to concentrate at first on folk-inspired stage works, rather than offering the public more abstract chamber music.

Once the walls of our theaters and the ears of our people have become attuned to folk music, it will be possible to move on to work of a higher order, music that is less closely earthbound — for then there will be no danger of its being uprooted. . . . [But] before we can hope to win the people for work inspired by their own voice, we must first arouse in them the consciousness of their own musical language. Otherwise nothing we might say in that language could be understood by them. This was the task I set myself when writing [the opera] *Háry János.*

This comic opera is based on a real person who lived in the early nineteenth century and fought in the Napoléonic Wars. Háry János gleefully embellished his exploits as he recounted them. His tales made him into the hero he never was in real life. Kodály described his protagonist in the preface to the opera:

Háry is a peasant, a veteran soldier, who day after day sits in the tavern, spinning yarns about his heroic exploits. The stories produced by his fantastic imagination are an inextricable mixture of realism and naïveté, of comic humor and pathos. . . . Though superficially he appears to be merely a braggart, essentially he is a natural visionary and poet. That his stories are not true is irrelevant, for they are the fruit of a lively imagination, seeking to create, for himself and others, a beautiful dreamworld. . . . He does not lie but creates legends. He is a poet. What he narrates never happened, but he has lived through it and so it is more true than reality.

Writing of the suite Kodály extracted from the opera, biographer László Eösze explains: "Out of these six pieces, with their sharp contrast of mood and treatment, what emerges is a convincing portrayal of Háry, the typical representative of the whole Hungarian peasantry. When he is writing [movements II, IV, and VI] of the great world to which the peasants are strangers, Kodály adopts a mocking, critical tone. But when they, the ordinary people, are his subject [movements I, III, and V], his confidence in their future touches his music with sublimity."

"A Fairy Tale Begins." The first movement begins with an orchestral outburst that represents a sneeze. According to Hungarian tradition, a story preceded by a sneeze is a fable and not to be taken literally. Afterward, the music settles down for a sustained prelude, the seriousness of which cannot be fully believed as long as we remember the sneeze.

"Viennese Musical Clock." Háry and his lady-friend Örzse are at the Imperial Court, staring in wonderment as the clocks perform music. The mechanical nature of the clocks is represented by the percussion section and by the regularity of the music's phrases.

"Song." The two lovers sing the Hungarian song, "This Side the Tisza, Beyond the Danube." The orchestra includes a Hungarian folk instrument known as a cimbalom, which is similar to the hammered dulcimer. (Kodály allows for the substitution of a harpsichord or piano.)

"The Battle and Defeat of Napoléon." This movement is a caricature of military music. The humorous incongruity of the last notes of the first tune indicate that Háry thinks the French army and its leader are ludicrous. The percussion and lower brass depict the battle. The low sliding sounds poke fun at the heroism of fighting. As Háry tells the story, he defeats the entire army singlehanded, and he kills Napoléon. The movement ends with a mock funeral march, whose melody is played by a most unsolemn instrument: the saxophone.

"Intermezzo." This movement is based on the vigorous rhythms of the *verbunkos,* a Hungarian soldiers' recruiting dance. The mockery of the preceding movement is replaced by a noble vision of national spirit.

"Entrance of the Emperor and His Court." Háry imagines that the members of the aristocracy have shed their false dignity and become fairy-tale figures. Their ceremonial entrance is caricatured in two march tunes (one in the winds, followed by another in the brass), neither of which is sufficiently serious for a real emperor or a real court.

Franz Liszt

Born on 22 October 1811 in Raiding, Austria, not far from Vienna.
Died on 31 July 1886 in Bayreuth, Germany.

Concerto Number 1 in E-Flat Major for Piano and Orchestra

Allegro maestoso
Quasi adagio. Allegretto vivace. Allegro animato —
Allegro marziale animato

Concerto Number 2 in A Major for Piano and Orchestra

Both concertos were begun in 1839. Liszt revised them continually for many years. He was pianist at the first performance of the First Concerto, at the Weimer Castle on 17 February 1855, with Hector Berlioz conducting. Liszt conducted the first performance of the Second Concerto at the Hoftheater in Weimar on 7 January 1857, with his pupil Hans von Bronsart at the keyboard. The composer continued to revise the A Major Concerto, which assumed its final shape only in 1861.

Liszt was a man of contradictions, many of which long served to obscure his true significance. He was an extraordinarily original artist, yet he composed outright potboilers as well as pieces of great beauty and sensitivity. That some of his more obvious works have frequently been heard on pops concerts has assured him a following, but such compositions represent only one side of his art. Many of his works are sophisticated, subtle, subjective statements by a composer far ahead of his time. His two piano concertos, composed virtually simultaneously over a period of some twenty years, exemplify this contrast. The First Concerto, an overt work, full of bravura and virtuosity, has been a traditional favorite with audiences as well as pianists. The less frequently performed Second, on the other hand, is more intimate and more personal. It shows the subjective side of Liszt's complex personality.

Liszt was the greatest pianist of his age. He virtually invented the kind of pianistic virtuosity that is still with us today. He thought up and perfected any number of dazzling keyboard techniques. As he had no models among pianists, he based his craft on that of the great violin virtuoso Niccolò Paganini. Paganini showed Liszt how to hold

345

an audience spellbound by sheer technique and how to cultivate a stage presence and a public personality that guaranteed an enraptured following. Like Paganini, Liszt had to write his own display pieces, because there was no previous music that called for the soloist to use his instrument in the way Liszt had taught himself to do. His early compositions are vehicles of virtuosity, and his early career was that of a traveling virtuoso performing keyboard acrobatics before enthralled crowds. It mattered little that these compositions were musically shallow. Their purpose was to display a new technique, and they succeeded completely in doing just that.

There are striking parallels here to certain types of show business celebrities today. A case can be made for a similarity with circus performers, but a more relevant parallel is with the stars of the rock and pop music worlds — virtuoso performers with an enormous following who compose their own music, tailored to show off their special talents. And, just as many of today's superstars of music are followed around on their concert tours by groupies, so Liszt had his entourage. Women idolized him in ways that were more like hero worship than artistic appreciation. There is a story, possibly apocryphal, about a lady who was so enamored of Liszt's persona that she kept against her breast for many months a cigar butt the great virtuoso had discarded.

Not surprisingly, Liszt had numerous affairs. Many were casual dalliances, but two were blatant scandals. In 1834 he entered into an impassioned relationship with the Countess d'Agoult, a rich married woman with two children. The composer and the countess lived and traveled together until 1844. They had three children, the second of whom, Cosima, was destined to leave her husband, conductor Hans von Bülow, in order to live with, have children by, and marry (in that order!) composer Richard Wagner. In 1848 Liszt began a long liaison with the cigar-smoking religious fanatic, Princess Carolyne Sayn-Wittgenstein, also married, which lasted until 1860.

Liszt was, as mentioned, a man of contradictions. At the height of his career as a concert pianist, he retired suddenly from public life. He was 37. Ironically, his retirement came at just the time when railroads began to make the life of a touring artist far easier. Nonetheless, Liszt never again performed in public. He continued to teach piano students, particularly enjoying the young women who came to learn from him, but he no longer accepted any fees for teaching. He devoted himself to composition, which he had neglected during the preceding decade.

Perhaps the biggest contradiction of all for Liszt was his increasing involvement with religion. In 1865 he received minor orders from the Roman Catholic church and became an abbé. He composed a number of religious works. In 1879 he was made Canon of Albano, which entitled him to wear a cassock. His religious feelings did not interfere with his continuing affairs of the heart. Perhaps his desire for the priesthood (he received four of the seven degrees) was one further instance of public posturing, but his religious feelings were quite genuine.

The late compositions of Liszt are forward looking. While Wagner had consciously striven for a "music of the future" that turned out to be very much a music of the present, Liszt actually anticipated several important features of twentieth-century music. Some of his late piano pieces display an almost Debussyan impressionism: they often contain unresolved dissonances that function as pure sonorities rather than participants in harmonic progressions. He even abandoned tonality. One of his late works is called *Bagatelle without Tonality* (this work was first published in 1956). He anticipated Schoenberg in the opening of his *Faust* Symphony, which is virtually a twelve-tone row. And, in many of his larger works, he developed a technique which nurtured the majority of composers of the early part of our century: thematic transformation.

This procedure, which is beautifully realized in the two piano concertos, involves the derivation of many different themes from one or two basic melodies. The result may be called a self-generating form — the possibilities for transformation of a given theme determine the character of subsequent sections. Thematic transformation lies between the traditional approaches of development and variation. It is akin to what Schoenberg called "perpetual variation." Composer Humphrey Searle describes the process of thematic transformation as follows:

> A basic theme recurs throughout a work, but it undergoes constant transformations and disguises, and is made to appear in several contrasting roles; it may even be in augmentation or diminution, or in a different rhythm, or even with different harmonies; but it will always serve the structural purpose of unity within variety. The technique was of supreme importance to Liszt, interested as he was in the "cyclic" forms and the problem of rolling together several movements into one.

In both of the piano concertos, the transformation technique dictates the form. The opening theme of the First Concerto, for example, appears throughout the work in many guises and thereby keeps the piece from rambling. This theme is not a good candidate to generate the entire piece, however, because it is too limited: the tonic note alternates with a note a semitone lower, and then a third note another semitone down is added. Then this figure is repeated a step lower. The essential shape, decorated downward motion by step, is important to the concerto. After this motive is stated at the outset in the strings, it is developed in a series of piano cadenzas alternating with brief statements in the orchestra. There is inevitably a more lyrical second theme. Although it is treated only briefly at first, we understand from its expansive shape and true melodiousness that it has great potential for later development. As this second idea contains undercurrents of the first theme, it is the first that seems to dominate the opening movement.

The second movement is really three movements in one. First comes an adagio based on a derivative of the first movement's lyrical theme. A significantly new treatment of this theme in the woodwinds serves as the beautiful transition to the second main section, a scherzo. The scherzo is based on yet another transformation of the lyrical theme. The final section, *allegro animato*, brings back the vigorous opening theme of the concerto, along with some of its derivatives from the first movement. As this section does not abandon the main theme of the middle movement, it serves to bring back together the main two ideas of the piece.

A consequence of this combination of themes is that the finale starts with melodic material from the lyrical theme cast in the vigorous rhythm and mood of the first theme. The first theme has the final word, however, in a *presto* coda.

Although the First Concerto is divided into three movements, the distinction between them is not as clearcut as in classical concertos. All the movements share thematic material, some passages turn up in more than one movement, and all three movements contain fast and vigorous music. Because of the pervasiveness of the two main melodic ideas, however, this complex form coheres beautifully. It serves as a vehicle for both rhapsodic invention and controlled unity.

The Second Concerto is divided into distinct sections but not separate movements. The first theme is stated and then developed extensively in the orchestra, accompanied by the piano. A subsidiary idea, a beautiful horn melody with a delicate filigree accompaniment in the piano, leads to a brief piano cadenza, which includes a transformation of the opening theme. Then comes the second main section, which is loosely related to the main theme: against a lumbering bass figure in the piano, the winds play this second tune. Next comes a totally new idea, which functions as the concerto's scherzo section. This idea is transformed into a transition to the slow section, in which the piano accompanies a new version of the first theme, this time in a solo cello. It is interesting how often the solo piano is cast in the role of accompanist. After the latest transformation is developed, a fast section functions as a development. It combines the lumbering bass figure and the scherzo rhythm from earlier. At the climax of this development, a march-like transformation of the first theme is played by the full orchestra with piano. This section, which seems to act both as the finale and as the recapitulation, presents yet another version of the main theme: a rhapsodic, halting, yet lyrical transformation in the solo instrument. After that, the piano and the orchestra drive the concerto forcefully toward its conclusion.

The Second Concerto is a brilliant example of Liszt's technique of thematic transformation and of his unique approach to form. This is a one-movement form which combines aspects of a four-movement concerto (first movement, scherzo, slow movement, finale) with a sonata-allegro form (exposition of main theme, exposition of contrasting theme, development section, recapitulation).

Les Préludes

Les Préludes was completed in 1851, although it originated several years earlier. Liszt conducted the Weimar Court Orchestra in the first performance on 23 February 1854.

Liszt's best known tone poem was named after a 375-line ode published in 1823 by French poet Alphonse de Lamartine. Despite the title, and despite Liszt's having subtitled his composition "After Lamartine," it was long believed that the music had nothing to do with the poem. The reason for the confusion lies with the origin of the music as a set of four pieces for male chorus, composed to poetry not by Lamartine but by an obscure poet named Joseph Autran. These choruses, called the *Four Elements,* share thematic materials with *Les Préludes.* But, as musicologist Alexander Main has pointed out, this fact proves only the tone poem's relationship to Autran's verses, not its lack of relationship to Lamartine's poem. Actually, some of the thematic material in the *Four Elements* was originally composed for neither Autran's nor Lamartine's lines. For example, the pervasive three-note motive first heard in the third measure of *Les Préludes* was used in at least three other works of Liszt, and it also opens the finale of Beethoven's last string quartet. César Franck later used it prominently in his Symphony in D Minor. Also, the gentle horn call in *Les Préludes,* used as well in one of the Autran choruses, originated in an opera by Donizetti.

Liszt composed the first of the four choruses for a concert in Marseilles in 1844. The remaining choruses were written somewhat later and may never have been performed during his lifetime. In 1848 Liszt's associate August Conradi orchestrated the accompaniments, and Liszt wrote to poet Autran about his intention of prefacing the set with an extensive overture. It is unclear whether or not this overture was actually composed, but Joachim Raff claimed to have orchestrated in 1850 a Liszt overture called *The Four Elements.* By this time Liszt had grown dissatisfied with the choruses, probably because of their mediocre poetry, and had decided against publishing or performing them. The overture orchestrated by Raff may have been, instead of the prelude to the choruses, Liszt's attempt to salvage some of the choral music in an orchestral format. In any case, Liszt was not totally pleased with the now independent overture, and he sought an appropriate literary source for inspiration as he reworked. He liked the melodies but apparently needed to associate them with a literary work in order to recast them in a convincing form. After trying unsuccessfully to interest Victor Hugo in supplying a text, Liszt turned to the works of his friend Lamartine. By 1851 the composer was referring to a *Meditation* Symphony, based on Lamartine. This "symphony" was probably *Les Préludes.*

Lamartine's poem is in four main sections, dealing respectively with love, destiny, war, and the countryside. Separating these four parts are three transitions. The poem is framed by an introduction and a conclusion that recalls the introduction. This form is clearly marked in the poem, as new sections bring new line lengths and also since most sections are set off by asterisks. Liszt based the form of *Les Préludes* directly on that of the poem. There are four main sections, each with a distinct mood. Most of them begin with a new transformation of the opening melody. These sections are separated by transitions. The whole is prefaced by an introduction and ends with a coda that recalls the introduction.

According to musicologist Main, not only the form but also the moods of the poem and music correspond. The poem's love section is paralleled by a sweetly melancholy violin and cello treatment of the main theme. The poem's harsh destiny is portrayed by a stormy allegro. The third main part of the music corresponds to the fourth section of the poem: the pastoral countryside is depicted by harp and horn figures over a drone. The poem's third part, war, is reflected in the fourth main section of the music, which is characterized by a march.

In addition, the transitional passages of both works correspond. For example, the trumpet call that leads to the final march section is inspired by the line, "It is the clarion's cry." This is not the only instance of instrumentation suggested by the poem. Throughout the poem are found references to lyre, harp, and lute — all plucked string instruments. Appropriately, Liszt features the harp in many passages and begins the tone poem with *pizzicato* strings.

One reason scholars mistakenly believed that *Les Préludes* was unrelated to the Lamartine poem was that Liszt prefaced the score with a brief program note, only loosely related to Lamartine and written not when the music was composed but for its publication five years later. Although apparently an afterthought, this program does serve as a guide to the music, and it does offer an explanation for the title:

> What is our life but a series of preludes to that unknown song, the first solemn note of which is sounded by Death? The enchanted dawn of every existence is heralded by Love, yet in whose destiny are not the first throbs of happiness interpreted by storms whose violent blasts dissipate his fond illusions, consuming his altar with fatal fire? And where is to be found the cruelly bruised soul, that having become the sport of one of these tempests does not seek oblivion in the sweet quiet of rural life? Nevertheless, man seldom resigns himself to the beneficient calm which at first chained him to Nature's bosom. No sooner does the trumpet sound the alarm than he runs to the post of danger, be the war what it may that summons him to its ranks. For there he will find again in the struggle complete self-realization and the full possession of his forces.

Edward MacDowell

Born in New York on 18 December 1860.
Died in New York on 23 January 1908.

◆ ◆ ◆

Concerto Number 2 in D Minor, Opus 23

Larghetto calmato
Presto giocoso
Largo. Molto allegro

The D Minor Concerto was begun in the winter of 1884–85 and finished in the spring of 1885. MacDowell was soloist when Theodore Thomas conducted the first performance on 5 March 1889 in New York.

In some ways it is ironic that Edward MacDowell has become known as the most representative nineteenth-century American composer. He was one of our truly important and influential composers, but his music does not sound particularly American, no doubt because of the many years he spent studying and composing in Europe.

MacDowell gave strong evidence of his musical talents when he was a child. He was given piano lessons while growing up in New York, but before long his parents felt that it was necessary for him to have a European education. Since they were people of means, MacDowell was able to set off for Paris, accompanied by his mother, at the age of 16. After two years at the Paris Conservatory, MacDowell moved to Germany for further study, and Mrs. MacDowell, believing that her son was then old enough to be on his own, set sail for New York.

MacDowell was 19 when he met Franz Liszt. He was one of several young participants in a concert of Liszt's music at the Hoch Conservatory in Frankfurt. At the age of 21 MacDowell became a piano instructor at the Darmstadt Conservatory, but he resigned after a year in order to devote more time to composition. He played his First Piano Concerto for Liszt in Weimar, receiving considerable encouragement from the elder statesman of German music. MacDowell subsequently dedicated the First Concerto to Liszt, who helped him secure European performances and publications of his works.

The composer married Marian Nevins in New York in 1884. The couple returned immediately to Germany, living first in Frankfurt and then Weisbaden. There he composed the Second Concerto, a big, romantic work in the tradition of the Liszt piano concertos. The

352

MacDowells met several American composers who were studying abroad. In 1888 one of them, Benjamin Johnson Lang, convinced them to move back to the States. The composer had lived in Europe for twelve years — almost half of his creative life. He had composed a lot of music in large and small forms, which displays the influence of Germans such as Schumann, Liszt, Wagner, and his teacher Raff.

Soon after returning to America, MacDowell played the new Second Concerto in New York and then in Boston. The piece received enthusiastic praise in the press, and conductor Frank van der Stucken promised to perform it at a concert of American music in Paris. MacDowell's reputation grew rapidly, and before long he was the most famous composer in the United States. He was living in Boston, where he had a number of private students and where he concertized frequently and composed intensely.

In 1896 he was invited to start a music department at Columbia University in New York. The university search committee had felt that he was "the greatest musical genius America has produced" and thus offered him a chair in composition, even though he was only 35 years old. He taught two music history courses, two theory courses, and a composition class. He insisted on rigorous training, but he also advised his composition students to listen to their native music and put it into their pieces. Syncopation, he claimed, was natural to Americans. He said that ragtime had influenced the scherzo of the Second Piano Concerto and that, had he lived longer in America, he would surely have made greater use of ragtime's rhythms.

Today these statements may seem odd. It is difficult to hear any hint of ragtime or any other American music in the concerto he composed in Weisbaden. Furthermore, now that we know the genuinely American music of such composers as Ives and Joplin, MacDowell's concerto sounds distinctly European. Its harmonies and melodies are taken straight from German romanticism. It was easier for MacDowell to speak out for American nationalism than to achieve it.

MacDowell's championing of American influences in music was laudable. He understood that, although there was a rich musical heritage in Europe, America was a different country with its own, albeit new, culture. He preached an indigenous music, but he was unable to compose it. A few years later he resented the fact that the music of a visitor — Antonín Dvořák, composer of the *New World* Symphony — was being presented to New York audiences as American national music. MacDowell failed to recognize the parallel to his early career, when he lived in Europe, wrote music that sounded European, and performed it there.

We have here in America been offered a pattern for an "American" national musical costume by the Bohemian, Dvořák. . . .

Before a people can find a musical writer to echo its genius, it must first possess men who truly represent it — that is to say, men who, being part of the people, love the country for itself; men who put into their music what the nation has put into its life; and in the case of America it needs above all, both on the part of the public and on the part of the writer, absolute freedom from the restraint that an almost unlimited deference to European thought and prejudice has imposed on us.

MacDowell did a lot for American music, but circumstances conspired to prevent his doing more. He could have influenced a whole generation of American composers from his position at Columbia, but he resigned after eight years because of a dispute with Nicolas Murray Butler, the new president of the university. MacDowell was frustrated by the poor preparation of his students, and he wanted Columbia to force secondary schools to train their students better in the arts. He proposed that any student poorly prepared in the arts be refused admission to Columbia, no matter how high his other qualifications. Butler saw this move as a threat to the enrollment numbers. The dispute was aired in the New York newspapers, much to the embarrassment of both parties.

After leaving Columbia MacDowell remained in New York. He became one of the founders of the American Academy of Arts and Letters, and he made plans to transform his summer home in Peterborough, New Hampshire, into an artists' colony. The MacDowell Colony is still flourishing today, providing artists with residencies of several months of distraction-free time in which to work. Soon after his resignation from the university, the composer began to show signs of mental illness. By the fall of 1905 he had regressed to a child-like state. He died three years later, at the age of 47.

MacDowell was something of a paradox. An enormously gifted composer, he made his mark and earned his reputation writing European music in Europe. Because of the support of Liszt, he was able to return to this country as a celebrity. His later compositions were all modest, yet in them he began to show some glimmers of a native art music. He strongly believed in indigenous American music, although he did not fully approve of nationalism. He eventually forbade, in fact, the performance of any of his compositions on all-American concerts. He felt that American music should have an identity, and that once it did it should rise above nationalism and take its rightful place alongside all the world's art music. Today MacDowell's beliefs are widespread, yet his music is far less known that it deserves to be. Yet his impact on American music — more through his founding of the American Academy and the MacDowell Colony than through his compositions — remains strong.

Gustav Mahler

Born on 7 July 1860 in Kalischt, Bohemia.
Died on 18 May 1911 in Vienna.

Das Lied von der Erde

Das Trinklied vom Jammer der Erde
Der Einsame im Herbst
Von der Jugend
Von der Schönheit
Der Trunkene im Frühling
Der Abschied

Das Lied von der Erde ("The Song of the Earth") was composed in the summers of 1908 and 1909. Bruno Walter conducted the first performance on 20 November 1911 in Munich.

European interest in the Orient arose in the seventeenth and eighteenth centuries, when increased contact with China resulted in an outburst of enthusiasm for Eastern art and philosophy. Voltaire and Leibniz, for example, were taken with Oriental ideas. Goethe tried to create a marriage between Eastern and Western thought in certain literary works. Mahler had a similar idea for *Das Lied von der Erde*, particularly in the last movement.

Western involvement with the East intensified toward the end of the last century. At that time many Europeans were traveling to China and publishing their accounts upon their return. Also significant were the International Expositions held in Paris in 1889 and 1900. These world's fairs had a considerable impact on European artists, many of whom were exposed to Oriental art and music for the first time. Mahler, in France on tour with the Vienna Philharmonic, went to several exhibits and performances. He was fascinated with the music he heard.

Translations of Chinese poetry began to appear toward the end of the century. When Mahler read Hans Bethge's *The Chinese Flute* soon after its publication in 1907, he immediately realized that his interest in the Orient now had a specific subject. He began to compose a setting of seven of Bethge's translations, to which he added some words of his own.

The texts of *Das Lied* are far removed from the ancient Chinese originals. Mahler adapted Bethge, who had translated into German from English and French translations of the Chinese. Thus the texts represent not so much ancient Chinese thought as Mahler's personal conception of a European interpretation of Chinese poetry.

In the first song the poet exhorts his listeners to give ear to life's shortness and sorrows. Then he deals in subsequent songs with themes of loneliness, youth, beauty, and drunkenness (this last representing life's immediate pleasures and pains). Thus the first five songs constitute an overview of the human condition, in preparation for the monumental sixth song, which addresses the parting from life.

Each of the three stanzas in "The Drinking Song of Earth's Sorrows" ends with the line "Dark is life, is death." Mahler set this line a semitone higher each time, resulting in a yearning intensity. The song portrays life as a brief battle from which wine offers the only respite.

The intimate lament "The Solitary in Autumn" is an evocation of loneliness. The poignant line "My heart is tired" reflects the world-weariness of the poem. The next three poems form the scherzo of this song-symphony, as Mahler called it. They are nostalgic glances at a happier past. "Of Youth" is untroubled and "Of Beauty" is almost carefree, except for the violent middle section depicting young horsemen. "The Drunkard in Spring" returns to the desperate gaiety of the opening movement: both are drinking songs. The poet seems to be saying, according to musicologist Burnett James, that youth passes and beauty vanishes, so why not drink and be merry?

"The Farewell," which is nearly as long as the other songs combined, is an essay in dualities: action vs. contemplation, elation vs. despair, life vs. death, East vs. West. The text consists of two poems by two different poets of the late T'ang Dynasty. By the addition of his own words, Mahler integrated the two texts, just as he connected them through a large orchestral interlude. According to Daniel R. Kuritzkes, the first poem

speaks in the first person of awaiting a friend at dusk. As night settles in, the speaker reflects on the beauty of the world, becoming impatient in his desire to share with his friend his intoxication with the earth. When the friend arrives, however, it is only to tell of his decision to part, to wander in the mountains, awaiting death. Though he too revels in the beauty of the spring, he sees it differently from the first friend, for he has become resigned to leaving it behind. For the waiting friend, earthly beauty is something of which he urgently needs to partake, to make his own for the short time he has to live with it. The second friend understands spring as a symbol of Earth's constant rebirth, reflecting the everlasting nature of the earth as compared to our transitory experience of it.

The two friends are allegorical figures, representing the differences between Eastern and Western thought. The cyclical nature of life, endlessly repeating itself as the seasons continually succeed one another, is an Oriental concept. To the Occidental mind, life is a unidirectional progression from birth to death. Mahler reflects the dichotomy between these two thought- and value-systems in the music of the sixth song. The Oriental mood is suggested by the use of the pentatonic scale (in a more pervasive manner than in the earlier songs, all of which have pentatonic motives or themes) and of certain instruments with Eastern connotations, such as the flute and the tamtam.

Mahler's invocation of the East goes deeper than these superificial references to Chinese culture. For example, the restraint with which he orchestrates the final song, with small instrumental groups creating various moods, recalls the manner in which Oriental artists apply their colors painstakingly and sparingly. Composer Richard Saylor's description of Eastern art applies remarkably well to the Oriental passages in "The Farewell": "Painting in China and Japan tends toward sparseness, ambiguity, monochromatic impressionism. Spaces are left purposefully open, inviting the viewer to fill in the meaningful emptiness. Symbols are used to express the inexpressible, to hint at the essence of a thing, to suggest ideas for contemplation."

The music in "The Farewell" plays Eastern and Western conceptions against each other. The Eastern idea of endless cycles and of immutability is contrasted with the Western notion of progress toward goals. The very idea of a dramatic confrontation between two different philosophies is, of course, thoroughly Western: Mahler remained, despite the Oriental influences, a Western artist. The Oriental passages lack extended development, since development moves music through time toward specific harmonic goals, or arrival points. Instead of harmonic motion there are pervasive drones that anchor us in the present moment. The result is a sense of stillness, of timelessness. One such passage is heard at the opening of the movement. When the voice first enters, it is marked "without expression." The sparse orchestration, speech-like voice, and harmonic stasis create a moment of contemplation (of the setting sun, according to the text), a moment out of time, a moment that does not participate in any musical progression.

This passage, like many later ones, simply stops (on a flute note). The music does not move toward this ending. There is no real cadence. In the Oriental view, events start and stop, but they neither originate from absolute beginnings nor move pointedly toward complete endings. Stopping in this seemingly arbitrary manner serves to cut the movement into isolated sections, each a moment unto itself.

The music evocative of Western values is quite different. It resembles other Mahler works and, significantly, the earlier songs in *Das Lied*. It is replete with surging climaxes, restlessly shifting levels of loudness, and rich orchestral colors. In the place of drones, the music acquires harmonic bass lines and complex chord progressions that propel it forward. A Western concept underlies the poet's inability to accept his friend's absence and later his friend's departure.

The Oriental mood returns as the friend awaits the final farewell. This stanza (which Mahler added to Bethge's text) represents the waiting friend's last attempt to view his situation from an Eastern perspective. The following passage, the final stanza of the first of the two poems, is a turbulent, impassioned rendering of the longing felt by the one friend for his comrade. This Western mood is underlined by involved rhythmic counterpoint. The soloist exclaims his lust for life: "O Beauty! O eternally loving — living — intoxicated world!"

What follows is an extended orchestral interlude, which separates the two poems. It gives listeners time to reflect on the ideas in the first half while preparing them for the change of philosophy in the second half. The second poem begins as if in a dream: the friend has settled down to await his companion in the stillness of the night. Before long the music builds toward an intense climax, after which the tamtam marks the return of the opening Oriental sound-world.

Mahler's own words bring the final section to a close: "The well-loved earth everythere Blooms in spring and grows green anew. Everywhere and always the horizon glimmers blue." According to Kuritzkes, the poet-composer

> looks back at the earth to celebrate its transcendant beauty, once more renewed with the blossoming of spring. In a verse which could have been bitterly ironic, Mahler rejoices in this rebirth even at the moment of . . . death. This is a dramatic, philosophical reversal of the end of the first poem, where the friend [is] unable to reconcile himself to the transience of his experience of earthly beauty. . . . Mahler realizes that life and death are only a natural part of the earth's cycle, not a unique, individual tragedy. It is this realization which allows the movement to conclude as it does.

The word *ewig* ("forever") is repeated nine times. The singer descends from the third scale degree to the second, then from the second to the tonic, again and again. The final time the voice stops on the second degree: no final resolution here, but rather the feeling that this music — like the cycle of life and death — continues eternally.

Mahler was able to make this ending work musically because the harmonic language has become thoroughly Oriental. No dominant-tonic cadence here, nor any final harmonic progression. Rather, the pentatonic scale, which symbolizes the Oriental way of thinking, becomes a pervasive, seemingly eternal sound. For the "ewig" motive to come to rest on the tonic would be too Western. Instead, it hangs in the air. The absence of a final sense of arrival is not a failure of the music to reach a goal. The very idea of the need to reach a goal has been supplanted by the timelessness of the East (at least Mahler's conception of the East), where there are no ultimate conclusions. Every ending coincides with a new beginning, in the never-ending cycle of life.

Symphony Number 1 in D Major

Langsam, schleppend. Im Anfang sehr gemächlich
Kräftig bewegt, doch nicht zu schnell
Feierlich und gemessen, ohne zu schleppen
Stürmisch bewegt

The First Symphony was begun in 1884 and finished in 1888. Mahler conducted the first performance in Budapest on 20 November 1889.

Despite his youth Mahler was not content with his position in Leipzig as opera assistant, even to such a distinguished older colleague as Artur Nikisch. The composer kept looking for a better position and kept trying to find interesting works he could direct in Leipzig. One opportunity arrived in 1886 when he met Baron Karl von Weber, grandson of composer Karl Maria von Weber, whose music Mahler greatly admired. Weber had in his possession the sketches of his grandfather's unfinished comic opera *Die drei Pintos*. Mahler was asked if he would be interested in completing the work.

At first Mahler was hesitant. Weber had sketched music for only seven of the 17 numbers in the libretto, and much of the music he had written appeared in an indecipherable shorthand. Mahler nonetheless studied the sketches and found that he *could* read the handwriting, so he agreed to the project. He was reluctant to compose his own music for the opera, except where absolutely unavoidable. Thus he incorporated music from other Weber pieces. He became obsessed with the work, even to the point of neglecting his conducting duties. But the project was good for him. It got him to concentrate his energies on composing, even though he was writing someone else's music.

Furthermore, the musical world's interest in the upcoming productions of *Die drei Pintos* proved a great boost to his career.

Practically every day he went to the home of Baron and Mrs. Weber in order to play at the piano what he had accomplished. A friendship grew between Mahler and the baron, and something more than friendship began between the composer and Mrs. Weber. They started a torrid affair. Although she was seven years older than Mahler and had a husband and three children, she seriously considered eloping with him. The lovers feared a scandal, but they found each other irresistible.

Despite the tensions he was causing in the Weber household, Mahler continued the practice of bringing his current work-in-progress to them for approval. Once the opera was finished, however, it became the First Symphony that he played for the Webers. One night he arrived at their house at midnight, carrying the newly completed first movement. He went to the piano, and the Webers stood at his sides to help him play the eight octaves of A that open the work. The composer later recalled, "All three of us were happy and enthusiastic. I don't think that I ever experienced such a pleasant hour with my First Symphony. Later we all went out together, filled with happiness."

Baron von Weber ignored as long as he could what was going on between his wife and the composer, but eventually his mind snapped. One day, while on a train to Dresden, he went on a mad shooting spree. He fortunately harmed no one as he repeatedly shot his revolver into the headrests between seats.

Mahler quarreled with the opera manager in Leipzig and was out of a job. Despite the fame *Die drei Pintos* had brought, he found it difficult to obtain a new position, in large part because of his scandalous affair with Marion von Weber. He also had problems trying to arrange a performance for the newly completed First Symphony, which most conductors considered too modern. The answer to both dilemmas came in 1888, when Mahler, at the age of 28, was appointed principal conductor of the Royal Budapest Opera.

After a year in the Hungarian capital, he was able to conduct the symphony. The reception was cool. The melodious first half was reasonably well received, but the mock funeral march and the turbulent finale presented the conservative audience with problems. There was some booing at the end.

The work was originally listed not as a symphony but as a symphonic poem in two parts. In this version the first part contained three movements and the second had two. Despite his calling it a tone poem, Mahler apparently had no particular program in mind. After the performance, though, he began to think that anything called a symphonic poem ought to have a story, so he added one. He later abandoned this idea, however, deciding that the work really was a symphony. The original titles of the movements were:

First Part: From the Days of Youth
    I. Spring without End
    II. Flora
    III. Under Full Sail
Second Part: Human Comedy
    IV. Funeral March in the Manner of Callot
    V. From Inferno to Paradise

The "Flora" or *Blumine* movement was eventually dropped. Mahler felt it was not sufficiently symphonic. It had, in fact, been taken from some incidental music he had previously written for a play. For a long time that movement was thought to be lost, but it turned up in 1959 and has occasionally been performed as part of the symphony. Critical opinion is divided, but the majority of commentators feel that the composer was correct in removing it. Others point to important thematic links between it and the finale.

This symphony was not really Mahler's first. There is evidence that he composed at least four others earlier and that their manuscripts may have survived until the Second World War. It is unfortunate that these early works were destroyed, but at least our knowledge of their existence helps to explain the experienced mastery evident in the First Symphony.

The symphony begins with one of the most extraordinary slow introductions in all of music. Quietly the strings, mostly in harmonics, intone the note A in many different octaves. This A is held, with slightly changing instrumentation, for the entire introduction — some four minutes of music. Against this veiled backdrop, various birdcalls and fanfares are heard. Finally the fast part of the movement begins, with a lovely lyrical theme (taken from one of Mahler's *Songs of a Wayfarer*). The four minutes of A has its effect, however. Although the movement is in D major, the fast section only touches that key briefly before going off into A major. The entire exposition is devoted to the one beautiful, peaceful theme, mostly centered on A. The development begins with a varied return of the mysterious opening. Then, once we are halfway through the movement, a fanfare-like theme is heard, finally in the long awaited key of D major. As the music develops and wanders through distant keys, the pervasive peacefulness is disturbed. At the end of the development, the music turns decidedly ominous, a mood that the two themes initially seem incapable of evoking. This turbulence is only temporary, however, as it is a preparation for the triumphant return of the second theme. The movement ends wittily, as the birdcalls from the introduction (which, incidentally, are included in both main themes) return with some urgency in *pizzicato* strings, trumpets, horns, and finally timpani. The timpani try to hammer home this simple motive, but silence keeps getting in the way. Finally the full orchestra joins in to bring the movement to a merry close.

The second movement is a scherzo. It continues the peaceful mood of the first movement, although it gets both more boisterous and, in the trio, gentler. The trio is a *Ländler*, an Austrian folk dance.

The slow movement's original title ("Funeral March in the Manner of Callot") refers to an etching by Jacques Callot (1592–1635). As Mahler explained,

> The external stimulus for this piece of music came to the composer from the parodistic picture, known to all children in Austria, 'The Hunter's Funeral Procession,' from an old book of children's fairy tales: the beasts of the forest accompany the dead woodsman's coffin to the grave, with hares carrying a small banner, with a band of Bohemian musicians in front, and the procession escorted by music-making cats, toads, crows, etc., with stags, roe deer, foxes, and other four-legged and feathered creatures of the forest in comic postures. At this point the piece is conceived as the expression of a mood now ironically merry, now weirdly brooding.

The funeral march is parodistic. At the beginning, for example, one string bass plays (to an accompaniment in timpani) a minor-key version of the folk song *Frère Jacques*. This solo is well within the range of the cello but rather high for the bass. The bass gives it a certain grotesqueness that is appropriate to Callot's etching. This tune is treated as a round, with more and more instruments joining in.

The loud opening of the last movement is notorious for its ability to startle an inattentive listener. During the premiere an elegantly dressed lady, who had been dozing during the quiet ending of the slow movement, was surprised by the outburst that begins the finale. She leaped out of her seat, scattering to the floor everything that had been on her lap. The author of this book witnessed a similar occurrence when he and his very pregnant wife sat in the front row at a performance of Mahler's First Symphony in a resonant gymnasium. Their unborn child (one of the dedicatees of this book) was startled by the sudden noise into jumping violently and kicking visibly.

The finale looks forward to Mahler's later symphonies in its dramatic contrasts, spectacular orchestration, and great length. Its mood is not far from that of the Fifth Symphony, for example. The innocence of the first two movements and the parody of the funeral march are left behind for this powerful, sinister, dramatic ending.

Symphony Number 2 in C Minor, *Resurrection*
Allegro maestoso
Andante moderato
In ruhig fliessender Bewegung
Urlicht —
Im Tempo des Scherzo

The Resurrection *Symphony was composed mostly during 1894. The first three movements were played in Berlin on 4 March 1895, under the direction of Richard Strauss. Mahler conducted the first complete performance on 13 December 1895, also in Berlin.*

There are some pieces of music that are so engaging, so electrifying, that they make the listener a part of them for their duration. "Music heard so deeply/That it is not heard at all, but you are the music/While the music lasts," as T. S. Eliot wrote in his *Four Quartets.* You must love such music or hate it. It is too powerful to foster indifference. Such works include the music dramas of Wagner, the symphonies of Mahler, the early ballets of Stravinsky, and the symphonies of Ives. It is no coincidence that these works were all created within the relatively brief span of fifty years, about a century ago. The controversy still rages over this music. Its supporters may never be reconciled with its detractors, since extreme musical expressions all but demand impassioned responses.

The years from 1865 to 1915 were a period of transition. The "laws" of musical sound, some of which had governed music since 1600 and others of which had never previously been questioned, were dying. Composers were disillusioned with tonality and were beginning to seek a new paradigm. The language of Bach, Mozart, and Beethoven was fine for those composers' times, but it could no longer speak directly to the concerns of late-nineteenth-century mankind. The world was becoming a new place, in need of new artistic expressions.

The interplay of old and new, the struggle between different values, gave a special richness to music composed during that half century. We can hear in some pieces written in 1865–1915 both the autumnal resignation of the old style and the excitement of a new language being born. The tension between a nineteenth-century sensibility and that of the oncoming century was mirrored in this unique body of music.

The symphonies of Mahler are typical of this age of transition. Late romanticism, which was in turn an outgrowth of the impassioned classicism of Mozart and Beethoven, nourished Mahler's strange genius. He, in turn, provided an impetus to the new age. His early symphonies are steeped in the mysticism of natural beauty. In his later symphonies we discover the roots of modernism in incongruous yet poignant juxtapositions of tragedy and comedy.

Mahler's symphonies are about life, death, and renewed life. The composer knew that his music was stretching the tonal system to its limits. He longed for the infinite, but the existing musical language had been created in a spirit of restraint. "A symphony must contain the world," he had said. But what *was* the world Mahler's symphonies were supposed to reflect? The cultural and political worlds of the Western world were splintering. The European social structure was soon to be destroyed by a World War. Mahler lived at the end of an age, and his music came at the end of a long and noble tradition. Thus it is fitting that there are funeral marches in his First, Second, and Fifth Symphonies; that his Sixth is the *Tragic*; that resignation tinges his Ninth and Tenth and the song-symphony *Das Lied von der Erde*. Mahler, the last great romanticist, sang a sad farewell to the romantic century.

Despite his preoccupation with death, Mahler was not fundamentally a pessimist. Despondency was too easy an answer. The composer, who struggled through massive symphonies in search for his God, knew that death was also rebirth. Then whom does he bury with these funeral marches? In the Second Symphony he bears the hero of the First Symphony to the grave, or so he said. What he may have meant was that he was burying his musical past. But in death there is hope for renewed life. Therefore the funeral march in the Second Symphony is the *first* movement: death as a beginning, not an ending. By the end of the work, a heavenly chorus has intoned the Resurrection. The Second, then, is essentially optimistic. It progresses from a song of death to a song of hope.

Mahler's later works were to be less obvious and more personal. He did not find his God, but he found the answer to his own anguished torments. The late symphonies are songs of resignation, that progress from turbulent beginnings to peaceful finales. Resignation can be as fulfilling as resurrection.

All of Mahler's symphonies express a single truth: ages change, societies and civilizations change, people change, art changes, but there is always the hope of the new mingled with the death of the old. The hero that Mahler continually buries in his symphonies is resurrected in new guise. The progression within the symphonies repeated itself in history, as Mahler's music pointed away from an old and soured romanticism toward a resurrection of the art of music. Mahler himself was too much a child of the nineteenth century to cross the line into outright modernism, but he understood the changing times with such extraordinary sensitivity that his music became, fifty years after its composition, a vital artistic experience.

Mahler knew that his time would come, and so it has. Now that we can understand how a man can search for God and find instead himself, how a man can reap inspiration and hope from death, we can appreciate Mahler's music. It was misunderstood and rejected in its time not so much because it was novel but because it consistently forecast the death of an age. But it also predicted the hope of a subsequent era, which is our era.

When Mahler wrote the Second Symphony, he was not yet vividly aware of his inner contradictions. He saw the life/afterlife problem more in religious terms than in the personal manner of his late symphonies. Nonetheless, these themes clearly underlie his feelings, as can be seen from what he wrote about the *Resurrection* Symphony:

> I have called the first movement 'Funeral Pomp.' . . . It is the hero of my First Symphony whom I bear to his grave, and upon the clear recollection of whose life I gaze from a higher vantage point. At the same time, there is the great question: "Why hast thou lived? Why hast thou suffered? Is all this only a great and ghastly joke?" — We *must* solve these problems in one way or another, if we are to continue living — yes, even if we are to continue dying! He in whose life this call has once resounded must give an answer; and I give this answer in the last movement.
>
> The second and third movements are designed as an interlude; the second movement is a recollection — a sunny scene, calm and untroubled, from the life of this hero.
>
> It must have happened to you once — you have borne a dear friend to his grave, and then, perhaps on your way homewards, there has suddenly appeared before you the image of a long-past hour of happiness, which now enters into your soul like a sunbeam — marred by no shadow — you can almost forget what has happened! That is the second movement. Then, when you awaken from this nostalgic dream and must return to life's confusion, it may easily occur that this perpetually moving, never ending, ever incomprehensible hustle and bustle of life becomes *eerie* to you, like the movements of dancing figures in a brightly lighted ballroom into which you must gaze out of the dark night — from so far that *you do not hear the dance music* any more. Life becomes senseless to you then, a ghastly apparition from which you, perhaps, recoil with a cry of disgust. This is the third movement! . . .

When I conceive a great musical idea, I always come to the point where I must make the Word bearer of the idea. . . . What happened to me with the last movement of the Second Symphony is simply this: I really looked through all the world's literature, even the Bible, to find the redeeming Word — and was finally forced to express my feelings and thoughts in my own words.

The way in which I received inspiration to this act is very indicative of the true nature of artistic creation. For a while I contemplated using a chorus for the last movement; only my concern that one might consider this a rather external imitation of Beethoven made me hesitate again and again. It was at this time that Bülow died and I attended the memorial services here in Hamburg. The mood in which I was sitting (in church), and thinking of the departed, was very much in the spirit of the work which I carried inside of me. At this point the choir from the organ loft intoned the Klopstock chorale *Aufersteh'n!* ["Rise Again!"]. Like lightning this hit me: everything became clear and distinct before my soul! The creative artist waits for this lightning — this is his "sacred conception."

What I had experienced on this day, I now had to create in tones. And yet, if I would not have carried the work in me — how would I have been able to experience it? After all, thousands were sitting with me in church at that moment. And this is the way it always goes with me: only if I experience, I compose; only if I compose, I experience.

From this extensive program, expressed in a letter to a friend, we can see Mahler's conflicts: life vs. death, death vs. resurrection, God in death vs. God in life, life vs. living, the necessity of living vs. the habit of living. Out of his relentless struggle to solve these conflicts was born a body of masterpieces which present extraordinarily varied approaches to persistent and gnawing problems. Mahler's vision of life and death can be accepted or rejected, but it cannot be ignored.

Symphony Number 3 in D Minor
Kräftig
Tempo di menuetto: sehr mässig
Comodo, scherzando
Sehr langsam, misterioso —
Lustig im Tempo und keck im Ausdruck
Langsam, rehevoll

The Third Symphony was begun on 5 June 1895 and completed on 6 August 1896. The second movement was first conducted by Artur Nikisch with the Berlin Philharmonic Orchestra on 9 November 1896. Movements II, III, and VI were played by the orchestra of the Königliche Kapelle, conducted by Felix Weingartner, on 9 March 1897 in Berlin. Mahler conducted the first complete performance at Crefeld, Germany, on 12 June 1902.

Mahler repeatedly wrestled with the problem of the Third Symphony's specific meaning. In his sketches and letters are found frequent descriptions of the composition. He often changed his mind on the programmatic significance of the work and on the number and order of movements. When the symphony was finally complete, Mahler decided to suppress all programmatic information, including even the descriptive titles he had given the individual movements. He feared that the piece might be misunderstood by listeners trying to hear correspondences between musical gestures and philosophical meanings. In one way the composer was correct: abstract musical significance is always more profound than extramusical ideas. But in another way it was unfortunate that he chose to hide his intentions, because the Third Symphony — more than most other pieces — is rich in specific references as well as purely musical significance. There are statements in this music of a philosophy of man and his relationship to nature, of the relationship between art and life, and even of the social equality of all people. These ideas are in the music, not merely associated with it, so that to ignore them is to miss an entire layer of meaning. By reading Mahler's letters and sketches and by studying statements recorded by friends, we can piece together a reasonably accurate picture of what the Third Symphony signified to the composer.

> That I call it a symphony is really incorrect, as it does not follow the usual form. The term "symphony" to me this means creating a world with all the technical means available. The constantly new and changing content determines its own form. In this sense I must always be reminded that I create my own original means of expression.
>
> The first movement, "Summer Marches in," should indicate the humorously subjective content. Summer is conceived as a conquerer advancing amidst all that grows and blooms, crawls and flies, hopes and desires, and finally everything we know by instinct (angels — bells — in a transcendental sense). Above all,

Eternal Love spins a web of light like rays of sun converging to a single burning point. It is my most personal and richest work.

This utterly original first movement, which was composed last, gave Mahler the most difficulty. He thought about it longest, had most doubts about it, and spoke and wrote most about it. He saw it as a "gigantic hymn to the glory of every aspect of creation . . . [and to] the miracle of spring, thanks to which all things live, breathe, flower, sing, and ripen, after which appear those imperfect beings who have participated in this miracle — the men."
This movement

is hardly music anymore, just the voice of nature: one shudders at this motionless, soulless material (I could have called this movement "What the Rocks Tell Me"), from which, little by little, life frees itself and finally conquers, developing and differentiating step by step: flowers, animals, men, right up to the kingdom of the spirit and that of the angels. In the introduction there is the scorched, brooding atmosphere of midday in summer, when all life is suspended and not a breath of wind stirs the vibrant, flamboyant air, drunk with sunshine. Life, the young prisoner of ever-motionless, inanimate nature, cries out in the distance and begs for freedom, until, in the . . . movement which follows the introduction, this life breaks out victoriously.

In march tempo, the first movement never stops advancing; as it approaches it becomes louder and louder, gathers strength, and grows like an avalanche until its din breaks above our heads in powerful rejoicing. . . . I would never have had the courage, I think, to finish this gigantic task if the other movements had not already been completed.

When you consider how much happens in [the opening movement], it seems concise, even though it equals a long symphony in length! There are so many forces at work! First the secret growth of nature, awakening from her slumber, throwing off her chains; then the approach of summer with her flowers; what life, these innumerable sounds! Then the battle against hostile forces. . . . It is a gigantic fresco, in contrast to the painted miniatures of the other movements. You cannot imagine the effort required to construct such a long movement, to support and control the whole edifice. And yet I needed this foundation, this colossal base on which to build the pyramid which, in the other movements, gradually tapers off, becoming progressively more transparent and more delicate!

The second movement, "What the Flowers in the Meadow Tell Me,"

> symbolizes that moment in evolution when the creation still cannot speak a word or make a sound. . . . It is the most carefree piece I have ever written. It is carefree as only flowers can be. Everything hovers in the air with grace and lightness, like flowers bending on their stems and being caressed by the wind. To my amazement I noticed today for the first time that the double basses play only *pizzicato*; they don't have a single bow stroke, and I don't use any deep and strong percussion. The violins, on the other hand, which have a solo, play animated, winged, and smiling motives.

The third movement, "What the Animals in the Forest Tell Me," was inspired by a childhood memory of the Iglau military band playing in Vlassim Park in Prague, where Mahler was struck by the "natural symphony" of birds and animals and by the sounds of a posthorn in the distance.

The fourth movement, "What the Night Tells Me," is a setting for contralto of some lines from Nietzsche's *Thus Spake Zarathustra.* The word "deep" recurs again and again in this text, and Mahler illustrates it with a low recurrent pedal note. The short phrases of the text lead to long pauses between the lines sung, thus contributing to the sense of isolation implicit in the words. Toward the end, at the line "But all joys want eternity," the music opens briefly briefly into a wonderful lyricism.

In the fifth movement, "What the Morning Bells Tell Me," the contralto is joined by women's and boys' choruses. The boys' chorus's "Bimm, bamm, bimm, bamm, . . ." is the sound of bells

The sixth movement, "What Love Tells Me," represents "the peak, the highest level from which one can view the world. . . . I could almost call the movement 'What God Tells Me' — in the sense that God can only be comprehended as Love. And so my work is a musical poem embracing all stages of development in progressive order. It begins with inanimate Nature and rises to the love of God!"

Mahler once said that for the opening movement he needed "a regimental band to give the rough and crude effect of my martial comrade's arrival." Thus the first movement's orchestration leans heavily toward the winds, brass, and percussion. Especially when we consider the augmented size of this part of the orchestra (eight horns, four trumpets, four trombones, five clarinets — including *two* piccolo clarinets, an instrument readily associated with the marching band), we understand that the orchestra virtually contains a military band.

The music itself includes fanfares, marches, flourishes, and drum cadences — not what we normally associate with symphonic music. Band music is not simply quoted; it actually is the basic thematic material that is developed in a thoroughly symphonic manner. The first movement thus invokes the march and bids it enter the world of the symphony. Mahler takes the vernacular and makes it the universal. The Third Symphony bridges the ever-widening gap between popular and art music. The marches and fanfares repesent the world of everyday experience — particularly for someone living in *fin-de-siècle* Vienna. Far from allowing this world to remain alien to the world of high art, Mahler — a great populist, despite his aristocratic position in society — refused to accept the distinction between the vulgar and the lofty. Both are part of life, and hence both should be components of art. The symphony thus seeks to diminish the distance between life and art.

Richard Strauss, who conducted the work, heard in the first movement "uncountable battalions of workers marching to a May Day celebration." May Day rallies were organized by Austria's Social Democrats as political demonstrations for the working class. These rallies expressed the same philosophy as Mahler's first movement: equality of the vulgar and the sublime, equality of the common people and the elite, equality of popular art and high culture. The marches played at the annual May Day demonstrations were the very type of music that infuses the symphony. In fact, the opening horn melody, which is based on a folksong, may have been played at these rallies (interestingly, this melody is also quite similar to the main theme of the finale of the First Symphony of Brahms, whom Mahler visited from time to time while working on his own Third Symphony). The symphony is not a picture of a specific event (such as a political demonstration), but its eqalitarian aesthetic has its origin in the same democratic ideas that were expressed at the rallies. It is as if, symbolically, the "workers marched to the rhythm of Mahler's music," as William J. McGrath explains in his fascinating book *Dionysian Art and Populist Politics in Austria*.

If a symphony begins with a forty-minute collage of marches and fanfares that presents an unparalleled vision of man and nature, where can it go from there? The Third is an evolutionary symphony, in the sense that it grows inexorably from this extraordinary opening through four intervening movements to a serene finale. Mahler, by his identification of the goal of this evolution with God and Love, seems to be saying that behind all the trivialities of mundane life (first movement), beyond the beauties of nature (middle movements), lies an eternal meaning that transcends all — and that meaning is Love.

Symphony Number 4 in G Major
Bedächtig, nicht eilen
In gemächlicher Bewegung, ohne Hast
Ruhevoll
Sehr behaglich

The finale of the Fourth Symphony was composed in 1892. The remaining movements were begun in the summer of 1899 and completed on 5 January 1901. Mahler conducted the first performance in Munich on 25 November 1901. He revised the symphony several times between 1901 and 1910.

In 1898 Mahler was named conductor of possibly the world's greatest orchestra, the Vienna Philharmonic. He retained this post for three hectic seasons, during which he had little time to compose. His creative work was accomplished during summer vacations.

At the end of his second season, Mahler took the Philharmonic on tour to Paris, where they performed as part of the World Exhibition of 1900. Although a musical triumph, the tour was in other respects a disaster. Advance publicity was virtually non-existent: no newspapers or critics received notification of the performance. The famous orchestra was all but lost in the multitude of events. The money that Viennese patrons had generously contributed proved to be far too little, and the orchestra members were nearly stranded in Paris. The Rothschild family in Paris came to the rescue with money for return tickets. As if to add the proverbial insult to injury, Mahler's name was misspelled on a poster. He was listed as *Malheur,* the French word for misfortune.

The exasperated composer was happy to forget about the Paris disaster when he arrived at his summer retreat a few days later. He had begun the Fourth Symphony the previous summer, and he was eager to devote his full efforts to that work.

The origins of the symphony go back to considerably earlier. The song which forms the fourth movement, "The Heavenly Life," was completed as an independent composition in 1892 and performed a few times. This lovely piece must have become very important to Mahler. It became the source of his Third Symphony, which was once planned to encompass seven movements, the last one being the song. There are thematic references in the Third's fifth movement to the "The Heavenly Life." Yet, by the time the Third was finished, the song was no longer part of it, although hints of it remain. The symphony had grown to enormous proportions: six movements lasting around a hundred minutes. To append this innocent ten-minute piece as epilogue would have been anticlimactic. Instead, "The Heavenly Life" became the finale of the Fourth Symphony.

Now Mahler faced an interesting compositional challenge. If he wanted to avoid the problem of anticlimax, he had to compose the Fourth in such a way that the song became an appropriate conclusion. The scope of the new symphony had to be modest, no small challenge for the composer of such extravaganzas as the Second and Third Symphonies. Mahler furthermore had to compose the first three movements so that they led convincingly to an already existing finale. What resulted was not only Mahler's most understated and, at least on the surface, simplest symphony, but also a work with a unique compositional strategy. Rather than building to a finale of huge dimensions, as Mahler had done, for example, in the Second Symphony, the Fourth becomes ever simpler and more modest. As musicologist Donald Mitchell explains,

> We ascend, as it were, towards the vivid images of heavenly life that are vouchsafed us in the finale, by means of a gradually *decreasing* complexity of forms and textures which Mahler most cunningly effects across the first three movements, so that by the time we have reached the long-drawn-out cadence with which the slow movement (in double variation form) ends, we are prepared musically and spiritually for the innocence — musical and spiritual — of the song that follows. Thus the interior poetic program of the work — a journey from formidable sophistication to a condition of simplicity — is spelled out for us by the evolution of the first three movements, through purely musical devices. The use of words in the finale comes as final confirmation, rather than clarification, of everything that has preceded the song.

Mitchell also believes that the "gradual reduction in complexity throughout the work [is in] preparation for the simplicity of the finale, the true innocence of a child's vision of paradise. Hence it was logical that the most concentrated and intricate musical thinking should be assigned to the first movement. It was undoubtedly this aspect of the Fourth that left its first audiences bewildered, confused, and hostile."

The symphony opens with a suggestion of simplicity fully appropriate to the song-finale, which is destined to use this same material: a brief introduction in flutes, clarinets, and bells leading to the main theme in violins. Mahler said of this theme, "On its first appearance it lies there as inconspicuously as the dewdrop on the flower before the sun shines into it. But as soon as a ray of light falls upon the meadow, it breaks up into a thousand reflections and colors in every pearl of dew, until a whole sea of light shines before us." Despite its superficial innocence, this melody's treatment throughout the sonata-allegro movement reveals its underlying sophistication. In this way Mahler establishes the work's unique aesthetic: the studied simplicity of the first movement's opening implies the innocence of the finale, but first these same ideas lead to a first movement of considerable subtlety. The remainder of the symphony allows the simplicity to penetrate beneath the surface, so that by the end simple innocence pervades the music.

The stages along this progression are interesting. The second movement is a grotesque scherzo, far removed from the old-world charm of the first. The movement contains a violin solo in which the concertmaster plays on an instrument tuned a step higher than normal. The result is a special sound, which Mahler associated with a street fiddle. He explained that the fiddle music "is the gruesome dance of death, led by a figure of popular demonology, *Freund Hein.* It is the mistuned fiddle of the skeletal figure of death which is heard at the opening of the movement. . . . It is a grisly, sudden feeling which comes over us, just as one is often panic-stricken in broad daylight in a sunlit forest. The scherzo is so mysterious, confused, and supernatural that your hair will stand on end when you hear it. But in the adagio to follow, where all this passes off, you will immediately see that it was not meant so seriously."

The peaceful yet poignant third movement is a set of variations on two themes. After the scherzo's C minor/major, the tonality returns to the first movement's G major. Near the end, however, there is a sudden expansive move into a bright E major, as the full orchestra blares forth material destined to be developed in the finale. This outburst acts like a catharsis. Afterwards the music remains in E major, a key that seems in its ethereal beauty to suggest an eternity beyond the scherzo's vision of death.

The finale repeats this progression of keys and hence of moods. Beginning firmly in the symphony's home key of G major, the song finally reaches E major when the soprano sings of the music of heaven. And there it ends, quietly in the depths of the orchestra. Only the harp and string basses can play the low E on which this music of innocence peacefully dies away.

Symphony Number 5 in C-Sharp Minor
Trauermarsch
Stürmisch bewegt
Scherzo
Adagietto
Rondo-Finale

*The Fifth Symphony was composed during the summers of 1901
and 1902. Mahler conducted the first performance in Cologne on 18
October 1904. He subsequently revised the symphony several times.*

Mahler's conducting responsibilities kept him from composing other
than during the summer months. Between the summers of 1901,
when he started the Fifth Symphony, and 1902, when he completed
it, he met Alma Schindler. She was half his age, but their attraction
was mutual and immediate.

Mahler's friends were skeptical about the depth of his interest in
Schindler. He was known to have had many affairs with young
women. He once had to keep such activities secret, but now that he
was the famous conductor of the Vienna Opera, he no longer had to
hide "indiscretions." Alma represented more than a casual dalliance
— she was beautiful, intelligent, and articulate, and she was a composer. Mahler soon became thoroughly infatuated.

Alma saw how temperamental and jealous the composer was. At
one point in their courtship, he did something that would make a true
feminist take up arms: he demanded that Alma give up composing.
While he was in Dresden to conduct, Alma sent a letter apologizing
that her composing had kept her from corresponding more. He replied that it was more important for her to write to him than to write
music. Her job was soon to be supervising a household, bearing children, paying the bills, copying *his* music, and standing by him in his
triumphs and failures. *His* job was to write music. Alma was upset,
but she wanted Mahler and she agreed. She stopped composing for a
while. But she never forgave him for his cruel demand.

Despite his reputation to the contrary, Mahler managed to convince Alma that, in his relations with women, he was innocent. He
claimed to have great fears about consummating their upcoming
marriage, since he was over forty. Alma could not understand his
doubts, but she agreed that they should become lovers immediately
and not wait until they were married. Alma's diary, after recording
in detail several passionate but failed encounters, states simply: "Joy
beyond all joy!" Soon, however, they were forced to acknowledge "the
hidden truth that exists behind the laws of bourgeois morality":
Alma was pregnant.

The couple was married on 9 March 1902. Mahler's life changed
in several ways: he broke off intimacies with other women, also broke
with his friends who had regarded Alma as beneath them socially,
and settled into a comfortable existence in which someone else took
care of his daily needs.

For the summer the newlyweds went to the country home Mahler
had recently acquired at Mayernigg. There the composer became

once again engrossed in his work on the Fifth Symphony, a work that represents as big a break with his past as did his marriage. Mahler withdrew from Alma, as he spent every day composing. She came to understand that she would always be second to his work.

At the end of the summer Mahler "premiered" the symphony at the piano for Alma. He worked on the orchestration in the fall, so that the work was finished at about the time their child was born. (Maria Anna Mahler was born on 3 November 1902 and died in 1907, leaving the composer with a crushed spirit from which he never recovered.) The orchestration proved to be only a preliminary draft, as Mahler continually revised it throughout his remaining years.

According to Alma, "From the Fifth onward, he found it impossible to satisfy himself; the Fifth was differently orchestrated for practically every performance." Mahler even went so far as to require an agreement from his publisher whereby any changes made in the symphony subsequent to its publication would have to be included in all future editions and added to any unsold copies already printed.

When Mahler conducted a preliminary sight-reading of the symphony in 1904, Alma listened.

> I had heard each theme in my head while copying the score, but now I could not hear them at all. Mahler had overscored the percussion instruments and timpani so madly and persistently that little beyond the rhythm was recognizable. I hurried home, sobbing aloud. He followed. For a long time I refused to speak. At last I said between my sobs: "You've written it for percussion and nothing else." He laughed and then produced the score. He had crossed out all the timpani with red crayon and half the other percussion instruments also. He had felt the same thing himself, but my passionate protest turned the scale.

A few months later the revised work went into rehearsal for its premiere. Mahler wrote to Alma,

> Today was the first rehearsal. It went off tolerably well. The scherzo is the devil of a movement. I see it is in for a lot of trouble! Conductors for the next fifty years will all take it too fast and make nonsense of it; and the public — what are they to make of this chaos of which new worlds are forever being engendered, only to crumble into ruin the moment after? What are they to say to this primeval music, this foaming, roaring, raging sea of flashing breakers? Oh that I might give my symphony its first performance fifty years after my death!

The performance went well, but Mahler was not totally pleased. He made "many important changes" in 1905, and then in 1906 reworked the score both before and after a performance in Amsterdam.

In 1908 he again revised it, this time for Vienna. Soon after he wrote, "I have newly revised my Fifth and should like to have a chance to conduct this quasi-novelty." The opportunity came for a performance in Munich, and Mahler demanded five full rehearsals so that he could consider the alterations he had made. He made further changes at each rehearsal.

Shortly before his death Mahler wrote to conductor Georg Göhler, "I have finished the Fifth. I actually had to reorchestrate it completely. I do not understand how I could have gone so completely astray — like a beginner. Evidently the routines I had established with the first four symphonies were entirely inadequate for this one — for a wholly new style demands a new technique."

What was this new style? Why did the Fifth cause Mahler such trouble? This symphony was his first not directly or indirectly concerned with the human voice: the Second, Third, and Fourth Symphonies actually use voice(s) and the First shares materials with two of Mahler's *Songs of a Wayfarer*. The Fifth was Mahler's first attempt at purely musical expression, without the mediation of a text that philosophized about love, death, or joy. The symphony does contain brief quotations from Mahler's songs, but they are incidental and disguised compared to those in the earlier works. Thus the Fifth is more abstract and, in its own way, more concise than its predecessors. And it is more contrapuntal. In the relaxed earlier symphonies, rich textures are built from harmonic frameworks. In the Fifth melodic lines are more basic than chords, and the rhythmic impulse is still more basic (consider the pervasive influence of the opening trumpet rhythm). We find Mahler beginning to explore the simultaneous combination of *independent* ideas. To preserve clarity he had to make the orchestration of such textures extraordinarily transparent, despite the large size of his orchestra. Mahler was apparently troubled by this need for clarity and only gradually came to understand how to achieve it; hence the repeated revisions.

Mahler once tried to explain to conductor Bruno Walter the source of his new contrapuntal language. They were at a country fair. Mahler called Walter's attention to the panorama of conflicting sounds — barrel organs, laughing, shouting, singing, shooting galleries, a military band. "Do you hear that? That's polyphony — and that's where I get it from. . . . That is how — from a lot of different sources — the themes must come, and like this they must be entirely different from each other in rhythm and melody — and anything else is only part writing and disguised homophony. What the artist has to do is to organize them into an intelligible entity."

Mahler tried to represent in symphonic music the wonderful jumble of sounds we encounter every day. In place of lyrical and dramatic music symbolic of lofty human emotions, he embraced the music and sounds of life. The songs and hymns to love and nature in the early symphonies gave way to earthier sources — the march and the dance.

It is instructive to compare the Second and Fifth Symphonies, since both begin with funeral marches. The Second proceeds from death to resurrection, as depicted in the quasi-religious finale, but the Fifth moves from death to life. The finale of the Fifth, despite its instrumental chorale, is a panorama of life, with all kinds of music, from the sublime to the mundane, from the profound to the vernacular, crowded into its borders. Both symphonies are affirmations, the Second of the human spirit and the Fifth of life itself. The difference is fascinating. It is hardly surprising that the new kind of music Mahler put into the Fifth should demand a new compositional technique.

The Symphony is divided into three parts. The first consists of the funeral march and the stormy allegro that seems to develop from its turbulence. The second is the scherzo movement, comprised of one *Ländler* after another. The last part includes the brief *adagietto,* which introduces the fifth movement — a collage of learned counterpoint (the movement can, up to a point, be analyzed as a fugue), folk-like tunes, sentimental melodies, and grand drama.

Composer-conductor Leonard Bernstein has written about the wonderful mixture of diverse elements in Mahler's symphonic music:

He took all (all!) the basic elements of German music, including the clichés, and drove them to their ultimate limits. He turned rests into shuddering silences; upbeats into volcanic preparations as for a death blow; *Luftpausen* became gasps of shock or terrified suspense; accents grew into titanic stresses to be achieved by every conceivable means, both sonic and tonic. *Ritardandi* were stretched into near-motionlessness; *accelerandi* became tornadoes; dynamics were refined and exaggerated to a point of neurasthenic sensibility. Mahler's marches are like heart attacks, his chorales like all Christendom gone mad. The old conventional four-bar phrases are delineated in steel; his most traditional cadences bless like the moment of remission from pain. Mahler is German music multiplied by *n.*

The result of all this exaggeration is, of course, that neurotic intensity which for so many years was rejected as unendurable, and in which we now find ourselves mirrored. And these are concomitant results: an irony almost too bitter to comprehend; excesses of sentimentality that still make some listeners wince; moments of utter despair, often the despair of not being able to drive all this material even further, into some kind of paramusic.

Symphony Number 6 in A Minor

Allegro energico, ma non troppo
Andante moderato
Scherzo
Allegro moderato

Mahler began the Sixth Symphony in the summer of 1903 and completed it in the summer of 1904. He conducted the premiere on 27 May 1906 in Essen.

The summer of 1904 was a happy and productive time for Mahler. He was secure in his job as music director of the Vienna Opera, probably the most prestigious post in the world for a conductor. From this position of power Mahler acted as he pleased: no more politics, no more artificial social graces to help his career, no more catering to musical inferiority. Furthermore, he had composed five large symphonies and was nearing completion of a sixth. His marriage to Alma Schindler had removed from him the burdens of daily living — she took care of his basic needs, which included even copying his music. He and Alma had one daughter, whom he dearly loved, and a second child was due.

Mahler was unaware of the clouds gathering. He remained oblivious to the cumulative effects of his cruelties toward Alma. He had demanded that she forsake composing, and she had acquiesced. He had demanded that she leave him alone to compose, and she did so. He had spent money lavishly on his own appearance but was unaware that she declined to attend social events because of her lack of suitable attire. Without complaint, she fulfilled the requirements of being the wife of a genius. Her rebellion was yet to come.

Nor could Mahler have known that his health was poor. A typical "Type A" personality, as ambitious and compulsive workaholics are called today, he was destined to die (not, as is generally accepted of heart disease, but of endocarditus) at the age of fifty. But in 1904 he was only 44 and at the height of his fame, and his marriage and family seemed secure.

Why, then, did he tempt fate? That summer he composed the pessimistic Sixth Symphony (which he originally subtitled *Tragic*) and also the *Kindertotenlieder* ("Songs on the Death of Children"). Why did Mahler set to music verses poet Friedrich Rückert had written to lament the loss of his child? Mahler took joy in his one daughter, to whom he was deeply attached, and in the birth of his second daughter on 15 July. Yet he wrote music of death. Alma was frightened when Mahler played the songs and the symphony at the piano. As he played the symphony, she heard its pervasive fate motive (the major-minor shift accompanied by drum beats) and understood its implications. But she could not understand *why*. Why was the composer, at his happiest time, voicing his darkest emotions?

Mahler's two daughters found their way into the symphony, but with tragedy. Alma later recalled the programmatic origin of the scherzo's changing meters: "In the [scherzo] he represented the unrhythmic games of two children, tottering in zigzags over the sand. Ominously the childish voices became more and more tragic, and at the end died out in a whimper."

When the symphony was finished, Mahler played it through for Alma. "Not one of his works came so directly from his heart as this one. We both wept that day. The music and what it foretold touched us so deeply. The Sixth is the most completely personal of his works, and a prophetic one also. . . . In the Sixth he anticipated his own life in music."

Alma's superstitions proved right. Fourteen months after the premiere of the Sixth, two days before his forty-seventh birthday, Mahler's elder daughter Maria died from scarlet fever. She was less than five years old, and the composer never recovered from her loss. At the same time, moreover, he suffered another blow. His controversial reign at the Vienna Opera had made many enemies for the tyrannical conductor, and he found he could no longer work there. He resigned. Four years later he was dead.

Alma always believed that he had foretold Maria's death in the *Kindertotenlieder* and his own end in the Sixth. Three times in the symphony's finale, a percussionist strikes a hammer. Mahler describes the sound as "short, mighty, but dull in resonance, with a *non*-metallic character; like the stroke of an axe." Alma understood these hammer blows as foreshadowing three fateful events of 1907 — Maria's death, Mahler's demise at the Vienna Opera, and the discovery by his doctor of his fatal heart disease. (Mahler's biographer, Henri-Louis de la Grange, has established as untrue the well-known story of Mahler's doom being forecast in 1907.)

On some level Mahler may have realized that he had been expressing a death wish in the Sixth. Normally a superb conductor, he had difficulty with the premiere. According to Alma, "Out of shame and anxiety he did not conduct the symphony well. He hesitated to bring out the dark omen behind the terrible last movement." After the performance, he was so overcome with emotion that he broke down and cried uncontrollably in the presence of Alma and a few close friends, including Richard Strauss. He began to fear the consequences of having composed music of death. Superstitiously he removed the third hammer blow from the finale. He had originally intended to portray himself as the tragic hero of the finale, "the hero on whom fall three blows of fate, the last of which fells him as a tree is felled." Now he was no longer sure he dared allow the third blow to strike.

The premiere was not totally successful. This strange, dark, massive work confused listeners. "My Sixth seems to be a hard nut which cannot be cracked by the weak little teeth of our critics," Mahler wrote. It took a long time for the symphony to gain the popularity it now enjoys. Amazingly, it had to wait until 1947 for its first American performance, and it was not heard in this country again until 1955, and next in 1964.

Mahler is generally acknowledged to have been one of the handful of truly great orchestrators. It may be surprising to learn that he always tinkered with his orchestrations as he heard them. Almost every time he rehearsed one of his symphonies, he made changes in scoring, dynamics, and even notes. While Mozart, for example, would produce a finished product with little effort, Mahler continually reworked details. The reason is that there were far more decisions to be made in putting together a Mahler score than a Mozart piece. The Mahler work is longer, the orchestra is much larger, the density and variety of textures is much greater, and there are far more notes. Mahler's revisions of his symphonies are similar to playwrights' changing their works after they have seen them on stage. The idea that every significant artist can produce a perfect product solely in his imagination, without having to experience it in the flesh, is a myth. The revisions made in the Sixth Symphony after early rehearsals and even after the premiere were quite extensive.

After he finished the Sixth, Mahler wanted to check the orchestration. He scheduled a rehearsal with the Vienna Philharmonic. Alma reported an amusing incident that took place at this rehearsal, which demonstrates Mahler's mania for perfection of detail. He was looking for the right sound for what eventually became the finale's hammer blows.

The notes of the bass drum in the last movement were not loud enough for him, so he had an enormous chest made and stretched with hide. It was to be beaten with clubs. He had this engine brought in before the rehearsal. The members of the orchestra crowded round the monster on the lighted stage — the rest of the house was in darkness. There was the breathless silence of suspense. The drummer raised his arm and smote: the answer was a dull, subdued boom. Once more — with all his strength: the result was the same. Mahler lost all patience. Seizing the bludgeon from the man's hand, he whirled it aloft and brought it down with a mighty whack. The answering boom was no louder than before. Everyone laughed. And now they brought out the old bass drum again — and the true thunder came. Nevertheless, Mahler had his chest dispatched at great cost to Essen [for the premiere], where it was again tried out and finally rejected as unfit for service.

Mahler once said, "A symphony must contain the world." The Sixth brings together many different facets of Mahler's world. The opening movement refers to Austrian marches, Mahler's personal life, simple religious ceremonies, and the peaceful countryside. March rhythms begin the movement, but they give way to a quasi-religious chorale, which serves as transition to a soaring, romantic theme. Alma tells us that this is her theme: "After he had drafted the first movement, he came down from the forest to tell me he had tried to express me in a theme. 'Whether or not I've succeeded I don't know. But you'll have to put up with it.' This is the great soaring theme of the first movement of the Sixth Symphony." These three very different kinds of music — macabre march, simple chorale, and love song — can readily coexist in a symphony that is a panorama of life. Another element enters in the development section. A pastoral image of the Austrian countryside is suggested by cowbells, string tremolos, and a simple, folk-like derivative of the Alma theme. All these different kinds of music are fragmented, juxtaposed, and dramatically opposed, until the Alma theme becomes triumphant, sweeping everything else away as it takes over the movement and brings it to a triumphant conclusion.

Mahler kept changing his mind about whether the scherzo or the andante should be the second movement. He originally planned for the scherzo to follow the opening movement, but even by the premiere he had changed his mind. In rehearsal he came to feel that the dynamic scherzo did not give sufficient relief after the powerful opening movement, and that the slow movement made the slow introduction to the finale seem excessive. But the score had already been printed with the andante following the scherzo. A short time later composer Alexander Zemlinsky prepared a two-piano arrangement, in which he followed Mahler's current wish and made the andante the second movement. Since Mahler had made several changes in orchestration during rehearsals, the score and the orchestral parts had to be reissued with all revisions included. This new version also placed the andante before the scherzo. And so the symphony remained, until the Mahler Society reprinted the score in 1963, with the scherzo preceding the andante. Editor Erwin Ratz suggested that, toward the end of his life, Mahler had reverted to the original order. But there is no proof of this assertion. Today the question remains unresolved, and we are apt to hear the symphony performed either way.

The scherzo is demonic and satirical. Even its seemingly gentler interludes, which Mahler labelled "grandfatherly," are diabolical, as they frequently change meter. The rhythms are also irregular, so we never know for sure when the next downbeat will arrive. The effect is an unsettling undercurrent beneath the otherwise placid interludes. Conductor Norman Del Mar, in his book on Mahler's Sixth, describes these interludes as "wearing mirthless grins as they strut about in deliberately affected mien though interrupted by repeated bursts of harsh laughter."

The andante is a straightforward movement, setting the stage for the complex drama of the finale. The slow movement presents lyrical themes, simple forms, and only rare hints of the passions of the other movements. Del Mar speaks of its "uniformity of mood" and "unsullied radiance."

The weight of the symphony falls in the finale. Although in some ways the Sixth is Mahler's most classical symphony, this emphasis on the finale is decidedly anti-classical. True, the Sixth does begin and end in the same key, does have the four standard movements of a classical symphony, does cast its outer movements and scherzo all in the key of A minor, and does use traditional forms (even including an indication to repeat the first movement's exposition). But, if we are listening to this work as an expansion of a classically proportioned symphony, we will not be prepared for the massive finale, by far the longest and most complex movement. It is in this extended drama that the tragic aspects of the symphony become most clear.

In order to make us listen intently, despite the emotional fatigue we may feel after three large movements, Mahler implies at the outset the size of the movement. He does so with an ethereal introduction that turns forceful. This passage is destined to return three more times, to mark the major divisions of the movement: at the beginning of the development section, at the start of the recapitulation, and at the final brief coda. At the beginning of the movement, this music serves as an introduction to an introduction. There follows a long, gradually building passage that contains small motives, hints of themes, and even a chorale — but no real theme. By the time the music reaches the *allegro energico* for the first theme, we have been listening several minutes. Thus we understand that this movement is unfolding on a vast scale.

The finale contains two references to fate. The fate motive from the first movement — a major chord sliding to a minor chord, to the accompaniment of drum beats — pervades the finale. Less emblematic than in the first movement, it is now fully integrated into the harmony and texture. The second reference to fate is the three (or, if Mahler's superstition is to be followed, two) hammer blows. The first two occurrences are at climactic points in the development section, the second being the climax of the entire symphony. The third time, the hammer sounds (or fails to sound) at the final statement of the major-minor fate motive: the two symbols of fate at last coincide. The orchestration at the final blow is less full than at the earlier hammer strokes. Alma explained, "Anyone who understands the symphony at all understands why the first blow is the strongest, the second weaker, and the third — the death blow — the weakest of all. Perhaps the momentary effect might be greater in the inverse order. But that is not the point."

What remains after the third hammer blow is a brief yet intense coda, based on fragments of main themes now stated in the depths of the orchestra. As this dirge dies down, the fate rhythm suddenly returns, but no longer with the major-minor shift. Norman Del Mar explains, "With a guillotine-like shock, the fate motive crashes out again, but . . . no longer [with] its major-minor alternation. For there is no longer any question of threat — the worst has happened; only the minor chord rings out. It is Fate that has triumphed as Fate always must."

Symphony Number 7 in E Minor
Langsam. Allegro risoluto ma non troppo
Nachtmusik I: Allegro moderato
Scherzo: Schattenhaft
Nachtmusik II: Andante amoroso
Rondo-Finale: Allegro ordinario

The Seventh Symphony was composed in the summers of 1904 and 1905. Mahler conducted the first performance on 19 September 1908 in Prague.

"My time will yet come," Mahler said. Many composers who fail to reach their contemporary audiences pin their hopes on posterity, of course, but Mahler was right. His time did indeed come, a half century after his death. During his lifetime his works met with indifference or hostility. After his death there were occasional performances by devoted conductors, but it was not until mid-century that audiences were really ready for Mahler's monumental, varied, impassioned, contradictory, even neurotic symphonies. Today performances are frequent, recordings are numerous, and people sport Tshirts that declare to the world "Mahler Grooves" and "Mahler Lives." This kind of popular acceptance may not be exactly what Mahler wanted, but there is no denying that his time has come. His music is as full of contradictions as is life in our complex culture. His symphonies place the emotional next to the commonplace, the religious alongside the sentimental, the complex against the simple, abstract structures with folk dances, and psychological introspection opposite mundane trivialities. The real appeal to our age is in the combination of such opposites, and in the way the music changes unexpectedly and dramatically from one pole to the other. Mahler's music thrives on contradictions. Today's listeners understand well the power of its oppositions.

Mahler had his private reasons for writing this kind of music. He was a deeply troubled man, insecure and self-confident at the same time, convinced of his immortality yet doubting his humanity. He knew that he was living at the end of an era, that a great cultural line from the renaissance to the age of modernism was reaching its dénouement. The romantic aesthetic was the final expression of this culture. Mahler's art was a product of romanticism's dying gasp. It could express the opulent, the overripe, and even the decadent. He would not live to see World War I bring to a final demise the romantic age, but he understood the impending doom of the values he had known. The contradictions of his times became the source of his music, as did the contradictions within himself.

Shortly before his death, Mahler spent an afternoon with Freud, trying to make some sense of his life. The composer and the psychoanalyst probed for the reasons behind Mahler's neuroses. They discovered one interesting source. In a classic Freudian encounter with his past, Mahler remembered a long-forgotten incident from his childhood. His parents frequently quarreled. One day the fighting became too much for the sensitive child. He escaped into the street, where he found a hurdy-gurdy playing an incongruously happy folk-tune. This confrontation between the impassioned and the commonplace became a source of his musical aesthetic.

Mahler, a man of contradictions that stemmed from deep-rooted personal and cultural conflicts, created a music that has found its widest audience among those who live in today's age of contradictions. Of all the Mahler symphonies, the Seventh surely has the greatest range of expression, the highest degree of discontinuity, the greatest conflicts. It is not surprising that the Seventh was the last to become popular, the last to yield its secrets to audiences. But now even its time has come. A few years ago it was neglected, even by conductors who specialized in Mahler. Not long ago Mahler's biographers were apologizing for it. Today it is understood as a work of great vision, an uncompromising statement on the conflict between two cultures: the dying romanticism of nineteenth-century Europe and the irrational world of the new century. The Seventh is a panorama of human emotions. It contains terror, joy, excitement, grief, and innocence, often within a few seconds of one another.

Let us consider some examples of the juxtapositions of contradictory moods in the symphony. The massive first movement begins with strings and winds playing the slow march rhythm that is destined to pervade the movement. The first march is funereal. Its melody is a tortured, irregular theme in the tenor horn. This instrument, rarely called for in symphony orchestras, is similar to the baritone horn or euphonium in this country. Thus it is an instrument associated more with outdoor brass bands than with symphony orchestras in concert halls. More march-like figures are added as the music builds. After a return to the opening, the tempo quickens for the main allegro. The music becomes dense and demonic. Then, incongruously, the violins play a lyrical, almost sentimental, sweeping theme against a counter-melody in the horns. After that, the march resumes as if there had been no interruption. From this point on the various themes, with their very different characters, are developed, juxtaposed, and combined. The music becomes frenzied. Then, a further incongruity: trumpet fanfares announce an almost pastoral treatment of the basic materials. Soon thereafter comes a return of the opening of the movement, but with everything transformed. This recapitulation is the most unsettling part of the movement, because nothing goes on for long before a wrenching contrast. This music of discontinuity drives toward a forceful conclusion, but with no real feeling of resolution.

The next three movements form a unit. The three character pieces comprise two "Night Music" movements flanking a scherzo. The second movement starts innocently with horn calls, but otherworldly elements soon enter. Clarinet fanfares, flute trills, string *pizzicati,* and sticks or branches in the percussion section all lead to an enormous downward splash. The horns relaunch the movement's opening, now even more shadowy in character. A new theme eventually arrives in the cellos, with extreme contrast. This lyrical, sophisticated tune is far removed from the haunted scherzo. Echoes of the opening bring back the first theme, now transformed under the influence of the second into a lyrical statement. The first theme dominates the movement, as it goes through an incredible variety of moods.

The third movement, the keystone of the symphony's arch form, is the true scherzo. It begins in a fragmented manner, with a different instrumental group on each beat of the 3/4 measure. It seems as if the orchestra is trying to establish a waltz-like continuity but cannot get together. Other fragments join in, and the texture becomes so elaborate that we do not realize it is essentially an accompaniment. Its function is clarified when a simple melody appears in the flutes and oboes. A contrasting theme, even more suggestive of a waltz, enters in the strings. These ideas are developed at length, until the trio section brings a slower waltz. Throughout the movement the melodies approach closer and closer to the popular music of Mahler's day, yet always maintaining contact with the smyphonic world by the use of fragmentary or dense accompaniments. The result is a troubled amalgamation of two musical cultures.

The fourth movement, "Night Music II," introduces two non-symphonic instruments into the orchestra: guitar and mandolin. This movement is delicately scored so that these soft instruments can be heard. It contains many fragments, some scherzo-like, some as shadowy as anything in earlier movements, some frankly sentimental. Much of the movement is an ever-changing mosaic of fragments. New ones are occasionally added and old ones are transformed, but only rarely is a long, uninterrupted melodic line heard. Close to the end, the orchestra becomes unexpectedly forceful. Then, as if to excuse itself for intruding on such a delicate movement, it settles back to chamber music.

The finale leaves behind the shadowy world of the three scherzos. It is the most problematic movement of this most problematic Mahler symphony. Its banalities, its frequent discontinuities, and its dissonant counterpoint have made it a challenging puzzle for performers and audiences alike. It asks our total involvement, and it asks that we accept whatever it throws at us next. Marked *allegro ordinario*, it presents a mixture of the familiar and the unfamiliar, jumbled together seemingly haphazardly. In reality it has a subtle logic, but the logic is not linear: new events do not necessarily grow out of earlier passages. The movement demands to be met on its own terms. It compromises nothing to expectation. As unusual as the symphony has been up to this point, its has not prepared us for such a powerful and unique conclusion. It would be impossible to trace here all the interruptions, all the juxtapositions of the vernacular with the sublime, all the vastly different kinds of music that come together. It is a veritable pageant of life. Some of its tunes and orchestrations sound close to the world of operetta, while others are of the most magnificent complexity. But what counts in all of this is the way these different moods come together. The context, even more than the extraordinary selection of materials, is what makes this movement uniquely challenging.

The finale in particular, although to some extent the entire symphony, brings to mind the late string quartets of Beethoven, which Mahler knew and admired. The quartets were slow to gain acceptance, not so much because of their alleged abstraction but, on the contrary, because of their use of familiar materials in unfamiliar contexts. And so the essence of the Seventh, particularly in its last movement, is the confrontation of vastly different kinds of music and musical values.

This extraordinary juxtaposition of opposites was unprecedented in 1905. But today it has become common, if not normative, not only in art but also in popular culture and in our very lives. Thus Mahler's music can be understood as wonderfully, ever fearfully, prophetic. And that is why a work like the Seventh Symphony, with all its contradictions and deliberate *non sequiturs*, can be deeply meaningful to us. Indeed, Mahler's time has come.

Symphony Number 8 in E-Flat Major
Hymnus: Veni Creator Spiritus
Final Scene from Goethe's *Faust*, Part II

Mahler sketched the Eighth Symphony between 21 June and 18 August 1906 and orchestrated it the following summer. He conducted the first performance in Munich on 12 September 1910.

When Mahler retired to his country retreat for the summer of 1906, he for once did not know what he was going to compose. He probably assumed that the new piece would be a large symphony, since his mature output consisted almost exclusively of large symphonies. But he had no program, no idea, no specific inspiration. He went to his studio the first day "with the firm resolution of idling the holiday away (I needed to so much that year) and recruiting my strength. On the threshold of my old workshop the 'Spiritus Creator' took hold of me and shook me and drove me on for the next eight weeks, until my greatest work was done."

The poem that seized Mahler's imagination was a hymn of Christian faith that the composer knew by heart. It had been written in the eighth century to celebrate the descent of the Holy Ghost upon the apostles at Pentecost. After completing his setting, the composer searched for music that would complement this massive first movement. He contemplated a four-movement symphony, in which the hymn was first, followed by two instrumental movements and a choral finale. But then a bolder idea came to him. The second, and final, part of the symphony would be an enormous setting of the final scene of Goethe's *Faust*. Mahler chose the portion of the verse play that describes the ascent of Faust's soul into Heaven. *Faust*, an extravagant dramatic poem in which Goethe attempted to fuse German romanticism and the classical spirit of ancient Greece, became the vehicle by which Mahler sought to integrate many sides of his musical personality into an enormous song of love. The humanism of *Faust* became a foil for the spirituality of the first movement's Latin hymn.

In a letter to his wife, to whom the Eighth is dedicated, Mahler explained his idea of love as expressed in the second movement: "In the discourses of Socrates, Plato gives his own philosophy, which, as the misunderstood 'Platonic Love,' has influenced thought right down to the present day. The essence of it is really Goethe's idea that all love is generative, creative, and that there is a physical and spiritual generation which is the emanation of the 'Eros.' You have it in the last scene of *Faust*, presented symbolically."

In the two parts of the Eighth, Mahler took two very different texts and set them to very different music. Yet there are connections, as musicologist David B. Greene explains.

> Simply by juxtaposing Goethe's text to Veni Creator, Mahler directs us to some aspects of his vision. Wherever the two texts refer to similar ideas, such as corporeality or light, Mahler links them by using the same musical motif. Indeed, motifs from Part One . . . so permeate Part Two that the listener is invited to hear the entire Part Two as projecting an idea similar to that of Part One, in spite of the conspicuous differences in atmosphere and structure. If the two parts interpret each other, Faust's redemption at the end of the second cannot be unlike the ecstatic combination of Veni I and Veni II at the end of the first. To be redeemed must mean to be unsurpassably fulfilled in a way that contributes to the glorification and enhanced awesomeness of that which is primal and ultimate, without subordinating human fulfillment to the ultimate or the ultimate to human fulfillment.

The Eighth is Mahler's only completely choral symphony. The Second and Third Symphonies begin, like Beethoven's Ninth, with large-scale instrumental movements, so that the human voice comes later, as a culmination. But voices permeate the Eighth from beginning to end. This different approach to the choral symphony led Mahler to a special musical language.

In a certain sense, the Eighth is a conservative piece, particularly in the first movement. If we compare the counterpoint of *Veni Creator*

Spiritus with that of the symphonies on either side of the Eighth, we understand the work's conservatism. Typically, Mahler's counterpoint, sometimes called "dissonant counterpoint," combines several disparate lines into a collage-like whole. But in the Eighth's first movement, the constituent melodic lines fit together in a more traditional way. They cooperate in producing straightforward harmonies. Donald Mitchell, the eminent Mahler scholar, attributes the language of *Veni Creator* to Mahler's study of Bach. He owned the complete works of Bach and studied them assiduously. Mitchell writes,

> The key to understanding the first movement of the Eighth Symphony is . . . by reading the movement as Mahler's tribute to one of Bach's great motets, probably *Singet dem Herrn*, whose vocal polyphony overwhelmed him and which he surely attempted to emulate in his symphony. . . . *Veni Creator Spiritus* is sensibly approached as a gigantic motet for solo voices, chorus, and orchestra — Bach seen through the occasionally distorting lenses of Mahler's creative spectacles. The Eighth Symphony's first movement is a vigorous celebration of the baroque as Mahler re-imagined it in 1906.

The form of the first movement is as rigorous as its counterpoint. There is an unambiguous recapitulation that organizes the movement in a manner that Mahler had abandoned after the Fourth Symphony. The late Mahler style is evident in the instrumental interludes, but for the most part the first movement — with its diatonic harmonies, rigorous counterpoint, and controlled form — is an unabashed look backwards. Even the treatment of the Latin text is typical of Bach. Mahler "presents the lines in an incredibly dense growth of repetitions, combinations, inversions, transpositions, and conflations," as program annotator Michael Steinberg explains.

The second movement reflects a more recent past: it refers to the operas of Wagner. Text setting is now straightforward, and the chromatic harmonic style is typical of the late nineteenth century. Although he had spent many years as an opera conductor, Mahler never composed a stage work, at least not in his mature years. The second movement of the Eighth Symphony is as close to opera as he would ever come, and that is quite close. There are characters, arias, a libretto, choruses, and even leitmotifs. Mitchell sees this movement in addition as

> a vast synthesis of many of the forms and media that Mahler had pursued since he first found his voice as a composer. . . . Thus, the setting of the last scene of Goethe's *Faust* represents

an amalgam of dramatic cantata, sacred oratorio, song cycle, choral symphony in the manner of Liszt, and instrumental symphony, the whole culminating in a final chorale (*Chorus mysticus*) modelled on the concluding chorale of the Second Symphony, though surpassing its precedent in size and ambition.

The Eighth occasionally unleashes torrents of sound, and it was part of Mahler's aesthetic intent to embody his hymn to the redemptive power of love in sonorities of appropriate dimensions. But the vast resources are, characteristically, more often deployed in the most delicate of instrumental effects and subtlest of nuances.

And thus the second movement is thoroughly Mahlerian in style as well as aesthetic. It is therefore misleading to think of the Eighth as a massive monolith, although it does require a thousand performers. There is actually only one instant where almost everyone is performing. The massive passagess are placed far apart. In between we find Mahler's typical music — sensitive, imaginative, sometimes delicate — whether in the service of a Bachian setting of a Latin hymn or of an operatic setting of Goethe's *Faust*.

Writing a symphony requiring a thousand performers is one kind of challenge. Getting it performed is another. Preparations began early in 1910, several months before the scheduled premiere. Because he was committed to conducting in New York for several months, Mahler entrusted Munich impresario Emil Gutmann with responsibilities for organizing the performance. The composer was afraid that the event might turn into a "Barnum and Bailey Show"; Gutmann, on the other hand, hoped it would.

While Mahler was in the United States, assistant conductors began to prepare the three choruses. Since a thousand qualified singers did not live in Munich, it was necessary to use groups from several cities. The *Singverein* practiced in Vienna, while the children's chorus rehearsed in Munich and the *Riedelverein* prepared in Leipzig. Mahler's protégé Bruno Walter trained the eight vocal soloists.

With Mahler conveniently out of the way, Gutmann tried to cut corners and to market the event with more of an eye to the box office than to artistic integrity. It was he who dubbed the work *Symphony of a Thousand*. He attempted to substitute an inferior second chorus from Leipzig for the prestigious Vienna *Singverein*. He tried to eliminate one of the three final rehearsals. And he announced to the public that rehearsals had begun when in fact the music was still being copied.

Toward the end of the summer, everyone came to Munich for the first full rehearsal. Mahler was concerned about the placement of the instrumental forces. The new Music Festival Hall was to be officially opened by the performance. In this large a hall it was essential to put the three choirs, enormous orchestra, extra bass (entering at the enormous endings of the two movements), and eight soloists where they could be heard, and where all performers could see the conductor. Mindful of every detail, the composer planned out the lighting for the performance, and he insisted that Gutmann somehow keep the streetcars passing by the hall from sounding their bells.

The performance was an event of signal importance. Musicians and celebrities from all over came to Munich to hear it: Arnold Schoenberg, Otto Klemperer, Anton Webern, Oskar Fried, Wilhelm Mengelberg, Siegfried Wagner (son of the composer), Alfredo Casella, Erich Korngold, Felix Weingartner, Leopold Stokowski, Stefan Zweig, Max Reinhardt, Thomas Mann, the Prince of Bavaria, the King of Belgium, and Henry Ford. An audience of three thousand heard 1030 performers: an orchestra of 171, the 250 singers of the Vienna *Singverein*, 250 members of the *Riedelverein* of Leipzig, 350 children from the *Zentral Singschule* of Munich, eight vocal soloists, and one conductor.

Although premieres of his gigantic earlier symphonies had usually met with indiffierence or hostility, by 1910 Mahler was a commanding conductor of international standing. Furthermore, thanks in part to Gutmann's publicity, the event was preordained to be a spectacle. In her reminiscences of her husband, Alma Mahler recalled:

> The dress rehearsal provoked rapturous enthusiasm, but it was nothing compared to the performance itself. The entire audience rose to its feet as soon as Mahler took his place at the conductor's desk; the breathless silence which followed was the most impressive homage an artist could be paid. . . . And then Mahler, god or demon, turned those tremendous volumes of sound into fountains of light. The experience was indescribable. Incredible, too, was the demonstration that followed. The whole audience surged towards the platform.

The composer-conductor received a thirty-minute ovation.

Bruno Walter added, in his memoirs, "When the last note of the performance had died away and the waves of enthusiastic applause reached him, Mahler ascended the steps of the platform, at the top of which the children's choir was posted. The little ones hailed him with shouts of jubilation, and, walking down the line, he pressed every one of the little hands that were extended towards him. The loving greeting of the young generation filled him with hope for the future of his work and gave him sincere pleasure."

One of the members of the audience was conductor Leopold Stokowski. Stokowski found the work overwhelming and resolved to direct it himself. He was 28 years old when he conducted the American premiere with the Philadelphia Orchestra. He had no one like Gutmann working for him. He himself had to raise $15,000 — quite a substantial sum in 1916 — to underwrite nine performances in Philadelphia and one more in New York. That Stokowski could find financial backing for a large artistic project was a revelation. By this venture he established the Philadelphia Orchestra as a credible institution in its city, and he taught America a lesson it has not forgotten: big art can be big business.

Symphony Number 9 in D Minor

Andante comodo. Allegro risoluto. Andante
Im Tempo eines gemächlichen Ländlers
Rondo-Burleske: Allegro assai
Adagio

The first sketches for the Ninth Symphony were made in the summer of 1908 in Toblach, Austria. The work was completed by 1 April 1910 in New York. Bruno Walter conducted the first performance at the Vienna Music Festival on 26 June 1912.

At rare times circumstances conspire to place an artist of sensitivity and vision at a cultural and philosophical crossroads that he uniquely understands and can express. The result can be a great work that speaks eloquently of its era to all future ages. Such a time was the end of the first decade of the present century, and such an artist was Gustav Mahler. The great work was his Ninth Symphony, a heart-rending farewell to nineteenth-century values and to a world of innocence, and simultaneously a vision of a future too terrible and too wonderful to imagine in 1910.

The Ninth is the middle work of Mahler's farewell trilogy: (1) *Das Lied von der Erde*, the song-symphony the composer refused to label Number 9 out of superstitious fear of death (Beethoven, Bruckner, and Schubert had died after nine symphonies), the last movement of which is "The Farewell"; (2) the Ninth, the most abstract of the trilogy and yet the most universal; and (3) the unfinished Tenth Symphony, over the manuscript of which Mahler wrote repeated cries of anguish at his impending death, yet which closes in a mood of tranquil acceptance of the inevitable. The Ninth is a work of parting not only because it repeatedly uses the farewell motive from Beethoven's

Les Adieux Sonata, but particularly because of its total range of expression. It is Mahler's farewell to his life with his wife Alma, with whom he had had a stormy relationship but for whom he had found renewed tenderness as he came to rely on her more and more during his final months. (He also came to understand his feelings for her better during a solitary psychoanalytic session with Freud.) It is a farewell to romanticism, which had grown overripe as the nineteenth century gave way to the twentieth. It is a farewell to the symphonic tradition (although subsequent composers have indeed written symphonies, after Mahler the form was no longer supreme and to utilize it was in some sense to invokve the past). Mahler brought the form that Haydn had first made viable to its emotional limits.

Mahler's world was changing. In a few years World War I would give horribly real expression to the tensions that Mahler understood instinctively. The War would bring to a final close the age to which Mahler was already saying good-bye. The musical statement of the end of that age was the demise of tonality, the logical system of goal-direction and dissonance resolution that had ruled music for three hundred years. Mahler's Ninth takes tonality to its outer limits as it creates almost unbearable tensions. But eventually, in accordance with the fundamental nature of the tonal system, these tensions do resolve.

The death of one era means the birth of a new one. Mahler's Ninth is the farewell of a dying artist in a dying age. The new age is best represented by the music of Mahler's younger colleague, Arnold Schoenberg. The new music is really no more dissonant than Mahler's (an important point to bear in mind). The crucial difference is that Schoenberg no longer believed in the aesthetic necessity of resolution. The conjunction between old and new, between farewell to the past and embracing of the future, is mirrored in the not very different music of Mahler and Schoenberg.

Before the Ninth can take leave of its special world, it must establish what that world is. The first movement does so on a lofty, abstract plane. It starts with the most elemental of sounds — a rhythmically repeated single note, suggestive of the first sound we ever hear, a heartbeat. Soon various fragments of sound appear: a simple harp motive, a horn fragment, a viola oscillation. Still no melody, no continuity. The violins enter with a fragmented line, more like a series of sighs than a true melody. The music is growing — gradually and inexorably — from the most basic sounds to a sophisticated musical statement.

As the symphony grows, more instruments join in, and contrapuntal tension increases. But the melodic material is still based on the original fragments, so that real continuity is not yet achieved.

When continuity does finally arrive, it is with the power of the full orchestra (marked by a cymbal crash). This sumptuous sound — densely contrapuntal and highly charged emotionally — is the goal toward which the music has been struggling. This is the world of romanticism to which the composer must now say farewell.

Several times the music reaches this goal, and several times it crumbles back to its fragmented origins. Twice (the second time triumphantly) the opening elemental rhythm interrupts and brings back nebulous wisps of sound. Only toward the end does resolution come. At last continuity is achieved, not by the full orchestra blaring forth its agonized cries but by an intimate and poignant duet for flute and horn. Now there is peace. When the fragments return after this duet, their inner tension is gone. They are consonant, gentle, touching, other-worldly. The music has gained with simplicity what was impossible with grandiosity.

If the first movement bids a tortured good-bye to the aesthetic turmoil of romanticism, the second says adieu to the very different world of Austrian peasant culture. The music is thoroughly continuous, and the continuity comes from two age-old folk dances, the *Ländler* and the waltz. Mahler subtly makes them a bit grotesque by unusual orchestration (notice in particular the use of contrabassoon, piccolo, and string bass), as if to indicate that the innocence of pre-twentieth-century Austria had already begun to sour.

The movement opens with a simple *Ländler* in moderato tempo, that seems to end over and over again, often with a version of the farewell motive from the first movement. As if to get out of this endless cycle of cadences, the music plunges suddenly into a demonic waltz — a waltz with none of the elegance of Johann Strauss' Vienna, but rather full of the conflicts of the twentieth century. Eventually a second *Ländler* comes along, in a slow tempo. The three dances alternate to the end of the movement. When the first *Ländler* returns in the middle, it has lost its folk-like naïveté, but when it returns at the end, it is again innocent. Or is it? Just before the close it turns suddenly sinister and shadowy, although it does end simply enough.

The inner tensions of the first two movements erupt with veritable violence in the third, and thereby the symphony is finally purged of its inner turmoil. Just as the second movement derives from the dance, so the third comes from the march. The music plunges headlong into the grostesque. The fragmentation of the first movement returns, as melodies often seem unable to go on for more than two bars without stumbling. Here Mahler comes closest to a twentieth-century sensibility. The music drives relentlessly, mercilessly, until — almost without warning — the mood changes to a sentimental serenity. After this extended slow section, the fury of the march returns to drive the music ruthlessly to the end.

It is a master stroke that a small but prominent motive from the middle section of the third movement, stated at first calmly but then mocked in the E-flat clarinet, is transformed into a principal motive of the poignant finale. It is in this movement, a broadly sweeping adagio, that Mahler makes overt his farewell. It is not a farewell of bitterness (as in the first movement), of nostalgia (as in the second movement), or of protest (as in the third). The composer has moved into a purely spiritual realm. It is as if he is accepting death, even welcoming it. The movement is bittersweet, intense, impassioned, and extraordinarily beautiful. And when it ends, it is with exquisite tenderness.

The Ninth Symphony was composed under the most trying of conditions, conditions that, in their own mundane way, also dealt with farewell — Mahler's farewell to his career as a conductor. He was generally acknowledged to be one of the great conductors. He spent the last three concert seasons of his life conducting in New York, first for the Metropolitan Opera and then for the Philharmonic. The Philharmonic had been in financial difficulties, and a wealthy lady named Mrs. George R. Seldon raised $90,000 from such donors as J. P. Morgan, August Belmont, Joseph Pulitzer, and Andrew Carnegie, to insure the continuation of the orchestra. The musicians had to agree to accept the governance of the wealthy patrons and to accept Mahler as their conductor, empowered to fire inferior players and hire new ones as needed. The orchestra members were not happy, because they had not been consulted over the choice of a conductor and because Mahler had never conducted them. But they had no choice. They were forced to accept the terms of the governing board or else the Philharmonic would surely fold.

Mahler announced his austere intentions to raise musical standards and to educate more than entertain the public. Some of his concerts in the 1909–10 season were very popular, but others were not. Critics objected strenuously to his unusual programming and to the liberties he took with certain works. At other times, paradoxically, they objected to his refusal to perpetuate liberties earlier conductors had taken. And there were objections to the large amount of contemporary music programmed — music by Strauss, Bruckner, Chabrier, Debussy, Enesco, and several others.

Mahler was an artist of utmost integrity, and he had a vision. He cared nothing for the opinions of the press, and he made no concessions to requests from the governing committee. He felt that the committee's demands ranged from stupid to naïve to arrogant, and he ignored them. He devoted all his energies to rehearsals and to putting the final touches on the Ninth Symphony.

Matters came to a head when the members of the committee attended a rehearsal of Beethoven's *Emperor* Concerto. Some of the ladies did not like the unusual approach (which was actually more faithful to what Beethoven had intended than previous New York performances had been). Harsh words were exchanged, and one of the ladies actually said to the most formidable Beethoven interpreter in the world, "No, Mr. Mahler, this will never do!" The fact that Mahler was highly respected as a conductor by musicians all over the world meant nothing to these small-minded, provincial board members. They felt they knew better. The committee quietly started a movement to have Mahler replaced for the next season. By April the composer was thoroughly tired of New York and its petty intrigues, and his health was not good. He had just finished inking the Ninth Symphony, and he happily left for his summer retreat in the Austrian Alps, where he worked on the Tenth.

The board decided over the summer to retain Mahler, but to do everything in its power to exercise direct influence over his programming. Mahler returned to New York in the autumn and continued his adventurous concerts — one of contemporary American music followed by another with Beethoven's Seventh Symphony somewhat re-scored. But he was weak and sick, and he was no political match for a determined board of directors. He had come to rely on the very generous salary he was receiving, because it was the only money he could leave to his family.

The board actually resorted to the underhanded by using the equivalent of a modern-day bugging device: a lawyer was hidden behind a curtain to copy down every word of Mahler's enraged statements as he was forced — yet again — to defend his artistic policies. He was defeated. He relinquished, in writing, his total control. He conceded to the board the right to approve or reject his programs. The ladies had won. Ignorance had won over art, wealth had defeated genius, the spirit of a great man had been broken.

Soon after this humiliating episode, Mahler directed what was to be his final concert. He became dangerously ill and was forced to cancel the remainder of his contract. This was a stroke of luck for the board members, who now, without a scandal, were rid of the irascible conductor. Mrs. Sheldon expressed praise for Mahler publicly and wished him a speedy recovery as he set out across the ocean for the final time. The search began for a successor, but word was out among conductors. No one would agree to work for the board that had destroyed, if not actually hastened the death of, Gustav Mahler. It was ten years before the New York Philharmonic could again secure the services of a first-rate music director.

The Philharmonic board is to be credited as well as blamed. It did save a dying orchestra, it did bring to New York a great conductor who raised the city's musical standards, and it did put much needed financial resources into Mahler's hands. That the board was also arrogant and ignorant is just as true, however. It is the American way: money buys power, in the arts as in every corner of society. Today, all that really matters is that Mahler was able to finish the Ninth Symphony (unfortunately, not also the Tenth). All the rest is just a tidbit of history.

◆ ◆ ◆

Symphony Number 10 in F-Sharp Major, performing version by Deryck Cooke

Adagio
Scherzo
Purgatorio
[Scherzo] —
Finale

Mahler began the Tenth Symphony in the summer of 1910; it remained unfinished at his death. The first and third movements, as edited by Ernst Křenek, were first conducted by Franz Schalk in Vienna on 14 October 1924. Several people subsequently made realizations or completions of the entire work. The most frequently performed of these is by Deryck Cooke. His first performing version of nearly the entire symphony was premiered by Berthold Goldschmidt and the Philharmonia Orchestra in a London BBC broadcast on 19 December 1960. Goldschmidt conducted the London Symphony Orchestra in Cooke's preliminary version of the entire symphony on 13 August 1964. Cooke continued to revise his work, completing it in 1975. The final version was premiered by Niklaus Wyss and the San Francisco Symphony on 28 January 1976.

Had Gustav Mahler lived to complete his Symphony Number 10, it would undoubtedly have become an historically significant work. It would have been both the ultimate distillation of Mahler's style and an important influence on the twentieth-century techniques it anticipates. It might have been the last truly romantic work by a major composer who did not have to decide deliberately either to adopt or to bypass twentieth-century atonality. As it is, however, the Tenth occupies a strange position in the transition from the nineteenth to the twentieth centuries. However great its influence might have been, it was in fact nil, because the work was all but unknown to Schoenberg, Webern, Stravinsky, and their colleagues at the time they were forging a new language.

Mahler began to sketch the symphony in the summer of 1910, while completing the Ninth. He intended to finish it the next summer, as his conducting duties always kept him from composing at other times of the year. But he died in the spring of 1911, leaving a partially completed work.

By the Tenth Symphony, Mahler's opulent style had undergone a refinement, a purification. His romanticism had become tempered by a degree of classical restraint. Gone were the earlier symphonies' cowbells, off-stage brass bands, hammer blows, and mammoth choruses. A chamber-like style of orchestration is apparent on many of the fully scored pages of the Tenth, and an economy of materials is evident as well. Much of the first movement, for example, grows directly out of the opening soliloquy for violas. Rigorous derivation of a large movement from a single line is a technique not only of past masters but also of twentieth-century twelve-tone composers. Thus the piece looks forward to an era Mahler would never know: highly chromatic melodic lines contain most of the twelve tones, non-structural pungent dissonances are added purely for effect, and the intense chord that forms the climax of the outer movements contains nine different tones (by comparison, a stringent dissonance for Beethoven would probably contain no more than five different notes). Mahler was clearly in touch with the future as well as the past.

Mahler was deeply disturbed at the time he sketched the five movements of this huge work. He morbidly feared that he was dying, yet he began to feel that he had never lived. "I have lived my life on paper," he wrote. When his wife, Alma, had a passonate affair with architect Walter Gropius (whom she eventually married after the composer's death), Mahler realized that his marriage had suffered, in part because of his neuroses. But how could he regain his wife's affections? How could he apologize for his cruelties to Alma? He could write a symphony around the themes of despair, regret, anguish, death, and resignation, and yet he could conclude it in an atmosphere of peace and hope. That he associated such emotions with the Tenth Symphony is evident to anyone who hears it. That he linked these feelings to Alma is clear from the manuscript, on which he scrawled impassioned outbursts, often addressed to her. Twice in the finale, for example, he wrote, "To live for you! To die for you! Almschi." This transcendent final movement, then, became his atonement for his life with Alma.

On the second page of the third movement, originally called "Purgatorio or Inferno," the tortured composer scribbled, "Death! Trans[figuration?]!" On the third page, "O God! O God! Why hast Thou forsaken me?" Later we find, "Mercy!" and "Thy will be done!" The title page of the fourth movement bears this inscription: "The Devil leads me in a dance; madness seizes me, accursed that I am, annihilates me so that I forget to be, so that I cease to exist, so that I dis . . ." At the drum beat that ends that movement, he wrote, "You alone know what it means. Ah! Ah! Ah! Farewell, my lyre. Farewell, farewell, farewell. Ah, well. Ah. Ah." Alma later explained that the source of that stark drumbeat, which also begins the finale, was the solitary drum accompanying the funeral of a fireman who had been killed near the Mahlers' New York hotel. The composer, watching from his hotel window, recognized in the fireman's funeral procession his own. Alma saw his face contort in anguish, as tears ran uncontrollably down his face.

In yet another way death was linked with the Tenth Symphony. The composer had always believed that he, like Beethoven, Schubert, and Bruckner, was destined to compose nine symphonies. He felt that if he could finish the Tenth he would have outsmarted death. This superstition caused him not to number the song-symphony *Das Lied von der Erde*. Thus the Ninth was really his tenth, and he boasted that he had outwitted death. But the superstition held: there are only nine numbered, completed symphonies by Mahler. Psychoanalyst Theodore Reik, in his book *The Haunting Melody*, explains that Mahler saw father images in the earlier composers who had died after nine symphonies. According to classical Freudian theory, the son has a deep-seated wish to replace the father, and so, according to Reik, Mahler subconsciously felt that to die after completing nine symphonies would be to displace and hence to equal the earlier masters. Mahler's superstition became a desire to meet the masters on their terms — a real death wish.

Mahler actually had a first-hand experience with Freudian analysis. He blamed himself for Alma's affair. When he came to feel the hollowness of his marriage, he sought the help of Freud himself. The two men spent an afternoon together in August 1910. Freud, who had little interest in music, was impressed by Mahler's quick grasp of psychoanalysis. Thus Freud felt he was able to accomplish some good, despite the impossibility of protracted treatment.

Under Freud's guidance, Mahler relived a traumatic childhood experience. His father had always been cruel to his mother. Once, during a particularly vehement clash between his parents, the young Mahler fled the house in terror. He came into the street, only to be greeted by a hurdy-gurdy playing the popular Austrian tune *Ach, du lieber Augustin.* This frightening yet ludicrous juxtaposition of the emotionally charged with the trivial left an indelible impression on the boy. During his afternoon with Freud, Mahler came to understand this incident as the source of the frequent conjunction of tragedy and amusement in his music. He felt that the intrusions of ordinary melodies — the so-called "banalities" of his music — were expressions of this youthful experience. Once he came to understand why the commonplace had become as meaningful to him as the profound or tragic, Mahler purged his style of this confrontation of opposites. The Tenth Symphony contains no stark juxtapositions of tragedy and farce.

Mahler was full of turmoil and energy as he raced to complete the Tenth Symphony. He felt fear of death, remorse for his one-sided life, a new understanding of his personality and of his music, regret for the way he had treated his wife, and resolution to make the next months atone for the mistakes of his life. It was a time for renewed life, yet it became a time for death. Instead of juxtaposing the sublime and the banal, the Tenth Symphony places tragedy next to tranquility, despair next to peace, and resignation next to rejuvenation.

A shroud of mystery descended over the Tenth Symphony after the composer died in 1911. Mahler's first biographer, Paul Stefan, wrote (about a work he had never seen) that it could never be performed. Arnold Schoenberg, in a memorial lecture, perpetuated Mahler's superstition about nine symphonies: "The Ninth is a limit. He who wants to go beyond it must die. It is as if something might be imparted to us in a Tenth for which we are not yet ready. Those who have written a Ninth have stood too near to the hereafter. Perhaps the riddles of the world would be solved, if one of those who knew them were to compose a Tenth. But that is probably never to happen." This superstitious fear of Mahler's Tenth was echoed by conductor Bruno Walter, who conducted the posthumous premieres of *Das Lied* and the Ninth but refused even to look at the Tenth. Mahler's friend and second biographer, Richard Specht, wrote that the Tenth "will never come to performance. Mahler asked that it be burnt after his death. His widow could not resolve to do this, . . . but it is quite impossible that anyone . . . could complete a score from his mute symbols." Alma decided to suppress the manuscript.

The sketches lay virtually unknown for several years. In 1924 Alma felt that the time was finally right to unveil Mahler's last symphony. She asked the young composer Ernst Křenek to prepare as much as possible of the work for publication and performance. Křenek made performing versions of the first and third movements. Alban Berg checked Křenek's work and offered several criticisms, which somehow never found their way into the published score. The two movements were conducted in Vienna by Franz Schalk and in Prague by Alexander Zemlinsky. Also in 1924 a facsimile of several of the sketches was published.

The performances and publications were controversial. Some people were awed by the majesty of the music, even in its incomplete state. Others felt that it was impossible to know how Mahler might have changed the work had he lived, and thus to perform it in its unfinished state was a travesty.

Several composers who knew Mahler's style well were approached about actually completing the five-movement symphony. Schoenberg, Berg, and Shostakovich all refused. An accomplished composer knows how hard it is to enter another composer's mind and art. Shostakovich's response was typical: "In spite of my love for this composer, I cannot take upon myself this huge task. This calls for deep penetration into the spiritual world of the composer, as well as his creative and individual style. For me this would be impossible." In the 1940s and '50s, however, several musicologists worked on reconstructing the Tenth Symphony — Frederick Block, Clinton Carpenter, Joe Wheeler, Hans Wollschläger, and Deryck Cooke.

Cooke had been asked by the British Broadcasting Corporation to write a booklet to accompany a series of Mahler centennial broadcasts in 1960. When he came to write on the Tenth Symphony, he was unwilling to base his remarks on the two published movements alone. He studied the facsimile of the sketches and discovered, as many others had, that all five movements existed in states near to completion.

Cooke recalled,

> It did not occur to me to try to *complete* the symphony, since it was obvious that no one could do this for Mahler. What seemed worth doing . . . was to give a radio talk on the Tenth during the centenary year, illustrating it with the two published movements, with the performable sections of the full-score draft of the second movement, and with the more fully textured parts of the short scores of the last two movements, scored by myself as closely to Mahler's orchestral style as I could manage. But, as I labored on this project, the manuscript yielded up more and more of its secrets. . . . I drew up far more of the draft in full score than I had originally thought possible. All but five or six minutes of the 75-minute whole was ready for performance.

After the broadcast, Cooke

began pondering over the omitted sections, trying to see if I could find some way of filling them out without interfering with

Mahler's basic conception. Meanwhile, however, Mrs. Mahler, who had answered the BBC's request for permission to broadcast the program by giving it her "blessing," now wrote to say that she had misunderstood their (entirely accurate) description of its nature and vetoed any further performance of the score. (This veto was entirely in principle, since she had heard neither the actual program nor a recording of it.)

Cooke continued to perfect his score, and numerous Mahler scholars tried to persuade Alma to reconsider. Finally she agreed to listen to a recording of the BBC program, and she was moved to tears. She wrote to Cooke, "I was so moved by this performance that I immediately asked Mr. Byrns to play the work a second time. I then realized that the time had come when I must reconsider my previous decision not to permit the performance of this work. I have now decided once and for all to give you full permission to go ahead with performances in any part of the world."

Shortly after writing this letter, Mrs. Mahler died. Her daughter Anna Mahler, going through various family papers, came upon 44 additional pages of manuscript that had previously been unknown. They enabled Cooke to complete a performing version of the entire Tenth Symphony, which was performed and recorded. Cooke continued to revise his work, finally completing his definitive score in 1975.

Cooke's version should not be thought of as a completed piece by Gustav Mahler, despite the fact that it contains no gaps. Nor is it an attempt to finish Mahler's work. Every measure contains music written by Mahler, but many passages have counterpoint added by Cooke. He finished much of the scoring, and he had to orchestrate part of the third and all of the fourth and fifth movements. It is difficult, when caught up in the intense emotional experience of listening to this music, to remember that it is not a finished piece. Yet, even though the orchestration in the final two movements lacks the composer's typical imagination and richness of color, the music is distinctly Mahler's, not Cooke's.

Cooke himself was sensitive to these issues:

> The present score is in no sense intended as a "completion" or "reconstruction" of the work. First of all, no completion has been necessary, in the usual sense — that is, free composition to fill gaps in the structure, as is Süssmayr's completion of Mozart's Requiem. Mahler's draft continues without interruption from beginning to end, even if the continuity is only tenuously preserved in places.
>
> Yet it is utterly impossible to "complete" the work, in the true sense. Mahler himself, in bringing it to its final form, would

have revised the draft — elaborated, refined, and perfected it in a thousand details; he would also, no doubt, have expanded, contracted, redisposed, added, or cancelled a passage here and there (especially in the second movement); and he would finally, of course, have embodied the result in his own incomparable orchestration. Obviously, he alone could have done all this: the idea that someone else can now reconstruct this process is pure illusion.

On the other hand, it would be wrong to say that the present score cannot claim to represent Mahler's Tenth Symphony in any sense whatsoever. It does, quite simply, represent the stage the work had reached when Mahler died, in a practical performing version.

There is certainly ample music to understand the striking originality of the work. The first movement, for example, attempts something virtually no other large romantic piece tries: to remain in one key for much of its length. About 80% of the movement is in the key of F-sharp (major or minor). Variety comes not from change of key but from an incredible richness of harmonies and dissonances within that one key. The second movement is just as experimental, but in the rhythmic domain. In much of the movement, there is a new time signature for nearly every measure. The first six measures, for example, are 3/2, 2/2, 2/2, 5/4, 2/2, 3/4. This kind of metric irregularity was unprecedented in tonal music; it seems more typical of Stravinsky than Mahler. The third movement's innovation is its brevity. This shadowy, fleeting movement lasts a mere 170 quick measures, in contrast to the first movement's 275 slow measures, the second movement's 522, the fourth's 578, and the fifth's 400. No music since Beethoven's late string quartets had attempted to combine short and long movements into a balanced whole. It is no surprise that, for the 36 years the symphony was known only by its expansive first and brief third movements, listeners could not understand how those two movements related to each other.

Perhaps because Mahler had not gotten as far in composing the last two movements, they are less overtly innovative than their predecessors. But their high degree of artistry is evident, despite the fact that Mahler left only an occasional clue to their orchestration. Thanks to Cooke's careful work in bringing all movements to a performable state, we are able to understand not only each movement but also the motivic unity and the progression of moods throughout the Tenth Symphony.

Felix Mendelssohn

Born on 3 February 1809 in Hamburg.
Died on 4 November 1847 in Leipzig.

◆　◆　◆

Concerto Number 1 in G Minor for Piano and Orchestra, Opus 25

Molto allegro con fuoco —
Andante —
Presto. Allegro e vivace

The First Piano Concerto was begun in Rome in the fall of 1830. The bulk of the compositional work was done a year later in Munich, where the work was finished in early October. The first performance was played by the composer there on 17 October 1831.

Mendelssohn was a child prodigy as a pianist as well as a composer. He appeared in concert from age 10. Although his earliest successes as a composer were for media other than the piano, it was inevitable that he would turn his attention to piano composition. He thought about writing a piano concerto while he was in Rome in the fall of 1830, a time when he began the *Italian* Symphony. He may have sketched some of the music, but, when he completed the work in Munich a year later, he referred to it as having been tossed off in a few days.

The concerto is dedicated to Delphine von Schauroth, a young pianist with whom Mendelssohn was infatuated. The composer wrote to his sister Fanny of his attraction for Delphine, although he sought to disguise the extent of his involvement by invoking a non-existent Scottish girl.

> Ministers and counts trot around her like domestic animals in the hen yard; artists, too, and other cultivated persons. Her mother is a baroness; she is an artist, and very cultivated. In short, I made sheep's eyes. We played Hummel's four-hand sonata beautifully, to the delight of the company; I melted and smiled and pounded and held the A-flat at the beginning of the last movement for her because "my small hand cannot reach it.". . . I run day after day to the museum and twice a week to Schauroth, where I stay for a long time. We flirt outrageously, but it is not dangerous, because I am already in love with somebody else. And that is a Scottish girl whose name I do not know.

Not only did the Scottish girl not exist, but also, according to Mendelssohn's diary, he went to visit Delphine far more often than twice a week.

Felix also confided to Fanny that Delphine "composed a passage for my G Minor Concerto, which makes a startling effect." Which passage it was that Delphine wrote we do not today know, but he must have been indeed taken with her to allow the intimacy of her contribution to his composition.

Mendelssohn played the first performance of the concerto at a concert on which he conducted his First Symphony and the *Midsummer Night's Dream* Overture. At the request of the King of Bavaria, who was in the audience, he also improvised at the piano on a theme of Mozart. The King was eager for Mendelssohn to marry Delphine, but the affair seems to have cooled when the composer left Munich a few months later. He continued to perform the concerto throughout Europe, to great success. Delphine herself eventually played the piece as well. Her final performance of it was at a Mendelssohn memorial concert, twenty years after his death. She was 56 years old.

Often essays in this book speak of concertos that, for one reason or another, are not virtuosic display pieces. The Mendelssohn First *is* a showpiece. Despite the lack of cadenzas, the piano is used in a dazzling manner, which is probably why its initial audiences were so taken with the work and why the foremost virtuoso of the day — Franz Liszt — readily added it to his repertoire. The concerto's bravura complements rather than displaces its substance.

The three movements are not separated by pauses, but rather the same brass fanfare serves as both transition to the second movement and introduction to the finale. The last movement also relates to the earlier movements by recalling some of their themes.

Concerto in E Minor for Violin and Orchestra, Opus 64
Allegro molto appassionato
Andante —
Allegretto non troppo. Allegro molto vivace

The Violin Concerto was begun in 1838 and completed on 16 September 1844. Revisions continued up to the first performance, which was given on 13 March 1845 by violinist Ferdinand David and the Leipzig Gewandhaus Orchestra, conducted by Neils Gade.

In 1840 Mendelssohn was "invited" — that is, summoned — to the court of the new King of Prussia, Frederick William IV. The King wanted to make patronage of the arts a major priority of his regime, and therefore he brought poets, painters, musicians, and intellectuals to Berlin. Frederick William meant well, but he was a dreamer who had more ideas than he could ever put into practice. He wanted Mendelssohn, for example, not only to become head of music at the Royal Academy of the Arts but also to start a new conservatory that would be the center of German musical life.

The composer's family urged him to accept the post. His mother, who was recently widowed and living in Berlin, was particularly eager for her son to return to the city where he had spent his childhood. Mendelssohn was reluctant, because he had never liked Berlin and because he was sure his liberal ideas would clash with the King's conservatism. Furthermore, he knew that he would have precious little time for composing the music he most wanted to write. One of his many projects was a concerto he had promised his old friend, violinist Ferdinand David. But in the end Mendelssohn accepted: when a King invites, a subject comes. The composer was excited about working in Germany's largest city, and he looked forward to performing with and composing for Berlin's large ensembles.

After complicated negotiations concerning his exact duties and title, Mendelssohn moved himself and his family to the Prussian capital in 1841. He took a leave of absence for one year from his position as conductor of the Leipzig Gewandhaus Orchestra. Concertmaster Ferdinand David, for whom Mendelssohn was writing the Violin Concerto, took over as conductor, succeeded, when the composer remained in Berlin, by Ferdinand Hiller and then Neils Gade (to whom fell the honor of conducting the premiere of the concerto when it was finally ready in 1845).

Once in Berlin, Mendelssohn encountered a series of frustrations. The orchestral musicians were not as accomplished as those in Leipzig, and they were hostile to him. In addition, the bureaucrats with whom he had to deal at court were evasive and uncooperative. Of the Minister of Arts, through whom all Mendelssohn's requests had to be channeled, the composer said, "He seems to have sworn death to every free intellectual endeavor. He is afraid of a mouse." Adding to Mendelssohn's unhappiness was the unexpected death of his mother in 1842.

The composer was overworked and depressed. He was required to teach, compose for the Royal Theater and for church services, and conduct an orchestra and a chorus. He also had to put up with official stupidity and insensitivity. For example, he was asked to set to music a "patriotic" poem that actually opposed German freedom (to his credit, Mendelssohn refused this task, although he did conduct the setting by one Konradin Kreutzer). His unhappiness took its toll on his music. During his years in Berlin he was required to write incidental music — mostly empty and now all but forgotten — for productions of Sophocles' *Antigone* and *Oedipus at Colonus* and of Racine's *Athalie*. The one exception was the wonderful music to Shakespeare's *A Midsummer Night's Dream*, which he had begun at the age of 17 and now completed on commission from the King. A courtier "complimented" the composer on his new piece: "What a pity that you wasted your beautiful music on such a stupid play!"

The King's plans for a new conservatory came to nothing. Mendelssohn had faithfully drawn up a series of well-considered ideas, but the King, like the true dilettante he was, had transferred his enthusiasm to other projects. The school idea was put "on hold" indefinitely. The composer wrote to a friend: "Grand plans, tiny accomplishments; huge demands, small achievements; sophisticated critics, miserable musicians."

Mendelssohn was ready to quit. But the King flattered him and charmed him into staying. His work load was lightened and he was given the freedom to travel. But the King turned out to be duplicitous — much of what he promised never materialized. Mendelssohn returned temporarily to Leipzig, where he did succeed in founding a new conservatory. This school, which had been planned some time earlier, fulfilled all the ideals that Frederick William had wanted for Berlin but was unwilling to implement. The stellar faculty included violinist David (who was still waiting patiently for Mendelssohn's Violin Concerto), composer Robert Schumann, and music theorist Moritz Hauptmann.

Mendelssohn returned to his official duties and unofficial frustrations in Berlin. He found the social environment at the court oppressive, and his health was beginning to suffer (he died three years later at the age of 38). King Frederick William pretended to be puzzled when he learned that his amply paid servant wanted complete freedom, but he finally acquiesced — on condition that Mendelssohn be available for future commissions and performances. The composer left Berlin for good in 1844, writing to a friend, "The first step out of Berlin is the first step to happiness." No longer required to compose patriotic works, church hymns, and incidental music, he was finally able to complete the work that he had begun six years earlier — the magnificent Violin Concerto.

Although Mendelssohn was himself a violinist and had previously written another violin concerto (at the age of 15), he repeatedly sought the advice of his friend David. As a result the E Minor Concerto is a masterful integration of virtuosity and musicality. It is full of melodic lines that spin seemingly effortlessly from the violin yet nonetheless exploit fully the technical potential of the instrument.

The finale in particular presents unabashed bravura and true melodiousness integrated in one of Mendelssohn's wonderfully impish scherzos. It is this combination of virtuosity and lyricism that has endeared the concerto to generations of violinists and listeners.

The concerto also has its share of innovations. Consider, for example, the manner in which the movements are linked together. A bassoon holds one note over from the last chord of the first movement, creating a harmonic link into the second movement. That movement goes without pause into a transitional section which ties it to the finale.

The first movement includes a written-out cadenza. Traditionally, the cadenza is left to the soloist to improvise, compose, or choose. It usually occurs just before the close of the first movement, at a point where the forward motion of the concerto stops for a while so that the soloist can show off his virtuosity. This extended, unaccompanied passage usually has little to do with the structure of the piece. Mendelssohn sought to integrate the cadenza into the form, so he placed it earlier in the movement. It serves as the transition from the development section to the recapitulation. Now that the cadenza has an important structural role, its form and harmonies could no longer be left to the whim of the soloist. Thus Mendelssohn wrote down exactly what the soloist should play, taking care (and asking David's advice) that it should nonetheless give the virtuoso ample opportunity to show off his skill. There is no cadenza in the second or third movements, but the perpetual motion of the finale gives the violinist constantly imaginative figuration that promises to dazzle and at the same time delight listeners.

The Hebrides Overture (*Fingal's Cave*), Opus 26

The first version of The Hebrides *was completed in Rome in December 1830. The first performance was given on 14 May 1832 by the London Philharmonic Society. The final version is dated 20 June 1832.*

Mendelssohn was in his early twenties when he began to travel extensively and chronicle his impressions of foreign lands in a series of compositions. In the summer of 1829 he visited Scotland, where he began to sketch what would become 13 years later his *Scottish* Symphony. While in Scotland he visited the Hebrides Islands, where he wrote the theme for his *Hebrides* Overture. Carrying with him sketches for the overture, he went the next year to Italy, where he began the *Italian* Symphony.

Several times the composer thought he had finished *The Hebrides,* only to feel subsequent dissatisfaction. There are altogether three different extant manuscripts of the finished work. They differ considerably. The piece was initially called *Overtüre zur einsamen Insel* ("Overture to a Lonely Island"). The first revision is entitled *Die Hebriden.* The final version, *The Hebrides,* is considerably shorter than its earlier counterparts. It was eventually published as the *Fingal's Cave* Overture.

In a letter dated 7 August 1829, the composer jotted down the theme which opens the overture. He wrote, "To make you understand how extraordinarily the Hebrides have affected me, I have written down this tune." This theme he later associated with Fingal's Cave, a grotto on the Hebridean island of Staffa, although he did not see the grotto until the day after he wrote the letter.

Mendelssohn wrote home from Italy on 30 November 1830 that he was working on the piece daily in order to finish it as a birthday present for his father. On 20 December, a bit late for the birthday, he said that the overture was done. But he wrote to his sister much later, on 21 January 1832, "I'm too fond of the piece to perform it in an imperfect state, but I hope to set to work on it soon and have it ready for England and Michaelmas. . . . The D major middle section is very silly. The whole so-called development tastes more of counterpoint than of whale oil, seagulls, and codliver oil, and it ought to be the other way around." The composer's friend, pianist Ignaz Moscheles, to whom the overture is dedicated, wrote, "The first version seemed so beautiful and well-rounded that I could not conceive of any change, and we discussed this point again today. However, he struck to his decision to change it." The first revision was used for the premiere on 14 May. Shortly afterward Mendelssohn made his final revision, which was published in April 1835 and is played today.

The overture is beautifully evocative. The sixteenth-note oscillations and arpeggios that pervade the composition suggest the wind and waves that must have impressed Mendelssohn in the Hebrides. Equally effective are the wisps of melody that form the main theme. Not until the second theme do we hear anything like a full-blown tune. When it arrives, this theme is especially engaging because of the previous absence of extended melody. This lyrical line, in the cellos and later the clarinets, is one of Mendelssohn's inspired ideas — simple and beautiful. The overture ends by evaporating rather abruptly into silence, as if the winds and tides at Fingal's Cave have momentarily died down, soon to return.

A *Midsummer Night's Dream* Overture, Opus 21

The Midsummer Night's Dream *Overture was composed between 8 July and 6 August 1826. It was first performed at Stettin on 20 February 1827, with Karl Löwe conducting.*

Although Shakespeare's plays had long been known in German-speaking countries, it was not until a new series of definitive translations appeared in 1801 that the English playwright began to be widely read in Germany. The new versions were tinged with romanticism and thus acquired widespread appeal among nineteenth-century German artists and intellectuals. Ludwig Tieck, one of the translators, called *A Midsummer Night's Dream* a "romantic masterpiece." And so the played seemed to Mendelssohn, who read the drama over and over in his garden. He was just 17 years old when he wrote to his sister Fanny, "I have grown accustomed to composing in our garden. . . . Today or tomorrow I am going to dream there the *Midsummer Night's Dream*. I have a lot of nerve!"

It is astonishing that a young boy could compose as polished and original a work as the *Midsummer Night's Dream* Overture. What is even more amazing is that the music captures perfectly the English spirit in Shakespeare's comedy. Mendelssohn had not yet visited England, nor had he traveled beyond his native land at all. His travelogue compositions, such as *The Hebrides* of 1830 or the *Italian* Symphony of 1833 or the *Scottish* Symphony of 1842, lay far in the future.

An adolescent composer, even one of such precocious genius as Mendelssohn, would likely show his latest work-in-progress to his teacher. And so the composer brought a sketch of the introduction and exposition of the overture to Adolph Bernhard Marx. Marx, who became Mendelssohn's friend in 1824, was a brilliant and articulate music theorist and historian, as well as something of a composer. He was working on his treatise *On Painting in Music* at the time he was Mendelssohn's teacher, and thus he was most interested in his student's programmatic overture.

Marx later recalled that "the introductory chords and the dance of the elves were just as we know them. Then, alas, there followed the overture proper — but I was unable to associate it with *A Midsummer Night's Dream*. As a faithful friend I felt in duty bound to tell the composer frankly what I thought. He was concerned, provoked, even hurt, and ran away without saying good-bye."

A few days later the composer sent a note of apology and asked Marx's advice on adjusting the overture to be more in accordance with the play. "I did not fail him," Marx wrote. I "hurried to his assistance and pointed out that such an overture must reflect faithfully and completely the drama of which it was to be prologue. Enthusiastically and with absolute devotion he took up the work again. Only the allusion to the lover's wandering in the first motive could be salvaged from the original version; everything else had to be rewritten. . . . I insisted on his saving a place for the jesters and even for Bottom's ardent braying. He followed my advice, and the overture took the form we know now."

When the overture was premiered, Marx published a most favorable review. Mendelssohn appreciated his friend's support and help, although the composer's father had doubts about the teacher. Abraham Mendelssohn said, "People who talk so aptly but produce nothing apt exercise a bad influence on productive talents." The composer and his teacher eventually had a falling out when Mendelssohn refused to perform a trivial oratorio by Marx in Leipzig.

We may well wonder what the original version of the overture was like. The sketches Marx criticized have not been preserved. But the final result, owing in small or large part to Marx's advice, is one of the masterpieces of romantic orchestral music. It is wonderfully evocative of the elfin world of Shakespeare's play, especially in the opening woodwind chords and the ensuing string *scherzando*. A delightful moment occurs when Bottom the bumpkin is represented by horn and ophicleide (an obsolete instrument that looked like a saxophone but with a cup mouthpiece; today the part is generally played on tuba) intruding loudly upon a delicate woodwind and string passage. Especially beautiful is the concluding transformation of the assertive main theme into a gracefully lyric melody in the violins.

The craft, originality, and maturity that Mendelssohn exhibits in this early piece are astonishing. In some ways he never went beyond what he achieved in his teens. His later works are sometimes more learned, yet his craft was fully developed by age 17. Thus when he was commissioned to provide additional incidental music for several scenes of *A Midsummer Night's Dream,* he was able with no effort to re-enter the musical counterpart of Shakespeare's fairyland that he had created 17 years earlier.

Symphony Number 3 in A Minor, Opus 56, *Scottish*

Andante con moto. Allegro un poco agitato.
Andante con moto —
Vivace non troppo —
Adagio —
Allegro vivacissimo. Allegro maestoso assai

The Scottish *Symphony was begun in August 1829 and finished on 20 January 1842. Mendelssohn conducted the first performance with the Leipzig Gewandhaus Orchestra on 3 March 1842.*

In his early twenties Mendelssohn started to chronicle his extensive travels in a series of orchestral compositions. Italy was responsible for the *Italian* Symphony, and Scotland inspired two different works — the *Hebrides* Overture and the *Scottish* Symphony.

The composer's first of nine visits to the British Isles began in April 1829. He had been encouraged by his composition teacher Carl Friedrich Zelter to get away from provincial Berlin and to see the world. His father concurred. Equally important was the young man's wish to be away from home and on his own. He went first to London, where he roomed with his friend Carl Klingemann. The British capital was at first confusing. "It is frightful! It is crazy! I am confused and mixed up! London is the most grandiose and complicated monster that the world has to offer."

He soon got used to London. His music was played and warmly received. A performance of his First Symphony made him the darling of the British public, and he henceforth thought of England as his second home.

In the summer he and Klingemann set off for a holiday in Scotland. They went first to Edinburgh, where they visited the ruins of the chapel in which Mary Stuart had been crowned. There the young composer was struck with the idea of recording his impressions of Scotland in a symphony. He wrote down the first 16 measures of the introduction, which contains the main melodic material of the opening movement.

The composer was enchanted with Scotland. He saw Glasgow, Perth, Inverness, and Loch Lomond, and he met Sir Walter Scott, all of whose novels he had read. His enthusiasm for Scotland is evident in this letter to his family:

Everything here looks so stern and robust, half wrapped in haze or smoke or fog. Moreover there was a bagpipe competition. Many Highlanders came in costume from church, victoriously leading their sweethearts in Sunday dress and casting magnificent and important looks over the world. With long red beards, tartan plaids, bonnets and feathers, naked knees, and their bagpipes in their hands, they passed quietly along by the half-ruined gray castle on the meadow, where Mary Stuart lived in splendor and saw Rizzio murdered. I feel as if time went very quickly when I have before me so much that was and so much that is. . . . In the twilight today we went to the palace where Queen Mary lived and loved. . . . The chapel beside it has now lost its roof, it is overgrown with grass and ivy, and at the broken altar Mary was crowned Queen of Scotland. Everything is ruined, decayed, and open to the sky. I believe that I have found there today the beginning of my *Scottish* Symphony.

The symphony was destined to wait a decade for completion. The following winter, Mendelssohn worked on it along with the *Hebrides* Overture and the *Italian* Symphony, while traveling in Rome and Naples. Since he was in Italy, it was perhaps natural that the *Italian* got the most attention. "Who can wonder that I find it difficult to return to my misty Scottish mood?" By the time the double bar was finally drawn at the end of the A Minor Symphony, the other travelogue works had long been completed. Thus, despite the confused numbering of Mendelssohn symphonies (in order of publication, not of composition), the *Scottish* was actually his last symphonic work to be completed.

The composer returned to Great Britain several times. In 1842, when he was in England to conduct the London premiere of the *Scottish* Symphony, the composer met the young Queen Victoria and Prince Albert. They were more nervous about meeting the famous composer than he was about spending an evening with royalty. He requested, and was granted, permission to dedicate the symphony to the Queen.

Just how Scottish is the Third Symphony? No folk tunes are quoted. Mendelssohn, in fact, disliked all folk music. Shortly after his visit to Scotland, he wrote, "No national music for me! Ten thousand devils take all nationality! Now I am in Wales, and, dear me, a harpist sits in the hall of every inn of repute, playing incessantly so-called national melodies, that is to say, the most infamous, vulgar, out-of-tune trash, with a hurdy-gurdy going on at the same time!"

Nonetheless, there is a certain Scottish folk flavor in the symphony, although it is muted and more on the surface than in the structure. As biographer Eric Werner explains, "In the whole first movement we breathe the heavy, thick air of a Scottish Highland mist; accordingly, it is massively orchestrated and darkly colored. In marked contrast to this, the scherzo . . . reminds us of the gay folk dances of the Scots, with their bagpipes. The theme is pentatonic, like Gaelic folk songs." Each phrase of this clarinet theme ends with a rhythm known as a "Scotch snap." Furthermore, the rushing chromatic waves toward the end of the first movement might be taken as representative of the howling north wind. Mendelssohn originally labelled the finale *allegro guerriero* — "fast and warlike." This marking, though eventually replaced with *allegro vivacissimo*, has led several commentators to view this movement as a picture of Highland warriors in full battle.

Still, it would be a mistake to hear too many direct references to Scotland in this music. Mendelssohn deplored music with explicit extramusical references. Many of the invocations of Scotland are more in the ears of certain prejudiced listeners than in the music. In fact, one rather perceptive listener — composer Robert Schumann — heard a performance of this symphony and, thinking it was the *Italian* rather than the *Scottish* (Mendelssohn published the work without subtitle), praised the gorgeous Italian imagery and called the work "so beautiful as to compensate a listener who had never been in Italy." So much for its unmistakable Scottish character!

Symphony Number 4 in A Major, Opus 90, *Italian*
Allegro vivace
Andante con moto
Con molto moderato
Saltarello: Presto

The Italian *Symphony was begun in Italy in 1831 and completed in Berlin in 1833. Mendelssohn conducted the first performance, with the London Philharmonic Orchestra, on 13 May 1833.*

For several centuries Italy was a mecca for composers from northern Europe. Particularly during the romantic era, a trip to the sunny south was all but required of any self-respecting artist. Composers flocked to Italy to find inspiration. Some of the more obvious results are Hugo Wolf's *Italian* Serenade, Tchaikovsky's *Capriccio Italien*, Berlioz' *Harold in Italy*, Liszt's *Venezia e Napoli*, and Mendelssohn's *Italian* Symphony.

Mendelssohn first visited Italy in 1830, when he was 22 years old. He was overcome by the beauty of the ancient Roman ruins, the Alban Hills, Venice, the Vatican, the Colosseum, and the Monte Pincio. His letters home speak rhapsodically of these sights, but he rarely mentions the Italian people. In fact, he spent most of his time in the company of Germans. He was untouched by the politics, society, or culture of Italy. Thus, although the inspiration behind the *Italian* Symphony was genuine, the Italy conjured up is a country as seen by a tourist. Only the finale, a folk dance called a *saltarello*, captures an authentically Italian flavor.

Although the composer had hoped to finish the symphony while in the south, the work took rather longer than expected. The incentive to finish the music came in the form of a commission from the London Philharmonic Society. Mendelssohn finally completed the symphony in Berlin two months before its 1833 London premiere.

Mendelssohn was never quite satisfied with the piece. In a letter written in 1834, he expressed displeasure with the middle movements, and he stated that he would have to alter virtually the entire first movement. In the revised score dated 1837 the changes are slight. Later there were more revisions, but the final score has apparently been lost. The version published in 1851, four years after the composer's death, follows the original score.

The first movement presents the conductor with an interesting dilemma. Mendelssohn indicated the customary repeat of the exposition section. Performers today generally feel free to observe or ignore exposition repeats. Choice is made on the basis of the performer's understanding of the pacing and proportions of the piece, the length of the concert, and even the nature of the concert. Scholars have long debated whether indications of such repeats were mere formalities left over from earlier baroque practices or whether composers really intended them to be observed. There are some pieces that seem too long if the repeat is taken, others that are unbalanced when it is omitted. For most works, however, the internal evidence is inconclusive. The choice of whether or not to repeat becomes one of artistic interpretation. In the *Italian* Symphony there is a "first ending" of the exposition that is completely omitted from the performance if the repeat is not taken. The presence of a first ending is not without precedent and does not therefore definitively require that the repeat be observed. In this symphony, however, the first ending contains some music heard nowhere else in the movement until the final few measures. This material is related to but distinct from the principal melodies of the movement. If the repeat is taken, the end of the coda is a reminiscence. Every other theme has already returned, and, when the one from the first ending finally does also, the movement is complete and can end. If, on the other hand, the repeat is omitted, the end of the coda is a fresh, new twist related to the main materials. Quite a difference!

The elegaic character of the second movement is established by the opening's stark two-voice counterpoint, which is somewhat unusual in music for full orchestra. For his third movement, Mendelssohn reverted to the classical period's minuet rather than utilizing the romantic era's preferred scherzo. This refined minuet is the epitome of classical restraint and elegance. The finale is really the symphony's scherzo. It is one of Mendelssohn's typically sprightly dance movements.

Mendelssohn's *Italian* Symphony is a work of considerable subtlety and originality. It adheres to formal procedures that are classical in spirit although sometimes in violation of strict classical forms. Its surface sound, with its brilliant orchestration, lovely harmonies, and charming tunes, is thoroughly romantic. Its unique blend of classicism and romanticism make it one of the jewels of the nineteenth-century symphonic literature.

◆ ◆ ◆

Symphony Number 5 in D Minor, Opus 107, *Reformation*

Andante. Allegro con fuoco
Allegro vivace
Andante —
Andante con moto. Allegro vivace

The Reformation *Symphony was composed in 1830 and first performed in 1832 in Berlin.*

It is ironic that the grandson of Moses Mendelssohn, who was considered by many to be the greatest Jewish intellectual of his century, should compose a symphony in honor of the tercentennary of the Protestant Reformation.

The Reformation was the religious movement that led to the establishment of Protestantism. Martin Luther led the rebellion against the spiritual, political, and economic domination by the Catholic church. In 1519 he openly defied the power of the Pope; in 1520 he publicly burned the Pope's order to excommunicate him. Luther had many followers, and the ensuing struggle between Catholics and Protestants was fierce. By 1530 the Lutherans had won the right to determine the religion of the people under their rule. Their beliefs were stated in a document presented at a meeting called in Augsburg by Emperor Charles V for the purpose of resolving the differences between Protestants and Catholics. Charles and the Catholics could not accept the ideas of Luther, and the split between the two divisions of Christianity became permanent. The document, known as the Augsberg Confession, became the fundamental statement of the Protestant faith.

Luther was at first interested in the Jews. In 1523 he wrote that Jews "are blood relations of our Lord. . . . We must exercise not the law of the Pope but that of Christian love and show them a friendly spirit." Unfortunately the condition of the Jews did not improve under the Reformation. Luther felt that treating Jews kindly meant converting them. When they resisted, his prejudices against them came forward. In 1542 he wrote, in anger, "If the Jews refuse to be converted, we ought not to suffer them or bear with them any longer." Thus the Jews remained in their ghettos, shut out not only from material well-being but also from the mainstream of European science, art, and culture. It was not until the following century that they were able to break through religious and class barriers to particiate in European intellectual life.

The figure most responsible for this breakthrough was Moses Mendelssohn. This philosopher became a close friend of dramatist Gotthold Lessing, who based his best-known play, *Nathan the Wise,* on Mendelssohn. German intellectuals were at first astounded but then intrigued by the fact that Lessing became closely involved with a Jew and wrote a play about him around the themes of freedom and tolerance. As a result Mendelssohn was accepted by the intelligentsia. His essay on immortality, written in German rather than Yiddish, was widely read; it made him a more respected philosopher than even Kant. He translated the Old Testament into German for the advantage of Jews whose Hebrew was not fluent. He believed that his people were foremost Germans and only secondarily Jews, and he felt that all religious rites should be conducted in the language of the people rather than in Hebrew. The main focus of Mendelssohn's life and work was to help his people leave their ghettos and join society as the equals of Protestants and Catholics. He did not live to see the actualization of this dream: he died in 1786, and the emancipation of Jews in Germany was officially decreed in 1812. But even then prejudice remained rampant.

One of the nine children of Moses Mendelssohn was Abraham, father of Felix. Although Abraham was only ten when Moses died, he accepted his father's Jewish liberalism. Thus at the age of 16 he joined the Society of Friends, dedicated to combating orthodoxy. Many of the members went so far as to have themselves baptized. When the official emancipation of Jews in Germany failed to rid the country of anti-Semitism, Abraham saw no contradiction in protecting his children by having them baptized as Protestants. Abraham's wife, in fact, had been a strong advocate of conversion for years. He even followed the expediency of having himself baptized several years later, but he continued to think of himself as a Jew.

Felix was raised a Lutheran. He, like his father, maintained important spiritual ties with Judaism, but his beliefs were thoroughly Protestant. He was a humanist who often defended Jews and was proud of his heritage, but he was also a devout Protestant who composed such statements of Christian faith as *Te Deum, Magnificat,* hymns, motets, cantatas, and the *Reformation* Symphony. It is indeed odd that the grandson of a Jewish philosopher should compose Christian music, but the liberalism of the grandfather did lead, albeit indirectly, to the conversion of the grandson.

Because of his faith the composer was eager in 1830 to participate in the tercentennary celebration of the Augsburg Confession. Although he was only 20 he composed a large and serious symphonic work, originally known as *Symphony for the Festival of the Reformation of the Church.* Much of the first three movements is derived from a religious motive known as the "Dresden Amen," a figure understood as a symbol of the Holy Ghost. The final movement is based on the well-known hymn "A Mighty Fortress Is Our God," which was written by Luther.

The celebration for which the symphony was written was cancelled. A year later the piece was rehearsed in Paris, but the musicians reacted so negatively that it could not be performed. It was evenutally played in 1832, but the composer had a low opinion of it. He called the first movement "a fat bristly animal." Later he said, "I cannot stand it any more and would rather burn it than any other of my pieces; it should never be published." Thus it was not printed until 21 years after Mendelsohn's death, when it had to be called Symphony Number 5, since symphonies composed later had already been published as Numbers 3 and 4.

Mendelssohn was deeply interested in the music of Bach, and the *Reformation* Symphony can be considered an homage to the older master's religious spirit and contrapuntal mastery. The chorale-like introduction, opening almost like a fugue, owes a lot to Bach. The Dresden Amen is heard twice in the strings just before the andante leads to the allegro. Bach-like counterpoint is heard in much of the first movement.

The second movement is the only part of the symphony that reflects Mendelssohn's typically light and delicate style. The movement is a scherzo, loosely derived (by inversion) from the Dresden Amen motive. The brief slow movement leads directly to the finale.

At the opening of the last movement, a solo flute intones Luther's hymn tune, which is developed in imitative counterpoint. Later in the movement the hymn returns in the brass, like a *cantus firmus.* The work ends with a full statement of the hymn, simply harmonized in chorale fashion.

Wolfgang Amadeus Mozart

Born on 28 January 1756 in Salzburg.
Died on 5 December 1791 in Vienna.

Concerto in A Major for Clarinet and Orchestra, K. 622
Allegro
Adagio
Allegro

The Clarinet Concerto was first sketched in 1789. It was completed in the middle of October 1791. It was presumably premiered by Anton Stadler, for whom it was composed.

The clarinet is a relative newcomer to the orchestral wind family. The instrument was invented in the early eighteenth century as a modernization of an old French reed instrument known as the *chalumeau*. The earliest known reference to an instrument named "clarinet" dates from 1716. Composers occasionally incorporated the new instrument into opera orchestras, but a number of years passed before it was used in chamber or orchestral performances. The early clarinet had few keys and was therefore not particularly agile. Thus the instrument was accepted only gradually. Furthermore, players were scarce. They were usually oboists who had hastily learned the new instrument.

The clarinet was particularly popular in Great Britain. One of the earliest clarinet recitals was given in Dublin in 1742, and J. C. Bach used clarinets for a London opera production in 1763. It is likely that the eight-year-old Mozart first encountered the instrument the next year during a visit to the British capital. He subsequently heard it in several other European musical centers, including (during a visit in 1777) Mannheim, where instrumentalists were particularly accomplished. Karl Stamitz, one of Mannheim's composers, wrote a number of clarinet concertos that foreshadow Mozart's use of dramatic skips. Although Mozart no doubt knew some of the Stamitz concertos, he rarely incorporated clarinets into his own music prior to his move to Vienna in 1781.

Mozart approached the clarinet cautiously. His early uses of it are not particularly idiomatic. The clarinet music in three divertimentos from the early 1770s, for example, sounds as if it could have been written for any treble wind instrument. Later on the composer used clarinets in place of oboes in some orchestrations. On the rare

419

occasions when he used both (as in the *Paris* Symphony of 1778), he usually relegated the clarinets to the role of unobtrusive filler.

Soon after moving to Vienna, Mozart met clarinetist Anton Stadler. Like the composer, Stadler was a Freemason. Although reportedly not as great a virtuoso as his contemporaries Tausch and Bähr, Stadler was known for the soft vocal qualities of his playing. Mozart found in Stadler a kindred spirit as well as a truly artistic musician. The clarinetist and the composer became close friends, and the influence of Stadler's musicality on Mozart's subsequent music was enormous. Stadler taught Mozart about the expressive subtleties of his instrument, and the composer produced several major works for him. Stadler's intimate tone and agility over the whole range of the instrument found their way into immortality through Mozart's music. The clarinetist taught his friend about large skips from one register to another, the repetition of a figure successively in different registers, the use of the low sounds for arpeggios, and alternations between high and low in order to make the clarinet sound like two instruments in dialogue.

The culmination of this happy collaboration was the Clarinet Concerto, written a few weeks before Mozart's death. In this work the composer perfected his conception of the clarinet idiom. He took full advantage of the clarinet's ability to play arpeggios, long-held high notes, singing melodies, and dramatic juxtapositions of register.

K. 622 had begun life in 1789 as a concerto in G major for basset horn, which is an alto clarinet on which Stadler excelled. Mozart had written basset horn parts for Stadler in a number of works, and now presumably he wanted to try it as a solo instrument. We do not know why the composer stopped after writing 199 measures and decided to recast the work for clarinet.

Had Mozart been composing for anyone but Stadler, he would have faced a problem. The basset horn's lowest note is written C (the actual sounding note is G, since the basset horn pitched in the key of G), but the clarinet generally goes down only to E (sounding as C-sharp on the clarinet in A). The lowest four notes in the solo part would have had to be rewritten when the basset horn concerto became a clarinet concerto. But Stadler had a special clarinet, sometimes known as a basset clarinet, with extra low notes. Its written range was the same as that of the basset horn. Mozart thus did not have to rework the solo part but only to change the key of the piece from G major to A major. But he inadvertently created a problem for later clarinetists, who did not have extended clarinets.

Since Stadler, who was not a particularly reliable fellow, lost the manuscript of the Clarinet Concerto, we can only guess what the original solo part was like. Prior to its publication the concerto was edited for performance on a standard instrument. The anonymous editor was not particularly skillful. Some passages that seem to suggest a low register move suddenly and inexplicably into a middle register, other passages are awkward for the fingers but would be easier if played an octave lower on an extended instrument, descending scales sometimes leap suddenly up, passages that contrast low and high registers sometimes move unexpectedly into a weak middle register, sometimes the range of the solo part conflicts with that of the orchestral instruments, and there is a curious extra measure in the first movement that can be explained only by lowering the solo part an octave in order to provide three repetitions of a figure in successively lower registers. These awkward passages have provided a dilemma for clarinetists. Since basset clarinets became obselete after Stadler's death, musically satisfying compromises must be found whenever the concerto is played on a modern instrument. In 1974 a reconstruction of the original version was finally published, and there has been an attendant revival of interest in the basset clarinet.

There is an interesting aspect of this problem that seems to have eluded musicologists who have studied Mozart's use of the clarinet. This concerns what clarinetists call the "break" — a discontinuity in tone quality between B-flat (the note produced when all holes are open) and B (the lowest overblown note, produced by closing all holes except the "register key"). Clarinetists have always deplored composers' seeming insensitivity to this discontinuity in sonority between adjacent notes — the thin sound of the B-flat versus the rich sound of the B. Even Mozart *appears* to have been guilty of such lack of concern, except when we consider the nature of Stadler's extended clarinet. On his instrument the notes B-flat, A, A-flat, and G could be produced either with most holes open or overblown with most holes closed. Stadler no doubt would have chosen the fingering that would produce the tone quality appropriate for a given passage, either to emphasize melodic continuity or to highlight contrast of registers. Thus most of the places that clarinetists may dismiss as poor uses of the break in the Mozart concerto would, no doubt, have sounded fine on the extended clarinet.

The Clarinet Concerto is Mozart's last completed work of major proportions. This fact has led some commentators to hear in it an autumnal quality. Other critics, ironically, hear no hint of grief or resignation. However we interpret its mood, the work is definitely one of Mozart's masterpieces, hardly the trifling showpiece that some of his earlier wind concertos are. The intimate character, the wealth of wonderfully melodic themes, the contrapuntal rigor, the adventurous modulations, and the magnificent treatment of the solo instrument all indicate that Mozart was working at the height of his powers, deeply inspired by the musicianship of his close friend. The concerto is a sublime work, far removed from the empty virtuosity of other clarinet concertos, such as those by Stamitz, Spohr, and Weber. It has a personality uniquely its own. It helped to establish the clarinet as a full-fledged member of the woodwind family, and it defined the clarinet idiom for subsequent generations of composers. Later composers who wrote extensively for the instrument in collaboration with virtuoso performers — Weber and Brahms are the prime examples — never went beyond the character that Mozart created under the influence of Stadler. It is only in the twentieth century that composers have devised new conceptions of the clarinet sound, thus finally breaking more than a hundred years of dominance by this one composition on the entire clarinet literature.

Concerto Number 1 in G Major for Flute and Orchestra, K. 313

> Allegro maestoso
> Adagio non troppo
> Rondo: Tempo di menuetto

Concerto Number 2 in D Major for Flute and Orchestra, K. 314

> Allegro aperto
> Andante ma non troppo
> Allegro

Concerto in C Major for Oboe and Orchestra, K. 314

> Allegro aperto
> Adagio non troppo
> Allegretto

The Oboe Concerto was composed in Salzburg in the summer of 1777. The oboist who performed it there was Giuseppe Ferlendis. The two Flute Concertos were composed in January or February 1778 in Mannheim. The Second Flute Concerto is essentially identical to the Oboe Concerto.

Both Mozart and his father were employed by Archbishop Colleredo of Salzburg. The Archbishop did not care for either of them, and they in turn disliked their positions. In 1777 the family decided that Wolfgang should make a tour of the musical capitals of Europe, in the hopes of making a better living through performing, teaching, and commissions. Leopold remained in Salzburg, so that there would be at least one stable income. Shortly before leaving, Wolfgang composed an oboe concerto for Salzburger Giuseppe Ferlendis.

Mozart had been welcomed at courts throughout the continent in earlier years, when he was regarded as a child prodigy, but now he was 21 and just another musician. His travels were a series of frustrations and disappointments. He failed to secure a position, and he received precious few commissions.

Mozart's mother accompanied him, since Leopold did not trust his son in such practical matters as finding lodging, packing properly, and arranging transportation. More to the point, Mozart's mother was to try to curb her son's penchant for pranks and bawdy behavior, neither of which would have helped get an appointment. They went first to Munich, and, when nothing developed there, they proceeded on to Mannheim. The Mannheim Orchestra was at that time renowned as the finest in the world. Mozart became friendly with several members of the orchestra, including flutist Johann Baptist Wendling and oboist Friedrich Ramm. The composer gave Ramm a copy of the concerto he had written a few months earlier in Salzburg. Ramm was delighted, and he performed the work in Mannheim on numerous occasions.

For a while Mozart thought he was going to receive an appointment at the court of Elector Carl Theodore, but nothing came of it. His spirits were as low as his finances. His friend, the flutist Wendling, helped by introducing him to a Dutch amateur flute player named De Jean. De Jean commissioned Mozart to write three "short and easy" concertos and four quartets for flute and strings.

The composer was eager to receive the 200 gulden he had been promised, but he was reluctant to undertake the rather large project of composing seven multi-movement pieces. One reason for his compositional lethargy was his dislike for the flute. Another was the amount of time he was spending trying to seduce soprano Aloysia Weber. She was never really interested in Mozart romantically, but he did not give up easily. (He eventually married her sister Constanze.) Leopold was furious when he learned of his son's lackadaisical attitude, despite the real threat of poverty. He wrote angrily, "Use your time to carry out the commissions quickly!"

Wolfgang responded defensively, "Here I do not have one hour of peace. I can only compose at night, and so cannot get up early. Besides, one is not disposed to work at all times. I could certainly scribble the whole day, but a piece of music goes out into the world, and, after all, I do not want to feel ashamed for my name to be on it. And, as you know, I am quite inhibited when I have to compose for an instrument which I cannot endure."

Having resigned himself to the lack of employment in Mannheim, Mozart made ready to move on to Paris. He told De Jean he would complete the commission there and send him the music, but the Dutchman was growing impatient. Mozart gave him what was finished: three of the four quartets and two of the three concertos. One of the concertos, the G Major, was neither short nor easy. The other concerto turned out to be a transcription, with only tiny alterations, of the oboe concerto which Friedrich Ramm had already been playing all over Mannheim. The third flute concerto was never composed. The Dutchman, none too pleased, gave Mozart only 96 gulden.

If De Jean received less music than he had bargained for, he received greater musical substance in the First Concerto than he may have expected. It is a major work. In its graceful use of the flute, we hear no traces of the composer's dislike of the instrument. Mozart was a thorough professional, able to put his prejudices aside in order to create a first-rate work — once he got around to writing it. Perhaps the slow movement's intensity was too much for De Jean, and perhaps the virtuosity in the finale — with its rapid runs and wide leaps — was too challenging for an amateur player. Even if De Jean could not do justice to the concerto, however, subsequent flutists surely have. It has taken its rightful place among the handful of important works for flute and orchestra.

De Jean must have felt more comfortable playing the Second Concerto. Since it was originally written for oboe, it does not utilize the flute's highest register (which is beyond the capabilities of the oboe). And, since Ferlendis, the oboe player for whom it was written, was not the most accomplished virtuoso, the concerto is not as dazzling as its companion in G major. But it is a beautiful and elegant work that is an important part of the flute repertory.

Both the flute and oboe versions of K. 314 were performed often in Mannheim and Paris. In 1783 Mozart presented a copy of the Oboe Concerto to the Esterházy oboist Anton Meyer, who played the work in Vienna. The score and parts were subsequently lost, however, only to be rediscovered in Salzburg in 1920.

How is it possible, we may well wonder, for essentially the same work to be successful as both an oboe concerto and a flute concerto? Both versions seem thoroughly idiomatic, and both seem to use the soloist in a natural and ingratiating manner. The answer is that Mozart's wind concertos are more concerned with lyricism in general than with the particular virtuosic capabilities of individual instruments. He had a sense of melody that transcended the differences between instruments. The notion that each wind instrument needs its own special kind of music, which only it can do well, was a later idea. Transcription was still common in the classical period, as it had been in the baroque. Mozartian melodic lines that sound well, as his invariably do, are attractive played on almost any instrument.

Concerto Number 1 in D Major for Horn and Orchestra, K. 412

Allegro
Allegro

Concerto Number 2 in E-Flat Major for Horn and Orchestra, K. 417

Allegro maestoso
Andante
Rondo

Concerto Number 3 in E-Flat Major for Horn and Orchestra, K. 447

Allegro
Romanze: Larghetto
Allegro

Concerto Number 4 in E-Flat Major for Horn and Orchestra, K. 495

Allegro moderato
Romanze
Allegro vivace

The First Horn Concerto was composed in Vienna in 1791, although the movements may have existed earlier as independent pieces. The Second Concerto was completed on 27 May 1783. Concerto Number 3 was probably written in Vienna in 1786 or 1787, although the slow movement dates from 1784. The Fourth Concerto was completed on 26 June 1786 in Vienna. The probable soloist for all four concertos was Ignaz Leutgeb.

Like his other solo wind-instrument music, Mozart's concertos for horn and orchestra were composed for one of his friends. The intended soloist was Ignaz Leutgeb. Mozart had known Leutgeb when they both lived in Salzburg. The composer had been employed by Archbishop Colleredo, in whose orchestra Leutgeb played. Leutgeb moved to Vienna in 1777, and Mozart followed in 1781. There the horn player tried to supplement his income by opening a cheese shop, with the help of a loan from Mozart's father.

Although the horn concertos written for Leutgeb suggest that he must have been an extraordinary performer, he was otherwise apparently an uneducated simpleton, who was often the butt of Mozart's practical jokes. The composer once admitted, "I can never resist making a fool of Leutgeb."

Mozart made fun of Leutgeb in several horn compositions. For example, the Quintet (K. 407) for horn, violin, two violas, and cello (an odd combination, since three of the five instruments share the middle register) is full of jokes at the expense of the horn player, whose limited instrument cannot play all the notes of the scale. Throughout the finale of the First Concerto, Mozart wrote numerous remarks, performance instructions, exclamations, and comments to Leutgeb. The composer included in the manuscript of this movement a drawing of Leutgeb playing the horn. The Second Concerto bears the dedication "W. A. Mozart took pity on that ass, ox, and fool of a Leutgeb, in Vienna, 27 May 1783." The manuscript of the Fourth Concerto was written with red, blue, green, and black inks, apparently to confuse the performer.

Because the system of brass-instrument valves had not yet been invented, Mozart wrote his horn concertos for the natural horn. This instrument was able to produce only certain notes, namely those in the overtone series of the instrument's fundamental pitch. This pitch is D in the case of the First Concerto, as the work is in that key, and E-flat for the other concertos. Since higher overtones are closer together than lower ones, the natural horn could play scale passages in the high register but only arpeggios in its low range. Additional notes could be produced by "stopping" the instrument: inserting the hand well into the bell in order to raise the pitch a half-step. Stopping also muffles the sound, however. Thus stopped notes stand out timbrally. Mozart tried to turn this limitation into an advantage, since in certain passages the special sonority of the stopped horn adds interesting accentuation. Leutgeb would have had to use a good many stopped notes in the *Romanze* of the Fourth Concerto, for example, since that movement is surprisingly chromatic. The effect of stopping is lost when the concertos are played on modern valve instruments, although the newer horns have far greater agility.

The history of the First Concerto is confused. It was once thought to have been written in 1782, with the second movement revised extensively in 1787. Recent research has suggested that this revision was in fact carried out after Mozart's death by an anonymous editor. Musicologist Alfred Einstein believed that the two movements originated in different pieces, since their orchestras differ: the bassoons of the first movement are omitted from the second. Another musicologist, Alan Tyson, has established the date of composition as 1791. Why the concerto has only two movements is an open question.

The Third Concerto has a subtlety and depth beyond what is found in the other concertos. The demands Mozart makes on Leutgeb are expressive as well as technical. Could the composer really have expected the man he ridiculed as a simpleton to have the emotional depth to project this work?

The limitations of the natural horn seem to have motivated certain alterations in the standard concerto form, particularly in the first movements. Since the instrument can play only some notes, a melody that can readily be performed in one key may be impossible in another. Thus Mozart had to change the normal pattern of key and theme relations, in order to assure that any tune he wished the horn to play would occur in an appropriate key. For example, the gentle second theme of K. 495, heard initially in the violins (joined after two measures by the oboe) just after the opening *forte* passage, is not given to the horn at the expected place. The natural horn cannot conveniently play it in the dominant key. Rather, the violins again take the tune when it comes in the dominant, while the horn accompanies. It is only much later, in the recapitulation, that the horn can at last play it — in the tonic. Similar adjustments to the standard sonata form occur in the other concertos.

The slow movements of the Second and Fourth Concertos are in B-flat major, while in the Third the *Romanze* is in A-flat. Because of the natural horn, the differences are considerable. Which scale degrees must be stopped differ (since all three concertos are written for horn in E-flat), and thus the slow movement of K. 447 has its own special mood, compared to that in two E-flat concertos (the First Concerto has no slow movement).

When the horn avoids stopped notes, it plays only notes of the overtone series. Overtone figures tend to sound like fanfares and hunting calls, since the traditional hunting horn is a valveless instrument. Thus it is not surprising to find hunting fanfares, particularly in the finales of all four concertos.

Concerto Number 9 in E-Flat Major for Piano and Orchestra, K. 271
Allegro
Andantino
Presto. Menuetto. Cantabile. Presto

The E-Flat Major Concerto was composed in January 1777. Mlle. Jeunehomme was probably the first performer, in Salzburg.

Mozart and his father Leopold were both employed by Archbishop Colloredo of Salzburg. Although for a time the elder Mozart was pleased with the post, he knew that his son was an exceptional talent deserving a major appointment in one of the musical centers of Europe, not in provincial Salzburg. Many trips abroad failed to find any offers of employment, however, and the father-and-son pair remained in the service of the Archbishop. Their situation deteriorated in 1776. In an attempt to economize, Colloredo closed his court theater. Furthermore, he became more exacting in the services he expected of his musicians. He began to resent the way Leopold was forever dragging his son off in search of better employment. He did not want his servants "running around like beggars."

The Archbishop's resentment soon turned to outright dislike. In a fit of anger he told Leopold that Wolfgang knew nothing about music and "ought to go to a conservatory in Naples in order to learn something."

Leopold planned another trip in March 1777. Wolfgang had recently completed — for a celebrated pianist named Mlle. Jeunehomme, who was visiting from Paris — the masterful Piano Concerto in E-Flat. The composer hoped it might help him secure a prestigious court or church post. He tried to sell the concerto to a publisher when he arrived in Paris 18 months later, but the publisher would not buy it, probably because the piece was too unusual. Biographer Alfred Einstein calls it "one of Mozart's monumental works, those works in which he is entirely himself, seeking not to ingratiate himself with his public but rather to win them through originality and boldness. He never surpassed it." Because of its power and uniqueness, Einstein calls the concerto "Mozart's *Eroica.*"

The Archbishop would not grant Mozart and his father leave to travel. He needed their services at upcoming ceremonies for the visiting Emperor. Leopold thought that perhaps Colloredo could be persuaded to allow Wolfgang to go while the elder musician remained behind. Wolfgang's mother could accompany him and try to keep the impulsive youth out of trouble.

Wolfgang petitioned the Archbishop to dismiss him so that he could travel. Colloredo's reply came swiftly: both father and son were fired. Leopold begged to be reinstated. The Archbishop accepted the elder composer's plea, but Leopold's self-esteem was considerably shaken. Wolfgang told his father to "laugh heartily and be jolly and cheerful and always remember, as we do, that [the Archbishop] is a jerk [actually, Mozart used a stronger word], but that God is compassionate." The young composer and his mother set off on what was destined to be yet another unsuccessful job hunt.

One aspect of the originality of K. 271 is the appearance of the piano in just the second measure of the piece. In his book on the Mozart piano concertos, Denis Forman suggests that Mozart's reason for this arresting opening may have been to get the attention of the Salzburg audiences and make them quiet down quickly. Although many later concertos bring in the solo instrument early, this practice was virtually unheard of in 1777. Beethoven subsequently did it in his Fourth and Fifth Concertos, but these pieces' openings work quite differently from the rapid dialogue of K. 271, in which the orchestra presents one motive and the piano answers with another. These two figure are repeated, and then the piano falls silent for the remainder of the orchestral exposition. This intrusion of the piano into the first orchestral *tutti* has consequences. Throughout the first movement the relationship between piano and orchestra often does not follow tradition. The piano re-enters, for example, a few measures before the end of the *tutti*. It plays a trill, followed by a brief solo, before the opening of the movement is restated. When the next orchestral *tutti* comes along, the piano interrupts it. The development section begins with a restatement of the opening dialogue. At the recapitulation, however, the roles are reversed: the piano plays the orchestra's motive, and the strings respond with the piano figure. The repetition of this dialogue returns to the original orchestration, however, with the piano extending its motive by an excursion into minor keys.

The beautiful slow movement is quite original in a different way. It is in a minor key, which was exceedingly rare for concertos in 1777. The beginning, with muted strings in canon over a pulsating bass, suggests opera. In the final measures biographer Einstein hears a distinct reference to recitative.

The finale's originality lies in the interpolation of a stately minuet — really a separate movement with four variations — into a brilliant rondo.

It would be a mistake to think of the concerto solely in terms of its innovations. It has a depth of feeling and an elegance of manner that are of far greater importance than its structural novelties. It is those qualities that have made the concerto endure.

Concerto Number 10 in E-Flat Major for Two Pianos and Orchestra, K. 316a (365)

Allegro
Andante
Allegro

The Concerto for Two Pianos was composed in Salzburg in 1779. Mozart and his sister Nannerl first performed the work there in that year.

In January 1779 Mozart returned to Salzburg from an extended journey to Munich, Augsberg, Mannheim, and Paris. He had been trying to find employment in those cities for the previous two years. All attempts had failed. His talents were no longer seen as those of an amazing child prodigy, and his lack of social graces was no longer cute. He now had to compete in a world full of talented musicians, most of whom knew how to behave around the aristocracy and nobility of Europe.

The journey had been filled with disappointments. Time after time Mozart failed to secure a position or to earn much money as a performer. Furthermore, he had found and then lost a woman he wanted to marry, and his mother, who had come with him, had died in Paris. On the other hand, the young man felt the excitement of being away from home and from his father's well-intentioned but sometimes oppressive dominance.

While in Mannheim and Paris, Mozart became acquainted with a new type of composition, known as the *symphonie concertante,* or concerto for more than one solo instrument with orchestra. The idea of multiple soloists in a concerto is reflected in the Concerto for Two Pianos, composed soon after Mozart returned to Salzburg.

After two more years in his native city, the composer moved permanently to Vienna, where he and his pupil Josephine von Aurnhammer frequently performed the Two-Piano Concerto. Mozart revised the orchestration to match the resources of the enlarged Vienna orchestra. The new version, with added clarinets, trumpets, and timpani, has not been preserved.

Although he had a low opinion of her pianistic abilities, he was willing to perform with von Aurnhammer (and also to dedicate to her six of his violin and piano sonatas). She, however, had other interests that Mozart, recently married, was unwilling to accommodate. The composer, who was not attracted to von Aurnhammer, described the aggressive pianist in a letter home: "If a painter wanted to portray the devil to the life, he would have to choose her face. She is as fat as a farm wench, perspires so that you feel inclined to vomit, and goes about so scantily clad that really you can read as plain as print: 'Pray, do look here.' True, there is enough to see, in fact, quite enough to strike one blind. But one is thoroughly well punished for the rest of the day if one is unlucky enough to let one's eyes wander in that direction."

Mozart conceived of the concerto form as an interplay and a dialogue, if not a confrontation, between soloist and orchestra. What happens to this idea when there are *two* soloists? Most of the *concertante* composers bypassed this question by writing lighthearted music that did not deal with the dramatic interaction or opposition between soloists. Although the Concerto for Two Pianos is carefree and happy on the surface, Mozart was not one to avoid compositional challenges. He realized that the dialogue principle could be transferred to the two solo instruments, although there was a danger of the orchestra becoming superfluous. His solution was to provide the soloists with a dialogue while relegating the orchestra — especially the winds — to a more background role than in his concertos for a single piano. He kept the orchestra small: pairs of bassoons (usually doubling the low strings), oboes, and horns; violins; and violas, cellos, and string basses all playing the same music. Mozart gives this orchestra plenty to do in *tutti* passages (although there are fewer measures devoted to the orchestra alone than in any other Mozart piano concerto), but once the pianos enter the focus is on them. They rarely accompany the orchestra, as often happens in concertos for one piano, and they do not share the orchestra's melodies as often as in the other concertos.

After the soloists enter the first movement on a four-octave trill followed by a run, they begin their dialogue. Everything the first piano says the second answers — by repeating, often with variations or elaborations. Notice how Mozart avoids the potential monotony of the dialogue format by constantly varying the length of time between responses, and also by overlapping. It is important that we hear the duetting with ample stereo separation or while carefully watching the pianists, in order to appreciate which pianist is playing at any given time.

The winds have somewhat greater prominence in the slow movement, with the result that the pianos are in dialogue less often. At times they combine as one cohesive instrumental unit. The dialogue principle returns to dominate the finale.

Concerto Number 14 in E-Flat Major for Piano and Orchestra, K. 449

Allegro vivace
Andantino
Allegro ma non troppo

The E-Flat Major Concerto was completed on 9 February 1784 in Vienna. Barbara Ployer played the premiere in that city probably in March 1784.

On 9 February 1784 Mozart began to keep a written record of all his compositions. The first entry was a piano concerto, later known as K. 449, completed that very day. Mozart kept the catalog up to date until about two weeks before his death. The listing filled 58 pages.

Mozart was at the height of his popularity at the time he started this diary. The Viennese public attended his concerts in great numbers, always eager to hear the latest concerto the composer had created to show off his own pianistic skills. He played frequently — 14 performances in 21 days during March 1784, for example — but nonetheless had time to compose 15 piano concertos within five years: three in 1782–83, six in 1784, three in 1785, and three in 1786. This remarkable series of works chronicles Mozart's development during this period far better than do his symphonies, sonatas, or quartets. Each concerto is a gem, different from the others because of its unique approach to the traditional form.

Much as he disliked doing it, Mozart was forced even from his first years in Vienna to supplement his income by teaching. One of his better students was Barbara Ployer, daughter of the agent of the Archbishop of Salzburg. As she wanted a piece for her own use as a soloist, she commissioned Mozart to write the E-Flat Concerto. Once she had premiered it, he was concerned over the future of the music. Since Babette had paid him handsomely for it, it rightly belonged to her. If Mozart did not have the work printed, however, Babette would have the only copy in existence. On the other hand, if Mozart were to have it engraved, he feared that the engraver would print extra copies and sell them himself. In the days before copyright protection, composers faced real problems in trying to earn money from their works. Mozart finally decided to have the music hand-copied for his own use. To ensure that the copyists did not cheat him, he made them work under his scrutiny at his house.

By the end of three months, Mozart had written three more piano concertos. He compared the four in a letter to his father: "I am curious to learn which of the three, in B-flat, D, and G, you and my sister like most. The one in E-flat does not at all belong to the same category. It is of a quite peculiar kind, composed rather for a small orchestra than for a large one." The orchestra includes only two oboes and two horns in addition to the strings. Mozart constructed the piece so that it could be played with or without the winds or even as a chamber quintet (piano, two violins, viola, and cello).

Concerto Number 17 in G Major for Piano and Orchestra, K. 453

Allegro
Andante
Allegretto. Presto

The G Major Piano Concerto was begun in late March 1784 and completed on 12 April 1784. Barbara Ployer was the pianist at the first performance at Döbling, Austria, on 10 June 1784.

Like most composers of today, Mozart was unable to earn a living just from his compositions. He was forced to secure his primary income from teaching, which he did not particularly like. Soon after moving to Vienna, he wrote to his father, "I could not get on at all without pupils, which is a kind of work that is quite uncongenial for me. . . . I am a composer and was born to be a *Kapellmeister,* and I neither can nor ought to bury the talent for composition with which God in His goodness has so richly endowed me."

He almost enjoyed working with his more talented students, however. One of his accomplished pupils was Barbara Ployer, daughter of the agent of the Archbishop of Salzburg. Mozart liked Babette, and he wrote counterpoint exercises for her lessons and composed two concertos for her to perform — the E-flat Major, K. 449, and the G Major, K. 453. She premiered the G Major at a concert in the country arranged by her father. She and Mozart played the Sonata for Two Pianos, K. 448, at the same concert.

A few weeks after completing the concerto, Mozart happened to hear a caged starling sing a tune very similar to the main theme of the concerto's finale. The composer was taken by this extraordinary coincidence and by the beauty of the bird's song. He purchased the starling and kept it as his pet. When it died, Mozart buried it and wrote a short poem for its gravestone.

To what extent did Mozart's intention to write for Babette Ployer influence the resulting composition? It is impossible to know, but we may speculate that the concerto's graceful, elegant character is appropriate for a feminine performer. We may also speculate that Mozart wanted to experiment with a different kind of concerto when writing for a performer other than himself. The G Major is quite unlike any of its predecessors, and Mozart may have felt that, should the concerto fail to please its audiences, the performer would have to share the blame. We may also suspect that, since the concerto contains few difficult passages, it was written for a less than professional pianist.

The first movement has been characterized as "full of hidden laughter and hidden sadness"; possessing a "continuous iridescence of feeling"; having a "wistful quality"; like a ghostly march. It is very special music, difficult to capture verbally. Without better knowledge of Barbara Ployer, we cannot know to what extent her personality influenced the music. But the movement does have a unique atmosphere.

The second movement begins with an unusual melody that seems at first unable to break away from its initial note, to which it inevitably returns five measures later. This phrase is followed by a dramatic pause — quite unexpected so early in the movement. That silence is an integral part of the theme. Every time the opening melody returns, it is followed by the pause. During the silence we await with suspense the continuation, never quite knowing what will happen next. Sometimes the music moves unexpectedly into a distant key. Sometimes it continues more normally. The last time the main theme is heard, after the cadenza, it is tamed. It no longer returns inevitably to its initial note and it no longer is followed by silence.

The finale is a set of variations on the starling theme, which many commentators find similar to Papageno's music in the opera *The Magic Flute*. The theme is in two halves, each repeated. The piano enters for the first variation, which is a direct ornamentation of the theme. In the second variation winds have the theme, accompanied by strings. For the third variation the winds ornament the theme to a repeated-note accompaniment in the strings; on the repeat of each half, the piano takes over the wind melody over an Alberti bass of continuous sixteenth notes. The fourth variation moves away from the tune into the mysterious key of G minor, with the orchestra playing first and the piano alone playing the repeats. The alternation of orchestra and piano continues in the forceful fifth variation, which returns to the major mode but remains far from the original version of the theme. The movement closes with a long coda, in which the operatic nature of the music becomes evident. Along with new melodies, the main theme is utilized, but not in a systematic manner: the coda is not a further variation. This good-humored final passage ends as piano and orchestra alternate at ever closer time intervals.

Concerto Number 19 in F Major for Piano and Orchestra, K. 459
>   Allegro
>   Allegretto
>   Allegro assai

The F Major Concerto was completed on 11 December 1784 and first performed shortly thereafter by the composer in Vienna.

If we listen in chronological order to the 15 piano concertos Mozart composed between 1782 and 1786, we hear the gradual deepening of his art. As the later concertos became more profound, they began to puzzle their intended audiences. Thus the form that had brought Mozart his greatest popular success also caused his downfall. The turning point is the Concerto in D Minor, the first one composed in 1785 — a brooding, impassioned work that must have perplexed some of its first listeners. The transition away from superficially appealing music came gradually, and the next concertos do not directly continue the *sturm und drang* (literally, "storm and stress") of K. 466. But the seed was planted, and it grew to produce the magnificent late music, in which Mozart — no doubt without consciously choosing to do so — evolved toward a more rarified style. This change in style brought a critical diminishing of the composer's popularity and with it a drastic lessening of his income.

The contrast between the type of music that gained Mozart a strong following in Vienna and that which lost him his admirers can be readily heard if we compare K. 466 with its immediate predecessor, the Concerto in F, K. 459, the last concerto of 1784. In the light-hearted gaiety of the F Major we hear no hint of the turbulence that was to emerge just two months later. K. 459 is in an obviously populist style; it is a piece made to appeal, which it does exceedingly well. It is also a magnificently crafted work — notice in particular the learned counterpoint in the finale — but complexities lie beneath its graceful surface. The F Major is one of the most charming and exuberant of the concertos.

The character of the concerto is established immediately by the march-like main theme. This melody is one of several, but it dominates the movement and thereby minimizes the sense of conflict between themes. Absent also is the dramatic confrontation between solo instrument and orchestra that is a source of tension in K. 466 and other Mozart concertos. Here the piano functions often as accompaniment to the orchestra, and the solo interludes tend to be short and unassuming: there is little outright virtuosity. The movement is urbane and elegantly polished, the epitome of the classical and a surefire success with the Viennese listeners who wanted to be entertained more than challenged in the concert hall.

The second movement is as graceful as the first. Ostensibly the slow movement, its tempo marking is *allegretto*. Again there is little conflict to disturb the music's gentle flow. Conflict appears at last in the finale — not an impassioned confrontation, but enough of a drama to make this movement the concerto's emotional center. The conflict is not so much between piano and orchestra, nor particularly between tonal areas, but actually between types of music. This allegro begins with an innocent melody in dialogue between the piano and the winds. Suddenly and unexpectedly, this simple tune is replaced by carefully worked-out, almost academic counterpoint in the strings and winds. Where does this music come from? It is unprecedented and unprepared. The carefree first theme returns as if nothing had happened, but we cannot forget the incongruous interruption. The remainder of the movement accomplishes the reconciliation of these two very different impulses. The two themes begin to invade one another and, despite a complex, almost fugal working out of the contrapuntal impulse, the two moods do eventually come together. After the cadenza, the brief close is devoted to the happy main theme, which now is unthreatened by the seriousness of imitative counterpoint. A work which begins without conflict ends by regaining its innocence.

Concerto Number 20 in D Minor for Piano and Orchestra, K. 466

     Allegro
     Romanza
     Allegro assai

The D Minor Concerto was completed on 10 February 1785 and first performed that same day by the composer in Vienna.

When Mozart moved from Salzburg to Vienna in 1781, he left behind the security of regular employment. He had been court organist for the Archbishop of Salzburg, but he felt the need for independence. His Vienna years were spent in the financially precarious position of a free-lance composer. At first his prospects were good. He was able to find a number of piano students, and he received several commissions and performing engagements. Mozart was much in demand as a piano soloist, and thus the decade in Vienna saw the composition of no fewer than 17 piano concertos, written mostly for his own use.

     The composer had scored one triumph after another by the time his father Leopold came from Salzburg for a visit in 1785. Leopold was overwhelmed by Wolfgang's successes. He wrote to the composer's sister Nannerl,

> From the fact that your brother pays 460 *gulden* rent, you may conclude that he has a fine lodging with all appropriate furnishings. . . . We went to his first subscription concert, where there

was a big crowd of distinguished people.... The concert was incomparable and the orchestra excellent. Besides the symphonies there were two arias sung by a woman from the Italian opera. Then there was a new, excellent concerto by Wolfgang, which the copyist was still working on when we arrived. Your brother had not even the time to play the rondo because he was still supervising the copying.

The new concerto was Number 20 in D Minor.

Of another of Wolfgang's many concerts, Leopold wrote, "Your brother played a wonderful concerto, which he had composed for Mlle. Paradis.... When your brother left the podium, the Emperor made a complimentary gesture with his hat is his hand and cried, 'Bravo Mozart!' When he came forth to play, he was applauded."

Just when he was at the height of this popularity, Mozart began to write a subtly different kind of music, particularly in his piano concertos. He had gained fame with a series of finely crafted, elegant, appealing works which posed no challenges to listeners. But, beginning with the D Minor Concerto, he turned his back on this socially popular idiom and began to compose more daring and experimental works. There has been considerable speculation on the reasons for these changes. Was Mozart disillusioned with music composed for social occasions? Was he deliberatety challenging a public whose adoration he had begun to take for granted? Did the changes come from an inner urge over which he had no control? The answer will never be known.

The results of Mozart's change in style are well documented, however. His popularity began to fall and with it his ability to earn a living. His last three symphonies and last two piano concertos were composed not in answer to commissions but on speculation. Mozart hoped (in vain, as it turned out) that they would eventually bring him some money. His struggle against poverty was continual. He composed prolifically, and often enough his music was applauded, but the deepening complexities of the late works certainly did not help his career. Luckily for future generations of listeners, Mozart did not — or could not — subjugate his artistic integrity to the demands of the marketplace. Even in specifically commissioned pieces we find the composer's strong personality asserting itself over the conventions of style.

This turn away from social music began with the D Minor Concerto. The public was divided. Some people loved the work, but other listeners were perplexed by its overt passions. A concerto was supposed to be an appealing showpiece for a performer's virtuosity, was it not? There was little precedent for such intense expression in a work for piano and orchestra. While only a few subsequent compositions of Mozart explore the brooding world of this concerto, the seeds of experimentation had been planted. The concerto looks forward to later masterpieces in specific ways — the key of D minor foreshadows the emotional depths of *Don Giovanni* and the small opening motive in the low strings presages the beginning of the *Jupiter* Symphony.

The concerto also looks forward to the romantic age, when overt emotionalism was to become no longer the exception but rather the norm. Few of the other Mozart concertos interested nineteenth-century composers or performers, who tended to dismiss them as superficial or anachronistic. But the D Minor was understood as a precursor of Beethoven's titanism. Had not Beethoven, after all, paid homage to this work by writing his own cadenzas for its outer movements? (Beethoven also learned from Mozart's only other minor-key piano concerto, Number 24 in C Minor, which became a model for Beethoven's Third Concerto.)

The tendency of the romantic century to "Beethovenize" Mozart (the term is borrowed from Mozart's biographer Hugh Ottaway) was based on a failure to understand the earlier composer's art. This is hardly surprising, since history is full of examples of new movements springing from misconceptions of past generations' achievements. The emotions of the D Minor Concerto are only half its story. The work is also elegantly restrained in a thoroughly classical manner. Its great power comes from the balance of passion and understatement. But the nineteenth century heard only the passions and thus conceived the work as a stepping stone to Beethoven's even more intense minor-key compositions.

Mozart scholar Alfred Einstein explains the sources of pathos and drama in this concerto:

This is the first work in which the *tutti* and the solo in the allegro are sharply contrasted, in a dualism there is no attempt to overcome. The orchestra represents an anonymous threatening power, and the solo instrument voices an eloquent lament. The orchestra never takes over the first theme of the solo part, a *recitativo in tempo*, or the second half of the second theme. The opposition of the two permits no reconciliation; it is only intensified in the development section. Nor does the reprise offer any solution: the *pianissimo* conclusion of the movement is as if the furies had simply become tired out and had lain down to rest, still grumbling, and ready at any instant to take up the fight again. And they do take it up again, in the middle section (in G minor) of the *romanza*, which begins and ends in such heavenly tranquillity. Mozart never included stronger contrasts within a single work, contrasts among the three movements as well as within each movement individually.... The finale contains chromatically intensified and refined passion and drama, announced at the very beginning in the rocket-like principal motive. But this time Mozart wishes to conquer his pessimism and despair. After the cadenza he turns towards the major, in a coda of enchanting sweetness, which represents at the same time an affecting ray of light and, in slight degree, a return to the social atmosphere of earlier works, the courtly gesture of a grand seigneur who wishes to leave his guests with a friendly impression. But this is not at all the childlike or grandiose optimism of Haydn or Beethoven.

◆   ◆   ◆

Concerto Number 21 in C Major for Piano and Orchestra, K. 467

Allegro maestoso
Andante
Allegro vivace assai

The C Major Concerto was completed on 9 March 1785 and first performed the next day by the composer in Vienna.

A few years after Mozart moved from Salzburg to Vienna, his father came for a visit. Leopold, who had always taken an active interest in Wolfgang's career, was eager to share in his son's newfound successes. Leopold set out from Salzburg on 28 January. He arrived on 11 February to find his fortunate son living in luxurious quarters. That same night Leopold attended a concert at which Wolfgang premiered "a new and very fine concerto." This work, K. 466 in D Minor, had been completed the day of the concert, and, as usual, there was no time for rehearsal. Nonetheless "the concert was incomparable and the orchestra played splendidly," Leopold wrote home.

Leopold had cause to be even more impressed the next day. Haydn came by to visit Mozart, and Leopold and Wolfgang joined the brothers Tinti in playing some of the string quartets Mozart had recently finished and intended to dedicate to Haydn. Haydn said to Leopold, "I tell you before God, as an honest man, that your son is the greatest composer that I know, in person or by name. He has taste and, added to that, the greatest knowledge of composition."

Leopold was to be dazzled yet again on the next day. Wolfgang played a concert in the presence of the Emperor, who waved his hat and shouted, "Bravo, Mozart!" And so it went. Leopold remained in Vienna another five weeks, exhilirated again and again by his son's successes.

On 10 March Mozart gave a concert for his own benefit. On it he played another new piano concerto, K. 467. This work, written only a month after K. 466, is totally different from it. Expansive rather than taut, full of military pomp rather than romantic passion, this concerto was an enormous success. Leopold expressed some doubts about its difficulty and about certain dissonances, probably in the slow movement, but the piece was well received.

The composer felt confident enough of his popularity to lessen his concerns for public taste in his concertos — the brooding nature of K. 466, the dissonances in K. 467, the minor mode in K. 466 and K. 491, and the minor-mode slow movements of K. 482 and K. 488 are examples of his growing independence from "social" music during his successful Vienna years.

Mozart's father left Vienna on 20 March, happy yet exhausted. He was never to see his son again, as Leopold died two years later.

Martial rhythms and emphasis on trumpets and drums set the tone for the first movement of K. 467. It contains no fewer than eight independent melodies, many with a highly rhythmic character and most rather short. The working out of this mosaic of varied materials requires a lengthy movement. There are some bold harmonic excursions that cloud the sunny world of C major — further examples of Mozart's growing disdain for popular appeal.

The slow movement contrasts with the martial first. It contains the lyricism that the opening movement pointedly avoids. Furthermore, the andante has its own special sound, created in part by the scoring — muted strings, frequent *pizzicato*, subdivided viola section — and in part by the pungent harmonies. These dissonances actually caused Leopold to suspect a copyist's error!

The finale reconciles the divergent moods of the other two movements. Based on a theme used earlier in the Concerto for Two Pianos, K. 365, this rondo has great sophistication and understated wit. Its elegant surface disguises considerable subtlety.

Concerto Number 22 in E-Flat Major for Piano and Orchestra, K. 482

Allegro
Andante
Allegro. Andantino cantabile. Allegro

Concerto Number 23 in A Major for Piano and Orchestra, K. 488

Allegro
Adagio
Allegro assai

Concerto Number 24 in C Minor for Piano and Orchestra, K. 491

Allegro
Larghetto
Allegretto

The Concerto K. 482 was finished on 16 December 1785 and first performed in Vienna by Mozart on 23 December. The A Major Concerto was completed on 2 March 1786 and premiered in Vienna a few weeks later, during one of Mozart's Lenten concerts. The C Minor Concerto was completed on 24 March 1786 and was first performed shortly thereafter by the composer.

In the winter of 1785–86, Mozart was busily involved with stage works. His principal project was *The Marriage of Figaro*. Three times he took time out from opera composition to compose piano concertos. The resulting works, far from being trifles used to relax and divert his energies from the more taxing dramatic work, are true masterpieces. The Concertos in E-Flat Major, A Major, and C Minor are among Mozart's greatest achievements, despite the fact that each was written within a few weeks *while* he continued to work on *Figaro*. This is truly astounding!

Both the E-Flat Major and the A Major Concertos represent the composer's temporary return to a popular style. Perhaps he felt that he had gone too far into subjective romanticism in his previous concertos, or possibly he sensed that public enthusiasm, upon which he depended for his livelihood, was diminishing. His return to music written with a nod toward the public was not an artistic compromise, however. Mozart's genius was broad enough to allow composing for specific tastes. As Mozart scholar Alfred Einstein explains, he met his public halfway without sacrificing his own individuality.

K. 482 in particular looks back to Mozart's earlier, less complex music, in particular the two earlier piano concertos also in E-Flat — K. 271 and K. 365 for two pianos. The finale of K. 482, like that of K. 271, includes a self-contained miniature movement. The horn motives in the first movement of K. 482 also recall its predecessor.

The work is Mozart's biggest piano concerto: possibly his longest, it is surely the most fully scored. The orchestra includes one flute, two clarinets (their first appearance in a Mozart concerto), two bassoons, two horns, two trumpets, timpani, and strings. We know from the outset that the concerto is conceived on a grand scale: the orchestral *tutti* contains a wealth of themes and motives, most of which are destined to be developed at length. When the piano finally enters, it is with still more new material, which eventually gives way to a restatement of the opening.

The atmosphere of the second movement is something quite different. Einstein describes the piece as "almost an exhibition of sadness, false consolation, despair, and resignation." This extraordinarily beautiful, intense, personal, and dissonant movement is one of Mozart's most memorable achievements. There is poignant string music, such as the opening for muted violins, and there is delectable wind writing, in particular a duet for high and low clarinets (during the variation for winds alone) and a dialogue between flute and bassoon. This music was certainly not conceived primarily as a bid for applause. Yet the first audience understood the movement's sublimities and demanded its repetition before the concerto could proceed. Such a procedure was acceptable in the eighteenth century, although Mozart concerto movements rarely evoked such enthusiasm.

The finale is a rondo with a 6/8 hunting-horn theme. This movement, like its predecessors, is painted on a broad canvas. Just when the movement seems about to end, it moves into a new key (A-flat major), meter (3/4), and tempo (*andantino cantabile*) for a complete contrast. The original music returns, with the hunting theme finally played by the horns at the end.

The mood of each of the three concertos is closely associated with its key. It may not matter to us (or at least to those of us who do not have absolute pitch) that K. 482 is in E-flat major or that K. 488 is in A major. But the choice of tonality mattered a great deal to Mozart. He did have perfect pitch, and he associated each key with a particular expression. E-flat major, A major, and C minor are each allied with a special mood in Mozart's mature works. A major, for example, suggests a certain tranquil beauty, common to such works as the Fifth Violin Concerto, the Piano Sonata K. 331, the Clarinet Concerto, the Clarinet Quintet, and the Piano Concerto K. 488. It is furthermore no coincidence that two of these well-known A major pieces feature the clarinet. The sound of that instrument seems to have contributed to Mozart's A major mood. It is significant, therefore, that K. 488 omits the usual oboes, whose sonority may have been too strident for this A major piece, in favor of clarinets, rarely used in Mozart's piano concertos (K. 482 also uses clarinet instead of oboes: the clarinet timbre has something to do with E-flat major as well as A major).

The slow movement of K. 488 is in F-sharp minor, a key represented nowhere else in the Mozart piano concertos. It too has a particular mood, which may be described as restrained passion. The movement is colorfully orchestrated, with delectable passages for the wind choir and for *pizzicato* strings. The closing, with high repeated notes in the piano, is particularly beautiful.

The finale returns to the mood of A major, although with a few reminders of the world of F-sharp minor. The movement is a rondo with many different themes.

The carefree gaiety of the E-Flat Concerto and unruffled grace of the A Major Concerto differ markedly from the tragic intensity of their successor in C minor. C minor was a vastly different key from E-flat major and A major for Mozart. Interestingly, the slow movement of K. 482 is also in C minor, and its mood is similar to that of K. 491. Although K. 491 was composed just a few weeks after K. 482 and K. 488, and although all three works were written under the influence of *Figaro*, a greater contrast could hardly be imagined. The E-Flat Major is forthright and assertive and the A Major is gentle and understated, while the C Minor is dark and brooding. As musicologist Einstein has written, the composer "evidently needed to indulge in an explosion of dark, tragic, passionate emotion." No record remains of how the C Minor Concerto's first audiences reacted to it, but they probably had difficulty assimilating the outer movements. This concerto is obviously not an example of Mozart's "social" music.

Composing K. 491 gave the composer some trouble, despite the fact that he completed it only twelve days after finishing the A Major. The original score contains numerous corrections, changes, and rewritings, including up to four reworkings of some passages. Such indecision is uncharacteristic of Mozart, who often composed an entire work in his head before setting it down — without need of revising — on paper.

Some commentators consider this concerto a precursor of nineteenth-century romanticism. Indeed it does display its emotions overtly, in its chromatic themes, adherence to the minor mode even in the finale, rich instrumentation, and passionate outbursts. It is more than an anticipation of a later aesthetic, however. It *is* a fully romantic conception. Just as Haydn wrote romantic music in his *Stürm und Drang* (literally, "storm and stress") period, so Mozart on occasion wrote music overtly expressive of the darker side of human feeling. Most of his pieces in C minor (and also those in G minor) share this atmosphere. It is no surprise that Beethoven, the composer who more than anyone expanded the romantic ideal in music, greatly respected this concerto. He studied it, performed it, and paid homage to it in his own Third Concerto, also in C minor.

The first movement has a wealth of thematic material, but it is dominated by its opening melody, an elaboration of a chromatic descent which contains hints of most of the movement's subsequent harmonic regions. This tune is decidedly non-pianistic and in fact is never heard unadorned or complete in the solo instrument. This theme is launched no fewer than three times in the orchestra prior to the entrance of the piano. Mozart's typical tonal strategy works powerfully here: the music refuses to leave the turbulent home key of C minor throughout the entire orchestral exposition. An undercurrent of tension mounts as we await, with growing impatience, tonal motion. The piano enters at long last, but not with the main melodic material. Once the piano breaks into rapidly moving sixteenth notes, we understand the solo instrument as catalyst. The sixteenths take the music away from the tonic toward the sunnier, less intense world of the relative major. There we remain, hearing several new thematic ideas which try to dispel the world of C minor. Excitment builds in the development section, but inevitably the music returns to the main theme in the original key. In most other minor-key concertos, material that originates in the relative major in the exposition returns in the happier key of the tonic major in the recapitulation and thereby lays to rest the movement's principal tensions. Not here! The recapitulation stays relentlessly in C minor. Once the cadenza ends, the coda brings the movement to a quiet end that suggests neither resolution nor relaxation.

The insistence on the minor mode in the first movement makes the major-mode opening of the slow movement extraordinarily beautiful. The utter simplicity of this first theme adds to its beauty. The poignant world of the first movement is not to be forgotten, as the music returns to C minor for the first of two episodes, featuring the woodwinds. The movement subsequently avoids C minor.

A halting yet somehow graceful C minor tune, that never goes more than four measures without stopping, opens the last movement. The pauses in the main theme are filled in a variety of ways in the ensuing variations: first with piano figurations, then bassoon arpeggios, etc. Unlike in most minor-mode concertos, the finale does not move decisively to the uncomplicated world of the tonic major. The music twice tantalizes us with almost carefree variations — one in the relative major, one in the tonic major — but it always returns from its journeys to the home key of C minor. And there it ends, with an almost dance-like variation that goes directly into a coda.

Concerto Number 25 in C Major for Piano and Orchestra, K. 503

Allegro maestoso
Andante
Allegretto

The C Major Concerto was completed on 4 December 1786 and probably performed the next day by the composer.

Mozart had moved to Vienna to seek fame and a livelihood from his music. For a time he was successful, but his fortunes began to change with the premiere of the opera *The Marriage of Figaro* in May 1786. There were now a number of factors creating difficulties for the composer. He was entering a period of compositional experimentation, of discovering new forms and procedures, with little regard for public reaction. The C Major Concerto, composed at the end of 1786, was in many ways an experimental work. It eschews lyrical melodies to a large extent (at least in the first movement), and it matches this melodic austerity with harmonic economy.

Frustrated over his dwindling reputation in Vienna, the composer thought of trying his fortunes in London, and even went so far as to ask his father to babysit for his children while he and his wife traveled to England. The elder Mozart remarked sarcastically, "Not at all a bad arrangement! They go off and travel — they might even die — or remain in England — and I should have to run after them with their children!" The trip never materialized. Mozart was forced to try to earn some money in Vienna, despite the decreasing number of subscribers to his concerts. He composed the C Major Concerto for a concert in December 1786 he hoped would bring in some money.

Surprisingly, considering the novelties in the concerto, the concert was a success. K. 503 actually became one of Mozart's most popular concertos, probably because of its grand gestures and heroic length. It is the only Mozart piano concerto that received several performances by different pianists while it was still quite new. Beethoven chose to play it at one of his first concert appearances in Vienna (his fondness for the work remained with him, if subconsciously: the entrance of the piano in the development section of his Fourth Concerto is directly modeled on the comparable place in K. 503).

The concerto is no longer among the public's favorites. Commentators have accused it of less than superb melodic inventiveness, and perhaps this fact is responsible for the relatively few performances given it today (many major American orchestras did not present the concerto at all until well into the twentieth century). The opening theme, for example, is not the kind of tune you walk out of a concert humming. Surely Mozart knew this. Why, then, did he choose to begin his longest and most elaborate piano concerto with a non-lyrical tune? It is impossible to know his reasoning, of course, but it is instructive to speculate. Perhaps, for a concerto in the most basic key of C major (no sharps, no flats), he wanted to explore a basic and simple relationship: the identity between melody and harmony.

In the opening theme the same notes make up both the fanfare-like motive and the chords under it. In other words, there are no "non-harmonic tones." A more famous example of this procedure is the opening of Beethoven's *Eroica* Symphony. That piece begins with two E-flat major triads, followed by a melody using only the notes of the E-flat chord. The Mozart concerto begins with a "melody" that uses just the notes of a C major triad; the harmony is also C major. This kind of subtlety, deriving from the very nature of classical tonality, may have been more meaningful and more striking to performers and listeners in the late eighteenth century than today, since by now we have heard many pieces that derive melodies and harmonies from the same source.

But why should Mozart want to begin a concerto in such a manner? Does the unity of melody and harmony compensate somehow for the purposeful melodic impoverishment? Most of the other Mozart piano concertos begin with (one of) their most memorable melodies. Since he usually counts on our recognizing this melody when it recurs later in the movement, Mozart wants initially to engage our attention with its attractiveness. In this concerto he catches our attention in another way: by the bold C major fanfare. This too will be readily remembered and recognized. Yet, intrigued by this special opening, we also await a truly lyrical theme. We do eventually get to hear one, and then another. Making us wait for tunefulness is an engaging compositional strategy.

Was this strategy Mozart's conscious intention? Probably not, as he wrote the concerto in only a few weeks, at the same time he was working on the *Prague* Symphony (completed only two days after he finished the concerto). He scarcely had time to get notes onto music paper, let alone to ponder subtleties of musical form. But his lack of conscious intention does not mean that the sophisticated strategy outlined above does not matter. Mozart's superb inner ear intuitively took care of the elegant structures which music analysts today study and praise.

In his wonderful book *The Classical Style*, pianist-critic Charles Rosen presents some fascinating ideas about the unusual thematic structure of this movement.

> The Concerto in C Major . . . is a magnificent and — to many ears — a cold work. Yet it is the one that many musicians (historians and pianists alike) single out with special affection. The unattractiveness for the public comes from the almost neutral character of the material: in the first movement in particular this material is not even sufficiently characterized to be called banal. An opening phrase built as a series of blocks from an arpeggio cannot be called even a cliché. It is conventional, highly so, but in no pejorative sense: it is merely the basic material of late eighteenth-century tonality, the bedrock of style. Even a later, more attractive theme in a military spirit is equally conventional in this sense: like bread, it cannot cloy.
>
> The splendor of the work and the delight it can inspire come entirely from the handling of the material. There are other concertos of Mozart in which the material is almost wholly conventional — K. 451, for instance, of which Mozart was so proud, and K. 415 — but none of them reveals the powers of K. 503. The different ideas in the first movement are treated in block fashion: in spite of the masterly transitions, we are conscious of the juxtaposition of large elements, and above all we are aware of their weight. Indeed, throughout this concerto, we are made to feel how much pressure the form itself can bring to bear even while using almost completely inexpressive ideas.

Cold? Completely inexpressive? These are strange words to describe music by Mozart. Perhaps Rosen exaggerates; perhaps better words would be "reserved" and "objective." But he does have a point. The concerto is incredibly far removed from, for example, the overtly emotional and deeply melodic Concerto in D Minor, K. 466. The amazing thing about the series of twelve piano concertos (of which K. 503 is the last) he wrote within the span of only three years is their variety. No two are alike structurally, dramatically, or melodically. Thus it is not surprising to find one concerto that attracts us not so much by the sumptuousness of its materials as by their elegant manipulation.

Interestingly, after the experiment of creating "tranquil power" (Rosen's term) by other than melodic means, Mozart lost interest to a large extent in the concerto form. He wrote only two more piano concertos in his remaining five years.

The melodic austerity of the first movement of K. 503 is underscored harmonically. This is not a movement where Mozart modulates wildly or widely, and the actual harmonies are quite restrained. The predominant color, as Rosen points out, comes from the juxtaposition of tonic major and tonic minor, along with the latter's relative major. Such relationships are not very dramatic nor very far reaching, but they are rich enough to make this music wonderfully expressive despite the patent inexpressiveness of some of its melodies.

Rosen comments:

> In general the lyricism of Mozart's works lies in the details, and the larger structure is an organizing force; in K. 503 the details are largely conventional, and the most striking expressive force comes from the larger formal elements, even to the point of pervading a heavily symphonic style with melancholy and tenderness. For the most part, too, this melancholy arises miraculously from the simplest of changes from major to minor. . . . The emotion is less poignant than in some of the other concertos, but it is the combination of breadth and subtlety that has made this work so admired.

Concerto Number 26 in D Major for Piano and Orchestra, K. 537, *Coronation*

    Allegro
    Larghetto
    Allegretto

The Coronation *Concerto was completed on 24 February 1788. There is no record of a performance at that time, but Mozart did perform it in April 1789 in Dresden.*

Mozart's relations with Archduke Leopold were never good. The composer's father tried in 1772 to secure for his 17-year-old son a position with the Archduke. A similar attempt a few months earlier had failed to get Mozart a job with Leopold's brother, largely because the Archduke's mother considered the Mozarts "useless people" and "beggars." Leopold followed his brother's lead by refusing the Mozarts' request.

The composer had no further dealings with Leopold until many years later. The Archduke succeeded to the Austrian throne when Emperor Joseph II died in 1790. Mozart had been receiving a small stipend from Joseph. The amount was not great, but the services Mozart rendered for this honorarium were minimal as well. He is supposed to have written on his tax return, next to the entry listing this income, "Too much for what I do; too little for what I could do!"

Mozart hoped not only to retain his stipend once Leopold was installed as Emperor but also to upgrade his position. He petitioned Leopold to be considered for the post of second *Kapellmeister,* a job that had been held by Antonio Salieri at Joseph's court. Mozart implied to his friends and creditors that he had a good chance of landing the job. As usual, Mozart was "building castles in the air," in the words of biographer Alfred Einstein. The composer went so far as to ask another Archduke to intercede in his behalf.

Leopold was not about to entrust the musical education of his children to someone with as questionable a reputation as Mozart's. The Emperor's Italian wife, furthermore, had dismissed Mozart's opera *La Clemenza di Tito* — performed a year earlier when Leopold was made King of Bohemia — as "German rubbish." Leopold offered Mozart no employment.

When Leopold was crowned Emperor in October 1790, an official delegation of musicians, headed by Salieri, was sent from Vienna to Frankfurt, where the coronation took place. This group pointedly did not include Mozart. He did not give up easily, however. He decided to go to the coronation on his own, in the hopes of finding some sympathetic employer among the many noblemen in attendance. The composer pawned his silver in order to buy a coach. He and his brother-in-law set off on what was to be one of his last journeys.

Mozart was optimistic, but for no justifiable cause. His letters to his wife show that he remained the impractical dreamer his father had always deplored: "I am firmly resolved to make as much money as I can here and then return to you with great joy. What a glorious life we shall have then!"

Mozart gave one concert in Frankfurt. Since the occasion was the coronation, he played a particularly festive work, the Piano Concerto in D. It had been composed over two years earlier, for a Lenten concert that had not taken place. Mozart had performed the piece in the meantime in Dresden. For Frankfurt he added trumpets and timpani, thereby justifying the nickname *Coronation* Concerto.

As was often the case with Mozart, the concert was an artistic success and a financial failure. He received no offers of employment, either from the new Emperor or from anyone else, and few people attended the concert.

The D Major Concerto was an appropriate choice for a celebratory concert. It is direct and approachable to the point of simplicity. The relationship between piano and orchestra is uncomplicated, as is the solo part itself. Actually, we do not know exactly what Mozart played when he was soloist, because the manuscript is not complete.

The composer never wrote out the piano music fully. The left hand is quite sketchy. He did not need exact notation to perform the work himself, and there is no evidence that he wanted anyone else to play it. In fact, by not filling in the solo line he protected himself against the work being copied, performed, or published by others.

The concerto first appeared in print three years after Mozart's death, in an anonymous edition that fills in — sometimes skillfully, sometimes not — the missing parts of the piano music. We will never fully know how Mozart intended the concerto to be played. Did he envision it as the simple and direct work we know, or did he ornament and elaborate it while he performed?

Concerto Number 27 in B-Flat Major for Piano and Orchestra, K. 595
Allegro
Larghetto
Allegro

Mozart's last piano concerto was completed on 5 January 1791. It was first performed on 4 March of the same year in Vienna.

Although the often-repeated story that Mozart died in poverty is an exaggeration, it is true that his popularity and hence his ability to earn a living slid steadily downward during his last years. While he composed twelve piano concertos between 9 February 1784 and 4 December 1786, he wrote only two more in his remaining five years. He was losing his public. People were less and less willing to pay to hear Mozart perform a new piano concerto. By the time of his last effort in the genre, K. 595 in B-flat, he could not afford to give an entire concert of his own. The last piano concerto had to be premiered on an "academy" given by clarinetist Joseph Bähr. In an advertisement for the concert, Mozart is given last billing, after Bähr and a singer.

Writers on Mozart are fond of characterizing K. 595 as his farewell concerto. Alfred Einstein, for example, calls it his "confession . . . that life had lost attraction for him." Einstein also mentions a "mood of resignation" and "the depths of sadness," and he believes that the finale's mood of "resigned cheerfulness . . . comes from the knowledge that this is the last spring." Biographer Hugh Ottoway describes "a veiled sadness that masquerades as gaiety." While not denying the autumnal qualities of this music, one cannot help wondering how latter-day commentators would understand K. 595 if

Mozart's health had improved, if he had lived another forty or fifty years, if he had composed another two dozen piano concertos.

What gives the concerto its special aura? After all, it is in B-flat *major*, without even a minor-mode slow movement. Yet the poignancy is unmistakable. The first movement sets the tone with its opening string undulations, preceding by a measure the main theme. This beginning is unusual for Mozart; the only other major work of his that starts in such a manner is the G Minor Symphony, K. 550. Once the music begins on this note of unrest, intensity repeatedly alternates with gaiety. Notice, for example, how the wistful opening theme is twice interrupted by brief wind fanfares. The happier passages are conventional, almost impersonal: fanfares, arpeggiations, and rapid scales over simple harmonies. This objective music is constantly supplanted by more personal music, characterized by distant modulations, excursions into the minor, intense chromaticism, and discontinuities.

The slow movement exhibits a quality peculiar to Mozart's last works: simplicity (the Clarinet Concerto is another prime example). Mozart's is a sophisticated art, and the apparent simplicity is actually based on considerable subtlety. The composer no longer wished to use his craft in a virtuosic manner, such as he did in the five-part counterpoint in the *Jupiter* Symphony or in the many fugues in earlier works. Here the surface appears straightforward, effortless. Contrasts are minimized. But the music has an inner depth precisely because of the sophisticated artistry that always remains half hidden.

The theme of the rondo pleased Mozart so much that he used it in another composition, the song *Sehnsucht nach dem Frühlinge* ("Longing for Spring"), composed a few days after the concerto. The last movement has many of the qualities of the first two. It includes two cadenzas, both written out by Mozart.

Concerto Number 3 in G Major for Violin and Orchestra, K. 216
> Allegro
> Adagio
> Allegro

Concerto Number 4 in D Major for Violin and Orchestra, K. 218
> Allegro
> Andante cantabile
> Andante grazioso. Allegro ma non troppo

Concerto Number 5 in A Major for Violin and Orchestra, K. 219

Allegro aperto. Adagio. Allegro aperto
Adagio
Tempo di menuetto. Allegro. Tempo di menuetto

The G Major Violin Concerto was completed on 12 September 1775 and first performed shortly thereafter in Salzburg. The D Major Concerto was composed and premiered in Salzburg in October 1775. The A Major Concerto was completed on 20 December 1775 and first performed shortly thereafter in Salzburg.

There have been at least eight violin concertos attributed to Mozart. The first five are totally authentic. They were composed in Salzburg between April and December 1775. Mozart was at the time leader of the Archbishop's court orchestra. Since there are no cadenzas extant for the Salzburg concertos, some scholars believe that Mozart composed them to perform himself: he would have improvised the cadenzas. Other musicologists believe that his assistant and eventual successor, Gaetano Brunetti, was the intended soloist. The latter theory is plausible, since Mozart hated to play the violin. He was an accomplished fiddler, but he preferred to appear as piano soloist or as violist in chamber concerts. In fact, though he was employed as concertmaster (leading violinist), his father Leopold felt he had to write to his son, rather sarcastically, "The fiddle is hanging up on its nail, I suppose." When Wolfgang left the service of the Archbishop, he never again performed in public on the violin.

Of the eight violin concertos, the Third, Fourth, and Fifth represent the earliest of Mozart's compositions to have remained in the standard repertory. The composer was only 19 when he wrote them. Concerto Number 6 appears to have been assembled by violinist J. F. Eck from some hasty sketches by Mozart; the crude second movement was completely fabricated by Eck. Concerto Number 7 is unmistakably Mozartian, but there have been several anonymous "improvements" added. A so-called *Adelaïde* Concerto, supposedly written at Versailles in 1766 (Mozart would have been only ten), was actually composed by twentieth-century violinist Fritz Kreisler, who frequently passed off his own works as newly discovered music of the old masters.

After using the first two concertos to learn the medium, Mozart wrote a third concerto that was suddenly mature, suddenly deep. Mozart scholar Alfred Einstein wonders, "What had happened in the three months that separate the Second from the Third . . . ? We do not know. Suddenly there is a new depth and richness to Mozart's language: instead of an andante there is an adagio that seems to have fallen straight from heaven." To help create the special character of this movement, Mozart replaces the oboes of the outer movements with a pair of flutes.

The composer's reaching for new heights of expressivity went hand-in-hand with innovation. Einstein cites the moment in the adagio when

> the solo returns once more to speak with poignant intensity; or when, in the rondo, the ending comes in the winds, or, in the same movement, humorous or homely and obviously French quotations occur; or when the recapitulation of the magnificent first movement is introduced by an eloquent recitative. Suddenly the whole orchestra begins to speak and to enter into a new, intimate relation with the solo part. Nothing is more miraculous in Mozart's work than the appearance of this concerto in this stage of his development; but just as miraculous is the fact that the two concertos that follow, the one in D in October and the one in A in December, are on the same high level.

The ending of the finale, to which Einstein alludes, is indeed special, with oboes and horns quietly playing a repeated-note figure. This utterly simple gesture beautifully concludes the gentle finale.

Mozart's art continued to deepen as he composed the next violin concerto, a mature and sophisticated work. The long, expressive melodies of its middle movement would seem to be beyond the grasp of the composer of the first two concertos. Likewise, the subtle form of the Fourth Concerto's final rondo, with its variety of tempos and moods, is far in advance of anything in the early concertos.

For many years it was believed that K. 218 was more than superficially indebted to a violin concerto by Luigi Boccherini, which Mozart supposedly heard in Florence in 1770. Mozart scholar Alfred Einstein, for example, suggests that the young composer subconsciously remembered Boccherini's concerto, which is also in D major, when he wrote his own Fourth Concerto five years later. Both concertos share not only key but also structure and even some themes. More recently, however, it has been established that this "Boccherini concerto" is, like Mozart's *Adelaïde* Concerto, a forgery. Instead of K. 218 being inspired by this spurious concerto, it seems that the Mozart work may have been the model for the fake! An anonymous eighteenth-century forger may have composed the work, taking Mozart's concerto as a model and attributing the spurious work to Boccherini. Thus a publicity-seeking soloist (possibly the forger himself) could have the honor of introducing and promoting a new work by a well-known composer.

The D Major Concerto, K. 218, is a gracious work. Although the opening fanfare may suggest otherwise, its prevailing mood is one of intimacy. Neither the exquisite lyricism of the slow movement nor the unexpected changes of meter and tempo in the finale can dispel this atmosphere. Even the different dances suggested in the last movement are elegantly stylized, so that the considerable contrast between them scarcely ruffles the calm surface. Of this movement Einstein wrote: "The rondo combines Italian and French elements, in that, as in the Third Concerto, it interpolates little humorous episodes containing references familiar to its listeners: a gavotte, and a musette mentioned several times in the Mozart correspondence as being of Strassburg." Rather surprisingly, the work ends quietly.

The subsequent concerto, in A Major, sparkles with the wit that is typical of Mozart at his happiest. This humor is conveyed by the lightness and airiness of the themes, yet it is also projected in a more subtle manner. The composer trusts that his listeners have heard enough music of the classical period to know what ought to happen in various parts of a concerto. He plays delightful games with these expectations. He frustrates our preconceptions of form, and he laughs at us — gently but surely — for trying to fit such a unique work into a stereotyped mold.

Consider the first movement. The orchestral exposition presents what seems to be the principal thematic material of the movement. Then the soloist enters not, as we might expect, with the first theme, but rather with an adagio that grows out of the arpeggiated triad at the end of the orchestral exposition. What is this, we may well ask. The only logical answer is that it functions like a slow introduction, displaced from its usual inital position to the interior of the movement. Once we understand this adagio as introduction, we naturally expect it to be followed by an allegro stating the main themes of the movement. But again we are fooled. There is an allegro, but the solo violin begins with a totally new theme. Or *is* that theme new? Underneath this violin melody the orchestra plays the material that we already heard at the opening, material we had initially taken to be the first theme, material which now turns out to be accompanimental to the main melody.

The second movement suspends wit in favor of a lyrical beauty that Mozart seldom equalled, even in his more mature works. It is ironic that when Gaetano Brunetti prepared to perform the concerto in Salzburg, he asked Mozart to provide an alternate slow movement because he found this one "too studied." The new movement, the Adagio in E major, K. 261, is a charming piece, but the original adagio belongs to the concerto.

Humor returns in the finale, and once again it is based on our expectations of form. The tempo and character suggest a minuet, but once we have heard the main theme followed by a subordinate theme followed by a return of the main theme, we suspect that the movement is a rondo. A brief minor-key outburst strengthens this impression, as does the subsequent return of the main theme. If this movement were simply a rondo, it would now begin drawing to a close. But it has been too brief. What happens next, however, is too different to sound like yet another subsidiary theme. The tempo and meter change, and we plunge into a "Turkish" march, which is long enough and replete enough with inner contrasts to be a separate movement. Now that our sense of form is thoroughly but delightfully confused, Mozart innocently brings back the minuet theme, with its original contrasting music, to round out the movement.

There is irony in the way the finale ends. The actual final phrase is softly understated, utterly lacking the bravura we might expect in a concerto ending. Furthermore, we have heard exactly this same music three times previously, each time followed by a brief pause and then a continuation. How are we to know that the last time is really final, until the ensuing silence turns out to be permanent? The conductor is faced with a decision. Should he or she perform this final phrase exactly as it had been played at its earlier appearances, so that we are caught off guard by the lack of subsequent music — a thoroughfully delightful witticism, but possibly a bit unsettling? Or should the ending be prepared by broadening the tempo, thereby diminishing some of the delicious humor but ending the piece more decisively? There is no right answer, but a choice must be made. Either way, the ending is appropriate to this lighthearted movement.

Serenade Number 9 in D Major, K. 320, *Posthorn*
Adagio maestoso. Allegro con spirito
Menuetto: Allegretto. Trio. Menuetto
Concertante: Andante grazioso
Allegro ma non troppo
Andantino
Menuetto. Trio I. Menuetto. Trio II. Menuetto
Presto

The Posthorn *Serenade was completed on 3 August 1779. Nothing is known of its first performance, which probably took place at an outdoor festivity in Salzburg that summer.*

In the late eighteenth century there was no clear distinction between popular and "classical" music, nor between music intended for indoor concerts and for outdoor entertainments, nor between chamber and orchestral music. For performance at social occasions, Mozart wrote pieces with such titles as Serenade, Divertimento, and *Cassation*. The forms were similar. Each is a series of loosely related, light-hearted, often lengthy movements. The differences lay more with how the music was used than with its character. If the suite was intended for outdoor entertainment at night, it was called a serenade; if it was to be played at an indoor affair or during the day, it was entitled a divertimento or a *cassation*. Some of the movements are dances (usually minuets), some are marches (played as the musicians entered and exited), some are *concertanti* for solo instrument(s) accompanied by the ensemble, and some are extended symphonic movements. As the serenades were generally not played through from beginning to end but rather used to fill gaps during the festivities, Mozart was not overly concerned with formal unity. Thus the serenades, etc., are generally collections of minimally connected movements.

The distinction between these entertainment suites and Mozart's symphonies of his Salzburg period is vague. Symphonies were intended for concert use, but several of the serenades (such as K. 320) include movements that are more sophisticated than anything the symphonies contain. Although some of the entertainment pieces are scored for chamber groups, others, such as the *Posthorn* Serenade, call for as full an orchestra as any of the early symphonies.

Serenades were a favorite type of popular music in eighteenth-century Germany and Austria. Just as virtually everyone today has a radio or record player to listen to popular music, in Mozart's day every member of the aristocracy employed an orchestra to play this music. It was heard in parks, in the streets, in the gardens of the wealthy, and during parties, dinners, wedding feasts, and anniversary celebrations. Usually an evening party began with a march (musicologists speculate that the two Marches in D, K. 335, were originally part of the *Posthorn* Serenade), performed by those musicians who could play while entering. Since the ensuing movements were heard at different times during the evening, serenades were not thought of as single continuous compositions, and hence they are often quite lengthy — far longer than any of Mozart's music for the concert hall. To entertain the party guests Mozart often included concerto-like movements, usually for solo violin with orchestra (in the *Posthorn* the *concertante* instruments are winds). At the end of the festivities, the musicians exited while playing a concluding march.

The orchestra in K. 320 includes, in the sixth movement, two unusual instruments: piccolo and posthorn. The latter, a primitive ancestor of the modern cornet, is used in no other Mozart composition. Probably the only other orchestral use of this folk instrument is in Mahler's Third Symphony. No one knows why Mozart included these two instruments, other than to please and interest his listeners. The orchestration of a serenade usually depended on practicalities — on just what instrumentalists were employed by the nobleman commissioning the work. Similarly, the number of movements was determined by the occasion. The nature of the festivity for which K. 320 was composed is not known, but the length of the music (even without the flanking marches) and the large ensemble suggest an important event. The *Posthorn* is one of Mozart's two most elaborate and symphonic serenades (the other is the *Haffner,* K. 250).

The seriousness of mood and sophistication of harmony in the slow introduction hardly suggest an outdoor entertainment, but the music turns into a carefree allegro after six measures. This allegro is marked *con spirito,* and it does indeed have high spirits, heard at the outset as an alternation of loud and soft measures. This contrast of dynamics pervades also the second theme, during which there is a crescendo for the whole orchestra — a rare device since, in the words of musicologist Alfred Einstein, Mozart "was as a rule much too distinguished a composer to stoop to" something so obvious. But this music was intended for the outdoors; furthermore, these dynamic contrasts just might, in Einstein's view, have been intended as a picture of the conflicts between Mozart and his hated employer, Archbishop Colloredo.

Extreme dynamic contrasts are heard also in the following minuet, which is a thoroughly charming movement. The ensuing andante begins the *concertante* section, in which the wind players are treated as soloists. There is a cadenza for the winds, in true concerto fashion, toward the end of the movement. The winds are also featured in the subsequent rondo, the middle movement of the serenade.

Despite the disjointed manner in which serenades were usually performed, Mozart shows some concern in K. 320 for overall form: the work is symmetrically organized. The central rondo is flanked by two slow pieces, the second and sixth movements are minuets, and the first and last are large-scale allegros.

After the two *concertante* movements comes a solemn *andantino* in D minor, followed by the second minuet. This movement has two trio sections, the second featuring the posthorn and the first possibly utilizing the piccolo. There is some confusion, since Mozart included a line in the score for piccolo in this section only, but he left the line blank. Most modern conductors assume that the piccolo is to play the melody along with the first violin but two octaves higher. The serenade concludes with a good-natured finale that has wonderful rhythmic vitality and some delightfully clever contrapuntal passages.

Symphonies concertantes

Symphonie concertante in E-Flat Major for Oboe, Clarinet, Bassoon, Horn, and Orchestra, K. 297b

      Allegro
      Adagio
      Andantino. Adagio. Allegro

Symphonie concertante in E-Flat Major for Violin, Viola, and Orchestra, K.364

      Allegro maestoso
      Andante
      Presto

The Symphonie concertante *for strings was composed in Salzburg in 1779. The* Symphonie concertante *for winds was composed between 5 and 20 April 1778 in Paris.*

The *symphonie concertante,* or by its more common but less accurate Italian name *sinfonia concertante,* has a curious history. The genre came into fashion rather suddenly around 1770, was for a decade the rage in musical circles, yet had virtually died out by 1830. During that half century approximately 570 *symphonies concertantes* were composed by about 210 composers, mostly working in or writing for Paris (hence the appropriateness of the French title).

A *symphonie concertante* is a two- or three-movement work for a group of soloists (usually two, three, or four, but possibly up to nine) and orchestra. Almost all examples are in a major key and are light-hearted (K. 364 is a partial exception). The solo group is treated somewhat like a single solo instrument in a classical concerto. Unlike in its baroque counterpart, the *concerto grosso,* the orchestra in the *symphonie concertante* more often accompanies than opposes the soloists. The emphasis is more on melody than on development, as most *symphonies concertantes* shun the intellectual (again, K. 364 is an exception).

Why did a new form come suddenly into existence? Musicologist Barry Brook, who has written extensively on the *symphonie concertante,* speculates that composers were trying to upgrade their social status. No longer content as servants of nobility, they sought to join the bourgeoisie. As they now had other means of income, they no longer had to rely exclusively on the patronage system. Many chose to make their living by composing, and they therefore sought to write the music performers wanted to play, audiences wanted to hear, and for which both were willing to pay.

Paris, the second largest city in the Western world at the time, boasted more concerts, composers, performers, engravers, and publishers than any other city. There was a large number of fine instrumentalists in Paris, who were eager to perform in a solo capacity. Composers took advantage of the situation by writing multiple concertos (thus satisfying several players and guaranteeing more performances) in a popular style (thus ensuring audience enjoyment). Success with players and audiences led to more commissions and performances: composers discovered the profit motive.

Mozart was always interested in ways to earn money, although he had a notoriously bad business sense. It is hardly surprising that he moved from Mannheim, where he had failed to find sufficient commission money, to Paris early in 1778. He was more than willing to jump on the bandwagon and compose *symphonies concertantes,* if there were patrons willing to pay for them. He had made valuable contacts in Mannheim, which was a center of orchestral music, and he had written two flute concertos on commission, but further sources of income had not materialized. Some of the Mannheim instrumentalists were also active in Paris, and they asked him to compose a *symphonie concertante* for them to perform there. Jean Le Gros, director of the *Concerts spirituels,* agreed to pay for the commission and to present the premiere.

Hoping to cash in on the popularity of the *symphonie concertante* genre, Mozart worked on other concertos for multiple soloists. In Paris he received another commission, from the Duc de Guines, for a work for flute, harp, and orchestra. A few months later he began, but never completed, a *symphonie concertante* for violin, piano, and orchestra, which he had intended to perform himself with Mannheim violinist Ignaz Fränzl. The work, the existing fragments of which suggest that it might have become a major piece, was probably not finished because Mozart was not willing to stay in Mannheim and Fränzl was not willing to move. Once he had returned to Salzburg, Mozart began but again did not complete a *symphonie concertante* for violin, viola, cello, and orchestra. The problem may have been the unlikelihood of a commission or a performance, or Mozart may have sensed the inherent compositional difficulties of a triple concerto. He also composed, probably to perform himself with his sister, a concerto (K. 365) for two pianos and orchestra: not quite the same thing as a *symphonie concertante,* since the two solo instruments are the same. (This concerto should not be confused with the earlier Concerto for Three Pianos and Orchestra — subsequently arranged for two pianos — a minor work Mozart composed in 1776 for three amateur pianists.)

Given the current popularity of such works, Mozart no doubt hoped for instant fame and fortune from his piece for flute, oboe, bassoon, horn, and orchestra, which had been commissioned for the Mannheim musicians. The players learned their parts and were eager to perform the new work. But the performance was cancelled, due to political intrigues. Giovanni Giuseppi Cambini, an Italian composer living in Paris, was one of the more prominent composers of *symphonies concertantes*: he produced over eighty of them in eight years. One of these works, scored for the same combination that Mozart employed, was performed only a week before Mozart delivered his finished score to the director of the *Concerts spirituels*. Cambini recognized Mozart's genius and probably wanted to forestall any unfavorable comparisons, so he prevailed upon Director Le Gros to suppress the work. The performers were furious. As Le Gros had paid for the commission, he owned the only copy of the score. In the days before Xerox, there was nothing Mozart could do.

Or was there? The composer left Paris in October 1778, having failed once again to secure adequate funds from commissions and performances. He wrote home, "Le Gros bought it from me. He thinks he is the only one to have it, but that is not true. I still have it fresh in my head and will set it down as soon as I am home."

The Le Gros manuscript has not survived, and it is not known whether Mozart ever rewrote the composition as planned. The early Köchel catalogs list the piece as missing. It was almost a hundred years before Mozart's biographer Otto Jahn unearthed a copy of a *symphonie concertante* by Mozart. This work is scored for oboe, clarinet, bassoon, horn, and orchestra — not quite the same combination as Mozart's missing score. The high quality of this work and its distinctly Mozartian flavor make its authorship unquestionable (as a recent computer-assisted stylistic analysis has proven), but no one knows whether it is the same as the Le Gros work or not, and, if it is, whether the new version was made by Mozart or someone else. The scoring is most skillful: the oboe part does not sound like a transcribed flute part, nor does the clarinet part seem like it was once for oboe. It is likely that the work Jahn discovered is in fact an arrangement of the lost composition.

Mozart did write one additional work for multiple soloists and orchestra, soon after his return to Salzburg. If it were not for this *Symphonie concertante* in E-flat, for violin, viola, and orchestra, the composer's contributions to the short-lived *symphonie concertante* genre would seem rather meagre. In addition to isolated *concertante* movements in earlier serenades and divertimentos, we would have only the compositions of 1778–79: two unfinished pieces, a flute-harp work for two amateurs, a concerto for two pianos that is not really a *symphonie concertante*, and a fine work for winds the original version of which is lost.

The composition of a *symphonie concertante* presents interesting challenges. It does not suffice to write a symphony featuring various instruments in solo capacities. The work must be specifically a concerto for the solo instruments. Each one must be treated equally and must be given idiomatic passages. In K. 297b Mozart sometimes treats the solo wind quartet as a group, at other times he features each individual soloist in turn, and elsewhere the quartet plays its own chamber music to orchestral accompaniment. It is no small feat to incorporate all these roles within a single work, and it is not surprising that the wind *symphonie concertante* is longer than most other Mozart concertos.

K. 364, the piece with string soloists, solves these challenges with even greater originality and beauty. It is a sublime composition that makes Mozart's earlier attempts at multiple-instrument concertos seem by comparison like apprentice works. It avoids certain problems inherent in the form by using only two instruments, not an entire solo ensemble like that in K. 297b: the violin and viola are neither identical (as in the two-piano concerto) nor vastly different (as in the flute-harp and violin-piano works). K. 364 shows that dialogues between two similar but distinct solo voices can be extraordinarily beautiful.

After an extended orchestral *tutti,* K. 297b introduces the solo quartet in typical concerto fashion. Each instrument plays virtuosic music uniquely suited to its capabilities. It is not difficult to hear hints of Mozart's solo concertos for oboe, clarinet, horn, and bassoon echoing in this music. The horn is used treacherously high, the different clarinet registers are contrasted, and there are passages of rapid runs: the Mannheim musicians for whom this music was probably written must have been accomplished players.

The first movement, as in any Mozart concerto, has a cadenza toward the end. It is fully written out: Mozart could hardly have expected his players to improvise together. The cadenza exploits the interaction of the four wind timbres.

The second movement is marked adagio, but musicologists suspect that it was originally an andante. Most *symphonies concertantes* have leisurely slow movements like this one, or else none at all. An adagio marking is out of character for this graceful, untroubled music.

The finale is a set of ten variations plus coda. The theme and each variation feature one or two instruments, answered by the full quartet. The contrast between winds used as solo instruments and as orchestral members is interesting. The theme features oboe and bassoon. The variations successively highlight clarinet answered by horn, bassoon, clarinet arpeggios answered by bassoon, oboe accompanied by bassoon, oboe answered by clarinet, oboe answered by clarinet in very rapid notes, the entire quartet, oboe playing wide arpeggios, each instrument in turn, and oboe accompanied by the others. The lighthearted coda is typical of the Parisian *symphonie concertante.*

When he decided to create a *symphonie concertante* for violin, viola, and orchestra, Mozart was apparently concerned about the inherent inequality of the violin and viola. The violin has a more penetrating sound and usually plays with greater bravura. To compensate, the composer wrote fewer virtuosic violin passages than in his violin concertos, and he indicated that the viola should be played *scordatura.* This means that the instrument's strings are to be tuned a half-step higher than normal, the result being a more intense tone quality. (Since modern violas use steel strings and since the modern orchestra tunes higher than Mozart's, the viola part cannot generally be played scordatura today.) To reinforce in the orchestra the equality he strove for between the two solo instruments, Mozart subdivided the orchestral violas throughout the work. Thus, in addition to the normal first and second violins, we find first and second violas.

The dialogue nature of the work is evident even before the solo instruments enter. The orchestral exposition is full of dialogues of its own: between sustained chords and arpeggiated figures, between winds and strings, between first and second violins, between horns and oboes, between loud and soft textures, between bass and treble sonorities. Thus, when the solo instruments finally enter, their dialogue is well prepared. They seem to converse: often one instrument picks up what the other has been saying, or repeats it with variations or extensions.

The emotional core of the violin-viola dialogue is the middle movement, a poignant and quite dissonant andante in C minor. Here each solo instrument spins out at length its impassioned line, and then the other instrument replies. Elsewhere their alternation is more frequent.

The elegaic mood of the andante is dispelled in the finale, which is essentially a carefree piece. The trills in the main theme and the quirky rhythms in the soloists' first tune help establish this mood, as does the often rapid exchanges later on between the two soloists.

Mozart may not have been interested in the *symphonie concertante* for very long, but his two contributions to the genre (plus the one by Haydn) tower above all others. Mozart's two efforts prove that a musical form born of the desire to court public taste can rise above mundane social purposes to produce truly wonderful music.

Mozart's *symphonie concertante* for violin and viola is undoubtedly the crowning achievement by any eighteenth-century composer in the genre. Other composers continued to write *symphonies concertantes* for a few more decades, but the form soon died, almost as quickly as it had been created. By the early nineteenth century virtuosos were becoming stars, unlikely to share their glamour. Each virtuoso wanted to be seen as a supreme artist, alone in the spotlight. Thus the *symphonie concertante* thus lost its social relevance. Occasional multiple concertos — such as Brahms' Double Concerto for violin and cello or Beethoven's Triple Concerto for violin, cello, and piano — continued to appear sporadically during the nineteenth century, but the age of the *symphonie concertante* had passed.

Symphony Number 25 in G Minor, K. 183

> Allegro con brio
> Andante
> Menuetto Trio. Menuetto
> Allegro

The "little" G Minor Symphony was composed, and presumably performed toward the end of 1773 in Salzburg.

Leopold Mozart frequently displayed the talents of his son in various cities. When Wolfgang was a teenager, Leopold was determined to make him still more famous, thereby hoping to secure for him an appointment to a noble's court. To these ends father and son made three trips to Italy between 1770 to 1773 and one to Vienna in 1773. The young composer was exposed to several different influences on these journeys.

Leopold was successful only in the first of his two endeavors — to make Wolfgang famous. On the first trip to Italy, Mozart was exhibited as a child prodigy. He performed and composed in Milan, Verona, and Mantua. He met the leading Italian composer, Giovanni Battista Sammartini, and imitated his style in a string quartet, written at an inn while the Mozarts traveled to Parma. At Bologna, Wolfgang met the composer and pedagogue Padre Martini, for whom he composed two fugues. At Milan the young composer received a commission for an opera. In Rome he heard a performance of Gregorio Allegri's *Miserere*, which he subsequently wrote down perfectly from memory, although he had heard it but once. This amazing feat had tremendous public relations value, and Leopold, always the enterprising publicity agent, played it for all it was worth. He was no doubt responsible for his son's receiving from Pope Clement XIV the highest class of the Order of the Golden Spur, an honor previously accorded only one other composer — the great sixteenth-century master Orlando di Lassus. For a boy of 14 to receive such recognition was indeed a coup. Furthermore, Leopold saw to it that Wolfgang was elected to membership in the *Accademia filarmonica* of Bologna, despite a rule requiring members to be at least 20. To qualify for admission, Mozart had to be shut up in a room in order to compose a choral work in sixteenth-century style.

The Mozarts' second trip to Italy, a year later, was not intended to show off a child prodigy but to fulfill commitments made during the first trip. Wolfgang was now a young professional, and he had a commissioned opera to be produced. *Mitridate* was so successful that it ran for 20 performances and resulted in a second opera commission. Mozart had successfully assimilated the popular Italian style. Leopold decided that they should remain in Milan, hoping to secure an appointment for Wolfgang from the Archduke. But no appointment was forthcoming, and father and son returned to Salzburg. The old Archbishop of Salzburg had died, and a new one was to be installed. The new man was, at least at first, lenient with Leopold, allowing him leaves of absence for his continued attempts to further Wolfgang's career. Thus the Mozarts were able to try their luck in Italy a third time.

Again Wolfgang was successful as an opera composer. *Lucio Silla* ran for 25 performances. He also composed several string quartets and symphonies, many of which display an Italian influence. The third Italian trip was a lot like the others: much success, no appointment.

During the period of his Italian trips, Mozart wrote 27 symphonies. Many of them are relatively modest apprentice works that he composed in an attempt to master the form he admired in the hands of J. C. Bach, Sammartini, and Haydn. Four of the seven symphonies of 1773 are essentially three-part Italian overtures that may have been composed in anticipation of further opera commissions from Italy. The remaining three symphonies, however, are more substantive works. They show a deepening of expressivity and a startling maturation. In these works Mozart was searching not only for mastery of technique but also for his own voice as a symphonist.

One reason for Mozart's newfound musical sophistication was the trip he and Leopold made to Vienna after returning from their third Italian sojourn. Again the purpose was to find Wolfgang a job, and again the result was failure. The young composer heard a lot of contemporary music, notably that of Haydn, in the city that was the musical capital of the world. He learned considerably from this exposure to the most up-to-date trends. It was not long before the influence of this study appeared in his own music. His finales begin to rival the weightiness of first movements, development sections became more complex, and codas became lengthier.

Haydn was at the time writing overtly emotional music. He had become dissatisfied with the shallow music appropriate to social occasions. He was affected by the literary movement known as *Sturm und Drang* — "storm and stress" — and he experimented with impassioned symphonies in minor keys (such as the *Trauersinfonie, La Passione,* and the *Farewell*). Other Viennese composers were writing similar music, and the visiting Mozart was impressed. After his return to Salzburg, he composed his own *Sturm und Drang* piece, his only symphony to date in a minor key.

The "little" G Minor Symphony — so nicknamed to distinguish it from the great G Minor, K. 550, of Mozart's maturity — throws the listener immediately into an intensely emotional world. The opening syncopations, followed by impassioned rising arpeggios and rapid turn figures, set the mood. Similarly powerful are the string tremolos and the sudden *fortissimo* intrusion of the bridge section. The andante is also agitated, though in a more subtle way: its harmonies are often decorated with dissonances and its rhythms are frequently upbeats yearning towards downbeats. Biographer Alfred Einstein describes the minuet as darkly fatalistic, contrasting with a trio "full of a typically G major sweetness." Like the first movement, the finale starts with a starkly unharmonized melody. Also like the opening movement, it has restlessly synopated rhythms. Both theme groups of this sonata form utilize the same melody, so that the music seems obsessed by it. Einstein mentions, in addition, a "thematic relation to the first movement, which is not so much to be observed on the surface as to be dimly felt. But the form of the symphony gains a new unity through it."

Symphony Number 29 in A Major, K. 201 (186a)
Allegro moderato
Andante
Menuetto. Trio. Menuetto
Allegro con spirito

The A Major Symphony was composed in January or February 1774 and first performed shortly thereafter in Salzburg.

Symphony Number 29 is one of a trio of symphonies that are considered Mozart's first mature efforts in the genre. The others (not numbered chronologically) are Symphony Number 28 in C Major, K. 200, and Symphony Number 25 in G Minor, K. 183. Previously his symphonies had been similar to three-part Italian opera overtures, but now a new depth of technique and feeling and a new level of sophistication became unmistakable in the work of the 18-year-old composer.

Mozart and his father had recently traveled to Vienna, looking unsuccessfully for employment as court musicians. Leopold was growing increasingly dissatisfied with the provincialism of Salzburg, and he sought better opportunities for himself and his son than those provided by his employer, the Archbishop.

Mozart heard a lot of impressive music in Vienna, and his art matured considerably as a result of this exposure. The three symphonies composed upon his return to Salzburg show the imprint of Vienna. Significantly, once he moved permanently to Vienna seven years later, these symphonies were among the few pieces from Salzburg that he felt still warranted performance. Mozart knew which were his mature works.

What aspects of the music point to Mozart's newly sophisticated technique? The contrast, at the opening of the first movement, between the falling octaves and the repeated-note figures indicates a wonderfully imaginative craft. Notice also the way this repeated-note idea pervades the movement, not only melodically but also in accompanimental figures. The powerful repeat of the opening idea by the full orchestra, intensified by imitative treatment of the main theme, is typically Viennese. Notice how often and in how many different ways Mozart uses the technique of imitation, particularly in the closing theme. Beneath the innocent surface of this music lies incredible technical prowess.

In the delicate second movement Mozart has the strings play with mutes. He learned this device from Haydn's middle-period symphonies, which he had heard in Vienna. The wind instruments (the orchestra has only two oboes, two horns, and strings) are used sparingly, so that the movement almost seems to belong to a string quartet.

The minuet, like the preceding two movements, uses repeated notes extensively. This time they cleverly become the closing figure, played in the winds. The almost violent contrasts of loud and soft are typical of Mozart's new style.

The first theme of the finale recalls the falling octaves of the corresponding theme of the first movement, and the ubiquitous repeated notes are heard much of the time in the lower strings. Notice the delightful way Mozart gets into the second theme, using grace-note figures that let the melody slip in almost unnoticed in the second violins. Later, the music's complexity and intricacy make the development section dramatically powerful, more like its counterparts in Mozart's final symphonies than in the ones he had composed just a few months earlier. The orchestration is spectacular at the end, when the horns gloriously take over the orchestra.

Symphony Number 31 in D Major, K. 300a (297), *Paris*
Allegro assai
Andantino
Allegro

The Paris *Symphony was composed and first performed in June 1778. The premiere was given in Paris at the* Concerts spirituels.

Because his father could not get leave of absence from his duties in Salzburg, Mozart's mother accompanied him on a long journey begun in March 1777. They went in search of employment for the young composer in a major musical center. He was rapidly growing intolerant of the provincialism of Salzburg, where both he and his father were servants of Archbishop Colloredo.

Mother and son went first to Munich. In a letter home the young composer recounted his interview with Elector Maximilian Joseph. Even Mozart's own account shows his social clumsiness — a "mixture of cocksuredness and pretended servility," as biographer Hugh Ottaway labels it.

Mozart wrote, "When the Elector came up to me, I said: 'Your Highness will allow me to throw myself most humbly at your feet and offer you my services.' 'So you have left Salzburg for good?' 'Yes, your Highness, for good.' 'How is that? Have you had a row with him?' 'Not at all, your Highness. I only asked him for permission to travel, which he refused. So I was compelled to take this step, though indeed I had long been intending to clear out.'" We can readily imagine the Elector thinking of Mozart walking out on him as well, should he refuse permission to travel!

The letter continues, "'Salzburg is no place for me, I can assure you.' 'Good heavens! There's a young man for you! But your father is still in Salzburg?' 'Yes, your Highness. He too throws himself most humbly at your feet. . . . My sole wish is to serve your Highness, who himself is such a great—.' 'Yes, my dear boy, but I have no vacancy. I am sorry. If only there were a vacancy—.' 'I assure your Highness that

I should not fail to do credit to Munich.' 'I know. But it is no good, for there is no vacancy here.' This said he walked away." Similar scenes were repeated in Augsberg, then Mannheim, and then Paris.

In Augsberg Mozart became quite friendly with a cousin of his, Maria Anna Thekla Mozart. From Mannheim he wrote her crude letters full of adolescent jokes about bodily functions. Also in Mannheim he became enamored of the young singer Aloysia Weber. He actually schemed to run off on a performing tour to Italy with Aloysia and her family. Mozart's mother was powerless to stop this harebrained plan. A stern letter from father Leopold at home in Salzburg brought Wolfgang back to his senses, however.

Although his mother had planned to return to Salzburg after Mannheim, she was no longer willing to trust Wolfgang on his own. So the two set off on a grueling nine-day journey to Paris. Leopold had written, "Off with you to Paris! Find your place among great people!" But all Wolfgang could find in Paris were meagre jobs teaching less-than-great pupils.

Although opportunities for composition were few, Mozart did receive a commission for a symphony. He planned it especially for Paris — for its orchestra and for its public. As the composer had hoped, the D Major Symphony was enormously popular. But still no serious offers of employment were forthcoming. Mozart was disheartened. Then he received a severe blow when his mother died. There was little left to do then but to return to Salzburg, where Leopold had managed to convince the Archbishop to employ Wolfgang once again.

On his way home the composer stopped off in Munich. He wanted to see Aloysia Weber again. Leopold was very concerned, especially now that Wolfgang's mother was no longer around to keep him from doing anything rash. Leopold need not have worried. Aloysia's singing career was moving ahead rapidly, and she had no intention of getting involved with an unemployed composer.

Mozart arrived home having little to show for his journey. His mother was dead and the family resources depleted, yet he had come up with nothing beyond a successful performance of the *Paris* Symphony, an unfulfilled flirtation with a singer, and an enjoyable time with a cousin to whom he could write smutty letters. Leopold was not pleased, and Wolfgang was depressed at the prospect of having to remain in Salzburg.

One advantage to the trip was that Mozart heard the renowned Mannheim Orchestra, famous throughout Europe for its precision, ability to make sudden changes of mood or dynamics, excellent wind section, and skill at making huge crescendos. The Mannheim composers — Johann Stamitz, Karl Stamitz, Franz Xaver Richter, Franz Beck, Anton Filtz, Christian Cannabich, Giuseppe Toëschi, Ignaz

Holzbauer, and Ernst Eichner — planned their symphonies to display the capabilities of this great orchestra. When Mozart heard some of their works, he was deeply impressed with the orchestra's virtuosity and also with the wisdom of designing a symphony for a particular ensemble.

When he arrived in Paris, he found another fine orchestra and another group of composers writing specifically for it. Thus, when he received a commission from Le Gros, the director of the *Concerts spirituels,* to compose a symphony for the Paris Orchestra, he designed it to show off that group. Thus the D Major became his first symphony to include clarinets. Since the ensemble had excellent strings, Mozart featured them. The symphony opens, for example, with a device that was the pride of the Paris Orchestra: a forceful string unison known as *le premier coup d'archet.* Mozart wrote home, "I have been careful not to neglect *le premier coup d'archet* — and that is quite sufficient. What a fuss the oxen here make of this trick! The devil take me if I can see any difference! They all begin together, just as they do in other places."

Another example of string emphasis is the opening of the third movement, with a contrapuntal duet of first and second violins alone. That movement's second theme starts similarly, with an imitative passage for the violins. In addition, Mozart wrote several string passages against sustained wind chords.

He not only composed specifically for the Paris musicians but also was accommodating enough to substitute a shorter slow movement when Le Gros complained about too many modulations. The original movement, which has been restored for modern performances, features the strings in sometimes rapid figuration.

In one sense, the composer's skill at writing for a particular ensemble, plus his willingness to compose a symphony to fit the tastes of the public (and of Le Gros), ensured success. Le Gros declared it the best symphony ever written for his series, and the audience loved it. In another sense, however, the work was a failure, for it did not succeed in attracting any noblemen interested in hiring the composer. The pattern that plagued Mozart his whole life was repeated: the music was a success, but the composer remained unemployed.

Symphony Number 35 in D Major, K. 385, *Haffner*

Allegro con spirito
[Andante]
Menuetto. Trio. Menuetto
Presto

The Haffner *Symphony was composed between late July and early August 1782. Mozart gave what was probably the first performance on 23 March 1783 in Vienna.*

Mozart lived in Vienna for the last ten years of his life. By the time he had moved there from his native Salzburg, he had already composed over forty symphonies — all his works in that genre save the final half dozen. He composed *no* symphonies specifically for Vienna, except possibly the last three (no one knows for what occasion or reason he wrote them). The other symphonies from his Vienna period are K. 385 (written for Salzburg), K. 425 (for Linz), and K. 504 (for Prague). Mozart's main instrumental output during the Vienna decade comprised piano concertos.

Not only was Symphony Number 35 not composed for Vienna, it was not even conceived as a symphony. In July 1782, while Mozart was involved in a time-consuming operatic project and in preparing for his wedding to Constanze Weber, he received a letter from his father. Leopold asked him to write a new serenade. Mozart's childhood friend Siegmund Haffner was to be elevated to the nobility. A new composition performed at the celebration in his honor would be appropriate. Mozart had once before written a serenade for the Haffner family, the wedding serenade now known as the *Haffner*, K. 250.

Mozart was much too busy to write the new piece, but he nonetheless felt that he should undertake the project. He wrote to Leopold on 20 July:

> I am up to my ears in work. By a week from Sunday I must arrange my opera for wind instruments. Otherwise someone will beat me to it and secure the profits instead of me. And now you ask me to write a new symphony too! How on earth can I do that? You have no idea how difficult it is to arrange a work of this kind for wind instruments, so that it suits them and yet loses none of its effect. Well, I will have to stay up all night, for that is the only way; for you dearest father, I will make the sacrifice. You may rely on having something from me in each mail delivery. I shall work as fast as possible.

On 27 July Mozart sent Leopold the opening allegro. "It has been quite impossible to do more for you, because I have had to write yet another serenade for wind instruments alone (otherwise I could have used the piece for *your* project as well). On Wednesday the 31st I shall send the two minuets, the andante, and the finale. If I can manage to do so, I shall also send a march. If not, then just use the one from my earlier Haffner music, which is quite unknown."

Not surprisingly, Mozart fell behind schedule. By 31 July he sent Leopold only a letter, but no music. "One cannot do the impossible! I won't scribble inferior stuff. So I cannot send you the whole symphony until the next mail day."

On 4 August the composer and Constanze were married. Somehow, at about the same time he sent off most of the serenade, except for the march, which followed on 7 August. The final piece consisted of an introductory march, an allegro, two minuets, an andante, and a finale. The date of the Haffner celebration is not known, and thus it is impossible to determine whether the serenade was ready in time for the festivities. It does seem unlikely that Mozart met his deadline.

Eventually he wanted the serenade returned for performance at one of his concerts. He may not have written symphonies for Vienna, but he often performed existing ones there. He wrote to Leopold, requesting the music, on 4 December, then again on 21 December, 4 January, 22 January, and 5 February. Leopold may have delayed returning the score to punish Wolfgang for failing to complete the serenade on time, or possibly for having married someone of whom he did not approve. Mozart was growing impatient: "My next concert is to take place on the third Sunday in Lent, that is, on 23 March, and I must have several copies made. I think, therefore, that if it [i.e., the orchestral material] is not yet copied, it would be better to send me back the original score."

By 15 February Mozart had received the music which he had written hastily and piecemeal six months earlier. "My new *Haffner* Symphony has positively amazed me, for I had forgotten every single note of it. It must surely produce a good effect."

In order to transform the serenade into a true symphony, Mozart dropped the march and one of the minuets, and he added pairs of flutes and clarinets to the outer movements. He conducted the work on his Lenten concert.

The concert program indicates the relative insignificance of symphonies in Vienna. The *Haffner* Symphony framed the evening, serving as prelude and postlude. The program began with the first three movements. Then came the music the public really wanted to hear: an aria from the opera *Idomeneo*, a piano concerto, a recitative and aria, the two concertante movements from the *Posthorn* Serenade, an aria from *Lucio Silla*, a fugue (performed because the Emperor was in attendance), piano variations on a theme by Gluck, and a recitative and rondo. After these vocal and instrumental display pieces, the concert closed with the last movement of the *Haffner* Symphony.

As this story implies, the difference between a serenade and a symphony, between entertainment music and concert music, between pop and classical music, was small. It is true that serenades did tend to include light music, but Mozart had yet to write any profoundly challenging orchestral pieces. The *Haffner* Symphony, for all its sophistication, was surely appropriate background music to a celebration. One could hardly say the same of Mozart's four last symphonies. Thus Symphony Number 35 comes near the end of a long series of light, elegant, brilliant multi-movement orchestral music composed for specific occasions. The only serenades that he was yet to write are the rather special parody called *A Musical Joke* and the incomparable *Eine Kleine Nachtmusik*. Among the remaining works called symphonies, only the very next one — K. 425, the *Linz* — retains the atmosphere of the early serenades.

The origin of the *Haffner* Symphony as a serenade certainly does not preclude compositional subtlety. Consider the opening of the first movement, which the composer wanted performed "with great fire." The theme is an elaboration of the simplest of ideas: a stepwise descent of the scale from the tonic. The descent seems to get stuck on the fourth degree for several measures, after which its continuation is disguised. Mozart found this idea rich enough to base the entire movement on it. He inverts the theme and plays it in imitation.

Perhaps the most interesting moment in the direct and graceful andante movement occurs when the first violins continually repeat the same note for several measures, while the second violins play the melody. The minuet, according to musicologist Alfred Einstein, is characterized by "strength, festivity, and masculinity in the main section, and the most delicate grace in the trio." The relationship of the symphony to Mozart's entertainment music is most obvious in the effervescent finale, which the composer wanted played "as fast as possible."

Symphony Number 36 in C Major, K. 425, *Linz*

        Adagio. Allegro spiritoso
        Poco adagio
        Menuetto. Trio. Menuetto
        Presto

The Linz *Symphony was composed between 30 October and 3 November 1783. The first performance was given in Linz on 4 November 1783.*

Mozart's father and sister were not too happy with his choice of a wife. They looked down on Constanze as intellectually and socially inferior. The composer knew how his father felt, but he nonetheless thought he should ask permission to marry Constanze. Leopold Mozart's grudging letter of consent arrived a day *after* the marriage.

The newlyweds, who were living in Vienna, were not too eager to visit Mozart's family in Salzburg. A trip was inevitable, but the composer kept postponing it for one reason or another: first it was the weather, then the lessons he had to give, then concerts, then Constanze's pregnancy, and finally Wolfgang's fear that he would be arrested, as soon as he set foot in his native town, for having left the Archbishop's service without permission two years earlier.

As they were approaching their first anniversary, the couple left their month-old son in a home for infants and set out for Salzburg. The visit, which lasted three months, was not easy. Leopold and Nannerl were coldly polite to Wolfgang's wife, but they obviously did not approve of her.

While in Salzburg, Mozart visited his old friend, composer Michael Haydn, younger brother of Franz Joseph. Michael was under pressure to complete six duos for violin and viola. Wolfgang, discovering that Michael was in poor health and thus unable to fulfill the commission, quickly wrote two duos himself and presented them to Haydn, who had only to add his name and give them to the Archbishop.

On the return trip to Vienna, Wolfgang and Constanze stopped off in Linz, where they were guests of Count Thun. The Count invited Mozart to give a concert. As he had no symphony with him, he had to compose a new one "at breakneck speed," as he wrote to his father.

Mozart had recently been studying Joseph Haydn's symphonies. One feature that particularly impressed him was a slow introduction before a first movement's main allegro. Mozart's *Linz* Symphony is his first to begin with a short adagio. The concert for Count Thun included, in addition to Mozart's new symphony and one of his piano concertos, a symphony recently composed by Michael Haydn. Mozart added a slow introduction to his friend's work. For a number of years, this symphony was thought to be entirely by Mozart. It was known as Mozart's Symphony Number 37 in G Major, K. 444.

Mozart managed to compose the *Linz* Symphony, write the introduction to Michael Haydn's symphony, and copy out the orchestral parts in about five days. There was little time left for the players to learn the music. It is quite possible that the concert was sight-read. In fact, rehearsals for orchestral concerts were an unusual luxury at the time!

When Wolfgang and Constanze arrived back in Vienna shortly after the Linz concert, they learned that their baby had died. In subsequent years they had five more children, only two of whom lived past infancy.

The symphony was introduced to Vienna a few months after its Linz premiere. Mozart then sent a copy to his father, who conducted it in Salzburg. A number of years later, Mozart was in Prague to supervise the premiere of his opera *Don Giovanni.* Count Thun, who had a residence in Prague in addition to his house in Linz, asked Mozart to conduct K. 425 with the Count's private orchestra. The composer also presented the symphony publicly with the Prague Opera Orchestra.

The adagio introduction to K. 425 is not the only aspect of the work that reflects Mozart's indebtedness to Joseph Haydn. The 6/8 slow movement is quite Haydnesque, except that the inclusion of trumpets and timpani creates an underlying intensity that is peculiarly Mozartian. The third movement is brief and direct, perhaps more so than Haydn would have permitted himself at the time. Musicologist Neal Zaslaw calls our attention to the trio section's "mock innocence." The *presto* finale's main theme could easily be taken to be by Haydn, although Mozart's contrasting material, chromaticism, and involved development are uniquely his own.

Symphony Number 38 in D Major, K. 504, *Prague*
    Adagio. Allegro
    Andante
    Presto

The Prague *Symphony was completed in Vienna on 6 December 1786 and first performed a month later in Prague, under the composer's direction.*

Although Mozart was one of the best known composers in Vienna, he was forced to share public attention with such lesser talents as Antonio Salieri and Padre Martini. Because of the competition, it became harder and harder for Mozart to secure performances and commissions. Thus he was interested when Count Johann Thun invited him to Prague early in 1787. The composer's recent opera, *The Marriage of Figaro*, had been performed with great success there, and many people were eager to meet him. Mozart and his wife Constanze accepted the invitation. He was accorded many honors upon his arrival in Prague. Everywhere he turned he met with great respect and admiration, and his concerts earned him considerable praise in the press and substantial sums of money.

We know a lot about Mozart's visit to Prague because of a long letter he wrote from there to his friend Gottfried von Jacquin.

I drove with Count Canal to the so-called Bretfeld ball, where the cream of Prague's beauties are usually gathered. That would have been your cup of tea, my friend! I mean, I can just see you after all the lovely girls and married women. Running after? Not a bit of it — limping after them. I did not dance and did not flirt. The former because I was too tired, the latter because I am a natural idiot. But I looked on with great pleasure while all these people skipped about, quite enraptured, to the music of my *Figaro* arranged for contradances and waltzes. For people here talk about nothing but *Figaro*. Nothing is played, sung, or whistled but *Figaro*. Nothing, nothing but *Figaro*. Certainly a great honor for me!

Mozart's weeks in Prague provided the greatest popular successes he was ever to know. On 17 January he attended a performance of *Figaro* during which the audience broke into spontaneous applause to welcome and honor him. Two days later he played a piano concert, during which he improvised for half an hour before an enthralled capacity crowd. The next day he conducted a performance of *Figaro*. He received a commission for a new opera for Prague, which turned out to be *Don Giovanni*.

Mozart wanted to introduce a new symphony to the Prague audiences. He had completed a three-movement work just before leaving Vienna. As it had not yet been played, he conducted the premiere in his host city. The symphony thus became known as the *Prague*.

The first movement begins with a lengthy slow introduction, quite unusual for Mozart. The opening figure, which presages the beginning of the *Jupiter* Symphony, is never heard again. Eventually, syncopated repeated notes are introduced. This is significant, because the same figure starts the allegro. It is not until the seventh measure of the allegro that the music settles down to tonic harmony and to a figure that is truly melodic. The unsettled rhythmic vitality of syncopation, derived from the introduction, is felt throughout the movement, except during the lyrical second theme. The development section is quite involved contrapuntally, starting out with a canon (at the unusual interval of the seventh) that is answered in almost fugal fashion by another canon (at the second). Parts of this movement are so complex that Mozart actually worked out the counterpoint in a series of preliminary sketches, which he rarely felt the need to do for other compositions.

The second movement, like the outer ones, is cast in sonata form. Right from the outset Mozart contrasts diatonic music (first two measures) with chromatic writing (second pair of measures), an opposition he develops throughout the movement. After the opening period there is a diatonic canon that recalls the imitative passages in the first movement.

The finale is related to the first movement because of syncopations in the third and fourth measures. The continued development of these rhythms makes this movement quite intense, despite its carefree tempo. Increasing the headlong intensity are powerful modulations in the development section. The syncopations disappear finally in the coda, so that the symphony can end happily.

The *Prague* Symphony is also known as the *Symphony without Minuet.* Several early symphonies of Mozart also have but three movements. The early works' structure is derived from the tripartite French overture. In K. 504, however, it is the compactness and seriousness of expression that preclude a dance movement. The *Prague* is more dramatic than its predecessors. It deals with larger contrasts and stronger oppositions: the first movement's fragmentary first theme vs. its lyrical second theme, the second movement's diatonicism vs. chromaticism, and the finale's frequent juxtapositions of strings vs. winds and of loud vs. soft textures. The drama is heightened by extensive counterpoint. Thus Number 38 goes beyond the lighthearted early symphonies, and even beyond the transitional *Haffner* and *Linz* Symphonies, in establishing the symphony as a major form.

◆ ◆ ◆

Symphony Number 39 in E-Flat Major, K. 543

Adagio. Allegro
Andante con moto
Menuetto: Allegretto. Trio. Menuetto
Allegro

The E-Flat Symphony was composed in a few weeks and completed on 26 June 1788. Nothing is known of the first performance, which took place after Mozart's death.

For the last years of his life, Mozart experienced constant financial difficulties. He had moved to Vienna to seek fame and a livelihood from his music, and for a time he was successful. His music was appreciated, he received several commissions, he had a number of students, and he was able to earn an almost adequate income from performing. But his fortunes changed quite suddenly in the winter of 1787–88.

There were a number of factors creating these difficulties, according to biographer Hugh Ottaway. Ottaway discounts the usual explanation of intrigues by Mozart's rivals, such as Salieri; he also feels that the often blamed "fickleness" of the Viennese public is too vague a concept. Rather, he lays much of the blame on the actual music Mozart was writing, which was less accessible than his earlier compositions. The composer, now in his mid-thirties, was becoming more mature and more profound. He had begun to move away from "social" music two years earlier with the brooding D Minor Piano Concerto. As his music reflected more and more his inner complexities, his style became too difficult to be assimilated on a first hearing. Listeners were puzzled, and before long their puzzlement turned to rejection. By the summer of 1789, Mozart was able to find only one sponsor for one of his subscription concerts, which had traditionally attracted a large number of patrons. He had not willed (nor possibly even welcomed) the change in his style, but an artist of integrity does not have total control over what he produces.

Ottaway also blames a growing prejudice in Vienna against Freemasonry. Mozart was a Mason, and many of his friends belonged to the order's radical fringe, the Illuminati. The Emperor ordered all lodges to submit lists of activities and members. Propaganda was distributed against them, and anyone who was a Mason was regarded with suspicion and distrust. Furthermore, Mozart's recent successes in Prague worked against him, since that city was thought of in conservative Vienna as a center of radicalism. Nonetheless, he was able to secure employment as "chamber composer" at the Emperor's court. This position proved to be little more than that of a servant, as the composer received a meagre salary for providing dance music for court balls. His new earnings were hardly enough to offset the diminishing of income from sponsors, concerts, and students.

Mozart was forced to borrow money. Again and again he approached friends and patrons during the remaining four years of his life. His letters were at first dignified and optimistic, but later they became desperate and pathetic. When the composer died, he left huge debts.

The financial situation first became critical in June 1788. Mozart attempted a series of subscription concerts that failed. His landlord demanded immediate payment, but the composer had no money. He was forced to move his family quickly to a cheaper lodging in a suburb. In a letter to a friend asking for money to pay his *new* landlord, Mozart wrote, "On the whole, the change is all the same to me; in fact, I prefer it. As it is, I have very little to do in town, and as I am not exposed to so many visitors, I shall have more time for work." It was depressing that he had "little to do in town": no concerts, no commissions, nothing. For the first time since his move to Vienna, Mozart had time on his hands.

What he did with this time was to compose three symphonies in rapid succession. They were completed respectively on 26 June, 25 July, and 10 August. They proved to be his last symphonies. Probably Mozart planned to use the new pieces in subscription concerts the following winter, but the concerts never materialized, no doubt because of lack of sponsors. A performance of any of these symphonies would surely not have helped improve Mozart's fortunes: it is hard to imagine the conservative Viennese enjoying works this intense, complex, contrapuntal, and dissonant (notice the pungent dissonances in the introduction of Symphony Number 39, for example). The music has since become, of course, among the most loved, most played, and most respected by any composer, but it was really music for another age — music tinged with the romanticism of the upcoming century. If the concerts for which the new symphonies were intended had taken place, they would no doubt have merely added to Mozart's unpopularity. Actually, he never even heard the E-Flat and C Major Symphonies, and possibly not the G Minor either. Thus this great trilogy, vastly important in the history of music and of mankind, made little impact on the life of its composer.

Each symphony of the trilogy has its own personality. The G Minor is shadowy and intense, the *Jupiter* is triumphant and powerful, and the E-Flat has breadth and sweep that foreshadow the symphonies of Beethoven, in particular the one in the same key (the *Eroica*). Of the three only Symphony Number 39 begins with a slow introduction. This introduction is on a grand scale, and it suggests right at the outset, with string scales alternating with orchestral chords, the dramatic contrasts that are to come. The symphony is often fully orchestrated, thus creating a ponderous sonority appropriate to the work's large scope. But it also contains passages of intimacy, as in the string melodies of the slow movement and the middle section of the minuet, in which two clarinets play a delectable duet (Mozart's sensitivity to the clarinet foreshadows his wonderful Clarinet Concerto). Only in the finale does the music allow itself some degree of abandon, but even there the grand drama is never left far behind. Notice, for example, the powerful pause just as the development section begins. This single-minded movement has only one real theme, which by its pervasiveness increases the music's intensity.

◆   ◆   ◆

Symphony Number 40 in G Minor, K. 550
Molto allegro
Andante
Menuetto: Allegro. Trio. Menuetto
Allegro assai

The G Minor Symphony, composed in a few weeks, was completed on 25 July 1788. The first performance probably took place on 16 April 1791 in Vienna, under the direction of Antonio Salieri.

The last three symphonies of Mozart were composed within the amazingly short period of two months. 1788 was a productive year for the composer, but even so the composition of three symphonies of major proportions during the summer months was extraordinary.

A certain mystery surrounds the creation of this music. It was unusual for Mozart to write orchestral pieces during the summer, since performances were not likely to be scheduled outside the regular concert season. Furthermore, the composer received no commission and no payment for these works, and at least two of them were never even performed during his lifetime. Why, then, did he write them? Some like to believe that they were their own justification, that Mozart had such an intense inner need to express himself that he could not wait for a convenient commission. This romantic notion may fit the impassioned nature of the music, but it is out of character for the composer. He was a craftsman who was trying, albeit unsuccessfully, to make a living from his compositions. He could hardly afford the luxury of Art for Art's sake, no matter how passionate his desire for self-expression.

A more likely explanation is that Mozart wrote the symphonies for concerts projected for the following winter that never materialized. His practicality is shown by the fact that, once a performance opportunity finally presented itself three years later, he readily re-scored the G Minor Symphony (adding clarinets and revising the oboe parts accordingly) and permitted an orchestra four times the intended size to play it. It may well be, as Mozart scholar Alfred Einstein says, that it is symbolic of the last three symphonies' "position in the history of music and of human endeavor" that they represent "no occasion, no immediate purpose, but an appeal to eternity." Nonetheless, this apparent purity of conception was nothing more than a coincidence. To believe otherwise is to allow our understanding of Mozart's artistic identity to be colored by romantic values of a later age.

The tendency to think of the G Minor, in particular, in romantic terms has been rampant. The work has provoked the most emotionally extravagant of criticisms throughout its two-hundred-year existence. That critics have heard very different meanings in this music reflects more on their own personalities than on the music, but it is nonetheless fascinating to contrast these interpretations. Is the G Minor tragic or comic, depressed or buoyant, impassioned or graceful?

Otto Jahn called it "a symphony of pain and lamentation" (1856), while C. Palmer called it "nothing but joy and animation" (1865). Alexandre Dimitrivitch Oulibicheff (1843) wrote of the finale, "I doubt whether music contains anything more profoundly incisive, more cruelly sorrowful, more violently abandoned, or more completely impassioned," while A. F. Dickinson (1927) felt that "the verve of this movement is tremendous. It is . . . the best possible tonic for the low in spirits." Georges de Saint-Foix wrote in 1932 of "feverish precipitousness, intense poignancy, and concentrated energy," while Donald Francis Tovey wrote at about the same time of "the rhythms and idioms of comedy." Robert Dearling called it "a uniquely moving expression of grief," while H. Hirschbach thought it "an ordinary, mild piece of music." While scholar Alfred Einstein found the symphony "fatalistic" and Pitts Sanborn thought it touched with "ineffable sadness," composers seem to have had happier opinions. Berlioz noted its "grace, delicacy, melodic charm, and fineness of workmanship"; Schumann found in it "Grecian lightness and grace"; Wagner thought it "exuberant with rapture."

What are we to make of this extraordinary variety of opinion? These disagreements would seem to indicate a work rich in meanings so abstract or so veiled that they appear different to different listeners. More interesting, perhaps, are the ramifications for performance, since playing the symphony necessarily involves interpreting it. Some conductors may choose to favor the passionate, others the graceful, qualities. There is no right answer, no one best way to interpret.

An interesting aspect of the interpretation of the G Minor Symphony is the choice of tempos. The first movement is *molto allegro* (very fast) while the finale is *allegro assai* (quite fast). These markings would seem to suggest that the last movement is slower, yet most conductors do the opposite. One reason that audiences continue to find the G Minor Symphony meaningful after thousands of performances is that it is capable of being presented and hence understood in many different ways.

Nothing is known of the audience reaction to the G Minor Symphony at the 1791 premiere, when Antonio Salieri conducted an orchestra of 180 musicians. Indeed, it is not even definitely confirmed that this performance took place. If it did, listeners were probably perplexed when they heard this music. Mozart, though trying to write music specifically for audiences, was inexorably drawn in his late works toward complexities and deep emotions that often puzzled his listeners. There is much in the G Minor Symphony that is unprecedented and that certainly does not seem calculated to appeal immediately. The soft opening, for example, is exceedingly rare for a classical symphony without slow introduction. The pervasive insistence in the first movement on short motivic figures rather than full-blown melodies contributes to the work's intensity, a feature that would surely have made for difficult listening in the late eighteenth century. Mozart's biographer Hugh Ottoway speculates that contemporary listeners would have found much of the symphony actually distasteful.

What was really unprecedented about this piece in 1788, what must surely have been incomprehensible to listeners in 1791, was its many levels of subtlety. The special mood — whether it is labelled intense or exuberant or whatever — is created by an almost excessive amount of time spent in the minor mode, and by certain powerfully abrupt changes of tonal area. Three of the four movements are in G minor; a more typical procedure in the classical era would have been to cast the later movements in the major, possibly to suggest a progression from tension to resolution. Even within the first movment the music hovers around G minor more than might be expected. The lyrical second theme (with winds and strings alternating), cast at first in B-flat major, comes back in the recapitulation not in the expected G major but, with surprising poignancy, in G minor.

This insistence on the tonic key is offset by certain dramatically sudden changes to distant areas. At the beginning of the development section, for example, the music moves quickly to the distant key of F-sharp minor, and from there begins the inexorable (and intensely contrapuntal) journey back to the tonic. (This intensity of counterpoint, incidentally, returns full force in the minuet, which is as far removed as imaginable from the elegant dance music that Mozart usually put into his third movements.)

The finale parallels the first movement. Again a lyric second theme, cast initially in B-flat major, becomes tragic and introspective upon its return in G minor. Again the beginning of the development is a moment of great drama. This time it is not a change to a distant key but rather a bold unison passage that seems to deny all keys. This celebrated phrase seems to approach twentieth-century atonality (we actually hear ten of the twelve tones one after another — disregarding a brief ornament — without duplication, a procedure suggesting Schoenberg more than Mozart).

Of what significance for an audience is all this analysis of key areas (and lack thereof)? Few listeners, other than trained musicians, are consciously aware of what keys a piece moves to and through. But the subtle use of tonal areas is what creates a composition's moods and what conveys its meaning. We all react to the emotional content of a work like the G Minor Symphony. Although we may disagree — as the critics quoted above surely do — about the meaning of its emotions, few would deny that the symphony expresses deeply human feelings. It is through a possibly subconscious hearing of the tonalities that we perceive these emotions. Everyone hears the *effect* of tonal contrasts even if few can name or consciously locate the key changes. In the G Minor Symphony the resulting emotional impact is unique, original, and overpowering.

Symphony Number 41 in C Major, K. 551, *Jupiter*
Allegro vivace
Andante cantabile
Menuetto: Allegretto. Trio. Menuetto
Allegro molto

The C Major Symphony was written in a few weeks and completed on 10 August 1788. Nothing is known of the first performance, which took place after Mozart's death.

The origins of Mozart's last symphony are shrouded in mystery. Although it was probably created for a concert that never materialized, no one really knows why the piece was written. Nor does anyone know how it came to be called, in the early nineteenth century, the *Jupiter*. Nothing is known of its first performance, except that it did not take place during the composer's lifetime. The music itself, however, is far from mysterious. The symphony does merit its nickname, because of both the Olympian heights of its compositional craft and its affirmative character. This character contrasts markedly with that of the Symphony Number 40 in G Minor, K. 550, completed three weeks earlier.

The contrast between these two symphonies is extraordinary. The G Minor is shadowy, intense, and introverted, while the *Jupiter* is optimistic, triumphant, and extroverted. K. 550 relies more on isolated motives and wisps of melody, while K. 551 contains a wealth of lyrical melodic lines. Symphony Number 40 hovers in the minor mode, while Number 41 remains (except in development sections) resolutely in the major. It is amazing that both pieces were written virtually together. This fact shows how wrong it can be to hear in the mood of a composition a direct statement of its composer's inner feelings. That Mozart could produce two such different works at the same time attests to the breadth of his artistic vision and to his ability to distance himself as composer from his feelings of the moment.

The symphony begins with a simple rising figure that Mozart had previously used in a number of pieces, notably the Piano Concerto Number 20 in D Minor. The concerto starts with a mysterious version of this motive, whereas the symphony's opening is forceful and positive. The simplicity of the motive is echoed in the harmonies, which involve little other than tonic and dominant (the two fundamental chords of all tonal music) for the first thirty measures. There are several melodies in this first movement, the most beautiful of which is no doubt the strings' closing theme. The composer had already used this tune in an Italian aria he had composed a few months earlier.

In contrast to the outer movements' forcefulness, the inner ones exhibit a restrained elegance, each in its own way. The lovely figurations in the slow movement, its integration of wind and string sonorities, and its stately melodies contribute to this special character. The minuet is equally dignified, but there is nonetheless subtle humor in its trio section. It begins with the most elementary of progressions: a simple dominant chord moving without embellishment to a simple tonic. Such a progression suggests not beginning but rather ending, since it is a typical cadential gesture of the classical period. In fact, this figure at first sounds like a reiteration of the end of the minuet proper. Mozart begins the trio with an ending. He then goes on to present the phrase whose ending we have just heard, after which the cadence figure returns. Is it now ending the first phrase or beginning the second? It actually has both functions, as Mozart plays again and again with beginning-ending ambiguity. This is a subtle satire, an exhibit of wit that requires of the listener a certain degree of sophistication. In order to appreciate the humor, we must understand the conventional ways symphonic sections begin and end.

The finale is the movement that no doubt led to the name *Jupiter*. It is a *tour de force* of contrapuntal writing. Throughout the movement we are treated to ingenious combinations of melodies with themselves (in imitation) or with other tunes. The culmination of these procedures is the coda, in which Mozart manages to play all the main tunes of the movement simultaneously in what amounts to five-part counterpoint. To create such a passage requires prodigious skill. Not many composers would have had the technique to do it. But Mozart makes it all seem easy. There is no hint of the labors of composition in this music. It flows effortlessly, and if we are not listening carefully we might miss the intricacy of the passage. Mozart's musicality disguises his technique, as the symphony ends with a triumphant proclamation of craft in the service of art.

Modeste Mussorgsky

Born in Karevo (later renamed Mussorgsky), Russia, on 21 March 1839.
Died in St. Petersburg (now Leningrad) on 28 March 1881.

Night on Bald Mountain

*Night on Bald Mountain was begun on 10 June 1867 and first com-
pleted on 23 June 1867. It went through numerous revisions and
was never performed during Mussorgsky's lifetime.*

Night on Bald Mountain is Mussorgsky's only orchestral work and,
apart from *Pictures at an Exhibition* for solo piano (the well-known
orchestral version was done by Ravel), the only instrumental work
among his slender output. *Night* has an extremely confused history.

The earliest reference to the demonic idea behind the piece dates
from Christmas Day, 1858, when the 19-year-old composer and his
brother sketched an outline for a three-act opera based on Gogol's *St.
John's Eve*. Nothing came of this idea, however. Two years later the
composer claimed to have been commissioned to set an act of Baron
Mengden's drama *The Witch* to music. The act was to depict a
witches' sabbat on St. John's Night. No other evidence of such a commission has been found, however. It was probably a piece of wishful
thinking on Mussorgsky's part. He never composed the music.

Mussorgsky was one of a group of composers known as the Russian Five. The further history of *Night on Bald Mountain* involves two
other composers of the Five — Mily Balakirev, the overbearing leader
of the group who encouraged its Russian nationalism, and Nicolai
Rimsky-Korsakoff, the conservative who eventually embraced the
more disciplined approaches he had learned from his Western European contemporaries. In April 1866 Mussorgsky wrote to Balakirev
that he was working on witches' music, in the form of a tone poem.
He did not complete the piece until more than a year later. At that
time he claimed to have composed it without sketches, directly into
the orchestral score, in two weeks. He was convinced of the success
of the work. He dedicated it to Balakirev, and he wrote about it to
Rimsky-Korsakoff: "On 23 June, on the eve of St. John's Day, I finished with God's help *St. John's Night on Bald Mountain* — a musical
picture with the following program: (1) assembly of the witches, their
chatter and gossip; (2) cortege of Satan; (3) unholy glorification of
Satan; and (4) witches' sabbat."

After a technical analysis of the work, the composer continued:

In my opinion *St. John's Night* is something new and is bound to produce a satisfactory impression on a thoughtful musician. I regret that distance divides us, for I should like us to examine the newborn orchestration together. . . . There is a book, *Witchcraft* by Khotinsky, containing a very graphic description of a witches' sabbat provided by the testimony of a woman on trial, who was accused of being a witch and had confessed love pranks with Satan himself to the court. The poor lunatic was burnt — this occurred in the sixteenth century. From this description I stored up the construction of the sabbat.

The passage from Khotinsky's book that excited Mussorgsky's imagination is as follows:

Sabbats, or festivities of the evil spirit, where sorcerers and witches gathered, usually took place on the heights of isolated mountains, such as Brocken or Brocksberg in Germany, Blokula in Sweden, and Bald Mountain near Kiev. More women than men attended these gatherings, and witches were more honored by the Devil. . . . He who smeared himself with a special ointment fell into a deep sleep. He then saw the Devil in the form of a black goat, seated on a stone or rotting tree stump. . . . The goat was worshipped in a most vile way. . . . Dances started in which men and women danced with each other, and also with the demons who made up the retinue of the Devil. The majority of these had the appearance of wolves, goats, toads, and all sorts of reptiles. They were at once transformed into handsome young men and became partners of the women who came to the sabbat. They usually danced back to back. At this point unspeakably vile things occurred. . . . Sabbats could occur any night and differed only in the character of the sins and vile things that took place there. However, they usually took place on Fridays, the eve before Saturday, and the main annual sabbat was celebrated on St. John's Eve. . . . At night the witches, hair falling over their shoulders, mount brooms, oven forks, spades, besoms, or whisk brooms, and fly up the chimneys to the sabbat on Bald Mountain.

Mussorgsky's letter to Rimsky-Korsakoff indicates his need to discuss the orchestration with a more experienced colleague. But first he had to send the score to Balakirev for approval and possibly for performance. Mussorgsky exulted in the success of his music, but when Balakirev responded, after a long delay, exultation turned to dejection. Mussorgsky's mentor was unable to appreciate the harmonic boldness of the work, and he expressed his disapproval openly. No performance was forthcoming. Rimsky-Korsakoff also did not think much of this strikingly original composition. Mussorgsky put the work aside and went on to other projects.

He took the composition up again in 1872. The director of the Imperial Theater commissioned four of the Russian Five to collaborate on an elaborate opera-ballet, *Mlada.* Mussorgsky and Rimsky-Korsakoff, who were sharing quarters at the time, were assigned the second and third acts. Mussorgsky was to provide a processional march, a lively market scene, and a fantastic scene for which he rearranged *Night on Bald Mountain,* adding choral parts. The collaboration did not work, and *Mlada* was abandoned. The second version of *Night* has been preserved.

In 1874 the composer started a comic opera *Sorochintsky Fair.* Although he never completed it, he did rework the chorus and orchestra version of *Night* for inclusion in the opera. This was the last version of the piece that the composer made. But the story does not end with Mussorgsky's death seven years later.

Rimsky-Korsakoff, who felt that *Night on Bald Mountain* had many marvelous effects, tried to resurrect it after his friend died. He probably used the final version, which was tamer than the version for orchestra alone. Rimsky claimed that the piece was originally for piano and orchestra, but his memory was notoriously faulty and no other evidence has ever surfaced to suggest the existence of such a version. He smoothed out many of the irregularities, and he improved the orchestration. In many ways his score is so far from the original that it is better called a fantasy on themes from *Night on Bald Mountain.*

The original score was finally published in 1968. It differs considerably from the Rimsky version. It demonstrates both Mussorgsky's originality and his inexperience with form and orchestration. It is played occasionally, but it has not superseded the well-known Rimsky fantasy. There is, furthermore, reason to doubt that it is actually the very first version, since it lacks an important theme that Mussorgsky quoted in the letter written to Rimsky shortly after the first completion of the piece.

Pictures at an Exhibition (orchestrated by Maurice Ravel)

Mussorgsky composed the piano piece Pictures at an Exhibition *in 1874. Ravel began his orchestration in May 1922 and completed it the following summer. Serge Koussevitzky conducted the first performance at the Paris Opéra on 19 October 1922.*

Victor Hartmann was an architect, watercolorist, designer, and friend of Mussorgsky. The composer not only was fond of Hartmann but also believed his friend had the vision to become a great Russian architect. Mussorgsky was devastated when Hartmann died of a heart attack at the age of 39. His grief was mingled with feelings of guilt, since he had recently been walking with Hartmann when the architect had a seizure and could not breathe. Rather than bring a doctor, Mussorgsky tried to soothe the stricken Hartmann: "Rest a bit, little soul, and then we will go on." Because of this incident Mussorgsky illogically blamed himself for Hartmann's death: "When I recall this conversation, I feel wretched that I behaved like a coward with a fear of sickness. This fear existed because I was afraid of frightening Hartmann, so I behaved like a silly schoolboy!"

Mussorgsky, who was not the most stable of people, sank into a deep depression. He was haunted by his friend's death and his irrational belief that he was partly responsible. He took to drinking, sold some of his belongings to gain income, suffered from hallucinations, disappeared for days at a time, was involved in a brawl, and was thrown out of his apartment.

Vladimir Stassov, friend of both Hartmann and Mussorgsky, was concerned for the latter's mental and physical health. He believed it might help the composer if he engaged him in some activity in Hartmann's honor. Thus he organized an exhibit of some four hundred of the artist's works. Mussorgsky attended the show and was moved by what he saw, but he was unable to compose a memorial piece for Hartmann until a few months later. When he finally set to work, he decided to write a piano suite in ten movements, each of which represented one of Hartmann's paintings. Only three of the movements correspond to pictures in Stassov's exhibit. The others were sketches and drawings Mussorgsky had seen at Hartmann's home. Linking all the movements was a "promenade" theme. "My own physiognomy peeps out through the intermezzos," explained Mussorgsky. Although *Pictures at an Exhibition* has an unmistakable grandeur, the composer was content to leave it as a piano piece. It is tempting to think, however, that he would have been pleased by the way Ravel orchestrated it a half century later.

Maurice Ravel was always less comfortable with the grand tradition of German masterworks, as exemplified in the music of Beethoven and Wagner, than with Spanish folk music, American jazz, Hungarian gypsy music, and Russian concert music. The Russians' natural mixture of folk elements into their serious music, their disregard for the Germanic tradition, the spontaneity of their art, and the wonderful colors of their orchestrations appealed to the Frenchman. He was especially drawn to the music of Mussorgsky, the least Western of the Russians.

Despite his enthusiasm, Ravel knew relatively little about Mussorgsky's music, and even less about the man. The original versions of most of the Russian's compositions were not known, since performances were usually of versions that had been "improved" by well-meaning friends, such as Rimsky-Korsakov. Ravel's friend, critic Michel D. Calvocoressi, shared his interest in Mussorgsky. Calvocoressi went to Russia in 1912 to collect material for a book on Russian music and to try to study the original score of Mussorgsky's opera *Boris Gudonov.* He found wonderful hospitality but little information in Russia. He never got to see the *Boris* manuscript, but he did find out quite a lot about the original piano score of *Pictures at an Exhibition.*

This information was to prove most helpful to Ravel when, a decade later, he undertook the orchestration of Mussorgsky's piano piece, on commission from conductor Serge Koussevitzky. Ravel was delighted with this assignment, not only because of his admiration for Mussorgsky but also since he had been having difficulties composing and sought an easier project that might unblock his creative impulse. The effort was, in this respect, unsuccessful, for Ravel composed nothing at all for the year following the completion of the *Pictures* orchestration. The composer wanted to be as faithful as possible to Mussorgsky's original, but all that was available to him was the published version, which had been heavily edited by Rimsky-Korsakoff. With the help of the materials Calvocoressi had brought back from Russia, Ravel was able to surmise much about Mussorgsky's original ideas.

Although Ravel never went to Russia, knew little about Mussorgsky's personality, and was only six years old when the Russian composer died, there was a remarkable affinity between the two men. As Victor Seroff, who has written biographies of both composers, points out,

> Both men, in regard to their art, were driven, as if possessed, to everything new, to progress — to quote Mussorgsky, "On to new shores! Fearless through storm, shallow water, and reefs — on to new shores!" Both men were freethinkers, negated dogma and tradition. To both artistic integrity was as their own flesh. Their personal lives remained an enigma to the rest of the world. Both composers preferred the company of men. With women their relationships remained those of adoring sons and devoted but platonic friends. Although, unlike Ravel, Mussorgsky was never suspected of homosexuality, both men remained adolescent in their emotional relationships. Ravel always spoke of seeking solitude, yet he was as much afraid of being alone as Mussorgsky,

who in the latter part of his life was terrified of spending a night by himself. Both men were the most sociable "animals," to quote Mussorgsky again; both loved homes, family, and children, yet neither ever married. For both the houses of their close friends were like their own homes.

Ravel was not the first to orchestrate *Pictures,* nor was he to be the last. Other orchestral versions exist by Mikhail Tushmalov, Henry Wood, Leonas Leonardi, Lucien Cailliet, Leopold Stokowski, Vladimir Ashkenazy, and others. These transcriptions are occasionally performed as curiosities, but only Ravel's orchestration has entered the standard orchestral repertoire. There are also versions for synthesizer, brass quintet, solo guitar, and rock group. This large number of arrangements of *Pictures* indicates the essentially orchestral nature of Mussorgsky's score.

Ravel was a superb and original orchestrator. It is remarkable that the *Pictures* scoring does not make the piece sound like a work of Ravel. He tried consciously to preserve Mussorgsky's sound and to orchestrate as the Russian might have done.

The following description of the promenade and the pictures is drawn from Mussorgsky's letters and other sources:

Promenade. Mussorgsky intended to portray himself and his impressions while walking in the gallery showing the Hartmann exhibit.

Gnomus. Hartmann's design of a small nutcracker, a children's toy made for a Christmas tree. The nutcracker is in the form of an evil gnome.

Promenade.

Il Vecchio castello. A watercolor of a troubadour singing before a medieval Italian castle.

Promenade.

Tuileries. Children Quarreling at Play. Hartmann's watercolor of one corner of the famous French garden.

Bydlo. The Polish word for "cattle." A drawing of two big oxen pulling a heavy peasant cart with two huge wheels.

Promenade.

Ballet of the Unhatched Chicks. Hartmann's design for costumes in the ballet *Trilby.* The chicks dance with only their legs sticking out from their shells.

Samuel Goldenberg and Schmuyle. Two pencil drawings, belonging to Mussorgsky, titled "Two Polish Jews — One Rich, the Other Poor."

Limoges: The Market. A picture of a French market.

Catacombs. A painting of Hartmann himself, accompanied by the architect Kenel and a guide with a lantern, exploring the catacombs of Paris.

Cum Mortuis in Lingua Mortua. The Promenade theme, labelled in the score "with the dead in a dead language." Mussorgsky wrote on the piano score, "Hartmann's creative spirit leads me to the place of skulls and calls to them — the skulls begin to glow faintly from within."

The Little Hut on Chicken's Legs. The home of the witch Baba Yaga in Russian fairy tales. She lives in a hut mounted on the legs of a giant fowl. Hartmann designed a clock face that represents Baba Yaga's ride on a broomstick.

The Great Gate of Kiev. Hartmann's architectural design for a structure to commemorate the day Alexander II escaped assassination in Kiev. The gate, which was never built, is pictured with a giant helmet on top.

Carl Nielsen

Born on the island of Fyn near Odense, Denmark, on 9 June 1865.
Died in Copenhagen on 3 October 1931.

Symphony Number 4, Opus 29, *The Inextinguishable*
Allegro —
Poco allegretto —
Poco adagio quasi andante —
Allegro

The Fourth Symphony was begun in 1914 and completed in January 1916. Nielsen conducted the first performance in Copenhagen on 1 February 1916.

The Fourth Symphony marked a turning point for Nielsen. He began to compose it when he gave up his post as opera conductor. In the Fourth he left behind the idyllic style best exemplified by the Third Symphony. He now embraced a more pungent, more dramatic idiom characterized by conflict. Possibly this sense of conflict came from his concern over the world situation: the Fourth was written during the early years of the First World War. When the symphony was premiered in 1916, it had an immediate impact. The composer's biggest success, it solidified his reputation as Denmark's greatest composer.

Although Nielsen did not believe in explicit program music, in which a composition depicts a story in some detail, he did often have a philosophical idea in mind while composing. In 1914 he wrote to opera singer Emil Holm about the Fourth Symphony:

> I can tell you that I am well under way with a new large-scale orchestral work, a sort of symphony in one movement, which is meant to represent all that we feel and think about life, in the most fundamental sense of the word — that is, all that has the will to live and move. Everything may be included in this concept, and music is a manifestation of life — more so than the other art forms, since it is either completely dead (when it does not sound) or completely alive — and thus it can express the concept of life right from its most elementary manifestation to the most sublime emotion.

In later correspondence, written after the completion of the *Inextinguishable* Symphony, Nielsen expanded on this idea.

491

The title *The Inextinguishable* is not a program but a pointer to the proper domain of music. It is meant to express the appearance of the most elementary forces among men, animals, and even plants. We can say, in case all the world was devastated through fire, deluge, volcanoes, etc., and all things were destroyed and dead, then nature would still begin to breed new life again, begin to push forward again with all the fine and strong forces inherent in matter. Soon plants would begin to multiply, the breeding and screaming of birds be seen and heard, man's aspiration and yearning would be felt. I have tried to represent these "inextinguishable" forces.

From these ideas we can learn the source of the conflicts in the symphony. Indeed, it contains more contrasts than any other Nielsen symphony. We also learn of the deeper aspects of the composer's love of nature. Nature for him was not simply woods, meadows, brooks, and wildlife. It represented a life force, indestructible even though an individual life can perish. A World War kills men but not man. And so, the pastoral beauty of nature conflicts in the symphony with the tension of destruction, but life survives. The work is optimistic: despite deep tensions, the forces of life — represented by consonant, diatonic music — triumph in the end.

The musical conflicts are not only between different moods and different styles but also between different tonal areas. The Nielsen Fourth is not so much in a key as "into" a key — E major. Nielsen's great originality lies in his approach to tonality. The symphony does not establish its key at the outset. Rather, E major is the goal of all the struggles. When it finally emerges toward the end of the first, third, and fourth movements, it does so with triumphant affirmation. This is a markedly different approach to tonality from that used by earlier composers. Most tonal music is in a key. It gains its drama from how that key, once established, is threatened, how the music moves away from it, and how it returns. The stability of the tonic is never in doubt. Rather, the interest lies in how the key is reachieved. In Nielsen's Fourth, however, the ultimate outcome is less sure, so that there is an undercurrent of unrest in even the most lyrical passages. The emergence of E major is an affirmation, not a reaffirmation.

Nielsen's idea of a one-movement symphony was not entirely lost when he completed the four-movement *Inextinguishable.* The movements follow one another without pause — a relatively common device in the nineteenth-century symphony. But Nielsen goes further. No movement other than the last really ends. The first disintegrates into a transition to the second. The second also falls away in preparation for the dramatic re-entrance of the high violins (which play mostly *pizzicato* accompaniments throughout the second movement) at the beginning of the third. The third is linked to the fourth by a virtuosic string transition.

In addition to the links between movements, Nielsen ties the symphony together by common thematic material, most notably the second theme of the first movement. This long, leisurely, lyrical melody, first heard in the clarinets, returns often throughout the remainder of the piece. Shortly after its initial development, it is relaunched in the clarinets, only to be interrupted, in a most dramatic and unexpected manner, by a consonant march-like transformation of itself. It is subsequently treated in a tense and dissonant manner in the brass. It is furthermore the last melody in the first movement. Its relationship to the folk-like tune of the scherzo, also in clarinets now joined by bassoons, is thus quite evident. Even the intense opening of the adagio is related to this melody. The tune returns in its original form when the finale triumphantly achieves the goal key of E major.

The most striking feature of the finale is the duel between two sets of timpani, which Nielsen indicates should be placed far apart from each other. Twice during the last movement, the timpani erupt into a fierce dialogue. Nielsen asks the percussionists to play in a menacing manner. The intrusion of the drum battle anticipates Nielsen's subsequent use of the snare drum as antagonist in the Clarinet Concerto and Fifth Symphony.

Nielsen provided a brief preface in the score of *The Inextinguishable*: "Under this title the composer has endeavored to indicate in one word what the music alone is capable of expressing to the full: *the elemental Will of Life.* Music *is* Life and, like it, inextinguishable. The title given by the composer to this musical work might therefore seem superfluous; the composer however has employed the word to underline the strictly musical character of his subject. It is not a program but only a suggestion of the right approach to the music."

Just as life persists, so the first movement's lyrical theme remains throughout and returns at the close to its original form. Just as life grows to order from chaos, so the symphony achieves the stability of E major by the end. Just as life's struggles are subsumed by Life itself, so the battling timpani in the finale are subsumed into the overall texture, as the music sweeps to its triumphant close.

◆ ◆ ◆

Symphony Number 5, Opus 50

Tempo giusto. Adagio non troppo
Allegro. Presto. Andante un poco tranquillo.
Allegro

The Fifth Symphony was composed between February 1921 and 15 January 1922. The composer conducted the first performance in Copenhagen on 24 January 1922.

The Fifth Symphony was conceived shortly after World War I. Although Denmark was not directly involved in that conflict, Nielsen cared deeply about wartime tragedies. Several commentators have traced the intensity of the Fifth Smphony directly to his feelings about war. While Nielsen denied any programmatic intent, the hostile confrontation of opposites in the symphony is undeniably warlike. While such a statement is too vague to tell us much about the composer's intentions or about his music, it is true that his large-scale works in the 1920s did break new ground and acquire a profundity only hinted at earlier. They are more tightly knit, more pungent, more polyphonic, and more dramatic than his pre-war pieces. Nielsen was also interested in composing music of outright simplicity, such as popular songs and hymns. The direct melodiousness in parts of the symphony can be linked with this gesture toward a general public. The uniquely powerful structure of the symphony comes directly from the interplay of a folk-like simplicity and the intensely dissonant symphonic style of Nielsen's post-war years.

The Fifth Symphony is cast in a unique form, appropriate to the dramatic idea of the work yet unlike the structure of a classical symphony. The symphony explores the confrontation of two moods, two personalities, two aesthetics: the consonant, harmonic, and reposeful vs. the dissonant, contrapuntal, and intense. Povl Hamburger, writing about Nielsen's symphonies, characterizes these tendencies as the constructive and the destructive: "The basic impulses seem to stem from the . . . idea of the struggle for life, the eternal conflict between constructive and destructive forces . . . , the conflict, the tension between barbarism and civilization, between chaos and order."

Similarly, composer Robert Simpson, in his seminal book *Carl Nielsen, Symphonist*, believes that the Fifth Symphony expresses "man's conflict, in which his progressive, constructive instincts are at war with other elements (also human) that confront him with indifference or downright hostility. Nielsen found he could best reflect this drama in a two-movment work, the first movement to contain the crux of the conflict itself, and the second to be a finale that would rise out of the ashes in a great fount of regenerative energy. Even this finale is not free of difficulties, but it is to prove irrestible in the end."

The first movement begins tentatively with a viola oscillation. This perpetual motion continues until it becomes an obsession. Melodies try to invade it, but they repeatedly fall into mere figuration.

The movement unfolds painfully slowly, building into a hypnotic terror. The destructive forces enter in the guise of a flurry of notes (initially accompanied by a cymbal roll) and, later, an obsessive snare drum rhythm. This militaristic music builds to an almost chaotic barbarism, which falls away before seeming to reach its full potential. A string adagio brings the constructive forces. The ensuing lyricism is a moving contrast to what has preceded it, but it does not succeed in simply replacing the opening restlessness. The destructive element intrudes, and a veritable battle breaks out. When the obsessive flurry returns in the winds, the adagio music passes from strings to brass in order to gain strength. This move precipitates further conflict, as the disturbing element now can invade the strings. The dark force brings back its ultimate weapon, the snare drum. At first its compulsive rhythm sounds at its own independent tempo, and then the drum's offensive culminates in the drummer's improvisation "as if at all costs to stop the progress of the orchestra." The lyrical adagio finally wins out, and the movement subsides almost peacefully with a clarinet cadenza. The clarinet is accompanied, however, by the unwillingly tamed snare drum, still obsessed with its destructive rhythm.

The reconciliation at the end of the first movement is an uneasy peace. A battle has been won, but not a war. The destructive forces have bowed too easily to admit total defeat. The second movement begins with a brisk allegro, far removed from the struggles of the preceding movement. Chaos creeps in and undermines this section, forcing it into directionless repetitions and an incredible *perpetuum mobile* in the strings. The section ends prematurely, giving way to a long transition to a fast fugue. The undercurrent of destructive forces comes to the surface when the clarinet and timpani interrrupt. The more the music tries to continue in the face of these obstacles, the more frantic it becomes, finally reaching a demonic frenzy and collapsing: another section ends prematurely. A second fugue, this one an andante, now tries to carry the music forward. It is intense and dissonant, but it is not destructive and hence it does not need to be destroyed. At last a synthesis is reached. The music transcends the battlefield to achieve a unity beyond the forces of construction and destruction. For the first time the symphony can move directly into a new section, without need of a mediating transition. The final section is an allegro that freely recapitulates the opening of the movement. This last part triumphantly carries the spirit of exaltation and synthesis.

Sergei Prokofiev

Born on 23 April 1891 in Sontsovka, Ekaterinoslav, Russia.
Died on 5 March 1953 in Moscow.

◆　◆　◆

Concerto Number 1 in D-Flat Major for Piano and Orchestra, Opus 10

Allegro brioso —
Andante assai —
Allegro scherzando

Concerto Number 2 in G Minor for Piano and Orchestra, Opus 16

Andantino. Allegretto. Andantino
Scherzo: Vivace
Intermezzo: Allegro moderato
Allegro tempestoso. Meno mosso. Allegro.
Moderato. Allegro tempestoso

The First Concerto was begun in 1911 and completed on 7 February 1912. The composer played the first performance in Sokolniki Park, Moscow, on 7 August 1912, with K. S. Sarajev conducting.

The Second Concerto was written in the winter of 1912–13. Prokofiev was pianist and A. P. Aslanov was conductor at the first performance, which took place at Pavlovsk on 5 September 1913. The work was revised in 1923. The composer premiered the new version in Paris, under the direction of Serge Koussevitzky.

As a student Sergei Prokofiev was something of an *enfant terrible.* He was brash and self-confident, and his attitude toward the conservatory education he was receiving and the classics it taught was less than reverent. His early compositions reflect his personality: they were and are bold, innovative, and at times harsh. Prokofiev had the confidence of youth, and he believed in his own talent. He wanted a career, and he used a combination of craftiness, notoriety, and aggressiveness to pursue his goal.

After a number of his works had been performed, Prokofiev felt that the next step in his growing career should be to have some music published. Conductor Serge Koussevitzky had established a publishing house in 1909, appointing an editorial board of such distinguished musicians as Scriabin, Rachmaninoff, and Nikolai Medtner. Prokofiev submitted some pieces to this panel and received the first of several rejections. Medtner commented, "If that is music then I am no musician." The young composer next approached the firm of P. I. Jurgenson, the most respected publishing house in Russia. Although Prokofiev included a recommendation from composer Sergei Taneyev along with his scores, the response was disheartening as well as maddening: the firm was "too busy to look at new work."

The obstinate composer decided that he would find a way to make Jurgenson look at his scores. He decided to enlist the aid of A. V. Ossovsky, a wealthy amateur musicologist. Prokofiev showed up at Ossovsky's house one day, got past the servants, and refused to leave until he had played some of his music. The composer's effrontery worked: Ossovsky was charmed (whether by the young man or his music we do not know) and wrote a strong letter of recommendation to Jurgenson. At about the same time Prokofiev performed some of his piano pieces at a concert. When they were well received, he told everyone to make sure that Jurgenson heard about his success.

Jurgenson could not resist this two-pronged attack. He sent for the composer, listened to his music, and offered him a contract on the spot. Somewhat to Jurgenson's surprise, the piano music he published sold quite well.

Now that Prokofiev was a published composer, he was able to secure prestigious performances. Thus he introduced his First Piano Concerto in 1912, simultaneously making his debut as a piano soloist with orchestra and as a concerto composer. He performed at a summer outdoor concert. The unsophisticated audience enjoyed the sight and sound of a pianist-composer who looked like a boy playing, with great verve, passages of the most amazing technical brilliance. Critical reaction, however, was mixed, with some particularly nasty reviews. One newspaper called the concerto "harsh, coarse, primitive cacophony scarcely deserving the name of music. In his desperate search for novelty utterly alien to his nature, the composer has definitely overreached himself. Such things do not happen with real talent."

Rather than be discouraged, Prokofiev began almost immediately to compose the Second Concerto. When he performed it, the critics were again harsh.

A youth looking like a Petersburg schoolboy appeared on the platform. It was Sergei Prokofiev. He sat down at the piano and seemed to be at one moment dusting the keyboard, at another to be tapping the notes at random in a sharp, dry manner. Some of the audience did not know what to make of all this. Indignant murmurs arose. Two people got up and hurriedly left, exclaiming, "Music like this is enough to drive one out of one's mind!"

More followed. The young pianist ended his concerto with a relentless discordant combination of brasses. The audience was scandalized, and most of them hissed. With a mocking bow Prokofiev sat down again and at once played an encore. There were exclamations from all sides: "To the devil with this futurist music! We came here to enjoy ourselves! The cats on the roof make more endurable noises!" But the modernist critics were in raptures. "Brilliant!" they cried. "What novelty! What temperament and originality!"

Another reviewer reported, "Prokofiev's concerto is cacophony which has nothing to do with the art of music. His cadenzas are insufferable. The concerto is filled to overflowing with musical mud, produced, one might imagine, by the accidental spilling of ink on music paper."

These negative reactions closed many doors to the aspiring composer, but he did not give up. He took solace in the fact that his compatriot Igor Stravinsky had suffered insults at the premiere of the *Rite of Spring* earlier the same year and yet seemed to be having a spectacularly successful career. Furthermore, Prokofiev felt that his concerto was more radical and more endurable than any of Stravinsky's music he knew! He continued to compose the agressive music that he believed was right.

And he continued to pursue his career. He tried to get conductor Alexander Siloti to program the Second Concerto, but Siloti resisted. With the help of composer Nikolai Miaskovsky, Prokofiev made the issue public. Siloti responded in the press, "I cannot invite Prokofiev to play his Second Concerto at my concerts, for the simple reason that I should have to conduct the orchestra and with such a work that is quite beyond me. After all, Debussy's music at least possesses a pleasant aroma. Prokofiev's stinks to high heaven."

The composer next decided to enter a competition for piano performance. He planned to play one of his own concertos.

While I might not be able to compete successfully if I played a classical concerto, I reckoned there was a chance that my own [First] Concerto might impress the examiners by the sheer novelty of the technique it demanded; they simply would not be able to make up their minds whether I was or was not playing it well! Again, if I played my own concerto and did not win the prize, the defeat would be less mortifying because no one would be able to decide whether I had forfeited the prize because my concerto was bad in itself or because I played it badly!

When he announced that he would play his own First Concerto ("the Second would have sounded too outlandish inside the hallowed walls of the Conservatory"), the jury balked. How could they assess the accuracy of his playing if they did not know the work? Whereupon the composer arranged for his publisher to provide scores for everyone in the audience to read. This gesture of brash overconfidence impressed the jurists, and — after much deliberation — they awarded the prize to Prokofiev.

Alexander Glazunov, chairman of the jury, represented the minority opinion. True, several years earlier he had helped a brilliant young boy of 13 pass the rigid entrance examination for the St. Petersburg Conservatory. True, he had been forgiving when a certain irreverent Conservatory student had purposefully added wrong notes to classical chamber pieces. But to have the effrontery to enter a piano competition with his own so-called concerto was too much! Glazunov told his fellow jurors that they would sanction "a harmful trend" if they awarded the first prize to a rebel and an upstart, to a young man who publicly expressed scorn for Mozart and Chopin. But Glazunov was overruled. At first he refused to announce the result, but finally, seeing the impossibility of his position, he told the waiting audience the name of the winner "in a flat, toneless mumble," as Prokofiev later recalled. The winner received a grand piano, the opportunity of performing his concerto at the Conservatory graduation ceremonies, and, from his mother, a trip to England.

When he arrived in London, Prokofiev met the Russian impresario Sergei Diaghilev, whose ballet troupe had made history by introducing spectacular new works by Stravinsky and Ravel. Diaghilev was a sophisticated man of the world, and Prokofiev was an outspoken young man with no sense of social manners. Nonetheless, Diaghilev was willing to listen to Prokofiev's music. The composer played the Second Concerto (in an arrangement for piano alone). One of Diaghilev's assistants murmured, "This young man is a wild beast." But Diaghilev saw the potential for yet another ballet novelty, and he commissioned the arrogant composer on the spot.

Prokofiev returned to the Second Concerto several years later. The original score had been burned in a fire, and he revised the piece as he wrote out a new score. He completed the revision just before moving to Paris in 1923.

He went to France in an attempt to make his career international. Paris was then the center of contemporary music, and Prokofiev knew of the reverence for Russian music harbored by Ravel (and, earlier, by Debussy). Although the suave French musicians had trouble at first with Prokofiev's blunt personality, they soon included him regularly in their social gatherings. He decided it would further his acceptance in France to play one of his most typically Russian works. His performance of the revised Second Piano Concerto was an enormous success. Parisians were excited to see as well as hear Prokofiev hammering out what they took to be the longest and most difficult cadenza ever written. The tremendous energy in the music, and in Prokofiev's performance of it, secured his reputation in Paris.

Listening to Prokofiev's first two piano concertos today, it is easy to hear the brashness and verve that excited their first audiences and horrified Prokofiev's learned professors and some of the stuffier newspaper critics. But we can also be amused by the thought that this music was condemned as cacophonic or talentless. What struck early listeners as cacophony today seems more like the unbridled exhuberance of youth. This is exciting, extroverted music.

Prokofiev wrote of the First Concerto:

> The conception is expressed in two ways: by some of the means used to combine piano and orchestra, and by the form — a sonata-like allegro with the introduction repeated after the exposition and again at the end, a brief andante, and a developmental scherzo with cadenza to introduce the recapitulation. This form was criticized at the time in some quarters as being no more than a succession of unrelated episodes, but in fact the episodes are held together quite firmly. The execution of the idea was an improvement on previous scores, and, except for a little minor retouching, I have left the work as I wrote it.

The concerto was originally conceived as a one-movement concertino. As the composer points out, the finished piece combines single-movement and three-movement form. The sections are played without pause, and the finale functions in many ways as recapitulation of the first movement. The andante is almost too brief to be an independent movement.

Within this brief concerto there is a wealth of imaginative, original ideas. The fully orchestrated introduction, for example, is full of life. The brilliant virtuosity of the ensuing piano solo is equally extroverted. It is difficult to understand how the lovely slow movement could have offended anyone. It is closer in mood to the lyricism of Rachmaninoff than to the quirky outer movements. The finale is full of wit, charm, and rhythmic drive. Prokofiev biographers Lawrence and Elisabeth Hanson hear, toward the end of the cadenza, a sarcastic reference to the Mozart piano sonatas that Prokofiev hated to play.

As brilliant as the First Concerto is, the virtuosity in the Second is at times staggering. Prokofiev was out to conquer the world as a pianist and as a composer. The extremely long cadenza in the first movement, for example, builds inexorably in intensity and technical fireworks. Every time we think the pianist can give no more, Prokofiev places new demands before him. And this is in the concerto's slow movement! By contrast, the cadenzas in the tempestuous last movement are points of repose in an otherwise relentless piece. The perpetual motion of the scherzo and march-like drive of the intermezzo add to the impression of barbarism. This is highly original music, and, like its 22-year-old composer, brash, irreverent, and aggressive. It is not surprising that a public nurtured on music by Rimsky-Korsakov and his successors would find this music baffling. Today, however, its dissonances are exciting, its power breathtaking, its aesthetic engaging.

◆ ◆ ◆

Concerto Number 3 in C Major for Piano and Orchestra, Opus 26

> Andante. Allegro
> Andantino. Allegro. Allegro moderato. Andante
>   meditativo. Allegro giusto
> Allegro non troppo. Meno mosso. Allegro

The Third Concerto was composed in Brittany during the summer of 1921, using materials that date back as far as 1911. Prokofiev was soloist when Frederick Stock conducted the Chicago Symphony Orchestra in the premiere in Chicago on 16 December 1921.

Prokofiev worked on the Third Piano Concerto over an extended period. One of the themes dates from 1911, but it was only in 1916 that he determined to include it in a piano concerto. At that time he sketched out two themes for the first movement plus a theme and two variations for the second. He set the work aside but returned to it in 1918. He then decided to incorporate some material from a discarded diatonic string quartet. The first two themes of the concerto's finale originated in the quartet.

While working on these materials, Prokofiev decided to leave Russia. He applied for a visa to visit America. The Soviet Commissar for Education was perplexed that the composer should want to leave his homeland so soon after the Russian Revolution, at a time that was being hailed as the beginning of a new age. But Prokofiev was apolitical, as indifferent to the Soviets as he had been to the Czarist aristocracy. The Commissar told the composer, "You are a revolutionary in music, we are revolutionaries in life. We ought to work together. But I shan't stand in your way if you want to go to America."

The Commissar was convinced that Prokofiev would be disillusioned by life in a capitalist country. He was not wrong. After a difficult journey, involving 18 consecutive days on an overcrowded train with little food and inadequate sanitation, the composer embarked on the long trip across the Pacific. He continued to work on the piano concerto throughout the journey. When he arrived in San Francisco, he was detained and interrogated for three days. The authorities were suspicious of any Bolshevik. Prokofiev was finally allowed into the country. He went to New York, since he had been told that any artist hoping to make an impact in America had to start in that city.

His reputation as a musical revolutionary had preceded him. Thus the New York press was disappointed in his first performance, of one of his milder works. "The lion of the musical revolutionaries roared as gently as the gentlest dove. We waited in vain for those manifestations of musical extremes for which he is so famous." Prokofiev decided to include bolder works on subsequent concerts. The fundamentally conservative New York reviewers were still not pleased: "Bolshevism in art." "The epitome of Godless Russia." "Like a charge of mammoths across some vast, immemorial Asiatic plateau." "Mendelssohn with false notes." "If that is music, I really believe I prefer agriculture!" "The recipe for this kind of composition is as simple as that for boiling an egg. Write anything that comes into your head, no matter how commonplace. Then change all the accidentals, putting flats in the place of sharps and vice versa and the thing's done."

Further discouraged by the cool reception his orchestral music received from the conductor of the New York Symphony, the composer decided to try his luck in Chicago. There he fared better. Frederick Stock conducted the Chicago Symphony in his *Scythian* Suite, which received an ovation from the public. But the critics were as harsh as in New York: "A materialism equally as ruthless as Bolshevism." "The red flag of musical anarchy waved tempestuously over the old Orchestra Hall yesterday as Bolshevist melodies floated over the waves of a sea of sound in breathtaking cacophony."

Because of his popular success and Stock's support, Prokofiev was commissioned to write an opera for Chicago. Returning to New York to work, he finished *Love for Three Oranges* in October 1919. But his music still was having little success in the United States. He later recalled,

As I wandered in the enormous park in the center of New York, looking at the skyscrapers which dominate it, I thought with cold rage of all the wonderful orchestras in America who cared nothing for my music and would not play it. I thought of the critics tirelessly repeating the old platitudes of "What a great composer Beethoven is!" and reacting violently to anything in the slightest degree new. I thought of the managers arranging long tours for pianists playing the same old hackneyed programs fifty times over. I had come here much too soon. The "child" [America] is not old enough to appreciate new music.

Prokofiev returned to Europe for the summer.

He came back to Chicago rejuvenated in the fall. He was full of high hopes for the premiere of *Love for Three Oranges*, in particular because huge amounts of money had been invested in the production. But the performance was repeatedly delayed, in part because Prokofiev demanded (and threatened to sue to obtain) additional financial compensation. By the time the dispute was settled, it was too late to mount the opera. Prokofiev went to California for the winter.

Mary Garden, who had sung in the premiere of Debussy's *Pelléas et Mélisande*, was named director of the Chicago Opera. A champion of new music, she insisted that the Opera's contract with Prokofiev be honored. *Love for Three Oranges* was going to be produced the next season. Pleased with this knowledge, Prokofiev returned to Europe for the summer. At the suggestion of Russian poet Constantine Balmont, he took up residence in Brittany. There he finally brought to completion the piano concerto about which he had been thinking throughout the many months spent in America. He had already composed almost all the thematic material. He had only to supply the third theme for the finale and a subordinate theme for the first movement. He then assembled the concerto from the materials he had been collecting. When he returned to Chicago the following autumn, he brought with him the finished score. Stock agreed to conduct it with the Chicago Symphony. Prokofiev was soloist.

The performance was a smashing success. The reason may have had more to do with the notoriety surrounding the upcoming opera premiere than with the merits of the concerto. The Chicago public was eager to see the man whose opera was due to open in two weeks. Chicagoans were fascinated with Prokofiev because of his refusal, widely reported in the press two years earlier, to accept the "generous" support of American capitalism. According to the *Musical Courier,*

Florida and California [orange growers] are engaged in a struggle for the exclusive program rights to advertise their respective favorite brands. The manufacturers of the California Sunkist oranges offer to supply the singers free with the succulent fruit, and the inventor of the Florida blood orange is willing to present one of them to every auditor every evening at the Chicago Opera, if the management will permit him to put up a lobby stand of the Florida bloods and placard it with a sign: "This succulent and healthful brand inspired Prokofiev and is used exclusively by him in this opera and at home."

Since the composer had refused to allow his music advertise oranges, he had become known as the man who had turned down a lucrative offer to promote his costly opera. Thus, when he stepped onto the stage to play his Third Piano Concerto, Prokofiev faced an audience who had come to see and hear the man who was willing to spend the Opera's money but unwilling to help it earn any.

Elated by the concerto's success, Prokofiev performed it in New York five weeks later. There the public was not particularly interested in the Chicago Opera, or in the huge amount of money that had gone into its production, or in the advertising schemes of orange growers. What they perceived was a young composer who had dared to introduce his concerto (and his opera) in a rival city. The performance was destined to be a failure. The composer recorded: "In Chicago there was less understanding than support; in New York there was neither."

The opera imitated the concerto. *Love for Three Oranges* was a triumph in Chicago but a disaster six weeks later when the production moved to New York. The composer wrote about the scathing reviews: "I felt as if a pack of hounds had been set on me and were tearing me to pieces. If the opera had not been particularly well understood in Chicago, it was at least their own production and had been spared. But New York did not feel like sparing anyone or anything. They said in effect: 'So, you had the nerve to show us something we hadn't thought of producing ourselves? Well, this is what we think of it!'"

Prokofiev had spent most of the previous four years in the United States. Disheartened, he returned to Europe in March 1922. "I was left with a thousand dollars in my pocket, a bad headache, and an overpowering wish to get away to some quiet place where I could work in peace."

On purely musical grounds, it is hard to understand how the Third Piano Concerto could have provoked unfavorable reactions. A delightful and approachable piece, it has justly become one of Prokofiev's most popular scores. Its rhythms are engaging, its tunes are attractive, and its orchestration is delightful.

Perhaps the most striking characteristic of the concerto is its variety, underlined by sudden jumps from one mood to another. The lyrical introductory andante, for example, has scarcely begun to develop when it is cut short by an allegro, dominated by an impish theme in the piano. The heavily rhythmic transition to the second theme is typical of Prokofiev's brash side, but the theme itself is thoroughly lyrical. The brief introduction is expanded when it is recapitulated, as is the transition to the main theme.

The second movement is a set of variations, each of which has a different character as well as tempo. Most variations are separated by a distinctive chord progression, first heard in the winds just before the piano enters. The first variation is given to the solo piano, with flute and clarinet sounding the theme at the end. The second variation is scherzo-like and the third is *allegro moderato*. Prokofiev marked the fourth variation *meditativo*. The fifth is another allegro. The movement closes with a varied restatement of the theme, in winds accompanied by piano.

Just as the middle movement is slow with fast interludes, so the finale is fast with slow interpolations. A slow passage in the winds introduces a new theme of considerable beauty. The theme given at the outset is particularly engaging, because it seems unable to decide where its downbeats occur. The conclusion is brilliantly orchestrated.

◆ ◆ ◆

Concerto Number 1 in D Major for Violin and Orchestra, Opus 19

    Andantino
    Scherzo: Vivacissimo
    Moderato

The First Violin Concerto was begun in 1915 and completed in the summer of 1917. It was first performed in Paris on 18 October 1923. Serge Koussevitzky conducted and Marcel Darrieux was soloist.

Sometimes a composer can't win. As a young man Prokofiev was dismissed as a musical radical. His biting dissonances and sarcastic gestures were condemned by audiences accustomed to music by Rimsky-Korsakoff and Rachmaninoff. In 1921 Prokofiev's ballet *Chout* nearly created a scandal in London. The composer was derided as a "musical bolshevist." When the First Violin Concerto was first heard in Paris in 1923, on the other hand, audiences and critics — who had learned (with difficulty) to appreciate the fierce dissonances and jagged rhythms of Stravinsky — dismissed the work as "too lucid" and "Mendelssohnian"!

The concerto was scheduled to be premiered in Petrograd soon after its completion. Political conditions prevented the performance, however. Prokofiev, who had previously been apolitical, was concerned over the Russian Revolution's threat to the arts. He obtained permission to leave the country, and he traveled to Siberia, Japan, and the United States, before settling in Paris.

He was eager for a performance of the Violin Concerto. Many prominent violinists refused to play it. Finally, Koussevitzky's concertmaster agreed to try it. The work's future was not enhanced by its lukewarm reception, caused in part by a fashionable premiere on the same program: Stravinsky's Octet. When Joseph Szigeti played the concerto at the International Society for Contemporary Music festival in Prague the next year, it was an enormous success. Szigeti went on to perform it all over the world.

Years later, in his autobiography, Prokofiev delineated four dominant trends in his music. All of them are found in the First Violin Concerto. They are (1) the lyrical, which concentrates on melodic lines; (2) the innovative, which he identified with strong emotions; (3) the toccata element, which consists of driving, motoric rhythms; and (4) the classical, deriving from his early exposure to Beethoven sonatas.

1. The lyrical element is noticeable immediately in the beautiful, arching opening line in the solo violin, which moves gradually to its highest register. This line colors the entire first movement, so that even when the music becomes more pungent, lyricism is never lost.

2. The second aspect of Prokofiev's style is heard in the many innovative passages in the first movement. The solo violin plays a *pizzicato* accompaniment to flutes and clarinet. Later the solo instrument strums four-note chords in guitar fashion — another original sound. The most unusual passage in the first movement is the long coda, which is beautifully coloristic. Rapid, high, soft, delicate motion in the violin and harp accompanies the main lyrical melody in the flute. Other delicate sounds enter — viola tremolos, piccolo, other winds, and finally all the strings — but the low register is carefully avoided in this ethereal music. This passage returns, thoroughly transformed to include low sounds, at the end of the third movement. There are also several innovative effects in the second movement: left-hand *pizzicati* in the midst of bowed passages, high harmonic *glissandi*, etc.

3. The entire second movement exemplifies the toccata element. Its eighth-note rhythms relentlessly build excitement until the abrupt ending.

4. Most of the themes in the finale — notably the opening bassoon melody as answered by the violin — exemplify in their classic gracefulness Prokofiev's fourth trait. What results is a restrained, carefully proportioned movement.

Both the violin and the orchestra play nearly constantly. Prokofiev achieves variety not by dialogue but by the contrast of many types of music. The concerto is alternately delicate, pungent, lyrical, powerful, and intimate.

Concerto Number 2 in G Minor for Violin and Orchestra, Opus 63
Allegro moderato
Andante assai
Allegro, ben marcato

The Second Violin Concerto was begun in 1935 and completed in August of that year. Robert Soetens played the first performance in Madrid on 1 December 1935, with Enrique Arbos conducting.

1934 was a year of indecision for Prokofiev. He spent a large part of it in Russia, yet respect for his work was becoming especially high in the West. He was elected to honorary membership in the Academy of Music in Rome. As a result of his growing fame, he was asked by a group of French musicians to compose a violin concerto for the famous virtuoso Robert Soetens. The composer was torn between remaining in the West to take advantage of his rising fame, and returning to the homeland he had left 16 years earlier.

He knew full well that to move back to Russia would affect his musical style, because the brilliant, hard driving, powerful works he had been writing while living in Paris would never satisfy Soviet artistic doctrines. Russian music was supposed to be readily accessible, melodic, and consonant. The Second Violin Concerto is a transitional work: the first movement was composed in Paris, while the remaining movements were written after Prokofiev's return to Russia. The concerto is typical of his final Soviet period, in that it is lyrical, tonal, relatively consonant, and simplified.

Despite returning to Russia, the composer was still able to make extensive concert tours. Consequently, the concerto was composed in hotel rooms in a variety of European cities. The premiere took place on Prokofiev's and Soetens' tour of Portugal, Spain, Morocco, Algeria, and Tunisia.

The composer liked Spain. The Spanish people displayed a great love of music. "Wherever I played, after every concert, whether in a café or during supper in a restaurant, they would ask me thousands of questions about the Soviet Union, about Soviet music. The Spaniards were particularly interested to hear about our unions of creative artists, composers' contracts, and the centralization of our concert institutions and orchestras."

When Soetens premiered the concerto in Madrid, Prokofiev was accorded a standing ovation by both audience and orchestra. Later a special delegation was sent to the composer to express appreciation for his having allowed the work to be played first in Spain.

The first movement is cast in a traditional sonata form, except that the usual opposition between a dramatic first theme and a lyrical second theme is not evident. Both themes are lyrical. Nonetheless there is drama, as well as excitement and virtuosity, in the transitional and developmental passages. As the development section is remarkably straightforward, it is easy to follow the two themes through their various transformations. Prokofiev's concern with accessibility is clear throughout the concerto.

The second movement, like the first, is predominantly lyrical, with the solo instrument seldom silent. Again Prokofiev makes the main theme's transformations easy to follow. Many of the textures derive from the opening opposition of *staccato* (short-note) accompaniment and *legato* (smoothly connected) solo line. At the very end these roles are reversed, as the violin plays a *pizzicato* accompaniment to the lyrical tune in the cellos, horns, and clarinets.

In contrast to the earlier movements, the finale is brash, a bit sarcastic, almost demonic — certainly not lyrical. As earlier, the solo instrument plays nearly constantly. Despite the lack of outright lyricism, the music is melodic, as befits a concerto by a proper Soviet composer. Dance rhythms abound, and several times the music almost becomes a waltz. There are also exciting rhythmic and metric assymetries, such as a passage in 7/4 time that is heard twice.

Prokofiev's Second Violin Concerto was written nearly twenty years after his First. Comparisons are instructive. What is surprising is that the two works are not more different, considering the avant garde music the composer was creating in the intervening years. Although there are certain stylistic differences, they share the aesthetic of lyricism contrasted with harshness. The First Concerto was composed while Prokofiev was preparing to leave Russia, the Second upon his return. Thus the two works form an appropriate frame to Prokofiev's Parisian period.

Lieutenant Kije Suite, Opus 60
Birth of Kije
Romance
Wedding of Kije
Troika
Interment of Kije

Prokofiev composed music for the film Lieutenant Kije *in 1933. He extracted the concert suite in 1934, completing the work on 8 July.*

"The air of foreign lands does not inspire me because I am Russian, and there is nothing more harmful to me than to live in exile. . . . I must again immerse myself in the atmosphere of my homeland. . . . I must hear Russian speech and talk with the people dear to me. This will give me what I lack here, for their songs are my songs. . . . I am going home." So said Sergei Prokofiev to a critic in Paris in 1933, after 16 years away from his homeland. The composer longed to return for reasons of nostalgia, not politics.

Prokofiev's return was a boon for Soviet cultural policy. Russia's leading composer, having lived in the West and having been a "decadent modernist," had seen the "evil" of his ways and come back to his rightful home. He had apparently given up the dissonances of his foreign works in favor of a populist style thoroughly appropriate for a Soviet artist. He said, upon his return, "In the Soviet Union music is addressed to millions of people who formerly had little or no contact with music. It is this new mass audience that the modern Soviet composer must strive to reach."

One way to reach a large audience was to compose music for the cinema. As the film medium was both sophisticated and popular in 1934, Prokofiev eagerly accepted several commissions to write for the movies. The first music he undertook after his return to the Soviet Union was for Alexander Feinzimmer's *Lieutenant Kije*, based on a satirical story by Yuri Tinyanov. The score's sarcastic wit and sly humor contribute considerably to the film's delightful mood. Interestingly, the *Lieutenant Kije* music was used a quarter century later in another film, the British satire *The Horse's Mouth*, starring Alec Guinness.

The *Lieutenant Kije* music is among the most successful film scores ever composed. Prokofiev subsequently created several other movie soundtracks. His success in the medium came from his thorough understanding of the relationship between image, characterization, and music. In 1940 he wrote, "The cinema is a young and very modern art that offers new and fascinating possibilities to the composer. These possibilities must be fully utilized. Composers ought to make a study of them, instead of merely writing the music and then leaving it to the mercy of the film people. Even the most skilled sound technician cannot possibly handle the music as well as the composer himself."

The story takes place during the reign of Czar Paul, the nineteenth-century monarch who harbored an obsession bordering on mania for military pomp and discipline. The character of Lieutenant Kije is born when the Czar thinks he overhears someone say *Parutchik Kije* ("Lieutenant Kije") when in fact the actual phrase is *Parutchik je* ("the lieutenant, however . . ."). As no one dares tell the Czar he has made a mistake, the name of the lieutenant is entered into the military register. An elaborate biography must be concocted for the imaginary Kije. His military records are forged, and his career is invented. He receives a commission and gets married. Kije's creators make the mistake of casting him as a hero. When the Czar learns of his brave deeds, he insists on meeting Kije. Before he can come before the Czar, the lieutenant is conveniently "killed" in battle.

The first movement of the symphonic suite tells the story of Kije's "birth." The character's military destiny is signaled at the outset by a distant cornet fanfare. The ensuing parodistic march (beginning with drum, piccolo, and flute) suggests that his military character was less than real, since his true birth was in the mind of the Czar. An andante presents Kije's soulful theme (flute and saxophone).

The second movement is a romance, implying that Kije has become mature enough to fall in love. Prokofiev wrote two versions of this movement, one for orchestra and one for baritone solo with instrumental accompaniment. In the latter version the baritone sings:

My grey dove is full of sorrow. She moans day and night for her dear companion who left her, having vanished from sight. She is forever growing sadder. She never stops moaning and groaning. She flutters from one branch to another, listening to every sound and looking for her friend. Tell your heart to be calm, not to be like a butterfly. Do not fear to look elsewhere. Tell me, why should you not look? Seek your friend elsewhere. What has your heart decided? Where will it rest? Do you think you should go now? Be calm, fluttering heart. My grey dove suffers and cries.

The third movement, "Kije's Wedding," begins with a welcoming chant in the brass. The wedding tune appears in the cornet. Vodka no doubt flows freely at this marriage ceremony, since the music lunges from key to unexpected key. Kije's theme is played by the saxophone.

The subsequent "Troika" depicts a ride in a three-horse sleigh, accompanied by bells. Again there is an alternate version with baritone voice: "A woman's heart is like an inn: all those who wish may go in. And those who roam about day and night go in and out. Come here, I say, and have no fear, whether you are married or not. I call to everyone, whether shy or bold: come here, I say. All who are about keep coming in and going out."

The finale, "Kije's Burial," recalls themes from earlier movements as the hero reviews his past life. These melodies are cleverly superimposed. The opening cornet fanfare returns to close the suite.

Romeo and Juliet, Opus 64

The ballet Romeo and Juliet *was composed in the spring and summer of 1935. The first performance was given in Brno, Czechoslovakia, in December 1938.*

When Prokofiev was approached about composing a ballet based on Shakespeare's tragedy of two young lovers, he hesitated. He was unsure whether the complex psychological content of the drama could be translated into a wordless medium. In addition, he was concerned because *Romeo and Juliet* had already been made into operas by 14 different composers, and it had served as the basis for Tchaikovsky's overture and Berlioz' dramatic symphony. He worked on a possible scenario with stage director Sergei Radlov. Prokofiev's notes show an unusually high degree of attention to the details of plot and to the interaction of stage action and music.

When they received the music, the ballet directors found it utterly unlike anything they had had to deal with previously. They pronounced it impossible to dance, and they canceled their contract with Prokofiev. Another objection they had was to one of the many changes Prokofiev had made in the story: he had substituted a happy ending. The composer later explained:

In the last act Romeo comes a minute too soon and finds Juliet alive. The reason for taking such barbarous liberty with Shakespeare's play was purely choreographic: live people can dance, but the dying can hardly be expected to dance in bed. . . . It is

interesting to note that, while in London they limited themselves to stating simply that Sergei Prokofiev is writing a ballet
Romeo and Juliet with a "happy ending," our Shakespeare scholars turned out to be more Catholic than the Pope and stormed
in defense of the maltreated Shakespeare. Actually I was affected by something else — someone had remarked that at the
end my music did not sound like "true happiness," and this was
true. Therefore, after discussing the whole problem with cho-
reographers, we found a way of ending according to the original
play, and I have rewritten the music.

Once the Bolshoi company had rejected the ballet, Prokofiev arranged some of the music as concert suites, which were performed
with considerable success in Moscow in 1936 and 1937. But still no
one would dare to undertake staging the dance. In 1937 a proposed
premiere in Leningrad was cancelled. Finally the ballet was produced in 1938, but not in Russia. A company in Czechoslovakia performed the work without Prokofiev's participation. This premiere
outside of Russia of a major work, commissioned by a Russian theater and composed by the leading Soviet composer, was a national
embarrassment. The Russians hastened to mount the ballet. Leonid
Lavrovsky, the new choreographer of the Kirov Theater of Leningrad,
started to confer with Prokofiev immediately.

Lavrovsky made many suggestions for changes, based on his
thoughts about the staging. Prokofiev resisted every new idea. "I have
written the exact amount of music that is necessary. And I am not
going to do anything more. It is done. The piece is ready. If you want
to produce it — there it is. If not, then not." But Lavrovsky soon
learned how to deal with the stubborn composer.

Prokofiev had written no dance music for the first scene, but Lavrovsky wanted dance, not music alone, to introduce the story. When
Prokofiev refused to write any additional music, the choreographer
decided to use a movement from one of the composer's piano sonatas.
Prokofiev found out about this only when he heard it in rehearsal.
Angrily, he refused to orchestrate the music. "Very well," replied Lavrovsky, "we will have to perform it on piano, and you won't like that!"
Prokofiev left the rehearsal in a huff, but he eventually relented and
orchestrated the piece.

The composer also had troubles with the dancers, who were
quite inexperienced with twentieth-century music. The ballerina
who was to dance the part of Juliet explained,

> We simply did not understand his music. We were disturbed by
> his weird orchestration and the frequent changes in rhythm,
> which made it difficult to dance. We were not used to such mu-

sic, and we were afraid of it. It seemed to us while we rehearsed the andante in the first act, for example, that it was better to hum to ourselves some other melodies, more tuneful music, and thus create our dances to our own music. But, of course, no one dared to say this directly to Prokofiev. He was much too severe, much too haughty-looking, and all our complaints were transmitted through Lavrovsky.

Tensions continued to mount during the rehearsals. The composer, whose previous experiences with dancers included working with the world's greatest dance company — Serge Diaghilev's Ballets Russes in Paris — could not believe the artistic naïveté of the Kirov company. At one point the dancers were unable to perform because they could not hear the orchestra. Prokofiev had scored thinly when the drama seemed to called for such an approach, but the dancers were used to reacting to heavily orchestrated accents. The composer refused to believe that the orchestra could not be heard. He was finally prevailed upon to listen from the rear of the stage rather than the front of the auditorium, and then he understood that the instruments really were too soft. He finally agreed to change some of the scoring.

As the performance date approached, the dancers felt no more comfortable with the music. There was serious consideration given to cancelling the premiere, but it did finally take place, on time, on 10 January 1940. To the amazement of the performers, musicians, choreographer, and composer, the work was an enormous success. It was quickly established as a major piece of Soviet art and as the first worthy successor to the ballets of Tchaikovsky.

Scythian Suite, Opus 20
The Adoration of Veles and Ala
The Enemy God and the Dance of the Black Spirits
Night
The Glorious Departure of Lolli and the Procession
of the Sun

The Scythian *Suite was begun in the summer of 1914 and finished late in 1915. Prokofiev conducted the premiere on 29 January 1916 in Petrograd.*

Sergei Diaghilev was only 23 years old when he declared, "I think I have found my vocation. Patronage. I have everything necessary for it except money, but that will come." He was right. He had imagination, magnetism, vision, business sense, and the ability to get even the most difficult of artists to produce at their highest level. Diaghilev was not an artist himself, but he left a considerable mark on early twentieth-century music, dance, and painting.

The impresario's most successful venture was the dance company he formed in 1910 under the name Ballets Russes. He had the good sense to launch the company not in his native Russia but in Paris, where the public was supportive of the arts. In the 15 years of its existence, the Ballets Russes performed in all the major cities of the Western world. It introduced major ballets by the leading composers of the day: Debussy, Stravinsky, Ravel, Strauss, Poulenc, Prokofiev, and many others.

Diaghilev preferred to discover composers rather than to turn to established names. His most remarkable success was Stravinsky, who composed his three most famous ballet scores for the Ballets Russes. Prokofiev knew this success story and wanted to be the next Diaghilev discovery. He went to London in the summer of 1914, where Diaghilev's company was performing. Prokofiev was intent on meeting the great impresario, and he was sure he could impress him even more than Stravinsky had.

The composer met Diaghilev in London and played for him his Second Piano Concerto. Diaghilev, taken with the music, offered to have it choreographed. Prokofiev realized he had succeeded with Diaghilev more readily than even he had hoped. Yet he was still a brash and cocky young man. He boldly told the impresario that he did not want his concert music used as a ballet. Prokofiev preferred to do an opera based on Dostoevsky's *The Gambler.* Diaghilev felt that opera was a dead form. The often heated exchanges between the two men went on for several months. Diaghilev was willing to bear with this impudent young man because he felt that Prokofiev could be molded into a fine composer; Prokofiev continued to negotiate because his respect for Diaghilev was increasing and he was sure that the association would lead to an enormous advancement in his career. The two men finally settled on the idea of a ballet on prehistoric themes.

Diaghilev engaged the young poet Sergei Gorodetsky to provide the scenario. Gorodetsky, turning to Scythian mythology for characters, produced a story called *Ala and Lolli.* The first scene shows the Scythians worshipping in a ritual dance the sun god Veles and the wooden idol Ala, who symbolizes the creative powers of nature. In the second scene the evil god Chuzhbog and his seven loathsome monsters perform a frenetic "Dance of the Evil Spirits." Chuzhbog plans to abduct Ala, with the help of the evil spirits. The abduction must take place in total darkness, because even moonlight renders Chuzhbog powerless. The fairy moon-maidens descend from the heavens to help Ala. When Chuzhbog makes his attack, the Scythian warrior Lolli comes to Ala's rescue. There is a fierce struggle, and, just as Lolli is at the point of death, Veles the sun god destroys Chuzhbog.

The barbaric theme of this ballet was typical of the period. Stravinsky's *Rite of Spring*, which Prokofiev saw in London, is just one of many examples of artistic interest in the animal wisdom of primitive man. Prokofiev claimed to be unimpressed by the *Rite of Spring*, but the influence on his Scythian ballet music is unmistakable.

Late in the summer of 1915, Prokofiev completed the piano score for *Ala and Lolli*. He went to Milan to play it for Diaghilev, who did not like it at all. The impresario rejected the music as uninteresting and found the plot contrived. Diaghilev did arrange for a Prokofiev concert in Italy, as a consolation, but the idea of producing the Scythian ballet was dead. The impresario urged Prokofiev to compose a new ballet, with distinctly Russian music and based on a Russian folk tale. As he offered the composer a written contract, Prokofiev returned to Russia still excited about working with him.

Once back in his homeland, the composer decided to turn *Ala and Lolli* into a concert suite. Conductor Alexander Siloti, who had previously been indifferent to Prokofiev's music, was taken with the raw power of this *Scythian* Suite, as it was now called. He arranged for Prokofiev to conduct the premiere, knowing full well that a scandal might erupt. First the orchestra revolted. One cellist was heard to say, "I'd never stand for this if I didn't have a sick wife and three children." The audience was shocked by the music. Siloti walked up and down behind the listeners, muttering gleefully, "That's it! Give them a slap in the face! Give them a good, hard slap!" The press reacted in kind, and a full-scale artistic scandal ensued, which made Prokofiev's name in Russia. There is nothing quite like controversy to promote an artist's career.

Prokofiev's desire to outdo the Stravinsky of the *Rite of Spring* is evident right from the extraordinary beginning of the first movement. The tempo marking of the first section, which portrays the invocation of Veles, is *Allegro feroce*. The music bursts forth with great force, with brass and percussion dominating. This fierce music does indeed rival the *Rite* in its extravagant orchestration and dissonant harmonies, but Prokofiev avoided the central element of Stravinsky's excitement: jagged rhythms and meters. This is textural music. Different layers of orchestral sonority contribute to a vastly colorful texture. Melody is minimized. The second half of the movement, representing Ala, is slower and quieter, with emphasis on more ethereal sonorities: flutes, high strings, harps, piano, and celeste.

The second movement is a ferocious march, depicting Chuzhbog and the seven monsters. The music is dominated at first by the low instruments, plus eight horns and four trombones. Prokofiev does experiment with some rhythmic asymmetries and changing meters in this movement, which serve to increase the excitement continually.

"Night" begins as an atmospheric piece, with the interwoven delicate filigree of violin trills, solo piccolo, harps, and piano. The density increases, but the music remains transparent. In the middle, however, the brass enter forcefully and the fierce mood of the earlier movements returns, as Chuzhbog tries to cast a spell on Ala.

The finale depicts the triumph of Lolli and Veles. It is marked *tempestuoso.* But the tempest subsides in the fast middle section, which is the only part of the entire suite that is decidedly melodic. The level of dissonance also lessens in this section, probably to symbolize the joy of victory. The final section is a gradual build to a powerful closing.

There is an amusing story surrounding an early performance, or rather non-performance, of the *Scythian* Suite. Serge Koussevitzky scheduled the work in Moscow for Christmas Day, 1916. There was a war going on, and many of the orchestra members were in the army. It therefore proved impossible to perform a work calling for such a large performing force. Koussevitzky substituted a piece by another composer at the last minute. The next day a Moscow newspaper carried a review of the concert by Leonid Sabaneyev, a critic who always despised Prokofiev's music. The reviewer provided several scathing comments on the suite, concluding with the observation that "the composer himself conducted the work with barbarous enthusiasm." Obviously Sabaneyev had reviewed the concert without attending and had not been informed of the program change. Prokofiev struck back with a scathing letter to the newspaper, and the critic was forced to resign.

Symphony Number 1 in D Major, Opus 25, *Classical*
    Allegro
    Larghetto
    Gavotta
    Molto vivace

The First Symphony was composed in the summer of 1917, although it uses music composed the previous year. It was completed on 10 September and first performed in Petrograd on 21 April 1918. Prokofiev conducted the Court Orchestra.

Like all Russians, Prokofiev was affected by the Russian Revolution of 1917. He was living in Petrograd, where anyone in the street could have become a target of soldiers' bullets. More than once he found himself diving for cover. One day he composed a piece while crouching behind a wall to avoid being shot. There was an attempt to draft him into the army, but, thanks to the intervention of writer Maxim Gorky, the composer was excused.

He decided to spend the summer of 1917 away from the dangers of war, in a small village near Petrograd. He purposely chose a residence without a piano. Up to that time he had almost always composed at the keyboard, but he had lately begun to suspect that his fingers were a limitation to his imagination. He decided that the best way to write a piece away from the piano was to compose for a medium that does not include the piano and to use a familiar style.

> Haydn's technique had become especially clear to me after my studies with [composer Nikolai] Tcherepnin, and in that familiar channel it was, I felt, much easier to venture into dangerous waters without the piano. It seems to me that, had Haydn continued to live into our time, he would have retained his own way of writing and at the same time added something "new.". . . I wanted to compose a symphony in a classical style, and as soon as I began to progress in my work, I christened it the *Classical* Symphony, first because it sounded much more simple and second out of pure mischief — "to tease the geese," in secret hope that eventually the symphony would become a classic.

Petrograd remained an armed camp. Nonetheless, the composer gave three concerts there the following spring. On the third he conducted the *Classical* Symphony. The Soviet Commissar for Education was in the audience, and Prokofiev was banking on the conservative symphony's making a favorable impression. The composer was eager to further his career abroad, and he had applied for a passport to America. The Commissar had the power to grant or deny this request. He was perplexed that Prokofiev should want to leave Russia, but he did give his permission.

If the *Classical* Symphony had been written a decade later, it could have been called "neo-classic." It does anticipate the neo-classic style of the 1920s through '40s, but there is a difference between Prokofiev's use of the past and that of Stravinsky, the leading neo-classicist. The difference is between parody and satire, between humor and wit. Prokofiev's humor is ironic. Claiming that the symphony was a composition in a style Haydn might have used if he were still alive in 1917, Prokofiev created a subtle burlesque on the music of the classical era. He did not so much delve into the past to find inspiration for the present, as Stravinsky was to do, but rather he poked gentle fun at the past. Prokofiev once wrote about Stravinsky's neo-classicism, "I could not approve of adopting the idiom of another man and calling it one's own. Admittedly I had written a *Classical* Symphony, but that was only a passing phase. In Stravinsky the 'Bachism' is becoming the basic form of his music. I love Bach and can see nothing wrong in composing according to his principles, but I don't think one should write stylized imitations of him. Stravinsky even imagines he is creating a new kind of music."

The *Classical* Symphony takes forms, melodies, phrase structures, and rhythms typical of classicism and twists them in humorous yet graceful ways. We can "hear" a hypothetical original version of the music lurking beneath the surface. In other words, it is as if we could remove the witticisms and discover a truly classical symphony. Prokofiev's son once remarked that his father first writes music and then "Prokofievizes" it. It is certainly possible to imagine such a compositional process producing the *Classical* Symphony.

This is "wrong-note" music. It is not full of the outrageous mistakes of, for example, Shostakovich's *Age of Gold* or Mozart's *A Musical Joke*. We smile more than laugh at the quirky turns of phrase and unexpected harmonies, because they are not so very wrong. Out of place in a symphony of Mozart or Haydn, these "wrong" notes gain in Prokofiev's hands an integrity and a rightness appropriate to 1917. They give the symphony its charm and grace.

The piece begins with a two-measure introduction to the main theme. For the first eight measures this theme sounds as if it could almost have been written by Haydn, except for the violins' quintuplet. But then the theme is repeated a step lower. In a truly classical piece such a repetition would probably take place a step higher, suggesting E minor. Prokofiev's step lower sends the music into the relatively distant key of C major. The difference is subtle, but it gives the symphony is unmistakably humorous atmosphere.

Other subtleties include the unexpected appearance of one-beat measures, some delightfully sudden modulations in the development section, and the clever manner in which the recapitulation arrives. In the symphonies of Haydn, the recapitulation returns both the main theme and the main key. But here Prokofiev gives a full-blown statement of the theme in the "wrong" key of C major. After eight measures, the repetition is no longer a step lower, as in the exposition, but now, in the more normal manner, a step higher. Thus, by a confluence of witticisms, we arrive back at the home key of D major.

The slow movement presents a lyrical melody in the high violins, after a four-bar introduction. This music is "too high" for an opening statement by Haydn, but the effect is more ethereal than humorous. Some unusual rhythms, plus a middle section that consists of continual short notes, add to the cleverness of this movement.

The third movement's humor lies primarily in its extreme brevity. In addition, its purposefully clumsy phrases and unexpected twists of harmony create a delightful parody of classical minuets. The fact that this gavotte is in 4/4 time, rather than the standard minuet's 3/4, adds to the sophistication. The entire middle section takes place over a single, unchanging harmony.

The effervescent finale abounds with subtle harmonic twists, unexpected modulations, and clever turns of phrase.

No successful musical joke is merely funny. Beneath the surface of the *Classical* Symphony lies an elegance and a humanity that go well beyond the work's gentle mockery. Otherwise, how could we return to it again and again? Once we know a joke's punch line, we can no longer laugh at it. There is something both enduring and endearing behind the *Classical* Symphony's parody of classicism.

Symphony Number 5 in B-Flat Major, Opus 100
Andante
Allegro marcato
Adagio
Allegro giocoso

The Fifth Symphony was composed in the summer of 1944. Proko-fiev conducted the premiere in Moscow on 13 January 1945.

Soviet artists have often had to cope with the fickleness of governmental approval. Virtually every Russian composer of the twentieth century has enjoyed periods of praise and periods of condemnation. During World War II, however, government officials had more pressing problems to deal with than the awarding or withholding of artistic approval. Furthermore, composers were valued citizens, especially at a time when it was necessary to keep public morale high. They were evacutated from dangerous parts of the country and put in a rest home at Ivanovo, where they were left to compose as they wished.

The composers at Ivanovo in 1944 included Shostakovich, Glière, Miaskovsky, Kabalevsky, Khachaturian, and a number of lesser known musicians. The more patriotic in the group worked on pieces commemorating the war amd celebrating the hoped for victory. Some of the others took advantage of their isolation from the fighting and their freedom from meddling officials to do some creative loafing.

Prokofiev joined this group in the early summer. Suddenly life at the rest home changed. He was a man of boundless energy, and he took command of the group. He made sure no one took the name "rest home" literally. He instituted evening sessions in which each composer was to show what he had accomplished that day. Prokofiev demanded hard work and productivity, and he lived up to his own high standards. During that summer he completed two of his most ambitious works — the Eighth Piano Sonata and the Fifth Symphony.

Neither of these pieces is overtly a war composition. In contrast to what the other composers at Ivanovo were writing, and in contrast to his own earlier symphonies, the Fifth has no program other than the vague idea that it is a hymn to the freedom of the human spirit. The composer "did not choose this theme deliberately, it just came into my head and insisted on being expressed."

Ironically, or perhaps inevitably, the Fifth Symphony became known as a celebration of victory. Its optimistic character is surely responsible for this association, but also an interesting coincidence surrounded its premiere. Just before the concert began, the victory of the Red Army was announced in Moscow. As Prokofiev raised his baton, distant cannons were heard saluting the victorious entry into Germany.

The premiere was a triumph for Prokofiev, but it also proved to be his last public appearance as a conductor. Three weeks later he suffered a slight heart attack at a party in his new apartment. He fell to the bottom of the stairs and suffered in addition a brain concussion. Although he lived another eight years, he never fully recovered. This previously always active, always youthful man was forbidden most of his favorite activities — he could not play chess, play the piano in public, stay up late, converse in an animated manner, walk fast or far, smoke, drink, drive, conduct, or travel. He was a different person when he returned the following summer to the rest home in Ivanovo. No longer was he seen on the volleyball court, walking briskly over hillsides, or making sure the other composers were working hard.

As Russia gradually returned to normal after the war, the government turned its attention toward Soviet art once again. At a meeting of the Central Committee of the Communist Party called by Stalin's henchman Zhdanov in 1948, Prokofiev, Shostakovich, and most other prominent composers received official condemnations for "modernist and formalist" tendencies and for falling under Western influences. It is fascinating to compare the reactions of Shostakovich and Prokofiev. The former had lived his entire mature life under the

Soviet system and, much as he may have disliked it, he knew nothing else. Prokofiev, on the other hand, had grown up under the Czars and had lived in the West for 16 years. Both composers had to accept Zhdanov's decree and publicly "confess" — that much was not open to debate. But Shostakovich apologized with humility while Prokofiev retained a degree of cynicism, a degree of defiance. He attended Zhdanov's "conference," but he refused to take part or even to watch. It mattered little that he had composed an obligatory *Hail to Stalin* cantata or a *Cantata for the Twentieth Anniversary of the October Revolution,* or that he was willing to simplify the harmony of his oratorio *Guard for Peace.* He was forced publicly to accept the criticism. There was no choice if he wanted to remain in Russia, and he was too deeply attached to his native land and too sick to consider leaving. Furthermore, he feared for the safety of his wife should he defy the Committee.

The Fifth Symphony was one of the few works not condemned. Thus it received the official if tacit approval of the Stalin government. That is no doubt why, when it was scheduled for a performance in Salt Lake City in 1951, an anonymous phone caller threatened the life of the conductor if the performance should take place. The work was played without incident. Prokofiev, upon hearing this bizarre story, wrote, "Why should a conductor be threatened with death for including this symphony in his programs? Could it be because the music is a hymn to the freedom of the human spirit? My Fifth Symphony was intended as a hymn to free and happy man. In my view the composer — just as the poet, sculptor, or painter — is duty bound to serve man, the people. He must beautify human life and defend it."

The Russian public, which had recently applauded the very compositions of Prokofiev that were condemned in 1948, refused to accept the sudden reversal of official judgement. The composer's last works downplay the sarcastic side of his musical personality, but it is impossible to say whether the reason is political compromise or inevitable stylistic development. Eventually even Stalin capitulated, by awarding the Stalin Prize to the composer in 1951.

Both Stalin and Prokofiev died on the same day in 1953. Two years later, the Soviet government officially reversed its sanctions against Prokofiev's music. The purge of 1948 was dismissed as "Stalinist excess." With the composer safely dead and unable to defy any official decrees, the government allowed his music once again to be the national treasure it deserves to be. Prokofiev's music was always true to the Russian spirit, whether such nationalism was officially recognized or not.

The impulse behind the first movement of the Fifth Symphony is pervasively lyric. All three main themes are long, singable melodies. The one non-lyric element, a brief scherzo-like idea, is deliberately underplayed. Even when the full orchestra plays loudly, one of the singing melodies soars above the texture. Even when the music is rigorously contrapuntal, the simultaneous melodic lines are still lyrical.

The scherzo is a complete contrast. It features ever-increasing energy, provided by motor rhythms that continue through most of the piece. The liberal use of percussion contributes to the movement's demonic character. The middle section is also rhythmic, with a catchy tune that swings with its syncopations.

The slow movement is, like the first, lyrical, but it builds tremendously in intensity.

The finale summarizes the other movements in many ways, the most obvious being the quotation of the first movement's main melody in the introduction. The music has motor rhythms like those of the second movement, although the result is now march-like rather than dance-like. The ever-increasing intensity recalls the third movement.

Symphony Number 6 in E-Flat Minor, Opus 111
Allegro moderato
Largo
Vivace

The Sixth Symphony was begun in the summer of 1944 and finished late in the summer of 1947. It was first played on 11 October 1947 by the Leningrad Philharmonic, conducted by Yevgeny Mravinsky.

The last two decades of Prokofiev's life were filled with conflict and contradiction. The composer had willingly returned to his homeland after 16 years abroad, in part because he believed in the Soviet people. He wanted to create music of and for that people. On the other hand, he resented government officials dictating to him and other composers just how and what they ought to write. While he fundamentally agreed with the spirit of the doctrine of Socialist Realism — to create art that has broad appeal, that reflects the strong spirit of the Soviets, and that helps to create and preserve national unity — Prokofiev was continually angered by officials who felt they knew better than artists how to achieve these goals. Thus, while he never abandoned his ideals of a populist music, he was nonetheless frequently under attack for writing the wrong kind of music.

In 1945, shortly after the premiere of the Fifth Symphony, the composer suffered a brain concussion and heart attack, aggravated by hypertension. He was never to recover from these illnesses. He spent the remainder of his life as a semi-invalid. His weakened health might have made Prokofiev particularly vulnerable to official pressures to compose party-line music, but in fact it had the opposite effect. What could the Central Committee deprive Prokofiev of that his poor health had not already destroyed?

It was difficult for him to compose, yet he was determined to do so. He was allowed a few hours a week to work, and he stole additional time for composition when the doctors and nurses were not looking. So it was that he was able to resume work on the Sixth Symphony in the winter of 1946–47. He finished the piece the following summer, three years after he had started it (he had composed the Fifth Symphony, while still in good health, in one month). He conceived the symphony as a hymn to victory, the victory of Russia over Germany in the recently ended war. The piece is not a joyful celebration, however, because of the huge cost of the victory. Prokofiev explained the somber mood as follows: "Yes, we are now rejoicing in our magnificent victory, but thousands of us have been left with wounds that cannot be healed — health ruined for life, dear ones gone forever. We must not forget this."

He also wrote, "The first movement is agitated, at times lyrical, at times austere; the second movement is brighter and more tuneful; the finale, rapid and in a major key, is close in character to my Fifth Symphony, save for reminiscences of the austere passages in the first movement. . . . I did not want the finale to be regarded merely as a gay appendage to the preceding movements."

The symphony's somber tone is established by the low, detached chords at the beginning. The main melodic line, in the violins, is initially fragmented, in order to continue the ominous mood. A second theme, in the oboes, completely avoids chromatic notes and remains firmly in B minor. After reminiscences of the main theme, the music turns into a march, characterized by continual eighth notes in the accompaniment. The tune is marked *lugubre*, perhaps to suggest a funeral march. The music drives inexorably toward a climax of considerable power. The intensity is magnified by the persistence of one repeated note, which eventually becomes the first note of a recapitulation of the diatonic second theme, in the solo horn.

The second movement as well has considerable power. The high woodwinds at the opening suggest an intensity bordering on chaos. A melody eventually emerges in trumpet and violins, which continues to build until the entire orchestra is playing, from its lowest to its highest registers. After new lyrical melodies, tension returns as a strange, fast figure interrupts in the low instruments, dominated by timpani. The alternation of serenity and intensity continues until, at the point of greatest tension, the opening of the movement returns. The movement, like the first, ends quietly, although there is little sense of calm after such restless intensity. One can imagine while hearing this music Prokofiev's war-inspired grief, and one can equally well understand why Soviet officials failed to find in it the requisite optimism.

The finale begins as if in another world. Here is the positive attitude, the joy, that the earlier movements courted but never achieved. This carefree mood is not without undertones of tension, however: the melody is repeatedly answered by an almost incongruous figure of repeated notes, eventually rising a fifth, in the low instruments. The discontinuity implied by this interruption casts its influence over the entire movement, so that even the lyrical second theme, the straightforward development, and the eventual combination of the two melodies never seem as free and happy as they might be in another context. After the development we expect a recapitulation. Instead, the music comes down to a bassoon and bass clarinet solo, after which a theme from the first movement reappears. Now Prokofiev's plan becomes clear. He teases us with uncomplicated materials and normal procedures, in order to set us up for the enormous impact of the ending. Never again do we hear the happy little tune of the finale. Instead, the intensity of the first movement returns, followed by the repeated-note figure of the finale, suggesting that the main tune is coming. But it never does. Instead, the symphony abruptly ends. If this is truly a victory symphony, then what triumphs is tragedy. If this is truly a war symphony, then the tragedy of death far outweighs the joy of victory.

The Sixth Symphony was first performed in Leningrad in October. Prokofiev defied his doctors by attending the premiere. It was later played in Moscow. In both cases public enthusiasm was great. But evil forces far beyond Prokofiev and his music were at work.

Russia had made a rapid recovery from the war, and Stalin was able to turn his attention to areas such as the arts. He decided to take a strong line. Prokofiev believed in a nationalist Soviet music, but he had also advocated that Russian composers travel to other countries to show the world the greatness of their music. Such an idea was opposed to Stalin's policies of isolationism and confrontation. A. A. Zhdanov, a stupid yet powerful lackey of the Stalin regime, was dispatched to do the dirty work: another purge.

Zhdanov and Prokofiev were formidable opponents, despite the composer's weakened health. Zhdanov was a war hero, and Prokofiev was an enormously popular and influential composer. Zhdanov called together the newspaper critics who had praised the Sixth Symphony and ordered them to publish a series of "second thoughts."

Now the music was condemned as too harsh, too dissonant, too violent, too morbid to celebrate a victory. The symphony was dismissed an incomprehensible, despite the fact that its audiences had always seemed to understand it deeply and immediately.

Next Zhdanov summoned all offending composers to a three-day "conference," during which they were lectured about the proper way to compose. Six composers were publicly ordered to attend. Their names were listed in order of "guilt": Prokofiev, Shostakovich, Khachaturian, Miaskovsky, Popov, and Shebalin. Prokofiev, despite his failing health, attended the meetings, but he defiantly sat throughout in silence, his back turned toward Zhdanov.

Zhdanov issued a decree that the six composers had "persistently adhered to formalist and anti-Soviet practices in their music, which is marked by formalist perversions and many undemocratic tendencies, including atonality, dissonance, contempt for melody, and the use of chaotic and neuropathetic discords — all of which are alien to the artistic tastes of the Soviet people. . . . [The music] represents a Russian version of present-day modernist bourgeois culture . . . ; it must be liquidated."

Apologies were demanded from each composer. Miaskovsky and Shostakovich were dismissed from their professorships; Shebalin was fired from his post as director of the Moscow Conservatory; Khachaturian lost his position as secretary-general of the Soviet Composers' Union. The latter was replaced by a party appointee who served as hatchet man for further condemnations, against music that included some of Prokofiev's most popular and harmless compositions.

Prokofiev had no official post to lose, but Zhdanov made threats on the life of Mrs. Prokofiev. The composer was forced to apologize. The continuing stream of condemnations of his most popular music was so ludicrous that it revitalized his creative efforts. He decided to play an enormous practical joke. He promised to write only music for the good of the Soviet people, which of course was what he had always done. It was his word against Zhdanov's. Who could prove whether or not a new work was anti-Soviet? Prokofiev, still enormously popular, had promised to compose only pro-Soviet music. Could Zhdanov claim that he was doing otherwise? Prokofiev had found the way to emerge victorious from Zhdanov's purge. He made few compromises in his subsequent music, but his public stance of penance made him immune from further condemnation. Audiences were encouraged to accept his music, which they had always done anyway. Prokofiev knew that he had outwitted Zhdanov, and his satisfaction gave him new energy to compose for another year, until a stroke made him an all but helpless invalid in 1949.

Sergei Rachmaninoff

Born on 2 April 1873 in Oneg, in the Novgorod district of Russia.
Died on 28 March 1943 in Beverly Hills, California.

◆ ◆ ◆

Concerto Number 1 in F-Sharp Minor for Piano and Orchestra, Opus 1

Vivace
Andante
Allegro vivace

The First Piano Concerto was begun in 1890 and completed on 6 July 1891. The first movement was performed in Moscow on 17 March 1892, with the composer at the piano and Vasily Safonov conducting the Moscow Conservatory Orchestra. In October 1917 Rachmaninoff started extensive revisions, which were finished on 10 November 1917. The first complete performance, featuring the composer and Modeste Altschuler conducting the Russian Symphony Orchestra, took place in New York on 28 January 1919.

Rachmaninoff was one of the most brilliant students ever to attend the Moscow Conservatory. He won highest honors in piano at the age of 18. The following year he graduated a year ahead of his class with the gold medal in composition. By this time he had written an opera (which was performed with great success the following year), the First Piano Concerto, a scherzo for orchestra, two tone poems for orchestra, a string quartet, several songs, some chamber music, and a lot of piano music. He impressed audiences with his virtuosity, and his reputation began to spread. At the age of 19 he happened to compose a piano piece that was destined to become one of the most played works of all time — the Prelude in C-sharp Minor. The prelude was an instant success and was soon being performed worldwide.

He performed the first movement of his First Piano Concerto with the orchestra at the Moscow Conservatory, and the reception was not particularly enthusiastic. The composer was disappointed, of course, but subsequently he was truly devastated when his First Symphony suffered a similar fate. This time the performance was at a professional rather than a school concert, and the reviewers were merciless. Rachmaninoff withdrew both works and went into a deep depression. He never returned to the symphony (the work was eventually reconstructed from orchestral parts discovered in Moscow in

1947), and he let the concerto lay dormant until he revised it extensively in 1917.

The composer's depression was so severe that he had to seek psychiatric help: he was unable to return to composing. His melancholia must have had deep roots, as he remained insecure for the remainder of his life.

To try to shake off his depression, Rachmaninoff went to Italy in 1906 and then to Dresden, where he remained for three years. During this period he resolved to revise the First Concerto. "There are so many requests for this concerto, and it is so terrible in its present form, that I should like to work at it and, if possible, get it into decent shape. Of course it will have to be written all over again, for its orchestration is worse than its music."

The composer made his first American tour in 1909 and then returned to Moscow in 1910. He was appointed conductor of the Philharmonic, and in that position he became the most powerful musical figure in Moscow. He moved again in 1913, this time to Switzerland and then to Rome. He retreated to Moscow at the outbreak of World War I in 1914. War came to Russia three years later in the form of the Russian Revolution, which overthrew the Czarist regime and established the Communist state. Rachmaninoff, who was an aristocrat and a landowner, realized that he was in danger. He made plans to leave Russia a third time.

As the Revolution was starting, Rachmaninoff was finally getting around to revising the First Piano Concerto. By this time he had composed the enormously popular Second and Third Concertos, and he was eager to make the First a worthy companion of those two giants.

The composer later recalled the difficult times during which he was rewriting the concerto:

> The outbreak of the Bolshevist upheaval still found me in my old flat in Moscow. I had started to rewrite my First Piano Concerto, which I intended to play again. I was so engrossed with my work that I did not notice what went on around me. Consequently life during the anarchistic upheaval, which turned the existence of a non-proletarian into hell on earth, was comparatively easy for me. I sat at the writing table or the piano all day, without troubling about the rattle of machine guns and rifle shots. . . . In the evenings, however, I was reminded of my duties as a "bourgeois" and had to take my turn with the other flatowners in conscientiously guarding the house and joining in the meetings of the house "committee.". . .
>
> The anarchy around me, the brutal uprooting of all the foundations of art, the senseless destruction of all means for its

encouragement, left no hope of a normal life in Russia. I tried in vain to find an escape. . . . Then an entirely unexpected event, which I can only attribute to the grace of God and which, in any case, was the happy dispensation of a well-disposed fate, came to our rescue. Three or four days after the shooting in Moscow had begun, I received a telegram suggesting that I should make a tour of ten concerts in Scandinavia. The pecuniary side of this offer was more than modest, and a year earlier I would not have thought it worth my consideration. But now I did not hesitate to answer that I was satisfied and would accept the engagement. This took place in November of 1917. I had difficulty in obtaining a visa from the Bolshevists, but they were not long in granting it, for at first these new masters showed themselves fairly obliging towards artists. Later I heard that I was the last to receive permission to leave Russia in a "legal" manner. . . .

I was aware that I was leaving Moscow, my real home, for a very, very long time — perhaps forever. I travelled to St. Petersburg by myself in order to make all the necessary preparations for the continuance of our journey. My wife, with the two girls, followed later, and together we took the train which carried us via Finland to the Swedish frontier. One circumstance brought home to me the grip of the Bolshevists: I was allowed to take with me only the most necessary articles and not more than five hundred roubles for each member of the family.

Rachmaninoff left behind many of his manuscripts and most of his personal fortune. He stayed in Scandinavia for a few months and then left for America, which became his new home. Soon after arriving in the United States, he began to concertize. At one of his first concerts he presented the thoroughly revised First Piano Concerto, still incongruously listed as Opus 1. "I have rewritten my First Concerto; it is really good now. All the youthful freshness is there, and yet it plays itself so much more easily. And nobody pays any attention. When I tell them in America that I will play the First Concerto, they do not protest, but I can see by their faces that they would prefer the Second or Third."

The new Soviet regime in Russia had no use for an expatriate who was more than willing to speak out publicly against the Revolution and the Communists. In 1931 the Soviet government instituted a boycott on performances of Rachmaninoff's music. He was dismissed as "an insignificant imitator and reactionary, a former estate owner who as recently as 1918 burned with a hatred of Russia when the peasants took away his land, and a sworn and active enemy of the Soviet government. . . . [His music represents] the decadent attitude of the lower middle-class and is especially dangerous on the musical front of the present class war."

Back when Rachmaninoff was a student, he had an enormous respect for Tchaikovsky, who in turn supported the young composer. It is not surprising, therefore, that Rachmaninoff's Opus 1 should show his indebtedness to the elder composer's piano concertos. In particular Tchaikovsky's First Concerto can be heard hovering over the opening movement. Both works exhibit a typically Russian brooding passion. Also, the virtuoso piano style of the Rachmaninoff concerto owes much to Tchaikovsky. Rachmaninoff's harmonic language is sometimes more adventurous than his predecessor's, but it is clearly an extension of Tchaikovsky's idiom.

The melodic lyricism of the slow movement and of the slow interlude of the finale also betray an indebtedness to Tchaikovsky. The remainder of the finale, however, is less derivative. Its syncopations and rhythmic flair are the product of a youthful temperament and of a composer who was clearly emerging as an independent artist.

Concerto Number 2 in C Minor for Piano and Orchestra, Opus 18

> Moderato. Allegro. Maestoso. Tempo I
> Adagio sostenuto. Più animato. Tempo I
> Allegro scherzando. Moderato. Tempo I. Presto.
> Moderato. Tempo I. Maestoso. Risoluto

Rachmaninoff began the Second Concerto in the late summer of 1900 and finished it on 21 April 1901. Alexander Siloti conducted the last two movements, with the composer as soloist, in Moscow on 2 December 1900. Siloti conducted the first full performance with the Moscow Philharmonic and with the composer again as soloist, on 27 October 1901.

Because of the successes of his early music, Rachmaninoff wanted to write a symphony. At its first performance, in 1897, the First Symphony confused the audience, the critics condemned it, and — most importantly — the composer himself realized that it was a failure. He could not stand listening to the rehearsals and performance. His embarrassment over the piece sent him into a deep depression, which was intensified by an unhappy love affair. He started to drink heavily and was unable to compose for the next three years.

Instead, he put his energies into playing concerts and conducting. When he led the London Philharmonic in his own music in 1899, the public was enthusiastic. The Philharmonic management wanted him to return the following season to play his First Piano Concerto, but the composer rashly promised a "new and better" concerto. During the ensuing months Rachmaninoff's depression did not abate. He felt under tremendous pressure to compose the new work. Finally, in desparation, he consulted Dr. Nikolai Dahl, a psychiatrist who specialized in treating alcoholics through hypnosis.

Dr. Dahl was also an amateur cellist. Because of his interest in music, he was willing to treat the impoverished composer without charge. Rachmaninoff went to the doctor daily. Seated in a comfortable armchair, the patient was readily hypnotized. Dahl tried to get him to sleep better, to be more alert during waking hours, to stop drinking, to improve his appetite, and to increase his desire to compose. "You will begin to write your concerto; you will work with great facility; the concerto will be of excellent quality, " the doctor intoned again and again. These post-hypnotic suggestions worked. Rachmaninoff did stop drinking, never to start again for the remainder of his life. And he did at last begin to compose, completing the concerto within a few months. Dahl did not, however, succeed completely in curing the composer's depression, which returned periodically.

The last two movements of the concerto were written first, after a summer in Italy. Rachmininoff decided, with some trepidation, to play them publicly. The performance, which took place the following winter, was his first triumph as a composer in years. Then he was inspired to write the first movement. He dedicated the concerto to Dr. Dahl.

The composer still had doubts. Five days before he played the first complete performance, Rachmaninoff wrote to his friend Nikita Morozov, "I have just played over the first movement of my concerto, and only now has it become clear to me that the transition from the first theme to the second is not good and that in this form the first theme is no more than an introduction — and that when I begin the second theme no fool would believe it to be a second theme. Everybody will think this the beginning of the concerto. I consider the whole movement ruined, and from this minute it has become positively hideous to me. I am simply in despair!"

Despite Rachmaninoff's misgivings, the premiere was a success, as were several subsequent performances. The Second Concerto has gone on to become one of the most played and enjoyed in the entire repertory. The popularity of the work raised Rachmaninoff's spirits. In this new mood of self-confidence he decided to marry Nataly Satin, his first cousin.

The opening of the concerto — the inexorably building piano chords that lead into a broadly lyrical theme in the strings and clarinet — shows Rachmaninoff as heir to Tchaikovsky's romanticism. Tchaikovsky, who had died a few years before Rachmaninoff wrote the concerto, imbued his music with a brooding lyricism, expressed in sweeping melodies full of melancholy and passion. We find this thoroughly Russian spirit not only in the opening theme but also in the second theme (heard when the piano first plays melodically), in the lovely main melody of the second movement (introduced in the flute soon after the beginning, but heard mainly in the clarinet before being taken over by the piano), and — most clearly — in the emotional second theme of the finale (introduced well into the movement by violas and oboe).

Another feature the music has in common with the concertos of Tchaikovsky is its predilection for using the piano as accompaniment to the orchestra. This texture is heard, for example, during the long first theme. Perhaps the accompanimental use of the piano can also be traced to Rachmaninoff's frequent appearance in concert, while working on the concerto, as accompanist to the great singer Fyodor Chaliapin.

Rachmaninoff handles the keys of the three movements in an interesting fashion. The outer movements are in C minor (the finale evenutally changes to C major), while the slow movement is in the distant key of E major. Although there is a definite ending to each movement, followed by the customary pause, Rachmaninoff starts each movement with a transition from the key of the preceding movement. The effect is to link the movements tonally, although they are otherwise separate. Thus, when the second movement begins, it starts exactly where the first movement ended and works its way to the proper key during its introductory five measures. Similarly, the finale begins in the previous key of E major and arrives in C minor in the seventh measure.

The emotional highpoint of the concerto comes close to the end. The second theme of the finale — the embodiment of soulful Russian romanticism — is at long last played by the full orchestra (just after a brief piano cadenza), accompanied by the piano. This unabashed appeal to the emotions is the climax of the concerto's sweeping lyricism. After this extravagant grandeur, the work ends with a straightforward coda.

Concerto Number 3 in D Minor for Piano and Orchestra, Opus 30

Allegro ma non tanto
Intermezzo: Adagio —
Alla breve

The Third Piano Concerto was composed during the summer of 1909. The composer played the first performance with the New York Symphony Orchestra conducted by Walter Damrosch on 28 November 1909.

Rachmaninoff composed his Third Concerto at his summer estate Ivanovka. He needed a new concerto to play on his upcoming tour of America. He had decided to come to the United States with some trepidation, since he did not particularly like Americans. He complained that all they ever thought about was business. Yet it was for business reasons that the composer planned his American tour: he wanted to raise money to buy a car. He was fascinated by the novelty of the automobile, and he loved to drive through the countryside.

Rachmaninoff was too busy writing the concerto to have ample time to learn to play it prior to departing for the New World. He therefore took along on the boat a dumb piano, upon which he practiced silently every day. By the time the ship landed in New York, he knew the solo part.

Rachmaninoff recorded the events surrounding the first performances of the concerto.

My Third Concerto was written especially for America, and I was to play it for the first time in New York under the direction of Walter Damrosch. . . . Immediately afterwards I repeated it in New York, but under Gustav Mahler. At that time Mahler was the only conductor whom I considered worthy to be classed with Nikisch. He touched my composer's heart straight away by devoting himself to my concerto until the accompaniment, which is rather complicated, had been practiced to the point of perfection, although he had already gone through a long rehearsal. According to Mahler, every detail of the score was important — an attitude which is unfortunately rare amongst conductors.

The rehearsal began at ten o'clock. I was able to join in at eleven and arrived in good time. But we did not begin to work until twelve, when there was only a half hour left, during which I did my utmost to play through a composition which usually lasts 36 minutes. We played and played. Half an hour was long past, but Mahler did not pay the slightest attention to this fact.... Forty-five minutes later Mahler announced, "Now we will repeat the first movement." My heart froze within me. I expected a dreadful row, or at least a heated protest from the orchestra. This certainly would have happened in any other orchestra, but here I did not notice a single sign of displeasure. The musicians played the first movement with a keen or perhaps even closer application than the previous time. I went up to the conductor's desk, and together we examined the score. The musicians in the back seats began quietly to pack up their instruments and to disappear. Mahler blew up.

"What is the meaning of this?"

The concertmaster: "It is after half past one, Maestro."

"That makes no difference! As long as I am sitting, no musician has a right to get up!"

During his American tour Rachmaninoff played his Second Concerto with the Cincinnati Symphony Orchestra, conducted by Leopold Stokowski. During a second American tour eight years later, he was offered the post of conductor of that orchestra. Although he desperately needed money (his financial resources had been confiscated during the Russian Revolution), he turned down this offer, as well as one from the Boston Symphony to conduct 110 concerts in 30 weeks. He felt he did not know enough of the orchestral repertory to become the regular conductor of a major orchestra.

Although he was eventually to settle in the United States, Rachmaninoff's impressions of this country during his first tour were none too favorable. He wrote home,

I am weary of America and I have had more than enough of it. Just imagine: to concertize almost every day for three months! I have played my own compositions exclusively. I was a great success and was recalled to give encores as many as seven times. This was a great deal, considering the audiences there. The audiences are remarkably cold, spoiled by the guest performances of first-class artists. Those audiences always seek something extraordinary, something different from the last guest soloist. Their newspapers always remark on how many times the artist was recalled to take a bow, and for the large public this is the yardstick of your talent, if you please.

The Third Concerto begins with a lyrical melody in the solo piano, accompanied by the orchestra. Joseph Yasser, an organist and musicologist who was a friend of the composer, believed that this distinctly Russian tune was derived from an ancient chant of the Russian orthodox church, sung in the Monastery of the Cross, near Kiev. Yasser wrote an involved article in which he set out to prove the liturgical source of the Rachmaninoff theme. The composer denied the influence, but Yasser went so far as to demonstrate that Rachmaninoff might well have heard the melody years earlier in Kiev and hence might have remembered it subconsciously.

As the first movement progresses, the piano comes to dominate more and more, culminating in an extensive cadenza. (Rachmaninoff actually composed two alternate cadenzas, one longer and harder than the other. As pianist he used both on different occasions.) The cadenza develops the main melodic material, so that the ensuing return to the opening of the concerto need not dwell on its themes very long. This return serves less as a full-fledged recapitulation than as an epilogue, after the increasing predominance of the solo instrument has run its course.

As if to compensate for the piano's prominence in the first movement, Rachmaninoff holds it in reserve until well into the lyrical second movement. The middle section of this movement is a scherzo, whose melody is a clever transformation of the first movement's main theme.

The rhapsodic finale is a study in piano textures. The solo instrument is treated with marvelous variety. Rachmaninoff's deep understanding of his instrument resulted in a most pianistic of movements.

Rhapsody on a Theme of Paganini, for Piano and Orchestra, Opus 43

The Rhapsody was composed between 3 July and 18 August 1934. The composer was soloist and Leopold Stokowski conducted the Philadelphia Orchestra at the first performance on 7 November 1934 in Baltimore.

Rachmaninoff was one of the world's great pianists. During his mature years he spent so much time concertizing that he was unable to compose regularly. Thus we find that in 1926 he wrote his Fourth Piano Concerto plus a work for chorus and orchestra, yet no more music was forthcoming until 1931, when he wrote a solo piano piece. Again he fell silent until the *Paganini* Rhapsody in 1934, after he which only two more works appeared — the Third Symphony in 1936 and the Symphonic Dances in 1940.

He was able to compose only in relative seclusion. Thus he felt the urge to take up his pen once again after he had moved into a new home on Lake Firwaldstadt, near Lucerne. He had supervised the building of this house, which he called "Senar" — a name derived from his and his wife's names: SErgei and NAtaly Rachmaninoff. He greatly enjoyed what time he could spend at Senar. He relaxed by motorboating, gardening, visiting with his children and grandchildren, and composing.

He wrote from Senar to his friend Vladimir Vilshau,

Two weeks ago I finished a new piece. It is called *Fantasy for Piano and Orchestra in the Form of Variations on a Theme of Paganini* (the theme on which Liszt and Brahms based their sets of variations). It is a very long piece, about twenty or twenty-five minutes. That is the size of a piano concerto. I am going to try it out in New York and London, so that I can make the necessary corrections. The composition is very difficult, and I should start practicing it, but with every year I become more and more lazy about this finger work. I try to shirk practicing by playing something old, something that already sits firmly in my fingers.

Rachmaninoff based his rhapsody not only on the music of Niccolò Paganini (1782–1840), the great violinist who in essence invented virtuosity, but also on Paganini's personality. In some of the variations Rachmaninoff alludes to the violinist's life and character. Rachmaninoff used not only the theme from the last of Paganini's 24 caprices for solo violin but also the ancient death chant *Dies irae* ("Day of Wrath"), which had already been quoted by Liszt in his *Totentanz* and by Berlioz in his *Symphonie fantastique.*

Rachmaninoff wrote to choreographer Mikhail Fokine in 1937:

Why not resurrect the legend about Paganini, who, for perfection in his art and for a woman, sold his soul to an evil spirit? All the variations which have the theme of *Dies irae* represent the evil spirit. Variations 11–18 are love episodes. Paganini himself first appears in the theme and again, for the last time, but conquered, in Variation 23. . . . The evil spirit appears for the first time in Variation 7, where . . . there can be a dialogue with Paganini about his own theme and the one of *Dies irae.* Variations 8, 9, and 10 are the development of the "evil spirit." Variation 11 is a turning point into the domain of love. Variation 12 — the minuet — portrays the first appearance of the woman. Variation 13 is the first conversation between the woman and Paganini. Variation 19 is Paganini's triumph, with his diabolic *pizzicato.* It would be interesting to represent Paganini with his violin — not a real violin, of course, but something fantastic. Also, it seems to me that the other personages representing the evil spirit at the end of the piece should be drawn as caricatures in their fight for the woman and Paganini's art. Definitely as caricatures, representing Paganini. They also should be with violins, but even more fantastic and grotesque.

In 1939 *Paganini*, a ballet in three scenes by Rachmaninoff and Fokine, opened in London. The scenario largely followed the composer's ideas.

The work opens with an introduction, based on the principal motive from the Paganini theme. After the introduction the music goes directly into Variation 1, in which the theme is broken up in a "pointillistic" manner. Only after this variation do we hear the entire theme. Rachmaninoff thus came up with an ingenious new way to treat the age-old form of theme and variations. He exposes the theme only after the first variation has been heard. The theme is unmistakable, as it is played by violins in unison, accompanied by the piano. Variations 2–6 work with this melody in its original tempo and mood. Variation 7 then introduces the *Dies irae* idea in the piano, while the bassoon and the *pizzicato* cellos play the Paganini theme. Variations 8 and 9 treat the theme ever more forcefully, and then the *Dies irae* returns explicitly in the piano in Variation 10.

The next variations are character pieces based on the Paganini tune. Variation 11 is an accompanied cadenza. Variation 12 is an eerie waltz in the minor. Variation 13 suggests a demonic waltz. Variation 14 is in the style of a march but still in the meter of a waltz, so that it sounds like a parade of three-footed soldiers.

The following three variations, beginning with the piano solo of Variation 15, are symphonic and virtuosic. Variation 18 brings a romantic outpouring reminiscent of Rachmaninoff's earlier music, such as the passionate Second Piano Concerto and Second Symphony. This *andante cantabile* theme is not, as some program notes claim, Rachmaninoff's own, but rather it is an inversion — an "upside-down" playing — of the Paganini melody.

The string *pizzicati* and violin runs in Variations 19 and 20 respectively suggest Paganini's prodigious performing technique. Variations 21 and 22 are scherzo-like. Variation 23 brings back the Paganini theme, and Variation 24 is the finale. As it approaches the end, the music pushes toward a typical grandiose conclusion, but at the last moment it wittily becomes a whisper and ends impishly with an echo of the introduction.

Symphonic Dances, Opus 45

Non allegro
Andante con moto (tempo di valse)
Lento assai. Allegro vivace

The Symphonic Dances was completed in a version for two pianos on 10 August 1940. The work was orchestrated between 22 September and 19 October 1940 and first performed on 3 January 1941 by the Philadelphia Orchestra and Eugene Ormandy, to whom the work is dedicated.

As is well known, music underwent a revolution during the first years of this century. Composers such as Schoenberg, Stravinsky, Ives, and Webern invented new sounds, new rhythms, and new compositional procedures. The revolution perpetrated by these men gathered momentum, and before long many composers were exploring the new sonic landscape: atonality, unresolved dissonances, irregular rhythms, open forms, etc.

Not every composer joined the revolution, however. Sergei Rachmaninoff was only one year older than Ives and Schoenberg, yet his music seems generations removed from theirs. He found the music of Debussy insincere and that of Stravinsky cerebral. Rachmaninoff remained a true conservative. He never went beyond the mild metric shifts, jagged rhythms, and chromatic harmonies of the Symphonic Dances. Even this piece, more adventurous than his earlier music, uses no devices that were not available to composers in 1900. Yet it was composed in 1940.

Rachmaninoff's career as a composer was not easy. He was rejected by his fellow composers, most of whom had eagerly embraced the new possibilities opened up by the twentieth-century revolution. He also felt isolated from other composers because, as a superb pianist specializing in the romantic literature, he belonged more to the world of performers. Furthermore, he was a sensitive person who often went into fits of despondency when his music failed to make a favorable impression. He found it difficult to compose. Rachmaninoff wrote only five major works from 1917, when he left his native Russia to live in the United States, until his death in 1943. He had created the bulk of his work while he was still able to remain aloof from the political and musical agitation throughout Europe. After the October Revolution had sent him traveling internationally, he must have realized how divorced he really was from contemporary composers. He took refuge in his brilliant career as a pianist, but he continued to compose occasionally.

The Symphonic Dances was written first in a version for two pianos, under the title *Fantastic* Dances. Rachmaninoff often played this version privately with his neighbor, Vladimir Horowitz. The composer tried to interest Michel Fokine, who had successfully choreographed the *Rhapsody on a Theme of Paganini,* in making a ballet out of the piece. Nothing came of this project, however. Rachmaninoff completed the orchestration in the fall of 1940. Although he was an experienced orchestrator, he did not hesitate to seek advice. He wrote to Harry Glantz, trumpet player with the New York Philharmonic, about the feasibility of one passage. He sought the advice of Broadway orchestrator Robert Russell Bennett on the use of the saxophone. He asked the distinguished violinist Fritz Kreisler to edit the string parts.

The first movement is characterized by driving rhythms, except in the lyrical middle section, which features a Russian-style melody for the alto saxophone. Toward the end there is a quotation from the composer's First Symphony, which was all but unknown in 1940. After its unfavorably received premiere in 1897, it had disappeared, not to be rediscovered until four years after the composer's death.

The second movment is a slow, halting waltz with shifting meters. The waltz replaces Rachmaninoff's typically sentimental slow movement.

The finale's syncopated rhythms are vaguely reminiscent of jazz. In this movement Rachmaninoff frequently quotes the ancient Gregorian chant *Dies Irae,* sometimes disguised. This melody had been used in Liszt's *Totentanz,* which Rachmaninoff had added to his repertory the previous season, and in Berlioz' *Symphonie fantastique.* Rachmaninoff himself had previously used this song of death in his own *Rhapsody on a Theme of Paganini* and Third Symphony.

The preoccupation with death implied by the *Dies irae* quotation is also suggested by the original movement titles, which the composer later withdrew: three stages of life represented symbolically by "Noon," "Twilight," and "Midnight." Significantly, Rachmaninoff omitted dawn — birth — and emphasized old age and death. After he finished the Dances he said, "It must have been my last spark." And so it was. Although three years remained to his life, he never again composed.

Musical values change, and Rachmaninoff may yet have the last laugh over those who dismiss a work such as the Symphonic Dances as outmoded. More and more composers of today, in particular several members of the avant garde of the 1950s and '60s, are returning to unabashed lyricism and tonality. The music of Rachmaninoff is beginning to seem prophetic rather than reactionary. History may eventually come to regard him as a precursor of the triumphant return to tonality.

Symphony Number 2 in E Minor, Opus 27

Largo. Allegro moderato
Allegro molto. Meno mosso. Allegro molto
Adagio
Allegro vivace

*The Second Symphony was composed between October 1906 and
April 1907 and orchestrated in the fall of 1907. The composer conducted the first performance in St. Petersburg on 8 February 1908.*

More than a decade separates Rachmaninoff's first two symphonies.
The reason is that the composer considered the First Symphony a
disaster and was reluctant to make a second attempt in the genre.
When the composer eventually decided, with some trepidation, to try
his hand once again at composing a symphony, he at first told no one.
He was living in Dresden at the time, far away from the distractions
of his hectic career in Russia. When his friend Alexander Siloti visited
him, Rachmaninoff confided that he was working on a symphony.
Siloti invited him to conduct it in St. Petersburg and, without waiting for a response, informed the press of the upcoming premiere. Another friend wrote from St. Petersburg, asking about the work. Rachmaninoff explained,

A month ago, or more, I really did finish a symphony, but to this
must be added the phrase "in rough draft." I have not announced it to "the world," because I want first to complete it in
final form. While I was planning the orchestration, the work became terribly boring and repulsive to me. So I threw it aside
and took up something else. Thus "the world" would not have
known, yet, about my work — if it hadn't been for Siloti, who
came here and pulled out of me news of everything I have done
and of everything that I am going to do. I told him that there
will be a symphony. That's how I've already received an invitation to conduct it next season! And news of this symphony has
flown everywhere. I can tell you privately that I am displeased
with the piece.

Later the composer wrote to his friend Nikita Morozov, "As for
the quality of these [recent projects], I must say that the worst is the
[Second] Symphony. When I get it written [and orchestrated] and
then correct my *First* Symphony, I give my solemn word — no more

symphonies. Curse them! I don't know how to write them, but mainly, I don't want to."

Despite his misgivings about the Second Symphony, and despite his insecurity as a conductor, Rachmaninoff did agree to lead the premiere in St. Petersburg. He also introduced the work to Moscow a week later and then to Warsaw. The public reacted enthusiastically, as it has continued to do down to the present day. The composer was been vindicated as a symphonist.

The famous German conductor Artur Nikisch, who often made guest appearances in Russia, was eager to perform the symphony. As sometimes happens with well-known conductors, Nikisch let his fame take the place of diligent work. Confident that the Moscow orchestra knew the work, as Rachmaninoff had already conducted it with that ensemble, Nikisch managed to direct the concert without having rehearsed the work at all. In fact, he had not even looked at the score! Had Moscow not already heard the piece well played, this disastrous performance might have condemned the Second Symphony to the same fate that the First had suffered.

After these early performances, Rachmaninoff revised the work for publication. He dedicated it to composer Sergei Taneyev. Some months later Rachmaninoff met Nikisch in London. The conductor asked, "So, how is *my* [!] symphony?" The composer replied that it was being published. Nikisch, assuming that the work was dedicated to him, scheduled it in Berlin and Leipzig. When the printed score became available, the conductor bought a copy, only to discover the title page headed "To Taneyev." The arrogant Nikisch thereupon cancelled the German performances, although the programs had already been printed. Rachmaninoff feared that this public rejection of the symphony by one of the foremost conductors in Europe would bode ill for the work's future. To his surprise, however, it was soon awarded the prestigious (and lucrative) Glinka Prize.

Despite Rachmaninoff's misgivings and Nikisch's vengeance, the Second Symphony has become Rachmaninoff's best loved purely orchestral work, far surpassing in popularity his other two symphonies.

The symphony is a large, brooding, romantic work, more closely related to the nineteenth than to the twentieth century. The orchestration throughout is lush and impassioned, with considerable activity in the inner parts of the dense counterpoint. An interesting feature is the frequency of sustained notes in the bass register. The result is slowly changing harmonies, which give the symphony an imposing, monolithic quality beneath its varied melodies and motives.

Like many large nineteenth-century symphonies, the Rachmaninoff Second is pervaded by a single figure. It is first heard at the very opening, in the low strings. Its identifying characteristic is the alternation of a note and another note a step lower. This motive is also present in the prominent violin theme, which answers the initial presentation of the motive.

The two opening ideas, which both contain the basic motive, are developed throughout the extensive introduction. When the allegro finally arrives, its violin theme contains the motive, as does the lyric second theme. One result of the first movement's obsession with this one figure is that it favors motives and their combination over full-blown melodies. We must wait for later movements to hear the overwhelming expressiveness of Rachmaninoff's lyricism.

The frequent upward surges toward climaxes in the first movement are balanced by the opening horn theme of the second movement. This scherzo tune has an essentially descending shape, as does its answer in the violins. A second theme in the strings (introduced and accompanied by wistful clarinet arpeggios) provides the long melodic line absent from first movement. Like the scherzo theme, this tune descends, at least at first. It changes direction, however, as it prepares for the return of the scherzo mood.

The spiky trio theme, a "perpetual motion" in staccato strings, is treated in a quasi-fugal manner. Two factors prevent it from functioning as a true fugue — the motivic repetition within the theme and the fact that subseqent entrances are in the same key. The scherzo returns after this brief polyphonic interlude.

The slow movement begins with a string melody of soaring romantic beauty — a love theme rivaling in passion that in Tchaikovsky's *Romeo and Juliet*. After just four measures, however, this theme gives way to a long clarinet melody — beautiful in its own way, but lacking the emotional fervor of the first melody. This second tune transfers to the strings in preparation for a relaunching of the opening melody. Again we are frustrated by hearing only four measures of this quintessentially romantic music. This time it is replaced by more active music. The music builds gradually toward a powerful climax. Notice the activity within the orchestral sonority as the climax approaches. After a pause, Rachmaninoff at last provides what the movement has been yearning for: a development of the opening theme. This takes place first in a series of solos for horn, violin, English horn, flute, oboe, and clarinet. The love theme, so long understated, at last pervades the music — even while other materials are recalled — until the end of the movement.

The expansive finale starts vigorously, but soon we hear a ghostly march based on the fundamental motive. There is also a lyrically romantic melody and a quotation of the lush theme from the slow movement. After the final, soaring statement of the finale's lyrical tune, a brief but excited coda ends the work.

Maurice Ravel

Born in Ciboure, Basses Pyrénées, France, on 7 March 1875.
Died in Paris on 28 December 1937.

◆ ◆ ◆

Alborada del gracioso

Alborada del gracioso *was composed for piano in 1905 and orchestrated in 1918. Rhené-Baton conducted the first performance with the Pasdeloup Orchestra on 17 May 1919 in Paris.*

Ravel was a member of a bohemian group of artists known as *Le Club des Apaches*. The Apaches, who formed in 1902, were outside the artistic mainstream. The name these promoters of the avant garde chose for their club is a French slang term for "rowdy young men." They disliked the operas of Wagner, which were enormously popular in Paris. They admired instead Debussy's *Pelléas et Mélisande.*

The Apaches held weekly meetings and attended concerts together. Because they wanted to be able to play music far into the night, composer Maurice Delage rented a garden cottage far from any house whose occupants might be disturbed. At their meetings the club members performed and discussed new music, read poetry, and argued their viewpoints until late hours. Ravel often stayed on after meetings, sleeping on a cot.

Poet Léon-Paul Fargue wrote the following description of Ravel during his early years in the Apaches:

> He joined us in our cafés and in our wanderings through Paris, and he shared our enthusiasms and crazes of the moment. Like us, he was determined to go to every performance of *Pelléas* to the last. . . . It seemed that everything was still to be done, to be invented, and everyone knew that, and that was in the air. We were happy, cultivated, and aggressive, especially at concerts where we never hesitated to demonstrate, red in the face and chin in the air like a drawbridge, the burning and spontaneous justice of our point of view.
>
> It was in this passionate atmosphere of conflicting ideas and sensations, during these crowded hours where everything was worth its weight in richness and dignity, that the works of Ravel took shape, silently, in his patient and heroic soul. Here there was no question of failure or mediocrity, of favor-seeking or jobbery, of music for drawing rooms or bars, or of music of

the type which panders to fashionable sentimentality. Only of works, in the purest sense of the term. . . . This man, who was profoundly intelligent, versatile, precise, and as learned as it was possible to be, and who did everything with a facility that was proverbial, had the character and qualities of an artisan — and there was nothing he liked better than to be compared to one. He liked doing things, and doing things well; everything that issued from his brain, whatever reservations the critics may have had about his inspiration, bears the stamp of perfection, a certain perfection. He knew that a thing — a poem, novel, picture, garden, love affair, or ceremony — all such events or dramas can have what is called "finish," to employ a term used in the workshop. And it was his passion to offer the public works where were "finished" and polished to the last degree.

In 1905 Ravel wrote a set of five piano pieces, known as *Miroirs* ("Mirrors"), each of which is dedicated to a different member of the Apaches. The fourth piece, *Alborada del gracioso,* was for M. D. Calvocoressi, the critic who was largely responsible for the group's interest in Russian music. Pianist Ricardo Viñes, another Apache, played the first performance, in 1906. Years later, after the Apaches had disbanded, Ravel orchestrated just the one movement.

The title can be translated "Morning Serenade of the Jester." A *gracioso* is a jester in Spanish comedy, analogous to the fool in Shakespeare's plays. Such a jester assisted musicians in performing an *alborada,* a serenade by a lover to his still sleeping sweetheart.

Boléro

The ballet Boléro *was composed between July and October, 1928. The first production was given at the Paris Opéra on 22 November 1928 by Ida Rubinstein's troupe. Walther Straram was conductor, Bronislava Nijinska choreographer, and Ida Rubinstein danseuse. Ravel conducted the first concert performance with the Lamoureux Orchestra in Paris on 11 January 1930.*

Ravel was at the height of his fame when he embarked on a four-month concert tour of North America at the end of 1927. Before leaving, he promised dancer Ida Rubinstein that, on his return, he would orchestrate some piano pieces from Isaac Albéniz' *Iberia,* which she wanted to use for a ballet on a Spanish theme.

The American tour was an enormous success. An all-Ravel program in Carnegie Hall, with the Boston Symphony conducted by

Serge Koussevitzky, received a standing ovation from the entire audience. "You know, this doesn't happen to me in Paris," commented the gratified composer. He visited 25 cities, where he played the piano and conducted his music. He was overwhelmed by his success, and he was enchanted with America. He wrote home,

> As soon as I settled down at the Langdon Hotel..., the telephone didn't stop ringing. Every minute they would bring me baskets of flowers and of the most delicious fruits in the world. Rehearsals, teams of journalists (photographs, movies, caricatures) relieving one another every hour, letters, invitations to which my manager replies for me, receptions. In the evening, relaxation: dance halls, Negro theaters, gigantic movie houses, etc. I hardly know New York by day, cooped up in taxis in order to go to appointments of all sorts. I was even in a film, with make-up two centimeters thick.

Ravel visited the home of Edgar Allan Poe, whose writings were particularly admired in France. He saw Niagara Falls and the Grand Canyon. He listened to jazz in Harlem with George Gershwin and Paul Whiteman. He posed for photographs with Douglas Fairbanks and Mary Pickford. He was intrigued by the fast pace of American life, by our huge cities, skyscrapers, and technology. He brought all manner of American gadgets back to France with him. And he returned with $27,000 in concert fees: the tour had made him a rich man.

Ravel returned to France at the end of April. He soon set to work on the Albéniz orchestration for Ida Rubinstein, only to be informed that conductor Enrique Arbós had already orchestrated this music and that copyright laws forbade anyone else from making a transcription of the same music. The composer was annoyed. "My season is shot to hell! These laws are idiotic! I need to work. It would have been mere play for me to orchestrate *Iberia.* Who the hell is this Arbós? And what am I to say to Ida? She will be furious!" When Arbós learned of Ravel's problem, he graciously offered to cede the rights to him, but Ravel was already resigned to having to compose his own music for Rubinstein's Spanish ballet.

One day he played a tune at the piano for critic Gustave Samazeuilh. "Don't you think this theme has an insistent quality?" the composer asked. "I'm going to try to repeat it a number of times without any development, gradually increasing the orchestra as best I can." Thus Ravel got his idea for the ballet score. At first he called it *Fandango* but he later changed to *Boléro,* despite the fact that the music has little in common with the Spanish folk dance of that name.

The ballet was a smash hit. It was set in an Andalucían inn. Several male dancers, costumed as gypsies, were sprawled about on chairs and the floor. In danced Rubinstein. At first she danced languidly, but then, as the music grew more intense, she mounted a table and moved with ever greater abandon, arousing the men. They gathered round the table and began to join the dance. Their frenzy mounted, climaxing in an orgiastic scene of great abandon and color.

The composer was convinced that the music could not succeed apart from the ballet.

> It is an experiment in a very special and limited direction and should not be suspected of aiming at achieving anything different from, or anything more than, it actually does achieve. Before the first performance I issued a warning to the effect that what I had written was a piece lasting 17 minutes and consisting wholly of orchestral tissue without music — of one long, very gradual crescendo. There are no contrasts, and there is practically no invention except in the plan and the manner of the execution. The themes are impersonal — folk tunes of the usual Spanish-Arabian kind. Whatever may have been said to the contrary, the orchestral treatment is simple and straightforward throughout, without the slightest attempt at virtuosity.

Ravel predicted that symphony orchestras would refuse to program *Boléro.*

But he was wrong. It soon was played by orchestras in many countries, and it became and has remained Ravel's most popular orchestral work. It was broadcast and transcribed for other media, and it even became the background for movies such as *Bolero* (1934), starring Carole Lombard and George Raft, and the recent *10,* with Dudley Moore and Bo Derek (in which Ida Rubinstein's sexual conception of the music is updated). The work made an extraordinary impact when Arturo Toscanini conducted its American premiere with the New York Philharmonic in November 1929.

Ravel was present when Toscanini brought his New York orchestra to Paris to play *Boléro* a few months later. At the end of the performance, the composer refused to acknowledge the conductor's gesture toward his box. Afterward the composer stormed backstage and confronted Toscanini: the tempo had been twice too fast. The conductor replied that a bolero is not a funeral march and that the audience clearly approved, since they had given the composer and performers a standing ovation. Ravel finally relented, saying, "You, but nobody else."

Serious musicians have tended to agree with Ravel that *Boléro* is an interesting and successful experiment but hardly a major work of art. Recent developments, however, may be changing that opinion. There is a new school of composers, inappropriately called "minimalists," who are exploring the hypnotic power of music of repetition and gradual change. Seen in the light of this new aesthetic, *Boléro* becomes no longer quirky but instead prophetic. Just like some of the recent music of Steve Reich and Philip Glass, Ravel's piece repeats the same melodies over and over, gradually changing them so that a trance-like intensity builds throughout the performance.

It is easy to describe how *Boléro* is put together. Throughout the entire piece there is an insistently repeated two-measure rhythmic figure, with a typical Spanish flavor. It is heard first in the snare drum, which is eventually joined by other instruments, until it pervades the orchestra by the end. This ostinato accompanies two themes, played throughout in alternation: theme 1 in flute; theme 1 in clarinet; theme 2 in high bassoon; theme 2 in small E-flat clarinet; theme 1 in oboe d'amore; theme 1 in trumpet and flute; theme 2 in tenor saxophone; theme 2 in soprano saxophone; theme 1 in piccolos, horn, and celeste; theme 1 in oboe, oboe d'amore, English horn, and clarinets; theme 2 in trombone; theme 2 in piccolo, flutes, oboes, English horn, clarinets, and tenor saxophone; theme 1 in piccolo, flutes, oboes, clarinets, and violins; theme 1 in piccolo, flutes, oboes, English horn, clarinets, tenor saxophone, and subdivided violins; theme 2 in piccolo, flutes, oboes, English horn, trumpet, and subdivided violins; theme 2 in piccolo, flutes, oboes, English horn, clarinets, trombones, soprano saxophone, subdivided violins, violas, and cellos; theme 1 in piccolo, flutes, four trumpets, soprano and tenor saxophones, and first violins; theme 2 in flutes, piccolo, four trumpets, trombone, soprano and tenor saxophones, and first violins. This list of the themes' changing instrumentation shows both the ingenuity of Ravel's combinations and the manner in which he composes the crescendo into the score. The music escapes its seemingly endless cycle by extending theme 2 on its final appearance and moving, for the only time in the piece, into E major. This move has the function of breaking the trance and allowing the work, shortly after it returns to the home key of C major, to end.

In some of the thematic statements that are presented by several instruments, the higher sounds double the lower ones not only at the octave but also at other intervals, so that the orchestration comprises harmonies moving in parallel. Interestingly, these chords sometimes approximate the natural overtone series. Thus Ravel's orchestration does more than simply distribute the notes of the tunes to various orchestral colors. He uses sonorities instead to create new timbres, by having high instruments reinforce the overtones of low instruments. For example, when two piccolos join a horn and celeste in theme 1, they play respectively in G major and E major, thus reinforcing the C major horn's second and fourth overtones. In a carefully balanced performance in an acoustically superior hall, we should hear not so much piccolos, horn, and celeste as a single, new, blended timbre. In this way Ravel plays the orchestra as an organist plays his instrument: constantly adding stops (i.e., instruments) to create new colors. Implicit in this procedure is an attitude toward composition as not simply the combining of sounds but also the creation of new sounds. This idea, like *Boléro's* hypnotic repetition, is prophetic. It looks forward a half century to the electronic age, when composers regularly approach composition as the invention as well as the manipulation of timbre.

◆　◆　◆

Concerto in D Major for Piano (Left Hand Alone) and Orchestra

The Piano Concerto for the Left Hand was begun in the fall of 1929 and completed in 1930. Paul Wittgenstein played the first performance with the Vienna Symphony Orchestra, conducted by Robert Heger, on 5 January 1932 in Vienna.

Pianist Paul Wittgenstein, brother of philosopher Ludwig Wittgenstein, enlisted in the Austrian army during World War I. He was wounded and captured on the Russian front. Because of his wounds, his right arm had to be amputated while he was in captivity. What might have proved fatal to the careers of many other pianists was only a setback for the enterprising Wittgenstein. After a period of recuperation at the end of the war, he set about commissioning several composers to write works he could play with only one hand. Among those who responded were Britten, Strauss, Hindemith, Prokofiev, and Ravel.

Ravel had recently begun to compose a different piano concerto, the G Major, when he received the invitation from Wittgenstein. Since the composer enjoyed working within artificial restrictions, he eagerly accepted the challenge of composing for a one-handed pianist. In order to learn how a full sound could be achieved using just the left hand, he studied Saint-Saëns' Six Etudes for the Left Hand, Czerny's Exercise for the Left Hand and 24 Etudes for the Left Hand, plus works of Alkan, Scriabin, and Godowsky.

Ravel interrupted work on the G Major Concerto to compose the Left-Hand Concerto. After it was completed, he and Wittgenstein introduced the work to a private gathering. First Ravel, who was less than a superb pianist, played the solo part alone — but using two hands. Then Wittgenstein played the solo part while Ravel accompanied him, performing a piano reduction of the orchestral score at a second piano.

Wittgenstein was not pleased. He found Ravel to be "not an outstanding pianist, and I wasn't overwhelmed by the composition. It always takes me a while to grow into a difficult work. I suppose Ravel was disappointed, and I was sorry, but I had never learned to pretend. Only much later, after I'd studied the concerto for months, did I become fascinated by it and realize what a great work it was."

A dispute ensued between the pianist and composer over the proper interpretation of the work. As a result of their quarrel, Wittgenstein premiered the concerto not in Paris but in Vienna, under the direction not of Ravel but of Robert Heger. Disagreements were settled, however, and a year later Ravel conducted the Paris premiere, with Wittgenstein at the keyboard. They were scheduled to perform the work again, in Monte Carlo, but Ravel, who was already suffering from what were to be his final illnesses — neurasthenia, ataxia, and aphasia — had to ask Paul Paray to step in as conductor.

Ravel soon also finished the G Major Concerto. He told his publisher that

> planning the two piano concertos simultaneously was an interesting experience. The one in which I shall appear as the interpreter is a concerto in the truest sense of the word: I mean that it is written very much in the same spirit as those of Mozart and Saint-Saëns. . . . The Concerto for the Left Hand Alone is very different. It contains many jazz effects, and the writing is not so light. In a work of this kind, it is essential to give the impression of a texture no thinner than that of a part written for both hands. For the same reason I resorted to a style that is much nearer to that of the more solemn kind of traditional concerto.

The jazz effects in the D Major Concerto came from Ravel's recent trip to the United States. He had met jazz conductor Paul Whiteman, and he had spent several evenings visiting jazz clubs in Harlem with George Gershwin. In an address he gave in Houston, he predicted that the future of art music in the United States depended on American composers' involvement with jazz: "May this national American music of yours embody a great deal of the rich and diverting rhythm of your jazz, a great deal of the emotional expression in your blues, and a great deal of the sentiment and spirit characteristic of your popular melodies and songs, worthily deriving from, and in turn contributing to, a noble heritage in music."

Ravel realized that there was something artificial about a European composer seeking inspiration in American jazz. He knew that American composers could understand jazz in a deeper way than he could ever hope to. Throughout his career, however, the Frenchman drew inspiration from foreign sources (such as the Viennese waltz, on which he modeled *Valses nobles et sentimentales* and *La Valse*), and he reveled in artificial challenges (such as composing a piano concerto for one hand). Therefore he readily adopted certain mannerisms from the jazz he had heard in New York and Hollywood.

Ravel was one of the great orchestrators of all time. His skill can be heard throughout the concerto, particularly in the fuller passages. But listen carefully to the extraordinary originality of the low, quiet opening — a sound unlike that in any previous music. The cellos and half the string basses sustain an open chord, which the other half of the basses arpeggiate across their open strings. Then a melody is added in the most unlikely of solo instruments — the contrabassoon. Ravel writes for this potentially cumbersome instrument with such ease and elegance that we (and the contrabassoonist!) are treated to the rare pleasure of hearing it sing, in both its lowest and higher registers, with a lovely lyricism.

As the orchestra builds, its sonority is constantly fresh and imaginative. The climax of this first large crescendo is the entrance of the piano in a cadenza. Now we hear Ravel's imagination for sonority transferred into one instrument alone. He manages, by careful use of the pedal to sustain chords and melody notes while vigorous accompaniment figures are played in a lower register, to make the solo writing sound like two-handed music. Indeed, much of this cadenza *looks* on the page as if it is intended for both hands, and indeed it sounds that way. It requires an exceptional pianist (just as it required an exceptional composer) to realize this challenging music.

After the orchestra develops the melody originally played by the contrabassoon, the piano plays another solo (with light orchestral accompaniment). This time the music is lyrical, but again it sounds as if two hands are playing, because there is a full-blown, continuous melody in the upper register and *simultaneously* an arpeggiated accompaniment in the low register. Again the pedal helps create the illusion of two hands, although this time the challenge is greater, because the pianist must project sustained lyricism while in fact his hand is constantly jumping from one part of the keyboard to another.

The second section of this one-movement concerto is a scherzo, ushered in by a rapid descent in the winds answered by a descending scale in the trombones. When the piano eventually introduces the main tune, we hear the concerto's striking kinship to jazz. Blue notes abound, such as the use of the raised and lowered third scale degrees simultaneously, or the lowered seventh degree. Later in the scherzo section, we hear a blues-inspired tune played by a high solo bassoon, sounding almost like a jazz saxophone. This melody becomes still slinkier when taken over by a trombone. What is distinctly not like jazz about this theme, however, is the way it is, in effect, played at a different tempo from its accompaniment. As Ravel subsequently develops the implied rhythmic complexities, in the full orchestra with piano, the music becomes quite involved and exciting.

The final section begins with a sumptuous restatement of the opening materials. A spectacular cadenza ensues, in which the pianist must move his hand up and down the keyboard in rapid arpeggiations and, at the same time, project a melodic overlay — quite a task even for two hands! After the cadenza, the opening music returns briefly once more, and then the concerto concludes impishly with a brief reminder of the scherzo.

Concerto in G Major for Piano and Orchestra
Allegramente. Andante. Allegramente
Adagio assai
Presto

Ravel began the G Major Piano Concerto in the fall of 1929 and completed it in the fall of 1931. He conducted first performance with the Lamoureux Orchestra and soloist Marguerite Long on 14 January 1932 in Paris.

Ravel was interested in the music of many countries, including Spain, Russia, and, starting around 1918 when several jazz musicians began to appear in Parisian clubs, America. Many European composers were interested in the new harmonies and rhythms they were hearing, and before long Ravel and others were incorporating into their own compositions references to jazz. Ravel's involvement with jazz reached its peak in his two piano concertos, written in 1929–31.

Ravel was eager to listen to jazz in its authentic setting when he toured the United States in 1927–28. He visited nightclubs in New Orleans and New York's Harlem. He was intrigued to learn that jazz had far less impact on concert music here than in Europe. The more removed a composer is from a particular culture, the more objective he can be about its music. Ravel discovered that most American composers (with a few notable exceptions) were condescending toward jazz, while European composers were fascinated by it. The latter approached it without prejudice but also with only superficial understanding of its social meaning. For Americans jazz was laden with cultural connotations.

One American composer who both understood *and* respected jazz was George Gershwin, who was equally at home in the worlds of jazz, popular, and symphonic music. He admired Ravel, and the Frenchman respected his *Rhapsody in Blue.* The two men met during Ravel's American tour, and they went to Harlem jazz clubs together. Gershwin asked if Ravel would accept him as a student. Ravel replied, "You would only lose the spontaneous quality of your melodies and end up writing bad Ravel." When he returned to Paris, Ravel began the G Major Piano Concerto, somewhat under the influence (at least in the first movement) of Gershwin's Concerto in F, composed five years earlier.

While working on the concerto, Ravel received a commission for another piano concerto from Paul Wittgenstein, a pianist who had lost his right hand during the war. Ravel worked on the two concertos simultaneously. They are companion pieces, both influenced by jazz, with the G Major showing the bright and the Left Hand Concerto the dark side of the composer's personality.

Although not a superb pianist, Ravel had planned to perform the G Major on worldwide tour. Because his health was bad, he instead entrusted the honor of learning the solo part to Marguerite Long, and he limited the tour to Europe.

The composer wrote that the piece is

> a concerto in the truest sense of the word — I mean that it was written in the same spirit as those of Mozart and Saint-Saëns. The music of a concerto should, in my opinion, be lighthearted and brilliant and not aim at profundity or at dramatic effects. It has been said of certain great classical concertos that they are written not 'for' but 'against' the piano. I heartily agree. I had intended to entitle this concerto *Divertissement.* Then it occurred to me that there was no need to do so, because the very title *Concerto* should be sufficiently clear.

The jazz influence is most evident in the first movement. Of its five distinct themes, the first (piccolo at the opening) suggests a Basque folk tune, the second (first time the piano plays alone) a Spanish influence, and the remaining three jazz — a blue-note motive in the E-flat clarinet, answered by the trumpet, immediately after the second theme; the subsequent piano solo, with its off-beat accompaniment; the following syncopated melody for piano with occasional sustained chords.

The middle movement, which is devoid of jazz syncopations, was consciously modeled on the slow movement of Mozart's Quintet for Clarinet and Strings. Of particular interest is the beautiful extended duet for English horn and piano that comes close to the end.

The use of jazz in the finale is more subtle than in the opening movement. It is mingled with suggestions of marches, folk tunes, and dances. This movement is lighthearted and brilliant.

The G Major Concerto is a fine instance of Ravel's delight in the surface of music. He unashamedly embraced superficiality, as he was uneasy with profundity. He believed that there is more genuine meaning in the surface sounds of a composition than in the ideas behind them. He lavished great care on his orchestrations, because orchestration is indeed the surface of music. And he was interested in the sounds more than the meanings of exotic music, such as jazz. The concerto is sophisticated, sincere, elegant, and subtle, but it is not profound nor does it try to be. It is this lack of pretension — unfortunately rare in twentieth-century music — that gives the concerto its youthful innocence (although in actuality it was Ravel's penultimate composition) and that endears it to us.

Mother Goose Suite

        Pavane of the Sleeping Beauty in the Woods
        Hop o' My Thumb
        Laideronette, Empress of the Pagodas
        Conversations of Beauty and the Beast
        The Fairy Garden

Ma mère l'oye *was first composed for piano four-hands between 1908 and April 1910. This version was premiered by Jeanne Leleu and Geneviève Durony on 20 April 1910 in Paris. Ravel orchestrated the suite in 1910. He added several new numbers to make it a ballet in 1911. Gabriel Grovlez conducted the first performance on 28 January 1912 in Paris.*

Maurice Ravel once said, "In art sincerity is hateful." This statement could easily have been the composer's motto, for he always felt the need to hide the true feelings behind his music. As a friend once said, "Everything in Ravel proves his wish to obliterate himself and to confide nothing. He would rather be taken for unfeeling than to betray his sentiments." He could not tolerate unreserved sentimental effusions or passionate gestures. He was deeply aware of the artifice of musical creation and of the necessity of separating art from life. For Ravel composition was a disconnected, isolated process. Only rarely does a hint of *personal* joy or sorrow find its way into his music.

Thus Ravel was a paradox: his artificiality was natural. Artificiality was his aesthetic. He loved the techniques of composition for their own sake, and he embraced them in the spirit of invention, not of expression. Examples of his music conceived with self-imposed limitations include *Boléro,* in which a melody is repeated with only slight variation throughout, and the piano version of the *Mother Goose* Suite, which had to be playable by children.

Ravel loved the innocent world of children. When he was with young people, he let his mask of artificiality slip to reveal his true warmth. Jean and Mimie Godebski were his close friends, despite their tender age. When their parents decided to start their musical education early, Ravel encouraged them by writing a four-hand piano suite that was within the range of their small hands and limited technique. This suite was based on five of the children's favorite fairy tales. The composer allowed himself to be less reserved than usual in this piece for and about children, and the result is arguably his warmest work.

The *Mother Goose* Suite proved too difficult for the Godebski children to perform in public. Instead, Jeanne Leleu and Geneviève Durony, age six and seven, respectively, premiered the piece at a concert of the Independent Musical Society. Ravel said of the piece, "My intention of invoking the poetry of childhood in these pieces naturally led me to simplify my style and thin out my writing."

After the premiere he wrote to one of the performers, "When you will be a great virtuoso and I either an old fogey, covered with honors, or else completely forgotten, you will perhaps have pleasant memories of having given an artist the very rare joy of hearing a work of his, of a rather special nature, interpreted exactly as it should be. Thank you a thousand times for your child-like and sensitive performance."

The movements are crystalline miniatures. Particularly the first, "Pavane of the Sleeping Beauty in the Woods," is unpretentious. Its mere twenty measures spin out a beautifully simple series of melodies, thinly accompanied and with only incidental chromaticism. The result is a child-like clarity.

The second movement, "Hop o' My Thumb," depicts an episode from the Charles Perrault story of Tom Thumb, who was lost in the forest. The movement is headed, "He thought he would easily find his way back by means of the bread crumbs which he had dropped as he walked along. But he was greatly surprised when he was unable to find a single crumb. The birds had come and eaten them all up." The crumbs are represented by a seemingly endless series of thirds in the violins. Tom is portrayed by the oboe. As he gets lost and confused, the measures stretch from 2/4 to 3/4 to 4/4 to 5/4. The birds who eat the crumbs are represented — quite literally — by violin harmonics and trills.

"Laideronnette, Empress of the Pagodas" derives from a tale by Countess Marie d'Aulnoy. According to the score, the empress "undresses herself and gets into her bath. Soon pagodas and pagodines begin to sing and play instruments. Some have theorbos made of walnut shells, others have viols made of almond shells, for the instruments had to be proportioned to their height." The Oriental setting of this story is suggested by the xylophone, wood block, and glockenspiel, and by the pentatonic flavor of the melodies.

The fourth movement is "Conversations of Beauty and the Beast," after Mme. Beaumont. A portion of the dialogue is quoted in the score:

"When I think of your kind heart, you do not seem so ugly to me."

"Oh, yes, my lady, I have a kind heart, but I am a monster."

"There are many men more monstrous than you."

"If I had wit, I would invent a fine compliment to thank you, but I am only a beast. Will Beauty be my wife?"

"No, good beast."

"I die content, since I have the pleasure of seeing you once again."

"No, dear Beast, you will not die but will become my husband."

The Beast disappears, and Beauty sees at her feet only a prince more beautiful than love. He thanks her for having broken his enchantment. Beauty is represented by a limpid waltz melody in the clarinet, and the Beast is a grumbling chromatic line in the contrabassoon.

The final movement is "The Fairy Garden," which is a gradual crescendo based on a beautiful, long, slow melody.

Pavane for a Dead Princess

Ravel composed the Pavane *as a solo piano piece in 1899. Ricardo Viñes played the first performance in Paris on 5 April 1902. Ravel orchestrated the work in 1910. This version was first conducted by Alfred Casella in Paris on 25 December 1911.*

During his student days Ravel often attended soirées at the homes of Parisian music patrons. These gatherings included informal performances of new compositions. One of the patrons whose salon Ravel attended was the Princess Edmond de Polignac, who commissioned the *Pavane for a Dead Princess,* a modest work for solo piano. Ravel no doubt composed the work hastily and with little thought to its future. It was salon music written for the present, not for posterity.

He was surprised, if not annoyed, at the subsequent popularity of this unassuming composition. It became his first widely known work, as it was frequently performed by amateur pianists. Had he written a dazzling display piece for the piano, only virtuoso soloists would have played it and performances would have been better. But salon music is intended for amateurs, and so it was performed, usually badly, countless times. As its popularity eclipsed that of his more substantial works, Ravel came to resent the *Pavane.* He wrote disparagingly of it in later years: "It is so much a matter of ancient history that it is time the composer handed it over to the critics. I no longer see its virtues from this distance. But, alas, I can perceive its faults only too well: the influence of Chabrier is much too glaring, and the structure is rather poor. The remarkable interpretations of this inconclusive and conventional work have, I think, in great measure contributed to its success."

Ravel was alluding not only to the outlandish descriptive interpretations the work elicited from critics but also, sarcastically, to the awkward performances the work usually received. One less than remarkable performance was given by a child, who plodded through at a hopelessly slow tempo and with no sense of lyricism. The composer told the pianist, "Listen, my child, what I wrote is a *Pavane for a Dead Princess,* not a *Dead Pavane for a Princess.*"

Ravel did perform the piece himself, as he was eager to keep it from being played only by amateurs. For a similar reason he decided to orchestrate the *Pavane,* some eleven years after composing it. The success of the composition continued to haunt him, however, as it rapidly became, and has remained, one of the most popular of orchestral works.

The *Pavane* was easily orchestrated. Since a pavane was a court dance of the renaissance often played on the lute, Ravel used a lot of staccato piano-writing to suggest that instrument. This music was transferred to *pizzicato* strings, which better than the piano can suggest the sound of the lute. Listen, for example, to the string accompaniment to the opening horn melody.

In calling the piece "pavane," Ravel was alluding to the solemn renaissance dance form. The remainder of the title, however, has no particular significance. Despite the fanciful stories that appeared attempting to attach a doleful story to the piece, the composer continued to maintain that he was merely attracted to the alliterative sounds in the name *pour une infante défunte.*

Rapsodie espagnole
Prélude à la nuit
Malagueña
Habanera
Feria

Except for the third movement, which dates from 1895, the Rapsodie espagnole *was begun in 1907. The four-hand piano version was completed in October of that year, and the orchestral score was finished on 1 February 1908. Edouard Colonne conducted the first performance on 15 March 1908 in Paris.*

Every young French composer wanted to win the Prix de Rome. Established in 1803 and discontinued in 1968, this prize was given annually to a composer under the age of thirty who was a French citizen. The award included a stipend for four years, the first two to be spent in Rome, the third in Germany or Austria, and the fourth in Rome or Paris; there was also the option of up to three additional years of support. The winner's only obligation was to compose. The long list of winners includes such distinguished composers as Berlioz (1830), Gounod (1839), Bizet (1857), Massenet (1863), Debussy (1884), and Ibert (1919). The list also includes names of many forgotten composers. But it does not include the name of Maurice Ravel, despite his five attempts to win the coveted award.

The Prix de Rome was given not for original composition but rather for demonstrated accomplishment in writing in traditional forms. Each applicant had to submit a fugue on a given subject, a cantata on a given text, and a choral work. As a young man Ravel was not particularly patient with such academic exercises, and he was careless in preparing these contest pieces. His entries have been preserved, and they reveal a surprising dryness and a number of outright errors. He surely had the ability to produce correct academic music, but he did not have the temperament. By the time he had failed several times to win the prize, Ravel was already a well-known composer. His repeated failures became a public scandal. The composer was thoroughly disillusioned with the jurors and disgusted with the selection process. After ignoring the competition in 1904, he decided to try one last time in 1905, just before reaching the age limit of thirty. By this time he had already composed several fine, original works, including the String Quartet, the piano piece *Jeux d'eau*, and the orchestral songs *Shéhérazade*. The jury looked at Ravel's required compositions and ruled that he did not have the technical proficiency even to be a finalist. This decision caused a furor that became front-page news. This *affaire Ravel* intensified when it was revealed that all six finalists were composition students of the same teacher at the Paris Conservatory, who was one of the jurors. There were personal attacks on the members of the jury, and there were countercharges. As a result, the entire selection process came under public scrutiny, the curriculum at the Conservatory was sharply attacked for its conservatism and for its emphasis on technique rather than art, and the director of the Conservatory and several faculty members resigned.

Ravel did not receive the Prix de Rome. But his career did benefit, immeasurably more than it would have had he won the prize, from all the publicity. He was perceived as an *enfant terrible*, an avant gardist who was locked in the perennial battle between academics preserving an outmoded tradition and artists of the new wave. Now everyone wanted to hear the music by the young man whom the French musical establishment had snubbed. His works were performed throughout western Europe, northern Africa, and the United States. He became known as one of France's leading composers, the likely successor to Debussy as France's greatest living composer.

Ravel responded to this attention with a flurry of compositional activity. One of his new works was the *Rapsodie espagnole*. This colorful picture of Spain delighted some listeners and infuriated others at its first performance. Some critics praised it, while others dismissed it as slender, inconsistent, laborious, and pedantic. At the premiere there were some audible protests after the second movement. One member of a group of Ravel's friends called the Apaches shouted out from the balcony, "Once more, for the public downstairs, which didn't understand!" Conductor Edouard Colonne obliged by repeating the movement, after which the same Apache shouted out, "Tell them it's Wagner and they'll love it!"

Such support of a new work, particularly in the face of negative reaction from a philistine audience, was typical of the Apaches, a close-knit group of "artistic outcasts," as they called themselves. The group, which had begun to meet after concerts in 1902, included composers, performers, poets, visual artists, critics, and intellectuals. They exchanged ideas on the latest creations in the arts, met regularly for long discussions, gave their members nicknames (Ravel's was "Rara"), and attended important performances together. Once, coming out of a concert, some of the group accidentally bumped into a man selling newspapers. He angrily called them "Apaches," a French slang term for "rowdy young men." The group liked the term and decided to keep it as their official name.

The Apaches' secret greeting was to whistle the opening theme of Borodin's Second Symphony. They chose this work because of their enthusiasm for Russian music. The Apaches also had an imaginary member named Gomez de Riquet. He was invented by Ravel in order to avoid tiresome would-be participants from joining the group. Whenever such a bore came to an Apache meeting, a regular member would conveniently "remember" that they had been asked for a drink at the home of the legendary Spaniard Gomez de Riquet. With great apologies the group departed, leaving the somewhat bewildered intruder behind.

Ravel was interested in exotic music. Thus we find the sounds of Hungarian folk music in his *Tzigane* and of American jazz in his Piano Concerto. In 1907 he was particularly interested in Spanish music. His two major works that year were the opera *L'Heure espagnole* ("The Spanish Hour") and the orchestral suite *Rapsodie espagnole* ("Spanish Rhapsody"). Actually, Ravel's deep interest in Spain dates from his earliest years. His hometown was near the Spanish border, and thus he grew up in the midst of the Basque culture. His mother had spent her youth in Madrid, and she often sang Spanish folksongs to her young son. It is not surprising, therefore, that Ravel's first work of any importance should be the Spanish dance *Habanera*, written for two pianos in 1895. He later transcribed this piece for orchestra, making it the third movement of the *Rapsodie espagnole*.

Ravel's understanding of Spanish music was more than superficial, as the *Rapsodie* shows. He penetrated the spirit of Spanish music far more deeply than such other non-Hispanic composers as Edouard Lalo in his *Symphonie espagnole*, Emmanuel Chabrier in his *España*, and Rimsky-Korsakov in his *Capriccio espagnole*. Ravel did not quote actual folk music, but he used Spanish modes, rhythms, percussion instruments, and melodic turns in such an authentic way that even as thoroughly Spanish a composer as Manuel de Falla was impressed.

The work consists of a prelude and three Spanish dances — *malagueña* (a popular dance that originated in Malaga), *habanera* (a slow dance that originated in Africa and was brought to Cuba), and *feria*.

Suite Number 2 from *Daphnis et Chloé*
Daybreak —
Pantomime —
General Dance

Ravel began Daphnis et Chloé *in 1909 and completed it on 5 April 1912. Pierre Monteux conducted the first performance in Paris on 8 June 1912, with Vaslav Nijinsky and Tamara Karsavina dancing the title roles. The Second Suite was extracted in 1913.*

The year 1909 saw some extraordinary new developments in European music. In Germany Richard Strauss' controversial opera *Elektra* met with wildly mixed reactions. In Vienna Arnold Schoenberg was composing his first music without key center. In Italy the first of several futurist manifestos was published, calling for the destruction of music as it had been known and its replacement by the noises of machines. And France received its first exposure to the revolutionary ballets of Sergei Diaghilev's Russian dance company.

The Russian craze was in full swing in Paris when Diaghilev's Ballets Russes first arrived. Thus arts patrons and artists alike were thoroughly captivated by the exoticism of the Russian's productions, and Diaghilev was frequently invited to attend aristocratic Parisian salons. There he found financial support for his troupe, and therefore he was able to bring elaborate productions to Paris for several seasons to come. In the salon of the wealthy patron Misia Edwards, Diaghilev met several important French artists, including Ravel.

The composer had long been intrigued with Russian music, but he felt it to be too undisciplined. Diaghilev shared Ravel's opinion. He sought in his ballets, and in the music for them, technical perfection as well as raw excitement. The impresario found in Ravel a sympathetic mind, a fellow perfectionist, and a composer of colorful orchestrations and exciting rhythms. A few months earlier Diaghilev had been approached by choreographer Michel Fokine, who wanted to do a ballet based on the third-century pastoral romance *Daphnis and Chloé*. Once Diaghilev met Ravel and got to know his music, he felt that he had found the perfect composer for Fokine's ballet.

Ravel and Fokine worked together on the scenario. Their collaboration was not easy. The composer recalled, "Almost every night, work until 3 a.m. What complicates things is that Fokine doesn't know a word of French and I know only how to swear in Russian. In spite of the interpreters, you can imagine the flavor of these meetings."

The composer explained his conception of the ballet: "It was my intention, when I wrote it, to compose a large fresco painting, less in keeping with antiquity than with the Greece of my dreams, which was more closely related to a Greece such as French artists had portrayed at the end of the eighteenth century. The work is constructed symphonically, on a very strict tonal plan, based on a small number of motives, the full development of which is assured by the symphonic unity of the whole."

As *Daphnis* was the largest work Ravel was ever to compose, it occupied him for some time. He completed the piano score in the spring of 1910, but the orchestration remained undone. Enough of the score was ready in 1911 for a suite extracted from the ballet to be performed in concert. This was the First Suite, which created a furor when premiered. Ravel continued to work on the ballet, totally re-writing the finale in 1911. The premiere was finally scheduled in 1912, but the music was completed and copied only a month before the opening. There were other difficulties that led to a less than ideal performance: choreographer Fokine had frequent disagreements with lead dancer Vaslav Nijinsky, the stylized sets and costumes con-ceived by painter Léon Bakst were aesthetically far removed from Ravel and Fokine's conception, and the dancers had had no prior ex-perience with the unusual five-beat meter of the final scene. They were able to keep the count only by repeating to themselves over and over the five-syllable name Ser-gei Dia-ghi-lev. Yet this same com-pany was destined to cope with the far more complex rhythms of Stravinsky's The *Rite of Spring* the very next season.

    Daphnis calls for an enormous orchestra and a wordless chorus. This large ensemble posed practical difficulties for taking the pro-duction on tour. Reluctantly Ravel agreed to make an alternative ver-sion without chorus, but only with the understanding that Diaghilev would hire a chorus whenever the ballet was presented in a major city. When Diaghilev brought *Daphnis* to London in 1914, he took the more economical route and omitted the singers. Ravel was incensed, and he wrote a "letter to the editor" to four London newspapers:

> My most important work, *Daphnis et Chloé,* is to be produced at the Drury Lane Theater on Tuesday, June 9. I was overjoyed and, fully appreciating the honor done to me, considered the event as one of the weightiest in my artistic career. Now I learn that what will be produced before the London public is not my work in its original form but a makeshift arrangement which I had ac-cepted to write at M. Diaghilev's special request, in order to fa-cilitate production in certain minor centers. M. Diaghilev prob-ably considers London as one of the aforesaid "minor centers," since he is about to produce at Drury Lane, in spite of his posi-tive word, the new version, without choir. I am deeply surprised and grieved, and I consider the proceedings as disrespectful to-wards the London public as well as towards the composer.

    Diaghilev replied defensively, and Ravel counter-rebutted. The result was that the London performance did omit the chorus, but Di-aghilev signed a contract agreeing to use voices in all subsequent pro-ductions. The version without chorus is usually employed when the final three scenes — "Daybreak," "Pantomime," and "General Dance" — are presented in concert as the Second Suite.

    The story: a band of pirates invades a peaceful Greece. They overpower a group of maidens, one of whom is Chloé, beloved of Daphnis. The invaders hold a victory celebration and force Chloé to dance. The god Pan sends satyrs and flames to the pirate lair. The pirates flee. The music of the Second Suite begins with daybreak following the pirates' night of terror.

Ravel's evocation of the peaceful beginning of a new day is masterful. The shimmering of harps and winds accompanies a slowly unfolding melody in the low strings. No noise is heard other than the murmur of streams accumulating from the dew running off rocks. Daphnis is stretched out before the grotto of the nymphs. Gradually daylight comes. Soon birdsongs are heard in three violins and a piccolo. An ornamented piccolo tune indicates that a shepherd is passing in the distance with his flock. A melody on the small E-flat clarinet portrays a second shepherd. A group of herdsmen appears looking for Daphnis and Chloé. They discover Daphnis and awaken him. As the string music becomes more definite, he begins his anxious search for his beloved. Finally she appears, surrounded by shepherds. To an impassioned theme in the strings, the two lovers embrace. The music becomes hushed as Daphnis notices Chloé's crown, indicating that his dream of Pan rescuing her has become a prophecy fulfilled. Finally the undulations that have been present from the beginning subside, and an oboe melody portrays the old shepherd Lammon. He explains that Pan saved Chloé because she reminded him of the nymph Syrinx, with whom he was smitten.

The second scene begins with a trio for oboes and English horn. Daphnis and Chloé mime the adventures of Pan and Syrinx. Chloé represents the young nymph wandering in the meadow. The strings answer, as Daphnis declares his love. The nymph pushes him away. He becomes more insistent. She disappears into the roses. Desperate, he uproots a few stems and makes a flute, on which he plays a melancholy air. Chloé appears and dances to this flute music. The music becomes energetic, and the dance becomes more animated. It suddenly breaks for a woodwind descent, as Chloé falls into the arms of Daphnis. After a silence, the music is slow and chordal. Before the altar of the nymphs and over two sacrificial lambs, Daphnis swears his faith. As the music becomes animated once more, in comes a group of girls dressed as bacchantes, dancing to tambourine music. Daphnis and Chloé embrace tenderly. Several young men arrive. The music builds to a brief climax and then dies down, as the "General Dance" begins.

The story is ended, and the final scene brings the main characters into a sweeping dance that rises to a stunning climax, a Dionysian celebration of physical love.

◆ ◆ ◆

Le Tombeau de Couperin
Prélude
Forlane
Menuet
Rigaudon

The piano version of Le Tombeau de Couperin *was begun in July 1914 and completed in November 1917. Marguerite Long played the first performance in Paris on 11 April 1919. Ravel orchestrated four of the six movements in June 1919. Rhené-Baton conducted the premiere with the Pasdeloup Orchestra in Paris on 28 February 1920.*

Ravel was devastated by the First World War. Although he had been exempted from military service many years earlier, he was determined to fight for his country. In 1914, at the age of 39, he enlisted. He was sent to the front, where on several occasions he was nearly killed. He saw some terrifying sights.

> I saw a hallucinating thing: a nightmarish city, horribly deserted and mute. It isn't the fracas from above, or the small balloons of white smoke which line the very pure sky; it's not this formidable and invisible struggle which is anguishing, but rather to feel alone in the center of this city which rests in a sinister sleep, under the brilliant light of a beautiful summer day. Undoubtedly I will see things which will be more frightful and repugnant; I don't believe I will ever experience a more profound and stranger emotion than this sort of mute terror.

The war years brought other problems. Ravel's health was not good, and he had to be operated on for dysentery in 1916. No sooner was his convalescence over than he learned that his mother, whom he deeply loved, was dying at age 76. He arrived home from the front just in time to watch her die. "Spiritually it is frightful. I had written her just a short while ago and received her pitiful letters that gladdened me so . . . and gave me such joy. I was still happy at that moment, in spite of the unutterable apprehension in my heart. I had no idea it would happen so soon. Now I am left in this dreadful despair, this anxiety in my thoughts." The loss of his mother was the severest blow of the war years. He returned to the front despondent and alone. Then, once again, he had to be hospitalized — this time for frostbite.

The composer became so depressed that he was unable to complete any music for the next three years, except for finishing the piano suite *Le Tombeau de Couperin,* which he had begun before the war. *Le Tombeau* turned out to be a tragic work, although its pathos is disguised by a seemingly objective surface. His next compositions (once he was finally able to return to work) also reflect the ravages of wartime tragedies.

Ravel decided to dedicate each of the movements of the new piano suite to a friend who had died in the war. The prelude was for Jacques Charlot, cousin of Jacques Durand, who had transcribed several of the composer's pieces. The *rigaudon* was in memory of Pierre and Pascal Gaudin, childhood friends of the composer. The minuet was for Jean Dreyfus, son of Ravel's godmother. The toccata was dedicated to Joseph de Marliave, husband of the distinguished pianist Marguerite Long, who premiered *Le Tombeau.*

Performing the piece that was dedicated to her dead husband was extremely difficult for Long, and she subsequently had to stop playing for two years. Ravel felt so strongly that she should be the work's primary interpreter that he refused to give the score to any other pianist until Long was able to play in public again.

Tombeau means "tomb." A *tombeau* in the baroque era was a piece written as an elegy for a particular person. Both François Couperin and his uncle Louis Couperin composed keyboard *tombeaux.* Ravel's title suggests an homage to one of these French composers, but which one? All Ravel would say was that the piece was a general tribute to eighteenth-century French music. Beneath the pleasant surface of this suite lies a series of painful laments — in part for those killed in the recent war but also (subconsciously at least) for the composer's mother.

Ravel sought to objectify these laments by casting the piece in a form something like that of the baroque dance suite. A *forlane,* for example, is a very old dance that originated in northern Italy; François Couperin wrote a forlane. A minuet is a popular stately dance usually included in dance suites. A *rigaudon,* an old dance from Provence, was used in a few dance suites of Rameau and Bach. Ravel adopted the rhythmic patterns of these dances, but the melodic and harmonic language of *Le Tombeau* is very much his own. The prelude, as well as the piano version's fugue and toccata, are non-dance numbers borrowed from the baroque keyboard suite.

Tzigane

Ravel worked on Tzigane *intermittently for about two years, completing it in its original form for violin and piano on 24 April 1924. The premiere took place two days later in London, with Jelly d'-Aranyi, violinist, and Henri Gil-Marchex, pianist. The orchestral version was completed the following July and first performed on 30 November 1924. Jelly d'Aranyi was again soloist, with Gabriel Pierné conducting the Colonne Orchestra in Paris.*

Ravel's spirit had been shattered by World War I. It was only with great difficulty that he returned to writing music. Painstakingly he completed his one compositional effort of the war years, *Le Tombeau de Couperin,* which had occupied him from 1914 to 1917. Then for two years he composed nothing substantial. He subsequently came out of his depression only long enough to write a cynical picture of pre-war Europe — *La Valse* (1919–20). After that it took him two full years to compose the wonderful Sonata for Violin and Cello, which is only 16 pages long.

Ravel was depressed, not only because of memories of war horrors but also because his mother, to whom he had been deeply devoted, had died in 1916. The composer never fully accepted her death. Furthermore, Parisian society, which had been devastated by the war, returned to its former vitality only after a difficult period of adjustment. Ravel was still at the center of musical activities. He was vice-president and then president of the Independent Musical Society, which presented concerts of contemporary music of all countries. But things had changed. He found that he no longer represented the avant garde, as he had before the war. He saw his position as a leader in new music taken over by a new generation — Stravinsky, Schoenberg, Prokofiev, and others. "The new sounds in the air," explains Ravel's biographer Arbie Orenstein, "were those of jazz, polytonality, and atonality, as the lush velvet of impressionism gave way to the hard steel which had been prophesied in the *Rite of Spring.*" Ravel was an active member of a group of artists and intellectuals that spent countless hours in Parisian cafés, exchanging lively opinions. The composer had a lot to think about: the cultural ramifications of the war, the new music he heard in the concerts his Society put on, the aesthetic implications of the new avant garde style, and the heady ideas picked up in cafés.

With great effort he managed to complete the Sonata for Violin and Cello, which had been "dragging on," as he put it, for a year and a half. After that, he settled into a long period of creative inactivity. He was supposed to be working on an opera, *L'Enfant et les sortilèges,* but instead he composed nothing other than a few small pieces and orchestrations of other composers' works (including Mussorgsky's *Pictures at an Exhibition*).

One evening in July 1922, Ravel attended a private concert where he heard the superb Hungarian violinist Jelly d'Aranyi perform his Violin and Cello Sonata. Later that evening Ravel asked d'Aranyi to play some authentic gypsy melodies. She obliged, and he kept asking to hear more. The "evening" continued until 5 a.m. Ravel, like such composers as Liszt, Brahms, and Dvořák before him, was fascinated by both gypsy folk music and the gypsy manner of violin playing. (Coincidentally, it was for d'Aranyi that Bartók was at this time writing his two folk-inspired violin sonatas.) The idea for *Tzigane* was born that night. A few days later Ravel sent a telegram to another violinist, Hélène Jourdan-Morhange, who had advised him while he was composing the sonata and who had recently premiered that work: "Come quickly and bring the Paganini Etudes with you." He wanted to learn as much as he could about violin virtuosity.

Ravel's mental block against composing did not disappear. It was two years before he actually completed his modest gypsy work for violin and piano, and then only two days before its first performance. Thus D'Aranyi had to learn the fiendishly difficult solo part in an amazingly short time, yet she succeeded in dazzling critics and listeners alike at the London premiere. A few months later Ravel orchestrated the work, and d'Aranyi again impressed the audience when she premiered the new version.

Ravel made a third version of *Tzigane,* for violin and an instrument called a "luthéal." This now forgotten instrument was attached to a piano to make it sound like a cimbalom, a Hungarian folk instrument similar to a hammered dulcimer. The luthéal soon lost what small appeal it had had, and this version of *Tzigane* is no longer played.

Although Ravel never fully recovered from his compositional lethargy, after the composition of *Tzigane,* he was finally able to undertake *and* complete a number of major works.

The title *Tzigane* means "gypsy." It refers both to the work's typically Hungarian rhythms and melodic figures and to its stylization of gypsy violin playing. The extraordinary demands on the soloist far exceed what a folk violinist could manage. Still, the flavor of folk music is always present. Ravel subtitled the piece *Rapsodie en Concert,* and he described it as "a virtuoso piece in the style of a Hungarian rhapsody."

The piece owes its style equally to its two inspirations: folk music and the spectacular violin writing of Paganini. For example, the opening unaccompanied cadenza, which occupies more than a third of the piece, explores the typically Hungarian harmonic minor scale while it exposes the violinist to ever greater technical demands. The melodic line moves gradually upward, although Ravel directs the soloist to remain on the lowest string (the G string) for a considerable time. Thus the sound gets more and more intense as the melodic line rises. When the other strings are finally used, it is for spectacular multiple stopping (playing several notes at once). After the orchestra enters, the work becomes an incredibly virtuosic concerto, in which all manner of violin tricks — perpetual motion, rapid harmonics, left-hand *pizzicati* in the midst of bowed arpeggios, quadruple stops, extremely high writing — are accompanied by Ravel's typically imaginative orchestration.

Valses nobles et sentimentales
La Valse

The Valse nobles et sentimentales *was composed in 1911 as a piano piece. Louis Aubert gave the first performance on 9 May 1911 in Paris. Ravel orchestrated the work in 1912, for use in the ballet* Adélaïde, ou le langage des fleurs. *Ravel conducted the Lamoureux Orchestra in the first performance of* Adélaïde *on 22 April 1912 in Paris. The first purely orchestral performance was given by Pierre Monteux and the Orchestra of Paris on 15 February 1914.* La Valse *was composed between December 1919 and March 1920, first as a two-piano work and then for orchestra. Ravel and Alfredo Casella premiered the piano version in Vienna on 23 October 1920. Camille Chevillard conducted the first orchestral performance with the Lamoureux Orchestra on 12 December 1920 in Paris.*

Nearly a decade separated Ravel's two large waltz compositions. Both works began as piano pieces and were then orchestrated. Both refer to the Viennese waltz. Both look to bygone eras: the *Valse nobles* to the refined world of early nineteenth-century Vienna, and *La Valse* to the imperial Viennese court of 1855. But there the similarities end. The two works are very different, in large part because of events that intervened between their composition. The First World War deeply affected Ravel in a personal way. He was in the army, by choice, and several times was nearly killed. His experiences in battle made an everlasting impression on him. In addition, he was devastated by the death of his mother during the war years. Thus, while the pre-war

Valses nobles is an elegant reinterpretation of Viennese dance music, *La Valse* is a bittersweet reminiscence of a world that had been destroyed by the war. In 1911 Ravel could be aloof, almost classical, in his view of the dance music of another age and another culture. But the Vienna of 1920 (where, ironically, Ravel and Alfredo Casella premiered the two-piano version of *La Valse*) had little in common with that of 1855.

Both orchestral waltzes look to the past, but from very different presents. In both cases, though, the way they distance themselves from their subjects exemplifies the objectivity in Ravel's art. It was typical for him to seek inspiration in another society (consider the influences of American jazz in the two piano concertos) or another time (ancient Greece is invoked in *Daphnis et Chloé*). In virtually every piece he set for himself boundaries within which, or against which, the music had to work. Examples of such self-challenges include making the piano version of the *Mother Goose* Suite playable by young children; modeling *Valses nobles et sentimentales* on two collections of Schubert waltes — *Valses nobles* and *Valses sentimentales*; and borrowing the waltz rhythms of Johann Strauss (hardly the most natural language for a Frenchman) for *La Valse*. The composer's genius worked best when confronting such artificial limitations. On the score of *Valses Nobles et sentimentales* he wrote, for example, "The delightful pleasure of a useless occupation."

Ravel embraced artificiality as an aesthetic principle. His belief in restraint, denying of personal feelings, and separating of art from life does not mean that his music is cold or insensitive. For Ravel feeling and artificiality were compatible. He did not avoid putting emotions into music: "The source of genius — that is, of artistic creation — can be made up only of instinct or feeling." What he denied was his own personal emotions. He readily put objective emotions, feelings derived from outside himself, into his compositions. *La Valse*, an elegy to an opulent way of life that had been destroyed by war, is ample evidence of Ravel's capacity for feeling. But the emotions in this music are not an expression of inner passions. Ravel hid his own feelings behind an exaggerated artificiality, behind an objectified interpretation of emotion in general. He did not so much remove personal expression from his music as camouflage it behind an effortless perfection and an almost indifferent politeness — both clear throughout the eight waltzes of *Valses nobles*. *La Valse*, on the other hand, is the least polite of his works. Yet even there we hear his attempt to remove himself.

The objectivity of *La Valse* is evident even in its title. "The definite article," writes critic Paul Griffiths, "is crucial. This is not just a waltz: it is a waltz about waltzing, a waltz that waltzes around itself, which may account for the frenzy to which it mounts until a momentary burst of quadruple time, coming after so much Viennese 3/4, administers the *coup de grace.*"

As early as 1906 Ravel had the idea of composing a work based on the waltzes of Johann Strauss. By the time he actually wrote *Valses nobles,* however, he had settled on a more remote model — the waltzes of Schubert. Strauss is more in evidence in *La Valse.* The Vienna of Strauss waltzes is as far from the Paris of 1920, however, as the music of Schubert is from that of *Valses nobles.*

The piano version of *Valses nobles et sentimentales* was given a curious premiere. It was presented at a concert of the Independent Musical Society, an organization which Ravel had helped found in 1909 as a protest against "those solid qualities of incoherence and boredom" in the Parisian musical establishment. The Society attracted an audience sympathetic to contemporary music. In 1911 the organization gave a recital in which the names only of the eleven pieces, but not of their composers, were listed in the program. The audience members were invited to fill out ballots, indicating who they thought the actual composers were. Although the audience of supposed new music enthusiasts jeered at the dissonances and alleged wrong notes of *Valses nobles,* the plurality named Ravel as the composer. Was he supposed to be flattered or insulted by the unfavorable reception and correct identification? Other composers who received several votes for authorship of *Valses nobles* included Satie and Kodály. Only two other pieces on the concert were correctly attributed.

Ravel later wrote:

> The title *Valses nobles et sentimentales* sufficiently indicates my intention of writing a cycle of waltzes after the example of Schubert. Following on the virtuosity that is the basis for [my] *Gaspard de la nuit,* I use here a distinctly clearer style of writing. This makes the harmony more concrete and causes the profile of the music to stand out. The *Valses nobles et sentimentales* was given its premiere at one of the concerts of the Independent Musical Society where the composers are not named, in the midst of protests and catcalls. The audience voted the authorship of each piece. By a small majority the paternity of the waltzes was ascribed to me.

The emotional trials of the war, plus deteriorating health, made it impossible for Ravel to compose for several years. The stimulus to return to work came in the form of a commission from Russian ballet impresario Serge Diaghilev. He asked Ravel for a short ballet to share the program with Stravinsky's *Pulcinella.* Ravel complied by writing

La Valse. When the composer played the piano version for Diaghilev, the impresario called it a masterpiece. "But it is not a ballet. It is only the portrait of a ballet." Diaghilev could not see any choreographic possibilities in the music. He felt he could not work with a composition that was this far removed from its subject matter, that was so objectified, so artificial. Ravel never forgave Diaghilev. *La Valse* was performed in concert version a few months later, and it was eventually produced as a ballet a decade later by Ida Rubinstein.

La Valse contains every element of a Strauss waltz except its gaiety. Instead, there is a sinister atmosphere that becomes frenzied by the end. The composer said of the piece, "I feel that this work is a kind of apotheosis of the Viennese waltz, linked in my mind with the impression of a fantastic whirl of destiny." An inscription at the head of the score reads: "Flashes of lightning in turbulent clouds reveal a couple waltzing. One by one the clouds vanish; a huge ballroom filled by a circling mass is revealed. The scene gradually becomes illuminated. The light of chandeliers bursts forth. An imperial court about 1855."

To his friend Maurice Emmanuel, Ravel wrote: "Some people have discovered in it an intention of parody, even of caricature, while others plainly have seen a tragic allusion — end of the Second Empire, state of Vienna after the war, etc. . . . Tragic, yes, it can be that like any expression — pleasure, happiness — which is pushed to extremes. You should see in it only what comes from the music: a mounting volume of sound, which in the stage performance will be complemented by lighting and movement."

Ottorino Respighi

Born on 9 July 1879 in Bologna.
Died on 18 April 1936 in Rome.

The Pines of Rome
The Pine Trees of the Villa Borghese —
The Pine Trees Near a Catacomb —
The Pine Trees of the Janiculum —
The Pine Trees of the Appian Way —

The Pines of Rome was composed in 1924. The first performance was conducted by Bernardino Molinari in Rome on 14 December of that year.

During his lifetime Respighi was the most successful and famous Italian composer of his generation. Because of his renown he was appointed professor of composition at the Conservatorio di Santa Cecilia in Rome in 1913. In 1924 he was made director of that prestigious institution, but administrative duties did not appeal to him. Fundamentally a simple man, he had neither the talent nor the inclination for such a position. Furthermore, as he was frequently invited to guest conduct in other countries, his professional and administrative careers were in conflict.

Respighi was eager to resign from both the directorship and his professorship. But the Cultural Minister of Rome understood the value of having such a distinguished personage at the helm of the conservatory. To prevent (or, as it turned out, to forestall) the composer's resignation, the Minister arranged for Respighi's teaching duties to consist of only one advanced composition lecture course, for which he was required to give forty lectures a year at whatever times suited him. Nonetheless, Respighi resigned two years later in order to devote himself to composition.

Despite his administrative responsibilities, the composer was able to complete what has destined to become his most popular orchestral work — *The Pines of Rome* — during his first year as director of the conservatory. The premiere took place in December. The Augusteo was packed. Respighi had predicted that the audience would balk at the first movement. "You'll see that the first part won't have a smooth passage and they'll boo!" he had told his wife. There was, in fact, considerable booing and hissing at the close of the first section, caused no doubt by the stridently discordant trumpets that blare forth repeatedly on a note foreign to the prevailing tonality (B-flat in the key of A major). The effect is like children's taunting "nyah!" (Respighi's program note mentions children shrieking). A friend of the composer had suggested a different ending, but Respighi replied, "Let them boo; what do I care?"

After this dissonant close of the first movement, the orchestra quiets down for a contemplative second movement. At the premiere the audience did likewise. As the piece progressed, the public became more and more intrigued. Even before the triumphant ending, wild applause swept the hall.

This pattern was repeated at the second performance, two weeks later. At the end of the first movement, someone shouted, "This must not go on!" But by the end there was again an extraordinary ovation. *The Pines* was subsequently performed widely, always to enthusiastic response.

Once Respighi had resigned from the conservatory, he was free to travel. He and his wife embarked on an American tour at the end of 1925. Shortly before their ship landed in New York, several reporters and photographers came aboard, demanding interviews and information. Elsa Respighi recalled, "We had prepared nothing, no photographs, no typewritten notes, nor could we think of any 'important' or 'amusing' incidents in our lives that our journalist friends so demandingly expected of us. From the gentlemen's astonished expressions we realized that we had failed in some vital duty — the payment of tribute to 'Her Majesty Publicity,' a goddess of first importance in the United States."

Respighi was scheduled to conduct *The Pines of Rome* with the Philadelphia Orchestra in January. He interrupted his rehearsals to go to New York, because conductor Arturo Toscanini had chosen to give the American premiere of that same work on his triumphant return concert after an extended absence from the United States. Elsa Respighi's reminiscences are particularly vivid:

It was an unforgettable evening. The hall [Carnegie], bedecked with Italian flags and banked with masses of flowers, held a large and distinguished audience, including leading personalities of the musical world and the most beautiful women in America wearing their richest jewels. The atmosphere was one of throbbing expectancy. Respighi and I had come from Philadelphia to attend the concert. Toscanini was given a great ovation for each item in the program, but after *The Pines of Rome* the applause was almost delirious. He had acknowledged the audience's tribute five or six times, and I was about to leave the box when a tremendous roar made me turn around in alarm. The whole audience was standing, the orchestra sounding the "salute of honor," and Ottorino, next to Toscanini, was bowing his thanks.

Respighi returned to Philadelphia the next day. Elsa relates that the composer at first

found working with Stokowski's orchestra, then at the height of its fame, a little difficult. The attitude of some of the players was one of ill-concealed mistrust, which worried the Italians in the orchestra but did not last long. With Olympian calm Respighi spoke to each player in his own language (there were Russians, Germans, Frenchmen, Italians, etc.), and soon they were all won over by his personality. The Philadelphia Orchestra had gone *en masse* to New York to hear *The Pines* conducted by Toscanini, and all the musicians came back eager and determined to give, if possible, an even better performance. Respighi's first concert took place on 19 January. The orchestra gave the same program in Washington, Cleveland, and Baltimore.

The following program note appears as a preface to the published score of *The Pines*:

The Pine Trees of the Villa Borghese. Children are at play in the pine groves of the Villa Borghese, dancing the Italian equivalent of "Ring around a Rosy." They play at soldiers, marching and fighting. They twitter and shriek like swallows at evening. They come and go in swarms. Suddenly the scene changes.

The Pine Trees near a Catacomb. We see the shadows of the pines, which overhang the entrance of a catacomb. From the depths rises a chant, which echoes solemnly, like a hymn, and is then mysteriously silenced.

The Pine Trees of the Janiculum. There is a thrill in the air. The full moon reveals the profile of the pines of Gianicolo's Hill. A nightingale sings.

The Pine Trees of the Appian Way. Misty dawn on the Appian Way. The tragic country is guarded by solitary pines. Indistinctly, incessantly, the rhythm of unending steps. The poet has a fantastic vision of past glories. Trumpets blare, and, in the grandeur of a newly risen sun, the army of the Consul bursts forth toward the Sacred Way, mounting in triumph the Capitoline Hill.

Respighi transformed this program into a vivid orchestral tapestry. The colors of *The Pines* are sometimes spectacular, sometimes intimate. The brilliant outer movements demonstrate how much Respighi learned from his composition teacher, Rimsky-Korsakoff. The inner movements, by contrast, show why Respighi is often called a "neo-impressionist": the influence of Debussy is frequently in evidence.

Surely the best known of the many wonderful timbres in *The Pines* are the bird sounds at the end of the third movement. After the return of the opening piano cadenza and clarinet solo, we hear not an orchestral imitation of birds (such as those at the end of the slow movement of Beethoven's Sixth Symphony or those in the introduction of Mahler's First Symphony) but actual birds recorded. Respighi indicates that a particular phonograph record should be played. While his idea may have been controversial in 1924, with purists decrying the intrusion of recorded sounds into the orchestra, what he did has turned out to be prophetic. As recording technology has become more sophisticated and more common in the later twentieth century, composers have often combined prerecorded sounds (or even sonorities produced electronically on the spot) with orchestral sounds.

Other special effects in *The Pines of Rome* include the distant trumpet in the second movement, and the addition of a second brass section at the conclusion of the final movement. Here Respighi calls for *buccine,* which are old brass instruments that apparently date back to Roman days. The composer suggests that they can be played on modern descendents, called *flicorni* — fluegelhorns, euphoniums, and tenor tubas. Respighi took full advantage of the sonic resources of the modern orchestra, and even added special sounds to it, in order to produce one of the most colorful scores of this century.

Albert Roussel

Born in Tourcoing, France, on 5 April 1869.
Died in Royan on 23 August 1937.

◆　◆　◆

Suite Number 2 from *Bacchus et Ariane*, Opus 43

The ballet Bacchus et Ariane *was composed in 1930. Philippe Gaubert conducted the first performance at the Paris Opéra on 22 May 1931; the choreography was by Serge Lifar. Suite Number 2, which is identical with the ballet's second act, was first performed in concert on 2 February 1934; Pierre Monteux conducted the Paris Symphony Orchestra.*

Roussel, an approximate contemporary of Ravel and Debussy, was an important figure in French music. An uncompromising, original, and talented composer, he is credited with reconciling two divergent trends in early twentieth-century music in his country: the impressionism of Debussy and the academicism of d'Indy. Although he was a teacher and counted among his students Satie, Varèse, and Martinu, Roussel's influence was small. His style was inimitable, and he left no disciples, although his art was highly respected during his lifetime. The ballet *Bacchus et Ariane* is one of the finest scores by a composer whose music deserves to be far better known.

Roussel came to composition probably later in life than any other major composer. Although he did show musical promise in his youth, he opted instead for a career as a naval officer.

The composer had a difficult childhood. His father died when he was one year old and his mother when he was seven. He was entrusted to the care of his grandfather, who was mayor of his hometown and thus had little time for the boy. Three years later the grandfather died, and Roussel went to live with an aunt, who arranged for piano lessons. Vacations spent at the seaside, plus reading the novels of Jules Verne, kindled in the boy a longing for the sea. Thus he enrolled as a naval cadet at the age of 18, and he graduated from the Naval Academy two years later as a midshipman. He later became a commissioned officer. In the navy he traveled extensively, particularly to the Far East. Whenever time permitted on these journeys, he tried to study harmony from a book, but he found it difficult to understand the technicalities of music without a teacher. He also tried his hand at composing and even had a few performances of his pieces.

574

A fellow naval officer offered to show some of Roussel's manuscripts to the famous conductor Edouard Colonne. His friend reported that Colonne had been impressed and had advised Roussel to give up his naval career and become a composer. In actuality, the friend had never shown the music to Colonne. The friend believed so strongly in Roussel that he invented the story of the conductor's praise in order to encourage Roussel to follow his musical instincts. Impressed by what he believed was an authoritative evaluation of his talents, Roussel sought out the director of the Roubaix Conservatory for a second opinion. This time the encouragement was real, and Roussel made his fateful decision. He resigned his commission in 1894 and went to Paris to study music. He was then 25 years old, an age by which most composers have finished their formal education.

Roussel's first musical success came three years later, when two of his works shared first prize in a contest. The following year he enrolled at the newly formed Schola Cantorum and became a student of composer Vincent d'Indy. He studied composition, orchestration, and music history from d'Indy for the next nine years, thus completing his education at the age of 38. All during these years Roussel spent his vacations on ocean voyages, to assuage his nostalgia for his former life. His love of the sea remained with him his entire life and became part of his identity as an artist. He once wrote to his wife:

> The sea, the sea! There is nothing more beautiful in the world, is there? And it is beside the sea that we shall fulfill our lives and that we shall sleep, so that we may still hear in the distance her eternal murmuring. . . . To contrive to evoke all the feelings which lie hidden in the sea — the sense of power and of infinity, of charm, anger, and gentleness — this must be the greatest joy that could be given in the world to an artist in the domain of his art. . . . Why should not music, which is infinitely suited to rendering that which is elemental and imprecise, convey [feelings for the sea]?

D'Indy appointed Roussel a professor at the Schola Cantorum, a position the composer held until the outbreak of the First World War. Despite health problems he was able to enlist in the wartime navy. By the end of the war, his health was so bad that he had to retire to the Brittany coast to convalesce. He continued to compose large works, and his reputation grew. In 1929 he was honored by a festival of his music in celebration of his sixtieth birthday. In 1931 he visited the United States for the premiere of his Third Symphony, commissioned by the Boston Symphony Orchestra. He was then the leading composer of France: Saint-Saëns, Fauré, Debussy, and Satie were dead, and the output of Ravel and d'Indy was at best intermittent. At the same time the premiere of *Bacchus et Ariane* secured Roussel's reputation as a composer of theater music.

Historian Rollo Myers has explained the special quality of Roussel's art:

> It is not only today that Roussel's music tends to be underrated and misjudged; he has always been a connoisseur's composer, and even in his lifetime and in his own country it was only a comparatively small minority of critics and practicing musicians who saw from the first that here was a new voice speaking with authority and with something new to say. Certainly Roussel himself did nothing to court popularity or make any concessions to the taste of the day. Indeed, he did not believe that music, as he conceived it, should, or even could, be popular; for him it was "the most hermetic and least accessible of all the arts"; and it was this conviction that led him to declare that "the musician, even more than the poet, is completely isolated from the world, alone with his more or less incomprehensible language." There might, he conceded, be one or two fine works written expressly for the people; "all the rest, taking into account the relations existing at present between music and the masses, must be destined for the ears of only a very small number."

This aristocratic attitude may seem at odds with the sumptuous beauty and elemental excitement of *Bacchus et Ariane*, but Roussel's uncompromising attitude is proof of the necessity of an artist's integrity. Roussel wrote what he had to write, and eventually public understanding developed. Today the music of Roussel is no longer challenging to the ears. We understand the dissonances of *Bacchus* as powerful expressions of the drama's underlying emotions. If outright popularity has continued to elude this music, the reason is no doubt its intellectual rigor and its uncompromising austerity. But the power of *Bacchus* cannot be denied. This is commanding music.

The Second Suite from *Bacchus et Ariane* is the second act of the ballet. In his biography of the composer, Basil Deane provides the following scenario and commentary:

> At the beginning of Act II Ariadne awakens and, finding herself alone, climbs to the summit of the rocks. Looking seaward, she discerns the receding sail of Theseus' galley. Terrified, she attempts to throw herself into the sea, but falls instead into the embrace of Bacchus. Together they resume their dream dance. Their lips unite in a kiss which releases a Dionysiac enchantment, whereupon the island comes to life, and vine-wreathed fauns and maenads spring from among the rocks, crowding the

scene. Two of them offer a golden goblet filled with grape juice to Ariadne. She drinks and, intoxicated, dances with mounting frenzy, first alone, then with Bacchus. The entire troop of followers joins in a Bacchanalia, while the god conducts Ariadne to the highest pinnacle and crowns her with a diadem of stars ravished from the heavenly constellations. . . .

Ariadne's repose is evoked by a texture of subtle transparency, and her terror by a modernized version of a time-honored device, a succession of chords of the diminished seventh. Ariadne's solo dance is an instance of Roussel's ability to coordinate different elements in a sustained rise to a climax. The increasing abandon of the dancer is depicted by an intensification of the melodic line, by means of chromaticism, a progressive accelerando, a crescendo from *pp* to *ff*, and the expansion of a restrained texture to the sonority of the full orchestra. The exultant energy of the lovers' *pas de deux* is matched by the swaggering 10/8 rhythm, and the concluding Bacchanalia sweeps forward with ever-mounting excitement to the final apotheosis of Ariadne.

Camille Saint-Saëns

Born in Paris on 9 October 1835.
Died in Algiers on 16 December 1921.

Concerto Number 2 in G Minor for Piano and Orchestra, Opus 22

Andante sostenuto
Allegro scherzando
Presto

The Second Piano Concerto was composed in the spring of 1868. Anton Rubinstein conducted the first performance, with Saint-Saëns at the piano, in Paris on 13 May 1868.

Saint-Saëns had an extraordinarily long and productive career. He was active as a composer for 83 years. He wrote his first composition, which is preserved in the Paris Conservatory, at age three, and he continued to compose virtually nonstop until the day of his death. His career as a pianist was equally impressive. He began giving informal concerts in his neighborhood at age four, he played his first public recital at age eight, and he remained an agile and active performer until his final day (when he practiced two hours in the morning before dying in the evening).

He composed incessantly and effortlessly. He had no trouble, for example, writing and orchestrating a massive oratorio in a week. He created well over three hundred works, many of major proportions. Saint-Saëns also immersed himself in archaeology, astronomy, botany, conducting, play-writing, musicology, teaching, poetry, and philosophy. He was a world-renowned celebrity, making frequent concert tours and being received everywhere with great enthusiasm and respect. He was one of the few living composers ever to have statues of him erected and streets named after him.

Saint-Saëns was a prodigious correspondent, often writing as many as two dozen letters in a day. These letters, like his music, reveal little of his inner feelings. He knew many of the world's great musicians from several generations. A close friend of Rossini, Liszt, and Berlioz, he lived long enough to know Stravinsky and Ravel. Saint-Saëns was a sarcastic atheist with a caustic wit, but he was also quite generous. Having accumulated considerable wealth from his spectacularly successful career, he often gave money away as "scholarships" to young composers.

Among the famous musicians with whom he was friendly was Russian pianist-conductor-composer Anton Rubinstein. When the two musicians first met in 1858, Saint-Saëns impressed Rubinstein by sight-reading at the piano the latter's enormous *Ocean* Symphony. Rubinstein in turn overwhelmed his French colleague with his piano playing. Saint-Saëns later recalled,

> With no other resource but himself and a piano, Rubinstein has packed the enormous *Théâtre de l'Éden* with quivering multitudes and filled it with such resounding and gradated vibrations as might have been those of an orchestra. And when he joined forces with the orchestra itself, what an astonishing role was played by the instrument at his fingers across that ocean of sonority! You can get an idea of it by imagining a flash of lightning through a strong cloud. How he made the piano sing! What magic did he possess to give those velvety sounds a lingering duration which they do not, cannot have under the fingers of any other?"

The two friends played duets together and collaborated on concerts.

> We were very close and often played duets together. The pianos that served as our battlefield had a rough time of it, and we took little pity on the ears of our listeners. Those were the days! We made music simply for the joy of it, and we never had enough. . . .
>
> One year he asked me to take the orchestra at a series of concerts he planned to give. I had conducted little as yet and hesitated at the task. In the end I agreed, and during those eight concerts I served my apprenticeship as a conductor. At rehearsals Rubinstein would hand me the manuscript scores he had scribbled, full of crossings-out, cuts, and what looked like intricate geometrical diagrams. I could never persuade him to let me see the music beforehand — it was too amusing, he said, to see me at grips with the difficulties! Moreover, when he played he took not the slightest notice of the orchestra which accompanied him, so that one had to follow him at risk, and occasionally there was such a cloud of sonority rising from the piano that I could no longer distinguish anything and had to rely on the sight of his fingers on the keyboard as my guide.
>
> After that magnificent season we happened to be at some concert or other in the *Salle Pleyel*, when he said to me, "I haven't

conducted an orchestra in Paris yet. Let's put on a concert that will give me an opportunity of taking the baton." "With pleasure." We asked when the *Salle Pleyel* would be free and were told we should have to wait three weeks. "Very well," I said, "in those three weeks I will write a concerto for the occasion." And I composed the G Minor Concerto, which accordingly had its first performance under such distinguished patronage.

Saint-Saëns was able to complete the concerto in the short time allotted, but he was unable to learn the piano part sufficiently. "I played very badly, and, except for the scherzo, which was an immediate success, it did not go well. The general opinion was that the first part lacked coherence and the finale was a complete failure." Nonetheless, the work went on to become the most popular and respected of Saint-Saëns' five piano concertos.

Rubinstein subsequently performed the concerto as pianist. He recalled that it "served me for many years as a first-rate warhorse! It has everything — dash and elegance, dazzling brilliance and temperament; it is good music, too, if not devoid of a certain banality."

Eventually the composer learned the piano part. In 1893 he played it at a London Philharmonic concert, where he shared the program with Tchaikovsky. Both composers were in England to receive honorary degrees from Cambridge University. Saint-Saëns heard and liked Tchaikovsky's Fourth Symphony, and the two men spent most of their time at a banquet honoring them talking about music.

In 1908 Saint-Saëns became the first famous composer to write music specifically for a film. Always interested in anything new, he was fascinated by the movies and eager to compose a chamber suite to be performed during Charles Pathé's *The Assassination of the Duke of Manners*. Soon silent films were produced at a rate faster than composers could create music for them, and pre-existing music often had to be used. The scherzo of the Second Concerto frequently accompanied comedies.

The concerto is truly a virtuoso's showpiece, as might be expected from a collaboration of two extraordinary pianist-composers. It also has a marvelous freshness and spontaneity that is no doubt a product of the rapidity with which it was composed. The virtuosity is immediately evident when the concerto starts with an elaborate cadenza. Through much of the first movement, the piano plays dazzling runs, arpeggios, and other figuration, culminating in a second cadenza. Virtuosity is present even in the hushed interlude that follows this cadenza, just before the end of the movement.

The wonderfully melodic scherzo is full of deft touches of orchestration. Notice in particular the imaginative use of timpani and the virtuosic passage accompanied by the entire string section playing tremolo. The lightness of this nonetheless dazzling movement is reminiscent of the best Mendelssohn scherzos.

The whirlwind finale is an amazing *tour de force* for the pianist. It is no wonder that Saint-Saëns had difficulty learning to perform this music in a short time. The soloist is rarely granted a respite from the continually varied demands on his technique. Yet the music never slips into empty virtuosity. It is always delightful, always elegant. As biographer James Harding concludes, "Those who criticize Saint-Saëns for his frivolity should try one day to write music as airy and sure-footed as this. They would not find it easy."

Concerto Number 4 in C Minor for Piano and Orchestra, Opus 44
Allegro moderato. Andante
Allegro vivace. Andante. Allegro

The Fourth Piano Concerto was composed in 1875. Saint-Saëns was pianist at the premiere, which was conducted by Edouard Colonne in Paris on 31 October 1875.

In February 1875 the 44-year-old Saint-Saëns married a 19-year-old woman named Marie Truffot. The marriage was doomed from the start, since the composer was often away on concert tours. He was unwilling to take time out even for a honeymoon. Soon after the marriage he wrote his Fourth Piano Concerto, which he performed at the end of October 1875. A week later he became a father. He loved his son deeply and resolved to be an important part of his life, but the lure of the concert stage continually took him away from home. He left for two months in Russia soon after André was born.

While in Russia, Saint-Saëns became friendly with Tchaikovsky. The two actually danced an impromptu ballet on the story of Pygmalion and Galatea, at the Moscow Concervatory.

Marriage did not change the composer's way of life. He did not allow the birth of his second son at the end of 1877 to interfere with his hectic social and musical life. Tragedy struck the family a few months later, when within six weeks André died falling from a fourth-story window and his brother died from an infantile disease. The already weak marriage could not survive the ensuing emotional stress. Although Marie and Saint-Saëns continued to live together for three more years, they drifted ever farther apart. Finally the composer left his wife in 1881. They never again saw each other, although no formal separation was declared. Marie did appear at Saint-Saëns' funeral in 1921. She lived with her unhappy memories until 1950, when she died at age 95.

The Fourth Concerto is typical of Saint-Saëns at the height of his compositional abilities. It is a well worked-out composition, based on attractive materials. Only in one section does it attempt to reach an emotional depth. It is surface music, music that glorifies its tunes for their own sake rather than probes them for inner meaning. Saint-Saëns is often mentioned as the spiritual father of Ravel, another French composer who elevated superficiality to an artistic aesthetic.

The concerto is cast in two movements, each of which is divided into distinct submovements. This form, which Saint-Saëns also used in his Third Symphony, derives from the music of his friend Franz Liszt, who was interested in combining one- and multi-movement forms. The first movement begins *allegro moderato*. Biographer James Harding calls this opening section "utterly characteristic of Saint-Saëns' personal brand of nostalgia. This feeling, a compound of worldly elegance and wry disillusionment, is by no means disagreeable, and when it is presented, as here, with all the composer's smooth technique, the effect is captivating." The second part of the first movement is an andante that features a chorale-like theme and considerable pianistic display.

The second movement begins with a scherzo-like allegro that utilizes a transformation of the first movement's opening theme. A second idea is based on an imaginative repeated-note theme. The second part is an andante that begins with a fugue and develops into a cadenza. It is the only passage in the concerto that suggests deep emotions. The final segment is a boisterous allegro based on a transformation of the chorale melody from the first movement's andante, now turned into a waltz.

In some of the concerto's harmonies and piano figurations, it is not difficult to hear echoes of the salon music that was popular in France in the late nineteenth-century. Saint-Saëns himself composed a fair amount of this pop music. Those who question the tastefulness of putting such progressions into a piano concerto should remember that Saint-Saëns was one of the few French musicians of his day who truly believed in Mozart and Beethoven. He worked tirelessly against public indifference to tradition's masterpieces.

A principle of alternation works throughout the concerto. It is established at the beginning, when the strings and piano alternate for several phrases before the piano finally plays *with* the orchestra. Even after everyone performs together, an alternation of types of phrases continues. Alternation goes on in the first movement's andante, as the opening piano runs switch off several times with a wind chorale. Later on in the section, piano scales alternate with rolled chords. At the beginning of the second movement, first strings and then winds accompany the piano.

Concerto Number 3 in B Minor for Violin and Orchestra, Opus 61

Allegro non troppo
Andantino quasi allegretto
Molto moderato e maestoso. Allegro non troppo.
Più allegro

The Third Violin Concerto was written in 1880 and first performed the same year by violinist Pablo de Sarasate in Paris.

Like most composers who write concertos for an instrument they do not play, Saint-Saëns relied on the advice of a virtuoso. Thus many of his works for solo violin were composed for and with the help of the incredible Spanish violinist Pablo de Sarasate. Prior to meeting Sarasate, Saint-Saëns had written one violin concerto, now known as the Second (because of its order of publication). He had received some advice from George Augustus Polgreen Bridgetower, a violinist who in his younger years had premiered Beethoven's *Kreutzer* Sonata. But Saint-Saëns' Second Concerto is a rather naïve work. It was only once he began working with Sarasate that he really learned how to write solo violin music.

Sarasate, whose full name was Martín Melitón Sarasate y Navascues, was a child prodigy. When he was five years old, he heard his father, a violinist and the bandmaster of the picturesque fortress town of Pamplona, struggling to master a difficult violin passage. The young boy played the passage flawlessly on his miniature fiddle. The father, humiliated yet proud, never again played the violin. But he recognized his son's talent and sent him to study with some of the greatest violin pedagogues in Europe.

Sarasate was eight years old when he played a concert than won him a scholarship to study in Madrid. Four years later Queen Isabella sent him to the Paris Conservatory to work with Delphin Alard. Sarasate graduated with outstanding honors at the age of 13! At the age of 15 he began to tour Europe.

Sarasate was annoyed by the trivial music he was forced to play. There had been too few worthwhile pieces composed for violin since the classical era. He sought to solve this problem by seeking out a famous composer in the hopes of having a concerto written for him. The first composer he approached was Saint-Saëns, who was then 24. Saint-Saëns later recalled his first meeting with the 15-year-old virtuoso: "Fresh and young as spring itself, the faint shadow of a moustache scarcely visible on his upper lip, he was already a famous virtuoso. As if it were the easiest thing in the world, he had come quite simply to ask me to write a concerto for him. Flattered and charmed to the highest degree, I promised I would, and I kept my word with the [First] Concerto in A Major."

Sarasate went on to become one of the great violin virtuosos of the nineteenth century. He became known for his technical brilliance, perfect intonation, pure tone, and effortless playing. He became the first world-class violinist to make commercial recordings, and his portrait was painted by no less an artist than James Abbott McNeill Whistler.

Saint-Saëns was a virtuoso of another sort: he was a brilliant and effortless composer. He created a great many works, in virtually all genres, with apparent ease. It is not surprising that the composer and the violinist were temperamentally well suited to one another, that they became good friends, and that Saint-Saëns wrote a number of pieces for Sarasate.

Four years after he met Sarasate, Saint-Saëns composed the *Introduction and Rondo Capriccioso*, conceived in a Spanish style specifically for his friend. This piece quickly became standard virtuosic fare, whether performed in the original version with orchestra or in the arrangement by Georges Bizet for violin and piano. Sarasate performed it widely, thus making Saint-Saës' name known in many countries. The composer acknowledged, "In circulating my compositions throughout the world on his magic bow, Pablo de Sarasate rendered me the highest of services."

Seventeen years later the composer again wrote for his friend, this time his most substantial piece for violin and orchestra, the Third Concerto. This work, more than any of his seven other pieces for violin and orchestra or the eight chamber works for solo violin, shows the brilliance, subtlety, and understanding that the composer learned from Sarasate.

Years later Saint-Saëns recalled his friendship with the violinist: "Those who used to come to my musical evenings in the old days have not forgotten the distinction my celebrated friend used to lend to them, a distinction such that for several years no other violinist would agree to play at my house. All were terrified at the idea of being compared with him. He distinguished himself not only by his talent but also by his wit and the inexhaustible verve of his conversation, which was ever lively and much to be relished."

Saint-Saëns' biographer James Harding provides the following delightful picture of the violinist:

> He was, like Saint-Saëns, absent-minded in the everyday routine of life and would blandly agree to play at three concerts on the same evening, forgetting to turn up at any of them, or would set off on a journey across the world without any luggage. Once he succeeded in the course of a fortnight in getting rid of 30,000 francs which he had left in a drawer for the benefit of any callers who happened to need a loan. But when he put down the cigarette that smouldered continually between his fingers, and played the violin, he was complete master in a sphere where no one else could touch him.

The fact that the Third Concerto was written by a true professional, who thoroughly understood what sounds most beautiful on the violin, is evident on every page of the first movement. Consider, for example, the passionate opening theme, an emotional melody that exploits the instrument's lower register with great power and expressivity. After the violin moves into its upper register, Saint-Saëns asks the soloist to play some double- and triple-stops — two or three notes played simultaneously. Not all multiple stops sound well on the violin, but the composer knew which ones carry strength and sonority. Toward the end of the movement, when the violin plays rapid virtuosic figures, we again hear the composer's mastery of violin writing. The ending is truly spectacular, as the violin rises higher and higher above the full orchestra, finally reaching virtually the upper limits of the instrument.

The second movement uses the violin almost exclusively as a vehicle of melodic expression. Even when it plays virtuosic figures, they are within the context of lyrical melodies. The end of this movement is particularly beautiful: the violin in harmonics, doubled by a solo clarinet two octaves lower, plays arpeggios with a haunting, ethereal sonority, as the oboe recalls the main melody of the movement.

The solo instrument opens the finale with the outright virtuosity that is absent from the middle movement. After this introduction the violin plays the main theme, suggestive of gypsy violin playing. The second theme, also played by the soloist, displays another facet of the violin: melodic lyricism. There is a chorale, followed by a passage in which the soloist accompanies the orchestra, again in virtuoso fashion. The concerto ends with a flourish that grows out of the second theme.

Symphony Number 3 in C Minor, Opus 78, *Organ*
Adagio. Allegro moderato. Poco adagio
Allegro moderato. Presto. Allegro moderato. Presto.
Allegro moderato. Maestoso. Allegro. Molto
allegro

The Organ *Symphony was composed in 1886. Saint-Saëns conducted the first performance, with the London Philharmonic Orchestra, on 19 May 1886 in London.*

Saint-Saëns voiced a complaint in 1871 that sounds very much like
the grumbling of composers a century later:

> Not so very long ago a French composer who was daring enough
> to venture onto the terrain of instrumental music had no other
> means of getting his work performed than to give a concert him-
> self and invite his friends and the critics. As for the general pub-
> lic, it was hopeless even to think about them. The name of a
> composer who is French and still alive had only to appear on a
> poster to frighten everybody away. The chamber music socie-
> ties, flourishing and numerous at the time, restricted their pro-
> grams to the resplendent names of Beethoven, Mozart, Haydn,
> Mendelssohn — and sometimes Schumann as proof of their
> audacity.

If the complaint seems like those of today, so did the solution. In
order to combat prejudice against contemporary French chamber
music, Saint-Saëns founded the Société Nationale de Musique, which
was similar in purpose and activities to many composers' organizations functioning today. The other leading members of the organization were César Franck, Gabriel Fauré, and Edouard Lalo. The Society met with unexpected success. Not only was it responsible for the
premieres of many fine new French compositions, but also it showed
the public that such music was worthwhile. As a result, modern
French music began to appear on other concert series. Before too
many years had passed, the Society had two hundred members,
many of whom met regularly at Saint-Saëns' house to discuss and
play new music.

As the Society grew, so did its bureaucracy. In 1876 composers
Vincent d'Indy and Henri Duparc were elected secretaries. D'Indy undertook the herculean task of putting the archives in order. Thus he
became an important member of the Society's administration. Once

in this position of responsibility, he made a bold suggestion: that music by foreign composers be included in the Society's concerts. Saint-Saëns was willing to allow music by Grieg, Tchaikovsky, and Glinka, but he balked at the suggestion of the composer who really interested d'Indy: Wagner. Saint-Saëns understood that to start playing the music of this cult hero would be to return to the state of affairs the Society had been founded to remedy. He feared that the magnetic musical personality of Wagner would eclipse the works of the members. D'Indy, a devoted Wagnerian, was enraged. The ensuing rift between him and Saint-Saëns was not to be healed.

Their disagreements escalated over the succeeding years, and each enlisted allies. The proponents of d'Indy's position were the composers most influenced by Wagner. They took as their leader César Franck. Franck had been a friend of Saint-Saëns and had dedicated his Quintet of 1880 to his colleague. But that piece also symbolized the rivalry between these two leading French composers: Franck's work had been inspired by his passion for a particular woman, to whom Saint-Saëns was also attracted. Saint-Saëns heard rumors that Franck's pursuit had been more successful than his own. His personal resentment of Franck fueled his professional jealousy: Franck had a circle of devoted disciples and students, while Saint-Saëns did not. And, a few years later, Franck's Symphony in D Minor, which owed quite a lot to Saint-Saëns' Third Symphony, eclipsed its model in popularity.

Saint-Saëns understood that he was in the minority in the Society, and that those under the spell of Wagnerian aesthetics were both more numerous and more powerful than his own allies. Saint-Saëns resigned in 1886. He felt the Society had done its work. His departure, after 15 years as president, marked the end of an era.

The year 1886 ended an artistic era for Saint-Saëns as well. He conducted the premiere of the composition that was destined to be his last effort in the symphonic genre: his Third Symphony. In his remaining 35 years, he composed only a few incidental orchestral works (in addition to several works for soloist with orchestra). He turned his attention instead to the theater, writing seven operas, a ballet, and incidental music to seven plays.

The Third Symphony (actually it was the composer's fifth, since two youthful works were never numbered) is in many ways conservative. It looks backward to the heroic symphonies of Beethoven, yet it all but ignores the new Wagnerian sounds that excited Franck and d'Indy. It was with no small sarcasm that composer Charles Gounod said, as Saint-Saëns mounted the podium to conduct the symphony, "There's the Beethoven of France!"

The *Organ* Symphony was first heard in London. It had been

written for the London Philharmonic, which managed to get it without paying a commissioning fee. Saint-Saëns had been invited to appear as guest conductor and piano soloist. He asked for a stipend of forty pounds. The Philharmonic responded that it was a non-profit organization with limited funds. Saint-Saëns was offered an honorarium plus the honor of writing a symphony for the occasion. Knowing that the orchestra was prestigious and that it was large, he agreed.

He dedicated the symphony to Franz Liszt, who died shortly after the premiere. Liszt's style of orchestration is echoed in the symphony. In particular, Saint-Saëns took from the Hungarian composer's tone poem *Hunnenschlacht* the idea of including an organ in the orchestra.

The symphony received splendid receptions at both its London and Paris premieres, but, apart for its influence on Franck, it had little subsequent impact on French music. Saint-Saëns understood that the Third Symphony represented a deadend. "I have given all that I had to give," he wrote. "What I have done I shall never do again."

The composer referred to himself in the third person in the extensive program note he provided for the London premiere.

This symphony is divided into parts, after the manner of Saint-Saëns' Fourth Concerto for Piano and Orchestra and Sonata for Piano and Violin. Nevertheless, it includes practically the traditional four movements: the first, checked in development, serves as the introduction to the adagio, and the scherzo is connected, after the same manner, with the finale. The composer has thus sought to shun in a certain measure the interminable repetitions which are more and more disappearing from instrumental music. The composer thinks that the time has come for the symphony to benefit by the progress of modern instrumentation.

Saint-Saëns went on to list every instrument in the work's large orchestra, and then to give a detailed analysis of the symphony.

The first of the symphony's two movements comprises an adagio (which Saint-Saëns called "plaintive") which leads to an allegro and, after a transition, to a full-fledged adagio (the composer described this section as "extremely peaceful and contemplative"). The second movement begins with the usual scherzo, complete with trio section. The second time the trio occurs, it becomes a transition (labelled "a struggle for mastery, ending in the defeat of the restless, diabolical element") into the final section: an introduction ("triumph of calm and lofty thought") to a fugal allegro. The organ helps delineate the implied four-part symphonic structure. It is silent in the first section, then enters at the start of the slow section. It is absent from the scherzo but marks the arrival of the finale with a massive C major chord.

Like Franck's Symphony in D Minor, Saint-Saëns' Third is a cyclic work. This means that certain important themes recur in different movements. It was appropriate for Saint-Saëns to omit formal recapitulations, since the main themes of the earlier sections recur in later sections. An additional source of unity is the symphony's rhythmic style. In many places a tune can be felt either with or against the beat. Only by listening carefully to the accompaniment can we sense the beat, but the accompaniment is sometimes ambiguous or even nonexistent. This situation occurs, among other places, at the start of the first *allegro moderato,* at the beginning of the scherzo, and at the transformation of the first movement's first theme that is heard soon thereafter. The allegro theme returns in the introduction to the finale and again toward the end of the symphony, each time with its relation to the beat changed. What was off the beat later falls on the beat.

The symphony contains many kinds of music, projecting many different moods. It is sometimes dance-like, sometimes intimate, and sometimes grandiose. It is a large, romantic work of a sort that was falling into disfavor in France. Yet it is a spectacular orchestral showpiece, and its return to popularity in the twentieth century is due largely to its ability to show off a virtuosic orchestra at its best.

Arnold Schoenberg

Born on 13 September 1874 in Vienna.
Died on 13 July 1951 in Los Angeles.

Concerto for Piano and Orchestra, Opus 42

The Piano Concerto was completed on 30 December 1942. Edward Steuermann was the pianist at the first performance and Leopold Stokowski conducted the NBC Symphony Orchestra in New York on 6 February 1944.

Schoenberg, like many German artists of his generation, was forced to flee his homeland in the face of Nazi oppression. The composer came eventually to Los Angeles, where a number of European intellectuals gathered as refugees from Hitler's Europe. This group formed a strong cultural underground. Los Angeles is also the land of Hollywood, and the imported culture mingled freely if uneasily with the denizens of Tinseltown. Barriers were not (and are not) respected in southern California, and people readily crossed over from the artistic and intellectual subculture to that of the entertainment industry.

Schoenberg knew academics, since he earned his living as a teacher at UCLA, but he also knew several Hollywood personalities. More than once he had to refuse financially attractive offers to write movie music, as he was temperamentally unsuited to the creation of soundtracks. Indeed, it would be hard to imagine a composer whose style is less likely to work for dramatic backgrounds. Schoenberg's music belongs in the foreground: it is intense, extremely emotional, and uncompromising.

One person who befriended the expatriate composer was George Gershwin, a composer equally at home with popular and concert music. Another friend who inhabited both worlds of music was Oscar Levant. Levant was a classically trained pianist and composer who played with jazz bands and wrote popular songs. He achieved prominence as a performer of Gershwin's jazz-inspired concert music. Levant wrote film scores and occasionally acted in movies, and he also composed symphonic music. He studied with Schoenberg briefly. In his *Memoirs of an Amnesiac* he recounts the origin of Schoenberg's Piano Concerto:

> After I had achieved a certain fame and notoriety, I revisited Schoenberg in California and I asked him if he would compose

a slight piano piece for me, for which I gave him payment. He was delighted.

When I returned to New York, there was correspondence and suddenly this small piano piece burned feverishly in Schoenberg's mind and he decided to write a piano concerto. He sent me some early sketches, and it is possible that in the main row of tones my name or initials were involved [this assertion is not true]. However, I wasn't prepared for a piano concerto, and in the meantime Han[n]s Eisler assumed the role of negotiator for Schoenberg. Among other things, the fee grew to a vast sum for which, as the dedicatee, I was promised immortality.

The negotiation had suddenly become frenzied, and the familiar father figure was suffocating me. I couldn't stand it and I sent a telegram withdrawing from the venture.

Eventually the piano concerto was performed by Leopold Stokowski and the NBC Symphony, with Edward Steuermann as soloist.

Several years later I was in Beverly Hills and encountered Schoenberg. After we had greeted each other, he asked "Are you composing?" And I replied, "I have forgotten how."

He insisted one never forgets.

In a spasm of goodwill, I said, "I owe you some money." He nodded in agreement and I gave him a check. He was very cheerful about the whole thing.

I didn't really owe him any money — it was just an excuse to ameliorate the old situation.

As I look back, I was shortsighted and perhaps should have behaved differently.

The concert where the concerto was first played was sponsored by General Motors. Critic-composer Virgil Thomson praised conductor Stokowski for performing a new work by one of the great living composers, and he thanked General Motors for backing a concert of which they could be truly proud. Thomson lauded Schoenberg for having written a deeply expressive romantic work, in the best traditions of Vienna and Bach. But all this praise was to no avail. The music had seemed strange to most listeners, and as a result of this performance Stokowski's contract was not renewed.

The Piano Concerto is one of the more approachable examples of Schoenberg's twelve-tone style. The fact that the work was written using the twelve-tone method literally makes no difference to the average listener. There has been so much erroneous information written about Schoenberg's compositional "system," however, that it is necessary to clear the air by mentioning a few things that twelve-tone music is and is not. Schoenberg's very beautiful music does not deserve to be condemned for reasons that have little to do with how it sounds and that are false.

Twelve-tone music is not mathematical music. It is not cerebral music. It is not music composed automatically or by anything other than the composer's musical talents and emotional expressivity. The use of a twelve-tone row guarantees nothing and precludes very little, but it does make possible new degrees and kinds of unity.

A row is a particular ordering of the twelve notes of the chromatic scale. Schoenberg chose one row for each composition, and he kept to that row — plus the basic transformations of it (such as playing it backwards, upside-down, or transposed higher or lower) — for an entire work. Melodies *may* come from statements of the row as a succession of notes. Harmonies *may* come from playing adjacent notes of the row simultaneously and/or playing two or more forms of the row at once. The row is usually *not heard* directly. Rather, its special sound colors the nature of the melodies and harmonies, so that different themes have basic characteristics in common. Since segments of a row may be freely repeated, it is not true (despite claims to the contrary by ignorant critics) that we must hear the other eleven notes before a tone may be repeated. A row is not a theme, not a melody, not a series of chords, and not a form. But it does influence all of these basic elements of musical expression.

Someone who has not composed twelve-tone music may think that the strict use of a row is a hopeless straitjacket for the composer. But such is not the case at all. The row is no more restrictive than the use of a generative theme in a Bach fugue or the adherence to a particular theme in a set of variations. To use the row musically requires a prodigious compositional technique. In the hands of second-rate composers, it can indeed become a substitute for imagination. But Schoenberg always used the row with integrity and to create beautiful music.

He thought of himself only as a composer, and he despised those music theorists who sought out the rows rather than the music in his compositions. He refused to teach his students twelve-tone technique, insisting instead that they master the traditional counterpoint of Bach and harmony of Brahms. Thus this man who has been labeled the great revolutionary of music was in reality a thorough conservative. He revered tradition and thought of his music as a logical extension of that of Mahler and Brahms. He wanted his tunes to be hummed like those of Tchaikovsky, and he sensed that allowing people to know about the twelve-tone method might preclude their hearing his lyricism.

He was right. He became a talked-about composer whose music was not played very much. His music has been the subject of more treatises than performances! Anyone today listening to the Piano Concerto without prejudice, without trying to find rows or hear techniques, knows what beautiful music Schoenberg could write.

This music is *not* easy to hear, however, for several reasons. (1) Prejudice against the misunderstood twelve-tone method is only one reason. (2) Schoenberg's music is also unrelievedly tense. It is not just that his dissonances do not resolve. With the twelve-tone technique every note is important (although not, as sometimes claimed, equally). Since every note belongs to at least one form of the row, no note is purely ornamental, and the result is an almost unbearable intensity. (3) Furthermore, none of the twelve tones is absent for long, since each transformation of a row is simply a rearrangement of the same twelve notes. Hence the intensity never lets up totally. (4) The most important factor that makes this music difficult, paradoxically, is its conservatism. The forms, the rhythms, and the phrases all suggest late romantic music. It is not impossible to hear the spirit of Brahms hovering over this music. But the harmonies do not behave the way Brahmsian chords do: they do not resolve. The gestures suggest a type of resolution that the harmonies rarely deliver, and the result is more unsettling than in more radical music that does not even suggest traditional procedures. It takes an effort for a listener to stop expecting Brahmsian gestures to act tonally.

These four factors make Schoenberg's Piano Concerto challenging. These factors have little directly to do with the twelve-tone system, however. Schoenberg's music is the way it is because of the personality of its composer — complex and uncompromising — not because of his compositional method. The composer's tonal music, from early in his career and also from late (the next piece after the Piano Concerto, for example, is a set of variations in G minor), is not very different from his twelve-tone music. It presents the same challenges, the same unremitting intensity, the same demands on the listener. This is music that requires an effort to hear, an effort it more than repays. It is not, however, the only music that requires effort: there have also been long periods of misunderstanding before audiences learned to appreciate Mahler or Ives or late Beethoven. We have learned to love that music, and we should also learn to love the highly emotional twelve-tone music of Arnold Schoenberg.

The Piano Concerto is cast in one long movement that is subdivided into four distinct sections, each of which is not quite independent enough to be a movement in itself. The first section opens with the piano alone, playing a slow dance-like theme reminiscent of an

Austrian *Ländler.* The theme pervades the first section, as the instruments of the orchestra gradually join the piano.

The second section is a frenzied, demonic allegro. Snare drum and xylophone join the orchestra to add to the excitement. Other special effects include *col legno* (hitting the strings with the wooden part of the bow), flutter-tonguing (wind and brass instruments' equivalent of strings' tremolo, and *sul ponticello* (bowing near the bridge on string instruments to produce a nasal sound).

The third section is an expressive adagio, into which the tensions of the previous scherzo continually intrude. The final section is a leisurely-paced rondo. Toward the end the theme of the first section returns, and then the music moves to a triumphant close.

Concerto for Violin and Orchestra, Opus 36
Poco allegro
Andante grazioso
Allegro

The Violin Concerto was begun in the summer of 1934 and completed on 23 September 1936. It was first performed by Louis Krasner and the Philadelphia Orchestra, conducted by Leopold Stokowski, on 6 December 1940.

The Violin Concerto was the first major work Schoenberg composed after immigrating to the United States. He, like many artists coming to America in the 1930s, was a refugee from Hitler's Germany.

When Hitler came to power on 30 January 1933, the anti-Semitism that had been growing in Germany suddenly became official policy. Schoenberg, a baptized Jew and a "modernist" composer, was in danger. His biblical opera-in-progress *Moses and Aaron* seemed suspiciously Jewish in Germany, and his uncompromisingly dissonant music was decidedly not what the Nazis wanted to uphold as *their* art. The composer soon learned that the government had "requested" the elimination of the "Jewish influence" at the Berlin Hochschule für Musik, where he taught. Schoenberg voluntarily resigned, hoping thereby to receive two years' severance pay: "One who, like myself, stands in an unassailable position in matters political and moral and who, by losing his field of activity, has been most deeply injured in his artistic and manly honor, should not on top of all that have his economic position endangered — indeed, threatened with disaster." He was granted a compensatory salary for only seven months. On 17 May he left Berlin.

He went to Paris, where he became involved with the Jewish community. He began to feel a strong solidarity with those who were being persecuted in Germany solely for their religious heritage. Thirty-five years after he had been baptized, he officially rejoined the Jewish faith. Painter Marc Chagall was a witness at the ceremony. He thereupon worked to start a Jewish Unity Party and a Jewish newspaper. "It is my intention to take an active part in endeavors of this kind. I regard that as more important than my art, and I am determined — if I am suited to such activities — to do nothing in the future but work for the Jewish national cause . . . [and] to persuade people to help the Jews in Germany." Schoenberg's conversion was greeted by a scathing article in a Vienna newspaper. The composer had made a stand that was viewed as anti-German; it was impossible to turn back.

After a few weeks Schoenberg left for the United States, to accept two concurrent teaching positions in Boston and New York. He was welcomed by musicians here, but he found the commuting depressing and the climate unhealthy. He spent the summer at the community of artists and religious leaders in Chautauqua, New York, where he began the Violin Concerto. He decided quite suddenly that autumn to move to Los Angeles, which became his home for the next 17 years.

Coming to Los Angeles after living most of his life in Vienna and Berlin must have been like traveling to another planet. He encountered people and customs that he found strange but strangely enchanting. He joined a growing community of major artists who had been compelled to leave Europe because of the Nazi threat. He also encountered Hollywood, with its other-worldly glitter and informality. For example, he once found himself at a dinner of ASCAP (American Society of Composers, Authors, and Publishers), the performing rights organization to which he had recently been elected. He was seated between two song-writers. To the German composer who allowed no one, save possibly his wife, call him by his first name, one of the song-writers said, "You know, Arnold, I don't understand your stuff, but you must be O.K. or you wouldn't be here."

Schoenberg considered writing music for the movies. A representative of producer Irving Thalberg once visited the composer to try to convince him to provide music for the screen version of Pearl Buck's *The Good Earth*. The emissary, trying to generate some excitement for the project, described the film: "Think of it! A terrific storm is going on; the wheat field is swaying in the wind, and suddenly the earth begins to tremble. In the midst of the earthquake, Oo-Lan gives birth to a baby! What an opportunity for music!" Schoenberg replied, "With so much going on, why do you need music?"

The composer preferred to spend his time on such serious works as the Violin Concerto and the Fourth String Quartet. But he did need a source of income, so he finally relented and went to see Thalberg. Hans Heinsheimer, in his book *Menagerie in F Sharp*, describes what happened:

> Thalberg kept Schoenberg waiting twenty minutes, but it shows the awe-inspiring grandeur of Hollywood, and of M.G.M. in particular, that Schoenberg, who had *never* waited for anybody in all his 61 years, *threatened to leave but actually did not.* . . .
>
> Finally the great Thalberg arrived and apologized to the great Schoenberg. Then he asked him what his terms would be for writing music to *The Good Earth*.
>
> "My terms are very simple," said Schoenberg. "I want fifty thousand dollars and an absolute guarantee that not a single note of my score will be altered."
>
> Here endeth the story and any relationship between Arnold Schoenberg and the moving-picture industry.

The composer was able to secure a teaching position at the University of Southern California. After a year he moved to UCLA, where he remained until retirement in 1944.

The extraordinarily difficult Violin Concerto was premiered in Philadelphia in 1940. The soloist was Louis Krasner, who a few years earlier had commissioned and performed the Violin Concerto by Schoenberg's former student Alban Berg. The composer was unable to travel to Philadelphia to hear the performance, but he learned that it would be broadcast in Los Angeles. He brought a small portable radio to his office at UCLA, only to discover at the last minute that the broadcast had been cancelled.

We hear a lot about Schoenberg as the great radical composer of the twentieth century. The real facts are more complex. While it is true that many of his early works, written in Vienna and Berlin in the second decade of this century, are unprecedented in their bold treatment of dissonance, the composer was fundamentally a traditionalist. His later works attempt an integration of his earlier radicalism with the traditions of German music. In his younger years he admired Wagner's experimental harmonies and Mahler's colorful orchestration, but in his later years he came to view himself as the successor to Brahms.

His later music is still dissonant, and the dissonances still do not resolve in the usual manner: Schoenberg's sound is not Brahms' sound. But the procedures are similar: the phrasing, the counterpoint, the form, and the rhythms. Schoenberg was a conservative like Brahms. Both composers responded to their own times but felt a deep nostalgia for an earlier classicism.

The Violin Concerto, for example, is a traditional work. What is conservative about it? There are hints of sonata form; there are long, beautiful melodies (such as the very opening solo violin line) and incisive motives; there are distinct themes; there is contrast; the soloist displays breathtaking virtuosity; there are recapitulations (consider the unmistakable return of the theme of the first movement late in the finale); there are wonderfully imaginative moments; the violin has a cadenza. All that is different from a nineteenth-century concerto is the tonal language — a big difference, to be sure. The music is undeniably dissonant, and that is why some listeners find the concerto difficult (even though it is a half century old and thus can in no way be called "new music"). Yet the music can also be forthright, engaging, and decidedly extroverted: listen to the march-like parts of the finale. Making the finale simpler and more straightforward than the earlier movements is a classical procedure, one more ramification of the concerto's underlying traditionalism.

Why did Schoenberg write dissonant music? Before this question can be answered, we must understand what dissonance is. A dissonance is not an unpleasant sound, but rather a tense sound that seems to need resolution. Virtually all music contains dissonances. In Schoenberg's Violin Concerto the dissonances rarely resolve, and that is what makes it different from tonal music.

Why, then, did Schoenberg write music in which the dissonances do not resolve? Part of the reason is that he was a severe person, and his severity shows through in his music. But there is a deeper reason. In the unresolved dissonances of a piece like the Violin Concerto it is possible to hear the *Angst* of our century. Schoenberg had lived through the death of one culture (the opulent, even decadent, late romanticism of the two decades surrounding 1900) and the birth of a new one. The tensions of his age erupted in one World War and, at the time he composed the concerto, were about to break out in another. Is it surprising that the music of an intense person who had lived through the most intense period in history should itself be intense? After all, Schoenberg's music, like all music, is a reflection of its times and its creator.

Yet its gestures do seem to belong to another era. The opening of the second movement, for example, is appropriately marked *grazioso*. The rhythms, the orchestration, and the melodies suggest a gracefulness such as we might find in Brahms or Mahler, but the underlying dissonant harmonies tell us that such gestures can no longer be as innocent as they were in 1890.

When the shape of the music implies resolution but the harmonies do not resolve, then tension is inevitable. As in all music, the degree of tension becomes greater or lesser as the music progresses, but the inevitability of unresolved dissonance requires a deep involvement from a listener. Thus the Violin Concerto can actually be more difficult to listen to than a lot of more recent music, in which not only the harmonies but also the rhythms, textures, themes, and forms are non-traditional. When everything is new, we do not expect anything as old-fashioned as resolution. When some things are new (dissonant harmonies) and some things are old (forms, rhythms, and gestures), it is difficult to give up expecting resolution. Nor should we, since the essence of Schoenberg's incredible intensity lies precisely in the disjunction between what is expected and what happens.

◆　◆　◆

Five Pieces for Orchestra, Opus 16
　　　　　　　Premonitions
　　　　　　　The Past
　　　　　　　Chord Colors
　　　　　　　Peripetia (Turning Point)
　　　　　　　The Obbligato Recitative

Schoenberg began the Five Pieces for Orchestra on 23 May 1909. He completed the work later that summer. Henry Wood conducted the first performance in London on 9 March 1912. Schoenberg subsequently revised the work, for a smaller orchestra, in 1947.

The years 1909–11 were a time of incredible cultural richness and artistic advancement in Vienna. It is impossible to pinpoint exactly when one era ends and another begins, but in these years we find Gustav Mahler composing his impassioned farewell to the nineteenth century, the Ninth Symphony. The same summer Schoenberg wrote his revolutionary Five Pieces for Orchestra, a work that offers an optimistic glimpse of the new century. Other composers of the older generation were also saying farewell in music. For example, Richard Strauss composed *Der Rosenkavalier*, an apotheosis of that symbol of nineteenth-century Vienna, the waltz. And other young composers, such as Alban Berg and Igor Stravinsky, were forging a new style.

The new music, with its total chromaticism, can be traced to Wagner's tortured music drama *Tristan und Isolde*. But the immediate ties between the old and the new were Mahler and Schoenberg. Mahler, who never abandoned tonality, supported Schoenberg, Berg, and Anton Webern, even though he was not sure he understood their music. They respected Mahler and learned tremendously from his music. The orchestration, frequent changes of moods, and contrapuntal richness of Schoenberg's demonic Five Pieces owe a lot to the older composer.

By the autumn of 1911, much had changed. Mahler was dead, and Schoenberg had left Vienna for Berlin. Strauss, although no one had yet realized it, was finished writing powerful operas. The last true voices of tonality were stilled. All that remained in Vienna were second-rate tonal composers who had either not understood or not accepted the artistic upheaval that had taken place. The younger composers had achieved their goal of finding a way to conceive music without tonal progression. What remained for them was to work out the implications of their new aesthetic.

It is possible to hear the thrill of discovery in the Five Pieces. Schoenberg may not have realized consciously the importance of the music he was composing, and he may not have foreseen that he was creating a new musical language that would influence most subsequent music. But the music is alive with a confident vitality. This music has the excitement of a major breakthrough. It remained for later generations to find links between its new style and tradition. Listening to it more than three-quarters of a century later, we can readily hear its relationship to late romanticism. The Five Pieces are not all that different from Mahler's Ninth: they share the same dynamism, the same coloristic orchestration, the same powerful dissonances. The difference lies with those dissonances: Schoenberg found that they did not have to resolve. He called this discovery — years later, after he had thought about it coolly — the "emancipation of the dissonance."

The concern for pure color — most apparent in the chordal, purposefully unmelodic third piece — is an additional source of the freshness of the new style. The idea came to Schoenberg in a discussion with Mahler. Schoenberg argued that it should be possible to construct a melody of timbres, a line in which each note is given to a different instrument. "I cannot unreservedly agree with the distinction between color and pitch. I find that a note is perceived by its color, one of whose dimensions is pitch. Color, then, is the great realm, pitch but one of its provinces. . . . If the ear could discriminate between differences of color, it might be feasible to invent melodies that are built of colors. But who dares to develop such theories?"

Schoenberg himself dared to develop not only the theories but also the music. In order to obtain a wide range of colors, he employed an enormous orchestra, including four flutes (two doubling piccolo), three oboes, English horn, five clarinets (including the rare contrabass clarinet), three bassoons, contrabassoon, six horns, three trumpets, four trombones, tuba, percussion, harp, celeste, and strings. Throughout the work the orchestral sonority shifts often, creating a tense restlessness and a kaleidoscope of colors.

Schoenberg was reluctant to give descriptive names to the individual pieces. His publisher felt that some suggestion of extramusical meaning would help the music. The composer knew there was quite enough musical meaning in the Five Orchestral Pieces without having to burden listeners with suggestions of additional significance. But, uncharacteristically, he relented. He wrote in his diary:

> Maybe I shall give in, for I have found that titles are at least possible. On the whole, unsympathetic to the idea. For the wonderful thing about music is that one can say everything in it, so that he who knows understands everything; and yet one has not given away one's secrets — the things one does not even admit to oneself. But titles give you away! Besides — whatever was to be said has been said, by the music. Why, then, words at all? If words were necessary they would be there in the first place. But art says more than words. Now, the titles which I may provide give nothing away, because some of them are very obscure and others highly technical. To wit:
>
> I. Premonitions (everybody has those).
> II. The Past (everybody has that too).
> III. Chord Colors (technical).
> IV. Peripetia (general enough, I think).
> V. The Obbligato (perhaps better the "fully developed" or the "endless recitative").
>
> However, there should be a note that these titles were added for technical reasons of publication and not to give a poetic content.

The first performance met with bafflement from the press and audience. Not too many people yet understood the new language. Now that many years have passed, we comprehend the new sounds and procedures much better. What is interesting is that the Five Pieces have lost none of their impact. They still proclaim the glory of a new music. It is no longer literally new, of course, but it retains its full excitement.

Pelleas und Melisande, Opus 5

Pelleas und Melisande was composed between 4 July 1902 and 28 February 1903. Schoenberg conducted the first performance in Vienna on 26 January 1905.

Schoenberg was 27 years old. He was a struggling composer, with high ambitions but few accomplishments and fewer prospects. He was earning a small income in Vienna by orchestrating other composers' operettas, but he was discouraged about his own career. He began to think about moving to another city.

In September 1901 a touring literary cabaret came to Vienna from Berlin. The musical accompaniment was to be conducted by Oskar Straus, whose uncle forbade his appearance because the performance fell on the Jewish Day of Atonement. Ernst von Wolzogen, director of the company, recalled that Straus "brought me a young musician of small stature, strong features, and dark hair, whose name, Arnold Schoenberg, at that time was completely unknown."

Wolzogen was impressed with Schoenberg's cabaret songs, and Schoenberg began to think that he might secure employment at the cabaret's home theater in Berlin. A move away from Vienna would be providential for another reason. Schoenberg was in love with Mathilde Zemlinsky, sister of his mentor and former teacher, composer-conductor Alexander Zemlinsky. Mathilde was several months pregnant. A move to Berlin promised both employment and avoidance of a scandal. The young couple married in October and moved to Berlin in December.

The cabaret promised artistic excitement and new ideas. One of its writers, Otto Julius Bierbaum, explained:

> In placing our art at the service of the music hall, our intentions are entirely serious. We are firmly convinced that the time has come for the whole of life to be permeated by art. Painters nowadays make chairs, and aim to make them not just the sort you can admire in museums but the sort you can park yourself in without discomfort to the portions of your anatomy concerned. In the same way we want to write poems that will not just be read amidst the bliss of solitude, but that can bear singing to a crowd hungry for entertainment.

These exciting ideas did not, in practice, lead to great artistic stimulation or professional success for Schoenberg. His situation was no better than in Vienna. As musical director of the cabaret, he made barely enough money to support his new family. He had to conduct, compose popular music, and — once again — arrange and orchestrate music by others. He is reputed to have turned out over six thousand pages of manuscript by 1903! Not much time remained for serious composition.

The most prominent composer in Berlin at the time was Richard Strauss. Schoenberg knew and admired several of Strauss' scores, and he was glad to meet Strauss in April 1902. The famous composer took an interest in the young man from Vienna. Knowing that Schoenberg was having financial troubles, Strauss helped him secure grants and extra jobs. Schoenberg copied the orchestral parts for Strauss' enormous *Taillefer.* Strauss found other copying jobs for Schoenberg, helped him secure a part-time teaching post, and nominated him for a Liszt Foundation Fellowship. Strauss' letter of recommendation requested that "a man, who lives in the most dire poverty and is *very* talented, be given urgently a scholarship of one thousand marks a year for some years. . . . You will find that his works, if a bit overcharged at the moment, show great talent and gifts."

Strauss helped Schoenberg artistically as well as materially. He called his younger colleague's attention to the symbolist play *Pelléas et Mélisande* by Maurice Maeterlinck. Strauss, unaware that Debussy's opera on the same text had recently been premiered in Paris, suggested that Schoenberg might want to compose an opera on *Pelléas.* Writing in 1950, Schoenberg recalled,

> I had first planned to convert *Pelléas et Mélisande* into an opera, but I gave up this plan, though I did not know that Debussy was working on his opera at the same time. I still regret that I did not carry out my initial intention. It would have differed from Debussy's. I might have missed the wonderful perfume of the poem; but I might have made my characters more singing. On the other hand, the symphonic poem helped me, in that it taught me to express moods and characters in precisely formulated units, a technique that my opera would perhaps not have promoted so well. Thus my fate evidently guided me with great foresight.

The tone poem *Pelleas und Melisande* was the only large-scale work Schoenberg completed while living in Berlin. It is surely no coincidence that in this, the only tone poem Schoenberg ever composed, he employed a technique from Strauss' famous tone poems of the 1890s: the use of short figures to characterize particular people, objects, emotions, or events, much in the way Wagner used leitmotifs in his operas. Strauss and Schoenberg were attempting to tell stories and to depict their emotional undercurrents in purely orchestral music.

In 1903 Schoenberg moved back to Vienna. He wrote to Strauss,

> Some friends have taken trouble on my behalf, so that I can earn my living here to a certain extent. Naturally I have no fixed employment, unfortunately, but I will have a lot of work from Universal Edition, the new Viennese publishing house, and if this goes only half way, it will at least be bearable. So I must say good-bye to you for a long time. I would like to take this oppor-

tunity to thank you, honored master, once again for all the help you have given me at a sacrifice to yourself in the most sincere manner. I will not forget this for the whole of my life and will always be thankful to you for it.

Schoenberg and Strauss remained on good terms for a number of years. However, once Schoenberg turned to composing atonal music, Strauss could no longer understand nor sympathize with Schoenberg's music. The two men went their separate ways, particularly in old age, when Schoenberg fled the Nazi terror by moving to America while Strauss remained in Germany. In 1946 Schoenberg wrote about Strauss, denying the allegation that the latter had been a Nazi and expressing sympathy for the way the war had ravaged the man's career and fortune. Schoenberg concluded, "I do not speak as a friend of Richard Strauss; though he was helpful to me in my youth, he has later changed his attitude towards myself. I am sure that he does not like my music and in this respect I show no mercy: I consider such people as enemies."

The unworldly atmosphere of Maeterlinck's play, which was first produced in 1893, inspired music by four major composers. In addition to Schoenberg's tone poem and Debussy's opera, we have incidental music by Sibelius and Fauré. According to Harry Neville, what attracted these composers was Maeterlinck's preoccupation

with the mystery that lies just beneath the surface of ordinary life; the facts of time and space have little influence on the movements of his characters. We seldom know who his pale knights, orphan princesses, and guardians of desolate castles may be; we are not told where they come from, nor where they go; their existence has nothing concrete about it. Through everything runs the suggestive symbolism of both action and setting. Overtones and implications say more than direct speech, symbols more than fact. Maeterlinck's subject is the mystery of fate, the power of destiny and of the subconscious, the intense but hidden inner conflicts of life.

In 1920 Schoenberg's student Alban Berg published an analysis of *Pelleas und Melisande* in which he identified twenty distinct themes used as leitmotifs. In 1949 Schoenberg himself wrote a similar analysis.

The work is cast in 17 short sections, which group into four larger units, roughly corresponding to the four movements of a symphony. It begins with an introduction describing how Golaud, step-brother of Pelleas, finds the strange, child-like Melisande weeping by a brook.

The bass clarinet, almost at the very beginning, presents the fate motive. Melisande refuses to identify herself, and she evades his questions. Her helplessness is represented by a descending oboe theme. Golaud's theme appears softly in the horns, as Melisande refuses to allow him to help her retrieve the crown she has lost in the brook. As his theme expands through the full orchestra, he leads her to his castle, where he weds her. After the music dies down, the trumpet sounds the theme of Pelleas, characterized as a youthful knight. His theme includes the two-chord motive of destiny. The return of Melisande's theme symbolizes her growing love for Pelleas.

The second section, a scherzo, depicts the scene in which Melisande, playing with her wedding ring by a well, loses it at the same instant that Golaud, riding far away, falls off his horse: the Golaud theme, in trombones and tuba, descends. Golaud begins to grow suspicious of Pelleas and Melisande. In a climactic scene, Melisande lets her hair fall from a castle window over the ecstatic Pelleas. This scene begins with flutes and clarinets in imitation. Harps join in, and two solo violins play Melisande's theme while a solo cello plays Pelleas' theme. As Pelleas and Melisande declare their love, Golaud's suspicions are realized. He leads Pelleas to the tombs beneath the castle. Trombone *glissandi* (used here for the first time ever in a symphonic work), muted horns and trumpets, and flutter-tongued flutes produce a suitably eerie texture. Pelleas fears Golaud's strange mood.

The third section, an adagio, starts with the love music of Pelleas and Melisande. The theme is a long, lyrical violin line. The love theme combines with the Pelleas and Melisande themes, as the music surges toward a climax. The couple embraces. Golaud's theme is heard as he rushes from the shadows and kills Pelleas. We hear the fate motive.

In the final section Melisande lies in her chamber, having given birth to a daughter. Golaud, still suspicious, questions her, but she denies that her love for Pelleas had been anything more than innocent. A chorale-like version of Melisande's theme, accompanied by a descending figure in the flutes and piccolos, is a premonition of her death. The servants fall to their knees as Melisande dies. The work ends with a recapitulatory epilogue.

Schoenberg concludes his analysis of the work with this statement: "The first performance, 1905 in Vienna, under my own direction, provoked great riots among the audience and even the critics. Reviews were unusually violent, and one of the critics suggested putting me in an asylum and keeping music paper out of my reach. Only six years later, under Oscar Fried's direction, it became a great success, and since that time has not caused the anger of the audience."

Verklärte Nacht, Opus 4

Verklärte Nacht was completed on 1 December 1899 in a version for string sextet. It was first performed on 18 March 1902 in Vienna by the Rosé Quartet. Schoenberg rescored the work for string orchestra in 1917 and revised the larger version in 1943.

Schoenberg occupies a curious position in music history. Regarded by many as the greatest composer of the twentieth century and as a vitally significant innovator, he has suffered neglect by many performers and indifference by audiences. The reasons for the relative rarity of Schoenberg performances are complex. His music is extremely difficult to perform, not so much technically as expressively, and it is most challenging to hear. Since it is extraordinarily rich in implications, which are fulfilled or frustrated on many levels and often much later in a piece, many hearings are necessary before a work opens itself to a listener.

Schoenberg lived a long time and underwent a fascinating development. His creative life is generally divided into four periods. During the first he was absorbed with the supercharged emotions of late romanticism. *Verklärte Nacht* ("Transfigured Night"), typical of Schoenberg's first period, was written in three weeks when the composer was 25. It sounds like Wagner or Mahler greatly intensified. As Schoenberg felt the need to introduce more and more expressive dissonance into his music, it became harder for him to resolve these dissonances convincingly. Therefore he abandoned resolution and, with it, the tonal system, which had formed the basis of virtually all Western music since about 1600. The composer entered his second and most radical period, the atonal. He wrote music full of the excitement of discovering and exploring a new world of sounds. Before too long, however, he came to need an organizing principle to replace tonality. He fell silent for seven years, during which he devised the twelve-tone system. Schoenberg used it to help reconcile the radicalism of his atonal music with the traditions of his past. The pieces of his third period use old forms, and they employ their tone rows in ways vaguely analogous both to traditional key centers and to old-fashioned thematic groups. Schoenberg looked back nostalgically to his early tonal music during his final period. He loosened the strictness of his twelve-tone writing and even composed some tonal music. Thus his final style embodied the integration of all aspects of his earlier styles, and it produced his great masterpieces: the Violin Fantasy, String Trio, and last choral pieces.

Although one cannot find in *Verklärte Nacht* all the directions Schoenberg was eventually to take, it is typical of the hyper-emotional personality of all his music. We hear passionate tugs at the limits of tonality, and we understand how the young composer would soon feel he had to go beyond the tonal system. In his later years he was once asked why he no longer wrote music like *Verklärte Nacht.* He replied, "I still do, but nobody notices."

The piece was originally conceived as a string sextet. Alexander Zemlinsky, Schoenberg's teacher and future brother-in-law, tried to get it performed, but the *Tonkünstlerverein,* the only professional ensemble in Vienna at the time, rejected it. One member dismissed the piece by saying, "It sounds as if someone had smeared the score of *Tristan* while it was still wet." Scheoberg later recollected with bitter irony that the work had not been accepted for performance because it contained one chord that was strictly forbidden by the rules of harmony. "It is self-evident: there is no such thing as the inversion of a ninth chord; therefore, there is not such thing as a performance of it. One cannot really perform something that does not exist."

When the first performance finally did take place, Mahler heard some rehearsals and was deeply affected. He became a champion of Schoenberg's work and remained his strong supporter throughout his remaining years, even when he found Schoenberg's subsequent pieces difficult to understand.

Verklärte Nacht was inspired by a poem from Richard Dehmel's collection *Woman and World.* Dehmel (1863–1920) was a poet who combined Nietzsche's ideas of the superman with the politics of socialism. His work was a powerful influence around the turn of the century. An extract from the poem is quoted in Schoenberg's score. Both the poem and the composition share an atmosphere of morbidity, typical of the late nineteenth century.

Henry E. Krehbiel paraphrased the fragment quoted by Schoenberg:

> Two mortals walk through a cold, barren grove. The moon sails over the tall oaks, which send their scrawny branches up through the unclouded moonlight. A woman speaks. She confesses a sin to the man at her side: she is with child, and he is not its father. She had lost belief in happiness, and, longing for life's fullness, for motherhood and mother's duty, she had surrendered herself, shuddering, to the embraces of a man she knew not. She had thought herself blessed, but now life had avenged itself upon her by giving her the love of him she walked

with. She staggers onward, gazing with lackluster eye at the moon, which follows her. A man speaks. Let her not burden her soul with thoughts of guilt. See, the moon's sheen enwraps the universe. Together they are driving over chill waters, but a flame from each warms the other. It will transfigure the stranger, and she will bear the child to him. For she has inspired the brilliant glow within him and made him, too, a child. They sink into each other's arms. Their breaths meet in kisses in the air. Two mortals wander through the wondrous moonlight.

Egon Wellesz, a student of Schoenberg, explained that *Verklärte Nacht* "is made up of five sections, in which the first, third, and fifth are of a more epic nature and so portray the deep feelings of people wandering about in the cold moonlit night. The second contains the passionate plaint of the woman, the fourth the sustained answer of the man, which shows much depth and warmth of understanding."

Franz Schubert

Born on 31 January 1797 in Vienna.
Died on 19 November 1828 in Vienna.

◆　◆　◆

Incidental Music to *Rosamunde*
        Overture
        Entr'acte
        Ballet
        Entr'acte
        Romanze
        Geisterchor
        Entr'acte
        Hirtenmelodien
        Hirtenchor
        Jägerchor
        Ballet

The Rosamunde *Overture was composed and premiered in 1820 to introduce the play* The Magic Harp. *The remainder of the* Rosamunde *music was composed in 1823 and first performed on 20 December 1823 in Vienna.*

Schubert, who rarely received commissions, was pleased to be asked to provide music to accompany Helmina von Chézy's play *Rosamunde,* which was going to be produced at the Theatre an der Wien in 1823. Perhaps he should have felt some hesitation, as the same author had provided the disastrous libretto for Weber's opera *Euryanthe* a few years earlier. But Schubert, no doubt enticed by the prestige of the performance, put together some eleven musical numbers. Although he had but three weeks in which to complete the project (the playwright had managed to write her text in just five days!), the music is indeed charming, and some of it is among his most beautiful. Particularly memorable are the first entr'acte and the final ballet.

Unfortunately, the play followed the precedent of *Euryanthe* and was a flop. It was performed only twice. Schubert never again completed a stage work. The text of *Rosamunde* is now lost. A synopsis has been reconstructed, however, and it indicates how ridiculous an affair it must have been. It involved a princess raised by a shepherd, a conveniently arranged shipwreck, hidden identities, a letter perfumed with poison, a daring rescue, a last-minute reunion, and a nefarious plot.

Since he had insufficient time to compose an opening orchestral number, Schubert used the D major overture he had composed in 1820 for his opera *Alfonso und Estrella*. As he hoped for future performances of both the opera and the play, however, he felt that they should not share an overture. Rather than compose a new opening for *Alfonso*, he returned the D major overture to its original work. He decided to replace it with a C major overture he had composed a few years earlier for a melodrama called *The Magic Harp*. *The Magic Harp*, which had a plot as ludicrous as that of *Rosamunde*, was unlikely to be revived. Schubert felt that his C major overture would be lost to obscurity unless he found it a more congenial home.

As it turned out, the entire drama was destined for obscurity. But the incidental music has survived without the play. The C major overture, which was never actually performed with the play, became known as the *Rosamunde* Overture. There is no musical connection between the overture and the remaining *Rosamunde* music.

The first time the overture appeared in print under its new title was in 1834, six years after the composer's death, in an arrangement for string quartet by one J. von Blumenthal. There had been a publisher's announcement in 1827 to the effect that the C major overture was to be brought out in a piano arrangement, presumably by the composer, as the overture to *Rosamunde*. But the music was never printed, and it has never been proven that Schubert made such a transcription.

The varied uses of the overture are typical of Schubert. He subsequently, for example, used the music from the last entr'acte in two other compositions: the slow movement of his A Minor String Quartet and the third of his Impromptus, D. 935. Similarly, the introduction and coda of the C major overture had previously been used (in D major) in the *Italian* Overture. It has been argued, although less than convincingly, that Schubert planned to use the first entr'acte, in B minor, as the finale of his *Unfinished* Symphony, in the same key.

Symphony Number 2 in B-Flat Major
                Largo. Allegro vivace
                Andante
                Menuetto: Allegro vivace. Trio. Menuetto
                Presto vivace

The Second Symphony was composed between 10 December 1814 and 14 March 1815. It may have been played shortly thereafter in Vienna, or its first performance may have taken place in London on 20 October 1877.

Schubert was not a professional composer. He wrote music for enjoyment and from an inner drive, but he rarely gave much thought to publishing, or to preserving his manuscripts for posterity, or to performing them beyond his circle of friends. In his young years he never made any money composing. Had he lived longer, his attitude toward professionalism would no doubt have changed, but he died at the age of 31. Thus all of his compositions are, in a real sense, early works. Had Beethoven died at the same age, he would have produced but one symphony.

Schubert's first orchestral music was composed for the student orchestra of the *Stadkonvikt*, a state-supported school that he had attended. Even after he had graduated, he continued to play viola at orchestra rehearsals. He was also active in a group known as the Society of Amateurs. This ensemble had grown from a family string quartet to include friends who played various instruments. The society members played symphonies of Haydn and Mozart, the first two of Beethoven, and whatever music Schubert wrote for them. The quality of performance was uneven: the society deserved its name.

The Second Symphony may or may not have been performed by the *Konvikt* orchestra or by the Society of Amateurs. In any case, the work quickly sank into oblivion, as Schubert went on to other compositions. He seemed to care little about his manuscripts once they had been played. Luckily, several of his friends thought enough of his music to make and keep copies. The symphony, like most of his music, remained unknown for years. It was rediscovered and given its first professional performance in 1877. It was first published in 1884. It was not heard in the United States until 1936!

Schubert was perennially poor. At times he had difficulty even paying for the music paper he needed for the large number of compositions that flowed effortlessly and seemingly spontaneously from his pen. At the time of his Second Symphony, he was earning a meager income assisting his father, who taught at a local school. He disliked this work, since it kept him from composing during the mornings. He performed his teaching duties mechanically. Nonetheless, he was able to write more music than ever before, in part because of his increased experience and in part because of the advancement of his technique that resulted from composition lessons with Antonio Salieri.

The composer wrote in all genres in 1814–15, although his attention was primarily on opera. His finest opera, in the opinion of Schubert scholar Alfred Einstein, dates from this time. It is *Claudine von Villa Bella*. Only one of its three acts survives today, because in 1848 the servants of Josef Hüttenbrenner, who had been a friend of the composer and who had kept several of his manuscripts, used the only copy of the score to light fires! It is only by sheer good fortune that the Second Symphony did not suffer a similar fate.

Schubert is sometimes criticized for a lack of conciseness. This charge is both true and unfair. Schubert did use the traditional forms of Haydn, Mozart, and Beethoven: sonata allegro, theme and variations, minuet and trio, rondo. But Schubert's aesthetic was different from that of his predecessors. Whereas their music is concentrated, economical, taut, and dramatic, his is leisurely and expansive. Schubert seems to have been more interested in his materials than in what happens to them. Because he had a wonderfully inventive imagination, he wrote the most exquisite of melodies and the most charming or poignant of harmonies. We do not even hear the looseness of form because always we appreciate listening to these wonderful tunes, progressions, and orchestrations one more time.

The Second Symphony exemplifies this aesthetic. The outer movements are quite long — over six hundred measures in the first, over seven hundred in the last. The inner movements are more modest, but they do contain frequent repeats. We can easily get lost in the outer movements' sonata forms: Schubert develops while still in the exposition, arrives in the apparently wrong key, lingers over phrases, repeats. The music would seem positively diffuse were it not for the very important fact that it is so beautiful! Schubert's lackadaisical approach to classical form works *only* because the melodies and harmonies keep our attention in themselves.

It may be argued that classical forms, particularly the sonata allegro, are inappropriate to the kind of music Schubert wrote. Perhaps this is true, since these forms are ingerently dramatic and Schubert's music is not. But there were no other forms available, and one could hardly expect a boy of 18, whose genius lay in melody and harmony, to revolutionize music by constructing new abstract structures. Had he lived a normal life span, perhaps he would have evolved new forms appropriate to his compositional aesthetic. There is some evidence that he was moving in that direction in his last symphony, which he left in a fragmentary state.

Schubert's adherence to classical forms in his youthful symphonies does not detract from the music. A piece like the Second Symphony works in spite of, not because of, its form — and this is what makes this music drastically different from that of Mozart, Haydn, and Beethoven. Schubert's Second succeeds because of it materials. When we listen to Beethoven, we feel excitement as we participate in the drama of conflicting themes and keys. When we listen to Schubert, our emotional responses come directly from the tunes, not from their opposition and resolution.

What this argument really says is that Schubert was the first great lyrical composer and the first thorough romanticist. His music is the first in which the beauty of each moment carries the meaning. Even as different a composer as Brahms appreciated this unique aspect of Schubert's art. He marveled at "the freshness and unconcern with which Schubert planned and even wrote [the Second Symphony]. . . . He took genuine delight in a broad, leisurely, musical means of expression which cannot dwell in sufficient detail on the material it contains."

Symphony Number 3 in D Major
Adagio maestoso. Allegro con brio
Allegretto
Menuetto: Vivace. Trio. Menuetto
Presto vivace

Schubert wrote the opening of the Third Symphony on 24 May 1815. He returned to the music and completed it between 11 and 19 July of the same year. Johann Herbeck conducted the last movement in Vienna in 1860. The first performance of the entire symphony was given in London by August Manns on 19 February 1881.

When Napoléon occupied Vienna in 1809, the beseiged city entered a period of considerable hardship. Once the conquerer was driven out in 1813, Vienna began to rebuild its economy. No one had much energy or resources to put into the arts at this difficult time. As a result, none of aristocracy maintained orchestras any longer. The only professional ensemble in town was the *Tonkünstlerverein*, which performed only a few concerts, mostly devoted to oratorios. There were few outlets for symphonies.

In part to counteract this lack of professional music-making, several amateur orchestras were formed. The Schubert family string quartet, for example, was expanded to become a chamber orchestra. The composer was violist, his two brothers violinists, and their father cellist. To this nucleus were added friends who played various wind and string instruments. As the orchestra could no longer fit comfortably into the Schubert home, the members assembled twice a week at the house of a local merchant. Under the direction of violinist Josef Prohaska, the orchestra played symphonies by Haydn, Mozart, Pleyel, Rosetti, and others. The group continued to grow and had to move several more times to still larger houses. Occasional public concerts were given from 1815 onwards.

Schubert enjoyed playing in this orchestra. He had for many years been a member of his school orchestra, and even now that he had graduated he continued to play with that group from time to time. Between these two ensembles he acquired a thorough exposure to the symphonic music of the day. He composed several orchestral works between 1813 and 1818 himself, including the first six symphonies. These pieces were rehearsed if not actually performed by one or the other of Schubert's two orchestras.

After the amateur orchestra disbanded, Schubert's early symphonies all but disappeared. The piano arrangements that appeared in the 1860s did not generate sufficient enthusiasm to warrant performance or publication of the orchestral versions. The late nineteenth century's attitude is typified by Brahms' reaction to an invitation in 1873 to conduct an all-Schubert concert. Brahms declined, saying that there were not enough suitable orchestral works of Schubert to fill a concert.

Interest in the early orchestral music surfaced at last in England, where the first five symphonies were given their professional premieres at the Crystal Palace Concerts between 1873 and 1881. The Third Symphony was the last in the series to be heard. Its 1881 premiere took place 66 years after it had been composed. Even after these London performances, however, the early symphonies were still not frequently played. It was only with the advent of recordings and broadcasts in the twentieth century, and with the proliferation of orchestras, that they became part of the standard symphonic repertory.

The odd-numbered early symphonies tend to be graceful and effervescent, while their even-numbered siblings strive for deeper expression. For example, the slow movement of the Third, which we might expect to be sober, is instead light and delicate. Its tempo is not adagio or even andante (although Schubert originally marked it *andante molto*) but allegretto. It is a direct ABA form, in which both themes are simple and lovely. They would hardly be out of place in the beautiful *Rosamunde* music.

The minuet has a wonderful rhythmic vitality. It is characterized by a strongly accented upbeat — a real foot-stomping rhythm. The trio is a graceful *Ländler*, an Austrian folk dance.

The finale of the Third suggests Rossini in its fast tempo and airiness. Musicologist Mosco Carner mentions the several "Rossini-isms to be found on almost every page. In addition to the all-pervading tarantella rhythm . . . , [the movement] is full of triad arpeggios followed by short scale passages, repetitions of simple cadences, unexpected and noisy *tutti* crashes, and frequent crescendos, all in the typical Rossini vein." This mercurial movement's perpetual motion precludes major contrasts. When the second theme group arrives, for example, it turns out quite similar to the first theme. Interestingly, its key is not the traditional dominant but rather the subdominant.

This is not the only instance in the Third Symphony of an unusual choice of key. The first movement's and the finale's second theme groups are both recapitulated in the subdominant, which is quite rare in the music of Mozart, Haydn, or Beethoven. Also, even less likely to occur in the classical period, the recapitulation of the first theme of the finale occurs in the dominant. Critics sometimes attack Schubert for such deviations from tradition, claiming that he did not understand the structural implications of the tonal system. Quite the contrary, Schubert knew exactly what he was doing. His use of tonality differs in fundamental ways from that of his predecessors. As Carner explains,

> The idea behind the classical practice of introducing, in the reprise, the second subject on the tonic was to indicate the solution of the harmonic conflict between the two poles of tonic and dominant, a conflict which imparted to the exposition some of its dynamic, forward movement. Schubert ignores that idea by frequently bringing back the second [or even the first] subject in a key other than the tonic and thus creates a tension of tonalities similar to that in the exposition. This seems to suggest that what mattered with Schubert was not so much the functional and structural significance of the keys as their more sensuous appeal as patterns of different harmonic color. In other words, the romantic feeling in Schubert's harmonic style began to affect even the basic tonal relations of classical sonata form.

Composing this spontaneous symphony gave Schubert little trouble. He wrote the opening 47 bars in one day, put it aside, and then returned to complete the work in little over a week. The manuscript shows evidence of rewritings in only two places: the main theme of the first movement was first given to strings, then to the oboe, before finally being assigned to the clarinet; and the themes of the second movement were originally quite different.

Symphony Number 4 in C Minor, *Tragic*

Adagio molto. Allegro vivace
Andante
Menuetto: Allegro vivace. Trio. Menuetto
Allegro

The Tragic *Symphony was begun in early April and completed on the 27th of that month in 1816. It may have been performed shortly thereafter by the amateur orchestra in which Schubert played viola. The first professional performance was conducted by A. F. Riccius in Leipzig on 19 November 1849.*

All of Schubert's symphonies prior to the *Unfinished* were the products of a man scarcely out of his adolescence. Schubert had an extraordinary facility and a marvelous talent, and thus he was able to compose an incredible amount of music. But we must remember that the bulk of this music was written by a youth and that none of it was composed by a mature man: Schubert died at the age of 31.

Thus we should not be surprised to find a symphony called *Tragic* that does not really explore the depths of the human spirit. Nor should we be surprised to hear more than mere hints of Beethoven in this music, just as the influences of Mozart and Haydn are strong in the next symphony. As the teenage Schubert studied the works of the composers he most respected, he assimilated their techniques and styles. His own lyric gift is also in evidence throughout the Fourth Symphony, but it was not until his later works that he succeeded in freeing himself from the sometimes overbearing influence of Beethoven.

Schubert lived in the same city as the composer whose genius he admired timidly and from afar. He never met Beethoven, but he knew his music. "Who can still do anything after Beethoven?" Schubert asked in apparent hopelessness. The two composers were quite different. Beethoven came directly out of the classic tradition of Mozart and Haydn, and thus his music is always tightly constructed. But Schubert was the opposite. His lyric muse never totally mastered classical form, and yet his music sings with as genuine emotions as does Beethoven's. The abundance of intensity in Beethoven's music pulled against the constraints of classical forms, but Schubert's emotions came naturally and struggle was foreign to his aesthetic.

At the time that he wrote the C Minor Symphony, Schubert was attracted to Beethoven's most emotional pieces. The Fourth Symphony is indebted to Beethoven's works in the same key: the Third Piano Concerto, Fourth String Quartet, *Coriolan* Overture, and Fifth Symphony.

The bold opening — a sustained C played by the full orchestra — suggests Beethoven (the *Coriolan* Overture begins in the same way), as does the beginning of the subsequent allegro. The repeated notes that occur in many passages sound at first like Beethovenian intensification, but then Schubert, thoroughly enjoying this particular sound, lingers over them and returns to them again and again. They lose some of their intensity and gain instead a thoroughly Schubertian gracefulness.

The Fourth Symphony is most enchanting when it is least like Beethoven, as, for example, in the beautifully lyrical slow movement. The form here is the simple alternation of two quite different ideas (the second, incidentally, is a transformation of the main theme of the first movement). When not trying to achieve a complexity comparable to Beethoven's, Schubert composed a movement of immediacy and charm that is, in its own way, still dramatic: notice the transition to the second theme and the sudden emergence of triplets in the coda.

The third movement returns to the world of Beethoven. Its intense chromaticism is unusual for Schubert, as are the complexities of meter. The manner in which he forces a 2/4 melody into 3/4 measures by starting on the third rather than the first beat is typical of Beethoven but rare in Schubert. The accompaniment subtly reminds us that 3/4 is the proper meter for a minuet (actually, the fast tempo makes this movement more like a scherzo, despite the indication *menuetto* — another Beethovenism).

Casting the finale in C minor rather than C major, but changing to the major for the coda, is a thoroughly Beethovenian idea. When Beethoven does something similar, the major mode comes as a catharsis, as a resolution won through struggle, while for Schubert it is simply a contrast. If Beethoven had written this symphony, he would no doubt have made all four movements drive toward the achievement of C major as a goal. Schubert is more leisurely in his approach: he likes his music to go from C minor to C major, and so he makes this move in the first as well as the last movement. He is unconcerned with the effect of the first movement's resolution on the finale: something which is worth hearing once is worth hearing twice. The finale has clear gestures toward Beethoven in its themes, but their development and modulations make the movement ultimately pure Schubert. Despite its restless beginning it acquires such good spirits by the end that we may wonder why Schubert chose to name the symphony *Tragic*.

◆ ◆ ◆

Symphony Number 5 in B-Flat Major
Allegro
Andante con moto
Menuetto: Allegro molto. Trio. Menuetto
Allegro vivace

The Fifth Symphony was begun in September and completed on 3 October 1816. Its only performance during Schubert's lifetime took place in the fall of 1816 in Vienna, under the direction of Otto Hatwig.

In marked to contrast to other Viennese composers, such as Haydn, Mozart, and Beethoven, Schubert worked in virtual obscurity. He was employed not as a musician but as an assistant schoolmaster. When he died he was almost unknown outside his circle of friends. His symphonies were performed, if at all, by the amateur orchestra in which he played viola. Most of the symphonies waited until years after the composer's death for a professional performance. The Fifth Symphony, for example, was heard once during Schubert's lifetime; the next performance took place in London in 1873!

His orchestra was important to the young composer. The ensemble's performance quality was uneven but probably as good as could be expected for a group of amateurs. By playing in the ensemble and hearing readings of his early symphonies, Schubert learned to orchestrate. His sensitivity to sonority is impressive. Practical experience was an excellent teacher.

Other than playing in the orchestra and composing, there was little enjoyment in Schubert's life in his nineteenth year. He disliked his job as a teacher, since it took away precious time from composing. And he longed for professional recognition, which continued to elude him. At the beginning of 1816 he applied for a position as Director of Music at a college in Laibach, a post that he would have found far more congenial than working in his father's school. Despite a strong letter of recommendation from his teacher Antonio Salieri, Schubert failed to get the job. It went instead to one Franz Sokol. His disappointments continued when a package of his songs that had been sent to Goethe was returned. He had set some of the poet's verses to inspired and original music, and he had hoped that Goethe would approve. The favorable opinion of this famous writer would certainly have helped Schubert establish professional credibility. But the music was returned without comment. There is no record of Goethe's ever having even mentioned Schubert's songs.

He resigned himself to remaining what he was: a poorly paid teacher and an unknown composer. He turned his attention back to composing, and he produced in rapid succession the Fourth and Fifth Symphonies.

Just as the Fourth is Schubert's attempt to assimilate the influence of Beethoven, so the Fifth confronts the music of Haydn and Mozart. The modest orchestra — with no clarinets, no trumpets, and no timpani — duplicates that of the original version of Mozart's G Minor Symphony. Appropriately, the minor-mode minuet seems to come from the same mold as that in the Mozart symphony (although the trio is pure Schubert). The graceful yet good-humored finale is a first cousin of Haydn's symphonic last movements, and the lovely slow movement seems equally indebted to both composers.

Musicologist Mosco Carner has written perceptively on the classical influences in the Fifth Symphony:

> Not only has he here completely mastered the classical style, but what is more important he now fuses the traditional idiom with a remarkable individual expression, and the result is a work in which Haydn's wit and Mozart's gracefulness and light touch combine in perfect union with the composer's happy flow of melody and exuberant expression. The Fifth is thus the most successful and most representative of Schubert's early symphonies. It was, to all intents and purposes, his conscious farewell to the two masters of his youth. For in the Sixth Symphony . . . Schubert aims at something bigger and more ambitious.

Symphony Number 6 in C Major
            Adagio. Allegro
            Andante
            Presto. Più lento. Presto
            Allegro moderato

The Sixth Symphony was composed between October 1817 and February 1818. The first performance took place in Vienna on 14 December 1828.

Almost all of the Schubert's symphonies were composed when he was quite young. It is not surprising to find in them more than a few hints of the music of his contemporaries and immediate predecessors. The music of Beethoven, Mozart, and Rossini (who was extremely popular in Vienna at the time) can be heard echoing in the Sixth Symphony. But maturity was beginning to come to the talented young composer: his own unique lyric gift is also in evidence throughout the Sixth.

It is fascinating to compare Schubert's songs with the symphonies composed at the same time. The songs are considerably more adventurous than the symphonies. In the songs of 1817–18 we find little influence of Beethoven, Mozart, Rossini, or anyone else. Schubert was already very much his own man as a 19-year-old songwriter.

Because he was surer of his accompishments in song, he hoped that his vocal music would help him establish some professional credibility. He set several Goethe poems. However, when he sent the songs to the poet, they were returned without comment. Further disappointment came when Schubert tried to have one of these Goethe songs published. At the urging of friends, the composer submitted *Erlkönig* to the firm of Breitkopf and Härtel in 1817. The editors knew of a Franz Schubert, but not the young composer from Vienna. Their Franz Schubert was a musician in Dresden. When they sent him the manuscript for confirmation, he wrote back: "With the greatest astonishment I beg to state that this cantata [!] was never composed by me. I shall retain the same in my possession to learn, if possible, who has so impertinently sent you that sort of rubbish and also to discover the fellow who has thus misused my name." The song was not published until 1821, and then by a different firm.

Schubert's professional disappointments were mirrored by personal frustrations. He had become friendly with a number of interesting and sophisticated people in Vienna, one of whom — Franz von Schober — tried to persuade him to give up teaching and move out of his parents' house. Schubert moved into the home of Schober's affluent mother, cut back on his teaching, and began to develop promising friendships with prominent musicians. But the arrangements did not work out, probably for financial reasons. By the fall of 1817 the composer was obliged to move back home and resume full-time teaching. He was destined to remain an obscure composer.

One of the works created at this time of depression was the sunny Sixth Symphony. As the last of his early symphonies, it is admittedly derivative, but nonetheless it foreshadows the sublimities that were to emerge in his final completed symphony, the *Great* C Major of 1825. There was a crisis in the making in Schubert's symphonic style, which can occasionally be heard beneath the surface of the otherwise untroubled Sixth. After that work, Schubert started but left incomplete no fewer than five symphonies, including the magnificent *Unfinished* in B minor of 1822. Perhaps the cause of his crisis and the reason he could not complete another symphony for seven years (a considerable period in the Schubert's short life) was that he realized he had to move beyond symphonies indebted to others but did not yet know how.

The shadow of Beethoven hangs over the introduction of the Sixth. The very opening, which leans immediately toward the subdominant, recalls Beethoven's First Symphony in the same key. Schubert's development section, in which wind instruments trade off a motive derived (by inversion) from the main theme, is also Beethovenian. Both themes in the bubbly exposition, however, owe more to Rossini. In the accelerated coda we can hear echoes of Mozart, in particular *his* great C major symphony, the *Jupiter*.

Where in all this mixture of influences is Schubert? The remaining movements are cast more distinctively in his own style. The composer of the second movement, with its lovely lyrical main theme and quicker middle section, is unmistakable. The scherzo is also typical of the composer, although the slower trio section is reminiscent of Beethoven. While the airy main theme of the finale may seem like Rossini on the surface, its development is thoroughly Schubertian. It may be coincidence or it may be prophetic that the coda treats the identical motive that pervades the finale of Schubert's later C Major Symphony.

The Sixth had to wait a decade for performance. In 1828 the Society of Friends of Music agreed to perform the *Great* Symphony (the nickname was bestowed many years later by Robert Schumann), completed three years earlier. But the work proved too difficult, and Schubert offered to substitute his earlier C Major Symphony. The performance did take place, on 14 December. But Schubert never heard it. He had died a month earlier.

Symphony in B Minor, *Unfinished*
Allegro moderato
Andante con moto

The Unfinished *Symphony was begun on 30 October 1822. By November of that year, the composer had completed two movements and started a third. He never completed the piece. Johann Herbeck conducted the first performance, in Vienna on 17 December 1865.*

Our understanding of the symphonic career of Franz Schubert has changed drastically in the past decade. We used to think that he had completed seven symphonies, and left two unfinished, between 1813 and his death in 1828. Now we understand that his seven finished symphonies span the years 1813–26 and that he also worked on six additional symphonies, all of which he left incomplete. The chronology is as follows ("D." numbers refer to Otto Erich Deutsch's catalog of Schubert's works):

1. Symphonic Fragment in D Major, D. 2B (1811)
2. Symphony Number 1 in D Major, D. 82 (1813)
3. Symphony Number 2 in B-Flat Major, D. 125 (1815)
4. Symphony Number 3 in D Major, D. 200 (1815)
5. Symphony Number 4 in C Minor, D. 417 (1816)
6. Symphony Number 5 in B-Flat Major, D. 485 (1816)
7. Symphony Number 6 in C Major, D. 589 (1817–18)
8. Symphonic Fragment in D Major, D. 615 (1818)
9. Symphonic Fragment in D Major, D. 708A (1821)
10. Symphonic Fragment (Symphony "Number 7") in E Major, D. 729 (1821)
11. Symphonic Fragment (Symphony "Number 8") in B Minor, D. 759 (1822)
12. Symphony "Number 9" in C Major, D. 944 (1825–26)
13. Symphonic Fragment (Symphony "Number 10") in D Major, D. 936A (1828)

Several things are remarkable about this list:

1. Schubert tried to compose a symphony at the early age of 14.

2. He had a strong predilection for composing symphonies in D major: six of the 13 symphonies are in that key. This fact led musicologists for a long time to mistake sketches of several different works for alternate versions of the same work.

3. Between the Sixth Symphony and the so-called *Great* C Major Symphony, Schubert started and later abandoned no fewer than four separate symphonies. Clearly he was having trouble completing a large, integrated, multi-movement work for orchestra.

4. D. 944, the *Great* C Major Symphony (usually numbered "9," although before the B Minor *Unfinished* had been discovered D. 944 was known as "7"), was not Schubert's last effort in the genre. That work previously had been thought to have occupied him during his last year, but recently uncovered evidence strongly implies that it dates from considerably earlier. The Symphonic Fragment D. 936A gives a quite different indication of Schubert's last thoughts on symphonic form.

5. There is no *Gastein* Symphony in the list. It was long believed that Schubert had completed a symphony between the Sixth and the

Unfinished (usually numbered "8", but according to the recent critical edition, which numbers only finished works, numbered "7"). The *Gastein* was supposedly lost by the Friends of Music in Vienna. For over a century music historians searched for this work, but to no avail. Now it has been established that the D. 944, the *Great* C Major, *is* the *Gastein* Symphony.

All this can be quite confusing. For a time the confusion was shared and debated only by academics. Recently, however, various musicologists have made performing editions of most of the fragments. It is becoming common to hear any of the works in the above list (except for D. 2B) in concert. All the mature fragments have been completed by at least one scholar, and all have been recorded more than once.

For years D. 615, D. 708A, and D. 934A lay largely unexamined in a single folder in the Vienna State Library. Those few musicologists who had been permitted a glimpse of the manuscript found sketches for nine different movements, which were assumed to have been intended for one, or possibly two, symphonies in D major. In preparation for Schubert anniversary celebrations in 1978, librarian Ernst Hilmar decided to have a closer look. He saw by the types of music paper used and on the basis of stylistic considerations that there were three different works in the folder, dating from three different periods in Schubert's short creative life — 1818, 1821, and 1828. Three different unfinished symphonies by Schubert, all different from the famous B Minor Symphony!

There is another mature unfinished symphony. D. 729 in E Major is an entire symphony of some 1300 measures, of which about 950 have only one line of music. Several people have harmonized and orchestrated this work: English composer J. F. Barnett in 1883, conductor Felix Weingartner in 1934, Swiss composer Emile Amoudruz in 1948, the Russians Leonid Butir in 1969 and Boris Spassov in 1978, and English musicologist Brian Newbould in 1978.

The remaining mature incomplete Schubert symphony is the well-known *Unfinished* in B minor, of which Schubert completed and orchestrated the first two movements. He sketched a scherzo, orchestrated its first two pages, and wrote the melody line of a trio. Brian Newbould suggests that the B minor *entr'acte* from the *Rosamunde* incidental music may have been intended to serve as the finale.

After working on the symphony for about a month in the autumn of 1822, Schubert put it aside in order to compose the well-known *Wanderer* Fantasy for piano. The following spring he was made an honorary member of the Styrian Music Society in Graz, one of the few honors he received during his lifetime. He wrote a letter of appreciation to the Society, in which he promised them as a token of his gratitude the manuscript "of one of my symphonies."

In September Schubert gave the unfinished score of the B Minor Symphony to his close friend Josef Hüttenbrenner, whose brother Anselm was a member of the Society. Anselm was a pianist and a mediocre composer. Apparently there was some misunderstanding, because Anselm never passed the score on to the Society. He kept it without telling anyone for forty years.

In 1860, 32 years after Schubert's death, Josef told the conductor Johann Herbeck about the piece. "My brother possesses a treasure in Schubert's B Minor Symphony, which we place on a level with any of Beethoven's. Only it isn't finished. Schubert gave it to me for Anselm as thanks for having sent him, through me, the Diploma of Honor of the Graz Musical Society." With difficulty Herbeck convinced Anselm, by then an old man, to allow the symphony to be performed. Herbeck had to promise also to perform one of Anselm's works. The performance of Schubert's two completed movements took place 43 years after they had been composed.

There has been a lot of speculation on why Schubert never finished the piece and why he never mentioned it, not even to his brother Ferdinand, who was compiling a complete list of Schubert's works. It has been suggested that the symphony really is complete in two movements. But, if so, why did Schubert sketch a scherzo, and why are the two movements in different keys? Perhaps Schubert simply lost interest in the project. Or perhaps he found he could not write a third movement that lived up to the first two. It has even been proposed that he did in fact complete the work but that the Hüttenbrenners lost half of it.

Inevitably, various people have finished the work. A contest was held on the hundreth anniversary of Schubert's birth offering a prize for the best completion. The situation is different from that related to, for example, Mozart's Requiem, Bach's *Art of the Fugue,* or Mahler's Tenth Symphony. Schubert did not leave the work unfinished because he died, and he did not leave a large enough portion of the last two movements to allow for simple completion by another hand. Not surprisingly, none of the completions by others has met with wide acceptance.

The *Unfinished* Symphony contains some of the most beautiful music ever composed, and it surely deserves the popularity it has earned in its two-movement state. Schubert was a supreme lyricist: witness the second theme of the first movement, one of the great tunes of all times. But he had trouble with large forms. He admired the symphonic drama that Beethoven had achieved, but his own development sections tend to be rambling and discursive. His melodic inventiveness all but makes up for this deficiency in most of his extended pieces. The B Minor Symphony, almost uniquely among his compositions, does not suffer from formal weaknesses. It is taut, dramatic, and logical. Both its poignant first movement and its bittersweet second are as well integrated and well paced as any of Beethoven's masterpieces.

The first movement contains a wealth of melodies. Even as the music grows from the depths, it is melodic from the beginning. The first idea, in cellos and basses alone, is destined to become important subsequently. Soon the violins enter with a second melody, followed by a poignantly songful theme in the oboe and clarinet. These three ideas constitute the first theme group. Despite their deep beauty and lyricism, they pale in comparison to the second theme, which begins in the cellos.

The overriding lyricism of the first movement is maintained in the second, which is based on two lovely melodies. The first is heard at the outset in the violins, and the second comes later in the clarinet. The pathos in the second theme is reminiscent of the first movement. The two themes alternate throughout the movement. The coda features a delicately slow-moving line for unaccompanied violins alternating with winds.

Symphony in C Major, *The Great*

            Andante. Allegro ma non troppo. Più moto
            Andante con moto
            Allegro vivace
            Allegro vivace

The C Major Symphony was probably begun in May 1825 and completed early in 1826, with subsequent revisions in 1826 or 1827. Felix Mendelssohn conducted the first performance with the Leipzig Gewandhaus Orchestra on 21 March 1839.

When did Schubert compose his last completed symphony, the piece generally considered his greatest orchestral work? For years scholars have believed the date on the manuscript, obviously written in Schubert's hand: "March 1828." As the composer always dated his scores according to when they were begun, not completed, this date seemed conclusively to place the C Major Symphony in his last months (he died in November 1828). Not so, say several present-day musicologists. For a variety of reasons, they now (since 1977) believe that the symphony was composed earlier.

Why should the date of composition matter? Schubert is acknowledged to be one of the truly great composers, and musicians, scholars, and listeners are usually eager to understand as much as possible about the life, development, and working methods of significant composers. Such knowledge helps in the understanding and enjoyment of their masterpieces. Whether the C Major Symphony represents a culmination of Schubert's development or an earlier stage is significant to a comprehension of his growth and of the interrelationship between his works.

Deciding a question of dating involves a considerable amount of detective work. As musicologist Robert Winter explains, four kinds of evidence must be examined: (1) biographical data, including letters to and from the composer, concert programs, newspaper articles, advertisements, publications, etc.; (2) internal evidence, such as progressive alterations in the composer's style; (3) changing handwriting characteristics of the composer and of the different copyists the composer employed, use of various kinds of ink, changes in notation and terminology in scores (e.g., "cembalo" vs. "fortepiano" vs. "pianoforte"), etc.; (4) characteristics of the music paper used, including watermarks, number of staffs, format of printed staffs, etc. The fourth type of evidence, and to a lesser extent the third, provides the most nearly objective data but paradoxically has been little used until recently. There is evidence, strong but not quite conclusive, of each type that contradicts the "March 1828" dating.

Stylistic data is seductive yet ambiguous. We are dealing with a difference of at most three years: everyone agrees the symphony was composed sometime between 1825 and 1828. How much could Schubert's style have changed in that time? True, three years does represent a significant period for someone who composed a thousand pieces yet died at the age of 31. But how sure can we be that two pieces using similar melodic motives originated at the same time? Schubert could have had similar melodic inclinations at different times. Also, to find that Schubert seems to have discovered a particular chord progression at one period does not prove that a work in which he fully exploited it was necessarily composed at the same time. In a fascinating article published in 1982, pianist Paul Badura-Skoda shows how stylistic data can be shown to "prove" different dates for the symphony. Another problem with style analysis is that we want to understand Schubert's stylistic development in context of his chronological development, yet, if the date of a major piece is in question, how accurate is our notion of his music's chronology?

Studies of paper type are particularly fruitful in dating the music of Schubert (and of his contemporary Beethoven), because, in Vienna in the first third of the nineteenth century, music paper was manufactured by hand and in a vast profusion of styles. Schubert habitually bought a supply of music paper, used it, and then bought more, rather than hoarding large amounts. Since the history and development of nineteenth-century paper manufacturing is reasonably well known, scholars can tell a lot about the chronology of Schubert's music by examining the types of paper on which it was written.

The manuscript of the C Major Symphony is, up to a point in the finale, written mostly on one type of paper, of which Schubert is known to have bought a hundred sheets to take with him on a summer trip in 1825. There are five other works, all dated in the summer of 1825, whose manuscripts were written exclusively on this type of paper. But there are two passages in the symphony — part of the coda of the first movement and virtually the entire trio of the third movement — written on a different type of paper. Furthermore, most of the last movement appears on a variety of paper styles. This variety is probably due to two factors: Schubert must have run out of the paper he had brought with him and been forced to buy the inferior grades available in the small cities he visited. Once he returned to Vienna, he probably had to use various remnants of paper he had lying around, since there was a paper shortage in Vienna in the winter of 1825–26. This latter deduction is confirmed by looking at the papers used by Beethoven at the same time. (Further confirmation — or refutation — awaits the examination of contemporary manuscripts by other Viennese composers.) The symphony ends with several pages written on a new high-grade paper, which is the same type the composer used for a number of compositions from early 1826.

The type of paper inserted into the first and third movements is identical to that used by Beethoven in September 1826. This fact suggests that these passages were revised after the symphony was finished. There is internal stylistic evidence to support this contention: the trio of the scherzo contains a chord progression Schubert apparently first used in 1826.

The chronology suggested by musicologist Winter is, then, as follows: Schubert began the symphony after leaving Vienna in May 1825. He worked on it while traveling to Gmunden and Gastein, among other places, that summer and completed it in early 1826. He made two significant revisions before presenting the score to the Friends of Music Society in Vienna in the fall of 1826. Interestingly, these dates coincide with those for the so-called *Gastein* Symphony, a work long believed to have been composed in the summer of 1825, presented to the Friends of Music in October 1826, and subsequently lost. Many musicologists now believe that the C Major Symphony *is* the *Gastein*, that it was never lost, and that earlier musicologists postulated the existence of another Schubert symphony because they believed the C Major dated from 1828.

What are we to make, though, of the "March 1828" date on the first page of the manuscript. One suggestion is that Schubert composed the symphony in 1825–26 and revised it in 1828, but the evidence of paper types seems to dispute this. None of the papers in the manuscript corresponds to those Schubert used in 1828. Furthermore, a complete set of orchestral parts plus copyists' receipts have recently turned up in the archives of the Friends of Music Society. These materials were dated in the summer of 1827, so we now know positively that the "March 1828" date is erroneous. Or do we?

If that date is wrong, how did it come to appear on the score? Careful scrutiny of the way Schubert wrote his 5's and 8's at this time indicates that the date may actually be "March 1825." This conjecture is strengthened by the fact that the top of the questionable numeral was cut off when the manuscript was bound, making even more plausible the possibility that the date reads "1825." On the other hand, the man who had the score cut to size and bound in the 1840s and was presumably the last to see the date intact, copied it as "1828" on the cover. Was he incorrect in his reading of Schubert's date? Even if we accept 1825 as the year in which the symphony was begun, what can we make of the "March" portion of Schubert's date? The type of paper used was not on the market in March and could have been available at the earliest in May. It is possible that Schubert mistakenly wrote "March" rather than "May," or, as Badura-Skoda suggests, that the partially lopped-off "8" in "1828" could be read not as "5" but as "6." This reading would make the date "March 1826," certainly possible from the point of view of paper types but unlikely considering Schubert's penchant for dating scores when he started, not finished, them. The problem of the notated date has yet to be solved.

The early performance history of the symphony is no less fascinating than that of its composition, but it is fortunately less shrouded in mystery. The work was not performed during Schubert's lifetime. It lay virtually unknown among the composer's papers for a decade. It was discovered by Robert Schumann, who came to Vienna on a musical pilgrimmage to visit the graves and habitats of the great composers. Schumann met Schubert's brother Ferdinand, who showed him a pile of manuscripts. "The riches that lay piled up there made me tremble with pleasure. Where to begin, where to stop?" Among the papers was the C Major Symphony. "Who knows how long it would have lain neglected there in dust and darkness, had I not immediately arranged with Ferdinand Schubert to send it to the management of the Gewandhaus Concerts in Leipzig, to the artist who himself conducts them (Felix Mendelssohn)." Mendelssohn loved the symphony and conducted it three times, but in a drastically cut version (which nonetheless gave rise to Schumann's famous remark about its "heavenly length").

The work at first proved difficult for critics and for other orchestras. When the Vienna Philharmonic performed it in 1839, only the first two movements were played. F. A. Habeneck had to cancel a performance in Paris in 1842 when his orchestra refused to rehearse beyond the opening movement. Similarly, a London orchestra was unable to master the symphony's difficulties when Mendelssohn tried to introduce it to England in 1844.

Despite its challenges, Schumann was outspoken in his praise. He had discovered the piece, and he was determined to see to it that it was properly performed and appreciated. "Deep down in this work there lies more than mere song, more than mere joy and sorrow, as already expressed in music in a hundred other instances. It transports us into a world where I cannot recall ever having been before." On another occasion he wrote, "Herein is revealed the finest technical skill, life in every fibre of the music, the finest gradations of coloring, and care for the minutest detail."

Schumann was no doubt reacting to many wonderful moments in the symphony: the extraordinary sense of satisfaction when the long, slow introduction finally achieves tonic harmony at the beginning of the allegro; the wealth of wonderful melodies, placed in transition sections as well as in expository passages; the subtle variations on these melodies, such as the addition of the trumpet to the second movement's oboe tune, thus transforming it into a processional; the Viennese elegance of the third movement's trio; the powerful trombones and the repeated-note motive in the finale; the wonderfully original modulations; Schubert's magnificently inventive sense of harmony, evident on almost every page of the score.

This symphony is sometimes given the nickname "The Great" — a difficult title to live up to but one that the C Major deserves in every way. Even if we can no longer dream about someone someday uncovering the long lost *Gastein* Symphony, we can be forever thankful that Schumann was able to rescue Schubert's C Major Symphony from a dusty pile of manuscripts in Ferdinand Schubert's rooms.

Robert Schumann

Born on 8 June 1810 at Zwickau in Saxony.
Died on 29 July 1856 at the Endenich asylum, near Bonn.

Concerto in A Minor for Cello and Orchestra, Opus 129
Nicht zu schnell —
Langsam —
Sehr lebhaft

The Cello Concerto was composed between 10 October and 24 October 1850. It was first performed on 9 June 1860 at the Leipzig Conservatory by cellist Ludwig Ebert.

Schumann's last professional position was as municipal music director of Düsseldorf. He was not particularly successful as a conductor, however, and was eventually asked to relinquish the post. Shortly after settling in his new city, Schumann composed the Cello Concerto, one of his last major works. The onset of a severe mental illness subsequently curtailed his compositional activities (he did write the Third Symphony soon after the concerto, and some chamber music the following year, but his previous feverish compositional pace was gone forever.)

The concerto is melodic throughout, with the cello always prominent and the orchestra usually used lightly. Thus the piece is not a dialogue or confrontation between soloist and orchestra. But a composer full of conflicts is sure to express them in some manner. The concerto's conflicts and contrasts are all found within the solo line. Schumann pits high cello against low cello, instead of placing the soloist in opposition to the orchestra. The result is taxing for the soloist: this, in contrast to the Piano Concerto, is a virtuoso's work.

The piece is cast in three movements connected by transitions. The bridge between the second and third movements is an elaborate recollection of the materials of the first movement. The finale is dance-like, while the other movements are lyrical.

Although the concerto was composed rapidly, Schumann continued to tinker with it for several years, right up until the time of his final hospitalization in the asylum at Endenich. He never heard a performance of it.

The exact nature of Schumann's mental illness has long puzzled historians. The development of his symptoms over his entire lifetime has been studied, and two conflicting theories have been advanced to account for his case history. One hypothesis holds that Schumann was a schizophrenic; the other opinion claims that he was a manic-depressive in his early years who later developed organic brain disease. As more has been learned about the nature of mental illness, the latter diagnosis has emerged as probably the correct one. Typically manic-depressive, Schumann had periods of high productivity associated with moods of elation (such as the two weeks during which he composed the Cello Concerto), and he had times (such as the "dark days" before he wrote the Second Symphony) in which he was so depressed that he composed nothing. During his "down" periods he would be silent for days. He sometimes had to spend weeks just to write a letter. At such times he was unable to focus his attention and appeared to others alarmingly distracted.

One person who was unnerved by the composer's inability to focus his mind was a man who came from Paris to ask Schumann some questions about performing one of his pieces. Instead of answering the young man's carefully phrased queries, the composer asked him, "Do you smoke?" The man replied in the affirmative, expecting that Schumann, who was smoking at the moment, would offer him a cigar. Instead, the composer remained silent. After an embarrassed interval, the man repeated his questions. Schumann again replied, "Do you smoke?" After a third attempt to elicit some musical information, the man left, badly shaken.

Extreme swings between concentration and distraction are typical of manic-depression, but not of schizophrenia. In addition, the fact that Schumann's repeated attacks did not lead to a deterioration of personality suggests a diagnosis of manic-depression. His final psychosis, which led to his admission to the mental hospital at Endenich, began in a state of extreme confusion, which is quite rare for schizophrenia. That illness progressed to a form of dementia typical of organic disease but unlike anything associated with schizophrenia. It is likely, therefore, that Schumann suffered from two, not one, disorders. His manic-depression should not have proved fatal and was, actually, an advantage. He could have lived to an old age, composing wonderful music during his elated phases — but for the onset of brain damage, probably caused by a venereal disease contracted in the promiscuous days of his youth. Schumann's syphilis had remained dormant in his body for twenty years, but then its symptoms became manifest and merged with those of manic-depression. His friends and family saw what seemed to be an intensification of his mental illness, culminating in premature death.

Some of Schumann's symptoms during his final three years were typical of syphilis of the nervous system. He began suddenly to have hallucinations. He imagined voices telling him his music was worthless. He wished to die. His wife Clara wrote in her diary of "the voices of demons, with horrible music. They told him he was a sinner, and that they wanted to throw him to hell. In short, his condition grew into a veritable nervous paroxysm; he screamed in pain, because the embodiment of tigers and hyenas were rushing forward to seize him." He was able to gain temporary relief by turning his attention to corrections in the Cello Concerto, but the psychosis worsened. He tried to commit suicide by throwing himself into the icy Rhine River. He was rescued. A few days later he entered the Endenich asylum, where he was destined to spend his final two and a half years.

During this time he never saw Clara. At first the doctors felt that the separation helped Schumann preserve some semblance of equilibrium. Later, they feared the effect of a reunion on Clara. Furthermore, she could not bring herself to see Schumann in what she thought of as a madhouse. She finally did visit him on the day before his death.

Schumann found hospitalization stressful. Separated from his wife and children, he was unable to compose, and finding himself in an asylum confirmed his lifelong dread that he was mad. As he came to feel that his situation was hopeless, he stopped eating. Despite force-feeding through a gastric tube, he became severely emaciated. When Clara finally did visit, he was so happy to see her, despite his weakened and demented condition, that he allowed her to feed him.

In his fascinating book *Schumann: The Inner Voices of Madness*, psychiatrist Peter Ostwald explains that "sudden feeding of patients who have lost a great deal of weight as a result of chronic starvation is known to induce neurocirculatory collapse, a physiological shock so severe that many cannot survive." Ostwald believes that Schumann intended to committed suicide by starving himself. When Clara came back into his life, however, he felt renewed hope and began to eat. But, ironically, eating hastened his death.

Concerto in A Minor for Piano and Orchestra, Opus 54
Allegro affettuoso
Intermezzo: Andantino grazioso —
Allegro vivace

Schumann began to sketch the Piano Concerto in 1833. He completed the first movement in 1841. The entire work was finished on 31 July 1845. It was first performed by Clara Schumann, with Ferdinard Hiller conducting, in Dresden on 4 December 1845.

If the history of nineteenth-century music had to be studied solely in terms of one instrument, that instrument would have to be the piano. The keyboard was the perfect medium for conveying the intimacy and passion, the subjectivity and the bravura, of the romantic spirit. The piano was also a perfect vehicle to display the virtuosic technical accomplishments of pianist-composers. Thus figures such as Chopin and Schumann, who were sensitive pianists but not virtuosos, did not produce the piano music most popular with their contemporaries. Virtuosity for its own sake was the accepted value. Composers like Schumann and Chopin, who used the piano for more intimate expressions, were destined to find less adulation than technical wizards, who were celebrities idolized in the way of today's rock stars.

Franz Liszt, for example, is remembered today because of his compositional talents, but in his day his dazzling keyboard displays made him famous. What of such other keyboard virtuosos as Kalkbrenner, Thalberg, and Henselt? Their empty, bombastic showpieces, written for the sole purpose of showing themselves off, died with them.

One of the most virtuosic of mid-nineteenth-century pianists was Clara Wieck. She, like most of her colleagues, had an underdeveloped musical taste. Her programs bypassed the substantial works of Bach and Beethoven in favor of the showpieces of virtuosity composed by Thalberg and Henselt. In 1840 Clara married Robert Schumann. The next year he composed a fantasy for piano and orchestra, which failed to receive either performance or publication, probably because of its lack of technical fireworks. Four years later, when Clara's fame was at its height, the composer added two more movements, and the result became known as the Piano Concerto in A Minor. Clara wrote in her diary, "I am very glad about it, for I have always wanted a large bravura piece by him. . . . When I think of playing it with orchestra, I am happy as a king."

But she was wrong to look for bravura in the concerto. Schumann continued Beethoven's trend away from empty virtuosity. As he once wrote, "My concerto is a compromise between a symphony, a concerto, and a huge sonata. I find that I cannot write a concerto for the virtuosi." Schumann allowed the soloist only one cadenza, in the first movement, and he wrote it out in full, probably to prevent the introduction of impromptu showing off by the soloist. This cadenza sounds more like part of a piano sonata than like a display piece.

The qualities which endear the work to us today are the very things which were most criticized when the piece was young: the democratic mixture of piano and orchestra and the avoidance of virtuosity. It should not be surprising that the concerto was not favorably received. After the first performance once critic described the "praiseworthy efforts of Mme. Schumann to make her husband's curious rhapsody pass for music." Liszt called it "a concerto without piano."

Under the guidance of her husband, Clara gradually turned toward more substantive music. As she continued to play the concerto, with ever greater conviction and understanding, it gradually won acceptance. After a performance in Prague in 1847, she wrote, "Robert's concerto gave extraordinary pleasure. I succeeded very well in it. The orchestra accompanied, and Robert conducted, *con amore*. And he was called out. This amused me a lot, for, when the public would not stop clamoring, I almost had to shove him out upon the stage, and the way he acted there was just too funny."

If the concerto does not have virtuosity and does not create a dramatic conflict between soloist and orchestra, wherein lies its appeal? It is the overriding lyricism that carries the music forward. In addition, the roles of piano and orchestra are many, from the dialogue that opens the concerto and returns for the outer sections of the slow movement, to the piano accompanying the solo winds in the second theme of the opening movement, to the orchestra accompanying the piano in the finale. These roles provide variety but not conflict.

Overture to *Manfred*, Opus 115

The music to Manfred *was composed in 1848–49. Schumann conducted the first performance of the overture in Leipzig on 14 March 1852. The complete work was staged later that year in Weimar, under the direction of Franz Liszt.*

Schumann suffered periods of severe mental imbalance. He was sometimes driven by inner urges that did not let him rest until he finished a composition. *Manfred*, for example, was composed at the constant urgings of inner voices. It was a particularly appropriate project for Schumann. He had just completed the opera *Genoveva*, which concerns a tragic woman. Now he felt the need to reconcile one of his major personality conflicts by putting his efforts into a dramatic composition about a male hero. Just as he was alternately dependent on others and independent of them, just as his behavior vacillated between isolation and intimacy, just as he invented two imaginary alter egos to represent opposing forces in his personality, just as he struggled with classicism vs. romanticism in his compositions, so Schumann suffered from a conflict of sexual identity. As a young man he had been intimate with both men and women, and now he sought to reconcile his ambiguity on an artistic level: an opera about a woman followed immediately (he actually began *Manfred* less than a day after completing *Genoveva*) by a dramatic work about a man.

Schumann identified with Lord Byron's Manfred, a melancholy hero full of inner turmoil. Byron's poem finds Manfred atop a cliff in the Alps. He feels intense guilt for having destroyed a woman whose faults were really his own. He is distracted by "a lovely sound, a living voice, a breathing harmony." Manfred contemplates escape through suicide. He realizes that, should he decide against jumping, he may be forced into madness. But he avoids both forms of self-destruction. The parallels between Byron's hero and Schumann are extraordinary, and it is no surprise that the composer was drawn to Manfred. As musicologist Frank Cooper explains, Schumann "knew all too well Manfred's dilemmas. He did not seek the madness Manfred sought — it sought, found, and possessed Schumann. His tragedy was to go mad while desparately trying to cling to sanity and to the art which sanity alone can produce. Perhaps that is why *Manfred* is so curious a creation."

Although Schumann composed 15 scenes, the music to *Manfred* is today known primarily through the overture. The hero's dilemma is symbolized by the very strange opening: three evenly spaced chords that appear in the score as syncopations but are hard to hear in that manner, since no one in the orchestra actually plays on the beat. The musician's dilemma is how to make these chords sound off the beat when the beat itself is inaudible. The three chords remain isolated from the ensuing elaborate slow introduction. Nor do they return in any overt way during the entire yearning, unsettled, romantic overture. Thus the music offers no solution, just as Byron's Manfred does not resolve his problems.

Overture, Scherzo, and Finale, Opus 52
Andante con moto. Allegro
Vivo
Allegro molto vivace

The Overture, Scherzo, and Finale was composed in January 1841. It was first performed on 6 December of the same year in Leipzig, under the direction of Ferdinand David. Schumann rewrote the finale in 1845.

Robert Schumann's instrument, the piano, was the natural vehicle for the romantic expression he put into his music. The piano is capable of great intimacy and considerable power. The composer readily mastered keyboard writing in his earliest works, yet he yearned for the more titanic expressive power of the full orchestra.

Schumann at first had had little experience composing for such a large ensemble. He felt none of the confidence he had with the piano. So it was that his first symphony, the so-called *Zwickau* Symphony, was never finished, despite the fact that one of its three movements was performed in 1832. The composer realized that it was necessary not only to learn orchestration but also to study the fundamental disciplines of music theory. Only with the craft provided by these rigorous studies could he hope to command such a large form as a symphony.

After subjecting himself to the rigors of this pedagogy, which Schumann undertook with dedication but little enthusiasm, he felt ready to try again to compose a symphony. The result was the Symphony Number 1, the *Spring* Symphony, composed (but not orchestrated) in just three days during January 1841. The First Symphony is an ebullient, fully romantic work that seems to have pleased its creator. But he still needed to compose along more classical lines. So, only two weeks after writing the symphony, he embarked on another symphonic project: an overture in E major.

The overture soon acquired a second movement and a finale. The composer at first called the three-movement piece *Sinfonietta*. When Felix Mendelssohn had conducted the premiere of the *Spring* Symphony, it had been an unqualified success, the only such success the composer was ever to experience with an orchestral composition. When, on the other hand, Ferdinand David premiered the three-movement work (now called *Suite*) half a year later, it drew little applause from the audience.

Schumann rewrote the finale of the E major piece a few years later, and the music was published in 1846 as Overture, Scherzo, and Finale. He wrote to his publisher, "The whole has a light, friendly character. I wrote it in a really happy mood." The work is a substantial composition, although it does not quite have the proportions of Schumann's symphonies. One can readily hear in this early work the composer's struggle to master classical forms and procedures while continuing to let his romantic imagination soar.

Romanticism is unmistakable right from the outset. The slow introduction begins with the alternation of two almost operatic motives. These yearning, emotion-laden figures serve to introduce most of the orchestral instruments, one by one. The ensuing allegro is more classically restrained, more objective. Its opening motive, vaguely reminiscent of the beginning of Mozart's G Minor Symphony, per-vades the movement. There is an elaborate transition, based on the introduction's first figure, which culminates in a climactic passage based on the introduction's second figure. This attempt to integrate the composition by using the same materials in difference contexts is an example of Schumann's desire to work with forms that are clas-sical in spirit. Although there is no formal development section, Schumann compensates with a long and involved coda.

Many commentators hear echoes of Mendelssohn in the scherzo. The two composers were in close contact, as they both lived in Leipzig at the time Opus 52 was composed. Schumann admired Men-delssohn's music, particularly his masterful handling of the orches-tra, and Mendelssohn frequently conducted his friend's music. While there are echoes of Mendelssohn's elfin scherzos in this movement, Schumann is more heavy handed. For example, the horn calls shortly after the opening are doubled by second violins and violas — some-thing a more experienced orchestrator, like Mendelssohn, would not have done. The trio is brief, like a parenthetical insert. There is a reason for this. Schumann is again trying to be classical in spirit. After the scherzo is heard a second time, the trio returns, this time with a dramatic transition to integrate it more fully with the scherzo.

The effects of Schumann's study of traditional musical disci-plines are most noticeable in the finale. After a few introductory chords, the movement becomes quite contrapuntal. It seems to be a fugue, with instumental groups entering one by one with the same material. The fugue turns out to be illusory, however. Nonetheless, the entire exposition is pervasively polyphonic. If this were a com-position by Mozart or Beethoven, we might expect the contrapuntal exposition to promise an elaborate development section. But Schu-mann was not such a thorough intellectual, and he let his innate ro-manticism take over in the development. Instead of increasing the contrapuntal complexities, he steadfastly avoids polyphony, as if to dispel the learned overtones of the exposition. The development is constructed almost entirely of dramatic block chords. There is one passage in which the string basses sustain their notes while eveyone else plays short notes — a scoring that belies the frequently heard charge that Schumann was not an imaginative orchestrator. The re-capitulation is again contrapuntal, but it is played over sustained bass notes which tend to obscure the independence of melodic lines. The extended coda is chorale-like: the counterpoint is gone for good.

Symphony Number 1 in B-Flat Major, Opus 38, *Spring*
Andante un poco maestoso. Allegro molto vivace
Larghetto —
Scherzo: Molto vivace. Trio I. Scherzo. Trio II.
Scherzo
Allegro animato e grazioso

The Spring *Symphony was composed between 23 January and 20 February 1841. Felix Mendelssohn conducted the first performance with the Gewandhaus Orchestra in Leipzig on 31 March 1841.*

Composition is the art of combining tones to make a coherent musical statement. Orchestration is the art of choosing the proper instruments to perform those tones. The skills of composing and orchestrating are not the same. In earlier periods composers often were quite indifferent to orchestration. Throughout history they have become more and more concerned with which instruments play which notes. In some music, mostly of recent vintage, composition and orchestration have merged, as it has become impossible to imagine certain types of music apart from their actual sonority.

Most composers, at least until recently, have composed first (usually with some notion of the eventual instrumental setting) and then orchestrated. Not surprisingly, there have been second-rate composers who were first-rate orchestrators and there have been fine composers, such as Robert Schumann, who never completely mastered the craft of orchestration. Since we tend to think of orchestration as secondary, conductors usually neglect well-scored trivia but perform excellent music the orchestration of which needs improving. Purists may object to retouching the works of masterful composers, but it is a common practice to make judicious improvements in performance.

There are several reasons why such changes are necessary; poor orchestration is only one possibility. The design of several instruments has changed over the years, so that their sound quality has been altered and their ability to play certain notes and figurations has improved. Also, the size of the orchestra has increased steadily, at least until the end of the last century. And concert halls have gotten larger, thus altering the typical acoustical environments in which we listen. Thus, the orchestras for which baroque, classic, and early romantic composers wrote are not the orchestras of today, and certain adjustments are necessary. But well-meaning alterations of a score can get out of hand. Many of the symphonies of Bruckner, for example, were all but destroyed by "improvements" incorporated with the best of intentions.

In the opinion of most (but, significantly, not all) conductors, Schumann was not a highly skilled orchestrator. No one claims that he was an incompetent, but his orchestrations — especially when compared to those of his contemporaries Berlioz, Wagner, and Mendelssohn — lack brilliance. The objection is to more than the lack of color. Many feel that Schumann's scoring is murky, unbalanced, and too much the same from passage to passage. The argument continues to rage over whether or not to adjust the orchestration in Schumann's symphonies and, if so, how drastically. Opinions range from that of, for example, conductor Robert Heger ("I have attempted to play the symphonies of Schumann entirely in the original and observed, to my surprise, that even this is possible") to that of conductor Jascha Horenstein ("Schumann's symphonies simply cannot be 'projected' and properly performed because of the composer's 'defective technique' or no technique at all in orchestration!") Two distinguished conductors, Gustav Mahler and Felix Weingartner, completely re-orchestrated the Schumann symphonies. Musicologist Asher George Zlotnik wrote an 874-page treatise on revisions in Schumann's orchestration! Clearly, this is no small problem for performers. Every conductor must decide how much retouching to employ, if any, and whether or not to follow one of the several available revisions made by conductors who respected the music and wanted to rescue it from its allegedly inept orchestration.

In his youth Schumann was interested more in literature than in music. He was a musical amateur, with little use for formal training. He dreamed of writing symphonies and he improvised them (at the piano), but he had neither the training nor the first-hand experience with an orchestra actually to write out his imaginary symphonies. Orchestration is a skill that is acquired mainly through experience, such as working with the orchestra as conductor, performer, or at least producer of concerts. It is difficult to study scoring only through instruction, because the discipline is primarily practical and since a typical musical education concentrates first on music theory (harmony and counterpoint). Schumann had no instruction at all until his twentieth year, and by then he was too old to work diligently in such theoretical areas, let alone on orchestration.

The composer realized his deficiencies and sought to correct them. He was 22 when he decided he really wanted to write a symphony. He started on a work in G minor (which he never completed), and he even secured a performance of the first movement. Then, a bit in a panic, he wrote to conductor Gottlieb Christian Müller, "I take the liberty of writing to ask you whether you feel inclined to give me lessons in instrumentation and assist me in revising a symphony movement of my own, shortly to be performed in Altenburg. I cannot tell you how much obliged I should be if you would do this, as I have been working quite in a way of my own, without any sort of guidance, and I am not at all confident of my abilities for symphonies."

The work was performed, and its deficiencies were obvious. Even Clara Wieck, who was to marry Schumann, complained about the scoring. The composer was intensely embarrassed by the performance. He wrote to his publisher, "I consider this art to be so difficult that it will take long years of study to give one certainty of mastery." Schumann revised the movement, but with little improvement. After a second unsuccessful performance he put the work aside and did not again attempt to write for orchestra for another eight years.

During this period he composed mostly piano pieces and songs. It is perhaps no coincidence that his subsequent orchestral works often sound like piano music transferred to the orchestra, rather than compositions indigenous to a large ensemble. He heard Berlioz' magnificently orchestrated *Symphonie fantastique* in 1835 and the newly discovered C Major Symphony of Schubert in 1839. The extraordinary sonorities of the latter inspired him to try again to compose a symphony, although he still had not studied orchestration. He composed and orchestrated his First Symphony in just one month in 1841. The manuscript shows numerous changes of instrumentation, testifying to repeated revisions almost every time Schumann heard the work (it received fifty performances during his lifetime). In later years the composer would no longer listen to suggestions for fixing problems in the First Symphony. Because of the steady worsening of the mental illness that would eventually kill him, Schumann became increasingly suspicious of even the most well-meaning critics. But this was not the case when the symphony was new.

Felix Mendelssohn conducted the premiere performance. At the first of three rehearsals, the opening brass figure sounded dreadful because the Leipzig Gewandhaus Orchestra had only natural horns and trumpets, not the newly invented valve instruments. Some of the notes sounded full and brilliant, as Schumann had expected, but some sounded muffled because they could be played only by "stopping" the instruments — done when players insert their hands into the ends of their instruments. Mendelssohn suggested playing the figure a third higher, an idea which Schumann readily accepted. The sonority was thus improved, but the motivic relationship between this opening fanfare and the subsequent allegro theme was obscured.

Schumann, a man easily discouraged, must have been devastated by such an obvious error in scoring having to be corrected at the beginning of the first rehearsal of his first completed orchestra piece.

Mendelssohn's suggested change created a problem for future conductors. Some, such as Mahler, have restored the original version, once valve instruments became widespread. But other conductors have preferred the Mendelssohn revision, because the higher version sounds more brilliant. When the score was published in 1853, valve instruments had become common, and thus Schumann could have requested his publishers to reinstate the original figure. But he allowed the symphony to be published with the revision, possibly because he had come to prefer it or possibly because he did not want to trouble the publishers.

The opening is but one example of Schumann's inexperience in orchestration. Elsewhere the violins are asked to play figures that are very difficult and that sound more like piano music than string music. Woodwind solos are often doubled by other instruments, to no apparent advantage. Sometimes these solos are buried because of overly thick accompaniments. Elsewhere the balances are poor. On the other hand, there are some passages where the scoring is quite imaginative: the trio of trombones in the transition from the second to the third movements, the string figurations in much of the slow movements, etc.

Conductor Erich Leinsdorf has summarized the problem with Schumann's orchestrations particularly well: "I am of the opinion that Schumann is one of the all-time geniuses. His entire musical picture and imagination were very much influenced by his pianism. His orchestral scores can be played as they have been written, I am sure, but the greatest effort in performing them thus, in the end, yields results which are less to the credit of this great composer than if judicious changes are made in his scoring."

"Think of it," Schumann wrote to critic Ernst Wenzel, "a whole symphony, and, what's more, a *Spring* Symphony — I can't believe myself that it's finished." It was appropriate for the composer to write a paean to spring, because he had the year before married Clara Wieck. He was deeply in love and profoundly happy in this union. "The period in which it was written influenced its character and partly made it what it is." Schumann's bliss and contentment are echoed in the buoyant good spirits of the symphony.

The composer wrote to conductor Wilhelm Taubert, "Try to inspire the orchestra with some of the spring longing which chiefly possessed me when I wrote the symphony in February 1841. At the very beginning I should like the trumpets to sound as if from on high, like a call to awaken. In what follows of the introduction there might be a suggestion of the growing green of everything, even of a butterfly flying up, and in the subsequent allegro of the gradual assembling of all that belongs to spring."

The inspiration for the *Spring* Symphony was one of Adolf Böttger's popular poems of spring and love. The final line of the poem could actually be sung to the opening melody of the symphony — *Im Tale blüt der Frühling auf* ("Spring unfolds in the valley"). Schumann at first gave descriptive titles to the four movements: "Spring's Awakening," "Evening," "Merry Playmates," and "Spring's Farewell." He subsequently did away with these titles, probably feeling that they offered a too restricted context in which to hear the music.

Symphony Number 2 in C Major, Opus 61
>Sostenuto assai. Allegro ma non troppo
>Scherzo: Allegro vivace. Trio I. Scherzo. Trio II.
>   Scherzo
>Adagio espressivo
>Allegro molto vivace

The Second Symphony was begun in December 1845 and completed on 19 October 1846. Felix Mendelssohn conducted the first performance with the Gewandhaus Orchestra in Leipzig on 5 November 1846.

Most of Schumann's early works were short piano pieces or songs — compositions that, true to the romantic spirit, conveyed particular moods. But eventually he needed to expand the scope of his output. To compose symphonies, concertos, overtures, and chamber music demanded that he confront the challenge of classical form. It was not easy for him to rethink his aesthetic along classical lines, particularly since he had not had a rigorous formal training. But he was determined to find a way to create unified and coherent larger works. What he wanted was to reconcile the lyrically expressive romantic concept of music that was natural to him with tradition's concern for structure. In other words, while content could define form in small pieces, large ones required a sophisticated architecture to make their content meaningful.

The classical and the romantic impulses were sometimes in conflict in Schumann's first efforts at large forms, such as the First Symphony. As musicologist Mosco Carner explains,

>Schumann's deliberate turn from the romantic miniature of his early period to the larger and stricter forms of the classical sym-

phony and chamber music — thus forcing upon himself a change of approach, style, and technique — could not altogether stifle his romantic Muse. In fact, it is in those very movements in which the romantic overcomes the neophyte to classicism that he made his individual contributions to the history of the nineteenth-century symphony. About the sincerity and nobility of his symphonic utterances there can be no doubt.

The decision to turn to large forms presented Schumann with two problems — how to sustain interest in an extended movement and how to make several movements add up to a meaningful whole. These problems were felt on every level. Even Schumann's approach to melody had to be changed. He had to compose themes capable of extended development; the typical epigrammatic tunes of his small piano pieces could not serve as symphonic material. It was not until the Second Symphony (chronologically the fifth of the six symphonies he at least began) that he achieved true symphonic development.

He accomplished this by forsaking external programs, such as the First Symphony's invocation of spring. For the Second Symphony he turned instead to an internal impetus. The symphony was a reaction to his recent recovery from a serious mental breakdown. He subsequently wrote, "I might indeed say it was the resistance of the spirit that was here at work and helped me to combat my condition. The first movement is full of this struggle, and in its character it is capricious and refractory." Later he added, "I sometimes fear my semi-invalid state can be divined from the music. I began to feel more myself when I wrote the last movement and was certainly much better when I finished the whole work. All the same, it still reminds me of those dark days."

Schumann suffered from a mental illness that came and went periodically throughout his life. Just prior to composing the Second Symphony, he had a particularly severe bout — his "dark days." He collapsed under the strain of intensive artistic activity. This breakdown was more severe than his first one had been, when he was 23. This time there was a strange irritation of his aural nerve, which caused Schumann to hear continuous ringing in his ears. Furthermore, every external noise turned into a definite pitch for him. He was constantly weak and disoriented. He wrote to Felix Mendelssohn, "Unfortunately, I have still not recovered my usual strength. Any sort of disturbance of the simple order of my life throws me off balance and into a nervous, irritable state. That is why I preferred staying at home when my wife was with you — much to my regret. Wherever there is fun and enjoyment, I must still keep out of the way. The only thing to be done is hope, hope — and so I will."

The composer's wife Clara felt that a complete change might help her husband, and so they moved to Dresden. In new surroundings he began to improve. Clara and Robert wrote fugues together and criticized each other's work; this diversion helped lead the composer back into music. By the summer of 1845 he was planning the new symphony. As he became engrossed in the actual composition of it, he often became exhausted and had to set it aside. He was in the middle of orchestrating the adagio in May 1846 when a new attack came upon him. Clara sent him to a country retreat with their two eldest daughters. The peaceful atmosphere worked a cure, but the symphony remained unfinished. Finally Schumann felt well enough to complete the work the following fall.

The extent to which Schumann *consciously* intended the symphony to reflect his (temporarily) successful struggle against his sickness is not known, but it is possible to understand the illness as the source of the music's inner meaning. Musicologist Brian Schlotel, for example, interprets the symphony as a direct outcome of the composer's determined effort to regain his health.

> It is this determination, sometimes fierce, sometimes prayerful, that lends the symphony its special characteristic, for transmuted by his genius the symphony takes on the universal significance of a struggle between light and darkness, represented in part by the two [simultaneous] opening themes. . . . After periods of conflict and periods of melancholy, the darkness lessens, the light increases, and in the last movement we can feel that the tides of misfortune have been pushed back, while with its final great "Amen" cadence the symphony ends on a note of spiritual hope.

Whether the relationship between the symphony and the illness was intentional or not, what matters is that the illness provided Schumann with exactly what he needed: a central unifying idea on which to base an extended composition. The symphony does not in any explicit sense chart the course of the disease. That would have been too obvious and too much like Schumann's earlier programmatic miniatures. Rather, it is a noble expression of the emotional experience of nearly going mad and of the victory over violent depression. The fear and denial of madness became the source of an integrated composition. The dramatic development from the first movement's struggle to the finale's victory is unique among Schumann's larger compositions. The Second Symphony makes him worthy to be called, as several scholars have labelled him, the first symphonist after Beethoven to make classical forms serve the romantic impulse.

The impetus behind the unity of the Second Symphony may have been extramusical, but the means are decidedly musical. The opening brass motive, for example, appears prominently in the second and fourth movements. In addition, all four movements are in the key of C — an unusual procedure. The reappearance of the lovely main theme of the slow movement as the second theme of the finale further integrates the work. Also, the manner in which the first movement's main allegro theme continually emphasizes the second beat of the 3/4 measures pervades the entire movement, including material related to other themes.

◆   ◆   ◆

Symphony Number 3 in E-Flat Major, Opus 97, *Rhenish*

Lebhaft
Scherzo: Sehr mässig
Nicht schnell
Feierlich
Lebhaft

The Rhenish *Symphony was composed between 2 November and 9 December 1850. Schumann conducted the first performance on 6 February 1851 in Düsseldorf.*

Like most nineteenth-century composers, Schumann was most comfortable composing programmatic music. The ties between literary and musical arts were strong during the romantic era, when composers readily sought inspiration in literature and other extramusical areas. There is a difference between what is an appropriate stimulus for a composer and what is useful information for a listener. Thus, Schumann hesitated to share with the public too much of the extramusical origins of his compositions. "We must not show our heart to the world. A general impression of a work of art is better. At least no preposterous comparisons can be made."

The *Rhenish* Symphony is based on a program, but only vague hints of its nature have been preserved, mostly in Clara Schumann's diaries. The composer apparently wanted to portray folk life on the Rhine, where he had recently moved to become Music Director of the city of Düsseldorf. The scherzo was inspired by a morning on the Rhine, and the fourth movement found its origin in the ceremony at which the Archbishop von Geissel was made Cardinal. That movement was originally titled, "In the Manner of an Accompaniment to a Solemn Ceremony."

If Schumann chose to repress his programs, is it fair for us today to ferret out references to what was in his mind and to share them with listeners? This is not an easy question. The middle three movements of the *Rhenish* Symphony seem wonderfully evocative, and it is only natural to wonder what is being evoked. The leisurely scherzo could readily call to mind a mist-enshrouded morning by the river, and the resonant chorale harmonies and rich counterpoint of the fourth movement do indeed seem to suggest a ceremony. But is this so because we know their inspiration or are such suggestions really in the music? The third movement seems equally evocative, but we do not know its programmatic origins. It is therefore harder to pinpoint the evocation. The three movements actually form a group of character pieces, much like those found in Schumann's piano music, and it is clear that their respective characters derive from more or less specific references.

The outer movements, on the other hand, are more abstract and symphonic. Schumann may well have had some programmatic reference in mind, but these movements seem less dependent on external characterization. They seem to deal with contrast and development of musical rather than literary materials.

The opening movement, for example, is a thoroughly symphonic sonata allegro form. The opening idea, particularly the very first melodic leap of a fourth, is the source of most of what follows. This opening has a wonderfully rhythmic vitality, coming in part from metric ambiguity: the music seems at first in two-beat and then three-beat patterns. There is a beautifully lyric second theme that again begins with a leap of a fourth. This melody is never allowed to go on very long before the broad first theme intrudes.

The three middle movements form a unit. The waltz-like scherzo has elements of both a dance movement's three-part structure and a slow movement's variation form. Next comes a simple song, too direct to be the real slow movement. Hence the need for five movements, the fourth of which is the real adagio.

Schumann used several devices in this movement to suggest the spaciousness of the Cologne Cathedral, where the "solemn ceremony" took place. Three trombones join the orchestra in this movement and remain for the finale. The rich brass writing is reminiscent of late renaissance cathedral music. Also, the composer employs polyphonic textures to suggest fifteenth-century music. Even the notation is somewhat archaic. Once the spacious, ceremonial character is established, the score employs the half-note rather than the more typical quarter note as the beating unit. The notation makes no difference to the listener, but it does convey to the conductor the reverential quality Schumann was seeking.

The finale returns to the symphonic world of the opening movement. The interval of a fourth figures prominently, as it does in every movement except the middle one. Toward the end the tempo broadens and there is a reference to the fourth movement's cathedral music.

The *Rhenish* Symphony was composed a few weeks after the Cello Concerto. Both works were written at incredible speed during Schumann's final burst of creativity. Despite their chronological proximity, the two pieces are quite different. The concerto is more rhapsodic, its movements are more closely linked, and its orchestration is more modest. The symphony, on the other hand, exhibits a sureness of orchestration sometimes absent from Schumann's earlier orchestral music. Furthermore, it shows a viable marriage between the lyric character piece that was the composer's natural mode of expression and the fully developed symphonic form for which he strove during most of his creative life.

Symphony Number 4 in D Minor, Opus 120
Ziemlich langsam. Lebhaft —
Romanze: Ziemlich langsam —
Scherzo: Lebhaft —
Langsam. Lebhaft

The D Minor Symphony was composed between May and September 1841 and first performed on 6 December 1841 in Leipzig. Schumann revised the work between 13 and 19 December 1851. He conducted the first performance of the final version on 30 December 1852 in Düsseldorf.

September 13, 1841, was a special day for Clara Schumann. Not only did she celebrate her twenty-second birthday, but also her first child, Marie, was christened. Furthermore, the previous day had been the first anniversary of her wedding. Her husband presented Clara with a special birthday/anniversary gift — the score of a new symphony, conceived as a portrait of his wife. The symphony, which eventually became known as Number 4 in D Minor, is pervaded by a melody which is a version of what Schumann called his "Clara" theme. He had previously used it in a number of other works: it first appears in the *Davidsbündlertänze*, a piano work written when Schumann first began to think seriously of marrying Clara.

The early years of Schumann's marriage were a period of intense compositional activity. He composed over 150 songs in 1840, which became known as his year of the song. 1841 was the year of the symphony — Schumann composed the First Symphony, the D Minor Symphony, and a work that is essentially a symphony without slow movement, the Overture, Scherzo, and Finale. The following year he concentrated on chamber music, completing three string quartets, the Piano Quartet, and the Piano Quintet.

During 1841 Schumann began the Overture, Scherzo, and Finale within days of completing the First Symphony. He went on immediately after finishing that work to what became the first movement of his Piano Concerto. No sooner was that movement completed than Clara recorded in her diary, "Yesterday he began another symphony. I have not heard anything of it so far, but at times I catch the sound of a fiery D minor in the distance, and I can see from the way he acts that it will be another work drawn from the very depths of his soul. Heaven is favorably inclined towards us, and even Robert cannot be more blissfully happy at his work than I am when he finally shows me what he has composed."

Before the year of the symphony had run its course, Schumann had not only completed three symphonies but also sketched another in C minor (which he never completed) and nearly finished a work for chorus and orchestra.

The D Minor Symphony (listed as Number 2) and the Overture, Scherzo, and Finale were introduced to the public at the same concert. The remainder of the program consisted of two piano works by Franz Liszt, one which Liszt himself played and one in which Clara joined him in a duet. Schumann had been looking forward to this concert, hoping it would help solidify his already growing reputation. But no one could compete with Liszt. Liszt was a commanding stage personality, and his performances of his own virtuoso keyboard works overshadowed Schumann's symphonies. The public seemed scarcely to notice the two orchestral works. Schumann's disappointment was made still more bitter by the fact that Clara, by performing the duet, had played an unwitting part in focusing attention on Liszt.

Although aware of his friend's personal magnetism as a performer, Schumann placed the blame for the public's indifference not on Liszt but on his own orchestral works. He withdrew the symphony and put it in his desk for a decade. He eventually re-orchestrated it and made a few small structural changes. His rescoring procedure was bizarre. He employed someone to recopy the original version of the string parts in some passages, leaving room on the paper for new wind, brass, and percussion music, which Schumann then filled in. Thus the rescoring does not affect the strings and does not allow them to respond to changes he made in the wind parts.

In May 1853 the thirty-first Lower Rhine Music Festival assembled an orchestra of 160 and a chorus of 490 to perform excerpts from Handel's *Messiah*, Mendelssohn's *Elijah*, and Gluck's *Alceste*. The distinguished violinist Joseph Joachim played Beethoven's Violin Concerto under Schumann's direction, and Hiller conducted Beethoven's Ninth Symphony. The festival opened with the new version of Schumann's Symphony in D Minor, now listed as Number 4 (Schumann had published two more symphonies since putting the D Minor aside in 1841). The festival closed with a work Schumann had composed especially for the occasion — *Festival Overture on the Rhine Wine Song*, for orchestra with chorus.

Although Schumann had acquired many years of experience as a conductor by the time he revised the symphony, in some ways the scoring is less successful than in the original version. It is thicker, less soloistic, and sometimes actually turgid. One Schumann scholar, Brian Schlotel, feels that the thicker orchestration was a direct result of Schumann's experiences on the podium: since he was not a particularly effective conductor, he may have decided (perhaps subconsciously) to write music that would "play itself" or even that would not suffer too drastically if various members of the orchestra did not attend rehearsals. On the other hand, there are decided improvements, both orchestrational and structural, in the new version. Brahms was the first of several musicians to prefer the original version, and he arranged, despite Clara's disapproval, for its publication thirty years after Schumann's death. Today most conductors use the final version, possibly incorporating some of the lighter scoring details of the original.

The "Clara" theme, which opens the symphony, returns in many guises throughout the piece. To unify a multi-movement composition in this manner was particularly popular among romantic composers, who took their cue from Beethoven (the four-note rhythmic figure that opens the Fifth Symphony, for example, recurs in all movements in various guises). As Schumann's slow introduction accelerates in its transition to the faster main portion of the first movement, the eight-note theme (a rising arpeggio followed by a descending stepwise motive) that is repeated again and again contains (notes 5–8) a fragment of the Clara figure. When this idea becomes the main theme of the allegro, a bond is established between the two sections of the movement. Since the secondary theme is virtually the same as the main theme but in another key, all the principle materials of the movement are generated by the opening melodic idea. Even a new lyrical melody which appears during the development section has embedded within it the Clara motive.

Another means Schumann employs to increase unity is having the movements played without pause. The somewhat inconclusive ending of the first movement propels us into the second, marked *Romanze*. After a plaintive melody in the oboe and cellos, the upper strings present the Clara theme much as it was first played in the first movement. The contrasting middle section features a solo violin decorating a new theme.

The vigorous scherzo theme also contains the Clara motive, this time played in inversion (upside-down). The trio section brings back the solo violin music from the second movement. At its end the scherzo slows down but does not really conclude. It fades into the slow introduction to the finale.

The finale begins with a new version of the end of the first movement's introduction, which contains the Clara motive. As in the first movement, this material also forms part of the main theme of the allegro. The development section begins with a fugato based on the second theme. In the coda the music gets progressively faster as it drives toward a triumphant ending.

It is an open question to what extent deriving different melodies from a common source motive actually unifies a composition. If the "same" symphony were performed with different melodies replacing Schumann's, but retaining the orchestration and the harmonic structure, would the piece be any less unified? Unity in music is created by far deeper and more complex means than simply using the same five-note figure in different contexts. In fact, some inferior pieces that do not seem particularly unified may nonetheless display careful derivation of melodies from earlier materials. Thus thematic consistency guarantees nothing. Why would Schumann bother with it, then? It does add extra interest, and it does provide listeners with something quite tangible to listen for while hearing the piece. The derivation of most materials of the Fourth Symphony from the Clara theme is fascinating to follow, but it is a mistake to believe that this derivation *creates*, rather than simply *reinforces*, structural unity.

Dimitri Shostakovich

Born on 25 September 1906 in St. Petersburg (now Leningrad).
Died on 9 August 1975 in Moscow.

Concerto Number 1 in E-Flat Major for Cello and Orchestra, Opus 107
Allegretto
Moderato —
Cadenza —
Allegro con moto

The First Cello Concerto was composed in the summer of 1959 for Mstislav Rostropovich, who played the premiere with the Leningrad State Philharmonic Orchestra, conducted by Yevgeny Mravinsky, on 4 October 1959.

Shostakovich's three visits to the United States took place under very different circumstances. The first, in 1949, came a year after the infamous purge in which the Stalin regime condemned the composer and five of his colleagues for adhering to "anti-Soviet practices in their music, which is marked by formalist perversions, dissonance, contempt for melody, and the use of chaotic and neuropathic discords — all of which are alien to the artistic tastes of the Soviet people." The music was dismissed as representative of decadent bourgeois culture. Shostakovich was forced to resign his professorship and to apologize publicly for his compositions. He was understandably perplexed the following year when Stalin personally telephoned him to ask him to represent Russia at the Cultural and Scientific Conference for World Peace in New York.

The composer had no choice but to go. He felt uncomfortable in a strange land, thrust into the limelight yet constantly watched by the Soviets. Most difficult for this intensely private man was having to play the scherzo from his Fifth Symphony on the piano before an audience of thirty thousand in Madison Square Garden. Also, Shostakovich feared that Stalin intended to show him to the world as a healthy celebrity and then have him quietly murdered upon his return. He was particularly worried when his scheduled concert tour of American cities was unexpectedly cut short by an order to return to Moscow.

650

He had always distrusted the West. Nothing happened during his 1949 visit to change his mind. His second visit, a decade later, took place under somewhat less tense circumstances. After Stalin's death in 1953, an official "thaw" began, under which the music of Shostakovich and other previously condemned composers was gradually restored to official favors. When Krushchev came to power in 1956, Stalin's crimes were made public. In 1958 the new leader issued a Party resolution, stating that Stalin's artistic judgements had been "subjective." The derogatory "formalist" label was officially lifted from the Soviet composers, and their earlier music was once again performed.

Soon after the Krushchev thaw, a group of American composers was invited to visit the Soviet Union. A few months later, Shostakovich and several other Russian musicians spent a month in the United States. Although the composer still felt uneasy in the West and still knew that every move he made was watched, he was able to visit different parts of the country and hear a lot of American music as well as several pieces of his own, including the First Cello Concerto.

The group traveled to New York, San Francisco, Los Angeles, Louisville, Washington, Boston, and Philadelphia, where the Philadelphia Orchestra accompanied Mstislav Rostropovich in the American premiere of the Cello Concerto. In each city the Russians met prominent leaders of artistic, social, and political groups. Sometimes the visiting composers were asked to compare musical life in the U.S.A. and U.S.S.R. Their answer struck several observers as well-rehearsed propaganda. The visitors denied that a political event, such as the end of the Stalin regime, could have any effect on what music was performed. They claimed that musical criticism, even when emanating from government officials, always serves to educate the public and help guide listeners' tastes. They felt that composers have an obligation to correct artistic errors pointed out by critics. The Russian composers praised the high quality of performances in America. They condemned atonal and experimental music as inimical to the spirit of the people. And so it went, city after city: cautious meetings between musicians representing two very different cultures with two very different political systems. Always the Russians were willing to answer questions, and always the answers seemed to come directly from Moscow.

Reporter Walter Arlen described the visiting Shostakovich as "highly nervous, a chain smoker with darting eyes and fidgeting hands, ill at ease and seemingly anxious most of the time." The composer certainly had reason to be anxious. He hated being in the spotlight and he hated being a political pawn, yet there he was for an entire month in a foreign country he did not understand, meeting celebrities, having his every word reported in newspapers, and knowing all along that everything he said had to be exactly what the Party wanted. His surveillance was not as tight as it had been during his previous visit, but he knew he was being observed. The performances he heard of his music, particularly the triumphantly received First Cello Concerto, must have been his only opportunity to feel himself.

Upon returning to Russia, Shostakovich wrote an article about his trip. He praised American musicians, thanked the United States for its hospitality, appreciated the warm response his music had received, and thanked Americans for their interest in the Soviet Union. He did criticized American universities for allowing composition students to write whatever they wished rather than insisting that young composers respect tradition and audience tastes: "'Freedom of choice' transforms into freedom to reject the serious creation society requires, to reject art with a content that would express the inner world of the human being."

We now know, thanks in large part to the posthumous publication of the composer's memoirs, that he was secretly very much in favor of artistic freedom of expression. We also know that several propagandistic articles that appeared under Shostakovich's name were written by others and not even seen by the composer prior to publication. We can only wonder what his true impressions of the United States were in 1959.

The composer's last visit took place in 1973. He wanted one final chance to learn more about this country, and he took the opportunity to travel to Northwestern University to accept an honorary doctorate. His health was very bad and the trip was exhausting, but his family wanted him to go because they had hopes that American doctors might produce miraculous cures for ailments the Russian doctors had pronounced hopeless. After two days in a Washington hospital, the composer began his return trip; the American doctors were as pessimistic as the Russians. Two years later the composer was dead.

The First Cello Concerto is one of Shostakovich's more serious and introspective works, although it is not lacking in the rhythmic vitality that characterizes his popular earlier music. The solo instrument opens the piece with a four-note figure that is destined to pervade the first movement. This brief motive contains intervals, rhythms, and mood suggestive of the entire concerto. Throughout the first theme, which grows out of this figure, the cello arches gradually upward into its penetrating high register and then gradually back down. The second theme, with its incessant rhythms underlying a song-like line, also unfolds along a grand arch upward and then downward.

The second movement begins with smoothly lyrical material quite foreign to the world of the first movement. The cello enters with a beautifully broad melody. A second theme continues this mood of subdued lyricism for a while, but eventually the music grows to a climax. The solo horn provides the transition to the marvelous coda, an ethereal passage in which the cello plays in high, pure harmonics to the accompaniment of muted violins, celeste, and low strings — a magical close to one of Shostakovich's most personal statements.

The third movement follows without pause. It is an extended cadenza for cello alone. Shostakovich has here, as in the First Violin Concerto, elevated the cadenza from its usual position of virtuosic parenthesis to a place of structural importance. It moves gradually from the lyricism of the slow movement through increasing virtuosity to reminiscences of the first movement.

The finale is a robust rondo, with an impetuous first theme and a dance-like second idea. Hints of the first movement's first theme become gradually move overt, until the actual melody is quoted. A fiery passage of great bravura closes the work.

Concerto Number 2 in F Major for Piano and Orchestra, Opus 102
Allegro
Andante —
Allegro

The Second Piano Concerto was composed early in 1957. Maxim Shostakovich, son of the composer, was soloist at the first performance on 10 May 1957 in Moscow; Nikolai Anosov conducted.

After the Second World War, Shostakovich and his music were out of favor. But when his chief antagonist, Joseph Stalin, died in 1953, the composer began to return to favor. That year he was able to write and premiere his Tenth Symphony, an intense work that could never have been performed while Stalin was alive. Although there were no repercussions, the Tenth *was* criticized. The one constant between the repression of 1948–53 and the liberalization of 1953–56 was Socialist Realism. The interpretation of this doctrine, by which the government sought to impose a forced optimism on Soviet art, had loosened somewhat, but the idea remained in force. An article in *Pravada* explained the new openness within the old strictures: "Socialist Realism offers boundless vistas for the creative artist and the greatest freedom for the expression of his personality, for the development of diverse art genres, trends, and styles. Hence the importance of encouraging new departures in art, of studying the artist's individual style, and . . . of recognizing the artist's right to be independent, to strike out boldly on new paths."

Shostakovich was cautious. After the complex and somber Tenth Symphony, he produced several lighthearted works, including the Second Piano Concerto. He had survived two purges and two rehabilitations, and he suspected more were to come. But he now understood how to survive. He wrote music that followed Socialist Realism, but he also created a lot of protest music, in which he disguised his anti-Party sentiments so that government officials would not recognize them. He lived another twenty years, during which he composed some of his most personal and austere music. There is always a political meaning in his major works, a meaning that Party officials would not have liked if they had understood it.

It was for his son Maxim that Shostakovich composed the Second Piano Concerto. Maxim was an advanced student at the Moscow Conservatory when he premiered the concerto the day of his nineteenth birthday. The work is infused with the spirit of youth. Its carefree outer movements and its intimate yet direct slow movement were obviously written specifically for a young performer. The piano writing, while sensitive and somewhat virtuosic, is playable by a young artist. Perhaps the composer was trying to recapture his own youth, when he too was an aspiring and accomplished pianist.

Maxim was interested in music from a very young age. Shostakovich told the story of how his three-year-old son used to enjoy the march theme from the Seventh Symphony. This tune was a favorite in the Shostakovich household, since it is similar to a melody in Franz Lehar's *The Merry Widow* that is sung in Russian to the words, "I'll go see Maxim." The family attended the Seventh Symphony's first rehearsals in order to hear how Maxim's tune sounded when played by an enormous orchestra. On one occasion Maxim starting "conducting" so vigorously that he had to be taken home. Today, more than forty years later, Maxim is a world-renowned conductor, particularly of his father's works.

The piano writing in the first movement of the concerto suggests various kinds of etudes that a young piano student has to master: toccata, fantasy, octaves, arpeggios, chromatic scales, chords, etc. The jaunty second theme has been likened to the American song, "What Shall We Do with a Drunken Sailor?" — surely a coincidental resemblance. The contemplative slow movement is scored modestly for piano and strings, with one passage for horn and piano. Notice the particularly beautiful entrance of the piano, when the music moves from C minor to C major. The jaunty finale is based on two themes, one that seems to get stuck on one note, and the other a dance-like tune in 7/8 time. There is an in-joke in this finale: immediately after the 7/8 passage, the soloist plays a passage from the Hanon five-finger exercises that virtually all pianists have to practice endlessly.

It is not quite fair to imply that the concerto is an example of Socialist Realism, although Soviet composers have always been encouraged to write for the young. It is really a non-political piece. But stylistically it is not far removed from, for example, the *Festive* Overture of 1954, since it too is direct and untroubled. But the concerto is more sophisticated, with a lot of clever wit in the outer movements. Socialist Realist music is not supposed to be humorous, so this lighthearted but not altogether innocent work stands apart from Shostakovich's pro-Party music.

Concerto Number 1 for Violin and Orchestra, Opus 77
Moderato
Scherzo: Allegro
Passacaglia: Andante. Cadenza —
Burlesque: Allegro con brio. Presto

The First Violin Concerto was composed in 1947–48. It was first performed on 29 October 1955 by violinist David Oistrakh and the Leningrad Philharmonic Orchestra, conducted by Yevgeny Mravinsky.

In 1979 the world's understanding of Shostakovich's career was substantially altered by the publication of *Testimony,* a book purporting to be a translation into English of memoirs the composer had dictated to Solomon Volkov. Throughout the book, the manuscript of which had been smuggled out of Russia, Shostakovich reveals his true opinions of the Soviets and their policies toward the arts. He shows his genuine concern over the injustices of the Stalin regime, which he was powerless to protest publicly. However he often raised his voice in indignation in the most private, but eventually most public, way — through his music. *Testimony* was greeted in the West as a revelation and in Russia as a hoax. Surely it was no coincidence that, two years later, something called the Progress Publishers of Moscow brought out *Dmitri Shostakovich: About Himself and His*

Times. This book is a collection of all the old pronouncements, purporting to be by the composer and full of praise for the Soviet system, translated into impeccable English.

It is fascinating to compare the two books' very different pictures of the events of 1948. It was in that year that Stalin appointed Andrei Zhdanov, a Communist Party leader known for his ruthlessness, to "look into" the matter of Soviet music. During the Second World War, Stalin had had to concern himself with more crucial matters than the arts. But after the war, according to *Testimony,* the leader worried more over symphonies and their dedications than over affairs of state. He was not pleased by the music his countrymen were turning out, and he called in Zhdanov. Unfavorable reviews began to appear. Works of Shostakovich that had previously been honored were now condemned. A full-scale purge was in progress.

Zhdanov drew up a list of composers who were guilty of writing music against the spirit of the Russian people. Shostakovich and Prokofiev headed the list. Zhdanov ordered all offending composers to a three-day "conference," during which their "crimes" were enumerated and public apologies were demanded. The threat was not veiled. A decree was issued stating that the composers had "persistently adhered to formalist and anti-Soviet practices in their music, which is marked by formalist perversions and many democratic tendencies, including atonality, dissonance, contempt for melody, and the use of chaotic and neuropathic discords — all of which are alien to the artistic tastes of the Soviet people."

About Himself and His Times is not so naïve that it fully accepts Zhdanov's condemnations of most of Shostakovich's music, but it does give a different view of 1948. The editors of the Soviet publication are hardly as cynical as the author of the memoirs: "As well as setting out some correct basic principles, the [Zhdanov] resolution contained some unfair and inexcusably harsh appraisals of the work of several major composers, including Shostakovich. . . . Shostakovich himself made a speech, in which, as always, he strove to derive benefit from any well-meant criticism, while at the same time renouncing none of his compositions."

Shostakovich's "speech" — actually the public apology demanded by Zhdanov — is reprinted in *About Himself and His Times*:

> The composer should be offended not by the criticism which he may receive but by the absence of criticism, because criticism can help him to advance and overcome his shortcomings, whereas the lack of criticism at best does not help him and, in all probability, even hampers his development. . . . There have

been many serious faults and failures in my work, although throughout my career I have thought about the people who listen to my music, about the people who bore me and nurtured me, and I have always striven to have the people accept my music. I have always heeded criticism directed against me and tried in every way to work better and harder. Now, too, I am paying heed to criticism and shall continue to do so in the future.

For the next few years the composer was exceedingly careful about his output. The compositions Shostakovich bought forth were ideologically unassailable — a feeble oratorio entitled *Song of the Forests*, choruses on words by revolutionary poets, and scores for patriotic films such as *Meeting at the River Elbe*, *The Fall of Berlin*, and a tribute to Stalin called *The Unforgettable 1919*. But Shostakovich also composed subversive music in private, pieces that would have been controversial had they been heard during the last years of the Stalin regime. The First Violin Concerto is one such piece. He kept its existence unknown for seven years, until the "thaw" following the death of Stalin removed his music from the Soviet blacklist. The concerto was finally premiered in 1955.

The official Soviet opinion on the two styles Shostakovich cultivated during the years of the Zhdanov Resolution is that the composer was struggling to purge himself of modernism and thereby to compose music for the people. In this view the secret works, like the Violin Concerto, are seen as holdovers from the "unfortunate" style that Zhdanov had attacked. As Boris Schwarz explains in his fascinating book *Music and Musical Life in Soviet Russia*, Shostakovich "wanted to be understood through his *best* efforts, not by 'writing down' to the people. The fallacy of Soviet aesthetics — in the narrow interpretation of Stalin and Zhdanov — is not so much that art must be understandable by the people, but that *all* art must be understood by *all* the people. That is an impossibility unless art is brought down to the lowest common denominator." Shostakovich was deeply concerned with making his music meaningful, but it is in serious works like the Violin Concerto that he sought to do so. In the public pieces of 1948–53, he wrote trivial music that could *please* anyone, especially the likes of Stalin and Zhdanov, but *move* no one.

The Violin Concerto was, in its own private way, subversive. The second movement uses the four-note motive D/E-flat/C/B. In German musical nomenclature, these notes are D/Es/C/H, which correspond to the composer's initials in German — D. Sch. It was contrary to the Zhdanov decree to put into music a motive proclaiming a composer's individuality, especially at the very time when the government was demanding music not of individual expression but of the people and for the state. That the meaning of the motive was encoded in German, the language of the recently defeated enemy, made the concerto politically dangerous. Small wonder that Shostakovich felt he had to keep the piece secret! At about the same time, the composer wrote a song cycle using Jewish folk texts. To use Jewish poetry in a Soviet composition was in effect to condemn Stalin's anti-Semitism. Shostakovich felt he had to protest the repressive ideology of the Stalin regime, and that he had to make his protest with the strongest communication of which he was capable — music. But he also knew that his protest music had to be suppressed, at least for the time being.

After the death of Stalin, Soviet artists were gradually returned to favor. The artists remained cautious if not suspicious, since official tastes were unpredictable yet carried tremendous importance. One of the first works Shostakovich composed after the thaw was the Tenth Symphony, an intense composition which uses the DSCH motive. Emboldened by the success of the symphony, Shostakovich decided to allow some of the secret music from the Zhdanov era be performed. The First Violin Concerto and the songs on Jewish poems were heard in 1955. It is rumored that there are other secret works from the years of repression that still have not been performed.

When violinist David Oistrakh premiered the Violin Concerto, there was little response. No official decree came from the government through the Composers' Union, and thus everyone was afraid to make a public stand for or against the work. Almost everyone. Oistrakh was devoted to the concerto, and he had no official connection with the government. *He* could dare to praise the work publicly. He wrote an article of extravagant appreciation for the concerto. He played it not only in Leningrad and Moscow but also on his first American tour, where it was a triumph in New York.

The composer's final act of defiance with regard to the Violin Concerto was to insist that it be known as Opus 77, so that the world would realize that it was composed at the time of the Zhdanov purge, and not as Opus 99, the number under which it was first published.

The concerto departs from the typical Russian display piece. Its symphonic scope and lack of virtuosity for its own sake are more typical of the German tradition. Its seriousness is apparent in the first movement, a contemplative nocturne. The violin enters after four measures and remains present for most of the movement. The impulse is lyric, as the solo instrument plays an incredibly long melodic line that rises gradually yet inexorably. The climax is reached as the violin plays double stops — two notes at once. While the movement is surely not overtly aggressive or harshly dissonant, it is easy to understand why Shostakovich feared that its gravity and emotional intensity, as well as its Germanic style, would not meet Zhdanov's requirement for music to uplift the masses.

The second movement is a typical Shostakovich scherzo, complete with rhythmic vitality and sarcastic humor — another quality that would not have passed the censors of 1948. The DSCH motive appears in various guises.

The third movement is a passacaglia, which is a baroque form in which a melody is repeated again and again, usually in the bass. The 17-measure theme is first heard in the low strings and then the tuba and bassoon, before the violin enters. At the climax of the movement, the passacaglia theme appears in the solo instrument, played in octaves.

The passacaglia leads to the concerto's only cadenza. It is an elaborate essay for violin alone, almost of the scope of a separate movement. Its slow build to overpowering intensity includes references to the DSCH motive. In traditional concertos the cadenza functions like a parenthesis in the musical development, a place where the piece stops for the soloist to show off. In the Shostakovich concerto this role is reversed, as the cadenza forms the emotional core of the entire work.

The cadenza leads directly to the finale, a burlesque that is like a second scherzo. Its folk-like melodies and dance-like rhythm border on the raucous and the grotesque — once again values at odds with Zhdanov's decree.

The concerto is not overtly political music, not music of outright protest, like the songs on Jewish texts. It is simply music, carrying a universal meaning rather than a message of defiance against the government. Yet its seriousness was enough to make it subversive in 1948. That fact testifies volumes about the repression of artists under Stalin. What Shostakovich felt he had to hide for seven years was nothing more than an honest, abstract piece of music — not a condemnation of Stalin or the Soviet system but a statement of human emotions, which are not always joyous. What Stalin and Zhadanov feared was that such music would expose the lie they were trying to force on the Russian people. The post-war years were not a time of joy. It was as foolish to try to promote false optimism by forcing composers to write, and people to hear, insipidly happy music as it was futile to try to suppress somber emotions by forbidding music of the sort found in Shostakovich's Violin Concerto.

Symphony Number 1 in F Minor, Opus 10

Allegretto. Allegro non troppo
Allegro. Meno Mosso. Allegro
Lento. Largo —
Lento. Allegro molto. Meno mosso. Allegro molto.
    Molto meno mosso. Adagio. Largo. Più mosso.
    Presto.

The First Symphony was composed in 1925. Nikolai Malko conducted the first performance with the Leningrad Philharmonic Orchestra on 12 May 1926.

Composer Alexander Glazunov, director of the Leningrad Conservatory, recognized the tremendous talents of the 13-year-old boy who auditioned for him in 1919. Glazunov admitted the young Shostakovich and recommended that he study piano and composition. For the next six years the youth excelled in both areas. For his graduation recital he performed one of the most challenging Beethoven sonatas, the Opus 106. Under the tutelage of Maximilian Steinberg, Shostakovich studied harmony, counterpoint, fugue, and orchestration. In his final years at the conservatory, he was permitted to compose original works, one of which was his senior project — the First Symphony.

When the symphony was premiered the following year, it made a tremendous impact. Suddenly the young composer was a nationally known celebrity. The piece was played in Leningrad and broadcast from Moscow. The following year it had several performances in other countries.

Prior to this newfound fame, Shostakovich's life had been difficult. Poverty affected most Russians in the early years of the Soviet regime, and the composer's family was no exception. His father died while Shostakovich was in school. Despite the demands of his studies, he was forced to earn money by playing the piano in a movie theater, called the Bright Reel. "My memories of the Bright Reel are not the most pleasant ones. I was 17 and my work consisted in providing musical accompaniment for the human passions on the screen. It was disgusting and exhausting. Hard work and low pay."

Shostakovich particularly disliked his boss, Akim Lvovich Volynsky. Volynsky was not only a theater owner but also head of a ballet school. Every day he went to his school "and looked at the girls with satisfaction. This was Volynsky's little harem. He was about sixty then. He was a short man with a large head and a face like a prune. . . . He gave his harem good publicity, by the way. He published *A Book of Rejoicing*, the title in capitals. And in rejoicing, Volynsky prophesied world fame for his protégées. Nothing came of it. It turned out that Volynsky's patronage wasn't enough; you needed talent as well."

After working in the theater for a month, Shostakovich went to see Volynsky about his wages.

He asked me, "Young man, do you love Art? Great, lofty, immortal Art?" I felt uncomfortable, and I replied that I did. That was a fatal mistake, because then Volynsky put it this way: "If you love Art, young man, then how can you talk to me now about filthy lucre?" He gave me a beautiful speech, itself an example of high art. It was passionate, inspired, a speech about great immortal Art, and its point was that I shouldn't ask Volynsky for my pay. In doing so I defiled Art, he explained, bringing it down to my level of crudity, avarice, and greed. Art was endangered. It could perish if I pressed by outrageous demands.

Shostakovich held his ground and demanded his money. "I hated Art by then. It made me sick. We were desperate for money, I had worked hard, and now they didn't want to pay me for that work. I was 17, but I knew that I was being cheated. . . . Had I worked so hard in order to support Volynsky's harem?"

The composer finally convinced Volynsky to pay part of what was due him, but he had to sue for the rest. Once the First Symphony catapulted Shostakovich to fame, he happily left his job at the Bright Reel.

Volynsky died a few months later, but the composer was nonetheless able to have his revenge. A memorial evening was planned to honor the departed ballet master. Since Shostakovich was known to have been associated with Volysky at the Bright Reel, the now famous composer was asked to share his reminiscences of the "great" man.

I was angry at first. But then I thought about it and decided: why not? Why shouldn't I appear with my reminiscences? I had a story to tell, and I went. . . . Naturally, my performance was out of tune with the other orators. They remembered primarily what an exalted personage Akim Lvovich had been. And here I was with my crude materialism, talking about money. One didn't bring up money on memorial evenings. And if one did, it was only to remind those present what a selfless man the dear departed had been. . . . I shared my memories. The audience was in an uproar, and I thought, even if you drag me off the stage, I'll finish my story. And I did.

The outspoken young man in this story resembles more his older compatriot Sergei Prokofiev than the shy and quiet Shostakovich of later years. The First Symphony, which owes more than a little to some of Prokofiev's early works, seems to reflect this same brash personality. Consider, for example, the humorous trumpet and bassoon duet at the opening, or its quirky answer in the solo clarinet. The music keeps starting and stopping, until finally a degree of continuity is achieved in the allegro. But still the music is jerky, with many unexpected turns. Continuity comes at last with the lyrical second theme, heard first in the flute and then in the clarinet. Since this melody is developed immediately and contrapuntally, we know that the music has settled down — at least temporarily.

The youthful energy returns in the development section, when an interesting passage for solo strings turns unexpectedly into a demonic march. Again the movement tantalizes us with fragments.

The second movement begins with one of Shostakovich's typical scherzo tunes. There is greater continuity here than in the first movement, despite the dry humor of the melody. This music breaks off for a slower, more lyrical, almost oriental theme. There is an exciting transition, featuring the piano, back to the scherzo. Later the two melodies are played simultaneously, despite one being in 4/4 time and the other in 3/4. The contrasting coda is announced by three massive piano chords.

When the third movement turns out to be slow and lyrical, we understand how the symphony has moved by stages away from its original discontinuities. The music builds in intensity and seriousness. Its emotional center — indeed, the heart of the entire work — is a long, high violin solo.

With its frequent changes of tempo, the finale brings back some of the quirkiness of the first movement. After the impassioned yearning of the slow introduction, clarinets usher in the allegro. No section is allowed to continue very long before there is a major contrast. By the time we hear the march-like ending, the movement has built up considerable nervous energy.

Shostakovich was dissatisfied with the First Symphony. As he began to become involved with overt artistic experimentation, he came to feel that the piece was too traditional. His Second Symphony is a thoroughly modernist work, and the opera *The Nose* of 1915 flouts operatic conventions at every turn. But it is the First Symphony, not these avant-garde experiments, that has endured. For a long while it was believed that the Soviets had suppressed the radical works of

Shostakovich's youth. But now, even after the Second and Third Symphonies and *The Nose* are available, most audiences and musicians still prefer the youthful vigor of the First Symphony.

Symphony Number 5 in D Minor, Opus 47

Moderato. Allegro non troppo. Largamente.
Moderato
Allegretto
Largo
Allegro non troppo. Allegro

The Fifth Symphony was composed in 1937 and first performed by the Leningrad Philharmonic Orchestra, conducted by Yevgeny Mravinsky, on 21 November 1937.

Soviet artists were first confronted with the doctrine of Socialist Realism in 1933. Initially a literary idea, it soon spread to the other arts. The Soviet Composers' Union printed an article that attempted to apply the concept to music: "The main attention of the Soviet composer must be directed towards the victorious progressive principles of reality, towards all that is heroic, bright, and beautiful. This distinguishes the spiritual world of Soviet man and must be embodied in musical images full of beauty and strength. Socialist Realism demands an implacable struggle against folk-negating modernistic directions that are typical of the decay of contemporary bourgeois art, against subservience and servility towards modern bourgeois culture."

It was not long before the Union of Composers' naïve interpretation ran up against the government's version of Socialist Realism. Shostakovich's opera *Lady Macbeth of Mtsensk* (the title character is not related to Shakespeare's) had been such a success at its 1934 premiere that it subsequently played over a hundred times to packed houses. But when Stalin came to a performance early in 1936, he left the theater in a rage. Soon an editorial condemning the opera and its composer appeared in the official newspaper *Pravda*. The article, apparently dictated by Stalin himself, was harsh:

The listener is shocked from the first moment of the opera by an intentionally dissonant, muddled flood of sounds. Fragments of melody, embryos of musical phrases, appear — only to disappear again in the crashing, grinding, and screeching. Following this "music" is difficult, remembering it is impossible. It is built on the premise of rejecting opera. . . . Here we have "leftist" confusion instead of natural, human music. . . . The danger of this trend to Soviet music is clear. . . . Leftist distortion in opera stems from the same source as leftist distortion in painting, poetry, teaching, and science. Petty-bouregois innovations lead to a break with real art, real science, and real literature. . . . All this is coarse, primitive, and vulgar. The music quacks, grunts, and growls, and it suffocates itself in order to express the amatory scenes as naturalistically as possible.

Stalin was objecting to the dissonance, although it was not excessive; he was taking exception to the portrayal of the masses as squalid, yet the libretto is essentially a dismissal of pre-revolution Russian morality. What no doubt most offended him was the work's blatant sexuality, which is capped by a rape scene in which the orchestral accompaniment is so suggestive that it has been called "pornophony." The important point is that Stalin felt he could condemn a work for its allegedly anti-social overtones. His power was more than that of a music critic: the threat to Shostakovich was quite real. Soon came another blow: a *Pravda* article opposed to his ballet music. The composer, expecting to be arrested, actually kept a small suitcase packed to take into imprisonment. He feared for his own safety and that of his newborn daughter.

Stalin was shrewd enough to understand the political power of art. Echoing the ideas of Socialist Realism, he demanded that music reflect and thus promote the optimistic spirit of the Soviet people. He was quite willing to destroy individual artists — whether literally or figuratively — who did not cooperate. He dismissed the music of Shostakovich as "formalist." The term, strictly speaking, refers to art in which there is more form than content, art that is impotent because it adheres to abstract rules but has no soul. But Soviet politicians used the word to refer to art that is contrary to the Party's purposes. In dismissing Shostakovich's music as formalist, Stalin meant that it was modernistic, decadent, overly Westernized — all qualities seen by the Soviet leader as in direct opposition to Socialist Realism.

Stalin stopped short of having the composer arrested, but Shostakovich knew full well that Stalin allowed the right to work only to those artists who submitted to his will. In the eyes of the government, Shostakovich was a disgraced composer. He kept largely to himself, composed little, and even cancelled the premiere of his Fourth Symphony (although it had had ten rehearsals) for fear that its harsh dissonances and complexities would anger Stalin even more. Shostakovich hid behind the excuse that it was an inadequate work, but, when he finally allowed it to be played in 1962, he did not change a single note.

The composer wrote next to nothing for well over a year. He finally summoned his courage to produce the Fifth Symphony. Its subtitle is ironic: "A Soviet Artist's Reply to Just Criticism." The work does strike out in a new direction, away from the complexities of the condemned works, but it does not totally embrace the forced optimism of Socialist Realism. The Fifth is a tragic work, yet the Soviets had demanded optimism in art. They denounced formalism, yet the Fifth is as rigorously formal as any Shostakovich symphony. They wanted folk music, but there is none in the symphony. The composer used the subtitle to conceal the fact that he had not capitulated, had not churned out to mindless political art.

An audience that included the most distinguished members of Soviet society gathered to hear the disgraced composer's "Reply to Just Criticism." Many expected a scandal that would seal his fate forever. But the symphony was greeted with an enormously favorable response. Many in the audience wept openly. They wept not only for joy but also in response to the essential Soviet tragedy expressed in the music. And they wept because they realized that, whatever *Pravda* said, Shostakovich was *their* composer.

Years later the composer recalled,

> I will never believe that there are only idiots everywhere. They must be wearing masks — a survival tactic that permits you to maintain a minimal decency. Now everyone says, "We didn't know, we didn't understand. We believed Stalin. We were tricked, ah, how cruelly we were tricked." I feel anger at such people. Who was it who didn't understand, who was tricked? An illiterate old milkmaid? The deaf-mute who shined shoes on Ligovsky Prospect? No, they seemed to be educated people — writers, composers, actors. The people who applauded the Fifth Symphony. I'll never believe that a man who understood nothing could feel the Fifth Symphony. Of course they understood, they understood what was happening around them and they understood what the Fifth was about.

Even the seemingly exultant finale does not negate the tragedy at the symphony's core. Shostakovich replied, again much later, to the criticsm that the finale is not an apotheosis: "The rejoicing is forced, created under threat, as in *Boris Godunov*. It's as if someone were beating you with a stick and saying, 'Your business is rejoicing, your business is rejoicing,' and you rise, shaky, and go marching off, muttering, 'Our business is rejoicing, our business is rejoicing.' What kind of apotheosis is that? You have to be a complete oaf not to hear that."

Yet the symphony was a critical as well as a popular suuccess. It was enthusiastically received by the makers of official opinion. Why? Were the Soviet officials too stupid to realize that Shostakovich had not really capitulated? Perhaps. Or perhaps Stalin felt he had proved his point by threatening Shostakovich and that now the composer was useful as a national asset. At any rate, the official approval of his music left Shostakovich free to compose as he wished — at least until the next purge.

It is clear today, now that we have read the composer's memoirs, that he never fully gave in to the demands of Socialist Realism. He allowed his verbal statements — many not even actually written by him — to be used as propaganda. But his musical statements were full of the truth as he saw it: the Soviet people were oppressed and their optimism was superficial. Again and again the composer spoke the truth in the veiled language of music. He compromised when necessary, by accepting mindless criticism, speaking propaganda, withdrawing compositions from performance, and even composing nationalistic fluff from time to time. But never did he compromise in his serious compositions.

The Fifth Symphony is not a "reply to just criticism." It is indeed a reply to criticism, but as the criticism was unjust the reply is all the more impassioned. Curiously, Shostakovich came close to revealing the truth. An article published shortly before the premiere contains the expected proclamation of optimism, yet the underlying tragic nature of the symphony is alluded to as well. The article is titled, "My Artist's Reply":

> The theme of my symphony is the development of the individual. I saw man with all his sufferings as the central idea of the work, which is lyrical in mood from start to finish. The finale resolves the tragedy and tension of the earlier movements on a joyous, optimistic note.
>
> We are sometimes faced with the question of whether tragedy is even a legitimate genre in Soviet art. Here, however, genuine tragedy is often confused with resignation and pessimism. I think that Soviet tragedy has every right to exist. But the contents must be suffused with a positive inspiration like, for instance, the life-affirming pathos of Shakespeare's tragedies.

The long first movement opens powerfully with imitative music in the strings. They dominate for quite some time, thereby establishing the large proportions of the movement. Gradually a simply repeated-note rhythm is introduced — a quarter followed by two eighths — which becomes the underlying pulse in the faster section. The development builds in density, intensity, and tempo. This grim march continues to intensify as the snare drum plays the basic pulse rhythm incessantly. A unison restatement of the opening theme by the full orchestra forms the huge climax.

The scherzo is in part a parody of a theme from the Fourth Symphony, which Shostakovich may have believed would never be performed. This grostesque music, with its clarinet trills, violin solos, and waltz-like trio, recalls Mahler at his most macabre. The movement has humor to match the first movement's intensity, but neither succeeds in relieving the underlying pathos.

The slow movement, like the first, gradually rises in intensity. There is a beautifully delicate middle section, in which oboe, clarinet, and flute in turn play a lovely melody to the simple accompaniment of a violin tremolo. This tune returns at the end with a beautiful new sonority: harp harmonics plus celeste accompanied by a high violin tremolo.

The finale was supposed to dispel the tragedy of the earlier movements, but, as the composer eventually admitted, its gaiety is too forced to replace the earlier brooding. The movement is full of nervous energy, as one idea follows another quickly. The timpani, which open the movement, bring it to a triumphant close. Perhaps this ending signifies Shostakovich's personal triumph over artistic repression.

Symphony Number 7 in C Major, Opus 60, *Leningrad*
Allegretto. Moderato. Adagio. Allegretto
Moderato, poco allegretto
Adagio. Moderato risoluto. Largo —
Allegro non troppo. Moderato

The Seventh Symphony was begun in August 1941 and completed on 27 December 1941. Samuel Samosud conducted the first performance with the Bolshoi Theater Orchestra on 5 March 1942 in Kuibyshev, Russia.

It was in 1941, shortly after the outbreak of war between Hitler's Germany and Stalin's Russia, that the city of Leningrad began to know fear. The war was raging on the borders of the Soviet Union, and every day more young men from Leningrad left for the front. Those who remained behind worked hard fortifying the city. Shostakovich, who had sent his family to the safety of their country home, worked along with the rest.

In July a massive evacuation of Leningrad began. Shostakovich refused to go. He asked instead to be sent to the front, but his request was denied. He then volunteered for the civilian guard, but again he was turned down. He finally enlisted in the civil defense firefighters and was assigned to protect the Leningrad Conservatory.

On 29 August the attack began. Hitler was determined to destroy Leningrad completely. Shells and bombs fell everywhere, on both civilian and military targets. The nine-hundred-day siege had begun. Several times Shostakovich was given the chance to leave, but he refused. He did his duty as a firefighter, and he worked on the Seventh Symphony. During air raids he carefully took his manuscript with him to the shelter. He composed intensely and incessantly.

In September the composer spoke to his countrymen by radio:

An hour ago I finished scoring the second movement of my latest large orchestral composition. If I manage to write well, if I manage to finish the third and fourth movements, the work may be called my Seventh Symphony. In spite of the war and the danger threatening Leningrad, I wrote the first two movements quickly. Why am I telling you all this? I am telling you this so that the people of Leningrad listening to me will know that life goes on in our city. All of us now are standing militant watch. As a native of Leningrad who has never abandoned the city of my birth, I feel all the tension of this situation most keenly. My life and work are completely bound up with Leningrad.

A month later, after he had finished the third movement, Shostakovich wrote:

While I was working on this music, Leningrad was converted into an impregnable fortress. . . . It was with a feeling of admiration and pride that I watched the heroic deeds of the people of Leningrad. Despite frequent air raid alarms, everyone went about his work with precision and efficiency. . . . I have still to write the finale of the symphony, but its general outlines are already clear to me. I could describe it with one word — *victory*. . . . Never have I dedicated any of my works, but this symphony, if my work meets with success, I intend to dedicate to Leningrad. Every note in it, everything I have put into it, is linked with my native city and with these historic days of its defense against the fascist barbarians.

His family was back in Leningrad, and the composer feared for the safety of his wife and children. He at last decided to obey orders from City Defense Headquarters and leave for Moscow. He took the score of the symphony, but little else, and left. But Moscow too was in danger, so the family moved on to Kuibyshev. The composer's wife wrote, "For a long time my husband could not reconcile himself in thought to the necessity of leaving Leningrad. The intense battle for existence waged by his native city, the particularly close companionship under strenuous wartime conditions — all this made him suffer keenly in the unaccustomed safety of Kuibyshev, far from the front lines." It was there, in a cramped apartment, that the symphony was completed in late December.

Shostakovich wanted it performed by the Leningrad Philharmonic, but the siege made that impossible. The premiere took place instead in Kuibyshev, in early March. The performance was repeated in Moscow at the end of the month. The impact there was so great that the air raid warden could not bring himself to interrupt the performance or even the ensuing twenty-minute ovation to announce that sirens were sounding. The people knew that this was a symphony of victory, a symphony for the survival of Leningrad. It gave them courage and confidence.

The work was performed in many countries. In England sixty thousand listeners cheered it. There was considerable competition for the first United States performance. Arturo Toscanini, conductor of the NBC Symphony, had the power and financial resources of the National Broadcasting Company behind him. NBC arranged for a plane carrying a microfilm of the score and parts to fly from Russia across Europe's battlefields to New York. Toscanini was able to perform the American premiere on 19 July 1942. This historically meaningful performance may not have been impeccable, but it was almost as important to Americans as the world premiere had been to Russians. Many years later Shostakovich said, "Toscanini sent me his recording [of his first performance] of my Seventh Symphony, and hearing it made me very angry. Everything is wrong. The spirit and the character and the tempos. It's a lousy, sloppy hack job." The work was performed 62 times and broadcast 1934 times in the United States during that first season.

American poet Carl Sandburg published an open letter to Shostakovich on the occasion of the American premiere:

All over America last Sunday afternoon goes your Symphony No. 7, millions listening to your music portrait of Russia in blood and shadows. . . . On a long battlefront sagging toward Moscow the Red Army fights against the greatest war machine that ever marched into any country. . . . The outside world looks on and holds its breath. And we hear about you, Dmitri Shostakovich — we hear you sit there day after day doing a music that will tell the story. In Berlin no new symphonies, in Paris, Brussels, Amsterdam, Copenhagen, Oslo, Prague, Warsaw, wherever the Nazis have mopped up and made new laws, no new symphonies. . . . Your song tells us of a great singing people beyond defeat or conquest who, across the years to come, shall pay their share and contribution to the meanings of human freedom and discipline.

The most moving performance took place on 9 August 1942. There were only 15 members of the Philharmonic left in Leningrad, but they resolved to perform the symphony dedicated to their besieged city. The word went out throughout Leningrad for all musicians, from whatever groups, to assemble. One of the organizers recounted, "My God, how thin many of them were! How these people livened up when we started to ferret them out of their dark apartments. We were moved to tears when they brought out their concert clothes, their violins and cellos and flutes, and rehearsals began." A score was sent from Moscow in a medical transport plane, and conductor Karl Eliasberg, upon seeing that a huge orchestra was called for, realized that he still did not have enough musicians. The military command agreed to release the needed players from the front lines. A special order was given to knock out the enemy guns near the concert hall, so that the music could be heard. The concert took place, and it was broadcast as a ray of hope to the citizens of Leningrad.

The broadcast was prefaced by a brief speech: "In a few moments you will hear the Seventh Symphony by Shostakovich, our great compatriot, performed in Leningrad for the first time. The very fact that the Seventh Symphony is being performed in besieged Leningrad is a testimony to the indomitable spirit of the people of the city and their pluck, to their belief in victory and their willingness to fight to the last drop of blood to win. Listen, comrades! Now we are switching over to the hall where Shostakovich's Seventh Symphony will be broadcast!"

While the symphony was still new, the composer made several statements about its meaning. The following description is combined from these different sources:

The first movement of the symphony tells of the happy, peaceful life of a people confident in themselves and in their future. It is a simple life, such as was enjoyed by thousands of Leningrad's volunteer fighters, by the whole city, and by the whole country before the war broke out. Then comes the war. I have made no attempt at naturalistic interpretation of the war by imitating the drone of aircraft, the rumbling of tanks, artillery, explosions, etc. I wrote no so-called battle music. I tried instead to give an emotional image of the war. The exposition tells of the happy life of the people. A central place is given to a requiem in memory of the heroes who sacrificed their lives so that justice and reason might triumph. A single bassoon mourns the death of the heroes. The requiem is followed by an even more tragic theme. I cannot describe it. Perhaps it is the tears of a mother, or even that feeling which comes when sorrow is so great that there are no more tears. These two lyrical fragments form the conclusion of the first movement. The closing chords resemble the din of distant battle, a reminder that the war continues.

The second movement is a lyrical scherzo recalling happy episodes of the recent past. It is tinged with melancholy. The love of living, the wonder of nature — this is the meaning of the pathetic adagio which is the third movement, the dramatic center of the symphony.

The finale is devoted to a happy life in the future, after the enemy has been crushed. A moving and solemn theme rises to the apotheosis of the whole composition — victory.

Many years later, long after the emotions of wartime had died down, the composer revealed a somewhat different idea behind the symphony:

Everything that was written about those symphonies [the Seventh and Eighth] in the first few days is repeated without any changes to this very day, even though there has been time to do some thinking. After all, the war ended a long time ago, almost thirty years. Thirty years ago you could say that they were miliary symphonies, but symphonies are rarely written to order, that is, if they are worthy to be called symphonies. . . . The Seventh Symphony had been planned before the war and consequently it simply cannot be seen as a reaction to Hitler's attack. The "invasion theme" has nothing to do with the attack. I was thinking of other enemies of humanity when I composed the theme. Naturally, fascism is repugnant to me, but not only German fascism; any form of it is repugnant. . . . Hitler is a criminal, that is clear, but so is Stalin. I feel eternal pain for those who were killed by Hitler, but I feel no less pain for those killed on Stalin's orders. I suffer for everyone who was tortured, shot, or starved to death. There were millions of them in our country before the war with Hitler began.

The war brought much new sorrow and much new destruction, but I have not forgotten the terrible prewar years. That is what all my symphonies, beginning with the Fourth, are about, including the Seventh and Eighth. Actually, I have nothing against calling the Seventh the *Leningrad* Symphony, but it is not about Leningrad under siege; it is about the Leningrad that Stalin destroyed and that Hitler merely finished off.

We can never know what the real story behind the symphony was. Perhaps Shostakovich really intended to depict Leningrad attacked by Hitler and only in later years sought to make the symphony's meaning more universal. On the other hand, perhaps he did feel while writing it that is was about murder and destruction in general, and he allowed it to be associated with the siege of Leningrad because in that way it could help uplift the spirits of an oppressed populace. The true story does not really matter, because the symphony stands as a work of art that transcends the particular meanings its creator may have had in mind.

The middle section of the first movement is one of the most notorious passages in all symphonic music. Some people find it a grimly relentless expression of war, while others find it excessively banal. Béla Bartók found it so ludicrous, when he heard one of the early New York broadcast performances, that he included a parody of it in his Concerto for Orchestra. Shostakovich has a snare drum play a military figure again and again for no fewer than 280 measures, while the orchestra repeats a march theme over and over, gradually increasing the instrumentation until the full orchestra, including an extra brass section, is playing. Shostakovich may have meant in this passage to depict hordes of German soldiers marching toward Leningrad, although he did deny any graphic representation of war. Perhaps, on the other hand, he had in mind the increasing terror of war in general. Whatever the programmatic intent, the passage is powerful — not subtle, not even really beautiful, but certainly gripping. The most chilling moment occurs when the snare drum suddenly disappears, leaving only uncanny reminiscences of it at the end of the first and middle of the third movements.

Another unusual feature of the symphony is the number of extended woodwind solos. These sparsely accompanied, often elegaic lines suggest the intimacy of chamber music within this expansive symphony. These solos occur in all movements but the last. They involve piccolo, flute, clarinet, oboe, English horn, bass clarinet, and bassoon. Just as the first movement's march is purposefully overstated almost to the point of terror, so the composer almost overdoes the woodwind solos in order to make us pointedly aware of the tragic nature of this "Victory Symphony."

Symphony Number 8 in C Minor, Opus 65

Adagio
Allegretto
Allegro non troppo —
Largo —
Allegretto

The Eighth Symphony was composed in the summer of 1943 at Ivanovo, the summer retreat of the Union of Soviet Composers. Yevgeny Mravinsky conducted the premiere in Leningrad on 4 November 1943.

The career of Dmitri Shostakovich was a constant struggle with the vicissitudes of Soviet governmental policy towards the arts. His music continually went in and out of favor, as he repeatedly came up against the doctrine of Socialist Realism.

An early formulation of Socialist Realism (still considered valid in Russia today) was made by author Maxim Gorky in his 1933 essay "On Socialist Realism." Gorky called for works that express the spirit of the people and speak directly to them. It was not long before the government saw the political advantages of such an attitude. Art could be used to impose the will of the state, but first the artists had to be made to cooperate. In 1934 Andrei Zhdanov, an official of the Communist Party, made an address in which he endorsed Gorky's concept. Zhdanov demanded "works attuned to the epoch" and art depicting "reality in its revolutionary development." The newly formed Union of Soviet Composers embraced this doctrine as a statement of aesthetic purpose. Composers were "encouraged" to accept the precepts of Socialist Realism. Actually, they were left with little choice in the matter.

A few years after Shostakovich publicly (but never privately!) accepted Socialist Realism, Russia became involved in World War II. The composer embarked on a trilogy of wartime symphonies. Much of the Seventh was actually composed in the middle of the seige of Leningrad. Its performance in war-torn Leningrad was an inspiration to the embattled Russian people, who found it possible to hear in the symphony a picture of Hitler's march on Russia and his ultimate defeat. After the war the Seventh was widely performed as a symbol of victory. The composer's intentions were complex and even contradictory, but as far as the public and Stalin were concerned the Seventh was an excellent example of Socialist Realism. Then came the Eighth Symphony, the middle member of the wartime trilogy.

The war was now in its third year, and the composer was deeply troubled by it. His concerns came out in the new symphony. He could not write a victory symphony when there was no victory. He said, "In this work there was an attempt to express the emotional experience of the people, to reflect the terrible tragedy of the war." The symphony is tortured, not triumphant. As musicologist Boris Schwarz explains, "The Eighth represents the matured thoughts, more bitter, more resigned, and more strongly yearning for peace — for true peace, not a noisy victory celebration." Such a somber, depressive work could hardly please the government, which was struggling to keep up the morale of the embattled Russians. But Stalin and his subordinates were too concerned with the war to worry about Shostakovich's obvious flaunting of official policy. Furthermore, the worldwide success of the Seventh Symphony guaranteed his safety, at least temporarily.

According to the composer, the Eighth Symphony was in reality "an attempt to express the emotional experience of the people, to reflect the terrible tragedy of the war." The depression of a people at war in their own land infuses every movement of the Eighth. Since it was not a triumphant symphony like its predecessor, the Soviets were not totally pleased with it. But the Seventh had brought worldwide notoriety to Shostakovich, and everyone was eagerly awaiting the next installment in the wartime trilogy. CBS radio, for example, paid the Russian government $10,000 for the first American broadcast rights to the Eighth!

The meaning behind the Eighth was apparent to listeners in the West. They understood this plea against the horrors of war. Although the new symphony was not as popular as the Seventh, it was more profound and more respected. This fact spelled trouble for Shostakovich at home: the work that was condemned in Russia for its overt pessimism was hailed in the West as an anti-war protest. The seeds were thus planted for the purge of 1948. Shostakovich himself tells the poignant story of the Eighth Symphony and how it led to his downfall:

> The war brought great sorrow and made life very, very hard. Much sorrow, many tears. . . . I had to write about it; I felt that it was my responsibility, my duty. I had to write a requiem for all those who died, who had suffered. I had to describe the horrible extermination machine and express protest against it. . . .

The Seventh and Eighth Symphonies are my requiem. I don't want to linger on the brouhaha connected with these works. Much has been written about it, and from an external point of view this is the best known part of my life. And, in the final analysis, this brouhaha had fateful repercussions for me. . . .

You would think that the news that your music is enjoying success would bring nothing but pleasure, but I didn't have complete satisfaction. I was happy they were playing my music in the West, but I would have preferred that they talk more about the music and less about tangential matters. . . .

Stalin was incensed. Wendell Wilkie came to Moscow, when he was a presidential candidate. He was considered a big shot who could do much. He was asked about the second front and he replied, Shostakovich is a great composer. Mr. Wilkie, naturally, thought that he was an extremely deft politician: see how he got out of that one. But he didn't think about the repercussions for me, a living human being.

I think that was what started it. They shouldn't have made such a fuss over my symphonies, but the Allies fussed, and fussed deliberately. . . . Stalin hated the Allies and feared them. He couldn't do a thing with the Americans. But almost immediately after the war he dealt cruelly with his citizens who had had relations with the Allies. Stalin transferred all his fear and hatred to them. This was a tragedy for thousands upon thousands. A man received a letter from America and was shot. And the naïve former Allies kept sending letters and every letter was a death sentence. Every gift, every souvenir — the end. Doom.

And the most loyal wolfhounds shared Stalin's hatred of the Allies. They felt the scent. They weren't allowed yet to attack and go for the throat. The wolfhounds merely snarled, but it was clear. [Composer Tikhon] Khrennikov was one of the wolfhounds. . . . [A musicologist] was giving a lecture on Soviet composers and, in passing, praised my Eighth Symphony. After his lecture Khrennikov came up to him, bursting with rage. He was almost shouting. "Do you know whom you were praising? Do you? As soon as we get rid of the Allies we'll put your Shostakovich under our thumbnail! . . ."

The success of the Seventh and Eighth Symphonies was like a knife in the throat of Khrennikov and company. They thought that I was blocking their light, grabbing up all the fame and leaving none for them. . . . My fellow composers wanted to destroy me. And every report of the success of the Seventh or Eighth made me ill. A new success meant a new coffin nail.

If the political situation were not tense enough, Shostakovich also had to put up with the jealousies of other, more powerful, composers. It is no surprise that he refused to disclose the specific program of the Eighth Symphony. Just its somber nature alone got him into trouble, which was compounded by its popularity in the West. Western listeners understood well the lament of the long opening movement, the sardonic bitterness of the second movement, the obsessive violence of the third movement, the relentless litany of the fourth movement, and the sometimes serene, sometimes powerful, sometimes tentative hopefulness in the finale. Stalin and his henchmen knew that the West understood the symphony and that no amount of critical disapproval in the Russian press would matter. More drastic steps had to be taken to prevent the composer from revealing his message of Soviet despair to the world. The purge of 1948 became an inevitability.

Stalin called in Andrei Zhdanov, who had articulated the Party's position on art back in 1934. Unfavorable reviews began to appear; compositions that had previously been honored were now condemned. The purge was in progress. Zhdanov drew up a list of composers who were guilty of writing music against the spirit of the Russian people. Shostakovich and Prokofiev were at the top of the list. Zhdanov ordered all offending composers to a three-day "conference," during which their "crimes" were enumerated and public apologies were demanded.

The Eighth Symphony came in for particularly severe criticism. One of Zhdanov's henchmen declared, "There are still discussions around the question of whether the Eighth is good or bad. Such a discussion is nonsense. From the point of view of the people, the Eighth is not a musical work at all; it is a 'composition' which has nothing to do with art whatsoever."

Zhdanov claimed that "all the newspapers printed letters from the workers, who all thanked the Party for sparing them the torture of listening to the symphonies of Shostakovich. The censors met the wishes of the workers and put out a blacklist, which named those symphonies of Shostakovich that were being taken out of circulation."

From the purge of 1948 to the thaw that followed the death of Stalin in 1953, Shostakovich wrote no symphonies. Instead he was forced to compose film scores and patriotic pieces (he did write some important works in secret). In order to survive, he pretended to obey the doctrine of Socialist Realism. His public music of 1948–53 was simple, direct, tuneful, and accessible. But it is works like the Eighth Symphony that have lasted.

◆　◆　◆

Symphony Number 10 in E Minor, Opus 93
Moderato
Allegro
Allegretto
Andante. Allegro

The Tenth Symphony was begun in July 1953 and completed on 27 October 1953. Yevgeny Mravinsky conducted the premiere in Leningrad in 17 December 1953.

Soviet composers have always been concerned about their music's meaning, partly because their government, particularly under Stalin, has taken an active interest in what Soviet art signifies to the people. Soviet officials do not speculate about abstract musical meaning; no one asks the philosopher's question: what do you mean by "meaning"? Symphonies are believed to say particular things, and those things are either healthy or not.

Thus, for example, Shostakovich's Seventh Symphony was presented to the world as an optimistic prediction of Russian victory in the war against Hitler. The composer's next three symphonies were likewise topical, as they were written during and just after the war. But the recognized meanings of the Eighth, Ninth, and Tenth Symphonies were not always acceptable. The composer related the history of those works in his memoirs, *Testimony,* dictated to and edited by Solomon Volkov.

When the Eighth was performed, it was openly declared counter-revolutionary and anti-Soviet. They said, why did Shostakovich write an optimistic symphony [the Seventh] at the beginning of the war and a tragic one now? At the beginning of the war we were retreating and now we're attacking, destroying the Fascists. And Shostakovich is acting tragic; that means he's on the side of the Fascists.

The dissatisfaction gathered and rose; they wanted a fanfare from me, an ode; they wanted me to write a majestic Ninth Symphony. It was very unfortunate, the business with the

Ninth. I mean, I know that the blow was inevitable, but perhaps it would have landed later, or less harshly, if not for the Ninth Symphony. . . .

When the war with Hitler was won . . . everyone praised Stalin, and now I was supposed to join in this unholy affair. There was an appropriate excuse. We had ended the war victoriously; no matter the cost, the important thing was that we won, the empire had expanded. And they demanded that Shostakovich use quadruple winds, choir, and soloists to hail the leader. All the more because Stalin found the number auspicious: the Ninth Symphony.

Stalin always listened to experts and specialists carefully. The experts told him that I knew my work and therefore Stalin assumed that the symphony in his honor would be a quality piece of music. He would be able to say, There it is, our national Ninth.

I confess that I gave hope to the leader and teacher's dreams. I announced that I was writing an apotheosis. I was trying to get them off my back, but it turned against me. When my Ninth was performed, Stalin was incensed. He was deeply offended, because there was no chorus, no soloists. And no apotheosis. There wasn't even a paltry dedication. It was just music, which Stalin didn't understand very well and which was of dubious content. . . .

I couldn't write an apotheosis to Stalin, I simply couldn't. I knew what I was in for when I wrote the Ninth. But I did depict Stalin in music in my next symphony, the Tenth. I wrote it right after Stalin's death, and no one has yet guessed what the symphony is about. It's about Stalin and the Stalin years. The second part, the scherzo, is a musical portrait, roughly speaking. Of course, there are many other things in it, but that's the basis.

According to *Testimony*, Stalin worried more over symphonies and their dedications than over affairs of state. Thus Andrei Zhdanov, a Communist Party leader known for his ruthlessness, demanded that composers write only pieces that would uplift the spirit of the Russian people and declare to the world the optimism of the Soviets. Any music that contained hints of darker ideas, such as much of what Shostakovich had written during the war, was suppressed. Musical meaning could indeed be a dangerous thing!

Once Zhdanov's criticisms became official, no one — save a few courageous composers — questioned his authority to state what Shostakovich's symphonies meant. According to the composer, Zhdanov declared that the goal of music was to give pleasure, while our music was crude and vulgar, and listening to it undoubtedly destroyed the psychological and physical balance of a man. . . . All the papers printed letters from the workers, who all thanked the Party for sparing them the torture of listening to the symphonies of Shostakovich. The censors met the wishes of the workers and put out a blacklist, which named those symphonies of Shostakovich that were being taken out of circulation. . . .

Altogether this was called: The Party has saved music from liquidation. It turned out that Shostakovich and Prokofiev had wanted to liquidate music, and Stalin and Zhdanov didn't let them. Stalin could be happy. The whole country, instead of thinking about its squalid life, was entering mortal combat with formalist composers.

Shostakovich wrote no more symphonies until after Stalin's death. No sooner had the dictator died in 1953, however, than the composer was at work on the Tenth, his grim portrait of Stalin. With both Zhdanov and Stalin dead (Zhdanov died in 1948, possibly murdered by a jealous Stalin who laid the blame to Jewish doctors), the composer felt no need to compromise his musical language. He courageously allowed the far from optimistic symphony to be performed, although he guarded its secret meaning.

The work met with opposition. It was criticized for its complexity, predominantly somber mood, and denial of heroism. The Soviet Composers' Union debated whether it was sufficiently optimistic. A ludicrous compromise was reached, as the symphony was officially labeled an expression of "pessimistic optimism." Once again a politically expedient meaning had been grafted onto a Russian composition.

Eventually more substantial meanings became apparent. It really matters little to us today whether or not the Tenth Symphony is a picture of the life and times of Stalin, whether it is pessimistic or optimistic, or whether or not it could uplift the souls of Soviet workers in 1953. A third of a century after the fact we can separate history and art, politics and music. Today we hear a powerful and beautiful symphony without needing to concern ourselves with its extrinsic meanings. Perhaps the recent upsurge in interest in the music of Shostakovich has occurred because we can at last hear the true significance that lies behind the superficial meanings assigned to it by critics, government officials, and even the composer himself.

The first movement of the Tenth Symphony offers a fine example of its intrinsic meaning. It is a powerful, inexorable build from a quiet beginning to a series of shattering climaxes. It moves by gradual transformation of materials, not by overt contrast. After the climaxes it gradually subsides, returning to its opening material. It is an integrated statement of the "dramatic curve": a rise to a climax about two-thirds through the piece, followed by a period of gradual resolution. As we follow this curve of tension, we need not know or care what extramusical message, if any, this intense music is supposed to express. It emotional strength is immediate and indepedent of political or social meanings.

The middle two movements are both scherzos, one harsh and grotesque, the other genial and graceful. The second theme of the third movement is based on a four-note motive (also used in the First Violin Concerto) that is Shostakovich's musical signature: DSCH (the German equivalent of our D/E-flat/C/B), standing for D. Sch — Dmitri Shostakovich, abbreviated in German. This is an example of extramusical meaning about which the composer chose to reveal nothing, although we can guess that he was defiantly proclaiming his artistic identity once he was no longer forced to create anonymous Socialist Realist music. Yet the intrinsic significance far outweighs the programmatic implications of this bit of musical cryptography.

The DSCH motive also appears several times in the finale, most interestingly in four timpani just before the end. The movement is infused with dance-like and folk-like elements — a further enigmatic meaning?

Jan Sibelius

Born in Tavastehus, Finland, on 8 December 1865.
Died in Järvenpää, Finland, on 20 September 1957.

Concerto in D Minor for Violin and Orchestra, Opus 47
Allegro moderato
Adagio di molto
Allegro ma non tanto

The Violin Concerto was composed in 1903. Sibelius conducted the first performance with violinist Viktor Novacek in Helsinki on 8 February 1904. The revised version was introduced in Berlin by violinist Karl Haliř and conductor Richard Strauss on 19 October 1905.

It is not surprising that Sibelius should have composed several works for the violin, since as a young man he aspired to be a violinist. He even performed the first movement of the Mendelssohn Concerto while a student in Vienna. "My tragedy was that I wanted to be a celebrated violinist at any price. Since the age of 15, I played my violin for ten years, practically from morning to night. I hated pen and ink, and unfortunately I preferred an elegant violin bow. My preference for the violin lasted quite long, and it was a very painful awakening when I had to admit that I had begun my training for the exacting career of an eminent performer too late."

Between the composition of his Second and Third Symphonies, Sibelius wrote his Violin Concerto for Willy Burmester, former concertmaster of the Kajanus Orchestra. Burmester delayed playing the work, however, and Sibelius instead arranged for a performance by Viktor Novacek. Novacek, who was less accomplished than Burmester, was not quite up to the fiendishly difficult passages that had been composed with a great virtuoso in mind.

Critic Karl Theodor Flodin, a long-time supporter of Sibelius, reviewed the new work.

It is clear that the composer did not want to write one of those violin concertos which are really nothing but orchestral works with an *obbligato* solo part. He knows the fate of these modern concertos — to be played once and then set aside. . . . So he chose rather the other alternative — to let the soloist remain sovereign ruler the entire time, with a display of traditional pomp and circumstance. But here he collides with the whole solid mass of what has been said before, written before, and composed before. Impossible to come up with anything really new. And on that hidden reef the ship has foundered.

The composer took this criticism to heart and rewrote the concerto, giving greater prominence to the orchestra. The new version was dedicated to a young Hungarian violinist, Franz von Vecsey.

Still another soloist premiered the revised concerto. Karl Halíř, a member of the Joachim Quartet, played the work in Berlin under the direction of Richard Strauss. Sibelius was flattered that the famous composer would show an interest in his work, and he appreciated the care with which Strauss rehearsed. "As an instance of Strauss's extraordinary conscientiousness in performing the works of other contemporary composers," wrote Sibelius, "it should be mentioned that he had three rehearsals with just the orchestra for practicing the accompaniment. But the Violin Concerto needs it." Many years later Strauss is reported to have said, "I know more about music than Sibelius, but he is the greater composer."

Sibelius once advised a student, "I warn you against long preludes and interludes. And this refers especially to violin concertos. Think of the poor public!" Indeed, the violin enters after less than four measures of string oscillations. It plays a long, rhapsodic line, the first of three themes. There is no formal development section in this movement, since each theme is carefully developed when first stated.

The adagio opens with wind duets. The violin enters with a long, lyrical line in the low register. After an orchestral interlude the solo instrument plays complex two-voice counterpoint, in which the two parts have quite different rhythms — a true test of the soloist's musicianship and technique.

The second movement's repeated-note syncopations are transformed into the finale's long-short-short rhythm (the timpani contradict constantly with short-short-long). As in the first movement, the strings begin their repetitive accompanimental figure alone for a few measures before the solo violin enters with the main theme. The rhythmic vitality of the second theme is enhanced by a constant interplay between 6/8 and 3/4 meters. At the recapitulation the full orchestra plays an exciting transformation of the opening. Virtuosic runs in the solo violin end this flashy concerto.

Symphony Number 2 in D Major, Opus 43

Allegretto
Andante, ma rubato
Vivacissimo —
Allegretto moderato

The Second Symphony was composed in Rapallo, Italy, in 1901. It was premiered in Helsinki on 8 March 1902, on an all-Sibelius concert conducted by the composer.

Sibelius is generally considered the conservative among composers of the early twentieth century. It is easy to understand why he has earned this label if we compare his Second Symphony with some music by his more overtly revolutionary contemporaries. We do not find experiments in dissonance like those of Schoenberg, extreme compression such as that created by Webern, collages of free associations found in many works of Ives, or experiments in jagged rhythms such as those of Stravinsky's *The Rite of Spring*.

But if we compare Sibelius' Second Symphony of 1901 with music written at about the same time by these same composers, quite a different picture emerges. The boldly new formal procedures of Sibelius are not matched in Schoenberg's *Verklärte Nacht* of 1899, Webern's youthful tonal works from the turn of the century, Ives' Schumannesque First Symphony of 1898, or Stravinsky's traditional and academic Symphony in E-flat of 1905–07.

It is only the later paths that these composers took that makes Sibelius seem, by comparison, the conservative. The difference between these self-styled radicals and Sibelius is the difference between novelty and originality. The works of the Finnish composer are no less original than those by the composers who forged the novel twentieth-century musical language. The music of Sibelius never leaves traditional tonality, but it amply proves that it remained possible to say strikingly original things in the old idiom.

It is interesting to compare the Second Symphony with the music of another twentieth-century "revolutionary": Bartók, the only modernist whose music Sibelius respected. The surface sounds of the two composers are very different, but there are parallels nonetheless. Both composers seem all but unwilling (or unable?) to write extended melodic lines. They give the listener fragments, possibly strung together but still heard as individual units. In addition both were nationalists. That Bartók's music sounds Hungarian is hardly surprising, since he strove for a national style based on folksongs. Sibelius, on the other hand, rarely if ever quoted actual folk tunes, but he was as deeply concerned with his music's cultural identity as was Bartók. His dark, brooding music sounds distinctly Finnish. It has been suggested that the nationalistic sound of certain music comes from the pitch and rhythm patterns of its composer's native language. It is possibly not just a coincidence that Bartók and Sibelius share a fragmentary style and that the Hungarian and Finnish languages are related linguistically.

The fragmentation in Sibelius' style is the source of his original formal procedures. He once wrote, "It is as if the Almighty had thrown down the pieces of a mosaic from Heaven's floor and asked me to put them together." The first movement of the Second Symphony is an excellent example. Although tonally a sonata form, this movement has an additional structural logic. It starts not with the normal exposition of self-contained melodies but rather with a series of seemingly unrelated fragments, wisps of melody, mere implications of themes. These units are usually based on repeated notes or on a single sustained tone, and they often contain internal repetition. This single-minded effect is odd, perhaps unsettling, but it is intriguing. We anticipate and expect eventual continuity. As the movement progresses, certain fragments emerge as more important, since they are heard more often. Traditionally a development section breaks apart long themes into their constituent motives. Here the themes are already fragmented, so Sibelius begins instead to extend and join the pieces. Eventually they are integrated and continuity is achieved. This process is, in a certain sense, the opposite of traditional symphonic development.

The slow movement also utilizes the procedure of fragmentation. It opens with a long line that is not a melody but rather an accompaniment. When the real melody finally enters on the bassoon, it turns out to be a series of fragments. Real lyricism does begin to assert itself, but individual motives undercut this attempt at continuity.

The scherzo is built from a fragment of greatest simplicity: a repeated B-flat followed by a turn around that note. When the trio section arrives, this simplicity is carried to an extreme. Instead of the richly melodic statement we might expect in a normal third movement, we hear a note — again B-flat — repeated nine times (in the oboe). Even when this "melody" finally moves, it repeatedly returns to the same B-flat. The obsession of the fragments with repeating or returning to the same note recalls the single-mindedness of the first movement.

The scherzo is linked directly to the finale, not by transition or by the elimination of the pause between movements, but by the undermining of the final return of the scherzo material. The solemn opening of the finale enters imperceptibly but then builds momentum, so that the trio material can no longer withstand the oncoming movement. The third movement never really ends but rather is replaced by the finale.

The last movement contains an enormous crescendo to a huge climax. This procedure requires continuity: the symphony at last achieves a flowing melodic line. But even this tune is a series of repeating fragments strung together. The language of fragmentation is too thoroughly integrated into the symphony to be shaken off, even by this continual accumulation of intensity.

The Second Symphony marks the end of Sibelius' early romantic period, in which he felt the strong influence of Tchaikovsky. His formal procedures, based on fragmentation and recombination, have their first mature statement in this symphony. He continued to explore the expressive potential of fragmentation in later works, even after he abandoned the romantic aesthetic. That he chose to use tonality rather than atonality, that he preferred regular to changing meters, that he continued to explore logic rather than collage — these aspects of his conservatism are undeniable. Nonetheless, in the next quarter century, before he mysteriously ceased composing thirty years before his death, he created a uniquely original body of music. Ironically, both the great popularity his music achieved in the 1940s and the neglect it suffered in the '60s retarded a full appreciation of Sibelius' unique genius. Now that his compositions have returned to the concert hall with some frequency, we can hear without prejudice their special and unique qualities.

Symphony Number 4 in A Minor, Opus 63
Molto moderato, quasi adagio
Allegro molto vivace
Largo
Allegro

The Fourth Symphony was composed between January 1910 and 2 April 1911 in Järvenpää, Finland. Sibelius conducted the first performance on 3 April 1911 in Helsinki. He revised the work during the next few weeks, completing the final version on 20 May.

Shortly before beginning work on the Fourth Symphony, Sibelius scribbled in his diary, "A change of style?" Around 1907 he had left behind the romanticism of his first two symphonies and embarked on a period of experimentation. He was searching for an appropriately personal mode of expression. His new style may have been in part a result of serious illness. The Fourth Symphony does not chart the course of the disease; the music has no programmatic aspirations similar to those in Schumann's Second Symphony or Beethoven's A Minor String Quartet, which were inspired by recovery from poor health. Sibelius did not consciously, or even subconsciously, base the emotional connotations of the symphony on his feelings about his illness. The relationship between the music and his health was actually more specific.

The composer had throat cancer. After he underwent surgery to remove the tumor, he was ordered to give up smoking and drinking, both of which he had relied on all too heavily. He was forced to confront the fear of dying without the help of the artificial stimulants to which his body was accustomed. Previously, his cigars and wine had helped him focus on his work. Now, distracted by fears of death and unable to find solace in smoking or drinking, he found it difficult to concentrate. His work habits became different, and so did the resulting music.

"Stop worrying and get on with work!" he wrote in his diary. "Perhaps you will live a long time yet." Actually, he was destined to live another fifty years — without the "help" of tobacco or alcohol. He confided to the diary what he would admit to no one: he was suffering withdrawal symptoms. "Have been in hell. It's difficult to learn to work without stimulus. Yet it's a must."

During the 15 months he worked on the symphony, he repeatedly recorded his anguish over his inability to concentrate. It is plausible that the fragmentary nature of the symphony is an at least indirect result of his mental state. On 16 August 1910 he wrote: "When will I get this development finished, be able to concentrate my mind and have the stamina to carry it all through? I managed when I had cigars and wine, but now I have to find new ways."

He was all too readily taken away from his work by other projects. Several times he allowed major interruptions to interfere with composing. At the beginning of 1910 he was so consumed with financial worries that he was unable to work. In May he took time out to write a set of songs. In late September he traveled to Christiana and Berlin to conduct concerts of his music. In November he agreed to write an orchestral song for singer Aino Ackté's upcoming tour of Germany. Only after this new piece had been widely publicized, after he had spent several weeks working on it, and after he had taken time out for another concert tour, did Sibelius realize that he would not be able to complete it on time. He withdrew from the project, causing the promoter's annoyance, his own anguish, and the singer's anger.

Upon hearing the news, Ackté wrote: "Herr Sibelius, I am not accustomed to being treated in this fashion and being made a laughing stock. It would have been more honest if you had said right at the outset that the idea of Sibelius concerts abroad does not appeal to you. You would have saved me a great deal of trouble . . . and I would have been spared this ridiculous and embarrassing position."

Sibelius acted as much a prima donna as did Ackté. He did not respond to her letter, but wrote instead to a friend: "I leave the diva Ackté to drown in her publicity." The composer was subsequently incensed to read in the press that he had "just completed a great symphonic poem for voice and orchestra, which expert opinion has declared to be technically remarkable in its handling of the orchestra as well as being an extraordinarily effective piece."

Sibelius' inability to work intensively on the symphony continued. He wrote in his diary, "Can I not really succeed in focusing my powers? I regard this as an absolute must. But how to achieve it? But, my friend, take comfort from the fact that you must work in your own way. The results would be improved tenfold were your working methods more rational."

There is nothing quite so potent as a deadline to get a composer going. As the new symphony was scheduled to be performed on 3 April 1911, Sibelius managed to get it done and copied — on 2 April!

He conducted the premiere as part of a concert devoted exclusively to his music. He saved the new symphony for the second half of the program, after several of his popular tone poems. The new language of the Fourth puzzled the audience. After the final chords had ceased, there was only silence. The listeners had so little understood the music that they did not know the piece had ended. Finally there was some applause: Sibelius' confused admirers were too polite to hiss or boo. But the composer knew the enthusiasm was not genuine. His wife later recalled, "People avoided our eyes, shook their heads; their smiles were embarrassed, furtive, or ironic. Not many people came backstage to the artists' room to pay their respects."

The press was as baffled as the public. One sympathetic reviewer tried to explain the piece by giving a detailed program, purporting to demonstrate how the symphony portrays a mountain scene. Sibelius was horrified. Although the symphony was in fact originally conceived amid the inspiring mountains of Finland, the composer had been trying to distance himself from what he viewed as outmoded pictoral music. He had sought a new, abstract style, and yet it was being interpreted in the most concrete terms. He had sought universal meaning, and a widely read critic was trying to attach to the piece a very specific significance.

Another critic responded in another newspaper that the true importance of the symphony was both its reaction against the musical experimentation prevalent in Germany and France and at the same time its distance from the past. With this attitude the composer heartily agreed. The critic saw the symphony as "a sharp protest against the general trend in modern music. . . . One composes automobile-symphonies nowadays and operas with deafening sonorities, works that demand an apparatus comprising a thousand performers, all this without any aim other than to astonish the listener with what is new and alien. . . . [The Fourth is] the most modern of the modern, and in terms of both counterpoint and harmony, the boldest work that has yet been written."

Sibelius himself voiced similar sentiments when he called the symphony "a protest against present-day music. It has nothing, absolutely nothing of the circus about it." Against what "present-day" music was Sibelius reacting? Modernism had not quite yet burst upon the musical scene. Schoenberg's Five Pieces for Orchestra, for example, had yet to be heard; his even more revolutionary *Pierrot Lunaire* was not yet composed. The unknown Webern was just beginning to explore an aphoristic style, and his equally unknown friend Berg was composing his first experiments in atonality. Stravinsky's most revolutionary pieces still lay ahead of him. His *Firebird* was premiered while Sibelius was working on the Fourth Symphony, but the Finnish composer probably did not hear it. The "modern" music he was reacting against was such opulent late-romantic creations as Mahler's gigantic Eighth Symphony and the tone poems and operas of Strauss. In 1911 Sibelius was actually quite close to modernists such as Schoenberg, Berg, Webern, and Stravinsky. The Fourth Symphony is every bit as startling in its originality as their works from the same period. It is only later developments that cast Sibelius in the role of a conservative. The Fourth Symphony is his boldest statement, his most extreme and most modern conception, while these other composers' works of 1910–11 are merely steps along a path that led them within a few years to a massive redefinition of music.

The Fourth Symphony shares with modernist music a concern for economy. One interval — a particularly unstable one — dominates the symphony. It is the tritone, so called because it encloses three degrees of the scale. The tritone is unstable because it is the only interval that is the same whether inverted or not. It pervades the symphony, sometimes isolated and sometimes, as in the main theme of the scherzo, embedded within a melodic line.

The first movement is fragmentary. Wisps of music come and go, with only an occasional hint of a real melody. The music suggests more than it states. It is like a shadow of a fuller bodied music, like a ghost of bygone romantic opulence. It is disembodied, floating, ethereal, unconnected: an utterly unique piece. This feeling is created in part by a vague sense of key. This is not atonal music, but the title page's indication "in A minor" is more a fleeting reference than an organizing principle.

The first movement seems to float not only because of its nebulous tonality but also because it continually disguises the beat. Thus, when the second movement offers a real melody, with a true pulse, the effect is like being brought back to earth after a journey to another world. This rhythmic scherzo is not nearly as abstract as the opening movement. There is a real theme, and a just as real contrasting theme, and they do have the character of a scherzo, but they do not add up to a normal scherzo with trio. The movement seems to evaporate in midstream.

The fragmented slow movement is almost as nebulous as the first, although it is marginally more melodic. Its form is as enigmatic as that of the second movement.

The fast tempo of the finale may suggest greater stability at first, but it is illusory. This kaleidoscopic movement contains many contrasts. The orchestral color is enriched by the addition of a glockenspiel, which is often prominent. As in the first movement, syncopations often disguise the beat.

The ending is extraordinary. The music does arrive convincingly in A minor, and the piece does end rather than simply stop. But the last sounds are neither loud nor soft. They are marked *mf — mezzo forte*, medium loud. Small wonder that the first audience did not realize that the piece had ended! This strange ending is not a mere detail or idiosyncracy. The Fourth Symphony is possibly the only well-known orchestral work that neither dies away nor builds to a triumphant close. The unprecedented *mf* close is symptomatic of the utterly unique vision of this most unusual of symphonies.

The composer characterized the Fourth as "a psychological symphony" and as a "spiritualized symphony." While working on it, he noted in his diary: "A symphony is not just a composition in the ordinary sense of the word; it is more of an inner confession at a given stage of one's life." If the Fourth is a true glimpse into Sibelius' inner self, then he must have been a very special person.

Symphony Number 5 in E-Flat Major, Opus 82
Molto moderato. Allegro moderato
Andante mosso, quasi allegretto
Allegro molto. Un pochettino largamente

The Fifth Symphony was contemplated as early as 1912 and first completed in 1915. This preliminary version was premiered by conductor Robert Kajanus on the composer's fiftieth birthday, 8 December 1915. Sibelius began to rewrite after this performance, finally finishing the work in 1919. Sibelius conducted that version in November 1919.

Although its positive tone may imply otherwise, the Fifth Symphony gave Sibelius more trouble than any other work. The first version, which took three years to complete, displeased him. He made extensive revisions after the premiere in late 1915. A second version was performed in 1916, but still the composer was not satisfied. He planned to have the work ready for a 1917 performance, but World War I and then civil war in Finland kept him from working on it. As these wars cut off Sibelius' income from his German publisher, he had to compose small piano pieces and songs in order to earn a living. He returned to the Fifth after hostilities ended. The work found its final form in 1919.

It is a total contrast to the inner, nebulous Fourth Symphony. With the Fifth, Sibelius went back to the energetic world of the Second, but with noticeably greater sophistication. Leaving behind the Fourth's experiments with vague tonality, he cast the diatonic Fifth unambiguously in E-flat major.

Sibelius was intrigued by the concept of a movement. To what extent is a movement an independent piece, and to what extent is it an integral part of a larger whole? The manner in which the Second Symphony's third movement melts into the finale is an early indication of Sibelius' concern with this question. His casting of the Seventh Symphony in one continuous movement is his final solution. In the Fifth, each of the two outer movements acts like two movements combined into one. The first movement was, in fact, two separate movements in the symphony's first version. In its final form, the first movement begins with an expansive section that is far too long, too involved, and too stable to be an introduction. Just as it approaches an expected recapitulation, it gives way to a scherzo. This new section is almost a waltz, except for rhythmic irregularities in the accompaniment. The two sections are closely integrated, with one beat of the first part's 12/8 becoming the scherzo's 3/4 measure. The result is a brightening of mood without a literal tempo change.

The finale also functions as two movements, but they interpenetrate one another more than in the first movement. The perpetual motion that begins the finale sounds like a second scherzo, in a fast 2/4 time. This music gives way to a slower passage in which the measures are consistently grouped in threes. This grouping makes the music sound now like a slow 3/2, even though, as in the first movement, the actual tempo has not changed. The scherzo returns, followed by a peroration in the slower tempo, now finally written in three-two time.

Between these two double movements lies the andante, an intermezzo that is essentially a set of variations on a simple theme.

The ending of the symphony is unusual. The slower idea of the finale takes over, gradually building in sound and intensity. The tension mounts to the breaking point, and then the music does just that: it breaks. A movement that has been characterized by continuous sound, particularly during the final build, at last admits silence. Sustained sound has become almost excessive. Several isolated, full, short chords punctuate the silence, as this most extraordinary of symphonies ends in a most extraordinary manner.

Symphony Number 7 in C Major, Opus 105

The Seventh Symphony was planned in 1918. Sibelius set to work in earnest while on a trip to Italy in March 1923; the piece was completed on 2 March 1924. The composer conducted the premiere in Stockholm on 24 March 1924.

Sibelius is not generally thought of as an innovator. He never indulged in the extravagantly original orchestral colors of Richard Strauss; he never experimented with new harmonies to the extent that Claude Debussy did; he was never interested in the emotionally charged dissonances of Arnold Schoenberg or the massive collages of Charles Ives (both of whom he outlived); he was never attracted to the exciting new rhythms of Igor Stravinsky. Yet, in his own quiet way, Sibelius was an original composer. His innovations were more subtle than those of his contemporaries. Sibelius experimented with form: using traditional sounds he found new ways to integrate large-scale compositions. His interest in new means of continuity and development is evident as early as the Second Symphony; it reaches its culmination in the one-movement Seventh Symphony.

Sibelius was not the only composer to recast a traditionally multi-movement form as one continuous piece. Several earlier composers wrote symphonies in which the individual movements are not separated by pauses (in Schumann's Fourth Symphony, for example, the beginning of one movement follows immediately the end of the preceding one). Eliminating a pause is a simple matter; replacing it with a transition (as in Beethoven's Fifth Symphony) is a more sophisticated procedure. Some composers went beyond inter-movement transitions and telescoped two movements into one (in Franck's D Minor Symphony the slow movement includes a scherzo interlude). Other composers tried to cast a traditional three- or four-movement form continuously: in Schubert's *Wanderer* Fantasy we hear opening movement, adagio, scherzo, and fugal finale compressed into a single piece; a similar procedure is found in Liszt's Second Piano Concerto and Schoenberg's First String Quartet and First Chamber Symphony.

These earlier pieces, though interesting and original, do not go as far as the Sibelius Seventh, which is a thoroughly symphonic composition in one continuous movement that does not readily subdivide into independent sections. It is a sweeping, concentrated, highly integrated work. There are elements of sonata form and of rondo form, but it is a useless mental exercise to try to make the Seventh fit such traditional molds. Several analysts have tried, and — significantly — they all came up with different ways to subdivide the symphony.

The composer was reluctant to call the work a symphony at first, so far removed is its structure from that of a typical classical symphony . At its premiere it was listed as *Fantasia sinfonica*. Only later did Sibelius realize that its scope warranted its inclusion in his symphonic canon. We should not be perplexed by the lack of common characteristics between a classical symphony and the Sibelius Seventh. What the music is counts far more than what the composer chose to call it. The word "symphony" originally referred to a form, but by 1924 it indicated more a genre. It suggested a degree of seriousness, a stature, a grandness, but no longer a structural mold.

Sibelius once spoke about the nature of a symphony with another composer who redefined symphonic form — Gustav Mahler. Sibelius later recalled that "contact between us was established in some walks during which we discussed all the great questions of music very thoroughly from every angle. When our conversation touched on the nature of the symphony, I said that I admired its style and severity of form and the profound logic that created an inner connection between all the motives. This was my experience in the course of my creative work. Mahler's opinion was just the opposite. 'No! The symphony must be like the world. It must be all-embracing.'" The severity, the restrictions, the tightly controlled structural logic of Sibelius' Seventh Symphony (qualities that necessitated a one-movement form) are the aesthetic opposite of the sprawling, visionary panorama of, for example, Mahler's Third Smphony. And both these symphonies are equally far removed from the classical forms of Mozart and Haydn.

Sibelius was correct to speak of an inner logic of motivic connection. The Seventh Symphony contains several independent motives, such as the rising scale that opens the work, that pervade the music. These motives are subjected to variation and development, but they are rarely expanded into complete melodies. The one outright melody is the powerful trombone solo that is heard in three different places. Each time it is treated in a magnificently contrapuntal fashion that leads to a wonderfully climactic intensification. Notice how, at its first appearance a few minutes into the symphony, the trombone sound cuts through the entire orchestra. And notice the wonderfully expansive music the orchestra is playing: after a certain tonal tentativeness, the music has at last reached its home key of C major with a wonderful sense of stability. The increasing complexity of the counterpoint on subsequent appearances of the trombone theme recalls the music of the sixteenth-century composer Giovanni Palestrina, whom Sibelius greatly admired and carefully studied.

Tapiola, Opus 112

Tapiola *was composed in 1926. Walter Damrosch conducted the world premiere with the New York Symphony Society on 26 December 1926.*

Sibelius was at the height of his professional career when he composed *Tapiola*. A few years earlier, for example, he had negotiated with George Eastman for a position as Professor of Composition at the newly formed Eastman School of Music in Rochester, New York. The composer, who had been in this country to receive an honorary doctorate from Yale University in 1914, demanded — and was to receive — the incredible salary of $20,000 for nine months, with half paid in advance, plus $12,500 for conducting concerts of his own music. The deal was concluded, but Sibelius backed out at the last minute, actually *after* the newspapers in Rochester had announced his impending arrival. He really had no interest in teaching.

Sibelius was riding the crest of worldwide fame when he suddenly stopped composing. When he completed *Tapiola* in 1926, he was 61 years old, yet in his remaining thirty years no music of major proportions appeared. After *Tapiola* he fell silent, except for an occasional small piece. As he ceased composing, he also became reclusive, curtailing his conducting and traveling.

No one knows why Sibelius stopped. Others have given up composing long before their deaths (Rossini, Glazunov, and Ives are prime examples), while some composers (most notably Verdi, Strauss, and Stravinsky) have produced some of their finest works in their eighties. It is fascinating to speculate on the psychological factors involved, but every composer has his own reason for composing or not composing. Did Sibelius lose his confidence? Did he feel that his life's work was complete? Did he believe that his tonal music was too old-fashioned compared to the atonality of Schoenberg, Berg, Stravinsky, and Bartók? Or did the composer's creativity simply dry up, replaced by a tragic sterility?

Throughout his late years there were continual rumors about an Eighth Symphony. In his 1931 biography of the composer, Cecil Gray writes, "The Eighth Symphony . . . has been completed and will probably be produced before this book sees the light." In 1932 the Sibelius Society in England announced that the Eighth would be included in a forthcoming series of recordings of the Sibelius symphonies. Also in 1932 the Eighth was promised to conductor Serge Koussevitzky, to conclude his Sibelius cycle with the Boston Symphony. In 1945 Sibelius told Basil Cameron that the work was finished; Cameron claimed to have seen the score. Yet no new symphony was published or performed. Some biographers have suggested that Sibelius actually did compose some of the work but then destroyed it because it did not measure up to his high standards.

A few years before his death, Sibelius was visited by Otto Andersson, Director of the Sibelius Museum, who gently broached the "forbidden question." Andersson had recently been to the United States, where many people had asked about the Eighth Symphony. "If I return to America, what shall I tell them?" Sibelius responded, "Yes, what shall you tell them? What shall you tell them?" After an embarrassed silence, the composer's wife said, "Tell Professor Andersson the truth. There is no Eighth Symphony." Sibelius responded, "That's right. There is no Eighth Symphony." And, once he had uttered those words, the face of the aged former composer brightened, as if a heavy burden had at last been removed.

The long silence of Sibelius' golden years is particularly mystifying in light of his last major work. If *Tapiola* had shown signs of a falling off of the composer's imagination or technique, then it might be understandable that he was reluctant to continue composing. But *Tapiola* is regarded by many as the greatest music ever to come out of Finland. It is wonderfully original and extraordinarily well crafted. Could it be that Sibelius was afraid that any subsequent piece would be destined to fall short of *Tapiola*?

The inspiration behind *Tapiola* is nature. Tapio is the god of the forest in Finnish mythology. Biographer Robert Layton likens the work to Debussy's *La mer*: "One does not have to have experienced the vast forests of Scandanavia, with all their variety of moods, colors, and sounds, their immense loneliness, their magic, terror, and majesty, for Sibelius' vision in *Tapiola* to make its impact. . . . It is as perfect an evocation of the forest as *La mer* is of the sea."

Sibelius prefaced the score with the following lines:

> Widespread they stand, the Northland's dusky forests,
> Ancient, mysterious, brooding savage dreams;
> Within them dwells the Forest's mighty god,
> And wood-sprites in the gloom weave magic secrets.

At the start, strings present a fragment — not enough music to be a full-blown theme, but too much to be only a motive. This seemingly unpromising figure is destined to pervade the entire work. It is a hallmark of Sibelius' command of compositional craft and of his unique vision that he is able to build an entire work from such an apparently nondescript fragment. Statements of this figure are separated by sustained chords or silences, which also carry implications for the work's future: it will involve monolithic sustained harmonies. Notice the bittersweet sonority of the basic figure when played by violas subdivided into four-part harmony.

Tapiola's great originality lies in the way it takes two simple ideas — a small figure and sustained chords — and builds from them an entire dramatic structure. The fundamental importance of these two ideas is made clear by the fascinating process of the opening section. The basic figure gradually recedes in prominence as the background chords come to the fore. The music suggests a visual analogy, an optical illusion in which figure becomes ground as ground becomes figure. Thus the entire opening passage is concerned more with the unfolding and transformation of sonorities than with such traditional elements as melody or rhythm.

Eventually high strings and winds usher in a sprightly, staccato, scherzo-like passage, based on the main figure. Even now, however, the chordal element is present, again relegated to the background.

The main figure eventually reaches a climactic statement in the brass, which in turn ushers in an allegro. Even the change of tempo, however, does not dispel the chords and their special atmosphere.

Intensity mounts. A second allegro arrives, this time with constant string tremolos. The strings produce an enormous crescendo, leading to the second triumphant brass statement of the main figure. From there to the end chords predominate, despite frequent appearances of variants of the main figure. By the end only chords remain.

The final sonorities are as unusual as is the idea of ending a piece with sustained chords. These chords are densely spaced at the bottom and more open at the top — the exact opposite of the way harmonies are traditionally scored. Thus ends an extraordinarily unique work — and a major compositional career.

Richard Strauss

Born on 11 June 1864 in Munich.
Died on 8 September 1949 in Garmisch.

Also Sprach Zarathustra, Opus 30

Zarathustra *was composed between 4 February and 24 August 1896. Strauss conducted the first performance on 27 November 1896 in Frankfurt.*

Glorification of the individual was a fundamental tenet of nineteenth-century German romanticism. In music this idea originated with Beethoven — both the man and his compositions. The first major composer to break away from the patronage system, he saw himself primarily as an independent artist and only secondarily as a servant of nobility. His music was expressive of individual emotions and values to an unprecedented degree. Subsequent composers emulated Beethoven the free-spirited artist as they attempted music of ever increasing individuality. The idiosyncratic musical personality of Berlioz, the megalomania of Wagner, and the unique world-view of Mahler are just some expressions of romantic individuality.

Romanticism was primarily a literary movement, although it affected all the arts. Philosopher Friedrich Nietzsche (1844–1900) was a romantic. He was deeply influenced by the ideas and the personality of Wagner, at first respecting and later rejecting the composer-dramatist's values. One of Nietzsche's major works is the book *Also Sprach Zarathustra* ("Thus Spake Zarathustra"), in which the ancient seer Zarathustra, or Zoroaster, delivers a series of pronouncements for mankind. Nietzsche glorifies the individual in the figure of the prophet and also in Zarathustra's concept of the *Übermensch,* or Superman — a recurrent theme throughout the book:

And Zarathustra spake thus unto the people: I teach you the Superman. Man is something that is to be surpassed. What have ye done to surpass man? All beings hitherto have created something beyond themselves: and ye want to be the ebb of that great tide, and would rather go back to the beast than surpass man? What is the ape to man? A laughing-stock, a thing of shame. And just the same shall man be to the Superman: a laughing-stock, a thing of shame. Ye have made your way from the worm to man, and much within you is still worm. Once were ye apes, and

697

even yet man is more of an ape than any of the apes. Even the wisest among you is only a disharmony and hybrid of plant and phantom. But do I bid you become phantoms or plants? Lo, I teach you the Superman! The Superman is the meaning of the earth. Let your will say: the Superman *shall be* the meaning of the earth!

Zarathustra's striving for perfection and transcendence is not really an idea of the sixth century B.C., when Zoroaster actually lived, but rather is related to the late nineteenth-century concepts of progress and the individual. To us such ideas may seem naïve, but a century ago they spoke of very real cultural concerns. They appealed to a composer such as Richard Strauss, who saw himself as a master craftsman transcending his past and leading music on to ever greater heights. He was the composer who in 1898 celebrated himself as genius in *Ein Heldenleben* ("A Hero's Life"). And it was he who dared to compose a symphonic poem around the figure of Nietzsche's hero.

What ultimately happened to the cult of the genius, to the adulation of the individual? In the twentieth century there was an inevitable reaction, as art became more objective. But there was also an intensification of the romantic ideal. It became an obsession, a neurosis, and finally a madness. Adolf Hitler saw himself as a Superman. He knew of Hegel's concept of "world-historical" individuals, "heroes" charged to carry out the will of the world. Hegel believed such persons were above common morality. Hegel's concept led to Nietzsche's, and Hitler identified both with the amoral world-historical hero of Hegel and with the Superman of Nietzsche. What had started as an idealization of the individual reached a *reductio ad absurdum* in the maniacal butcher of twentieth-century Europe. Nietzsche's philosophy and Strauss' musical interpretation of it (both of which appealed to Hitler) were but steps along the way, innocent in themselves yet, seen in retrospect, inevitable components in the destruction of the very culture that had produced them.

Today, Strauss' *Zarathustra* has a new meaning. It is a symbol no longer of the Superman, but of knowledge and mystery. The source of this symbol is not a book written in 1884–85, but a Hollywood film of the late 1960s. Stanley Kubrick's *2001: A Space Odyssey* used as a recurrent leitmotif the opening twenty measures of the tone poem. The music is associated with a mysterious monolith that appears on earth in prehistoric times, on the moon at the beginning of the space age, and on Jupiter in an infinity beyond time. The monolith seems to contain all knowledge of the past and future, of good and evil. The popularity of this movie, and of the music associated with it, has replaced Strauss' dated symbolism with something appropriate to the late twentieth century. One possible conclusion to draw from this un-expected dénouement of *Zarathustra's* musical story is that Strauss' composition *is* philosophical, but that the philosophy it "expresses" is actually *independent* of the music. Perhaps *Zarathustra's* philosoph-ical meaning comes from its cultural context, from how particular cultural values — whether of late nineteenth-century German roman-ticism, mid-twentieth-century European tyranny, or late twentieth-century American science fiction — interpret it.

But just how philosophical *is* Strauss' tone poem? The composer, who was known to brag that he could portray anything in the or-chestra, understood that music is not a medium of philosophy. It could reflect the mood of Nietzsche's work and the character of Zar-athustra, and it could even depict a series of events. But there is no way music can convey complex ideas. Strauss realized music's limi-tations: "I did not intend to write philosophical music or portray Nietzsche's great work musically. I meant rather to convey in music an idea of the evolution of the human race from its origin, through the various phases of development, religious as well as scientific, up to Nietzsche's idea of the Superman. The whole symphonic poem is intended as my homage to the genius of Nietzsche, which found its greatest exemplification in his book *Also Sprach Zarathustra*."

According to Strauss' biographer, conductor Norman Del Mar, the tone poem responds to the book in three ways. (1) Strauss selected eight of Nietzsche's eighty chapter headings to suggest sections of the music. Each chapter is Zarathustra's brief discourse on a particular idea. (2) The opposition found throughout the book between immut-able nature and the progress of man is symbolized by the conflict between two keys, the "natural" key of C major (no sharps, no flats) and the distant B major. (3) The evolution of man from primitive being to Superman became the metaphor for the form of the entire tone poem.

Strauss prefaced the score with the opening of Nietzsche's book:

When Zarathustra was thirty years old, forsaking his home and the lake by his birthplace, he took to the mountains. There he enjoyed his loneliness, communing with his soul, and did not tire of this for ten years. But at last a change was wrought in his heart, and one morning he arose with the dawn and, turning to the Sun, addressed him thus:

Thou tremendous star, where would be thy happiness if thou hadst not those to whom thou givest light?

For ten years thou hast mounted to my cave and wouldst have been saturated with thy light and thy path, had it not been for me, my eagle, and my serpent.

But we awaited thee every morning and, having taken from thy overflow, we blessed thee for it.

Behold! I am weary of my wisdom, like a bee who has gathered too much honey. I need hands outstretched to partake of it.

I wish to lavish my knowledge on the earth, until the wise shall again rejoice in their folly and the poor in their riches.

Therefore I must descend into the depths, as thou dost in the evening, when thou disappearest behind the sea yet still sheddest light on the underworld, thou exuberant star!

The men to whom I descend say thou dost set, and I must set also. Therefore bless me, thou tranquil eye, which can yet look without envy on an almost intolerable happiness.

Bless the cup which will overflow, so that the golden water streams from it, carrying everywhere the reflection of thy bliss.

Behold! This very cup shall again become empty, and Zarathustra shall again become a man.

Thus began the descent of Zarathustra.

The music begins in the depths of darkness, with a low rumble in string basses, contrabassoon, organ, and bass drum. Then comes the sunrise, as four trumpets intone the Nature theme: a simple three-note rising figure. After day breaks with a tremendous C major cadence, the orchestra begins to sound the Spirit motive: also a rising figure, this time four notes of a triad. Significantly, the key shifts to B minor. After the Spirit motive is expanded to a complete theme in *pizzicato* low strings, two horns intone a quotation from the Gregorian chant Credo. This statement of belief is ironic, representing the dreaded (to Nietzsche and Strauss) dogma of the church, which supposedly has prevented man from spiritual evolution.

The strings begin an adagio that corresponds to Zarathustra's pronouncement "Of the Backworldsmen." This title plays on the more common name, "backwoodsmen." Nietzsche depicts the naïve religious faith of simple people as an impediment to spiritual growth. Zarathustra states that he once believed in God, and that then he saw the world as "colored vapors before the eyes of a divinely dissatisfied one. . . . The God whom I created was human work and human madness, like all the gods!" God and the heavenly world were created by weak and perishing men. The backworldsmen believe in God as salvation because their bodies are sickly, whereas Zarathustra preaches the healthy body as the true meaning of the earth. Strauss' music is an expression "of devout fervor, depicting the naïve emotional comfort through belief in a benevolent divinity, however man-inspired," according to Del Mar.

After an ecstatic climax, we arrive at a section entitled "Of the Great Longing." According to Del Mar, Strauss is suggesting "the Spirit of Man's first yearning towards self-emancipation from ignorance and narrow-minded superstition. . . . But Man's first bid for spiritual freedom [the Spirit motive is heard in bassoons and cellos, again in the key of B minor changing to B major] immediately brings him into conflict with Nature on the one hand [the English horn and oboes sound the Nature motive, stubbornly suggesting the key of C] and his self-imposed religious dogma on the other [the horns again sound the Credo quotation, and the organ quietly intones another liturgical melody, the traditional Magnificat]." Zarathustra proclaims the independence of the soul, to which man has given all.

After rushing figures in the strings, winds, and harps, a section called "Of Joys and Passions" commences. The music attempts to illustrate Zarathustra's ideas on how passions lead to virtues. "Once hadst thou passions and calledst them evil. But now hast thou only thy virtues: they grew out of thy passions. Thou implantedst thy highest aim into the heart of those passions: then became they thy virtues and joys. . . . All thy passions in the end became virtues, and all thy devils angels. . . . Man is something that hath to be surpassed: and therefore shalt thou love thy virtues — for thou wilt succumb through them." During the Joys and Passions music, the trombones blare forth a new motive, the Satiety theme.

The return of the Spirit motive in the low strings, as other instruments continue the Joys and Passions music, announces the section entitled "The Song of the Grave." Zarathustra cries out against lost youth and proclaims the triumph of the will.

The music dies down for a section labelled "Of Science." Strauss depicts learning with a learned fugue. Suggesting the keys of both C and B, incorporating the Nature motive, and containing all twelve tones of the chromatic scale, the fugue subject is stated again and again in the low strings. Subsequently, the music incongruously suggests a dance, but, after interruptions by the Nature theme, the fugue resumes, accompanied by rushing figures. The resumption section is called "The Convalescent."

Zarathustra sheds all external values and looks within himself for perfection. This intense search causes a catharsis, described with extraordinarily rich orchestration. The prophet must recover. Now he understands his mission on earth, and he descends once again from his cave to proclaim the Superman.

The ensuing section, "The Dance Song," grows out of the Nature motive. Nietzsche's chapter tells how Zarathustra comes upon some maidens dancing. He sings to them of the fickleness of wisdom and of life itself. The music is, surprisingly, a Viennese waltz, which is developed at great length. Perhaps Strauss is trying to suggest, beneath this incongruous facade, that the Superman is not a lofty or abstract being but resides within ourselves even in our most mundane activities. The music remains firmly in the key of C until it finally slips to B and then back: this waltz belongs to both nature and the human spirit.

The waltz builds to the final, climactic section — "The Song of the Night Wanderer" (Nietzsche's preliminary title for his penultimate chapter; he later renamed it "The Drunken Song"). Del Mar explains, "Zarathustra is surrounded by his disciples and interrupts their joyful dancing and demonstrations of affection by passing through a kind of drunken fit. He recovers just as the Great Bell begins to toll and quietly interprets the solemn strokes by rhapsodizing line by line around the poem 'O Man, Take Heed'":

> O man! Take heed!
> What saith deep midnight's voice indeed?
> "I slept my sleep —
> "From deepest dream I've woke, and plead: —
> "The world is deep,
> "And deeper than the day could read.
> "Deep is its woe —,
> "Joy — deeper still than grief can be:
> "Woe saith: Hence! Go!
> "But joys all want eternity —,
> "— Want deep, profound eternity!"

The tone poem closes with a peaceful coda, disturbed only by the Satiety motive. The tonality is B major, the key of man's progress toward the Superman, but chords belonging to C major, the key of unchangeable nature, begin to intrude toward the end. The actual ending is an astonishing stroke of musical imagination. *Pizzicato* C major arpeggios in the low strings alternate with sustained B major chords in the high winds and strings. Isolated C's have the final word, but ultimate resolution is denied.

Del Mar again: "Nietzsche ends on a note of climax with the idea of 'Eternal Recurrence.' Zarathustra emerges from his cave in the last lines, glowing and strong in the spirit of a new dawn for his life's work. Such a conception has no place in Strauss' musical scheme, and he closed his tone poem in a mood of utter tranquillity, but showing the conflict between Man and Nature basically unresolved and as irreconcilable as the two nearest and yet harmonically so distant keys of B and C."

Death and Transfiguration, Opus 24

Death and Transfiguration *was begun late in the summer of 1888 and completed on 18 November 1889. Strauss conducted the first performance at Eisenach on 21 June 1890.*

Love and death (in addition to being the subjects of a Woody Allen film) are two passions that captured the imaginations of many artists in the nineteenth century. It was a time of overt emotions, a period of confrontation with the darker side of the human psyche, an era when passions ran high (in the arts, although certainly not overtly in Victorian society). The end of the century saw the beginning, in the work of Sigmund Freud, of a series of extraordinary theories of the mind. Freud postulated the pervasiveness of sexuality and of the death wish: love and death. Thus it is hardly surprising to find a composer such as Strauss, growing up in the emotionally charged atmosphere of the late nineteenth century, expressing comparable themes in his first two mature compositions. *Don Juan* is based on a character who pursued his passions but eventually succumbed to his inner wish for destruction; *Death and Transfiguration,* his next major work, takes as its theme a dying man who recalls the great loves in his past. (Interestingly, Strauss turned to a third human emotion — humor — for his next tone poem, *Till Eulenspiegel.*)

For a long time it was believed (and even reported in Strauss biographies) that *Death and Transfiguration* had been inspired by the composer's bout with a serious illness. But, in fact, the illness came several months after the completion of the music. The literary program actually came into existence not only after the illness but also several months after the composition of the tone poem, when Strauss asked his friend Alexander Ritter to write a poem to convey the meaning of the music. This overblown program-in-retrospect tells us less about the music than does Strauss' own explanation in a letter:

> The idea occurred to me to represent the death of a person who had striven for the highest ideal goals, therefore very possibly an artist, in a tone poem. The sick man lies in bed asleep, breathing heavily and irregularly; agreeable dreams charm a smile onto his features in spite of his suffering; his sleep becomes lighter; he wakens; once again he is racked by terrible pain, his limbs shake with fever — as the attack draws to a close and the pain subsides he reflects on his past life, his childhood passes

before him, his youth with its striving, its passions, and then, while pain resumes, the fruit of his path appears to him, the idea, the Ideal which he has tried to realize, to represent in his art, but which he has been unable to perfect, because it was not for any human being to perfect it. The hour of death approaches, the soul leaves the body, in order to find perfected in the most glorious form in the eternal cosmos that which he could not fulfill here on earth.

When Strauss' biographer Norman Del Mar compared this program with the music, he found that the tone poem quite carefully reflected the intended meaning. His description of *Death and Transfiguration* appears in the published score:

The work begins with ... the sporadic pulse and heart-beat of the ill man being suggested by an irregular figure given alternately to strings and timpani. The sighs of the sufferer are also graphically portrayed by the strings, together with a pathetic little upward twist on the flutes. The color then changes and the figure on the bed takes on a human personality. New themes are presented on flute and oboe, after which the music of suffering returns. A modulation brings the warmer colors back; the sufferer is still smiling gently as he remembers scenes of his childhood. . . .

Suddenly the sufferings take a violent turn and the ill man can be heard writhing in agony. The music paints vividly his struggles with the savage onslaught of his affliction. . . . A climax is built up, at the peak of which the principal subject of the allegro is announced in tones of stern resolution. This defiant gesture represents the invalid's determination to withstand the threatening approach of death. . . . With a superhuman effort the invalid summons his remaining strength and the most important motive of the work is heard for the first time, the theme of the artist's Ideology. . . .

[There ensues] a series of tableaux representing the different phases of his life beginning with his childhood, portrayed by themes from the introductory section of the work. The personality of the man is shown to be guilelessly present already in the child.

A short burst of pain, and . . . [then] a picture of the dashing young fellow he has now become, full of hope and vigorous aspiration. This tableau ends in a tremendous sweep on the violins which plunges the music headlong into a furiously passionate love-scene. Higher and higher it soars until the sheer memory causes the invalid the most terrible heart palpitations. . . .

There is a brief pause; then gently and with trepidation the dying man tries to evoke the fervent memories once more, but each time he brings on the fearful hammer-blows in his chest. . . . [He recalls] the magnificent moment when his ideals first present[ed] themselves to him in all their glory. There are three widely spaced statements of the Ideology theme as the artist's vision strengthens until, at the third statement, it boils over into an ecstatic afterphrase.

But the effort has been too great and the whole vision drains away, leaving nothing behind but the scene of the invalid in his bed. . . . The palpitations return with renewed ferocity, and with an upward slither the music fades as death brings relief to the sufferer; the moment of expiry is marked by the entry of the tamtam. . . .

Little by little out of the obscurity the opening figure of the Ideology theme emerges on each of the four horns in turn. . . . It is joined by the oboe melody from the introduction, now on the strings in an ever-increasing weight of radiant sound, indicating that the qualities which are in us from childhood endure to the Hereafter. . . .

The strings soar ever higher, there is a brief pause, and at last the Ideology theme is proclaimed in full as the transfigured soul realizes in the afterlife the aims which could never be accomplished during its earthly existence.

Don Juan, Opus 20

Don Juan was begun in either the fall of 1887 or the spring of 1888; it was completed on 30 September 1888. Strauss conducted the first performance in Weimar on 11 November 1889.

Strauss was 20 years old when he received his first big break. Totally unexpectedly, conductor Hans von Bülow invited him to become assistant director of the Meiningen Orchestra. Although Strauss had had little conducting experience and the position was without pay, he readily accepted. He had already composed a good deal of music cast in traditional forms. His move away from home and away from the dominance of his conservative father, a famous horn player, marked a turning point. He found himself influenced less by the absolute music of Brahms and Schumann and more by the avant garde program music of Wagner and Liszt. He also gained the freedom to live his own life, which meant love affairs. The romantic yearnings of this fiery youth surfaced both in his relations with women and in the new kind of music he began to compose. These two tendencies toward the passionate — sensual and musical — converged in his first truly major composition, *Don Juan,* an extravagant song of love.

His first great love was Dora Wihan-Weis, wife of his friend, cellist Hanuš Wihan, and four years his senior. The young Strauss was tormented by his desire for Dora, but he restrained his passions out of respect for Wihan. He went into a deep depression, but news that the Wihans' marriage was failing brought him out of it. It is difficult to reconstruct the exact events of the passionate affair between Dora and Richard, since she requested that all his letters be destroyed after her death in 1938. Three letters survived accidentally, and there is also a small correspondence extant from Dora to Richard. From these materials, circumspect and discreet though they are, it seems that a deep love developed between the two, which was consummated after the Wihans divorced. Strauss' behavior toward Dora caused some embarrassment, which his father was quick to point out. More than once the composer and Dora made plans to spend time together in Italy — a blatant admission of their affair that was sure to create a scandal in those staid times.

Dora was on the rebound from a marriage; Strauss was experiencing his first love. Since they were looking for different things, it was inevitable that the affair should end. Strauss found other women to love, notably Pauline de Ahna, whom he subsequently married. The importance of the affair with Dora was that the composer discovered intense desire, of which he sang in *Don Juan.*

Once Strauss moved to Meiningen, he stopped composing sonatas, quartets, concertos, and symphonies. He turned his attention to programmatic orchestral works. The first two, *Aus Italien* and *Macbeth,* are only partial successes, but the next one, *Don Juan,* is a masterpiece. He thought through his new aesthetic carefully and explained it to conductor von Bülow, who was not particularly sympathetic, having himself moved in the opposite direction, from adulation of Wagner and Liszt to championing of Brahms.

Strauss wrote to the conductor:

The only way a *self-reliant forward* development of instrumental music is possible is in carrying on from the Beethoven of the *Coriolanus, Egmont,* and *Leonore III* Overtures, of *Les Adieux,* from late Beethoven in general, all of whose works in my opinion could hardly have come into being without a pre-existing poetic model. . . . If one wants to create a work of art the mood and structure of which are of a piece and which is to make a vivid impression on the listener, then the author must also have had a vivid image of what he wanted to say before his inner eye.

This is only possible as a consequence of fertilization by a poetic idea, whether appended to the work as program or not. In my opinion it is a purely artistic process to create a new form to correspond to each new poetic model; making the form a beautiful one, complete and perfect in itself, is of course very difficult, but that makes it all the more stimulating. Making music according to the rules of form as set down by Hanslick [an influential critic who hated the music of Wagner but revered that of Brahms] is in any case no longer possible. From now on there will be no more beautiful but aimless phrase-making during which the minds of both the composer and the listeners are a complete blank, and no more symphonies.

What took the place of the symphony was the symphonic poem, a genre invented by Liszt some 35 years earlier. Liszt's twelve symphonic poems are based on myths, plays, pictures, poems, or ideas. As enthusiasm for literature grew during the second half of the nineteenth century, other composers experimented with literary music. Paradoxically (since his orchestral works are actually more symphonic than Liszt's), Strauss changed the name of the form to "tone poem."

Don Juan was the composer's third tone poem. The subject is the erotic legend about the woman-hating seducer who ultimately welcomes death. Of the many versions of the Don Juan story, Strauss chose the incomplete play by Nicolaus Lenau, a German poet who died in 1850. In the play Don Juan leads a life of worthless sensuality. When he dies at the end, it is really a victory because he can at last escape from his boring and destructive life. The "hero" indulges in virtually every form of depravity in his search for the ideal woman. Every successful seduction turns out to destroy someone or something. Don Juan is deeply troubled by his cruelties. His self-hatred is compounded by his frustration over rejection of his philosophy — the glorification of each moment as it happens. His discontentment leads him to further exploitations and adventures, with less and less regard for his own safety. By the end his greatest desire is to die at the hands of an enemy. Lenau conveys Juan's emotions through a series of incidents that Strauss translates into music: the tone poem depicts love scenes, a carnival, and Juan's final duel.

Although Strauss wanted the details of the program kept from the audience, he did feel it important for the orchestra musicians to understand what was depicted in the music. It is not difficult to discern the outlines of Lenau's play in Strauss' music. Biographer Norman Del Mar's interpretation appears in the published score:

The principal subject is a composite theme, all the major features of which are later isolated and extensively developed. This profusion of ideas together presents the figure of Don Juan himself in all his passionate glory and lust for life.

A further theme, first introduced in the bass instruments, carries the music impetuously forward and leads to the hero's first flirtatious exploit. . . . The theme of its heroine is purely capricious and not even the indication *flebile* (plaintive) can suggest that her heart has been touched.

Yet the chromatically descending figure with which she parts from Juan was intended by Strauss to represent "a feeling of satiety in Juan's heart," indicating that an emotional attachment has existed between them. . . .

With an impatient flourish he tears himself from this unsatisfactory mistress, turns around, and is immediately spellbound at the appearance of a new beauty. Don Juan is deeply stirred and their love scene follows. . . .

The music rises to a climax of unbearable intensity, subsiding abruptly as the cellos softly interpose Don Juan's opening motive like a question. He has awakened from the oblivion of love and although his mistress attempts to make his dreams continue, they no longer have the power to hold him. In a moment Don Juan is out of reach and away in search of further adventures.

His themes [build] to a pitch of frenzy; then suddenly there is a halt and a new courtship begins. This time the girl's capitulation is less immediate and Don Juan's wooing takes on a note of yearning intensity until gradually he overcomes her pitiable resistance and she finally succumbs altogether [in] . . . one of the great love songs in all music.

Strauss now offers a new, heroic Don Juan motive in four horns. [At a Masked Ball] there is a new glittering theme which together with Don Juan's horn motive — now on glockenspiel and trumpet — sweeps the music into a powerful series of majestic statements, gaining progressively in force and momentum until at the climax it falls with a torrential sweep into a terrible pit. . . .

Don Juan's morale has suddenly reached rock-bottom. The ghosts of his three former mistresses flit across his consciousness. In his despondency he has taken to wandering through churchyards and . . . [invites] to dinner the statue of a distinguished nobleman he has killed. . . . The statue does not come; it is the nobleman's son, Don Pedro, who intrudes upon the Supper Scene. He challenges the invincible libertine to a death duel. . . .

Don Juan, with Pedro entirely at his mercy, realizes that victory is worthless and voluntarily delivers himself to the sword of his adversary. There is a pale minor chord into which the trumpets jab out the dissonant note representing with horrible clarity the mortal thrust, and with a descending series of shuddering trills Don Juan's life ebbs away. The work ends on a note of blankness, which is the more devastating for the closeness with which it follows on the heels of a scene of unparalleled splendor and exultation.

Don Quixote, Opus 35

Don Quixote *was begun on 10 October 1896 and completed at 11:42 a.m. on 29 December 1897. Franz Wüllner conducted the first performance in Cologne on 8 March 1898.*

Virtually everyone who thinks about music has an opinion on program music (that which tells a story or paints a picture) vs. absolute music (that which does not). Richard Strauss was no exception. He often expressed himself on the subject, and he seemed not particularly concerned with the consistency of his opinions:

"I am a musician first and last, for whom every program is merely the stimulus to the creation of new forms, and nothing more."

Program music: real music! Absolute music: it can be put together with the aid of routine and rule-of-thumb technique by everybody who is at all musical. First: true art! Second: artificiality!

"I don't like programs at all. They promise one person too much, they exercise too great an influence on another, a third protests that the program has stifled his own imagination, a fourth would rather not think at all than try to rethink what someone else has already worked out."

"To me the poetic program is no more than the basis of form and the origin of the purely musical development of my feelings — not . . . a *musical description* of certain events of life. That would be quite contrary to the spirit of music. Nevertheless, in order that music should not lose itself in pure willfulness and wallow out of its depth, it needs certain formal restrictions, and these are provided by a program. To the listener, too, such an analytical program should not be more than a pointer which can be used by those who so desire. Those who really understand how to listen to music probably don't need it at all."

"Do you know what absolute music is? I don't."

"I want to be able to depict in music a glass of beer so accurately that every listener can tell whether it is a Pilsner or Kulmbacher!"

"I regard the ability to express outward events as the highest triumph of musical technique. . . . To be able to reproduce trifling sounds so that the listener can be in no doubt about their nature requires great artistic technique."

"In *Don Juan* I have illustrated one of the seducer's victims with such accuracy that everyone must be able to see that she has red hair!"

Quite an assemblage of opinions! Some of the time Strauss was being facetious, although it is amazing how many critics have taken seriously his boasts about being able to depict beer and redheads in the orchestra. But, despite Strauss' penchant for off-the-cuff remarks and self-contradictions (once he claimed, "*everything* can be portrayed in music"; another time he said, "it is not true to say that *everything* can be translated into the symbolic language of music"), there is a consistent philosophy behind the remarks quoted above. Program music does exist; programmatic composers do use extra-musical stories and images as inspiration; worthwhile program music can be appreciated without the aid of the program; even absolute music depends on a program that comes from the composer's inner emotions.

The perennial controversy surrounding program music intensified when Strauss' highly pictoral tone poems first began to be widely heard. The literalness of the bleating sheep in *Don Quixote*, for example, sparked a sharp debate that tended to eclipse rather than focus on the real issues of program music. Instances of such literal transference of natural sounds into the orchestra are relatively rare, even in *Don Quixote*. Yet virtually all the music in this most programmatic piece by music's most programmatic composer has some direct referent in Cervantes' novel.

The critical questions are: Do we need to know the story to appreciate the music? Is it fair to listen just to the music? If we are going to try to hear the music in terms of the story, how carefully ought we to associate events in the music with those in the novel? Strauss believed that the program was mainly a stimulus to his imagination, that the music should and could stand on its own, and that the listener need not know the program. He published the orchestral score of *Don Quixote* without literary explanation. Yet, when we do take the trouble to trace the origins of each event in the music, we can appreciate the wit, the characterization (developed as carefully as in many an opera), and the subtlety of Strauss' art in a far deeper way. Is listening without following the program any less incomplete than hearing an opera without knowing the libretto?

There are no easy answers. These problems become even more difficult for practical reasons. How is a listener to appreciate *all* the subtle interrelationships between story and music except by following an annotated score? It is customary to follow librettos while listening to operas, especially when they are performed in a foreign language, but few concertgoers bring along scores. Listening guides to such works as *Don Quixote* do not even usually exist in convenient format. One could easily give up on learning the fascinating characterizations and illustrations of Cervantes' story, since the music is rich enough in beautiful melodies and sonorities to hold anyone's interest. Yet listening to *Don Quixote* as absolute music is missing half the fun.

Hence the following guide. It is more detailed than is customary in this book, and each listener, of course, has the choice of whether or not to use it while listening. The description is adapted from the composer's program and from the biography by Norman Del Mar.

According to Cervantes, Don Quixote was an impractical man, a dreamer, who loved knight errantry "so much that he entirely forgot his hunting and even the care of his estates. So odd and foolish, indeed, did he grow on this subject that he sold many acres of cornland to buy these books on chivalry to read, and in this way brought home every one he could get."

In the introduction the hero is represented by three distinct themes, showing three sides of his personality. The first, marked "in a knightly and gallant manner," opens the composition; the second, played by the second violins, represents Quixote's courteous and gentlemanly manner; the third, in the solo clarinet, depicts his oddly twisted naïveté. The violas take up the first Quixote theme, which degenerates into aimlessness, as he reads his books and daydreams.

A gentle oboe melody portrays the Lady Patron to whom Quixote wants to dedicate his exploits. This melody at first lacks passion and has a certain dream-like quality: it represents Quixote's fantasy of an idealized woman. A muted trumpet fanfare stands for Quixote's imagined victory over some giant or monster, portrayed simultaneously by tubas and string basses. After this "battle," Quixote pretends that the lady swoons in love and gratitude; for the love duet, the oboe theme is played with the first Don theme in strings. He proclaims his devotion to her (horns), and she accepts him (solo violin). A love serenade ensues, but it is broken off suddenly as Don Quixote remembers that he is still in his study, reading. He reads on and gets involved in his fantasies once again. He imagines adventures of ever greater complexity. With a loud, dissonant interruption he comes suddenly back again to reality. He is drunk with wished for adventures and decides he will actually turn Knight Errant. Thus ends the introduction.

Strauss next presents the themes he will use for the following variations, each of which represents a different adventure. First we hear the solo cello, the instrument consistently identified with the hero, present the melody of "Don Quixote, the Knight of the Sorrowful Countenance." This tune is derived from the opening Quixote themes and from one of the themes heard while he was reading: the misguided knight is trying to turn into reality the very things about which he had been reading. Then the tuba and bass clarinet present the first of three themes for Sancho Panza, Quixote's faithful, long-suffering, and far more practical friend. First Sancho is shown as little more than a simpleton; the second theme, in the solo viola (Panza's instrument), describes the rapid and often idiotic wagging of his tongue; the third, a purposefully simplistic triadic figure (also in the solo viola), suggests Sancho's habit of talking nonsense with the solemn air of uttering profound truths. Now that we have met the two protangonists, we accompany them on their adventures, in the form of loose variations on their themes.

Variation I. Quixote's and Panza's themes are heard simultaneously (solo cello and bass clarinet respectively) as they set out together. Drifting above them, in winds and violins, is the Lady Patron's melody: they have not yet met their Dulcinea, but they are convinced they will. Quixote sees an evil "giant" — it is really a windmill! With a rush in the full orchestra, he attacks. He misses and falls (descending run in harp and solo cello). As he hesitatingly tries to pick himself up, the Don prays quietly to his imagined Dulcinea (the Dulcinea theme fragmented in the solo cello). With Sancho Panza's help he remounts his horse and prepares for further adventures (the solo cello becomes more continuous and restates the Quixote themes).

Variation II. The energetic music shows the two heroes in full strength and high spirits. Don Quixote has found the power of three men (his theme is played by three cellos). Woodwinds and brass flutter-tonguing, quietly at first, represent the bleating sheep that Quixote mistakenly takes to be a hostile army. Viola tremolos and trills represent the clouds of dust raised by the sheep, and shepherds' pipes are heard in the distance (played by flute, English horn, bass clarinet, and bassoon). The Don attacks the sheep.

Variation III. The knight and squire are having a conversation. We hear their themes in dialogue. Panza (solo viola) prattles on, as Quixote (solo violin) finds it harder and harder to get a word in edgewise. When Sancho finally has to stop for breath (a brief silence), the Don speaks quickly and impatiently (solo cello). But Sancho goes on, again constantly interrupting Quixote. Finally Don Quixote takes over the dialogue and, with the orchestra singing out his themes, tells of giants he will slay, maidens he will rescue (the Dulcinea theme is woven into the orchestral fabric), and kingdoms he will conquer. As Quixote's fantasies subside, his squire suddenly asks an impertinent question (bass clarinet). The Don answers angrily (violins, horns, and woodwinds).

Variation IV. Don Quixote rushes forward, leaving Sancho Panza behind (the orchestra plays rapidly and forcefully the Don's theme, but not Sancho's). Suddenly the knight hears a distant procession singing a religious chant (brass chorale). The strings play an excited version of Quixote's theme, to show that he is attacking. He wants to rescue a maiden, but she turns out to be a statue of the Virgin Mary that the penitents are carrying. He is knocked down (the string figure descends), and the procession resumes as the Don remains senseless on the ground (low sustained note in the cellos and string basses). Sancho arrives (bass clarinet and tuba), and Quixote revives. Sancho falls asleep (descending scale in bass clarinet and tuba). We hear his two snores (descending figures in tuba and then contrabassoon).

Variation V. While Panza sleeps, Don Quixote sits by the fire and reflects on his adventures and dreams of future conquests. This extended variation for solo cello includes Dulcinea's theme, as Quixote still wishes for a maiden to rescue and love. After the love theme, we hear a rush of sound in the violins, harp, and winds, depicting the night winds.

Variation VI. The knight and squire set off in search of Dulcinea. Quixote orders Panza to find her, which he cannot do, since neither of them knows what she looks like or where she lives. In desparation Sancho tries to convince Quixote that a brash stable girl who comes by is really Dulcinea under a spell (jaunty and rhythmically irregular oboe tune). The solo cello plays an annoyed version of Quixote's theme, and then Sancho pays his respects to the wench (tuba and solo viola). The viola continues as Sancho explains they were looking for Dulcinea (a fragment of the Dulcinea theme becomes the ending of the viola solo). The bewildered girl runs away (the jaunty oboe tune returns), as the Don remains behind, confused (fragments of the Quixote themes). He is at last alone and wistful.

Variation VII. Quixote and Panza are guests of a Duke and Duchess, who convince them they must go on a long journey through the air on a flying horse. They are blindfolded and put on a toy horse, and they really believe they are flying. The magical flight is graphically depicted by rushing figures in the entire orchestra. Strauss calls for a wind machine in the percussion section. The fact that the two heroes are not really flying is indicated by the constant low drone in the string basses.

Variation VIII. Gentle undulations in strings and winds, which include the Quixote themes, indicate that the knight and his squire are on a boat trip. Quixote is convinced that the boat will take them to some important adventure. Instead of finding a mission, however, they come dangerously close to a watermill (the orchestra gets loud) and are saved only when their boat capsizes. They manage to get out of the river and beat their clothes to dry them (*pizzicato* chords in low strings). A woodwind chorale indicates their prayer of thanks for having been spared.

Variation IX. The Don is excited because he sees two monks seeming to lead a coach containing a lady. He is convinced that the monks are enchanters bearing off a princess. The monks, in quasi-religious tones, explain who they are and that they have nothing to do with the lady (duet for two bassoons). Quixote does not believe them, and he interrupts to send them packing (forceful statement of his theme in strings).

Variation X. A neighbor of Don Quixote's, concerned for his safety as he goes about the countryside having harebrained adventures, disguises himself as the Knight of the White Moon (brass and woodwind fanfare). He challenges Don Quixote to a duel. The Don cries out as he is defeated: his single cello is no match for the Knight's full orchestra. The victorious Knight demands that Don Quixote remain at home for one year. The Don and Sancho begin their long march home (full orchestra, with incessant drum beat). They pause for a moment, as Don Quixote thinks about becoming a shepherd (the shepherd pipe tune from Variation II is recalled).

Epilogue. Quixote is weary when he arrives home. His theme is given by the solo cello in a plaintive version. This beautiful melody, and its ensuing development, indicate that the Don has lost his madness for adventure. Death is near. But, before slipping into eternity, Don Quixote recalls his life as it once was: his three themes are played as they were at the beginning of the work. With a final sigh (the solo cello descends an octave into its lowest register), he dies.

Ein Heldenleben, Opus 40

Heldenleben was begun in Munich on 8 August and completed in Berlin on 27 December 1898. Strauss conducted the first performance on 3 March 1899 in Frankfurt.

Richard Strauss was the most famous and most controversial of German composers at the close of the nineteenth century. His "cacophonous" tone poems excited and infuriated audiences. Critics frequently abused Strauss, yet the public found the music strangely electrifying. The composer knew that he was the most talked about figure in music, and he was confident of his genius. To glorify himself and vengefully to caricature his adversaries, the critics, he composed the autobiographical *Ein Heldenleben* ("A Hero's Life").

The self-conscious grandeur of *Heldenleben* is evident even in the composer's original reason for wanting to write it: to compete with Beethoven's heroic work, the *Eroica* Symphony (both are in the key of E-flat). Strauss created an imaginary hero, but he drew characteristics, supporting characters, and adventures from his own life. He told French critic Romain Rolland, "I do not see why I should not compose a symphony about myself. I find myself quite as interesting as Napoléon or Alexander." Strauss sought to portray a "general and free ideal of great and manly heroism . . . , that heroism which describes the inward battle of life and which aspires through effort and reunification towards the elevation of the soul."

As early as 1904 Rolland recognized that *Heldenleben* was actually symbolic of decadence. "The Hero's victory had made him aware of his strength: his pride is now boundless. He exalts himself, no longer able to distinguish between reality and his grandiloquent dreams, just like the nation which he represents. There are germs of disease in Germany: a delirium of arrogance, a belief in self and contempt for others. . . . Germany had hardly become a world power when it found the voice of Nietzsche. . . . The grandiose music of Richard Strauss now has that appearance."

Ein Heldenleben is divided into six sections, which correspond to the outlines of sonata form:

1. The Hero — first theme.
2. The Hero's adversaries (critics) — transition
3. The Hero's companion (wife) — second theme
4. The Hero's deeds of war — development
5. The Hero's works of peace (and struggles in the face of continued criticism) — recapitulation (with added episode)
6. The Hero's retirement from the world and the fulfillment of his life — coda.

The Hero's theme, which opens the work, is a long and broad melody in strings and horns. After this soaring tune is heard several times in different guises, the section ends with a dramatic pause, as if the Hero is waiting for the onslaught of his adversaries.

The critics depicted in the second section seem, especially in comparison with the Hero's lofty theme, puny and petty. Woodwind figures, purposefully ugly, abound. There are many critics, and they are all trivial. After the premiere of *Heldenleben*, Strauss wrote to his father that the real critics "spit poison and gall, principally because on reading my program note they believed that they could see themselves identified with the really hatefully portrayed 'grumblers and antagonists' and that I myself am meant for the Hero, which last is only partially true." The Hero's theme returns, as he confronts the adversaries. They in turn renew their attack, but the Hero breaks away, just as his companion makes her first appearance.

Strauss uses a solo violin for the Hero's wife. There is a long series of cadenzas, separated by orchestral interludes, which are intended to show the many sides of the companion's character. Strauss admitted that he meant to portray his own wife.

> It is my wife I wanted to show. She is very complex, very feminine, a little perverse, a little coquettish, never like herself, at every minute different from how she had been the minute before. At the beginning the hero follows her and gets into the mood in which she has just been singing; she keeps going farther away. At last he says, "No, I am staying here." He remains wrapped in his own thoughts, back in his own mood. Then she comes to him. For the rest, this long and fully developed section serves as an interlude, as a contrast between the two noisy outbursts of the opening and of the battle.

Eventually during this section we hear music of passion followed by a beautiful love theme.

At the end of the companion section, there is a faint echo of the critics' music, followed by a call to battle from three off-stage trumpets. The Hero rises in response. The battle section has long been celebrated in the symphonic literature for its grotesquely chaotic character. Strauss purposefully courts ugliness. The section is pervaded by percussion, by a distorted version of one of the critics' themes in the trumpet, and by snatches of various other themes that place the Hero and the critics in fierce struggle. Love themes suggest that the companion is a source of inspiration to the Hero. The Hero's theme soars forth at last to signal his victory.

The Hero's works of peace turn out to be quotations from Strauss' earlier compositions: *Don Juan, Also Sprach Zarathustra, Death and Transfiguration, Macbeth, Don Quixote, Till Euglenspiegel*, the opera *Guntram*, and the songs *Befreit* and *Traum durch die Dämmerung*. Interspersed with these quotations are the Hero and the companion music.

The final section beautifully depicts the peacefulness of the Hero's retirement.

The egocentricity of *Heldenleben* does not hide the fact that it is a product of its times. Only a hyper-romantic artist such as Strauss could be so vainglorious as to parade himself before his public in an ostentatious forty-minute work for enormous orchestra. The glorification of the artist as genius was a romantic notion, unknown before Beethoven. The late nineteenth century saw an exaggeration of artistic subjectivity, which brought with it the seeds of its own dissolution. There was a certain decadence in the conceit of a composer like Wagner, who proclaimed himself the creator of the music of the future. Wagner's egomania spread as romanticism turned overripe, and Strauss became the successor to Wagner's aesthetic. *Ein Heldenleben,* one of the last truly romantic works by the last truly romantic composer, represents the limits (as well as the strengths) of artistic subjectivity.

Strauss himself eventually realized the decadence into which romanticism had fallen. He came to dislike *Heldenleben,* probably more for what it represented that for what it was. The composer had the integrity to remove himself from the mire of a dying aesthetic. After one further attempt at self-proclamation, the even more blatant *Domestic* Symphony, he turned to the more objective genre of opera.

Heldenleben is a product of its locale as well as its times. Strauss' egomania parallels that of Germany. What began in the early nineteenth century as a revolt against classical restraint, a direct appeal to the emotions, a glorification of the genius, and a newfound freedom reached an ignoble dénouement in the figure of Hitler. The arts could travel just so far and no farther along such a long and strange route. Nations do not have the self-awareness of artists. The German romantic culture could not recognize its excesses, and so it continued toward an ultimately distorted aggrandizement of the self. *Heldenleben* tears at the limits of musical romanticism, yet Strauss knew he had to turn his back on the decadence he so eloquently expressed. Listening to *Heldenleben* today, we hear not so much the composer's autobiographical Hero as the impending death of an opulent culture.

The overblown romanticism of *Heldenleben,* its undercurrents of egomania, and its deliberate courting of the grotesque (the critics' music) and the harsh (the battle) are typical of late romanticism. The music reflects the values of late nineteenth-century Europe. The aesthetic of the work is the exaggeration that precedes the death of an age. Yet Strauss was a great composer, and *Heldenleben* is a beautiful work. One need not accept its premises to enjoy its sounds.

The work is a statement of a philosophy gone sour. Strauss did not negate the problems inherent in his culture, but rather he met them head-on by giving them a deeply felt musical expression. He battled the contradictions of his age, and he won. Thus Strauss really *is* the hero of *Ein Heldenleben,* in a sense more real than what the program implies. While *Heldenleben* is decidedly a period piece, it, like all great art, has significance for all periods.

Metamorphosen for 23 Solo Strings

Sketches for Metamorphosen *date back to 1943. The actual composition was begun on 13 March 1945 and finished on 2 April of the same year. Strauss supervised the final rehearsal, and Paul Sacher conducted the first performance with his Collegium Musicum in Zurich on 25 January 1946.*

Richard Strauss was not political. Political events affected him only to the extent that they affected the performance of his music. Yet no one living in Germany in the 1930s and '40s could maintain total indifference to the Third Reich. Strauss at first accepted the Nazis: he, like many of his compatriots, ignored the ever-escalating atrocities. Finally he acknowledged the horrors of Hitler, as he felt the destruction around him in a deeply personal way. This octogenarian's political awakening and his newfound sensitivity to the world around him had an impact on his music. After a couple of decades that had produced rather arid compositions which were pale shadows of his exciting tone poems of 1888–1904 and operas of 1905–1914, Strauss began to compose genuinely personal and emotional music. His astonishing late works, particularly *Metamorphosen* and the Four Last Songs, are profoundly expressive of the composer's sunset years and, as he saw it, the dying years of a great culture.

As biographer George Marek explains, "Strauss was not a Nazi. He was not an anti-Nazi. He was one of those who let it happen. He was one of those who played along. He was one of those who thought, 'Well, they don't practice as viciously as they preach.' He thought so until the hoodlums touched him personally."

At first Strauss welcomed Hitler, feeling that the new government would support German art. The leaders of the Reich were interested in Strauss. They understood the political importance of art. They knew that having important artists in their camp helped to legitimatize their rule both in Germany and before the rest of the world. Strauss was asked to meet with Hitler and his deputies Hermann

Göring and Joseph Goebbels. In 1933 Strauss accepted the post of president of the official agency with jurisdiction over all German music: the *Reichsmusikkammer.* The composer addressed the first meeting of this body: "After the assumption of power by Adolf Hitler, much has been changed in Germany, not only politically but also in the realm of culture. Already, after a few months of the National Socialist government, it has been able to call into being a body such as the *Reichsmusikkammer.* This proves that the new Germany is unwilling to let artistic matters slide, as it did more or less up to now. It proves that new ways and means are determinedly sought to make possible a new vigor in our musical life."

In fairness to Strauss, it must be mentioned that few Germans recognized the dangers of Nazism in the early '30s. Hitler was acclaimed amid high hopes for the future. But, as the months wore on and ever more repressive policies were put into effect, people began to realize the underlying threat of Hitler and his henchmen. But not Strauss. At least not openly. The composer took his position with the *Reichsmusikkammer* seriously, but in so doing he was forced to act politically. Every act of a public official is a political act, and Strauss was, after all, an official of the Hitler regime.

When Goebbels denounced composer Paul Hindemith for showing "signs of an un-German attitude," Strauss sent Goebbels a telegram congratulating him on the "weeding out of undesirable elements." When conductor Bruno Walter, a Jew, was forced by threats of violence to cancel an appearance with the Berlin Philharmonic, Strauss replaced him, purportedly for the sake of the orchestra members. When Italian conductor Arturo Toscanini refused to conduct a performance of Wagner's *Parsifal* in Hitler's Germany, Strauss substituted for him, for the sake of Wagner's music. When Hitler's official newspaper condemned author Thomas Mann for writing an article on Wagner that was not totally adulatory, Strauss joined a group of German artists who signed an open letter supporting the newspaper's position. Most of Germany's great musicians fled their homeland in the 1930s, many settling in the United States. Strauss remained.

But he knew what was happening. He was too old to leave behind his country, his possessions, his life as he had lived it. He continued to cooperate with the Nazis out of fear for the safety of his family. He even composed a piece in honor of the Japanese royal family in exchange for a promise that his daughter-in-law and grandsons would not be harmed.

It was not too long before Strauss personally felt the oppression of the Hitler regime. He was forced to cancel a performance in Salzburg because the Nazis did not at the time care for Austria. He was actually asked to prove that he was an Aryan artist with professional credentials (he listed as references Mozart and Wagner). His librettist, Stefan Zweig, had great troubles in Germany because he was Jewish, and the composer was henceforth unable to work with him. Strauss saw great monuments of German culture destroyed, and at last he felt the full impact of the current madness. The destruction of the opera houses in Berlin, Dresden, and Vienna in 1945 touched the aging composer in a personal way, more than had the murders of millions of innocent but anonymous people during the previous decade. He wrote to critic Willi Schuh, "The burning of the Munich Court Theater, where *Tristan* and *Die Meistersinger* received their first performances, where I first heard *Freischütz* 73 years ago, where my father sat at the first horn desk for 49 years — it was the greatest catastrophe of my life; there is no possible consolation, and at my age no hope." Strauss began to pull together some recent compositional sketches for a work called *Sorrow for Munich*, which eventually became *Metamorphosen*.

To another friend the composer wrote,

> The flower of German music, which had bloomed for two hundred years, has been withering away, its spirit caught up in the machine, and its crowning glory, German opera, cut off forever; most of its homes are reduced to rubble and ashes, and some of those not destroyed are already degraded as cinemas (the Vienna State Opera). My life's work is in ruins; I shall never again hear my operas. . . . In poor Munich the house in which I was born by the lovely Court Church of St. Michael has already been bombed. In short, my life is at an end.

In was in this mood of despair that Strauss composed *Metamorphosen*. Although he never divulged its exact program, it is not difficult to understand its expressive intent. Most of his major works are programmatic, as he felt that he could not write without some definite idea in mind. One of the main themes, heard when the violas first enter shortly after the beginning, is taken from the funeral march in Beethoven's *Eroica* Symphony. Strauss was not consciously aware of this derivation at first, but when he did understand it he quoted the exact theme near the end, in the cellos (in combination with the derived version). He marked this final passage, "In Memoriam." There is another quotation, related to King Mark's lament from Wagner's *Tristan und Isolde*. The original words are, "To what avail thy countless deeds of faithful service?" While he was working on *Metamorphosen*, Strauss wrote to a friend, "I am inconsolable! The Goethe House, the most sacred place on earth, destroyed! My lovely Dresden — Weimar — Munich, all gone!" Thus the new composition became a memorial to the cultural monuments destroyed in Hitler's war.

The day before Strauss finished the composition the Russians marched into Vienna. Three days later the Americans took Nuremburg and the Russians attacked Berlin. Two weeks later Hitler killed himself. By the end of the month the war was over. *Metamorphosen*, a requiem to a great civilization that had succumbed to a temporary madness, was created amidst the final days of that madness. The depth of the tragedy infuses the music. Strauss may have been slow to acknowledge the truth about his Germany, but the music shows with utter clarity that in his soul he understood. Strauss' compositional powers returned in full force in his late years to give profound expression to his grief — indeed, to the grief of the whole world — over the Third Reich's destruction of human life and and culture. The composer may have been politically naïve, but events conspired to force him, and his music, into the real world, and in the process he became a greater composer than he had been for many years. In the highest sense *Metamorphosen* indeed *is* a political work, albeit from the pen of a composer who had spent decades virtually innocent of the world.

The use of strings to project a long, intense, chromatic movement is reminiscent of some of Mahler's late works (also conceived as a farewell to life and to a dying culture), such as the first movement of the Tenth Symphony or the last movement of the Ninth. Mahler uses full orchestra, but the predominance of strings in an emotional movement foreshadows *Metamorphosen*. Another antecedent is Schoenberg's *Verklärte Nacht* for string orchestra, one of his early tonal works composed before he "emancipated the dissonance." These works from the first decade of this century were products of late romantic hyper-emotionalism. *Metamorphosen*, on the other hand, was written at mid-century, long after the demise of romanticism. Thus there is a distinct difference. Strauss, like Schoenberg and Mahler, was bidding farewell to the nineteenth century, but he did so at a distance. Strauss himself had outlived by several decades most other romantic composers. He was writing an impassioned adieu at the same time that Bartók was composing his *last* works, Stravinsky was nearing the *end* of his neo-classic period, Messiaen was working on the massive dissonances of his *Turangalîla* Symphony, John Cage was experimenting with putting objects inside of grand pianos, Pierre Boulez was exploring mathematically predetermined music, and electronic music was in its infancy. *Metamorphosen* is a farewell not to a dying era of music but to one long dead. Hence the poignancy is even greater than in Mahler or Schoenberg.

Strauss composed as if none of the innovations of the twentieth century had taken place. Except for the grief over the collapse of Germany that forms the work's emotional core, *Metamorphosen* could have been written in 1910. The tortured chromatic harmonies, the long arch that builds intensity inexorably toward two climaxes before finally disolving slowly into tranquillity, the ever denser counterpoint, the perpetual variations (metamorphoses) of the main themes — these are the expressions more of a late romantic than of a modernist.

Despite the conservatism of the harmonies in *Metamorphosen*, it is innovative in one sense: its scoring for 23 solo instruments. *Metamorphosen* is thus a paradox. A work profoundly in touch with its times politically, a heartfelt response to events taking place while the piece was being written, it utilizes nonetheless a musical language that belongs to a bygone era. Yet, within this paradox of using an old language to express new thoughts, Strauss created a second paradox. He composed, within the limitations of the late romantic style, an original and even innovative work. Its novelty may have arisen superficially from his decision to write for 23 solo strings, but fundamentally the originality of *Metamorphosen* comes from the composer's awareness of the tragedy surrounding him. His perspective was unique, for he was the only composer of substance who had remained in Hitler's Germany. In becoming politically aware, Strauss became what he had not been since 1915: a composer with a powerful and original vision of his world.

Till Eulenspiegel's Merry Pranks, Opus 28

Till Eulenspiegel was begun in 1894 and finished on 6 May 1895. Franz Wüllner conducted the first performance in Cologne on 5 November 1895.

Till Eulenspiegel was born at Kneitlingen in Brunswick, Germany, around 1300 and died at Möllen, near Lübeck, in 1350. Till had no respect for class boundaries, and his free life-style typified a new social movement toward greater self-assertiveness among the lower classes. His legendary escapades were no doubt exaggerated by the time the first printed account of his life appeared around 1500. In these tales everyone from kings down to peasants became victims of Till's pranks. Till assumed the roles of various tradesmen and he often played practical jokes on others, yet he always survived by means of trickery or quick wit. He died not on the gallows, as Strauss would have it, but from the plague. As with Don Quixote (who also inspired a Strauss tone poem), beneath the sometimes grim humor of the Eulenspiegel character lies some perceptive satire on human nature.

Strauss contemplated a one-act opera on Till in the summer of 1894. Despite many sketches of the libretto, the opera was never writ-

ten, in part because Strauss found it difficult to create a stage character of dramatic substance for Till, and partly because he was discouraged by the recent failure of his opera *Guntram.*

The composer had already had considerable success as a composer of orchestral tone poems. His craft as an orchestrator was second to none, and his abilities to depict realistic scenes almost graphically were little short of astonishing. Although regularly condemned
by the most influential critics, he enjoyed great notoriety. The public
was always eager to hear the newest orchestral creation by this most
advanced of composers. Therefore Strauss decided to cast the Till legend in the medium he knew best. *Till Eulenspiegel's Merry Pranks, after
the Old Rogue's Tale, Set for Large Orchestra, in Rondo Form,* as he
titled the finished work, became what many consider the composer's
masterpiece of orchestral writing.

Strauss used a classical form — the rondo — much as he had
used sonata form in *Don Juan* and *Death and Transfiguration* and was
to use variation form in *Don Quixote.* A rondo contains a main theme
that alternates with a series of subordinate themes. This form is appropriate for Till because it allows his melodies to return after each
episode, so that we know he has emerged intact from his latest adventure. There are actually two different tunes associated with Till:
the opening "Once upon a time there was a roguish jester..." melody in the violins and the subsequent horn tune, labelled by Strauss
"... named Till Eulenspiegel." Throughout the work Strauss treats
these themes, as well as the subsidiary ideas, with utmost variety,
transforming them in any number of different ways.

The entire tone poem is based, often quite literally, on the adventures of Till. Strauss was reluctant to divulge the exact nature of each
passage, since there were no fewer than 26 explicit references.

> It is impossible for me to give a program to *Eulenspiegel*: what
> I had in mind when writing the various sections, if put into
> words, would often seem peculiar and would possibly give of-
> fense. So let us this time leave it to the audience to crack the
> nuts which the rogue has prepared for them. All that is neces-
> sary for the understanding of the work is to indicate the two
> Eulenspiegel themes, which are run right through the work in
> all manner of disguises, moods, and situations, until the catas-
> trophe, when Till is strung up, after sentence has been passed
> on him.

To limit the program in this manner is to deprive the audience of the
delight of following the story as told in detail by the music. Strauss
subsequently provided a detailed program guide, which can give a
thoroughly enjoyable picture of Till's pranks. The fun starts with Till's
horn theme, just after the beginning. Notice its subtly irregular

rhythm, as its main motive is repeated always in a different relation-ship to the beat: Till was indeed an unpredictable fellow.

After the orchestra develops this tune into a full climax, the small D clarinet presents a mocking transformation of the opening tune, which Strauss labels, "That was a rascally scamp!" The subsequent galloping rhythm in the strings suggests that Till is riding off in search of new adventures. After the galloping idea is developed, the music dies down to a tremolo on the violas accompanying a simple transformation of the opening theme in the low strings: "Just wait, you hypocrites!" Then an upward rush in clarinets, with a loud cym-bal crash, signals the next adventure: "Hop! On horseback straight through the market women." In the midst of the ensuing chaos, "Off and away in seven-league boots."

There is a brief pause, as Till is hidden in a mouse hole. Dissonant minor seconds suggest that he is chuckling. He gradually emerges and prepares for his next adventure: "Dressed as a priest he oozes unction and morality." This is depicted by a wonderfully lyrical new theme in the violas, clarinets, and bassoons. The rogue peeps out of the diguise, as we hear his motive briefly in the small clarinet. A chro-matic triplet figure in the brass intrudes ominously: "He is seized with a horrid premonition as to the outcome of his mockery of reli-gion." A long descent in the solo violin indicates that Till has removed his disguise.

The subsequent return (in accordance with rondo form) of the opening Till theme is in a romantic guise: "Till exchanges courtesies with beautiful girls." The second Till theme is transformed: "Glowing with love, Till woos a girl." Till is rebuffed, and the music shows his outrage. "A refusal is always a refusal," Till thinks, and he leaves fu-rious, swearing vengeance on all mankind.

The next adventure, announced by new material in the bassoons and bass clarinet, is Till's meeting with the pedagogues. This jerky motive represents questions that Till poses. "After he has propounded to these philistines a few absurd theses, Till leaves them in astonish-ment to their fate." The music builds in complexity to depict the scholars' deliberations, which become ever more convoluted. The first Till theme is heard, indicating that he has revealed himself. The music builds to a climax — a held note with trills — which Strauss calls "Till's great grimaces." The music then dissolves into the sim-plest of tunes, thoroughly banal, as Till walks away whistling. The whistling tune evaporates, and there is a "fleeting and ghostly" inter-lude.

The recapitulation now brings Till back in his true character, with his horn theme. The music builds in seeming recklessness until the inevitable happens: Till is arrested. To depict this Strauss interrupts the orchestra with a loud snare drum roll, followed by powerful low chords. Till tries to remain nonchalant, as his familiar motive in the small clarinet indicates: "He whistles to himself indifferently." But his whistling becomes more desparate, and the premonition music from his episode impersonating the priest returns. Then, with a powerful descending major seventh, sentence is pronounced: Death by hanging! The hero makes one last attempt to whistle his tune (small clarinet), but the theme is transformed into an ascending figure: "Up the ladder to the gallows. There he dangles. The breath leaves his body. A last convulsion. Till's mortal self is finished." For an epilogue Strauss returns to the opening "Once upon a time" music, as if to suggest that the story of Till is, after all, just a fairy tale.

The composer supposedly once claimed that he could depict anything in music, and *Till Eulenspiegel* surely attests to his ability to invoke fear, chaos, and gallows humor as well as the hero's specific escapades. Rarely does one encounter a purely instrumental composition that is as explicitly programmatic as *Till* and at the same time as satisfying in purely musical ways as well.

Igor Stravinsky

Born on 17 June 1882 in Oranienbaum, Russia.
Died on 6 April 1971 in New York.

◆ ◆ ◆

Apollon Musagète

Apollon Musagète *was composed in Nice between July 1927 and
January 1928. It was first performed at the Library of Congress,
Washington, D.C., on 27 April 1928. Stravinsky revised the work in
1947.*

By 1920 Stravinsky was acknowledged as a leader of the avant garde.
When his very next piece turned out to be a reworking of some music
by the eighteenth-century composer Giovanni Pergolesi, the musical
world was amused. Was the great innovator playing games? As it
turned out, Stravinsky was completely serious. All his music for the
next thirty years became an attempt to reinterpret the past in terms
of the present. From earlier music this neo-classic music, as it is
called, borrows traditional forms, simple chords, straightforward
melodic formulas, and modest orchestrations. Yet it uses these devices in modern ways.

By the mid-1920s the emergence of Stravinsky's neo-classic sophistication was complete. In *Apollon Musagète*, for example, listeners heard not the vivid colors of the *Rite of Spring* or even the
varied timbres of the *Symphonies of Wind Instruments* but simply a
string orchestra. They heard triads, the basic chords of the classical
period, that refused to behave as they ought. Stravinsky's neo-classicism was music about other music. It demanded sophistication
from its listeners, who had to know Stravinsky's models in order to
understand how he transformed them.

The public was confused. It seemed that the composer had suddenly turned his back on avant-garde experimentation and gone
"back to Bach." Gone were the massive dissonances, the exciting folk
tunes, and the irregular rhythms. All that remained, it seemed, were
pale imitations of the music of many pasts. Listeners heard (or
thought they heard) modernizations of Bach's *Brandenburg* Concertos
(in the *Dumbarton Oaks* Concerto), Mozart's piano sonatas (Piano
Sonata), Haydn's symphonies (Symphony in C), nineteenth-century
French ballets (*Jeu de cartes*), Verdi operas (*Oedipus Rex*), medieval
music (Mass), and even the music of Broadway (*Scènes de ballet*).

726

What listeners actually heard were not imitations, nor even always homages, but demonstrations of how the sounds of old music could be made new.

Stravinsky entered his neo-classic phase because it was a necessary expression of who he was: a man critically (in both senses of the term) aware of his culture and its history. He continually absorbed ideas, art, and music of all ages. Everything that went into his inquiring mind came out in his music, still recognizable but thoroughly "Stravinskyized."

But his former admirers and present critics understood only his apparent revocation of his Russian style. Stravinsky must have enjoyed confounding those who *thought* they understood him. Although he was following a logical and necessary development, in their eyes he was instantly transformed from a radical to a reactionary. He abandoned the revolutionaries, leaving them without a general. He became the darling of the conservatives, who gleefully pitted him, the savior of music from the threats of atonality, against the "enemy," Arnold Schoenberg.

Some *still* believe that Stravinsky forsook his personal voice from 1920 on by artificially adopting other composers' styles. People who think that do not really understand Stravinsky's art. *All* his music has a degree of artifice. *All* his music refers to other music. Yet his music is nonetheless an intensely personal expression of *one* musical personality.

Those who find the essential Stravinsky in the *Rite of Spring, Firebird, Les Noces,* or *Petrouchka* mistake the exceptions for the rule. Stravinsky was mostly an Apollonian — restrained, cool, classical. It is a source of considerable misunderstanding that some of his best known works are Dionysian — impassioned, exciting, extroverted. *Apollo,* on the other hand, shows his Apollonian nature.

Like the early ballets, *Apollon Musagète* is distinctly sectional. Stravinsky's concept of mosaic form works as well in a ballet that refers to eighteenth- and nineteenth-century French music as it does in the more abstract works of the Russian period. The composer explained that he wanted "to compose a ballet founded on moments or episodes in Greek mythology, plastically interpreted by dancing of the so-called classical school."

Stravinsky's explanation continues,

I chose as the theme Apollo Musagetes — that is, Apollo as the master of the Muses, inspiring each of them with her own art. I reduced their number to three, selecting from among them Calliope, Polyhymnia, and Terpsichore as being the most characteristic representatives of choreographic art. Calliope, receiving the stylus and tablets from Apollo, personifies poetry and its rhythm; Polyhymnia, finger on lips, represents mime. . . . Finally, Terpsichore, combining in herself both the rhythm of poetry and the eloquence of gesture, reveals dancing to the world, and thus among the Muses takes the place of honor beside the Musagetes.

After a series of allegorical dances, which were to be treated in the traditional classical style of ballet . . . , Apollo, in an apotheosis, leads the Muses, with Terpsichore at their head, to Parnassus, where they were to live ever afterwards. I prefaced this allegory with a prologue representing the birth of Apollo.

Stravinsky goes on to explain the neo-classic aesthetic of the ballet.

When, in my admiration for the beauty of line in classical dancing, I dreamed of a ballet of this kind, I had specially in my thoughts what is known as the 'white ballet' in which to my mind the very essence of this art reveals itself in all its purity. I found that the absence of many-colored effects and of all superfluities produced a wonderful freshness. This inspired me to write music of an analogous character. It seemed to me that diatonic composition was the most appropriate for this purpose, and the austerity of its style determined what my instrumental ensemble must be. I at once set aside the ordinary orchestra because of its heterogeneity, with its groups of string, wood, brass, and percussion instruments. . . . I chose strings. . . .

The original purpose of strings was determined in the country of their origin — Italy — and was first and foremost the cultivation of *canto,* of melody. . . . It seemed to me that it was not only timely but urgent to turn once more to the cultivation of this element from a purely musical point of view. That is why I was so much attracted by the idea of writing music in which everything should revolve about the melodic principle. And then the pleasure of immersing oneself again in the multi-sonorous euphony of strings and making it penetrate even the furthest fibers of the polyphonic web! And how could the unadorned design of the classical dance be better expressed than by the flow of melody as it expands in the sustained psalmody of strings?

In his book of essays *The Poetics of Music,* Stravinsky offers two ideas that beautifully express the classical elegance and restraint of *Apollon Musagète:*

1. "The clear integration of a work of art and its crystallization demand that all the Dionysian elements, which stimulate a composer

and set in motion the rising sap of his imagination, be adequately controlled before we succumb to their fever, and ultimately subordinated to discipline: such is Apollo's command."

2. "Contrast is everywhere. One has only to take note of it. Similarity is hidden; it must be sought out, and it is found only after the most exhaustive efforts. When variety tempts me, I am uneasy about the facile solutions it offers me. Similarity, on the other hand, poses more difficult problems but also offers results that are more solid and hence more valuable to me."

Concerto in D for Violin and Orchestra
Toccata
Aria I
Aria II
Capriccio

The Violin Concerto was composed between 27 October 1930 and 4 September 1931. Stravinsky conducted the first performance with violinist Samuel Dushkin and the Berlin Radio Orchestra on 23 October 1931.

In his *Autobiography* Stravinsky relates the origins of his Violin Concerto:

While at Mainz and Wiesbaden I frequently saw [publisher] Willy Strecker. He talked to me a good deal about a young violinist, Samuel Dushkin, with whom he had become very friendly and whom I had never met. In the course of our conversations, he asked me whether I should care to write something for the violin, adding that in Dushkin I should find a remarkable executant. I hesitated at first, because I am not a violinist, and I was afraid that my slight knowledge of that instrument would not be sufficient to enable me to solve the many problems which would necessarily arise in the course of a major work specially composed for it. But Willy Strecker allayed my doubts by assuring me that Dushkin would place himself entirely at my disposal in order to furnish any technical details I might require. Under such conditions the plan was very alluring, particularly as it would give me a chance of studying seriously the special technique of the violin. When he learned that I had in principle accepted Strecker's proposal, Dushkin came to Wiesbaden to make my acquaintance. I had not previously met him or heard him play. All I knew was that he had studied the violin and music in general in America, where, in his early childhood, he had been adopted by the American composer Blair Fairchild, a man of great distinction, rare kindness, and a mind remarkable for its delicate sensibility.

From our first meeting I could see that Dushkin was all that Willy Strecker had said. Before knowing him I had been a little doubtful, in spite of the weight that I attached to the recommendations of a man of such finished culture as my friend Strecker. I was afraid of Dushkin as a virtuoso. I knew that for virtuosi there were temptations and dangers that they were not all capable of overcoming. In order to succeed they are obliged to seek immediate triumphs and to lend themselves to the wishes of the public, the great majority of whom demand sensational effects from the player. This preoccupation naturally influences their taste, their choice of music, and their manner of treating the piece selected. How many admirable compositions, for instance, are set aside because they do not offer the player any opportunity of shining with facile brilliancy! Unfortunately, they often cannot help themselves, fearing the competition of their rivals and, to be frank, the loss of their bread and butter.

Dushkin is certainly an exception in this respect among many of his fellow players, and I was very glad to find in him, besides his remarkable gifts as a born violinist, a musical culture, a delicate understanding, and — in the exercise of his profession — an abnegation that is very rare. His beautiful mastery of technique comes from the magnificent school of Leopold Auer, that marvelous teacher to whose instruction we owe the great majority of leading violinists."

Stravinsky consulted composer Paul Hindemith, who reassured him that his not playing the violin would actually be an advantage. His inexperience would make him "avoid a routine technique and would give rise to ideas which would not be suggested by the familiar movement of the fingers." That is curious advice, coming as it did from a composer who prided himself on being able to play all orchestral instruments yet whose orchestration is never as colorful or assured as Stravinsky's.

Dushkin recounted his collaboration with the composer:

During the winter I saw Stravinsky in Paris quite often. One day, when we were lunching in a restaurant, Stravinsky took out a piece of paper and wrote down [a] chord . . . and asked me if it could be played. I had never seen a chord with such an enormous stretch, from the E to the top A, and I said "No." Stravinsky said sadly, *"Quel dommage"* [what a pity]. After I got home I tried it, and, to my astonishment, I found that in that register the stretch of an eleventh was relatively easy to play, and the sound fascinated me. I telephoned Stravinsky at once to tell him that it could be done. When the concerto was finished, more than six months later, I understood his disappointment when I first said "No." This chord, in a different dress, begins each of the four movements. Stravinsky himself calls it his "passport" to that concerto. . . .

Whenever he accepted one of my suggestions, even a simple change such as extending the range of the violin by stretching the phrase to the octave below and the octave above, Stravinsky would insist on altering the very foundations correspondingly. He behaved like an architect, who, if asked to change a room on the third floor, had to go down to the foundations to keep the proportions of the whole structure.

The composer wrote the following program note on the concerto:

The Violin Concerto was commissioned for Samuel Dushkin by his patron and — in that worst year of the depression, 1931 — my "angel," the American gentleman Blair Fairchild. Fairchild had discovered Dushkin and his talent for the violin at an early age and had sponsored his education and career thereafter. . . .

The first two movements of the concerto and part of the third were composed in Nice, but the score was completed in La Vironnière, a château near Voreppe which I rented from a country lawyer who looked and dressed exactly like Flaubert. I loved this house and especially my attic workroom, with its wide and wonderful view of the valley of the Isère. The only disadvantage of my life there was that I had to drive all the way to Grenoble to buy groceries, so I eventually had to move.

The Violin Concerto was not inspired by or modeled on any example. I do not like the standard concertos — not Mozart's, Beethoven's, Mendelssohn's, or even Brahms'. To my mind, the only masterpiece in the field is Schoenberg's, and that was written several years after mine. The titles of my movements — Toccata, Aria, Capriccio — may suggest Bach, and so, in a superficial way, might the musical substance. I am very fond of the Bach Concerto for Two Violins, as the duet of the soloist with a violin from the orchestra in the last movement of my concerto may show. But my concerto employs other duet combinations too, and the texture is almost always more characteristic of chamber music than of orchestral music. I did not compose a cadenza, not because I did not care about exploiting the violin virtusoity but because the violin in combination was my real interest. But virtuosity for its own sake has only a small role in my concerto, and the technical demands of the piece are relatively tame.

The ballet *Balustrade* (1940) by George Balanchine and Pavel Tchelichev, and with the music of my Violin Concerto, was one of the most satisfactory visualizations of any of my theater works. Balanchine worked out the choreography as we played my recording together, and I could actually watch him imagine gesture, movement, combination, composition. The result was a dance dialogue in perfect coordination with the dialogues of the music. The dancers were few in number, and the whole second Aria was performed — and beautifully performed — as a solo piece, by Toumanova. *Balustrade* was produced by Sol Hurok, that master judge of the box *populi* (I imagine *Balustrade* must have been one of his few misjudgements in that sense). The set was a very simple while balustrade across the back of the dark stage. The costumes were sinuous and sexually suggestive patterns of black and white.

The Violin Concerto is a good example of Stravinsky's neo-classic style. He uses certain classical harmonies, motives, violin figures, and forms, but in a thoroughly contemporary manner: he places old sounds in new contexts. For example, the beginning of the first movement (after the two-measure introduction) uses an innocently diatonic motive. But listen carefully to the rhythmic and harmonic context. Although the motive itself could have been written by Haydn, the constant alternation of two accompanying chords — one a simple triad, the other mildly dissonant — could have been composed only by Stravinsky. Also, the subtle rhythmic irregularities within a constant pulse are distinctly his.

Why did Stravinsky write this kind of music? It is not a return to classicism, as some contemporary critics believed. Rather it brings together two eras that have no direct historical contact and thus makes an artificial amalgamation of styles. Stravinsky's neo-classic music is an idiosyncratic view of the classical age by a modern composer. It is not a speculation on how a classical composer might have composed in 1930. It attempts to show how melodies, harmonies, motives, rhythms, and forms of the past can be used in the present.

The music of neo-classicism comments on earlier music. It is art about art. In order really to understand the Violin Concerto, a listener has to have heard a lot of classical-period music, so that when Stravinsky uses, for example, a triad in a non-triadic context the listener will understand what is new and what is old.

The neo-classic attitude of the Violin Concerto is particularly evident in the recapitulations. In each of the four movements, the opening material returns toward the end, as in most classical-period pieces. But Stravinsky makes each recapitulation just another event, not the culmination of a drive toward resolution. The existence of each return is classical, but its effect is not.

Another neo-classic procedure is harmonic. In tonal music chords always progress to other chords, thereby increasing or decreasing tension. The Violin Concerto uses harmonic progression only sometimes. Elsewhere Stravinsky reiterates a single chord, or alternates two chords, so that harmonic motion is stopped. The purpose is to focus our attention on the clever and exciting rhythms. The most obvious example of this kind of music is in the final section of the last movement, where the music drives to its conclusion by rhythmic, not harmonic, means.

Stravinsky's blend of old and new is unique, and he is rightly thought of as the leader of the neo-classic movement. Virtually all major composers went through a neoclassic phase in the 1930s and '40s. Composers who had been radical experimenters in their earlier years felt a need to integrate their new discoveries with tradition. The very things they had rebelled against in the 1910s they now approached. For Stravinsky, neo-classicism lasted from around 1920 to around 1955. During those years he wrote some extremely sophisticated and beautiful music, of which the Violin Concerto is a particularly gracious example.

The Firebird

The Firebird *ballet was begun in November 1909 and completed on 18 May 1910. The first performance took place at the Paris Opéra on 25 June 1910, by the Ballets Russes. The choreography was by Mikhail Fokine, the scenery by Alexandre Golovine, the costumes by Golovine and Léon Bakst, and the conductor was Gabriel Pierné. The principal dancers were Fokine, Tamara Karsavina, and Alexis Bulgakov. Stravinsky subsequently extracted several different suites for concert performance.*

Serge Diaghilev and his Ballets Russes had an enormously successful debut performance in Paris in the summer of 1909. Diaghilev and his chief choreographer, Mikhail Fokine, began to make plans for future performances in the city that most appreciated their talents. Fokine felt it necessary to add to their repertory a ballet on a Russian folk subject. After reading several folk-tales, he decided that the legend of the Firebird could be adapted to the dance. He worked out a scenario in which Katschei the Immortal, one of the most fearsome ogres in Russian folklore, is defeated by the Firebird.

Then came the crucial question of who was to be the composer. Rimsky-Korsakoff would have been the logical choice, since he had written an opera on the subject of the Firebird a few years earlier, but he had died unexpectedly in 1908. Nicholas Tcherepnin and Sergei Vassilenko were considered, but Diaghilev decided to commission Anatol Liadov, who had written a number of orchestral works based on fairy tales. Liadov proved to be a slow worker, however, and reportedly was just buying the music paper at the time Diaghilev had hoped to receive a finished score.

Diaghilev and Fokine had recently heard a concert that included two works that greatly impressed them: *Scherzo fantastique* and *Fireworks* by the relatively unknown young composer Igor Stravinsky. And so the commission went to Stravinsky. The composer was flattered to receive what turned out to be the first of several commissions from the great impresario. Stravinsky willingly interrupted his work on an opera, *The Nightingale*. He composed rapidly. Diaghilev was pleased by his cooperation, and he was especially happy with the music. Clearly in the popular tradition of Rimsky-Korsakoff, who had been Stravinsky's teacher, *Firebird* was nonetheless boldly original and extremely colorful. The composer was not completely comfortable writing descriptive music, but he knew the importance of the commission and produced exactly what Diaghilev needed. The ballet, while not typical of Stravinsky, became (and remains) his most popular work. At three different times in his later life, he returned to *The Firebird* to extract concert suites from it. These suites are performed far more than the complete ballet score.

An amusing story shows how popular the work has become: a stranger once came up to the composer and asked if he were indeed the famous composer, Mr. Fireberg.

As soon as the score was ready in piano reduction, the company began to rehearse. Many people heard Stravinsky play the exhilarating new music at the piano. A typical reaction was that of French critic R. Brussel, who had been invited by Diaghilev to hear the ballet score. "The composer, young, slim, and uncommunicative, with vague meditative eyes and lips set firm in an energetic-looking face, was at the piano. But the moment he began to play, the modest and dimly lit dwelling glowed with a dazzling radiance. By the end of the first scene, I was conquered; by the last, I was lost in admiration."

Ballerina Anna Pavlova was originally cast in the title role, but she found the music incomprehensible. She was replaced by Tamara Karsavina, whose knowledge of music was only rudimentary. She had to rely on the composer for help.

> Often he came to the theater before a rehearsal began in order to play for me, over and over again, some particularly difficult passage. I felt grateful, not only for the help he gave me but also for the manner in which he gave it. For there was no impatience in him with my slow understanding, no condescension of a master of his craft towards the slender equipment of my musical education. It was interesting to watch him at the piano. His body seemed to vibrate with his own rhythm. Punctuating staccatos with his head, he made the pattern of his music forcibly clear to me, more so than the counting of bars would have done.

Finally the company was ready for Paris. There were rehearsals with the orchestra, and at last the performance. It was the first great triumph for Stravinsky, and it solidified the reputation of the Ballets Russes. Diaghilev went on to commission two more major ballets from Stravinsky, *Petrouchka* and the *Rite of Spring,* plus several smaller works. He also sought out other leading or promising composers, including Debussy, Ravel, Falla, and Prokofiev.

Stravinsky faced a compositional challenge in the *Firebird.* How could he musically differentiate the natural (Ivan, the Princess, the finale's hymn of rejoicing) from the magical (the Firebird, Katschei)? His idea, derived from Rimsky-Korsakoff's opera *The Golden Cockerel,* was clever. The natural characters and scenes were composed in a diatonic style, while the supernatural were interpreted with chromatic music.

The orchestration in *Firebird* is spectacular. Although he was still in his twenties, Stravinsky was already a master of scoring. The famous passage of natural harmonic string *glissandi,* at the end of the introduction, is one of the most beautiful sonorities in the piece. Some of the other well-known effects, such as trombone and French horn *glissandi,* were added only when Stravinsky made the second *Firebird* Suite in 1919. The colorful orchestral and rhythmic drive of the Infernal Dance foreshadow the brutally primitivistic world of the *Rite of Spring,* composed three years later.

Petrouchka

The Shrove-Tide Fair. The Magic Trick. Russian
    Dance
Petrouchka's Room
The Blackamoor's Room. Dance of the Ballerina.
    Waltz of the Ballerina and the Blackamoor
The Shrove-Tide Fair. Dance of the Nursemaids.
    Peasant with Bear. Gypsies and a Rake Vendor.
    Dance of the Coachmen. Masqueraders. Scuffle
    of the Blackamoor and Petrouchka. Police and
    the Juggler. Apparition of Petrouchka's Ghost

*Petrouchka was begun in August 1910 and completed in May 1911.
It was first performed by the Ballets Russes at the Théâtre du Châ-
telet in Paris; the orchestra was conducted by Pierre Monteux. Stravinsky continually revised the orchestration from 1915 to 1946; his
final thoughts are known as the "Revised 1947 Version."*

Serge Diaghilev's dance company, the Ballets Russes, often performed in Paris. During its second season in the French capital,
Diaghilev introduced a new ballet with music by an unknown Russian composer: Igor Stravinsky. *The Firebird* was a hit, and Diaghilev
immediately made plans for new Stravinsky ballets. The impresario
enthusiastically endorsed the composer's ideas for a dance depicting
pagan rites in prehistoric Russia. But Stravinsky chose to write a
different piece first.

The composer recalled in his *Autobiography,*

Before tackling the *Rite of Spring,* which would be a long and
difficult task, I wanted to refresh myself by composing an orchestral piece in which the piano would play the most important part — a sort of *Konzertstück.* In composing the music, I
had in mind a distinct picture of a puppet, suddenly endowed
with life, exasperating the patience of the orchestra with diabolical cascades of *arpeggi.* The orchestra in turn retaliates with
menacing trumpet blasts. The outcome is a terrific noise which
reaches its climax and ends in the sorrowful and querulous collapse of the poor puppet. Having finished this bizarre piece, I
struggled for hours, while walking beside Lake Geneva, to find
a title which would express in a word the character of my music
and consequently the personality of this creature.

One day I leapt for joy. I had indeed found my title — *Petrouchka*, the immortal and unhappy hero of every fair in all countries. Soon afterward Diaghilev came to visit me at Clarens, where I was staying. He was much astonished when, instead of sketches of the *Rite*, I played him the piece *Petrouchka*. He was so much pleased with it that he would not leave it alone and began persuading me to develop the theme of the puppet's sufferings and make it into a whole ballet.

Diaghilev brought together many of the leading talents of the day to produce the ballet. Scenario and decor were by Alexandre Benois, Mikhail Fokine was choreographer, Pierre Monteux conducted, sets and costumes were by Anisfeld, and dancers included Karsavina, Orloff, Cecchetti, and Nijinsky. The orchestra found the dissonances hard to understand and the dancers had difficulty counting the irregular rhythms, but the production was an enormous success. Despite his previous unfamiliarity with pantomime, Nijinsky was particularly spectacular in his role as the puppet. The renowned actress Sarah Bernhardt said of his portrayal of Petrouchka, "I'm afraid, I'm afraid — because I have just seen the greatest actor in the world."

After the triumphant Paris performances, the Ballets Russes toured Europe and the United States with its production of *Petrouchka*. The dance company needed twelve train cars to transport the elaborate scenery and costumes and the large personnel around the country. The receptions the work was accorded on this tour were not always favorable.

It may seem amazing today that such a tuneful piece as *Petrouchka* was once thought fearfully dissonant and dangerously revolutionary. The most famous dissonance is the "Petrouchka chord," a combination of C major and F-sharp major triads first heard in the clarinets just after the opening of the second scene. This strident sonority, which returns periodically throughout the remainder of the ballet, represents Petrouchka's insults to his audience. The reappearance of the chord at the end of the ballet signifies that Petrouchka's ghost is still delivering mocking insults.

Despite this and other dissonances, and despite jagged rhythms and irregular meters, *Petrouchka* has remained one of the most popular of twentieth-century compositions. Part of the work's appeal derives from its singable melodies. Many of these tunes did not originate with Stravinsky. There are Austrian waltzes, a French music hall song, and at least five Russian folk melodies. These quotations of popular music must have helped *Petrouchka's* early audiences assimilate this sometimes craggy score, but such references are for the most part lost on American audiences of today. The tunes that Stravinsky quoted are so typical of his own melodic style that most listeners simply assume he wrote them.

The original scenario of *Petrouchka* has been pieced together by Stravinsky scholar Eric Walter White:

> [*Scene I.* The Admiralty Square, St. Petersburg, during the 1830s.] Crowds of people are strolling about the scene — common people, gentlefolk, a group of drunkards arm-in-arm, children clustering around the peep-show, women round the stalls. A street musician appears with a hurdy-gurdy. He is accompanied by a dancer. Just as she starts to dance, a man with a musical box and another dancer turn up on the opposite side of the stage. After performing simultaneously for a short while, the rivals give up the struggle and retire. Suddenly the Showman comes out through the curtains of the little theater. The curtains are drawn back to reveal three puppets on their stands — Petrouchka, the Ballerina, and the Blackamoor. He charms them into life with his flute, and they begin to dance. . . .
>
> [*Scene II.*] Petrouchka's Cell. While the Showman's magic has imbued all three puppets with human feelings and emotions, it is Petrouchka who feels and suffers most. Bitterly conscious of his ugliness and grotesque appearance, he feels himself to be an outsider, and he resents the way he is completely dependent on his cruel master. He tries to console himself by falling in love with the Ballerina. She visits him in his cell, and for a moment he believes he has succeeded in winning her. But she is frightened by his uncouth antics and flees. In his despair, he curses the Showman and hurls himself at his portrait, but succeeds only in tearing a hole through the cardboard wall of his cell.
>
> [*Scene III.*] The Blackamoor's Cell. The Blackamoor, clad in a magnificent costume, is lying on a divan, playing with a coconut. Though he is brutal and stupid, the Ballerina finds him most attractive and successfully uses her wiles to captivate him. Their love-scene is interrupted by the sudden arrival of Petrouchka, furiously jealous. . . .
>
> [*Scene IV.*] The Fair. It is evening, and the festivities have reached their height. A group of wet-nurses dance together. A peasant playing a pipe crosses the stage leading a performing bear. A bibulous merchant, accompanied by two gypsies, scatters handfuls of banknotes among the crowd. A group of coachmen strike up a dance and are joined by the nurses. Finally a

number of masquerades — including devil, goat, and pig — rush onto the scene while Bengal flares are set off in the wings. . . .

Petrouchka rushes out from behind the curtain, pursued by the Blackamoor whom the Ballerina tries to restrain. The Blackamoor strikes down Petrouchka with his scimitar. . . . Petrouchka dies, surrounded by the astonished crowd. (In the commotion the Blackamoor and Ballerina have disappeared.) The Showman is fetched, and he reassures the bystanders that Petrouchka is nothing more than a puppet with a wooden head and a body stuffed with sawdust. The crowd disperses as the night grows darker, and the Showman is left behind. But as he starts to drag the puppet off the stage, he is startled to see Petrouchka's ghost appear on the roof of the little theater, jeering and mocking at everyone whom the Showman has fooled.

There is universal significance to the puppet-character, made of straw and sawdust yet with the capacity to love. He is to the Russians what Pierrot is to the French, Punch to the English, and Pinocchio to the Italians — a not-quite-real being whose tragedy is his very real passions, which make him yearn for an unattainable human life. The significance of the character is beautifully elucidated by literary critic Wallace Fowlie:

Only a straw-stuffed puppet, this modern hero! His soul is so tiny that we might almost say he has no soul at all. The flat bright colors of his costume are the simple basic passions which he has learned by rote and which he typifies under the white grease paint. But his mouth is human in its tortured line and his eyes have at times the light of all of man's prayers and loves. Human in his final convulsions and in his death, he appears only as a caricature of man in his life, an hallucinated clown whose jerkiness and animation depict the comic of passions. The crowd must forget the tragedy of passions. He is the will of the crowd. He is the tawdry projection of the crowd's willful flight from reality. He is the soul of the crowd when it has no courage and no heroism. Petrouchka is the reminiscence of what was human.

Yet the passion of all past heroes is in the puppet. Petrouchka is in love. Within the sawdust of his awkward body, there is a grain of life which has all the swelling recklessness and all the trembling blindness of Antony and Othello. . . . The divine in him, which is the force of his love, beats against the sawdust walls of his limp body, as he beats against the fictitious cardboard walls of his cell. For there is no greatness, no dignity in his world: the planks he parades on are barely nailed together and the rope which pulls the faded stage curtain seems to break at each night stand. Integrated, pure, tragic, his love for the insipid Ballerina dominates the show, melts the grease paint, releases his spirit in its dance before the ideal. . . .

Petrouchka's love is the pure symbol of tragedy: rapid, powerful, crushing. His movements are as futile as the first words of Phèdre. He is already, at the beginning of each performance, in the domain of death. His daily ritual is a flight from the vocation of mimicry and humor into a personal experience of love. There he lives as he had never lived in his showman's trade, and there he dies because of his infidelity to the lesser life.

◆　◆　◆

The Rite of Spring
The Adoration of the Earth
The Sacrifice

The Rite of Spring *was begun in the summer of 1911 and completed on 8 March 1913. The work is dedicated to Nicolas Roerich. The first performance was conducted by Pierre Monteux in Paris on 29 May 1913.*

Occasionally — very occasionally — circumstances conspire to bring together the right artist, the right intellectual climate, and the right external stimuli to produce a work so revolutionary, so powerful, so deeply reflective of its times that mankind can never be the same again. Such a work is the *Rite of Spring*. Even those who have never heard this work are touched by the raw emotions it exposes, because it reverberates in much of the music, popular as well as concert, heard today. Its techniques of discontinuity and juxtaposition, furthermore, are reflected in all art media and in popular entertainment as well.

Like many revolutionary works, the *Rite* takes its inspiration from extramusical sources. Composers, particularly in the experimental second decade of this century, frequently found that unusual texts, plots, or scenarios suggested novel approaches to composition. While it is surely true that Stravinsky's earlier ballets, such as *Petrouchka* and *Firebird*, point the way to the *Rite*, his wish to depict ancient pagan rites helped to create a unique musical language. After composing the *Rite* the composer moved on; such music cannot be repeated. Its influence can be felt in some subsequent Stravinsky compositions, but never again did he recapture (nor try to recreate) the frenzied ritualistic music of the *Rite of Spring*.

During the spring of 1910, Stravinsky had a fleeting vision: "I saw in my imagination a solemn pagan rite: wise elders, seated in a circle, watching a young girl dance herself to death. They were sacrificing her to propitiate the god of spring." He mentioned this image to his friends, painter Nicolas Roerich and impresario Serge Diaghilev. Diaghilev immediately seized on the idea for a ballet, and he asked Roerich and Stravinsky to work out a scenario.

Stravinsky's preliminary version of the scenario has been preserved: "It represents pagan Russia and is unified by a single idea: the mystery and great surge of the creative power of spring. The piece has no plot, but the choreographic succession is as follows:

First Part: The Kiss of the Earth. The spring celebration. It takes place in the hills. The pipers and young men tell fortunes. The old woman enters. She knows the mystery of nature and how to predict the future. Young girls with painted faces come in from the river in single file. Games start. The spring Khorovod [mock abduction of the bride]. The people divide into two groups, opposing each other. The holy procession of the wise old men. The oldest and wisest interrupts the spring games, which come to a stop. The people pause trembling before the great action. The old men bless the spring earth. The kiss of the earth. The people dance passionately on the earth, sanctifying it and becoming one with it.

Second Part: The Great Sacrifice. At night the virgins hold mysterious games, walking in circles. One of the virgins is consecrated as the victim and is twice pointed to by fate, being caught twice in the perpetual circle. The virgins honor her, the chosen one, with a marital dance. They invoke the ancestors and entrust the chosen one to the old wise men. She sanctifies herself in the presence of the old men in the great holy dance, the great sacrifice.

Many factors contribute to the exciting language of the *Rite*. The orchestral palette is vivid, colorful, and imaginative — from the pungent opening bassoon in its highest register, to the ensuing dense combinations of wind figurations, to the soaring horns of the "Ritual of the Ancients." The tonal language is also unique. The *Rite* is full of simple, folk-like melodies, often with not more than four or five different notes. These tunes are usually accompanied by less straightforward combinations of notes: biting dissonances or shimmering textures.

Despite its unique approach to melody and harmony, the music is primarily rhythmic. At times the rhythm is elemental, as in the repeated string chords with horn accents that open "The Auguries of

Spring" or the eleven powerful drum and string strokes that separate the "Mystical Circles of the Young Girls" from the barbaric "Glorification of the Chosen Victim." Almost everywhere the rhythm is exciting and irregular, particularly in the "Sacrificial Dance." Stravinsky chose simple melodies and slowly changing harmonies to help the listener focus on the inexorable rhythms. He constantly changes the repeated melodies and rhythms, often only slightly, so that we never know which variant to expect. Thus we are caught up in the excitement of the unpredictable and are continually assaulted by the unexpected. It is no wonder that the music, and the ballet that went with it, provoked violence at its first hearing.

Diaghilev knew that the *Rite* was going have a major impact. As he wanted the ballet to be as compelling as the music, he engaged the great Nijinsky to do the choreography, despite the dancer's inexperience directing and despite his ignorance of even the fundamentals of music. Stravinsky worked closely with Diaghilev and Nijinsky because he was particularly concerned about the relationship of the dance to the music. The composer had specific images in mind, and he jotted down in the score instructions to Nijinsky. According to Stravinsky scholar Jann Pasler, these choreographic directions

> reveal the extent to which Stravinsky composed with visual images in mind . . . and the way in which these images become associated with musical ideas. . . . Stravinsky's choreographic directions reveal *exactly* how he wished the dance to reinforce his musical design or move in counterpoint. Most important to him was that the musical and choreographic rhythms correspond. . . . However, according to Stravinsky's notes, the dance is not always to be in synchrony with the music. At times the dance was for him another dimension of the music, one with its own sense of time. . . .
>
> Dancers were not accustomed to such precise instructions from a composer, nor to such unusual music. Grigoriev writes that the company called the *Rite* rehearsals "arithmetic classes because, owing to the total absence of tune in the music, the dancers had to time their movements by counting the bars."

Not surprisingly, the rehearsals presented great difficulties for the dancers. Not only did they have to relate to music of unprecedented complexity, but also they often had to dance independently of that music. It is hardly surprising that Nijinsky demanded 120 rehearsals.

Despite the dancers' difficulties and comparable problems with the orchestra musicians, Diaghilev's Ballets Russes company was finally able to present the work in Paris. The riot the first performance provoked is by now legendary. During the orchestral introduction, the audience laughed and protested. Several eyewitness reports testify to the pandemonium once the curtain rose. Carl van Vechten related that the audience began "to make cat-calls and to offer audible suggestions as to how the performance should proceed. The orchestra played unheard, except occasionally when a slight lull occurred. The young man seated behind me in the box stood up during the course of the ballet to enable himself to see more clearly. The intense excitement under which he was laboring betrayed itself presently when he began to beat rhythmically on top of my head with his fists. My emotion was so great that I did not feel the blows for some time."

Romola Pulsky, later to marry Nijinsky, reported, "One beautifully dressed lady in an orchestra box stood up and slapped the face of a young man who was hissing in the next box. Her escort arose, and cards were exchanged between them." Jean Cocteau observed the old Countess de Pourtalès stand up and cry out, "This is the first time in sixty years that anyone has dared to make fun of me!" Because the orchestra could not be heard over the audience commotion, Nijinsky stood backstage and shouted the counts to the bewildered dancers.

When, fifty years later, the manuscript score of the *Rite* was returned to Stravinsky, he wrote across the final page, "May whoever listens to this music never experience the mockery to which it was subjected and of which I was the witness in the Théâtre des Champs-Elysées, Paris, Spring 1913."

The favorable reception subsequently accorded the *Rite* remains a footnote to the story of its scandalous first reception. The Nijinsky choreography was received calmly and enthusiastically at the two remaining Paris performances and at all seven London presentations.

After the summer of 1913, the Nijinsky choreography was retired from the Ballets Russes repertory, never to be danced again (there has been a recent attempt to reconstruct it, however). This is unfortunate, since its conception was deeply linked with Stravinsky's compositional ideas. In 1914 Pierre Monteux, who had conducted the premiere, directed the *Rite's* first concert performance. On this occasion the composer was carried from the hall in triumph on the shoulders of the crowd. The future of the work was sealed: although it has been revived as a ballet (usually with choreography) a number of times, the work has survived mainly in the concert hall. Stravinsky actually came to prefer this more abstract manner of presenting the piece, despite the effort he had put into coordinating the dance with the music. He decided that the dance was expendable, perhaps because the music is so physical that it demands active participation from each listener.

Song of the Nightingale

Song of the Nightingale *was composed in 1917. Stravinsky completed the score on 4 April in Morges, Switzerland. The music is based on the opera* The Nightingale, *composed in 1908–14. The first performance of the tone poem was conducted by Ernest Ansermet with l'Orchestre de la Suisse Romande in Geneva on 6 December 1919.*

While he was still a composition student of Rimsky-Korsakoff, Stravinsky had the idea of basing an opera on Hans Christian Andersen's fairy tale *The Nightingale.* The composer worked out the libretto in 1908 and showed the completed first act to his teacher a few months later. Rimsky approved. Before he had the opportunity to work on the remaining two acts, however, Stravinsky received a series of ballet commissions: *Firebird, Petrouchka,* and *Rite of Spring.* These works catapulted the young composer to worldwide fame. In the process of writing them, he evolved his first mature style, which is colorful, sometimes dissonant, rhythmically irregular, and melodically indebted to Russian folk music.

One result of his new-found fame was more commissions. In 1913 the Free Theater of Moscow made a generous offer to Stravinsky to complete *The Nightingale.* He was reluctant to return to the opera, since his style had undergone such a radical change in the intervening four years. The large fee was tempting, however, and the composer rationalized that the lack of action in the first act set it apart dramatically and thus a different kind of music might be appropriate. The 45-minute opera was completed in 1914 and produced not in Moscow (the Free Theater had collapsed) but at the Paris Opéra.

Stravinsky was not completely satisfied. He was still bothered by the four-year gap between the composition of Acts I and II. In addition, he was dubious of opera in general. In a 1913 interview he claimed, "I dislike opera. Music can be married to gesture or to words — but not to both without bigamy. That is why the artistic basis of opera is wrong." Many years later he wrote, "Perhaps *The Nightingale* only proves that I was right to compose ballets since I was not yet ready for an opera."

Early in 1917 the impresario Sergei Diaghilev suggested producing *Nightingale* as a ballet. The composer was interested. "I had been thinking of making a symphonic poem for orchestra by combining the music of Acts II and III of *The Nightingale,* which were homogeneous, and I told Diaghilev I would place that at his disposal if he cared to make a ballet of it. He warmly welcomed the suggestion, and I adapted a scenario from Andersen's fairy story to serve the purpose."

The resulting work, *Song of the Nightingale,* omits all of Act I and parts of Acts II and III; other portions are recomposed. The voice of the Nightingale is replaced by solo flute and solo violin.

Because of the war, the production of the ballet was delayed until 1920, when it was presented by Diaghilev's Ballets Russes at the Paris Opéra. Choreographer was Leonide Massine and set designer was Henri Matisse. In the meantime a non-staged orchestral premiere in 1919 had provoked a Swiss audience to violent protests.

Stravinsky's scenario for the ballet, adapted from Anderson, is as follows:

The Festival in the Emperor of China's Palace. The palace is festively adorned in honor of the Nightingale that sings so sweetly. The walls and the flooring, which are porcelain, gleam in the rays of thousands of golden lamps. The most glorious flowers are placed in the passages. There is a running to and fro and a draft, so that all the bells ring loudly. The Nightingale is placed on a golden perch, and a Chinese March signals the entrance of the Emperor.

The Two Nightingales. The Nightingale sings so gloriously that tears come into the Emperor's eyes. The lackeys and chambermaids report that they are satisfied too; that is saying a good deal, for they are the most difficult to please. Envoys arrive from the Emperor of Japan with the gift of a mechanical nightingale. As soon as the artificial bird is wound up, it sings a song. Its tail moves up and down and shines with silver and gold. It has just as much success as the real one, and it is much handsomer. But where is the living Nightingale? No one has noticed that it has flown away out the open window. The fisherman is heard out of doors, singing for joy because his friend has returned.

Illness and Recovery of the Emperor of China. The poor Emperor can scarcely breathe. He opens his eyes and sees that it is Death who sits upon his chest and has put on his golden crown and holds in one hand the Emperor's sword and in the other his beautiful banner. And all around, from among the folds of the splendid velvet curtains, strange heads peer forth. These are all the Emperor's bad and good deeds. They tell him so much that the perspiration runs from his forehead. The mechanical bird refuses to sing. Then the little live Nightingale is heard singing outside the window. As it sings the spectres grow paler and paler. Even Death listens and says, "Go on, little Nightingale, go on!" And Death gives up each of its treasures for a song and floats out the window in the form of a cold white mist. The Emperor falls into a sweet slumber. The sun shines upon him through the window. He awakens refreshed and restored. A Funeral March is heard as the courtiers come in to look at their dead Emperor. They stand astounded. The Emperor says, "Good morning!" Meanwhile, the friendly Nightingale has flown back to the fisherman, who is heard singing his song once more.

Song of the Nightingale is typical of Stravinsky's early ballets, although it belongs more to the coloristic world of *Firebird* than to the violent world of the *Rite of Spring.* Like the better known ballets, it is a mosaic of different sections with rarely a transition between them. The pentatonic scale (e.g., the black notes on a piano) is frequently used to underline the Chinese setting.

Stravinsky was a master orchestrator, capable of creating spectacular combinations of orchestral timbres. His imagination for sonority is heard on every page of *Song of the Nightingale,* from its initial powerful upward surge for horns, piano, and harps to its serene concluding trumpet solo supported by harps and strings. Whether writing a transparent soloistic or a fully orchestrated texture, Stravinsky's inventiveness continually provides new sonic experiences. The Nightingale's violin solo, high on the the G string, is but one example of his keen sense of sonority.

A mosaic form is appropriate not only because of the episodic nature of the ballet but also because of the style of the orchestration. When sonorities progress one to the next, we tend to respond more to this motion than to the constituent sounds. When, on the other hand, a composer wants us to hear sounds for their own inherent beauty, he minimizes progression to and from other timbres. What results is a series of interesting sonorities which do not move, either by transition or transformation, to other textures.

The mosaic approach to form is one of the far-reaching innovations of such early twentieth-century composers as Stravinsky, Debussy, Satie, and Ives. It is no coincidence that these composers stood, by birth and by choice, outside the mainstream Germanic tradition of tightly knit forms that always progress. *Song of the Nightingale* may not have been Stravinsky's most influential composition, but it typifies a new aesthetic that came to mean more and more to subsequent composers.

Symphonies of Wind Instruments

Stravinsky began to sketch the Symphonies of Wind Instruments *in 1918. The work was completed on 20 November 1920. Serge Koussevitzky conducted the first performance in London on 10 June 1921. The composer revised the piece in 1945–47.*

Stravinsky's revolutionary ballet the *Rite of Spring* rocked the musical world in 1913. It was hailed or damned as barbaric music, as music out to destroy music. It is, in fact, nothing of the sort. It is a sophisticated piece that presents a highly disciplined picture of pagan rites. It is exciting because it is controlled. It is memorable not for destroying its heritage but for breaking new ground.

Stravinsky soon realized what few others understood: the exciting, folk-inspired music of the *Rite* was a deadend. In the colorful Russian works he continued to create for the next few years, the underlying sophistication became more and more apparent. The final Russian work is the extraordinary *Symphonies of Wind Instruments,* surely one of Stravinsky's great masterpieces. Although cut from the same cloth as the *Rite,* it is an austere essay in, rather than a vivid panorama of, Russian nationalism.

Stravinsky himself appreciated how different the *Symphonies of Wind Instruments* was from his earlier works. Writing in his *Autobiography* about its initially unfavorable reception, he said:

> It is futile to look in it for passionate impulse or dynamic brilliance. It is an austere ritual which is unfolded in terms of short litanies between different groups of homogeneous instruments. I fully anticipated that the cantilena of the clarinets and flutes frequently taking up their liturgical dialogue and softly chanting it would not prove sufficiently attractive for a public which had so recently shown me its enthusiasm for the "revolutionary" *Rite of Spring.* This music is not meant to "please" an audience, nor to arouse its passions. Nevertheless, I had hoped that it would appeal to some of those persons in whom a purely musical receptivity outweighed the desire to satisfy their sentimental cravings.

The composer explained that "the title given to this short composition must not be taken in the usual sense of the word. There are various short sections, a kind of litanies, in close tempo relations, succeeding one another, and some rhythmic dialogues between separate woodwind instruments, such as flute and clarinet.... The whole structure of this work required a special title."

Symphonies, like much of Stravinsky's music, is frequently characterized as static. This term is not pejorative. His compositions often consist of isolated sections that explore at length one harmony, orchestral sonority, or melodic motive. Each such passage is a frozen, unchanging, static moment. The dynamism of *Symphonies'* form comes from how each static section relates to the next. These "litanies" are comprised of several distinct types of music — fanfare, chorale, folk-like tunes, etc. — that follow one another with little or no transition. The effect is like a mosaic of potentially independent musics. Coherence comes not so much from how one section leads to the next, as in traditional tonal music, but in the appropriateness of each subsequent section as contrast.

It is fitting that Stravinsky's most extreme statement of the aesthetic of discontinuity should appear in a work dedicated to the memory of Debussy. Stravinsky owed to Debussy not only his colorful orchestrations but also the aesthetic of stasis. Debussy's music, like Stravinsky's, focuses on each moment in time more than on the way one event progresses to the next. These two composers were friends, and they maintained a deep respect for one another. Each dedicated music to the other. Upon hearing of Debussy's death in 1918, Stravinsky immediately sketched the fanfare that was destined to open the *Symphonies of Wind Instruments.* After he had been working on themes for the piece for two years, he received a request to contribute a composition to a special issue of *La Revue musicale* in memory of the French composer. Stravinsky took one of the themes with which he had been working, a chorale, and made it into a somber piano piece. This piano chorale eventually became the final section of *Symphonies.*

Symphony in C

Moderato alla breve
Larghetto concertante —
Allegretto
Largo. Tempo giusto, alla breve

The Symphony in C was begun in the fall of 1938 and completed in Hollywood, California, on 19 August 1940. The title page states: "This symphony, composed to the Glory of God, is dedicated to the Chicago Symphony Orchestra on the occasion of the Fiftieth Anniversary of its existence." Stravinsky conducted the first performance in Chicago on 7 November 1940.

Although one would hardly suspect it from listening to the work, the Symphony in C was composed at a particularly difficult period for Stravinsky. He began the work in Paris the fall of 1938. He later recalled:

> The entire first movement was written there, in my Rue St. Honoré apartment, but in November I interrupted the work for a quick tour of concerts in Italy. When I reached Rome, however, a call from my elder son in Paris informed my that [my daughter] Mika's [tubercular] condition suddenly had become very grave, and the next day, November 30, calling Paris myself from the Turin railway station, I heard the terrible news that she was dead. It is no exaggeration to say that in the following weeks I was able to continue my own life only by my work on the Symphony in C. But I did not seek to overcome my grief by portraying or giving expression to it in music, and you will listen in vain, I think, for traces of this sort of personal emotion.
>
> And only three months later our house was again a morgue. Catherine, my wife, died on March 2, 1939. Then, both because I could not remain in those surroundings, and because I had been warned again of the seriousness of my condition, I moved to Sancellmoz, the sanatorium where my wife and Mika had been, and where my daughter Milena . . . was to spend the next six years. I remained in this boring and not at all Magic Mountain during the next five months, except for short absences, one of which was to attend the funeral of my mother, who died on June 7.
>
> For the third time in six months I heard the long Requiem service, walked in the fields beyond Paris to the cemetery of St. Geneviève, dropped a handful of dirt into an open grave. For the third time I saved myself, or at any rate recovered, by composing. The second movement, begun at Sancellmoz toward the end of March, was completed there in August. I do not think its classic formalities betray any more of my personal feelings of sorrow than did those of the first movement. . . .
>
> The upheaval caused by the war, though neither tragic nor terrible in my case, was nevertheless a difficult environment for composition. The third movement, composed in Cambridge, Massachusetts, and the fourth movement, composed in Hollywood, are very different in spirit from the first two, the European half, and, I fear, the symphony is divided down the middle. For one thing, the first movement is the only large one in the whole inventory of my mature works with no change of meter,

whereas the third movement's metrical irregularities are among the most extreme in any of my compositions.

In the preceding account Stravinsky's grief over the deaths of his daughter and mother appears strangely greater than that for his wife. In fact, by 1939 Catherine Stravinsky was his wife in name only. He had been having an affair for well over a decade with Vera de Bosset. The affair was no secret from Catherine, and she and Vera had actually become friends. Vera was the only true love in the composer's life. She was his nearly constant companion for fifty years. Catherine's death made it possible for the two to marry. When Stravinsky moved to the sanatorium at Sancellmoz after Catherine's death, Vera joined him there. When he moved permanently to the United States the next year, Vera soon followed. They were married in 1940 in Massachusetts, where Stravinsky was lecturing at Harvard and working on the third movement of the symphony. That summer they moved to California, which was to become the composer's longest permanent residence; there he finished the symphony.

Stravinsky's account of the Symphony in C continues:

What can one say about a score that is so unmysterious and so easy to follow at all levels and in all of its relationships? The answer is that critics (who must also earn their livelihood) will find a great deal of nothing to say, finding factitious comparisions with other music, then drawing attention to the severity of the diatonicism while tracing the development of the motive in the first movement and accusing me, in it, of consistency (which I dislike because only mediocre composers are consistent, as only good ones are capable of being very bad). They will also uncover my supposed use of Italianate song-and-accompaniment in the second movement, and of fugato in the last two movements, and discover the existence of a suite-of-dances in the third movement and of flirtations with ballet in other movements.

The composer might also have mentioned the solo winds in the second movement, which evoke eighteenth-century *symphonies concertantes*, and the sonata form in the opening movement.

Such references to earlier styles and forms is typical of Stravinsky's music between 1920 and 1955, his so-called neo-classic period. The neo-classic works were at first scorned: it appeared that the composer was turning his back on the colorful, folk-inspired, exciting styles of *The Rite of Spring* and *Petrouchka*. His rapprochement with the past was seen as a retrogression, a cautious backing away from his notorious avant garde style. In place of the barbarism of the *Rite* audiences in the '20s, '30s, and '40s heard the studied sophistication of works like the Symphony in C and the Violin Concerto. In actuality the composer was not backing away. He had realized that the primitivism of the *Rite* and the colorful panorama of *Petrouchka* were limited and that it was necessary to grow in new directions. There are occasional reinterpretations of tradition in several of these early pieces (the waltz in *Petrouchka*, for example, is thoroughy neo-classic); Stravinsky chose in his later years to develop extensively this hitherto all but unnoticed aspect of his style.

Neo-classic music reinterprets the sounds, procedures, and forms of classical-period music. Stravinsky's neo-classicism is not a return to the past, nor is it an attempt to suggest how Haydn, for example, might have written in 1940, nor is it a pastiche of quotations. It is an homage to tradition. The Symphony in C is Stravinsky's vision of the symphonies of Haydn and Beethoven; it is not an imitation but a personalized commentary. It is like some paintings of Picasso: the subject is recognizable, but instead of being represented realistically it is distorted through the filter of the artist's own personality. Stravinsky, like Picasso, transformed his subject matter as he reinterpreted it. A Picasso face is nothing like a face we have ever seen, but it is face nonetheless; the Symphony in C is nothing like a Beethoven orchestral work, but it is a classical symphony nonetheless.

The Symphony in C evokes the classical era by its title, its modest (by Stravinsky's standards) orchestra, the metric regularity of its outer movements, its diatonic passages, its use of traditional forms, and its seemingly simple harmonies. But Stravinsky adopts nothing from the past without changing it: the traditional orchestra produces his unique sound, the regular meters contain his typical irregular rhythms, the diatonicism does not add up to tonality, the classical forms are used as abstract molds which are filled with non-classical procedures, and the harmonies do not relate to one another in the typical manner. By comparing the symphony with the orchestral style of the late eighteenth century, we understand the nature of musical classicism; by noting how traditional elements can behave in non-traditional ways, we learn to hear what is truly distinctive about the eighteenth-century manner. The Symphony in C is music about other music.

In earlier music harmonies progress to other harmonies. Stravinsky's sounds, by contrast, often do not progress but rather remain static or simply alternate. His sonorities can seem frozen in time rather than moving through time. Thus the use of sonata form in the first movement is not organic. Sonata form is traditionally concerned with the opposition of two forces, represented not only by contrasting themes but also by different keys. The reconciliation of these forces is the goal of the form. But instead of dramatic opposition, the Symphony in C presents simple juxtaposition. Because the harmonies do not progress, they do not conflict; because they do not conflict, the essential motion of the sonata form — the drive toward the recapitulation — is absent. The recapitulation of the opening material simply happens, rather than being the culmination of the entire movement.

In a fascinating article on the symphony, B. M. Williams writes, "Whereas the romantic composer, like Beethoven, uses sonata form to comment upon personal and public emotions and to catch up his listener in a continuum of swiftly changing events, [Stravinsky's music] is closer to the truly static arts of sculpture and architecture than to music which is dynamic, whose parts are constantly on the move in the kaleidoscope of change." By freezing harmonies, melodies, and sections in static non-progressions, Stravinsky divorced classical sounds and forms from classical meaning. He allowed us to hear simple triads, diatonic tunes, and sonata forms in a pure state, not in the service of tonal progression. Thus the Symphony in C is indeed a sophisticated work. Although it can be appreciated for its attractive tunes, catchy rhythms, and sparkling orchestration, there is a deeper level. By hearing it as Stravinsky's idiosyncratic view of the symphonies of Haydn and Beethoven, we can understand it as an historical anomaly: a direct contact between eighteenth- and twentieth-century styles without reference to the intervening historical continuity.

Symphony in Three Movements
Allegro
Andante. Interlude —
Con moto

The Symphony in Three Movements was composed between 4 April 1942 and 7 August 1945. Stravinsky conducted the first performance with the New York Philharmonic on 24 January 1946.

Stravinsky wrote the following commentary on the Symphony in Three Movements:

The symphony was written under the impression of world events. I will not say that it expresses my feelings about them, but only that, without participation of what I think of as my will, they excited my musical imagination. And the impressions that activated me were not general, or ideological, but specific: each episode in the symphony is linked in my imagination with a specific cinematographic impression of the war.

The finale even contains the genesis of a war plot, though I accepted it as such only after the composition was completed. The beginning of the movement is partly and in some inextricable way a musical reaction to the newsreels and documentaries I had seen of goose-stepping soldiers. The square march beat, the brass-band instrumentation, the grotesque crescendo in the tuba, these are all related to those abhorrent pictures. . . .

March music predominates until the fugue, which is the stasis and the turning point. The immobility at the beginning of this fugue is comic, I think — and so, to me, was the overturned arrogance of the Germans when their machine failed. The exposition of the fugue and the end of the symphony are associated in my plot with the rise of the Allies, and the final, rather too commercial, D-flat sixth chord — instead of the expected C — in some way tokens my extra exuberance in the Allied triumph. The [rhythmic] figure was developed from the rhumba in the timpani part in the introduction to the first movement. It is somehow, inexplicably, associated in my imagination with the movements of war machines.

The first movement was likewise inspired by a war film, this time of scorched earth tactics in China. The middle part of the movement was conceived as a series of instrumental conversations to accompany a series of cinematographic scenes showing the Chinese people scratching and digging in their fields. The music for clarinet, piano, and strings, that mounts in intensity and volume until the explosion of three chords . . . and that then begins all over again, was all associated in my mind with this Chinese documentary.

The formal substance of the symphony — "Three Movements" would be a more exact title — exploits the idea of counterplay between several types of contrasting elements. One such contrast, the most obvious, is that of harp and piano, the principal instrumental protagonists. Each has a large *obbligato* role and a whole movement to itself, and only at the turning-point fugue, the Nazi *queue de poisson,* are the two heard together and alone.

But enough of this. In spite of what I have said, the symphony is not programmatic. Composers combine notes. That is all. How and in what form the things of this world are impressed upon their music is not for them to say.

About the genesis of the second movement, Stravinsky wrote: "I was often in company with Franz Werfel. As early as the spring of 1943, the distinguished poet and dramatist tried to encourage me to write music for his *Song of Bernadette* film. I was attracted by the idea and by his script, and if the conditions, business and artistic, had not been so entirely in favor of the film producer, I might have accepted. I actually did compose music for the 'Apparition of the Virgin' scene, and this music became the second movement of my Symphony in Three Movements."

Stravinsky also remarked that the first movement was originally conceived as a concerto for orchestra, and the third movement was once thought of as a piano concerto. The sketches for the piece do not bear these claims out, however.

The symphony begins with a vigorous flourish that has puzzled many commentators by its lack of subsequent integration in the movement. Robert Craft, the conductor who for many years functioned as Stravinsky's assistant, explains that the sketches show that this figure was composed next to last. The movement is extremely rhythmic throughout. The rhythms are asymmetrical and fascinating. To help us focus on them, Stravinsky kept the melodic material minimal and changed harmonies slowly. What resulted is a mosaic of rhythmic gestures. Within each section the harmony is reiterated or alternated, and the texture is relatively constant. Ever new rhythmic permutations are played out. For example, after the opening flourish concludes, there is a brief passage with a simple repetitive rhythm in the clarinets, which accompany several statements of an important motive in the horns. Then, without warning, the harmony, texture, and rhythm shift. While the low strings repreat the horn motive seemingly endlessly (thereby rendering the harmony unchanging), the upper strings, joined by the piano and then the winds, play irregular variations on a simple rhythmic figure. Just as suddenly as it began, this section gives way to another, in which the full orchestra develops rhythmic variants of the basic motive. The ending is quite unusual: the entire orchestra holds a beautifully spaced C major seventh chord, while only the bass clarinet reiterates a repeated-note rhythm.

The second movement is discontinuous, but in a less aggressive manner than the first. It is more melodic, less single-minded in its rhythms, and less harsh in its harmonies. But the emphasis on rhythm persists. The most striking section is the one in which solo strings and harp (in the recapitulation it is winds and harp) play a simple figure in rhythmic unison. A brief interlude connects the second and third movements.

The finale reverts to the rhythmic excitement and harmonic

stasis of the first movement. The form is again a series of disconnected sections. The first, for full orchestra, gives way unexpectedly to a scherzo-like passage that begins with only two bassoons. At the center of the movement is the "comic immobility" of the fugue. The curiously static subject appears in the piano, with some help from the trombone. Exhilarating rhythms push the movement to its close.

The Symphony in Three Movements typifies most of the music Stravinsky wrote between the early 1920s and the mid-1950s. In this so-called "neo-classic" style the composer took models, usually but not always from the past, and made them his own. Some of his models were specific pieces by other composers, but most were general types, particular styles, or specific forms. He recomposed the music so that it became thoroughly modern and uniquely personal. Stravinsky's neo-classic music is not imitative. Rather, he tried to show how early compositional devices and idioms can still be used in the twentieth century. This is sophisticated music, because it is making a statement on other music. To appreciate its neo-classicism fully, you have to be familiar enough with the models to understand to what extent Stravinsky is adapting them and to what extent he is injecting his own personality into them.

Neo-classic music is sometimes called music criticism in notes rather than words. When Stravinsky used classical harmonies in non-classical ways, he was making a commentary on what tonality is and what it is not. When he used forms that imply motion but froze them through the use of static harmonic plateaus, he was pointing out the arbitrariness of musical motion.

Stravinsky's models included Verdi operas, French ballet music of the nineteenth century, classical piano concertos, the Bach *Brandenburg* Concertos, the music of Broadway, and medieval masses. The Symphony in Three Movements is special among the neo-classic works, because its model is the composer's own early music. He was looking back with the sophistication of maturity to the excitement of youth, particularly as embodied in the *Rite of Spring*. It is surely no coincidence that, just prior to composing the symphony, he was at work on a revision of that early ballet.

There are many features the symphony has in common with the early ballet music: non-developmental ostinatos, discontinuous forms, static harmonies, permutational rhythms, harsh chords, and brilliant scoring. But it would be a mistake to think of the symphony as a return to an earlier style. Stravinsky was viewing that style from a distance. He was making a statement about ostinatos, discontinuities, harmonic stasis, etc., rather than embracing them anew. He was showing how these elements can be tamed in order to create that most classical of forms, a symphony. If the Symphony in Three Movements is not quite as exciting as its model, that is purposeful. Stravinsky stepped back from the immediacy of the early style to give a sophisticated version of it, two-dimensional but subtle. The excitement in the symphony is only on the surface. Beneath it lies a cool elegance, whereas the excitement in the *Rite* is total, even if less sophisticated.

◆   ◆   ◆

Symphony of Psalms

Exaudi orationem meam, Domine
Expectans expectavi Dominum
Alleluia. Laudate Dominum

The Symphony of Psalms *was begun in January and completed on 15 August 1930. It is "composed to the glory of God and dedicated to the Boston Symphony Orchestra." Ernest Ansermet conducted the first performance with the Brussels Philharmonic on 13 December 1930. The Boston premiere took place six days later, under the direction of Serge Koussevitzky.*

In 1929 Serge Koussevitzky comissioned Stravinsky to compose a symphonic work to celebrate the upcoming fiftieth anniversary of the Boston Symphony Orchestra. The composer decided to pursue an idea he had had in mind for some time: a psalm symphony. He later recalled that he

chose Psalm 150 in part for its popularity, though another and equally compelling reason was my eagerness to counter the many composers who had abused these magisterial verses as pegs for their own lyrico-sentimental "feelings." The Psalms are poems of exaltation, but also of anger and judgement, and even of curses. Although I regarded Psalm 150 as a song to be danced, as David danced before the Ark, I knew that I would have to treat it in an imperative way. . . .

The first movement, "Hear my prayer, O Lord," was composed in a state of religious and musical ebullience. The sequences of two minor thirds joined by a major third, the root idea of the whole work, were derived from the trumpet-harp motive at the beginning of the [last movement's] allegro. . . .

The "Waiting for the Lord" Psalm makes the most overt use of musical symbolism in any of my music before *The Flood.* An upside-down pyramid of fugues, it begins with a purely instrumental fugue of limited compass and employs only solo instruments. The restriction to treble range was the novelty of this initial fugue, but the limitation to flutes and oboes proved its most difficult compositional problem. The subject was developed from the sequence of minor thirds used as an ostinato in the first movement. The next and higher stage of the upside-down pyramid is the human fugue, which ... represents a higher level in the architectural symbolism by the fact that it expands into the bass register. The third stage, the upside-down foundation, unites the two fugues. . . .

Psalm 40 is a prayer that a new canticle may be put into our mouths. The Allelujah is that canticle. . . . The *Laudate Dominum* was originally composed to the words of the *Gospodi Pomiluy*. This section is a prayer to the Russian image of the infant Christ with orb and scepter. I decided to end the work with this music, too, as an apotheosis of the sort that had become a pattern in my music since the epithalamium at the end of *Les Noces*. The allegro of Psalm 150 was inspired by a vision of Elijah's chariot climbing the Heavens; never before had I written anything quite so literal as the triplets for horns and piano to suggest horses and chariot. The final hymn of praise must be thought of as issuing from the skies, and agitation is followed by "the calm of praise," but such statements embarrass me. What I can say is that in setting the words of this final hymn, I cared above all for the *sounds* of the syllables, and I indulged my besetting pleasure of regulating prosody in my own way.

Stravinsky wanted to create a work in which the orchestra and the chorus were equal partners. This wish led him to choose an unusual orchestra: five flutes, five oboes, no clarinets, four bassoons, a full brass section, two pianos, no violins, no violas, cellos, string basses, harp, timpani, and bass drum. The resulting sound is special; almost any measure of the *Symphony of Psalms* is recognizable just on the basis of its sonority.

The work exemplifies the composer's second-period style, sometimes called neo-classicism. Gone are the barbaric rhythms and pungent dissonances of the *Rite of Spring*. The neo-classic style is more refined and more subtle. In this idiom Stravinsky purposefully returned to chords, melodic figures, forms, and procedures of earlier eras, from medieval to late romantic styles. He used them in thoroughly personal and contemporary contexts. He used old sounds and made them behave in new ways, and he used new sounds within old forms. The resulting music is sophisticated: you must know the style being referred to if you are to appreciate fully Stravinsky's reference to it.

In some neo-classic pieces the composer actually recomposed existing works. *Pulcinella*, based on music Stravinsky believed was by Pergolesi, and *The Fairy's Kiss*, based on lesser known works of Tchaikovsky, are two examples. Most of the neo-classic music is more general, however. In the *Symphony of Psalms* there are references to tonal sounds, fugal procedures, and ancient chant melodies, but these diverse sources are thoroughly integrated into Stravinsky's personal rhetoric.

A typical example is the very first chord. In one sense it is simply an E minor triad, a sound that had been heard in countless pieces throughout the baroque, classic, and romantic periods. But this particular E minor chord is unlike any pre-twentieth-century triad. It is spaced not, as used to be normative, with notes close together at the top and far apart at the bottom, but rather with notes close together at the top and bottom yet far apart in the middle. This makes a big difference in the sound. We immediately recognize that this chord is a modern version of an age-old sonority. In addition, there are far more G's than E's in the chord, which surely would be a taboo if this were really a tonal triad.

This isolated chord is not merely an unusual sound. Its structure implies the tonal conflict of the first movement: E minor, the expected key given that the chord is an E minor triad, gives way to G major, since the note G is over-emphasized in the chord.

The use of fugue in the second movement is another instance of the neo-classic aesthetic. Fugue is a form that grew to its height during the baroque period. Its logic is rooted in tonality. Stravinsky adapted the form, and he used melodic lines that suggest tonal fugues, but he did not allow the harmonies to progress as they would in a truly tonal fugue. Instead, there are long stretches of harmonic stasis, despite the constant motion of notes.

The underlying stasis comes to the forefront in the coda of the last movement. Here Stravinsky composed one of the most beautiful passages in all music. Over a constantly repeating bass figure of four beats, a three-beat figure repeats over and over, with some variation. The notes scarcely change, the harmonies remain frozen, but the interaction of three- and four-beat patterns keeps our interest. The effect is extraordinary: a musical vision of eternity. The irony is that this serene yet tense passage sets the words, "Praise Him upon the loud cymbals; praise Him upon the high sounding cymbals. Let every thing that hath breath praise the Lord." The *Psalms* orchestra does not even have a cymbal!

The unchanging music of this coda perhaps symbolizes the eternity of God. The very last chord, which consists of C's in all registers plus a few high E's that sound more like overtones than separate pitches, may represent the purity of God. The proportions of the work (the three movements are in the approximate duration ratio 1:2:3) may suggest the Trinity. Stravinsky would no doubt have denied all such symbolism, since he did not believe in the ability of music to express anything other than music. But the *Symphony of Psalms* is one of the supreme creations of Western art, and, like much great art, is deeply religious, more so than its creator may have realized.

> People will always insist upon looking in music for something that is not there. The main thing for them is to know what the piece expresses and what the author had in mind when he composed it. They never seem to understand that music is an entity of its own apart from anything it may suggest to them. In other words, music interests them in so far as it touches on elements outside it while evoking sensations with which they are familiar. Most people like music because it gives them certain emotions, such as joy, grief, sadness, an image of nature, a subject for day-dreams, or — still better — oblivion from "everyday life." They want a drug — "dope." It matters little whether this way of thinking of music is expressed directly or is wrapped up in a veil of artificial circumlocutions. Music would not be worth much if it were reduced to such an end. When people have learned to love music for itself, when they listen with other ears, their enjoyment will be of a far higher and more potent order, and they will be able to judge it on a higher plane and realize its intrinsic value. . . . All these considerations were evoked by my *Symphony of Psalms* because, both by the public and the press, the attitude I have just described was specially manifested in regard to that work. Notwithstanding the interest aroused by the composition, I noticed a certain perplexity caused, not by the music as such, but by the inability of listeners to understand the reason which had led me to compose a symphony in a spirit which found no echo in their mentality.

Today, nearly sixty years after the symphony's completion, we understand very well its objectivity, an objectivity that reaches a higher plane of meaning than many subjective artistic statements. And the symphony does indeed find an echo in our mentality. We understand that the work is not Stravinsky's personal expression, but it is nonetheless a statement of faith. Its objectivity, reinforced by Stravinsky's denial of any personal message, makes it all the more universal. It has become a timeless statement on mankind's praise of God. The timelessness of its faith emerges in utmost simplicity in the changeless music of the coda.

Piotr Ilich Tchaikovsky

Born on 7 May 1840 in Votinsk, Russia.
Died on 6 November 1893 in Saint Petersburg.

Concerto Number 1 in B-Flat Minor for Piano and Orchestra, Opus 23

Allegro non troppo e molto maestoso. Allegro con
  spirito
Andante semplice. Prestissimo. Andante semplice
Allegro con fuoco

*The First Piano Concerto was composed late in 1874. It was or-
chestrated in January 1875. The first performance given was by
Hans von Bülow and the Boston Symphony Orchestra, conducted
by Benjamin Johnson Lang, on 25 October 1875 in Boston. Tchaikovsky revised the work in 1876 and again in 1889.*

The first of Tchaikovsky's three piano concertos has become enormously popular, overshadowing his later efforts in the genre. Tchaikovsky's friend Nicolai Rubinstein, a prominent pianist and conductor, would surely have been surprised to learn that this work was
destined to become the world's most popular piano concerto. Rubinstein was a powerful man in Russian musical circles, and it was
natural for Tchaikovsky to show him the concerto. The composer
hoped for some practical suggestions on the piano writing, since he
was not himself a virtuoso, and he hoped to interest Rubinstein in
performing the work. On Christmas Eve in 1874, Tchaikovsky met
with Rubinstein and his housemate, the critic Nicolai Hubert, at the
Moscow Conservatory. Tchaikovsky played the concerto, which was
finished but not yet orchestrated, at the piano. Rubinstein's reaction
was extremely negative, and Tchaikovsky, who was a very sensitive
man, was deeply insulted. When he described the event three years
later in a letter to his patroness, Nadezhda von Meck, his anger and
hurt were still smoldering. He could scarcely refer to Rubinstein by
surname, but rather called him R, R-ein, Nicolai Grigoryevich, N. G.,
or even His Excellency:

> I played the first movement. Not a single word, not a single re-
> mark!. . . Oh, for one word, for friendly attack, but for God's sake
> one word of sympathy, even if not of praise. Rubinstein was
> amassing his storm, and Hubert was waiting to see what would

happen and whether there would be a reason for joining one side
or the other. Above all I did not want sentence to be passed on
the artistry. My need was for remarks about the virtuoso piano
technique. R's eloquent silence was of greatest significance. He
seemed to be saying, "My friend, how can I speak of detail when
the whole thing is antipathetic?" I fortified myself with patience
and played through to the end. Still silence. I stood and asked,
"Well?" Then a torrent poured from Nicolai Grigoryevich's
mouth, gentle at first, then growing more and more into the
sound of Jupiter. . . . It turned out that my concerto was worthless and unplayable; passages were so fragmented, so clumsy, so
badly written that they were beyond rescue; the work itself was
bad, vulgar; in places I had stolen from other composers; only
two or three pages were worth preserving; the rest must be
thrown away or completely rewritten. "Here, for instance,
this — now what's that?" (He caricatured my music on the
piano.) "And this? How could anyone. . . ." Etc., etc. The chief
thing I can't reproduce is the *tone* in which all this was uttered.
In a word, a disinterested person in the room might have
thought I was a maniac, a talentless senseless hack who had
come to submit his rubbish to an eminent musician. Having
noted my obstinate silence, Hubert was astonished and shocked
that such a ticking off was being given to a man who had already
written a great deal and given a course in free composition at
the conservatory, that such a contemptuous judgement without
appeal was pronounced over him, such a judgement as you
would not pronounce over a pupil with the slightest talent who
had neglected some of his tasks — then he began to explain N.
G.'s judgement, not disputing it in the least but just softening
that which His Excellency had expressed with too little ceremony. . . .

I left the room without a word and went upstairs. In my
agitation and rage I could not say a thing. Presently R-ein joined
me, and seeing how upset I was he asked me into one of the
distant rooms. There he repeated that my concerto was impossible, pointed out many places where it would have to be completely revised, and said that if within a limited time I reworked
the concerto according to his demands, then he would do me the
honor of playing my thing at one of his concerts. "I shall not
alter a single note," I answered. "I shall publish the work exactly
as it is!" This I did."

Tchaikovsky dedicated the work not to Rubinstein, as he had
planned, but to the German pianist-conductor Hans von Bülow, who

performed it on a tour of the United States. Von Bülow sent what is thought to have been the first cable ever from Boston to Moscow, in order to tell Tchaikovsky of the great success of the work.

Rubinstein was a solid musician, and he considered himself Tchaikovsky's friend. He may have acted boorishly (although we have only Tchaikovsky's possibly exaggerated account of the incident), but he felt that his criticisms were justified. Whether or not the work is vulgar is still an open question. Works of art whose emotional appeal is as immediate and obvious as in this concerto are bound to offend some sensibilities, while they excite and uplift others. Rubinstein's claim that the work was badly written for the piano was probably true; Tchaikovsky himself revised the work twice, following suggestions of various pianists concerning the feasibility and effectiveness of the solo part. Rubinstein's charge that the composer stole from other composers is surely unfounded. The piece is as purely Tchaikovskian as can be, although there are several folksongs used in the work. There are Ukranian tunes in the outer movements, and the middle section of the second movement is based on the French song *Il faut s'amuser, danser et rire* ("Amuse Yourself by Dancing and Laughing"). This song was a favorite of singer Désirée Artôt, whom Tchaikovsky had wanted to marry a few years earlier.

Rubinstein came to regret his harshness and apologized to Tchaikovsky. He conducted the first Moscow performance of the concerto, and in later years often performed the work as soloist. The two men remained on good terms for many years.

There is something very unusual about the structure of this concerto. Perhaps Rubinstein's criticisms were based in part on his failure to appreciate the uniqueness of the structure. Musicologists are still debating the effectiveness of the atypical form of the first movement. After the famous dramatic horn beginning in the tonic key of B-flat minor, there is a large introductory section based on a beautifully lyrical melody in the strings, accompanied by huge chords in the piano. This melody is perhaps the most memorable in the entire concerto; it has been popularized countless times in recent years. What is unusual about this movement is that this introductory section is cast in the "wrong" key of D-flat major and that the music is so beautiful and engaging that it hardly seems to function as an introduction at all. It does not lead to the main body of the movement, because it is self-contained. By comparison, the main material (introduced in the piano in fast two-note groups) seems pale. It is true that the lyrical second theme is also very beautiful, but nothing happens in this movement that can rival the introduction. We expect such special music to return, perhaps grandly in the coda. But it never does, not in this movement and not in either of the subsequent movements. It remains a magnificent memory.

Is this a compositional problem? The debate continues, and probably always will. It is not preordained in the heavens that all melodies must be recapitulated, nor is it the law that all beautiful melodies must be heard more than once. That we as listeners want to hear the introduction music again is undeniable, but the real criterion of success is whether what actually happens is of sufficient beauty to keep our interest. And surely there is a wealth of attractive music in this concerto. It is really unfair to criticize the work for failing to be like other pieces. It is a unique artistic expression and must be judged on its own terms. Whether or not a particular listener finds it successful, one interesting fact remains: the gorgeous melody that most people identify with *the* Tchaikovsky Piano Concerto is the introductory theme, not one of the principal melodies that is developed.

Both the second (a combination of slow movement and scherzo) and third movements are quite brief. Lacking the extended development of the first movement, they are based more on alternation and juxtaposition than on extension and transition. The combined duration of the latter movements is considerably less than that of the opening movement alone.

The finale is continually exciting rhythmically. The main theme is dance-like, and it has some delightful ambiguities. It seems unable to make up its mind whether it is in 3/4 or 6/8 and, in either case, just where the first beat of the measure falls. This uncertainty pervades the movement and holds our interest. Even the lyrical second theme, another one of Tchaikovsky's apparently endless supply of beautifully expansive romantic melodies, often seems about to slip from 3/4 to 2/4.

Concerto in D Major for Violin and Orchestra, Opus 35
Allegro moderato. Moderato assai. Allegro giusto
Canzonetta: Andante —
Allegro vivacissimo

The Violin Concerto was composed between 17 March and 11 April 1878 at Clarens, on Lake Geneva, Switzerland. Adolf Brodsky was the soloist when Hans Richter conducted the first performance in Vienna on 4 December 1881.

One of the most difficult periods in Tchaikovsky's stormy life was the time of his marriage to Antonina Milyukova. The 37-year-old composer was in love with the idea of marriage, but certainly not with the persistent if not obsessive Antonina, whose only goal in life was to wed her famous teacher. Tchaikovsky, who longed for the intimacy of a home life and who wanted to convince the world (if not himself) that he was heterosexual, found himself ensnared in the trap Antonina cunningly had laid. Always kindhearted and generous, the naïve Piotr Ilich found it easier to succumb to a marriage he dreaded than to break off the engagement. The advice of his friends and siblings went unheeded as Tchaikovsky entered into a travesty of a marriage. He was able to stand living with Antonina only nine weeks. He left her, his spirit crushed and his creativity damaged.

His only salvation was his mysterious patroness Nadezhda von Meck, who was to remain his confidante, support, and friend for many years, although the two were never to meet. Nadezhda did not chide Tchaikovsky for seeking love in a loveless marriage. She had been hurt both by the composer's having kept silent about the marriage until the last moment and by the thought that he would even consider sharing his innermost soul with another woman. But she hid her pain and came to Tchaikovsky's rescue. She sent him money for his much-needed escape. He accepted her generous gift and fled the Moscow apartment Antonina had set up as a love nest. He remained out of Russia for several months, and he buried himself in work. This activity proved therapeutic. As he composed, he regained his sanity, his humanity, and his self-respect. And, in the process, he became a mature composer. He completed three important works — the Fourth Symphony, the opera *Eugene Onegin,* and the Violin Concerto — before returning to Moscow.

The concerto was intended for the great virtuoso Leopold Auer. It was another violinist, however, who had helped Tchaikovsky with the technicalities of writing for the violin. Yosif Yosifovich Kotek, a former student of the composer, was employed by Nadezhda von Meck. He had played an important part in establishing the friendship between Tchaikovsky and the wealthy patroness. Auer looked at the concerto once it was finished, and he promptly declared it unplayable. He not only refused to perform it himself, but he actively campaigned against other Russian violinists' attempting it. Thus Kotek refused to play it, as did Emile Sauret. The work sat idle for almost four years before Adolph Brodsky cautiously decided he would play the premiere, not in Moscow but in Vienna.

Viennese audiences were traditionally conservative, and critics in that city could be venomous. The orchestra was poorly prepared, and furthermore the concerto was unusual in many ways. The result was a riot. Half the audience hated the work's audacious novelities and the other half was excited by its gypsy rhythms. Critic Eduard Hanslick wrote one of his more vitriolic reviews:

The Russian composer Tchaikovsky is surely not an ordinary talent, but rather an inflated one, with a genius-obsession without discrimination or taste. Such is also his latest, long, and pretentious Violin Concerto. For a while it moves soberly, musically, and not without spirit. But soon vulgarity gains the upper hand and asserts itself to the end of the first movement. The violin is no longer played; it is pulled, torn, drubbed. The adagio is again on its best behavior, to pacify and to win us. But it soon breaks off to make way for a finale that transfers us to a brutal and wretched jollity of a Russian holiday. We see plainly the savage vulgar faces, we hear curses, we smell vodka. Friedrich Vischer once observed, speaking of obscene pictures, that they stink to the eye. Tchaikovsky's Violin Concerto gives us for the first time the hideous notion that there can be music that stinks to the ear.

Violinist Brodsky was challenged, not discouraged, by such a reaction. He pledged to perform the concerto forever. He had somewhat better success in London, and he won open admiration for the work in Moscow. Leopold Auer finally admitted his error and became, in his old age, a champion of the concerto which he had vehemently opposed. But by then he had retired from playing, and he never performed the Tchaikovsky Concerto. He did teach it to his students, who included such giants of the violin as Jascha Heifitz and Mischa Elman.

Why was a concerto that is today readily mastered by virtually every serious violinist at first considered so difficult and so unusual? It is true that the composer's incorporation of the type of gypsy violin playing he had heard in the Cossack camps around Moscow into a work for the concert stage was unusual. It is also true that the form is not standard. The lyrical opening melody, which sounds like the statement of a principle theme, is never heard again in the concerto (interestingly, Tchaikovsky used the same procedure with the opening of his First Piano Concerto). But these strokes of originality should hardly turn leading violinists away from the piece. Rather, the problem lay in the concept of idiomatic violin music.

Violin technique is always changing. Today's students routinely master yesterday's most fiendish difficulties. It is not only violinists who are responsible for this constant expansion of technical prowess, however. When a composer writes a difficult new piece, he may inadvertently ask the soloist to do new, possibly unheard of, virtuosic feats. Since such technical feats will not have existed in previous music, soloists may not know how to perform them. And the music will therefore be pronounced impossible, or at least not characteristic of the instrument. But if the work in question has real musical merit, as the Tchaikovsky Concerto certainly does, then some courageous and adventurous violinist will eventually find a way of achieving what the composer wants. Then other violinists will see that what they had thought impossible can actually be done, and they too will want to perform the piece. Thus, before too long, the work will have entered the repertory of several soloists, and its technical demands will no longer seem unidiomatic. The concept of what is characteristic for the violin will have changed a bit, as the impossible becomes "merely" the virtuosic. History has repeatedly demonstrated this fact, as major concertos by several composers have forced performers to expand their technique and with it their concept of what constitutes good violin music. The Tchaikovsky concerto was neither the first nor the last to extend the practical limits of violin playing.

Francesca da Rimini, Opus 32

Francesca da Rimini was composed between 7 October and 17 November 1876. It was first performed on 9 March 1877 in Moscow. Nikolai Rubinstein conducted the Russian Musical Society.

Francesca da Rimini is second only to Tchaikovsky's *Romeo and Juliet* as a depiction of soaring passion. The intensity of the music, its sweeping drives toward climaxes, and its lyric love songs are so immediate, so unmistakable that we are either swept up in the passion or embarrassed by it. There is no mistaking the emotions in this music, no hiding behind listening to notes. Anyone who has known passionate desire recognizes of what this music sings. We may call it tawdry or beautiful, we may dismiss it as nineteenth-century sentimentality or we may hear it as an extraordinary song of love, but we cannot deny the meaning of Tchaikovsky's tone poem. This is program music at its most explicit.

How did the composer come to write music of such unabashed passion? The answer may seem surprising, for this is not music composed by a lovesick romantic about his desire for his beloved beauty. In fact, Tchaikovsky was a homosexual, and *Francesca* was created as a final desperate attempt to convince both himself and his public that he was not.

Sexual preference is personal, especially for someone living in as repressive a society as that of late-nineteenth-century Russia. If Tchaikovsky had not tried so desparately and so publicly to disclaim his homosexuality, we would hardly be concerned about it. Nonetheless, despite considerable evidence to the contrary, several of Tchaikovsky's biographers still want to deny his proclivities. Some want to refute the "dreaded affliction" to which the cryptic "x x x" in his diaries obviously referred.

Tchaikovsky needed love, and he wanted desperately to have a home and family. He did not willingly admit that these goals were impossible. He was well into his thirties, and he still hoped that his old schoolboy habit was nothing more than a passing fancy. But he felt the pressure of growing suspicion, and he felt his uncontrollable drives assert themselves more and more strongly. He tortured himself with despair and alcohol. Finally, in 1875, he made two big steps to try to deny the truth.

First he decided to marry. He did not love Antonina Milyukova, and he found the thought of living with her somewhat repellent, but he went through with the marriage nonetheless. After nine weeks he could stand in no more. The home he had longed for, the stability he needed, and the love he wanted were mocked by this marriage. It took him a year to recuperate.

His second step was to compose the great love epic, *Francesca da Rimini.* Perhaps he identified with Francesca's temptation toward illicit love, or perhaps he poured out his own passion into a music whose program disguised it as a song of heterosexual desire. But he must have realized subsonsciously the hopelessness of what he was attempting: he felt compelled to surround his love music with music descriptive of Hell. It was ironic yet appropriate that he should compose love music that was also death music at the time of his impending marriage.

According to Tchaikovsky, the work is divided into three sections: (1) introduction: the gateway to the inferno ("leave all hope behind, ye who enter here"); (2) Francesca tells the story of her tragic love for Paolo; (3) the turmoil of Hades and the conclusion.

The outer sections set the mood for the central movement, which is the heart of the piece. The dissonant chromatic harmonies of the opening section yearn for resolution. Tension mounts, but release always eludes the music. Often the music moves over long-held or continually reiterated bass notes: we feel the desire to move on, to reach a goal, but the music denies the needed resolution. The accumulation of tension finally leads into the middle section, where the long, lyric love melody is heard. Now the piece is more consonant, as it sweeps us along irrestibly.

The story of the love of Francesca and Paolo is from the Fifth Canto of Dante's *Inferno.* Francesca, daughter of the Prince of Rimini, is promised in marriage to Giovanni Malatesta, an ugly yet famous soldier. Francesca instead falls in love with Paolo, Giovanni's younger brother. Giovanni surprises the lovers in an embrace and slays them.

Francesca's soul goes to Hell, to join the souls of others who in their lifetimes had abandoned themselves to sensual pleasure. These souls are punished in eternal darkness by raging tempests, meant to remind them of how in life they had given in to the tempest of lust.

In order that his audiences explicitly understood the heterosexual intent of the music's passion, Tchaikovsky prefaced the score with a careful explanation of why Francesca was in Hell. He then quoted several lines from the *Inferno* in which Francseca describes her love for Paolo.

Romeo and Juliet

Romeo and Juliet *was composed in the latter months of 1869. It was first performed on 16 March 1870 by the Russian Musical Society, conducted by Nicolai Rubinstein, in Moscow. Tchaikovsky thoroughly revised the work in 1870 and again in 1880.*

Composer Mily Balakirev (1837–1910) was something of a busybody. He was not content simply writing his own music. He wanted a hand in the creation of music by several other composers as well. Thus he became the leader of the group of Russian nationalists known as The Mighty Five, and also he befriended Tchaikovsky and gave him many detailed suggestions about various compositions. Not only did he take an active role in the creation of *Romeo and Juliet,* but also many years later he provided a program and specific compositional advice on the *Manfred* Symphony.

Balakirev wrote to Tchaikovsky in the fall of 1869, suggesting the composition of an overture based on Shakespeare's *Romeo and Juliet.* Balakirev included some music he felt appropriate for the opening; he described exact working methods to help Tchaikovsky find inspiration; he prescribed the tonalities for the various sections of the piece. Tchaikovsky was young, impressionable, and unsure of himself. He appreciated Balakirev's interest, rather than resented the interference. Tchaikovsky went so far as to submit the completed composition to Balakirev for corrections.

Balakirev liked much of the work, but he criticized the first theme. It reminded him of a Haydn quartet whereas he felt it should have the "old-world catholicism" of a Liszt chorale. He did not like the slow introduction at all. He did not approve of the ending. Tchaikovsky meekly made the revisions, although he himself eventually became dissatisfied and worked extensive changes of his own.

It is not surprising that Tchaikovsky readily complied with Balakirev's suggestion for a piece based on Shakespeare's love-tragedy. The subject was appropriate, because the composer himself was at the time involved in a hopeless love. A few months earlier he had fallen under the spell of singer Désirée Artôt, whom he had seen playing Desdemona. Tchaikovsky had not yet acknowledged his homosexuality, and he was eager to meet this enticing lady. He did see her frequently, and he began to talk about marriage. Had the marriage actually taken place, it might have been as disastrous as Tchaikovsky's eventual union several years later, which lasted only nine weeks. But Artôt herself prevented these difficult issues from ever coming up by marrying instead a Spanish baritone named Mariano Padilla y Ramos.

Artôt seems to have liked Tchaikovsky and been attracted to him as an artist, as she enjoyed "collecting" admiring young men. Tchaikovsky, on the other hand, had really thought he was in love. He did grieve for his lost love, but not as deeply as one might expect from such a hyper-sensitive romantic. He identified with the ill-fated Romeo and thus poured his unhappiness and love-longings into the *Romeo* Overture. It is true that, shortly after completing the work, he went to see Artôt-Padilla perform again. He sat throughout the performance staring at her through opera glasses, the tears running down his cheeks. Composing *Romeo* must have been a sufficient catharsis, though, as the composer subsequently resumed his normal life without undue grief.

Balakirev wrote him, upon receiving the finished score, with praise but also a rather unkind irony: "It is simply fascinating. I often play it and should like to hug you for it. In it is the tenderness and longing of love, and much more that ought to go straight to the heart of the immortal Albrecht. When I play this I visualize you wallowing in your bath with Artôt-Padilla herself rubbing your stomach ardently with fragrant soap suds." Surely Tchaikovsky was pleased with Balakirev's praise; his reaction to the reference to his non-affair, however, is not recorded.

The overture adheres to the outlines of sonata form more than to the plot of Shakespeare's play. Hence it is not very specific as program music. Nonetheless, certain themes do represent various characters and episodes in the drama. The andante introduction, with its church-like harmonies, depicts Friar Laurence. The ensuing allegro, with its fast scales and rhythms, represents the feuding of the Capulets and the Montagues. The love theme, which is one of Tchaikovsky's most inspired romantic melodies, refers to the doomed love of Romeo and Juliet. The work ends with the deaths of the protagonists.

Musically as well as programmatically the overture revolves around the love theme. Tchaikovsky keeps us waiting suspensefully long before allowing us to hear it in its full glory. First we hear Friar Laurence's music — sustained chords in the winds with various accompaniments of harp arpeggios, string lines, and string *pizzicati.* After this slow introduction has gone on quite a while, the first theme of the central section bursts in. This frenetic music, with its angular rhythms, represents the feuding families. After considerable forcefulness has developed, there is a transition — as is proper in sonata form — to the love theme. At first it is scored modestly, yet imaginatively, with muted violas and solo clarinet. No sooner have we heard this sensual theme than it disappears, to be replaced by an almost inconsequential oscillation in the violins: Tchaikovsky is now tantalizing us, because we know the beauties he is capable of giving us. At long last this interruption builds up to a renewed statement of the love theme, this time fully extended. But again the scoring is less sumptuous than we might expect. If ever a melody cried out for a treatment by a full string section, it is this romantic Romeo-Juliet tune. But not yet. This time it is given to flutes and oboes, with a beautiful counterpoint in solo horn and with strings relegated to the role of accompaniment.

And that is all we get to hear of the love theme until much later, because now the music goes on to the development section, concerned mainly with the Capulet-Montague theme and the Friar Laurence melody. Considerable excitement leads to the recapitulation. After the first theme is restated, Tchaikovsky gives us not the love theme but its inconsequential sequel. Then, at long last and with tremendous impact, we hear the love theme as we always knew it would be: played by full strings accompanied by the other instruments. This is a moment of extraordinary beauty, not only because of the opulent sound but also because we have been made to wait to hear it for about 15 minutes of this 20-minute piece.

A coda follows these extended statements of the love theme. The coda uses all the main ideas of the piece and builds in intensity, almost approaching chaos. There are two interruptions, no doubt intended to depict the deaths of the two lovers. First the orchestra breaks off suddenly, except for the sustaining bassoons, trombones, and basses. There is a sudden dramatic short chord in the full orchestra: Romeo dies. The music starts up again and then dies down. Suddenly there is a fierce timpani roll: Juliet dies. Over a funereal drum beat, tortured reminiscences of the love theme are heard. The Friar Laurence music returns much as it first was, as an epilogue. There is a final reference to the love music.

The unabashed romanticism of *Romeo and Juliet* seems excessive to some listeners, while others enjoy wallowing in its shameless sentimentality. But there is more to this piece than its surface drama. There is a sophisticated sense of form, which is probably the underlying reason why listeners, whether or not they are drawn to obvious expressions of love and death, continually return to this music. The piece is a lush example of program music, although it owes to Shakespeare only the inspiration of a plot outline. As an artistic statement it is thoroughly rooted in the nineteenth, not the seventeenth, century.

◆　◆　◆

Symphony Number 4 in F Minor, Opus 36

Andante sostenuto. Moderato con anima
Andantino in modo di canzone. Più mosso. Tempo I
Allegro. Meno mosso. Tempo I
Allegro con fuoco. Andante. Tempo I

The Fourth Symphony was composed between May 1877 and 7 January 1878. Nicolai Rubinstein conducted the first performance in Moscow on 22 February 1878.

Tchaikovsky resented having to earn his living by teaching students who cared little for music and had no talent.

Although it is a dreary business to have been forced to explain to my young men's class for 11 consecutive years what a triad consists of, at least I have had the consolation of feeling that I am ramming essential knowledge into them because they intend to take up music as a profession. But the young women's classes! Heavens above! Out of sixty or seventy only five at most will even make musicians. The rest come to the conservatory to fill in time or from motives that have nothing to do with music. They are not less intelligent or less hard-working than the men. Rather the opposite — but they all come to grief the moment that are unable to apply a rule mechanically or use it by rote. I often lose patience — and my head — with them and go quite frantic with rage.

The composer was too naïve to understand that his fits of rage actually made him more intriguing to that group of students who came to study "from motives which have nothing to do with music." Tchaikovsky was a handsome bachelor, and his passionate music attracted many young women to his lectures. They found his anger sexy. But he scarcely noticed them, even when he occasionally received love letters from the young ladies in his classes. One such woman was more persistent that the rest. Antonina Milyukova was obsessed by her professed love for the composer, and she was determined at all costs to become his wife. When he received a letter from her, he hardly remembered who she was, despite the fact that she had graduated scarcely five months earlier. Antonina declared her love and admiration and begged to see him. To his everlasting regret, Tchaikovsky answered the letter and consented to the meeting.

Perhaps the composer was willing to meet this somewhat unbalanced young woman because of his decision two years earlier to marry. He had had no one in particular in mind as a mate, but he longed for the warmth of a home life and he was eager to dispel the mounting rumors that he was homosexual. The rumors were, of course, true. The composer had never really considered what a union with a woman might entail. His desire for marriage was nothing more than a fantasy, but he decided, rather impetuously, to act out his fantasy when the opportunity presented itself in the person of Antonina Milyukova.

Antonina was not the only woman to come into Tchaikovsky's life while he was beginning work on the Fourth Symphony. Nadezhda Filaretovna von Meck was a widow in her mid-forties, with a dozen children, a love of music, and a lot of money. She knew and admired Tchaikovsky's music, and she wanted to know its composer. She began with some modest commissions and casual correspondence. The composer responded openly and warmly, fulfilling the commissions promptly and answering the letters. From these beginning grew one of the oddest and most celebrated friendships in history. Nadezhda and Tchaikovsky exchanged some 1100 letters, but they never met. At first she might have been looking for a mate, but she backed off when she learned of the composer's homosexuality and of his involvement with Antonina. Later the two had exchanged such intimacies in their letters, sharing their inmost thoughts and emotions, that they could not bear to see each other.

Von Meck became Tchaikovsky's patroness. She supported him with commissions, then with loans which he was not expected to pay back, and finally with a regular monthly allowance. The composer felt that she was a true friend. He never thought of her as a potential spouse, and he always considered her as more than a source of the funds he needed to support his mismanaged life.

He did not at first tell Nadezhda about Antonina. He was looking for a graceful way out of his involvement, but he was no match for the determined young woman. He even confessed his homosexuality to her, but she replied that she would marry him to "reform" him and that she did not really care if their marriage became only a friendship. She was carefully concealing her own secret: she was a nymphomaniac who had had countless affairs. Tchaikovsky was not to discover the truth about their sexual incompatibility until his wedding night.

The composer finally wrote to Nadezhda about the marriage, only three days before the wedding. His letter is full of self-justification and helplessness. Von Meck was too proud a woman to show her hurt. She was insulted that he had waited so long to tell her, that he was marrying another despite all their shared intimacies, and that he felt trapped by a marriage that had not yet even taken place. She kept her annoyance to herself as she answered his letter in supportive terms. She even sent more money.

After nine devastating weeks of this unconsummated marriage, Tchaikovsky's nerves were frayed. With Nadezhda's money he went away, retreating from an impossible situation. Only then could he work on the Fourth Symphony. He wrote Nadezhda a detailed account of the horrors of his married life. This long letter is filled with revulsion, pity for Antonina, self-reproach, and longing for death. As the school year was about to begin, the composer was forced to return to Moscow, where his wife awaited him in their newly decorated apartment. All the tensions and grief returned. He attempted suicide and contemplated murder. Tchaikovsky's mental state was so acutely disorganized that he was granted a leave from the conservatory. He moved out of the apartment, never again to live with Antonina, and he buried himself in his work on the symphony.

Antonina refused to grant Tchaikovsky a divorce because, under Russian law, adultery was the only permissible cause. She felt that, should Tchaikovsky admit publicly to adultery, her name would be sullied. For the rest of his life Tchaikovsky lived in fear that Antonina would blackmail him. Actually, it was Antonina who committed adultery. From 1879 on she took several lovers and bore them numerous children, all of whom she gave up for adoption. She was certified insane in 1896 and institutionalized until her death in 1917.

The composer's road back to mental stability came from composition. He worked intensely on the symphony, which he dedicated to Nadezhda von Meck. She had stood by him throughout the difficult period of his marriage, she had never chastened him for his stupidity in allowing himself to get involved with Antonina, and she had supported him financially the whole time. The dedication solidified the friendship.

Although the initial public reception of the new symphony was lukewarm, Nadezhda was deeply moved. She asked Tchaikovsky for

the program of the work he always referred to as "our symphony."
His reply sets out in some detail just what was in his mind as he
wrote the piece. He wanted the program to remain private, but because of his letter to Nadezhda it is invariably reprinted in concert
guides (such as this one!). Herein lies a warning to all programmatic
composers: any time a program is written down, even if in a private
letter or diary, it eventually becomes public knowledge and is thence-
forth always quoted in concert notes.

The introduction contains the germ of the entire symphony,
without question its central idea. This is Fate. . . . One must submit to it and take refuge in futile longings.

The unconsolable, hopeless feeling grows stronger and more
consuming. Would it not be better to turn away from reality and
immerse oneself in dreams?

Oh joy! A sweet, tender vision has appeared. A blessed, luminous being flies by and beckons somewhere.

How wonderful! How distantly already sounds the impor-
tunate first theme of the allegro. Little by little dreams have
completely enveloped the soul. All that was gloomy and joyless
is forgotten. Happiness is here; it is here!

But no! They were only dreams, and Fate awakens us
harshly. And thus all life is an incessant shifting between grim
reality and the waves hither and thither until the sea swallows
us. . . .

The second movement of the symphony expresses another
phase of longing. This is the melancholy feeling that suffuses
you toward evening when you are sitting alone, weary from
work. . . . It is pleasant to remember one's youth and to regret
the past, but there is no wish to begin again. Life has tired you
out. It is pleasant to rest and cast a glance backward. Many
things flit through the memory. There were happy moments
when young blood pulsed warm and life was gratifying. There
were also moments of grief, of irreparable loss. It is all remote
in the past. It is both sad and somehow sweet to lose oneself in
the past.

The third movement expresses no definite sensations. It is a
capricious arabesque, fleeting apparitions that pass through the
imagination when one has begun to drink a little wine and is
beginning to experience the first phase of intoxication. The soul
is neither happy nor sad. You are not thinking of anything; the
imagination is completely free and for some reason has begun
to paint curious pictures. Among them you suddenly remember
some *muzhiks* on a spree, and a street song. Then the discon-

nected images that pass through our heads as we begin to fall asleep. They have nothing in common with reality, they are strange, exotic, incoherent.

The fourth movement. If you cannot discover the reasons for happiness in yourself, look at others. Get out among the people. Look, what a good time they have, surrendering themselves to joy! A picture of popular merriment on a holiday. You have scarcely had a chance to forget yourself when indefatigable Fate appears once more and reminds you of herself. But the others pay no attention to you. They do not even turn around, do not even look at you, do not notice that you are alone and sad. Oh, how gay they are! How fortunate they are that their emotions are direct and uncomplicated! Upbraid yourself and do not say that all the world is sad. Strong, simple joys exist. Take happiness from the joys of others. Life is bearable after all.

Symphony Number 5 in E Minor, Opus 64

Andante. Allegro con anima
Andante cantabile, con alcuna licenza.
Moderato con anima. Tempo I. Allegro non
troppo. Tempo I
Valse: Allegro moderato
Andante maestoso. Allegro vivace. Molto vivace.
Moderato assai molto maestoso. Presto.
Molto meno mosso

The Fifth Symphony was begun in May 1888 and completed on 26 August 1888. The composer conducted the first performance in St. Petersburg on 17 November 1888.

Once Tchaikovsky's fame was well established, he felt he should solidify his reputation by making an international tour. He was practically the first Russian composer to make such a trip. He spent the winter months of 1887–88 traveling to Berlin, Leipzig, Hamburg, Prague, Paris, and London. He was an ambassador for Russian music. In each city he conducted his own works and those of his compatriots (despite the fact that he was, by his own admission, little more than competent on the podium). He met several leading composers, including Brahms, Grieg, Fauré, Massenet, Gounod, Dvořák, and the young Richard Strauss. During his tour he was constantly busy and unable to compose or to guard his cherished privacy. But he also enjoyed being the center of attention wherever he went. He described his tour, in a letter to his patroness Nadezhda von Meck, as "torments, terrors, agitations, but also, I must add in truth, *joys.*"

When he returned to Russia in May, he moved into a new house in the country. There he kept to himself, enjoying walks in the woods, gazing at his pond and island, and working in his garden. Thus did he put behind him the hectic months of his European tour. "I have won a certain amount of fame, but I ask myself again and again, what is it all for? Is it worthwhile? My answer is, a quiet life without fame is infinitely preferable."

Before long, he felt the inevitable need to compose. He created the Fifth Symphony during the spring and summer months. Tchaikovsky left no detailed program for the Fifth, as he had for the Fourth, written a decade earlier. All that survives is a scrap of paper, with a partial program for the first movement: "Introduction: complete resignation before Fate, or, which is the same, before the inscrutable predestination of Providence. Allegro: (1) Murmurs, doubts, plaints, reproaches, against x x x. (2) Shall I throw myself into the embraces of faith???"

Thus the Fifth, like the Fourth before it and the Sixth after it, was concerned with Fate. But Fate is more personal, less abstract, than in the programs of the other works. Tchaikovsky speaks of his own faith, and he employs the mysterious symbol "x x x," which he repeatedly used in his diaries when referring to his carefully guarded secret: his homosexuality. Perhaps the "x x x" in the program refers to this proclivity, of which he was ashamed, or perhaps it refers to a particular lover.

While he was working on the symphony, Tchaikovsky was pleased with it. But after he had conducted it in St. Petersburg and Prague, he had doubts. He wrote to Nadezhda von Meck, "I have become convinced that this symphony is unsuccessful. There is something repulsive about it, a certain excess of gaudiness, insincerity, and artificiality. And the public instinctively recognizes this. It was very clear to me that the ovations I received were directed at my previous work, but the symphony itself was incapable of attracting them or at least pleasing them. The realization of all this causes me an acute and agonizing sense of dissatisfaction with myself. Have I already, as they say, written myself out, and am I now only able to repeat and counterfeit my former style? Yesterday evening I looked through *our* Fourth Symphony! What a difference, how much superior and better it is! Yes, this is very, very sad!"

Tchaikovsky's greatest talent was his gift for melody, and nowhere is it more apparent than in the Fifth Symphony. Is this lyricism what embarrassed the composer, what he meant by the work's "gaudiness"? As we listen to its beautiful, romantic, lush melodies, we may find it hard to understand his dissatisfaction. We may also come to some degree of comprehension of the work's unknown program, for many of its themes seem to be unabashed songs of love. The composer did write over the opening horn melody in the second movement, in a combination of Russian and French, "O, that I love you! O, my love! O, how I love! If you love me —." We need not know the object of this love to feel Tchaikovsky's passion. It is no surprise that this melody, plus several others from the symphony, have been used for popular songs in recent years.

Like the Fourth Symphony, the Fifth is introduced by a Fate motive that is destined to return in subsequent movements. In this work the motive is more interior, more subtle, than in the Fourth. It is heard first in two low clarinets. The main body of the first movement is more brooding than lyric, more triumphant than intimate, although the second theme does have hints of subsequent lyricism. But Tchaikovsky is really saving the love songs for the second movement.

There are no fewer than three different romantic melodies in the slow movement. The first is heard at the beginning in the horn, an instrument that is prominent throughout the movement. Before long the oboe enters with a second melody, of equal beauty. A third lovely melody forms the middle section. It is first heard in a version ornamented by a trill-like figure in the clarinet, answered by the bassoon. It is only once the theme has been passed to the strings that its true passion can be felt. Development of this third theme is interrupted by a forceful return of the Fate motive, after which the first theme returns. This theme and the second one are played by the full orchestra, with a sweeping passion that seems at last to fulfill their expressive potential. That Tchaikovsky thought of the themes of this movement as intensely expressive can be seen from the care with which he marked them, continually instructing the players exactly how to render each melody on each successive occurrence. Subtle changes of tempo, character, and mood are indicated by terms such as *dolce con molto espressivo, animando, sostenuto, con noblezza, con desiderio, cantabile, con anima, con desiderio e passione, con tutta forza,* and *dolcissimo.*

The third movement, a waltz reminiscent of Tchaikovsky's ballet music, carries the lyricism of the second movement in a new direction. The middle section uses a contrasting, sprightly theme. The Fate motive makes an appearance just before the end, in the low clarinets and bassoons.

In the finale the Fate motive is at last integrated into the movement. No longer merely quoted, it pervades the music. The slow introduction is based on it, but it continually reappears later. When it is heard in the exposition (and again in the recapitulation), it does not interrupt the main themes so much as complement them. After a dramatic false ending, the *maestoso* coda at last casts the Fate motive triumphantly in the major.

◆ ◆ ◆

Symphony Number 6 in B Minor, Opus 74, *Pathétique*
Adagio. Allegro non troppo
Allegro con grazia
Allegro molto vivace
Adagio lamentoso

The Pathétique *Symphony was composed between 16 February and 31 August 1893. The composer conducted the first performance in Saint Petersburg on 28 October 1893, a week before his death.*

The way we listen to Tchaikovsky's Sixth Symphony is undoubtedly influenced by its subtitle, *Pathétique*. It does not seem to matter that the composer first wanted to call it *Program* Symphony (though he refused to divulge the nature of the program), nor does it matter that he wanted the title *Pathétique* withdrawn after the premiere. We know the piece as "The Pathetic," and there is no way to deny the connotations of that word. Actually, the title was suggested by Tchaikovsky's brother Modeste, who had at first mentioned "Tragic," which the composer rejected. The Russian word Modeste used was *patetichesky*, which means more "passionate" or "emotional" than "pathetic" or "pitiable." There is, according to Tchaikovsky's biographer John Warrack, a hint of the idea of suffering in the Russian term, so that "the work is Tchaikovsky's symphony of emotional suffering."

The composer was probably what today would be diagnosed as a manic depressive. While he was at work on the symphony, he was not, contrary to what we might expect, in a dark mood. He wrote to his friend Bob Davidov, "You cannot imagine what bliss it is to be convinced that my time is not yet over and that I am still able to work." He believed that the *Pathétique* was his finest composition. He had good reason to be in high spirits: his health was good, his fame was widespread, and he was in great demand as a conductor. His good mood lasted despite the lukewarm reception the Sixth Symphony received when he conducted the premiere.

But then, inevitably, depression returned. According to Soviet musicologist Alexandra Anatolyevna Orlova:

It seemed Tchaikovsky was paying too much attention to the nephew of Duke Stenbock-Thurmor. He was a nice young man, and Tchaikovsky took a liking to him. Whether anything [homosexual] went on between them is unknown; what is known is that the Duke wrote a letter [of complaint] to the Czar and gave it to the Chief Prosecutor of the State, Nikolai Borisovitch Yakobi. Yakobi had been a classmate of Tchaikovsky's at the St. Petersburg College of Law. Public airing of the issue could have meant deprivation of all civil rights, exile in Siberia, or worse. All his life Tchaikovsky lived in fear of people learning his secret. Nothing could have been worse than exposure. . . .

Yakobi could not very well prevent an official complaint from reaching the Czar. Yet this disgrace, he felt, would reflect not only on Tchaikovsky but on the whole College of Law. He decided to call a "court of honor," made up of his classmates — all those still living. . . . Tchaikovsky himself was [among the eight] present. . . . When everyone had left, Yakobi told his wife what had gone on and instructed her never to tell anyone. He called it a "judgement" on Tchaikovsky and said that they had asked for his death. So in one sense it wasn't really suicide but murder. They condemned him, and they did it in a terrible way. He was to take his own life. And he had to do it in such a way that nobody would know."

Thus, scarcely a week after the premiere of the Sixth Symphony, the composer lay dead. An elaborate cover-up convinced the world that the cause of death had been cholera. So rigid was the secrecy that the truth, if that is what it is, has come out only relatively recently. The story of the composer's suicide is not universally accepted.

Tchaikovsky was a man of honor, and he never questioned his obligation to carry out the suicide. He was a hypersensitive neurotic as well, and one can well imagine his suffering, determination, and morbidity as he took the poison that had been passed to him in secret.

The last symphony seems to be an expression of his hypersensitive nature. Probably that is why he chose not to reveal the program. But it is not too difficult to follow the emotional states portrayed in this music. The adagio finale is an almost hysterical account of "emotional suffering," but the lugubrious first movement, with its bittersweet second theme, as well as the asymmetrical rhythms of the waltz and the forced gaiety of the march, do not succeed in hiding the tragic undertones of the whole work. Tchaikovsky's language is one of immediacy, not subtlety, and nowhere is his emotionalism more personal than in the *Pathétique*. His sentimentalism was symptomatic of his era. Today the excesses of late romantic art can be appreciated in their historical context. We have known, in the wars of the twentieth century, a deeper and far more devastating hysteria than is depicted in the Sixth Symphony. The unbridled outpouring of this music, especially in its last movement, is tolerable today because it does not seem to portray the deepest possible human despair. Although the composer may have intended high tragedy, the music itself does not attempt such lofty heights. It is over-effusive, unsubtle, impulsive, yet it is immediate and spontaneous — it is, in a word, human. We can cry at it, and the crying can be beautiful, because we recognize ourselves: self-pitying, alternately laughing and weeping.

The *Pathétique* starts from the depths of the orchestra, with the quietest of sounds. String basses accompany one low bassoon, playing the mournful introductory melody. This tune also forms the basis of the faster main part of the movement. The slow unfolding continues, as instrumental colors are added and motion continues to accelerate. The orchestra gets louder, eventually cresting with a rapid passage for everyone, still based on the main theme. The second theme at last makes its appearance. As is often the case in the music of Tchaikovsky, it is a melody of haunting beauty and great lyricism. Tchaikovsky lingers over this tune, which seems tinged with sadness and regret. After it is played by the clarinet, the music gets as slow and soft as it was at the beginning: the bassoon solo is actually marked *pppppp*. The full orchestra suddenly intrudes, beginning the development section.

The second movement is the famous waltz that is not quite a waltz. Waltzes are supposed to be in 3/4 time, but this one is in 5/4. You would have to have two and a half feet to dance to it! Yet, it does not sound clumsy. It is graceful and urbane; you almost do not notice its strange meter. This is an extraordinary accomplishment for Tchaikovsky. Few compositions with five beats in a measure sound as natural. Part of the reason is that the phrase structure is doggedly regular, as if to compensate for the continual irregularity of measures divided into unequal halves (2 + 3 beats). There is a trio section in the middle, and it also is in 5/4 time. This trio is noteworthy for its continual pulse on the note D in the bassoons, string basses, and timpani.

The third movement, a march, retains some of the rhythmic irregularities of the waltz: there is ambiguity over whether beats are subdivided into two or three parts.

The almost optimistic mood of the march is shattered by the finale. Listen carefully to the emotion-laden opening in the strings. It is not quite what it seems to be. The melody that you think you are hearing is actually not played by any one instrumental group.

Rather, in every other chord the first violins are on top, while the second violins have the melody note in the intervening chords — a most unusual scoring. It is hard to understand why Tchaikovsky wrote such a strange scoring. Perhaps he was after an antiphonal effect, if the first and second violins in his orchestra were seated on opposite sides of the conductor. If that was his reason, it must be considered a miscalculation: recent psychological research has demonstrated that we perceive melodic continuity in one ear even when notes are actually presented alternately to one ear and then the next. Perhaps Tchaikovsky was seeking a troubled continuity, a threatened lyricism.

After the first of two climaxes the opening music returns, this time orchestrated in a more normal fashion. After the second, smaller climax the main theme is never heard again. It is replaced by a variant of it, which turns out to be, almost incongruously, the theme from the trio of the waltz. It is as if Tchaikovsky is saying that the deepest tragedy lurks behind the least likely facade. The music gets lower and slower, until just bassoons and low strings remain. The symphony returns to the depths from which it came.

Heitor Villa-Lobos

Born on 5 March 1887 in Rio de Janeiro.
Died on 17 November 1959 in Rio de Janeiro.

◆ ◆ ◆

Bachianas Brasileiras, Number 5
Aria
Dansa

The first movement of the Bachianas Brasileiras Number 5 *was composed in 1938. Bidú Sayão sang the first performance, with Burle Marx conducting, at the New York World's Fair on 4 May 1939. The second movement was added in 1945.*

"I do not believe in music as culture, or education, or even as a device for amusement or for quieting the nerves, but as something more potent, mystical, and profound in its effect. Music has this power to communicate, to heal, and to ennoble, when it is made a part of man's life and consciousness." This statement by Brazilian composer Heitor Villa-Lobos may be taken as his personal aesthetic. He elaborated, "I do not know what the word inspiration means. I create music out of necessity, biological necessity. I write because I cannot help it. I follow no style or fashion. My artistic creed is *la liberté absolue.* When I write, it is according to the style of Villa-Lobos."

At a very young age Villa-Lobos began to study the cello, which remained his primary instrument. He was also fascinated by street musicians. After the death of his father, he lived with his aunt, a pianist who often played Bach's *Well-Tempered Clavier.* The composer enjoyed improvisations and dances played by amateur musicians in Rio de Janeiro nightclubs. These diverse influences — cello music, the compositions of Bach, and Brazilian folk music — later combined in Villa-Lobos' unique compositional style.

At the age of 18 he sold some rare books left to him by his father in order to gain money for travel. For the next seven years he saw much of Brazil. As he traveled he wrote down and studied folk and popular music. At the age of 25 he returned to Rio eager to study composition and cello, but he found himself temperamentally ill-suited for the regimentation of formal schooling. He dropped out of school and studied on his own, first the composition treatise by French composer Vincent d'Indy and then the scores of the masters. His love for the music of Bach, whom he called "a mediator between all races," was solidified at this time. While he was educating himself, he earned his living playing his cello in cafés and cinemas.

He began to compose voraciously. Many of his early works were bold, brash, and unconventional. Although his more unusual compositions met with confusion when heard, his talent was never in doubt. His reputation solidified, and he was able, thanks to help from pianist Artur Rubinstein, to obtain financial support from several patrons.

He went to Paris, where he lived from 1923 to 1930. There Villa-Lobos found himself in the midst of an artistically sophisticated climate, where avant garde art was invariably greeted with excitement, interest, and controversy. His spontaneous compositions provoked great interest among the intellectual elite. As his music was widely performed, he became a celebrity in frequent demand in the salons of Paris. The music he composed in France was a boldly innovative amalgamation of Brazilian folk elements and the concert tradition.

When he returned to Brazil in 1930, Villa-Lobos found that a nationalistic movement in the arts was underway. Although previously an iconoclast, he became an important member of the cultural establishment. Despite his own lack of formal education, he was made an official advisor to the government on music education. He oversaw the teaching of music to both children and adults. His enthusiasm and creativity were boundless. He reorganized the music curricula in primary and technical schools; he advised concert organizations; he instituted vigorous programs to safeguard the traditions of popular music. He also arranged concerts in remote villages, often himself participating. When villagers, who had probably never heard of such a thing as a concert, failed to show up, Villa-Lobos would make speeches on the significance of art. When he told the peasants that hearing music was more important than attending soccer games, he was on occasion pelted with potatoes and eggs.

His compositions of this period were less advanced than his earlier works. As he participated in the Brazilian nationalist movement, the composer sought a less revolutionary style. The *Bachianas Brasileiras* suites, which date from this time, are tonal and not particularly dissonant. In these works Villa-Lobos tried to combine what he felt was the essentially folkloric spirit of Bach with the genuine folk music of the Brazilian people. He believed there was a natural affinity between these two different musics, since in both several independent melodies are heard simultaneously.

In 1944 Villa-Lobos made the first of several annual visits to the United States, where he rapidly gained a loyal following. His reception was the reverse of what it had been in Paris twenty years earlier. As his conservative later music was not controversial, it was readily accepted by unadventurous audiences in this country, but the intelligentsia dismissed it as facile and geared down to popular tastes. His last works were conventional and rarely nationalistic.

Villa-Lobos is reputed to have composed over two thousand works. Many of them were experimental, such as his notorious *New York Skyline,* in which he placed a picture of tall buildings on a graph that he then transferred to music notation. Much of his output is folk-inpired, such as the *Bachianas Brasileiras* suites, composed between 1930 and 1945.

Each of these nine pieces uses a unique ensemble and consists of two to four movements. The first movement generally bears a title reminiscent of Bach, such as Aria, Prelude, Fantasia, or Toccata. The remaining movements refer to popular Brazilian forms. According to Burle Marx, conductor of the first performance of the *Bachianas Brasileiras* Number 5, these suites "are not so much evocations of Bach in a contemporary manner as an attempt to transmit the Bach spirit — which to Villa-Lobos is the universal spirit, a source and end unto itself — into the soul of Brazil. . . . His admiration for Bach has not led him to imitation, but rather to a rendering of his style in the Brazilian idiom."

Two of the *Bachianas Brasileiras* use an orchestra of cellos. The composer had previously made some imaginative transcriptions of fugues from Bach's *Well-Tempered Clavier* for cello ensemble. From that endeavor he learned to associate the music of Bach with the special timbres of a homogenous group of cellos.

The variety of sonorities in the *Bachianas Brasileiras* Number 5 is extraordinary. The work is scored for soprano (in the first of movement only) and an ensemble of at least eight cellos. By contrasting the instruments' high vs. low registers, *pizzicato* vs. bowed playing, and melodic vs. accompanimental figures, the music produces a wonderfully rich palette of sounds.

The aria movement was composed in a single morning in 1938. The second movement was added seven years later. In the first of three sections of the aria, the soprano vocalizes on the neutral syllable "ah." The second section is a syllabic, unornamented setting of a poem by Ruth V. Corréa. The music of the opening section returns at the end, but now the soprano is instructed to hum. The second movement is more vigorous.

Antonio Vivaldi

Born in Venice, probably on 4 March 1678.
Died in Vienna on 26 or 27 July 1741.

◆ ◆ ◆

The Four Seasons, Opus 8

> Concerto Number 1 in E Major for Violin and
> Orchestra, *Spring*
>> Allegro
>> Largo e pianissimo sempre
>> Danza pastorale: Allegro
> Concerto Number 2 in G Minor for Violin and
> Orchestra, *Summer*
>> Allegro non molto
>> Adagio. Presto
>> Presto
> Concerto Number 3 in F Major for Violin and
> Orchestra, *Autumn*
>> Allegro
>> Adagio
>> Allegro
> Concerto Number 4 in F Minor for Violin and
> Orchestra, *Winter*
>> Allegro non molto
>> Largo
>> Allegro

The Opus 8 Violin Concertos were published in 1725 and most likely composed a number of years earlier.

Vivaldi's Opus 8 consists of twelve concertos for violin and orchestra, of which the first four comprise *The Seasons.* These concertos, each purporting to describe a season of the year, are the crowning achievement of Vivaldi's experiments in pictoral music.

Descriptive music was particularly popular in the baroque period, in both operas and instrumental music. Composers, in trying to create as exact a portrayal as possible of their subjects, were responding to the aesthetic of the "natural." Eighteenth-century philosophers called for all the arts to imitate nature in as precise a way as possible. In some of the more extreme statements of this position, absolute music was dismissed as meaningless. The simplistic formulations of one representative aesthetician strike us today as the exact opposite of defensible musical values: "We have good imitations of storms, thunder, and the like, from several musicians. It is only a question of following this plan and not permitting oneself any vague or undefined compositions. It is necessary to get down to detail in art and always have in view a model to copy. There is no expression at all without depiction."

This attitude, as Vivaldi scholar Marc Pincherle points out, is the reverse of latter-day composers' beliefs about program music:

> Their first care is apology, or, even more likely, denial. They never intended to describe; at most they intended to suggest certain states of mind as they would appear when transferred to the lofty realms of pure music. You are given, for instance, a work [Honegger's *Pacific 231*] whose content arises from the remote evocation of a locomotive, though you claim to identify in it the shudder of the train as it pulls away, the increasingly noisy rattling, and the thousand familiar sounds rendered with a hallucinating mastery, right down to the end of the run where the brakes are applied for the last time. Already Beethoven had written of the *Pastoral* Symphony, "More expression of feelings than depiction," while having a quail and a cuckoo sing forth with a pretty good likeness.

However, in the baroque era, composers and audiences alike valued accuracy of representation. Thus Vivaldi prefaced each concerto of *The Seasons* with a poem (translated below), to which the music carefully corresponds. In addition, he included specific quotations from the prefatory poems at strategic points in the scores. The mood of each concerto is established in its introductory orchestral passages, while specific tone painting is reserved for the solo sections.

That Vivaldi was able to compose imaginative, original, and wonderfully fresh music within the restricted aesthetic of literal representation testifies to his inordinate skill as composer and orchestrator. His success at tone painting in *The Four Seasons* was immediately appreciated by audiences, nobility, and the press. The *Spring* Concerto became a particular favorite of several violinists, and it was published in arrangements for hurdy-gurdy, musette, and flute. In the days before copyrights, appropriating another composer's work was an act of homage, not of thievery. Thus Michel Corrette paid *Spring* a great compliment by transforming it into a large sacred composition, as did Jean Jacques Rousseau in his unlikely mutation of it into a solo flute piece.

The popularity of *The Four Seasons* naturally impressed subsequent composers. These concertos thereby contributed to the growing interest in music descriptive of nature and country life. The pastoral tradition culminated in Haydn's *The Seasons* and Beethoven's *Pastoral* Symphony.

Spring. "Spring has come, and the birds greet it with happy songs, and at the same time the streams run softly, murmuring to the breathing of gentle breezes. Then the sky is cloaked in black, and thunder and lightning come to have their say. After the storm has quieted, the little birds return to their harmonious song." The opening sets the carefree mood. The subsequent passage for three solo violins is the joyful song of three birds greeting spring. The orchestra returns, and then it softly depicts the murmuring streams and gentle breezes. Loud tremolos portray thunder and lightning. In the ensuing solo, the trills are the little birds singing after the storm.

"Here in a pleasant flowery meadow, the leaves rustle sweetly and the goatherd sleeps with his faithful dog by his side." The second movement begins with the rustling of leaves in the orchestral violins accompanying the dream-like melody of the sleeping goatherd in the solo violin. The insistent rhythm in the violas depicts the dog's barking.

"Nymphs and shepherds dance to the festive sound of the shepherd's pipe beneath the beloved spring sky, decked out in its brilliance." The finale is a shepherd's dance, its drone suggesting bagpipes.

Summer. "In the season made harsh by the burning sun, men and flocks languish and pine trees are hot. The cuckoo unlocks his voice, and soon songs of the turtledove and goldfinch are heard. A gentle breeze blows, but unexpectedly the north wind seeks a quarrel. The shepherd weeps because he fears the dreaded storm and his destiny." As in the previous concerto, the mood, in this case languid, is suggested by the orchestral opening. The first solo, with its rapid repeated notes, is the cuckoo. After a return of the opening, the violin plays the songs of the turtledove and, with the rapid alternation of two high notes, the goldfinch. The orchestra then quietly depicts the gentle breezes. The music suddenly becomes loud and fast, portraying the north wind, which is interrupted by the opening theme, followed by the solo violin depicting the shepherd's fear. The north wind resumes to close the movement.

"Fear of lightning and thunder, plus a furious swarm of flies and hornets, prevents the shepherd from resting." The plaintive opening melody is the shepherd's fear, which is followed immediately by rapid, low repeated notes, suggesting the swarm of insects. The violin theme continues, showing the impossibility of rest. These elements alternate throughout the movement.

"Alas, his fears are justified. Thunder and lightning fill the sky, and hail brings down corn and grain."

Autumn. "With songs and dances the peasants celebrate the joy of a fine harvest. They enjoy their drunkenness and then fall asleep." The rhythmic opening is the harvest, with its songs and dances. The rapid second solo for violin depicts the peasants' intoxication. One last violin run — one final drunken prank — and then the soft, lyrical violin melody just before the final reprise of the harvest theme portrays sleep.

"Everyone leaves off singing and dancing. The fresh air is pleasing, and the fall atmosphere lulls everyone into a contented sleep." The subdued second movement captures this peaceful mood. The slow-moving cello line shows the sleeping drunks.

"At daybreak the hunters go forth to hunt with horns, guns, and dogs. They find a wild beast, who flees. The hunters follow its tracks. Exhausted and terrified by the loud noises of guns and dogs, the wounded beast tries to escape, but it is overwhelmed and dies." The vigorous opening music suggests horn calls. Later, the sparsely accompanied violin triplets show the beast's frenzied escape. The ensuing rapid orchestra music shows its fear. Just prior to the final return of the hunt music, we hear the animal's exhaustion in rapid violin lines leading to sustained notes.

Winter. "To tremble in the icy snow; to be buffeted by the wild wind; to stamp one's frozen feet; to feel the excessive cold make one's teeth chatter." The opening dissonant repeated notes set the mood. The rapid solo violin figuration is the blast of icy wind. These two motives alternate, until the repeated notes intensify, signifying the stamping feet. Later, soft tremolos indicate chattering teeth.

"To spend quiet and happy days before the fire, while outside everyone is soaked by rain." The slow movement's sustained viola notes, beneath the nostalgic violin melody, portray contentment.

"To walk carefully on the ice, going slowly for fear of falling; to slip and fall sharply to the ground; to run hastily on the ice until it cracks and opens; to hear the south wind, the north wind, and all the other winds in battle. Such is winter, but even so what joy it brings!" The finale's opening violin solo depicts walking on the ice. The music slows down to show the fear of falling. Then rapid descending figures indicate that someone has indeed fallen. The solo violin depicts getting up again. Silences alternating with rapid figures portray the ice cracking. The fast unaccompanied violin figures, punctuated by orchestral tremolos, are the different winds.

mother envisions the youth becoming more manly and growing in strength: he is driven to accomplish important deeds. He gains for himself a place among men. But then comes a moment of contemplation. A nameless desire captures the youth's heart as he wanders alone (forest sounds and birdsongs and the theme of love and unity from *Siegfried*). Passion awakens in him, and he feels for the first time soul-wearying pains. His passion grows until finally love makes him happy. The highest sound of joy signals the full happiness of his life in love. Birdsongs foretell success (from *Siegfried*), and gladness is expressed along with feelings about the innocent childhood of the soul ("From the Time of Youth, a Song Ever Sings in Me"). . . . The mother awakens from her reverie and turns again to the slumbering child. She gives thanks for her happiness and prays for heaven to bless her son. Once again the lullaby is heard, along with the theme of holiness. Suddenly the haunting forest horns and birdsongs return. Does the boy dream of his future? No, he sleeps quietly with a happy smile. . . . After a final loving kiss from the mother, the future hero rests in the care of God.

Richard Wagner

Born on 22 May 1813 in Leipzig.
Died on 13 February 1883 in Venice.

Siegfried Idyll

Siegfried Idyll *was completed on 4 December 1870. Wagner conducted the first performance in his home near Lucerne, Switzerland, on 25 December 1870.*

Cosima Wagner was 33 years old on Christmas Day, 1870. She awakened to the sounds of music playing — new, wonderful, unfamiliar music performed by a chamber ensemble. Cosima later wrote in her diary,

> As I awoke my ear caught a sound, which swelled fuller and fuller; no longer could I imagine myself to be dreaming; music was sounding, and such music! When it died away, Richard came into my room with the children and offered me the score of the symphonic birthday poem. I was in tears, but so was all the rest of the household. Richard had arranged his orchestra on the staircase, and thus was our Triebschen [their Swiss villa] consecrated forever. . . . After lunch the orchestra came into the house downstairs, and now the *Idyll* was heard once again, to the profound emotion of us all.

The music of *Siegfried Idyll* was written to express Wagner's happiness in his marriage to Cosima, in his new retreat on the shore of Lake Lucerne, and in his young son Siegfried. The composer had found peace, however temporarily, after struggling against public scandal.

Cosima had been the source of the scandal, which nearly ruined his career. She was the second of three illegitimate children of composer Franz Liszt and the Countess Marie d'Agoult. When Cosima first became interested in Wagner, she was married to conductor Hans von Bülow, to whom she had borne two daughters. Wagner was friendly with and professionally involved with the conductor. Von Bülow had directed many important performances of Wagner's music, including the premiere of *Tristan und Isolde,* and Wagner had used his influence with the King to help retain von Bülow in a position of importance in Munich.

At first Wagner hesitated to start an affair with Cosima, because he knew it would eventually mean ruin for von Bülow. But desire and selfishness got the upper hand. Wagner, who was separated from his wife Minna, invited the von Bülow family to spend part of the summer of 1864 with him. Cosima and her children arrived a week before the conductor. During that week Wagner and Cosima consummated their love. The lovers confessed to von Bülow when he arrived. He suffered greatly, but he was a weak man who knew that his career was in the hands of the influential composer. The conductor had no control over his wife's behavior. They stayed with Wagner for much of the summer, wanting to keep up appearances and avoid a scandal. Cosima shared the affections of both men. This unconventional arrangement seemed to inspire Wagner to begin a string quartet (a most unusual genre for him), which was eventually incorporated into *Siegfried Idyll.*

Cosima became pregnant. Her daughter Isolde was born in April 1865, but she was not sure who was the father. As the girl began to grow, her features took on a resemblance to those of the composer. Over the next several months, Cosima lived alternately with Wagner and von Bülow, the former for love and the latter for appearances. It was essential to try to keep the affair a secret from the King. All of Munich gossiped about the paternity of Isolde. Wagner told outright lies in order to remain in the King's good graces.

The composer bought the estate Triebschen in Switzerland in the spring of the following year, and that summer he attempted once again to silence the gossip by inviting the entire von Bülow family. The conductor still felt he had no choice but to accept the invitation. Wagner and Cosima continued to deny their affair to the King, even as Cosima was carrying the composer's second child. When von Bülow left at the end of the summer, Wagner actually managed to convince the King that Cosima had stayed behind only because he was better able to care for her than her husband.

In February 1867 Cosima gave birth to a daughter, Eva. She still claimed publicly that von Bülow was the father, and the conductor even hastened to see the child just on the chance that she might be his. The following April Cosima returned to von Bülow, although she made sure that his quarters had a room for her frequent guest. The two men still continued to share her.

By the following year it became impossible to maintain the preposterous ruse any longer. Bülow conducted the premiere of *Meistersinger,* but he was soon to be humiliated publicly. Cosima again joined Wagner for the summer at Triebschen, this time without her husband. Wagner had found another conductor whom he could trust to present his works, and Cosima wrote to Bülow that she would re-

turn to him no longer. She was again pregnant, although she deni＿ it at first. She discussed the possibility of divorce. The conductor w＿ reluctant. He no longer believed she would live with him again, ｂ＿ he knew that the scandal surrounding a divorce would mean the ｅ＿ of his conducting in Munich.

In June 1869 Siegfried Wagner was born. The press reported ／＿ Wagner's mistress had given birth again. Von Bülow's recent re＿ of *Tristan* was praised in the newspapers for the devotion the co＿ tor had brought to the work of his wife's lover. There was n＿ dignity nor hope left for von Bülow. He sent his daughters to liv＿ their mother and Wagner, and he resigned his post as condu＿ Munich. Because of the scandal, Wagner was banished from ｌ＿ social and musical circles. He was not allowed to supervise th＿ ich premieres of his first two *Ring* operas. The scandal also da＿ the career of Cosima's father, Liszt. Finally von Bülow agree＿ divorce, and Wagner (whose first wife had conveniently di＿ Cosima were married on 25 August 1870. For their first Chri＿ a married couple, Wagner presented Cosima with *Siegfried I*＿

The composition uses themes from the third act of the o＿ *fried* and also the cradle song "Sleep, Baby, Sleep." Wagner＿ the work only for his family and friends, but, because of＿ difficulties, he was forced in 1878 to publish it, in a versi＿ orchestra. It is the only symphonic composition of Wagner＿ He also published a detailed program:

> The first ninety measures of *Siegfried Idyll,* in order to s＿
> purity and holiness of the child's soul, use Brünhild＿
> from the opera *Siegfried* ("From Eternity to Eternity A＿
> mother, near his little bed, sings the boy to sleep wit＿
> He falls asleep, during the soft, intermittent horn＿
> mother notices that he is asleep, but she continu＿
> though halting several times. A series of trills ..＿
> that] the boy is now deeply asleep. The mother gaz＿
> fully upon her beloved child and dreams about his＿
> seems touched by a shiver as she thinks about the ur＿
> who will grow from this boy — arpeggios in the＿
> envisions (when the meter changes to 3/4) a hand＿
> flowering youth. This is Siegfried's theme of glory＿
> era ("Siegfried, Thou Glorious Protector of th＿
> sounded by an interplay of flutes, clarinets, an＿
> scending clarinet run expresses the mother's de＿
> strings pick up the theme. . . . It is combined wi＿
> sic: in the mother's soul her remembrance of the＿
> and of her cares joins with this vision of matur＿

Anton Webern

Born in Vienna on 3 December 1883.
Died on 15 September 1945 in the village of Mittersill, near Salzburg.

◆ ◆ ◆

Six Pieces for Orchestra, Opus 6

Langsam
Bewegt
Mässig
Sehr mässig
Sehr langsam
Langsam

Five Pieces for Orchestra, Opus 10

Sehr ruhig und zart
Lebhaft und zart bewegt
Sehr langsam und äusserst ruhig
Fliessend, äussert zart
Sehr fliessend

Variations for Orchestra, Opus 30

Six Pieces for Orchestra was composed in the summer of 1909. The first performance was conducted by Arnold Schoenberg on 31 March 1913 in Vienna. Webern re-orchestrated the work in the summer of 1928. This revised version was first heard under the direction of Hermann Scherchen in Berlin on 27 January 1929. Webern also made a version for chamber ensemble of ten players, for a performance in 1920. As that perfromance was cancelled, the chamber version was first played on 16 March 1970, when Friedrich Cerha conducted the ensemble Die Reihe *in Vienna.*

Five Pieces for Orchestra was composed between 28 June 1911 and 6 October 1913. It was performed in an arrangement for five instruments in Vienna on 30 January 1920, under the composer's direction. Webern conducted the first orchestral performance with the Tonhalle Orchestra in Zurich on 22 June 1926.

Variations for Orchestra was composed between April and 25 November 1940. Hermann Scherchen conducted the first performance in Winterthur on 3 March 1943.

The concert season 1912–13 brought before the European public some of the most startling original music of all time. New orchestral compositions of Webern, Stravinsky, and Debussy offered unprecedented sounds and aesthetics. Also heard for the first time was Schoenberg's song cycle *Pierrot Lunaire,* in which he introduced *Sprechstimme,* a technique of vocal production that is half song, half speech. Debussy's orchestral work was the ballet *Jeux,* a new departure into the world of fragmented, nondevelopmental forms. Stravinsky's work was the notorious ballet *Rite of Spring,* whose barbaric rhythms revolutionized music. Webern's contribution was the intense yet intimate Six Pieces for Orchestra, in which he first applied his aesthetic of the miniature to the full orchestra. Stravinsky's and Webern's pieces, both scored for enormous orchestra, provoked riots; Schoenberg's and Debussy's met with indifference. On the other side of the Atlantic, Charles Ives was quietly composing his possibly even more revolutionary music, such as *Three Places in New England.* A new era of music was born. There was no turning back, at least not for the next seventy years.

One aspect of the new style was its reaction against romanticism. Webern was not the only composer to turn to the miniature in order to get away from the overblown statements of such late romantics as Wagner, Bruckner, Strauss, and Mahler. No other composer explored the world of the aphorism as thoroughly as Webern did. Yet his aesthetic was not totally anti-romantic. Rather than deny the extreme emotions of late nineteenth-century music, he sought to condense those expressions into tiny pieces laden with meaning.

The reaction against romanticism was manifest in a dislike for descriptive titles. We even find such innocuous titles as "symphony" and "suite" appearing less frequently. The modernist composers were content calling their more abstract pieces simply "piece." Consider this list of some of the music they composed between 1908 and 1919:

Webern — Six Pieces for Orchestra
    Four Pieces for Violin and Piano
    Five Pieces for Orchestra
    Three Little Pieces for Cello and Piano
Schoenberg — Three Piano Pieces
    Three Little Pieces for Chamber Orchestra
    Five Pieces for Orchestra
    Six Little Piano Pieces
Berg — Four Pieces for Clarinet and Piano
    Three Pieces for Orchestra
Stravinsky — Three Pieces for String Quartet
    Three Pieces for Clarinet

Such titles are the epitome of objectivity and of anti-romanticism, even though the music in these works is sometimes intensely expressionistic.

Of these composers, Webern was the most committed to the miniature. Most of the Six Pieces for Orchestra, for example, require little over a minute to perform. They avoid any overt repetition, and they scarcely allow themselves any time for development in the usual sense. As Schoenberg once wrote about his student Webern, "Anyone can stretch every glance into a poem, every sigh into a novel. But to express a novel in a single gesture, a joy in a breath — such concentration can only be present in proportion to the absence of self-pity."

Webern provided the following program note for Opus 6:

> The pieces ... represent short song forms, in that they are mostly tripartite. A thematic connection does not exist, not even within the individual pieces. I consciously avoided such connections, since I aimed at an always changing mode of expression. To describe briefly the character of the pieces (they are of a purely lyrical nature): the first expresses the expectation of a catastrophe; the second the certainty of fulfillment; the third the most tender contrast; it is, so to speak, the introduction to the fourth, a funeral march; five and six are an epilogue: rememberance and resignation.

The emotion in Webern's music does not come out and wash over the listener, the way it does with late romantic music. You must enter into the special world of this music, and you must concentrate on its compressed language. Webern discovered that power and beauty can reside in a single note, carefully placed within the time and space of a composition. He discovered that beautiful melodies — *singable* melodies, for much of Webern's music is vocal — need have only a few notes. Since his music demands intense concentration, he felt that repetition was unnecessary: if you are listening carefully, you will hear it all the first time. And he realized, as some of his followers did not, that you cannot maintain intense listening for very long. That is why his compositions must be brief.

But are they really so short? If we measure duration by the clock, Webern's pieces *are* tiny. But they contain such concentrated expression that they can seem long. There are no dead spots, no static areas, few repeats, few transitions. Symptomatic of the discrepancy between actual and experienced duration in Webern's music are his attitudes toward length. When he was composing the Variations for Orchestra, for example, he estimated its length at 15 minutes; for the published score he revised the estimate down to nine and a half minutes; in performance the piece lasts about seven minutes. Yet it *seems* to take a quarter of an hour.

The outward events of Webern's life were not particularly exciting. His life was as interior as his music. His music was rarely performed and all but unknown to the general public. Indicative of his obscurity was his remark upon completing the Variations for Orchestra: "Thus another opus has been brought to completion. For the time, probably scant notice of it will be taken." Most of his performances, like those of composers today, were given not by mainstream organizations but by groups specializing in new music, such as Schoenberg's Society for Private Musical Performances in the 1910s and '20s and the International Society for Contemporary Music (ISCM) in the 1920s and '30s.

If performances of Webern's music were rare in his younger years, they were virtually non-existent in Hitler's Germany and in the besieged Austria. His situation was always precarious during the war. It became critical when the Russians overran Vienna in 1945. Webern fled with his wife and three surviving children (his son Peter had been killed in the war) to the mountain town of Mittersill.

Before leaving his home in Vienna, Webern buried beneath his garden house some of his most valued possessions. These remained unharmed when the invading soldiers took over the abandoned house, but they inflicted senseless damage on what remained in sight. Scores, books, and correspondence were strewn about the yard; Webern's cello was kicked in; his personal papers were used for kindling. Eventually Hermine von Webern, widow of the composer's son, was able to salvage much of these materials. But Webern never saw them again. A few months after moving to Mittersill, he was shot to death by an American soldier who mistakenly thought himself threatened by the composer.

After the war, Hermine stored Webern's mementos in her mother's attic, where they remained for twenty years. In 1965, while researching his massive biography of the composer, Hans Moldenhauer heard that Hermine might have a bust of Webern. He sought her out, and she led him to the attic. There they discovered not only the statue but also many scores from which the composer had conducted, his books, relics from his childhood, letters, and — carefully preserved but hitherto unknown, even to Hermine — a large stack of manuscripts. These scores and sketches contained not only well-known pieces but also previously unheard of works, some from Webern's student years and some from his maturity. In one afternoon in 1965 the known output of Anton Webern doubled!

Because of Moldenhauer's discovery, we now know that Webern

composed 18 orchestral miniatures in 1911–13, from which he sub-sequently selected five pieces for Opus 10. His procedure is telling: pieces which focus on exquisite details rather than on goal-directed progression can be mixed and matched, because there is no overall continuity to determine each movement's contribution to the whole.

The genesis of these 18 works is interesting. In the summer of 1911, two years after completing the Opus 6 orchestra pieces, Webern wrote to Schoenberg, "I have already written two orchestra pieces. They are very brief. Nothing long occurs to me. There will be a num-ber of short pieces that I shall call Chamber Pieces for Orchestra in order to indicate that they should not be played in a large hall. Until now the instrumentation has been very small. . . . In a large hall one would hardly be able to hear anything of the music." By the begin-ning of August there were seven pieces. Webern then turned his at-tention first to other works, then to a job conducting theater music, then to recovering from a series of illnesses, one of which required psychiatric treatment, and finally to the writing of a stage play called *Dead*. He returned to the orchestral miniatures in the fall of 1913. By December he had written eleven more pieces, one with voice. He sent four of them to Schoenberg, who responded by offering to conduct them. This performance never took place, however. None of the pieces was heard until 1920, when Webern made an arrangement of five of them for a small ensemble. This group, listed as Opus 10, was played at a concert of the Society for Private Musical Performances. The orchestral version of the Five Pieces had to wait another five years for performance. Webern conducted it at the 1926 ISCM festival in Zürich.

Webern's music, like that of many other composers, can be di-vided into three distinct style periods. His earliest music is tonal, but his predilections for brevity and transparency are already evident. His second period began as Webern completed four years of study with Schoenberg. Following the model of his teacher, Webern com-posed music with no key centers. Lacking large-scale organizing prin-ciples, this music is necessarily brief. The extreme is the fourth of the Five Pieces, Opus 10, which contains only six measures and lasts about twenty seconds. This piece, like all the middle-period music, is transparent and fragile. Every wisp of sound carries tremendous meaning.

The third period is characterized by strictly twelve-tone proce-dures. Webern learned the twelve-tone technique from his teacher, although his use of it is very different from Schoenberg's. Their dif-ferences are, in fact, of greater consequence than their similarities. The twelve-tone method provided Webern with the organizing principle missing in the middle period. Thus the late music is more expansive, more directed, and more dramatic. The Variations for Orchestra dates from this final period.

Much of Webern's music, particularly twelve-tone compositions like the Variations, is conceived contrapuntally. His interest in strict counterpoint dates from his student years. After preliminary studies in Latin, Greek, literature, mathematics, philosophy, cello, and piano, Webern earned a doctorate in musicology under Guido Adler at the University of Vienna. For his dissertation he studied and edited the *Choralis Constantinus* by renaissance composer Heinrich Isaac (1450–1517). From his historical studies Webern developed an abiding interest in canonic procedures.

A later generation of composers studied, imitated, and expanded Webern's compositional techniques while all but ignoring his music's human qualities. The post-Webernians, as they are called, were fascinated more by his means of expression than by the expression itself. As they generalized his twelve-tone ideas and glorified his canons, they inadvertently created a false impression of Webern's music as objective and impersonal. Quite the contrary: his music is a deeply emotional and subjective expression of a unique personality. Objectivity *is* a feature of some early twentieth-century music (Stravinsky's, for example), but not Webern's. When he conducted or coached performers in his own music, for example, he spoke to them always of beauty, nuance, and meaning, never of technique. His scores are full of expression markings and expressive tempo changes.

Glossary

List of foreign and musical terms used in this book, with brief definitions.

ABER   but

ABSOLUTE MUSIC   music whose meaning is abstract, as opposed to program music, which tells a story or projects an image

ACCELERANDO   get faster

ACCIDENTALS   sharps, flats, or naturals

ADAGIETTO   short movement in adagio tempo

ADAGIO   slow; a slow movement

AD LIBITUM   at liberty, may be omitted

AEOLIAN   mode similar to the minor (e.g., the white notes on a piano from A to A)

AFFETTUOSO   tenderly

ALLA   in the style of

ALLA BREVE   counted with two beats per measure, each beat represented by a half note

ALLEGRETTO   moderately fast; moderately fast movement

ALLEGRO   fast; a fast movement

ANDANTE   moderately slow, at a walking tempo; a moderately slow movement

ANDANTINO   not quite as slow as andante (since Mozart); somewhat slower than andante (before Mozart); movement in *andantino* tempo

ANFANG   beginning

ANIMATO   animated

ANTIPHONAL   sounding in alternation from opposite sides of a performing space

APERTO   broad

APPASSIONATO   passionately

ARCH FORM   symmetrical form in which the outer sections are similar, the penultimate section resembles the second section, etc.

ARIA   piece for accompanied solo voice (or for an instrument treated like a voice)

ARPEGGIO   presentation of a chord one note at a time, usually from bottom to top

ASSAI   very

ATHEMATIC   having no consistent melodic theme

ATONALITY   principle of organization of some twentieth-century music according to notes and intervals but not key centers

ATTACK   beginning of a sound

AUGMENTATION   presentation of a theme twice as slow as normally; opposite of diminution

AUSDRUCK   expression

AUSSERST   extremely

BAR   measure

BARLINE   line separating measures in a score

BAROQUE   period roughly between 1600 and 1750

BASS   lowest sounding part

BEDÄCHTIG   deliberately

BEHÄGLICH   leisurely

BEN   well

BERCEUSE   cradle song

BEWEGT   with motion

BOURRÉE   stately old French dance

BREIT   broad

BREVE   short

BRIDGE   transition, particularly in sonata form

BRIO   vigor, spirit

BUFFO   comic

B.W.V.   catalog listing for Bach's music

CADENCE   ending of a musical phrase

CADENZA   virtuosic passage for an unaccompanied soloist, usually in a concerto

CANON   composition in which two or more voices overlap by playing the same melody at different times

CANTABILE   in a singing fashion

CANTATA   composition for solo voice(s), orchestra, and possibly chorus

CANTUS FIRMUS   fixed melody, often taken from another source, that is the basis of a composition

CAPRICCIO   free, fanciful, possibly virtuosic piece

CELESTE   an instrument with a piano-style keyboard and a bell-like timbre

CHACONNE   composition in which a short bass theme is repeated again and again throughout

CHAMBER   for a small ensemble and/or performance space

CHORD   simultaneous sounding of three or more notes

CHROMATIC   using all twelve notes per octave of the scale (i.e., both black and white keys on the piano); opposite of diatonic

CLASSIC   restrained, carefully structured; opposite of romantic

CODA   ending section

COL LEGNO   played with the wood rather than the hairs of a bow

CON   with

CONCERTANTE   piece, movement, or passage featuring a solo player or group of soloists

CONCERTINO   group of soloists; short work in concerto style

CONCERTO   composition for a soloist with orchestra

CONCERTO GROSSO   baroque composition for small group of soloists accompanied by a larger orchestra

CONSONANCE   stable, restful sound; opposite of dissonance

CONTINUO   in baroque music, instruments playing the bass line and the harmony implied by it, usually cello, bassoon, and/or string bass plus keyboard

CONTRAPUNTAL   featuring counterpoint

COUNTERMELODY   melody played simultaneously with the main melody

COUNTERPOINT   simultaneous setting of two or more melodic lines against each other (almost all music includes counterpoint)

COUNTERSUBJECT   countermelody introduced in a fugue while the second voice enters with the main theme

COURANTE   running dance

CRESCENDO   gradual increase of loudness

CYCLE   group of related pieces, usually songs

D.   catalog listing of the works of Schubert

DEVELOPMENT   section where the conflict between keys and themes erupts, possibly with great excitement, and where fragments of melodies are used rather than full tunes

DIATONIC   using primarily the seven tones of the major or minor scale (e.g., white keys on a piano), without chromatic additions; opposite of chromatic

DIMINUENDO   get gradually softer

DIMINUTION   playing a theme twice as fast as normally; opposite of augmentation

DISSONANCE   restless, unstable, tense sound in need of resolution

DIVERTIMENTO   piece in several movements with a light character

DOCH   nevertheless

DODECAPHONY   twelve-tone music

DOLCE   sweetly

DOMINANT   chord on the fifth step of the scale, which is used to imply motion to the tonic

DORIAN   mode produced by white keys on the piano from D to D

DOTTED RHYTHM   long note followed by short note in the ratio 3:1

DOUBLE FUGUE   fugue with two subjects

DOUBLE STOP   simultaneous sounding of two notes on a string instrument

DOUBLING   performing the same melody by two or more instruments or voices at once

DRONE   sustained sound

DUPLE   divided in half

DYNAMICS   indications of loudness

E   and

EILEN   to hurry

ETUDE   study, exercise

ETWAS   somewhat

EXPOSITION   first large section, in which the main themes are presented

EXPRESSIONISM   highly emotional, often morbid, German art and music of the early twentieth century

FALSE RECAPITULATION   return to the main theme (usually not in the tonic) within sonata form development section

FANTASIA   composition in free form; medley

FANTASTICO   with free play of fancy

FEIERLICH   festive; solemn

FERIA   Spanish dance

FERMATA   indication that a note or chord is to be held an indefinite time

FEURIG   ardently

FF   fortissimo

FINALE   last movement

FLAT   indication to lower a note by a semitone; playing somewhat under the proper pitch

FLIESSEND   flowing

FLUTTER-TONGUE   intense sound created on a wind or brass instrument by buzzing the tongue against the mouthpiece or reed

FORLANE   Venetian dance

FORTE   loud

FORTISSIMO   very loud

FUGAL ENTRY   appearance of the main melody in a fugue

FUGATO   fugue-like passage

FUGUE   highly developed composition in which some of the instruments begin in imitation

FUNÉBRE   funereal

FUOCO   fury

FUOCOSO   with fury

GAMELAN   Indonesian percussion orchestra

GAVOTTE   French court dance

GEBRAUCHMUSIK   music composed for amateur performers

GEMÄCHLICH   comfortable

GEMÄSSIG   moderate

GEMESSEN   precisely; somewhat heavy

GIGUE   rapid dance

GIOCOSO   playfully

GIUSTO   with precision

GLISSANDO   continuous sliding from one note to another

GRAVE   extremely slow

GRAZIA   grace

GRAZIOSO   gracefully

HABANERA   slow Cuban dance

HALF STEP   semitone

HARMONICS   pure overtones produced usually on a string instrument

HARMONY   sounding of several notes together to form chords, and the relationship between those chords (almost all music has or at least implies harmony)

IM   in the

IMITATION   answering of a melody with the same melody in another instrument slightly later, as in a canon

IMPRESSIONISM   trend in French art and music of the late nineteenth and early twentieth centuries that reflects the artist's impressions of natural phenomena

INDETERMINACY   leaving some aspects of a composition to the performer's choice

INTERMEZZO   interlude

INTERVAL   pitch distance between two notes

INTRADA   introduction

INVERSION   melody played upside-down

JUST INTONATION   system of tuning instruments according to pure intervals, resulting in very consonant sounds but severely limited possibilities for modulation

K.   catalog listing of Mozart's works, comparable to other composers' "opus"; named for Köchel, who first catalogued Mozart's music

KECK   impudence

KEY   mechanism on a wind instrument for opening and closing holes; tonal center of a piece, *e.g.*, C major

KEY SIGNATURE   sharps or flats indicating in which key the music is to be performed

KRAFT   force

KRÄFTIG   forcefully

KRAFTVOLL   forcefully

LÄNDLER   Austrian folk dance in moderately slow triple time

LANGSAM   slow

LARGAMENTE   broadly

LARGHETTO   quite slow

LARGO   extremely slow

LEAP   sudden move from a low to a high note, or *vice versa*

LEBHAFT   lively

LEGATO   smooth

LEGGIERO   delicately

LEITMOTIF   motive that characterizes a person, place, idea, or emotion

LENTO   slow

LIBRETTO   script of an opera

LUSTIG   merrily

MA   but

MAESTOSO   majestically

MALAGUEÑA   popular Spanish dance

MARCATO   marked

MARCIA   march

MARZIALE   martial

MASS   Roman Catholic liturgical ceremony

MÄSSIG   moderate

MEASURE   unit of time, bounded by barlines

MEHR   more

MENO   less

MENUETTO   minuet

METER   pattern of strong and weak beats that creates measures

METRONOME   machine that ticks at a specific tempo, designated in beats per minute

MICROTONE   note that is not one of the twelve notes of the chromatic scale but fits in between two of them

MINUET   dignified dance

MISURATO   measured

MIT   with

MODE   scale other than the typical major or minor

MODERATO   moderately

MODULATION   change of key

MOLTO   very

MORENDO   dying away

MOSSO   motion

MOTIVE   short figure with a specific shape that can be recognized in a variety of contexts

MOTO   motion

MOTTO   important motive

MOVEMENT   quasi-independent piece, part of a larger work

MUSETTE   bagpipe-like instrument; dance used in baroque suites

MUSICOLOGIST   music historian

NACHTMUSIK   night music

NATURAL   cancellation of a sharp or flat

NICHT   not

NON   not

NON-HARMONIC TONE   note conflicting with prevailing harmony

OBBLIGATO   ornamental, accompanying solo part

OHNE   without

OPEN STRING   string on violin, viola, cello, or string bass played without placing finger on it

OPUS   work; catalog number

ORATORIO   large (usually religious) concert work for soloists, chorus, and orchestra

OSTINATO   melodic figure that repeats again and again

OVERTURE   orchestral introduction to an opera; single-movement orchestral composition

PANDIATONICISM   free mixture of all seven notes of a diatonic scale

PARALLEL FIFTHS   two voices a fifth apart moving in the same direction (traditionally forbidden)

PARALLEL HARMONY   progression in which all voices move the same amount in the same direction

PARALLEL MAJOR   major key with same tonic as a given minor key

PARALLEL MINOR   minor key with same tonic as a given major key

PAS DE DEUX   dance for two performers

PASSACAGLIA   composition that uses an ostinato throughout

PASSEPIED   lively old Breton dance

PASTORALE   composition suggestive of country scenes

PEDAL POINT   note sustained, usually in the bass, during a passage

PENTATONIC   five-note scale (e.g., the black notes on a piano)

PERPETUUM MOBILE   rapid piece or passage with relentless repetitive rhythm, that seems as if it will never end

PESANTE   heavily

PHRASE   unit of music that could be sung in one breath or that is analogous to a sentence in spoken language

PIANISSIMO   very soft

PIANO   soft; large keyboard instrument (abbreviation for pianoforte — "soft-loud")

PIÙ   more

PITCH   note or tone

PIZZICATO   playing a string instrument by plucking the strings with the finger

POCHETTINO   very little

POCO   little

POLACCA   Polish dance

POLYPHONY   simultaneous combination of different sounds

POLYRHYTHM   simultaneous use of contradictory rhythms or meters

POLYTONAL   in more than one key simultaneously

PP   pianissimo

PRESTISSIMO   extraordinarily fast

PRESTO   very fast

PROGRAM MUSIC   music that tells a story or paints a picture, as opposed to absolute music

QUADRUPLE FUGUE   fugue with four subjects

QUARTER-TONE   note midway between two adjacent pitches

QUASI   as if, like

QUINTUPLET   group of five notes

RECAPITULATION   restatement of a section heard earlier

RECITATIVE   musical declamation that is half spoken and half sung

REGISTER   how high or low sounds are

RÉJOUISSANCE   joyful composition

RELATIVE MAJOR   major key with same key signature as a particular minor key (e.g., G major is the relative major of E minor)

RELATIVE MINOR   minor key with same key signature as a particular major key (e.g., C minor is the relative minor of E-flat major)

REPEATED NOTES   identical pitches sounded successively

RETROGRADE   theme played backwards

RHAPSODY   composition in free form with many changes of mood

RICERCAR   fugue

RIPIENO   accompanying orchestral body in a concerto grosso

RISOLUTO   with decision

RITARDANDO   slowing down

RITMICO   rhythmic

RITORNELLO   refrain

ROCOCO   florid, ornamented music; the period (roughly between baroque and classic) when such music was written

ROLL   rapid, repeated strokes on a percussion instrument

ROMANCE   romantic composition

ROMANTIC   concerned with the overt expression of emotions; opposite of classic

ROMANZA   romantic composition

RONDO   form in which a main theme alternates with a series of subsidiary themes

ROW   see tone row

RUBATO   flexible tempo, freely accelerating and decelerating

RUHEVOLL   peaceful

RUHIG   peaceful

RUN   rapid sequence of notes going up or down

SARABANDE   stately Spanish dance

SCHATTENHAFT   shadowy

SCHERZANDO   playful; section in the manner of a scherzo

SCHERZO   fast, light-hearted piece

SCHLEPPEND   dragging

SCHNELL   fast

SCORDATURA   tuning the strings of a string instrument in an unusual manner

SCORE   printed music that shows what all the instruments are playing; to orchestrate

SEHR   very

SEMITONE   half step, distance between two adjacent notes

SEMPLICE   simple

SEMPRE   always

SEQUENCE   repetition of a figure successively higher or lower

SERIALISM   careful ordering of pitches (or durations, timbres, loudness, etc.), in certain twentieth-century music

SHARP   indication to raise a note by a semitone; playing slightly above pitch

SKIP   motion from one note to a distant note; opposite of step

SONATA   integrated three- or four-movement instrumental work for a small number of performers

SONATA FORM   form often used in first movements, comprised of exposition, development, and recapitulation

SOSTENUTO   sustained

STACCATO   short

STEP   motion for a note to an adjacent note; opposite of skip

STETS   continuously

STOPPED   sound produced, usually on French horn, by inserting hand into bell

STRETTO   overlapping of a fugue subject

STÜRMISCH   stormily

SUBITO   suddenly

SUBJECT   main melody of a fugue

SUITE   series of loosely related movements, often drawn from a larger composition

SYMPHONIE CONCERTANTE   classical-period composition for a small group of soloists accompanied by a larger orchestra

SYMPHONY   sonata for orchestra

SYNCOPATION   rhythm resulting from playing accented notes on unaccented beats

TAMTAM   large, gong-like instrument

TANTO   so much

TEMPERAMENT   system of tuning

TEMPO   speed

THEME   melody that forms the basis of (part of) a composition

THOROUGH BASS   bass line plus numerical symbols to indicate to a keyboard player the harmonic structure of a baroque composition

TIMBRE   tone quality

TIME SIGNATURE   numerical indication of the number of beats per measure and the rhythmic value of the note representing one beat

TOCCATA   virtuosic, improvisatory piece

TONAL   having a tonic

TONALITY   system of musical logic in which each chord has its own inherent degree of stability and in which one chord

THE TONIC   has ultimate stability and thus is the goal of motion

TONE POEM   programmatic orchestral piece in one movement

TONE ROW   particular ordering of the twelve notes of the chromatic scale, which is used to generate all melodies and harmonies in a twelve-tone composition

TONIC   stable note or chord in tonal music; key of a piece; see "tonality"

TONIC MAJOR   major key with same tonic pitch as a particular minor key (e.g., F major is the tonic major of F minor)

TONIC MINOR   minor key with same tonic pitch as a particular major key (e.g., D minor is the tonic minor of D major)

TRANSPOSITION   restatement higher or lower

TRAUERMARSCH   funeral march

TREMOLO   rapid repeat of a note or chord

TRIAD   fundamental chord of tonal music (e.g., do-mi-sol)

TRILL   rapid alternation of a note and another note a step away

TRIO   piece for three players; middle section of a scherzo or minuet

TRIO SONATA   baroque composition for two solo instruments and continuo

TRIPLE FUGUE   fugue with three subjects

TRITONE   interval containing three whole-steps, e.g., F to B or B to F

TROPPO   too much

TUTTI   passage with everyone playing

TWELVE-TONE   music that uses all notes of the chromatic scale as potentially equal in importance, usually by means of a tone row

TWELVE-TONE ROW   same as "tone row"

UN   a

UND   and

UNISON   simultaneous sounding of the same note or melody by several instruments

VARIATIONS   ornamented or otherwise altered repetitions of a theme

VIERTEL   quarter; quarter note

VIOLA DA GAMBA   archaic viola held between the legs

VIVACE   lively

VIVACISSIMO   very lively

VIVO   lively

WHOLE TONE   six-note scale with no semitones; interval, equivalent to two semitones, between some adjacent notes of most scales

ZART   tenderly

ZEITMASS   tempo

ZIEMLICH   tolerably

ZU   to

Bibliography

The following bibliography lists books recommended for supplemental reading. These are the sources most often consulted in the preparation of this volume, although there were many additional ones as well. As this list has been kept brief, there is no attempt at comprehensiveness. But each book listed below is one of the better books available for the general reader. There may well be other good sources on a given topic, but the bibliography tries to avoid the poorly written, the out-of-date, the inaccurate, and the useless — of which there are, unfortunately, quite a number in print. Many books have been published more than once, sometimes in different editions and sometimes even by different publishers. Recent publications are more likely to be found in bookstores or are at least may be ordered; earlier publications are more likely to be found in libraries. Only one publication is given for each book; that should be sufficient information to track it down, even if that exact edition is not eventually located. The standard reference book on music is the twenty-volume edition of *Grove's Dictionary of Music and Musicians*.

BACH
Geiringer, Karl. *Johann Sebastian Bach: The Culmination of an Era.* Oxford University Press (1966).
Wolff, Christoph, et al. *The New Grove Bach Family.* Norton (1983).

BARBER
Broder, Nathan. *Samuel Barber.* Schirmer (1954).

BARTÓK
Stevens, Halsey. *The Life and Music of Béla Bartók.* Oxford University Press (1953).
Ujfalussy, József. *Béla Bartók.* Crescendo (1972).

BEETHOVEN
Forbes, Elliott (ed.). *Thayer's Life of Beethoven.* Princeton University Press (1967).
Solomon, Maynard. *Beethoven.* Schirmer (1977).

BERG
Grun, Bernard (ed.). *Alban Berg: Letters to His Wife.* St. Martin's (1971).
Monson, Karen. *Berg.* Houghton Mifflin (1979).

BERLIOZ
Barzun, Jacques. *Berlioz and the Romantic Century.* Columbia University Press (1969, two volumes).

BORODIN
Abraham, Gerald. *Borodin: The Composer and His Music.* AMS Press (1976).
Leonard, Richard Anthony. *A History of Russian Music.* Macmillan (1957).

BRAHMS

Gál, Hans. *Johannes Brahms: His Work and Personality.* Knopf (1963).
Geiringer, Karl. *Brahms: His Life and Work.* Houghton Mifflin (1936).

BRUCKNER

Watson, Derek. *Bruckner.* Dent (1975).

CHOPIN

Gavoty, Bernard. *Frederic Chopin.* Scribner (1977).
Marek, George R., and Gordon-Smith, Maria. *Chopin.* Weidenfeld and Nicolson (1978).
Zamoyski, Adam. *Chopin: A New Biography.* Doubleday (1980).

COPLAND

Copland, Aaron. *Copland on Music.* Doubleday (1960).
Copland, Aaron. *Music and Imagination.* Harvard University Press (1961).
Copland, Aaron, and Perlis, Vivian. *Copland: 1900 through 1942.* St. Martin's/Marek (1984).

CORELLI

Pincherle, Marc. *Corelli: His Life, His Work.* Da Capo (1971).

DEBUSSY

Lockspeiser, Edward. *Debussy: His Life and Mind.* Cassell (1962, two volumes).

DVOŘÁK

Clapham, John. *Antonín Dvořák: Musician and Craftsman.* Faber and Faber (1966).

ELGAR

Kennedy, Michael. *Portrait of Elgar.* Oxford University Press (1968).

FALLA

James, Burnett. *Manuel de Falla and the Spanish Musical Renaissance.* Gollancz (1979).

FRANCK

Vallas, Léon. *César Franck.* Oxford University Press (1951).
Davies, Laurence. *César Franck and His Circle.* Houghton Mifflin (1970).

GLAZUNOV

Abraham, Gerald. *On Russian Music.* Johnson Reprints (1970).

GRIEG

Horton, John. *Grieg.* Dent (1974).

HANDEL

Keates, Jonathan. *Handel: The Man and His Music.* St. Martin's (1985).
Láng, Paul Henry. *George Frideric Handel.* Norton (1966).
Weinstock, Herbert. *Handel.* Knopf (1959).

HAYDN

Geiringer, Karl. *Haydn: A Creative Life in Music.* Norton (1946).
Robbins Landon, H. C.. *Haydn: Chronicle and Works.* Indiana University Press (1976, five volumes).

HINDEMITH
Hindemith, Paul. *A Composer's World.* Anchor (1961).
Skelton, Geoffrey. *Paul Hindemith: The Man Behind the Music.* Gollanz (1975).

HONEGGER
Honegger, Arthur. *I Am a Composer.* St. Martin's (1966).

IVES
Burkholder, J. Peter. *Charles Ives: The Ideas Behind the Music.* Yale University Press (1985).
Perry, Rosalie Sandra. *Charles Ives and the American Mind.* Kent State University Press (1974).
Rossiter, Frank R. *Charles Ives and His America.* Liveright (1975).

JANÁČEK
Horsbrugh, Ian. *Leoš Janáček.* Scribner's (1982).
Vogel, Jaroslav. *Leoš Janáček.* Norton (1981)

KODÁLY
Young, Percy M. *Zoltán Kodály: A Hungarian Musician.* Benn (1964).

LISZT
Searle, Humphrey. *The Music of Liszt.* Dover (1966).

MACDOWELL
Gilman, Lawrence. *Edward MacDowell: A Study.* John Lane (1908).

MAHLER
Cardus, Neville. *Gustav Mahler: His Mind and His Music.* Gollancz (1965).
de la Grange, Henri-Louis. *Mahler.* Doubleday (1973, first of projected three volumes; all three published in French).
Gartenberg, Egon. *Mahler: The Man and His Music.* Schirmer (1978).

MENDELSSOHN
Marek, George R. *Gentle Genius: The Story of Felix Mendelssohn.* Funk and Wagnalls (1972).
Werner, Eric. *Mendelssohn: A New Image of the Composer and His Age.* Free Press of Glencoe (1963).

MOZART
Einstein, Alfred. *Mozart: His Character, His Work.* Oxford University Press (1945).
Ottaway, Hugh. *Mozart.* Wayne State University Press (1980).
Hildesheimer, Wolfgang. *Mozart.* Farrar, Strauss and Giroux (1982).

MUSSORGSKY
Seroff, Victor. *Modeste Mussorgsky.* Funk and Wagnalls (1968).

NIELSEN
Simpson, Robert. *Carl Nielsen, Symphonist.* Crescendo (1979).

PROKOFIEV
Hanson, Lawrence and Elisabeth. *Prokofiev: The Prodigal Son.* Cassell (1964).
Robinson, Harlow. *Prokofiev.* Viking (1987).
Seroff, Victor. *Sergei Prokofiev: A Soviet Tragedy.* Funk and Wagnalls (1968).

RACHMANINOFF
Bertensson, Sergei, and Leyda, Jay. *Sergei Rachmaninoff: A Lifetime in Music.* George Allen and Unwin (1965).

RAVEL
Orenstein, Arbie. *Ravel: Man and Musician.* Columbia University Press (1975).

RESPIGHI
Respighi, Elsa. *Ottorino Respighi: His Life Story.* Ricordi (1961).

ROUSSEL
Deane, Basil. *Albert Roussel.* Barrie and Rockliff (1961).

SAINT-SAËNS
Harding, James. *Saint-Saëns and His Circle.* Chapman and Hall (1965).

SCHOENBERG
Rosen, Charles. *Arnold Schoenberg.* Viking (1975).
Stuckenschmidt, H. H. *Arnold Schoenberg: His Life, World, and Work.* Calder (1977).

SCHUBERT
Brown, Maurice J. E. *Schubert: A Critical Biography.* St. Martin's (1958).
Einstein, Alfred. *Schubert: A Musical Portrait.* Oxford University Press (1951).
Wechsberg, Joseph. *Schubert: His Life, His Work, His Time.* Weidenfeld and Nicolson (1977).

SCHUMANN
Ostwald, Peter F. *Schumann: The Inner Voices of a Musical Genius.* Northeastern University Press (1985).
Taylor, Ronald. *Robert Schumann: His Life and Work.* Granada (1982).

SHOSTAKOVICH
Roseberry, Eric. *Shostakovich: His Life and Times.* Hippocrene (1982).
Schwarz, Boris. *Music and Musical Life in Soviet Russia, 1917–1970.* Barrie and Jenkins (1972).
Shostakovich, Dmitri. *Testimony: The Memoirs of Dmitri Shostakovich.* Harper and Row (1979).

SIBELIUS
Johnson, Harold E. *Jean Sibelius.* Alfred A. Knopf (1959).
Layton, Robert, *Sibelius and His World.* Viking Press (1970).
Tawaststjerna, Erik. *Sibelius.* University of California (volume 1, 1957; volume 2, 1986; third volume projected).

STRAVINSKY
Pasler, Jann (ed.). *Confronting Stravinsky.* University of California Press (1986).
Stravinsky, Igor. *Poetics of Music.* Vintage (1947).
Stravinsky, Vera, and Craft, Robert. *Stravinsky in Pictures and Documents.* Simon and Schuster (1978).

STRAUSS

Del Mar, Norman. *Richard Strauss: A Critical Commentary on His Life and Works.* Barrie and Rockliff (1962, three volumes).

Krause, Ernst. *Richard Strauss: The Man and His Work.* Colet's (1964).

Marek, George R. *Richard Strauss: The Life of a Non-Hero.* Simon and Schuster (1967).

TCHAIKOVSKY

Hanson, Lawrence and Elisabeth. *Tchaikovsky: The Man behind the Music.* Dodd Mead (1966).

Warrack, John. *Tchaikovsky.* Scribner's (1973).

VILLA-LOBOS

Appleby, David P. *The Music of Brazil.* University of Texas (1983).

VIVALDI

Kolneder, Walter. *Antonio Vivaldi: His Life and Work.* University of California (1970).

Pincherle, Marc. *Vivaldi: Genius of the Baroque.* Norton (1957).

WEBERN

Moldenhauer, Hans and Rosaleen. *Anton von Webern: A Chronicle of His Life and Work.* Knopf (1979).

WAGNER

Gutman, Robert W. *Richard Wagner: The Man, His Mind, and His Music.* Harcourt Brace World (1968).

Stein, Jack M. *Richard Wagner and the Synthesis of the Arts.* Greenwood (1973).

von Westernhagen, Curt. *Wagner: A Biography.* Cambridge University Press (1978, two volumes).

General Topics

CONDUCTING AND PERFORMING

Cone, Edward T. *Musical Form and Musical Performance.* Norton (1968).

Wooldridge, David. *Conductor's World.* Praeger (1970).

GENERAL HISTORY AND HISTORY BY PERIODS

Bukofzer, Manfred E. *Music in the Baroque Era.* Norton (1947).

Einstein, Alfred. *Music in the Romantic Era.* Norton (1947).

Grout, Donald Jay. *A History of Western Music.* Norton (1980).

Mellers, Wilfrid. *Romanticism and the Twentieth Century.* Essential Books (1957).

Pauly, Reinhard G. *Music in the Classic Period.* Prentice-Hall (1965).

Revitt, Paul. *Nineteenth-Century Romanticism in Music.* Prentice Hall (1965).

Rosen, Charles. *The Classical Style.* Norton (1972).

MUSIC APPRECIATION AND INTRODUCTION TO MUSIC

Bernstein, Leonard. *The Infinite Variety of Music.* Simon and Schuster (1966).

Bernstein, Leonard. *The Joy of Music.* Simon and Schuster (1959).

Kerman, Joseph. *Listen.* Worth (1972).

Komar, Arthur. *Music and Human Experience.* Schirmer (1980).

Schwartz, Elliott. *Music: Ways of Listening.* Holt, Rinehart and Winston (1982).

MUSIC AESTHETICS AND THE MEANING OF MUSIC

Finkelstein, Sidney. *How Music Expresses Ideas.* International (1970).

Kramer, Jonathan D. *The Time of Music.* Schirmer (1988).

Meyer, Leonard B. *Emotion and Meaning in Music.* University of Chicago Press (1956).

Small, Christopher. *Music, Education, Society.* Schirmer (1977).

Three Classics in the Aesthetics of Music, containing "Monsieur Croche, the Dilettante Hater" by Claude Debussy, "Sketch of a New Aesthetic of Music" by Ferruccio Busoni, and "Essays before a Sonata" by Charles Ives. Dover (1962).

THE ORCHESTRA AND ORCHESTRATION

Carse, Adam. *The Orchestra from Beethoven to Berlioz.* Broude (1949).

Carse, Adam. *The Orchestra in the Eighteenth Century.* Heffer (1940).

Read, Gardner. *Style and Orchestration.* Schirmer (1979).

TWENTIETH-CENTURY MUSIC

Battcock, Gregory (ed.). *Breaking the Sound Barrier.* Dutton (1981).

Griffiths, Paul. *Modern Music: The Avant Garde since 1945.* Braziller (1981).

Meyer, Leonard B. *Music, the Arts, and Ideas.* University of Chicago Press (1967).

Peyser, Joan. *The New Music: The Sense behind the Sound.* Delacourte (1971).

Rockwell, John. *All American Music.* Knopf (1983).

Salzman, Eric. *Twentieth-Century Music: An Introduction.* Prentice Hall (1974).

Yates, Peter. *Twentieth Century Music: Its Evolution from the End of the Harmonic Era into the Present Era of Sound.* Pantheon (1967).

Richard Wagner

Born on 22 May 1813 in Leipzig.
Died on 13 February 1883 in Venice.

◆　◆　◆

Siegfried Idyll

Siegfried Idyll *was completed on 4 December 1870. Wagner conducted the first performance in his home near Lucerne, Switzerland, on 25 December 1870.*

Cosima Wagner was 33 years old on Christmas Day, 1870. She awakened to the sounds of music playing — new, wonderful, unfamiliar music performed by a chamber ensemble. Cosima later wrote in her diary,

> As I awoke my ear caught a sound, which swelled fuller and fuller; no longer could I imagine myself to be dreaming; music was sounding, and such music! When it died away, Richard came into my room with the children and offered me the score of the symphonic birthday poem. I was in tears, but so was all the rest of the household. Richard had arranged his orchestra on the staircase, and thus was our Triebschen [their Swiss villa] consecrated forever. . . . After lunch the orchestra came into the house downstairs, and now the *Idyll* was heard once again, to the profound emotion of us all.

The music of *Siegfried Idyll* was written to express Wagner's happiness in his marriage to Cosima, in his new retreat on the shore of Lake Lucerne, and in his young son Siegfried. The composer had found peace, however temporarily, after struggling against public scandal.

Cosima had been the source of the scandal, which nearly ruined his career. She was the second of three illegitimate children of composer Franz Liszt and the Countess Marie d'Agoult. When Cosima first became interested in Wagner, she was married to conductor Hans von Bülow, to whom she had borne two daughters. Wagner was friendly with and professionally involved with the conductor. Von Bülow had directed many important performances of Wagner's music, including the premiere of *Tristan und Isolde*, and Wagner had used his influence with the King to help retain von Bülow in a position of importance in Munich.

789

At first Wagner hesitated to start an affair with Cosima, because he knew it would eventually mean ruin for von Bülow. But desire and selfishness got the upper hand. Wagner, who was separated from his wife Minna, invited the von Bülow family to spend part of the summer of 1864 with him. Cosima and her children arrived a week before the conductor. During that week Wagner and Cosima consummated their love. The lovers confessed to von Bülow when he arrived. He suffered greatly, but he was a weak man who knew that his career was in the hands of the influential composer. The conductor had no control over his wife's behavior. They stayed with Wagner for much of the summer, wanting to keep up appearances and avoid a scandal. Cosima shared the affections of both men. This unconventional arrangement seemed to inspire Wagner to begin a string quartet (a most unusual genre for him), which was eventually incorporated into *Siegfried Idyll.*

Cosima became pregnant. Her daughter Isolde was born in April 1865, but she was not sure who was the father. As the girl began to grow, her features took on a resemblance to those of the composer. Over the next several months, Cosima lived alternately with Wagner and von Bülow, the former for love and the latter for appearances. It was essential to try to keep the affair a secret from the King. All of Munich gossiped about the paternity of Isolde. Wagner told outright lies in order to remain in the King's good graces.

The composer bought the estate Triebschen in Switzerland in the spring of the following year, and that summer he attempted once again to silence the gossip by inviting the entire von Bülow family. The conductor still felt he had no choice but to accept the invitation. Wagner and Cosima continued to deny their affair to the King, even as Cosima was carrying the composer's second child. When von Bülow left at the end of the summer, Wagner actually managed to convince the King that Cosima had stayed behind only because he was better able to care for her than her husband.

In February 1867 Cosima gave birth to a daughter, Eva. She still claimed publicly that von Bülow was the father, and the conductor even hastened to see the child just on the chance that she might be his. The following April Cosima returned to von Bülow, although she made sure that his quarters had a room for her frequent guest. The two men still continued to share her.

By the following year it became impossible to maintain the preposterous ruse any longer. Bülow conducted the premiere of *Meistersinger,* but he was soon to be humiliated publicly. Cosima again joined Wagner for the summer at Triebschen, this time without her husband. Wagner had found another conductor whom he could trust to present his works, and Cosima wrote to Bülow that she would return to him no longer. She was again pregnant, although she denied it at first. She discussed the possibility of divorce. The conductor was reluctant. He no longer believed she would live with him again, but he knew that the scandal surrounding a divorce would mean the end of his conducting in Munich.

In June 1869 Siegfried Wagner was born. The press reported that Wagner's mistress had given birth again. Von Bülow's recent revival of *Tristan* was praised in the newspapers for the devotion the conductor had brought to the work of his wife's lover. There was neither dignity nor hope left for von Bülow. He sent his daughters to live with their mother and Wagner, and he resigned his post as conductor in Munich. Because of the scandal, Wagner was banished from Munich social and musical circles. He was not allowed to supervise the Munich premieres of his first two *Ring* operas. The scandal also damaged the career of Cosima's father, Liszt. Finally von Bülow agreed to the divorce, and Wagner (whose first wife had conveniently died) and Cosima were married on 25 August 1870. For their first Christmas as a married couple, Wagner presented Cosima with *Siegfried Idyll.*

The composition uses themes from the third act of the opera *Siegfried* and also the cradle song "Sleep, Baby, Sleep." Wagner intended the work only for his family and friends, but, because of financial difficulties, he was forced in 1878 to publish it, in a version for full orchestra. It is the only symphonic composition of Wagner's maturity. He also published a detailed program:

> The first ninety measures of *Siegfried Idyll,* in order to sing of the purity and holiness of the child's soul, use Brünhilde's theme from the opera *Siegfried* ("From Eternity to Eternity Am I"). The mother, near his little bed, sings the boy to sleep with a lullaby. He falls asleep, during the soft, intermittent horn notes. The mother notices that he is asleep, but she continues to sing, though halting several times. A series of trills . . . [indicates that] the boy is now deeply asleep. The mother gazes thoughtfully upon her beloved child and dreams about his future. She seems touched by a shiver as she thinks about the unknown man who will grow from this boy — arpeggios in the strings. She envisions (when the meter changes to 3/4) a handsome man in flowering youth. This is Siegfried's theme of glory, from the opera ("Siegfried, Thou Glorious Protector of the World"), as sounded by an interplay of flutes, clarinets, and oboes. A descending clarinet run expresses the mother's delight; then the strings pick up the theme. . . . It is combined with the holy music: in the mother's soul her remembrance of the boy's childhood and of her cares joins with this vision of maturity. . . . Now the

mother envisions the youth becoming more manly and growing in strength: he is driven to accomplish important deeds. He gains for himself a place among men. But then comes a moment of contemplation. A nameless desire captures the youth's heart as he wanders alone (forest sounds and birdsongs and the theme of love and unity from *Siegfried*). Passion awakens in him, and he feels for the first time soul-wearying pains. His passion grows until finally love makes him happy. The highest sound of joy signals the full happiness of his life in love. Birdsongs foretell success (from *Siegfried*), and gladness is expressed along with feelings about the innocent childhood of the soul ("From the Time of Youth, a Song Ever Sings in Me"). . . . The mother awakens from her reverie and turns again to the slumbering child. She gives thanks for her happiness and prays for heaven to bless her son. Once again the lullaby is heard, along with the theme of holiness. Suddenly the haunting forest horns and birdsongs return. Does the boy dream of his future? No, he sleeps quietly with a happy smile. . . . After a final loving kiss from the mother, the future hero rests in the care of God.